MW00397939

EUROJAZZLAND

EURO

NORTHEASTERN UNIVERSITY PRESS

BOSTON

JAZZLAND

Jazz and European Sources, Dynamics, and Contexts

EDITED BY

LUCA CERCHIARI, LAURENT CUGNY, & FRANZ KERSCHBAUMER

Library of Congress Cataloging-in-
Publication Data
Eurojazzland: jazz and European
sources, dynamics, and contexts / edited
by Luca Cerchiari, Laurent Cugny, and
Franz Kerschbaumer.
p. cm.
Includes bibliographical references and
index.
ISBN 978-1-58465-864-1 (cloth: alk. paper)
ISBN 978-1-61168-298-4 (ebook: alk. paper)
1. Jazz—Europe—History and criticism.
I. Cerchiari, Luca. II. Cugny,
Laurent. III. Kerschbaumer, Franz.
ML3509.E9E97 2012
781.65094—dc23
2012014094

5 4 3 2 1

CONTENTS

3 parts

← Ed.

← Ed.

LUCA CERCHIARI

INTRODUCTION

t is curious that a comprehensive book on jazz in Europe still doesn't exist. There are hundreds of titles dedicated to the history of jazz and African American music in the United States, but none to its European counterparts. Some recent jazz histories also deal with Europe (and others with Asia, Africa, and Oceania, in that jazz is correctly regarded as an international sonic language), but just in a brief synthesis. In fact, the subject matter is so broad, in historical, geographical, and cultural terms, that such an enterprise would require years of research and an international committee of authors. The bibliography on regional histories and single musicians is quite a rich one, with more or less one hundred titles (among biographies are represented some of the most important European jazzmen ever—Django Reinhardt, Stéphane Grappelli, Martial Solal, Jean "Toots" Thielemans, Jan Garbarek, George Shearing, Ian Carr, Joachim Kühn, Albert Mangelsdorff, Gorni Kramer, Giorgio Gaslini, Enrico Rava, Joe Zawinul, Willem Breuker, Tete Montoliu). Almost every European country has produced a serious book on its own jazz history, and in some cases (France, England, Germany, Italy, Spain, Russia) more than one. A major problem is the language: whereas in the United States the common ground is English, in Europe, though English is also the language of the jazz community, almost every country speaks something different. Europe has also recently become, in geopolitical terms, a larger entity: the European Community, at present, includes twenty-seven countries, while new nations are waiting to be admitted to the Brussels-Strasbourg organization.

In any case, be it the result of the research of a committee of authors, or the effort of a single scholar, the history of jazz in Europe has yet to be effectively written. For the present publication we have chosen a different approach, a theoretical one. The idea of this book—not a history of jazz in Europe, but a series of essays dedicated to the complex, broader subject of the relations between Europe and jazz—came to me in 2008, when I invited my French colleague Laurent Cugny, professor at the University of Paris IV, to lecture at the University of Padua. We then met with our third editor, Franz Kerschbaumer, professor at the Austrian Graz University of Music and Dramatic Arts, and approved our project, which intended to co-opt several scholars, both from Europe and from the United States. Thanks to Friedrich Körner (and then to Kerschbaumer), Graz has become, since 1969, an international center for jazz research, besides offering a jazz program for instruments and related musical disciplines. In fact, courses in jazz musicology and history, since the seventies—sometimes in connection with disciplines like ethnomusicology, anthropology of music, or popular music, sometimes not—have been proposed and taught by an increasing number of universities and conservatories, not to mention private seminars, schools, and associations founded all around Europe, a list of which, and their related courses, would probably amount to a surprisingly high number. This academic network, or, better, these separate entities, sometimes connected and sometimes not, have so far produced a meaningful amount of research, developing with scientific purposes and methodologies a field that was at first approached, in the late twenties, by jazz critics both in Europe and in the United States, in some cases with relevant results (historiography, criticism, discography), in others with a limit of perspective that for a long time confined jazz to a status of lesser importance, unrelated to general musicological matters and to other cultural disciplines.

The many different relations between Europe and jazz can be divided into different categories, as we have done, choosing three main ones for the organization of this volume. The first concerns Europe as a source of jazz. Jazz has always been regarded as a typically twentieth-century expression of the broader African American contribution to world music history. The African and American roots of jazz have been thoroughly investigated; the European ones much less, although few current books have not forgotten to quote the European contribution to this music. Some relevant exceptions are such brilliant and innovative volumes as *Origins of the Popular Style*, by Peter van der Merwe (New York: Oxford University Press, 1989), *The Cambridge Companion to Jazz*, edited by Mervyn Cooke (Cambridge: Cambridge University Press, 2003), and *Cross the Water Blues: African American Musicians in Europe*, edited by Neil A. Wynn (Jackson, MS: University Press of Mississippi, 2007). Perhaps this situation is due, on one side, to the abovementioned limits of perspective of early jazz criticism (see, in this book, Laurent Cugny's contribution to this field) and, on the other, at least in part, to the so-called Afrocentric point of view. It is perplexing that white Americans have neglected for decades a meaningful part of their own roots, which include, in essence, the whole tradition of written and orally transmitted musics of the entire European continent. Melody, harmony, scales and modes, notation, rhythm, timbre, form, and even improvisation have much to do, in jazz, with European musical roots, as do instruments. Besides the banjo and the xylophone, which come from Africa, and the drums, which are the result of an American "assembly" of previous elements, all the most popular instruments in jazz are, in fact, European instruments: the saxophone, just to name one of the most popular, was patented before the second half of the nineteenth century by Belgian instrument maker Adolphe Sax. Some have been "reinvented" by jazz in terms of solo performance (winds and reeds, cornet, trombone, bass, harmonica), while others have been developed by this music in terms of peculiar performance techniques and styles (piano, guitar, trumpet, violin, flute). Some of the European instruments have been employed in a typically European way by European jazz (accordion, bass, violin; on bowed instruments, see Vincent Cotro's contribution). A specific tradition, in jazz, is the orchestral one. The so-called modern jazz big band, as we know it, is a new kind of instrumental entity consisting of four sections (trumpets, trombones, reeds, and the rhythm section) conducted by a director-arranger who is in general a piano or wind player. European jazz has contributed in its own way to orchestral jazz, either with specifically "European" arrangements and musics or with directors whose styles, performance attitudes, and gestures often differ quite a lot from those of their American colleagues (Europeans such as the German Alexander von Schlippenbach, the Swiss George Gruntz, the Italians Gorni Kramer and Giorgio Gaslini—Davide Ielmini's chapter in our book is devoted to Gaslini—the Austrians Mike Mantler and Mathias Rüegg, the British Mike Westbrook, Mike Gibbs, and Graham Collier, the French André Hodeir and François Jeanneau. These European orchestral contributions sometimes involved theatrical elements, offering a new, fascinating approach to the sonic theory and practice of jazz performance, at the same time evoking ideological debates and sociological values. As Joachim Ernst Berendt correctly pointed out in his world-famous *Jazzbook*, our continental jazz orchestras expressed a typically European feature, the idea of "collectivism."

Concerning musical cultures, every single European country has contributed to shape American jazz, which is—as we know—the result of many diasporas. We do not only have a Latin tinge (see Bruce Raeburn's essay), but also a British one (see Franz Kerschbaumer's chapter on the Celtic musical roots of jazz), an Italian one, a French one, a Mitteleuropean one, a Northern European one, a Balkan one, a Mediterranean one (and what about migrating cultures, strongly related with Europe, such as the Jewish and the Gypsy ones?). This aspect is also reflected in the European side of the jazz repertoire (see my chapter, in the book), a small but really meaningful body of work, consisting of several ethnic and urban melodies. Some have survived for centuries and circulated through publishing and sub-publishing means and exchanges (or, later, through discographical transmission); some were picked up by American musicians touring Europe in the twentieth century and brought to success in the United States, where a few became standards (Louis Armstrong has been, in this, a major "collector" and interpreter). Other melodies belong to the pre-jazz period and were absorbed by both secular and sacred African American styles and genres. These dynamics refer to the so-called popular style. Of course, American jazz, but especially European jazz, has much to do with European ethnic music, or folklore. A complete or even partial study of ethnic sources, in European jazz, has yet to be written; probably it will develop when ethnomusicologists and scholars of African American music start to cooperate with a precise, scientific research plan. The field is broad, and the topic fascinating, since it implies melodies and dances from all parts of the Old World. A minor but relevant connection between European folk roots and jazz concerns the pizzicato with the bass: its typical use in jazz probably derives from Eastern European ethnic and popular band traditions.

But jazz is also strictly related with classical music, or better, with the written side of European "art" music (see, in this book, Martin Guerpin's contribution). The contacts between these two genres have been and are more frequent and more relevant than one may think. Many features of the European classical styles of the seventeenth, eighteenth, nineteenth, and twentieth centuries were absorbed into the African American idiom (and, of course, in the American one). We may at first think about piano style and repertoire, which is of course a broad area of inheritances and exchanges. But if one considers, for example, a minor category like the recordings of the fifties (such as those of Charlie Parker, Clifford Brown, or Helen Merrill *with strings*), one finds another European retention: the orchestral strings, probably inspired to this peculiar aspect of jazz recordings by Hollywood film music, a music genre literally "invented" in California by "diasporic" European composers like Franz Waxman or Erich Wolfgang Korngold, who were raised within the Austro-German school of the first half of the twentieth century.

Improvisation has always been regarded as one of the essential and most peculiar features of jazz. But improvisation didn't start at all with jazz: European classical music is so rich in terms of improvisation that we could probably infer that jazz improvisation mostly comes from the European tradition. *Discanto* from the Middle Ages; Renaissance *diferencias* for string instruments; *basso continuo*; Baroque trumpet cadenzas; classical virtuosi solo parts for harpsichord, violin, or piano (impromptus, fantasias, and so on); Operatic bel canto vocal solos; Romantic improvisations for organ or, again, piano; twentieth-century aleatory music: here is a broad background to which jazz has often been connected, and from which, in part, its improvisational techniques and attitudes come. In the past centuries, composition and improvisation were, in classical music, two complementary sides of the same musical activity, in the sense that composers (Mozart, Paganini, Liszt, Thalberg, just to name few) used to improvise and then, often, transcribed their ideas on paper, and often improvised on popular or well-known melodies on their instruments, for the pleasure of their audiences. The concept of "virtuoso," to quote a famous series of Pablo albums recorded by guitar player Joe Pass in the 1970s, comes from the European tradition, where virtuosos used to compete in specific public contests; something similar happened in New York and elsewhere with the so-called "chases" during the bebop era, the forties, and

x

before. The composer and interpreter had often been the same musician, in Europe, until the first half of the eighteenth century, before the two things split into separate roles. Jazz is one of the few contemporary musics that has been able to keep alive this creative tradition, and, of course, to develop it in a special, personal way. While it is true that all composers in jazz are also instrumentalists and interpreters of their own music, it is also true that the instant composing process of jazz instrumentalists/soloists, while unique, at the same time was already known in the Classic and Romantic periods of European "art" music. During the twentieth century, the exchanges between the two genres have been frequent. European composers have influenced jazz, and jazz and African American music have influenced, or inspired, European composers: on one side we may remember the cases of Scott Joplin (who appreciated Wagner and wrote two operas, the lost *A Guest of Honor* and the published and recorded *Treemonisha*, but also a ballet, a musical comedy, and a symphony), James Price Johnson (who wrote a symphony), Duke Ellington (who arranged compositions by Grieg and Tchaikovsky), Charlie Parker (who had contacts with Edgard Varèse and Stefan Wolpe), Woody Herman (Stravinsky wrote *Ebony Concerto* for him, while Herman recorded Aram Katchaturian's *Sabre Dance*), John Lewis (who loved Bach and Baroque music in general), Bill Evans (who played piano works by Granados), George Russell (who used Greek modes to define his Lydian chromatic concept of tonal organization), Miles Davis (who listened to Ravel and recorded Rodrigo's *Concierto de Aranjuez*), Anthony Braxton (who quoted Schoenberg and Stockhausen), and many more. On the other those of Anton Dvorak, Claude Debussy, Igor Stravinsky, Ernst Krenek, Kurt Weill, Paul Hindemith, Francis Poulenc, Maurice Ravel, Darius Milhaud, Erwin Schuloff, George Antheil, Frederick Delius, Bohuslav Martinů, Dmitri Shostakovich, Bruno Maderna. Even American composers, by the way, have been influenced by jazz, or pre-jazz forms: let's name at least Louis Moreau Gottschalk, Charles Ives, John Alden Carpenter, Leonard Bernstein, Henry Cowell, and Marc Blitzstein; George Gershwin has been influenced by African American music (ragtime, spiritual songs, blues) but has also shaped, with his songbook, a meaningful part of the jazz repertoire, based on the interpretations of such tunes as "I Got Rhythm," "The Man I Love," "Embraceable You," "Lady be Good," and "Summertime." A more recent category of musicians interested in performing at the same time American jazz and European art music belongs to the second half of the last century: it includes such wonderful instrumentalists—and sometimes also composers—as the Europeans André Hodeir, Michel Portal, Jacques Loussier, Giorgio Gaslini, Enrico Pieranunzi, Stefano Battaglia, Friedrich Gulda, Mike Westbrook, Graham Collier, Mike Gibbs, Jan Garbarek, Markus Stockhausen, and the Americans John LaPorta, André Previn, Clare Fischer, Bill Smith, Lennie

Niehaus, Bob Cooper, William Russo, Keith Jarrett, Chick Corea, Richard Beirach, Wynton Marsalis, and Tom Scott (Benny Goodman and, of course, some pianists, including Thomas "Fats" Waller, were among the pioneers in this category).

It was a European classical musician, Swiss conductor Ernest Ansermet, who was first among his peers to write—in 1919—an important appreciation on jazz. He described in enthusiastic terms Creole clarinet and saxophone player Sidney Bechet, at that time touring Europe with Will Marion Cook's Southern Syncopated Orchestra. Ansermet's article, published by the magazine *La Suisse Romande*, started a cultural perspective on African American music and jazz that would first involve criticism (1930–70) and later, musicology. Literature and poetry were, in the twenties, receptive as well, as seen in the writings of the founder of Futurism, the Italian writer, poet, publisher, rabble-rouser (and many other things) Filippo Tommaso Marinetti, or the many poems and magazines dedicated to poetry, which in the same period were inspired (both in the titles and in the rhythm of lines and stanzas) by early jazz. This is to say that European ideas and authors very much contributed to a cultural approach to African American music and jazz that in some ways differs from the American one but that is nevertheless complementary. Single countries or, better, single cities, were relevant as well in terms of a "cultural environment"; in some cases (Paris's Montmartre, Montparnasse, and Saint-Germain-des-Prés, London's Soho, Berlin's Friedrichstadt, Milan's Navigli, and so on) even single city quarters (with their social and ethnic exchanges, architecture, performing arts) were very important. Paris, Brussels, London, Berlin, Moscow, and then Copenhagen, Oslo, Amsterdam, The Hague, Munich, Barcelona, Madrid, Rome, Milan, Perugia, Montreux, all became perennial or seasonal-specific jazz environments (and to some of these cities or quarters, just to name a single musician, John Lewis has dedicated some of his beautiful compositions). One could not think of the history of jazz without Paris, where, in the twenties, George Gershwin premièred his famous *American in Paris*, where several clubs managed by African Americans were born (let's remember Le Grand Duc and Chez Bricktop, opened by expatriate Chicago singer Ada Smith), and where African American dancer Josephine Baker, in 1925, was enthusiastically welcomed with the *Revue Nègre*. This show, which featured young jazz master Sidney Bechet (whose later residencies in Germany and Russia had a strong musical impact on these countries), was one of the many American revues that helped spread in Europe the recently born syncopated genre (going back to *In Dahomey*, by George Walker and Bert Williams, music by Will Marion Cook, published in London as early as 1903). In fact, in the long term, Paris would become even more important, in some aspects, than Chicago, Los Angeles, San Francisco, New Orleans, or Kansas City. Since the seventies, New York and Paris have actually been the two main jazz centers in *yup* the world. Hundreds of American jazzmen have recorded their *In Paris* LP or CD (a precise list is yet to be established, but no other European city has had such a privilege). And it was in Paris that the biggest record series ever dedicated to a jazz city was conceived and produced: *Jazz in Paris* (Universal Music France) has so far proposed more than 150 titles (most of them reprint, on CD, meaningful and sometimes "lost" recordings from the thirties, forties, and fifties of French and American jazzmen); the whole series has so far sold, in the world, more than two million copies. Curiously, nothing equivalent has yet been done in the United States, even if one may argue that dedicating an extended record series to New York or to Los Angeles could be regarded as nonsense, since jazz record production, in essence, was mainly developed in these two cities, after 1935. *hrm - so what does this mean?*

The role of Europe in the cultural appreciation of jazz has thus been relevant, and not only in the area of criticism and musicology. Different disciplines related to European culture have been employed to offer new and sometimes original points of view on this music: literary and visual arts studies, sociology and political sciences, anthropology, philosophy, historiography, psychology, linguistics and semiotics, media studies. Of course, since so much has been written, and so many debates and discussions were started in magazines and newspapers, and later in books and essays, jazz criticism (which owes much to France and something to Belgium, and later to England, Italy, Germany, and other countries, besides the United States) has been a typically European feature. After the pioneering articles and essays of Alfredo Casella, Robert Goffin, Alfred Baresel, André Schaeffner, Hilton Schleman, Giancarlo Testoni, Hugues Panassié, and Charles Delaunay, the post-1945 contributions of Joachim Ernst Berendt, Arrigo Polillo, Franco Fayenz, André Hodeir, Lucien Malson, Philippe Carles, Pawel Brodowski, Iain Lang, Steve Lake, Stuart Nicholson, Alyn Shipton—just to name few writers from different countries—have added something to our knowledge of this music, and helped the enjoyment of it in a different way. We are proud to offer, in this book, different points of view and approaches (see the chapter by Laurent Cugny on the controversial Euroamerican appreciation of jazz in early criticism, and Tony Whyton's essay on the more recent European contributions to this area of studies). Europe has also done very much in favor of jazz in terms of concerts and festival promotion, and in media production (radio, television, cinema, records). The public radio and television system has been a major force, especially from the mid-fifties to the eighties, in spreading the knowledge of this music and helping American and European musicians to perform: some were invited to play in radio or TV orchestras for long periods, weeks or months, and of course this also greatly helped the interactions and relations between American and European musicians. Just think about, in the sixties, George Russell's fruitful Scandinavian experience, or Ben Webster's in Denmark, and those of John Tchicai, Roswell Rudd, and Steve Lacy in Italy, twenty years later. In the field of cinema (a new media that was born in Europe at the end of the nineteenth and beginning of the twentieth century, but like the phonograph record received powerful new energies from its American life), in connection with jazz, Europe has offered wonderful creations. In the fifties, sixties and seventies, some of the best filmmakers— from Louis Malle to Michelangelo Antonioni, from Jean-Luc Godard to Roman Polanski—have employed jazz in their soundtracks, which were in some cases expressly commissioned to famous musicians like Miles Davis, John Lewis, Art Blakey, Michel Portal, Martial Solal, Giorgio Gaslini, Gato Barbieri. In the eighties a French filmmaker, Betrand Tavernier, produced one of the finest masterpieces of jazz-and-film history, the award-winning *Round Midnight*. Record production has been equally important: consider the pioneering role of the French label Swing, the first "indie" in the world dedicated to jazz (founded in the mid-thirties and directed by critics Hugues Panassié and Charles Delaunay, who also recorded many sides for the label in New York) and the case of Manfred Eicher's German label ECM, which since 1969, in sonic and graphic terms, changed the American tradition of jazz record production, introducing a new, "northern" and abstract, refined aesthetic paradigm. Germans and German Americans have always been important in jazz record production: just consider the work of Otto Heinemann with Okeh, and that of Alfred Lion and Francis Wolff with Blue Note; in Germany, in the sixties and seventies, Saba and then MPS, ECM, Japo, FMP, and Enja were equally relevant in documenting American and European jazz, including the avant-gardes, free jazz, and creative music. But the Germans, as Rainer Lotz has taught us, were equally active even in the pre-shellac era: cylinders and music boxes of German production documented ragtime, for example, even more than in the United States, while North and South America imported regularly this European production of African American music. Of course, the transatlantic topic is broader, since one may cite the Polish American brothers Leonard and Philip Chess and their renamed Chicago blues label, or the Turkish American brothers Ahmet and Nesuhi Ertegun, who started Atlantic Records in New York. Concerning ECM, the "European landscape," and other cultural topics, including contemporary exchanges between the musics of the Old and New Worlds, you may read Arrigo Cappelletti's, Jürgen Arndt's, and Herbert Hellhund's personal contributions in this volume.

Of course, jazz criticism and the peculiar attention of the media toward jazz started when American musicians intensified, in the late twenties and especially in the thirties, their concert tours in Europe, where African American music had circulated much more than we knew, in terms of stage performances and sound carriers, even before jazz: on this point, see Rainer Lotz's contribution. This was also the beginning of European jazz: musicians who had up to this point approached the new music thanks to records and the radio had the chance to learn directly from their masters and to mix—"alive"—with their living models. Louis Armstrong, Coleman Hawkins, and Benny Carter started playing with local musicians, even for long periods (see Catherine Tackley's chapter on Carter's experience in the United Kingdom), in the thirties, and later invited some of them to the United States: this was the case with Django Reinhardt, one of the most respected fathers of European jazz. In the same period a transatlantic trend of exchanges between the two worlds began. It is true that many American jazzmen found a new home in Europe: some went to Europe for months, some for years, some decided to move permanently to France, England, Denmark, or Germany. Duke Ellington is an example, and his longtime relation with France is brilliantly portrayed, in this book, by John Edward Hasse. In this long list of American musicians visiting Europe—more than one hundred names—we can at least select Sidney Bechet, Adelaide Hall, Milton "Mezz" Mezzrow, Valaida Snow, the already mentioned Hawkins and Carter, and then Kenny Clarke, Ben Webster, Art Farmer, Phil Woods, Steve Lacy, the Art Ensemble of Chicago, Mal Waldron, Dee Dee Bridgewater, David Murray, and Kurt Rosenwinkel. But the flow also went the opposite way: just consider the cases of Stan Hasselgard (Sweden); Toots Thielemans and Bobby Jaspar (Belgium); Spike Hugues, George Shearing, Marian McPartland, John McLaughlin, and Dave Holland (Great Britain); Jean-Luc Ponty, Michel Petrucciani, and Jacky Terrasson (France); Jutta Hipp and Karl Berger (Germany); Jan Hammer (Czechoslovakia); Gábor Szabó (Hungary); Ursula Dudziak (Poland); Valery Ponomarev (Russia); Joe Zawinul (Austria); and Enrico Rava and Roberta Gambarini (Italy). In our book, scholar Mike Heffley deals with the European expatriates McPartland, Zawinul, Berger, and Joseph Schillinger (the latter a very important, and quite unusual, Russian American scientist, composer, and music pedagogist; in a way also the founder of Boston's very famous Berklee College of Music). One of these trends of "Euro-American" musical migrations contributed in substantial ways to the development of the American jazz-rock style, or fusion, at the end of the sixties, which would probably have been different without the musical inventions and sounds of the Europeans John McLaughlin, Dave Holland, Miroslav Vitous, Joe Zawinul, and Jean-Luc Ponty. Moreover, in terms of style, it is unquestionable that two very different ones, the so-called Dixieland revival and free jazz, had, in Europe, a very peculiar and relevant development, both for aesthetic and sociopolitical reasons. See, on this point, the chapter by Alyn Shipton, and that by Ekkehard Jost, one of the few European scholars in the field of jazz research (after Goffin, Delaunay, and Panassié, the latter of whom also had a relevant role in the Euro-American Dixieland revival movement) whose books have been translated in the

United States. And what about the English writer, piano player, and record producer Leonard Feather, who, like Goffin, moved to the United States just before World War II? Feather, who had already started a jazz career in London in the second half of the thirties (on this point see, again, Catherine Tackley's chapter), didn't come back, and became American, while Belgian jazz writer, lawyer, poet, and amateur trumpet player Robert Goffin went back to his native country right after the war. Feather and Goffin, by the way, in 1942 started in New York—at the New School of Social Research—the very first university course dedicated to jazz, while the first conservatory jazz department was founded as early as 1929 in Frankfurt, Germany, by Bernhard Sekles and Mátyás Seiber, a former student of Zoltán Kodály; this pioneering enterprise was closed by the Nazis in 1933. Another European, the Austrian Dan Morgenstern, like Leonard Feather would become after World War II an American citizen, and an almost equally famous jazz critic (but also, later, a renowned archivist). Polish jazz writer, bass player, and organizer Jan Byrczek would have done the same in the seventies; after trying his hand at different activities in his country (including starting the Warsaw-based magazine *Jazz Forum*), he expatriated with success to the United States, only to return to Europe some years later, finally establishing a sort of permanent intercontinental existence between Poland and the United States.

The discourse on jazz and Europe or European jazz should obviously start, before any cultural and critical theory, from music. As I stated, it is not the purpose of this book to trace a transnational history of jazz in the Old World, which still waits to be written. Nonetheless, as an introduction, some essential information is needed. After a pioneering period of concerts and tours by American musicians, who were also active, and appreciated, as members of stage productions (revues, musical comedies, and the like), and after the spreading of the new African American music through the new media of the radio, the cylinder, and the shellac record (a problematic diffusion, since a very limited amount of authentic pre-jazz and jazz on 78 rpm records arrived in Europe, with a consequent misunderstanding, by many, of the artistic values and features of this novelty), the turning point of European jazz may be regarded, in fact, as the foundation, in Paris in 1934, of the Hot Club de France. HCF meant at the same time the actual club activity (the enthusiastic, nonstop Panassié-Delaunay contribution of the monthly magazine *Jazz Hot*, meetings of the associates, Swing label recordings, books) and the foundation of the now-viewed-as-classical quintet formed by Stéphane Grappelli (violin) and Django Reinhardt (guitar), plus a totally uncommon, original combo of other string instruments, two guitars and a bass. In terms of style and instrumental blend, it might be true that Grappelli, a classically trained French musician of Italian descent, and Reinhardt, a self-taught virtuoso of Belgian Manouche gypsy origin, were influenced by the original group led in the United States, in the mid-late twenties, by Joe Venuti (by the way, an Italian American) and Eddie Lang (another Italian American, his actual name being Salvatore Massaro). But similarities only concerned the lead instruments and the melodic approach to improvisation: it is unquestionable that Grappelli's and Reinhardt's quintet of the HCF had an additional, different flavor either in the melodic lines of the violin, played by Grappelli with a uniquely sweet European "perfect pitch," or in the uncommon, fanciful counterpoints of the two background guitars; or, again, in the typically Manouche, almost danceable rhythmical warmth and brilliance of Reinhardt's harmonic style, in his masterly melodic inventions, and in the nostalgic, Romantic spirit of his original tunes.

European jazz grew consistently after 1945, developing separately, or mixing, the "surplus value" introduced by Grappelli and Reinhardt, folk roots and "art" music, and later creating further mixtures, like the case of British jazz rock and progressive styles, where American jazz merges with rock and/or classical music elements (Soft Machine; Nucleus; Hatfield and the North; Robert Wyatt; Emerson, Lake, and Palmer; and so on), or single experiments consisting of new stimulating crossovers of jazz and ethnic roots (Zbgniew Namislowsky, Gianluigi Trovesi, Tete Montoliu, the post-Reinhardt Manouche jazz French guitar school, Michel Portal, Edward Vesala, Jan Garbarek, Arild Andersen, and so on), or of jazz and European "highbrow" avant-garde music. But it is probably with "art music" and its multifaced traditions that European jazz developed its own specific features. As Swiss trumpet player Franco Ambrosetti recently pointed out to me, it is true that, in terms of instruments, the piano has been one of the driving forces of European jazz. Henri Renaud to Martial Solal, Michel Petrucciani to Jacky Terrasson, Giorgio Gaslini to Franco D'Andrea, Enrico Pieranunzi to Renato Sellani, Krzystof Komeda to Wyacheslav Ganelin, Misha Mengelberg to Joachim Kühn, Bobo Stenson to Esbjorn Svensson, George Shearing to Tete Montoliu, the classical keyboard looks like a favorable "place" to experiment with new sounds, recall classical atmospheres and authors (from Chopin to Schumann, Debussy to Schoenberg), and simply speak the international language of jazz accompaniment and "solo flight." Piano players, guitar players (after Reinhardt, some basic names are René Thomas, Franco Cerri, Philip Catherine, John McLaughlin, Allan Holdsworth, Derek Bailey, Christian Escoudé, Marc Ribot, Bireli Lagrene, Volker Kriegel, Gábor Szabó, Attila Zoller, Terje Rypdal), arrangers, composers, the already noted violin players (which have a specific "French school" but also count single masters from other countries, such as Svend Asmussen or Michael Urbaniak), and of course several important reeds, trombone, and trumpet players, bassists (Niels-Henning Ørsted Pedersen, Dave Holland, Miroslav Vitous, George Mraz, Giovanni Tommaso), drummers (above all, Daniel Humair, who like German saxophone player Hans Koller must also be remembered as an excellent painter), and female singers, especially after 1960, have actually been the most original contributors to this stream of contemporary jazz. European jazz has developed a personal, peculiar sound, which, like it or not, is something completely different from the African American sound.

But all this, and much more, is the subject matter of another book, yet to be written—the long-awaited *History of Jazz in Europe*. We look forward to it.

I

EUROPE AS A SOURCE OF JAZZ

FRANZ KERSCHBAUMER

1 / THE INFLUENCE OF CELTIC MUSIC ON THE EVOLUTION OF JAZZ

The aim of this chapter is to add to the body of research into the development of jazz (and of traditional American popular music) by focusing on musical roots originating in northwestern Europe, an aspect that the literature has until now largely passed over.

The intention is not to diminish the significance of African American contributions to the birth and development of jazz. Rather, it is to complement these contributions by examining roots and affinities in European, Celtic music.

ok

The author has undertaken structured listening to numerous recordings, primarily of traditional Scottish and Irish music but also including Swedish folk music, to explore the European origins of jazz and early North American folk music. This process, together with often untapped evidence from the literature, has led to the following conclusions.

listening-based.

Irish-Scottish Music

Irish and Scottish music, as a part of the Celtic culture that spans Ireland, Wales, parts of Scotland and England, Brittany (Bretagne) in France, and Galicia and Asturias in Spain, was one of the seedbeds for American and British popular music and early jazz. The music of Scotland and Ireland in particular has a shared history and development, to the extent that individual musical forms cannot always be isolated from one another. In general, Irish melodies and harmonic structures exerted a strong influence on British and "imparted" American popular music. Scottish fiddle music, through the medium of "hillbilly music," made a decisive mark on American country and country-and-western music as well as the cakewalk, ragtime, Cajun, and small American string bands so central to the birth of jazz.

In addition to their African influences, the origins of jazz and North American folk, dance, and popular music can be understood in relation to migration from Northern Europe:[1] the majority of immigrants to the United States in the nineteenth century, a decisive period for this phase of musical development, came from Ireland, Scotland, Great Britain, Germany, and Scandinavia. Before 1820, these U.S. immigrants—largely Scottish-Irish—settled mainly in the southern Appalachians, bringing their Anglo-Scottish traditions with them and living in relative seclusion as so-called hillbillies.

eek.

[handwritten: what?]

As has been documented on numerous recordings, traditional Irish-Scottish music[2] of the nineteenth and twentieth centuries (two of the primary forms of which are jigs and reels) evinces the following "jazz-intrinsic" characteristics:

1. The "Scotch snap," typical of this music's melodic rhythm, is fundamental to a) fiddle music, for example "To Answer the Peacock" (CD: *To Answer the Peacock, Music for the Scottish Fiddle*; Brian McNeil. FMS Records 2084, p & c 1998, LE 1 as well as b) vocal music, as in "Comin' thro' the Rye" (CD: *Songs of Scotland*; Marie McLaughlin, Malcolm Martineau, with Isobel Frayling-Cork. Hyperion CDA67106, c 1999, LE 2). In the United States it led during the nineteenth century, as syncopation developed in the cakewalk, ragtime, and other styles, to offbeat phrasing in jazz.

2. Eighth notes, as later featured in jazz improvisation, appear as the rhythmic (or "motoric") normal value; phrasing (articulation) is ternary or in triplets, often with a two-beat feeling (accents on the second and fourth quarter notes) and with a latent offbeat articulation. A significant example is "The Fairy Reel" (CD: *Shetland Fiddle Music*; Scottish Tradition Series, vol. 4, School of Scottish Studies: University of Edinburgh; Greentrax Recordings 9004, c & p 1993, LE 3).

3. A strong affinity with the blues genre can also be discerned insofar as particular Scottish-Gaelic songs, besides featuring blueslike agogics, already exhibit a blues tonality, with minor sevenths and approximate minor thirds (the blues scale, C–D–E♭–F–G–B♭–C) as well as the downward singing of the tetrachord that is also characteristic of the blues—for example in "It's Time for Me to Rise Up" (CD: *Music from the Western Isles*; Scottish Tradition Series, vol. 2, Greentrax Records CDTRAX 9002, recorded in the Hebrides, c 1992, LE 4). In his 1992 book *Origins of the Popular Style: The Antecedents of Twentieth-Century Popular Music*, Peter van der Merwe examines these same wide-ranging genotypical connections between Irish-Scottish folk music and popular music (blues, ragtime, etc.), offering various musical/structural analyses.[3]

[handwritten: bit what about flat 5!? but what the]

4. "Diddling," a traditional solo vocal form originating in northeast Scotland, has a phrasing and articulation similar to jazz and as such can be seen as an early version of scat singing. The double-time phrasing technique so often heard in jazz since about 1925 is also practiced in this music, for instance in "Diddling & Mouth-Organ" (CD: *Bothy Ballads, Music from the North-East*; Scottish Tradition Series, vol. 1, Greentrax Recordings CDTRAX 9001, c & p 1993, LE 5).

5. Rifflike call-and-response structures common to Gaelic vocal groups, and sung over accented drum patterns, bear a marked similarity to their African analogues (for instance, the call-and-response phrases of the Yoruba people) and point forward to stomp patterns and the whole practice of riffing in jazz. One example is "One Day as I Roamed the Hills" (CD: *Waulking Songs from Barra*; Scottish Tradition Series, vol. 3, Greentrax Recordings CDTRAX 9003, c & p 1993,

LE 6). (This CD includes seven typical examples of these labor songs, recorded between 1965 and 1967 by the Danish musicologist Thorik Knudsen.)

6. Drum patterns with offbeat accents, as can be found in swing drum solos (for instance those of Gene Krupa), are also evident in Irish and British pipe-and-drum formations, for example "Boil the Breakfast Early" (CD: *The Best of the Chieftains*; Columbia 4716662, p 1992 Sony Music, recorded in the late 1970s, LE 7). The 1-4-7 accenting typical of Cuban music can be heard in "Suite de l'Oust et du Lie," a full series of circle dances also called "Rondes de Loudeac" and comprising a ronde, a baleu, a re-ronde, and a riquegnée (CD: *Pipes & Drums from Celtic Brittany, Bagadu du Moulin Vert*; ARC Music, EUCD 1508, p & c 1999, LE 8).

From these examples we can conclude that the aforementioned elements of jazz exclusively attributed until now to African traditions must also be viewed geno- and phenotypically in the context of the Irish-Scottish tradition.

Minstrel Shows, Cakewalk, and Ragtime

Black slaves on southern U.S. plantations began adapting the harmonies, melodies, and Scotch snap rhythm of the Scottish immigrants they worked with as early as the eighteenth century. This process had a significant effect on the creation and development of the cakewalk, ragtime, and also the blues. The American musician and musicologist Karl Koenig, in his publication *Walking the Gloryland: A History of the Cakewalk*, dealt in detail with the relationship between Scottish fiddle music and African American folk music. He writes: "The plantation Negro adapted a new style of music using the European concept of harmony and meter and within this musical system developed his own creative talents that resulted in styles like the cakewalk."[4] In Koenig's opinion, syncopation was probably not of African origin; in Africa the predominant rhythmic systems are multirhythmic, polyrhythmic, and polymetric.[5]

Moreover, comments Giles Oakley in his book *The Devil's Music: A History of the Blues*, in the chapter entitled "From Minstrels to Ragtime": "Slaves on the old plantations had absorbed many kinds of European music—Wesleyan hymns, Scottish and Irish fiddle music and ballads of all kinds. Transformed and shaped by their own African traditions, this music became the basis of the nigger minstrel shows." Oakley also talks of "the quaintest dances imaginable, accompanied by fiddlers and plantation songs."[6]

The cakewalk—music for minstrel shows—was made up largely of Irish-Scottish melodies; the (accompanying) bands usually included two or three fiddles and often several banjos. Many minstrel show tunes are adapted from Scottish or Irish jigs and reels, relying on the fiddle and its specific technique. The

[handwritten: minstrel shows definitely used European music, that's convincing]

FRANZ KERSCHBAUMER

directors of minstrel shows were often Scottish themselves. It is no accident that notable proponents such as James Scott, Budd Scott, and Scott Joplin themselves point to a Scottish connection and Scottish roots for the cakewalk and its descendant, ragtime. Many traditional jazz musicians played in, and were influenced by, minstrel and vaudeville shows. Both Bunk Johnson and W. C. Handy directed and played in minstrel shows, while the vocalist Noble Sissle and pianist Eubie Blake performed in vaudeville and accumulated their early musical experience there.

The cakewalk, an early form of ragtime with its typical, Scotch snap–derived syncopation and offbeat phrasing, was also played on the banjo—at first as an accompaniment to minstrel shows and later also in a solo setting, a development that led to ragtime and jazz. Documentation of this trend can be found in the recordings of the banjo player Vess L. Ossman from July 19, 1900. The piece "A Coon Band Contest" (from the CD *Ragtime*, Jazz Tribune n 42, Ragtime (1900–1930), CD 1, RCA LC 0316, Compilation BMG France, p & c 1995, LE 9), for example, showcases Ossman's virtuoso playing technique and clear ragtime structures.

The Scotch snap was also used and further developed in wind ensembles. The bands of John Philip Sousa brought the cakewalk to worldwide popularity in pieces such as "Silence and Fun" by Sousa's Band, recorded in New York on October 25, 1905 (ibid., LE 10) and the Six Brown Brothers' "Bull Frog Blues," recorded in New York on June 19, 1916 (CD: *Ragtime*; CD 2, ibid., LE 11).

Cajun Music

Another major contributor to the spread of European folk music in the United States was Acadian culture. The Cajuns are descended from these French settlers, who came from Normandy (and Bretagne) and settled in the region of Canada then known as Acadia, now Nova Scotia and parts of New Brunswick. Since the mid-eighteenth century the Cajuns have been found mainly in Louisiana, where they have cultivated a musical culture strongly influenced by the English during their time in Canada. This was another route by which Scottish fiddle music came to Louisiana, already a French colony, and to the rest of the American South. This helped to pave the way for an early fusion of Irish-Scottish music and Nordic swing with the music already heard in and around New Orleans. Cajun music, which is seen as a branch of country music, counts among its identifying characteristics the accordion, brought to America by German or French immigrants. At the end of the nineteenth century, Creole accordionists began to import offbeat rhythms and a blues quality into Cajun music. This influence can be heard in the piece "Lake Arthur Stomp" (LP: *Musica dei Cajuns della Louisiana: Louisiana Cajun French Music*; Albatros, USA Folk & Blues, LE 12).

6

Collaborations between early jazz musicians such as Buddy Bolden and New Orleans Cajuns provide evidence of a musical exchange. In his autobiography, the New Orleans bassist Pops Foster also describes playing hillbilly music—including a piece called "Chicken Reel"—and schottisches for the Cajuns near Fort Barrow, all part of his normal dance repertoire.[7]

String Bands and Brass-and-String Bands: One Conduit for the Emergence of Jazz

String bands were the preferred dance bands in the southern United States during the nineteenth and early twentieth centuries. While brass bands performed mainly at parades, concerts, political rallies, and so on, the majority of dance jobs fell to string bands, consisting of anything between two and ten musicians playing a variety of instruments. One or more violins, double bass, mandolin, guitar, or banjo were featured alongside either flutes or various brass instruments. Some bands used the wind section of the group for open-air events, with the strings taking over when the party moved indoors. This practice suggests a musical/structural relationship between the two sets of musicians.

The names used for these varying ensembles were somewhat haphazard: depending on the engagement, they might call themselves a string band, string orchestra, brass and string band, and so forth. As Karl Koenig notes: "Every early brass band contained a string band within its organization. . . . They were not 'brass band' musicians, or 'classical' musicians, nor just 'dance' musicians, but musicians that were capable of playing all styles. They played the style of music that the job demanded. . . . The technique of improvising was not stressed at the beginning of jazz. It was merely used to fill parts that could not be played as heard or remembered after hearing a new piece."[8]

These dance and all-purpose bands were hired for various events. The leaders were often trumpeters or violinists who generally played the given melody "straight."

One common term for these bands was "brass and string band": New Orleans was home to the Magnolia Brass and String Band in 1852, the Union Brass and String Band in 1860, the Clinton Independent Brass and String Band in 1870, and the New Orleans Brass and String Band in 1871, among others.[9]

Around 1890 a standard instrumentation emerged, with the violin as lead, accompanied by flute, cornet, clarinet, trombone, piano, bass, and drums. This signaled an evolution toward jazz band instrumentation. The most common format for seven-man ensembles at the birth of jazz after 1890 was violin, cornet, trombone, clarinet, bass fiddle, guitar or banjo, and drums; here, too, the violin was the lead voice. Violinists could read music and as such tended to be the musical leaders as well. According to Danny Barker, the "violinist played an important part in the first jazz bands: first—he added dignity; second—he played the lead; most times he was also the instructor as musical knowledge and technique was not too fine in many of these bands."[10]

The following bands held to this basic, later-New Orleans jazz instrumentation including violin: the Tio-Doublet Orchestra (or String Band) (1888–90); the Magnolia Orchestra (also occasionally known as the Magnolia String Band or Brass and String Band) (1891–1914); the Jimmy Palao Band (around 1900); the Woodland Band of LaPalace (including Kid Ory, trombone and other instruments, around 1905); John Robichaux's Orchestra (sometimes with two violins, 1895–1927); the Silver Leaf Orchestra (1897–1917); the (Original) Olympia Orchestra (1900–1915); the Imperial Orchestra (1901–8); the Superior Orchestra (1908–13); the Peerless Orchestra (1911–13); the Original Creole Orchestra (1913–17); the Tuxedo Orchestra, the Superior Band of New Orleans (with Buddie Johnson, trombone, Bunk Johnson, trumpet, Big Eye Louis Nelson, clarinet, Billy Marrero, bass, Walter Brandy, drums, Peter Bocage, violin, Richard Payne, guitar) and numerous others.

This type of ensemble was also used a great deal in vaudeville, as in a band that included Clarence Williams (vocals, piano), John Lindsay (bass), Jimmy Noone (clarinet), Bebe Ridgley (trombone), Oscar Celestin (trumpet), Tom Benton (guitar or mandolin), Johnny St. Cyr (banjo), and Armand J. Piron (violin), around 1914, or the King Oliver Band (around 1922).[11]

New Orleans string bands, later often referred to as jazz bands, included the following: the Excelsior String Band (Economy Hall, December 17, 1881); the String Band of the Excelsior Brass Band, which went by the name of Professor Baquet's String Band; the Eagle Band (1907); the Bud Scott String Band; the Italian String Band (around 1880); the Tio-Doublet Orchestra (1888–90); the Magnolia Orchestra (1891–1914); the Robichaux Orchestra (1895–1927); the Silver Leaf Orchestra (1901–8), and so on.[12]

As Karl Koenig notes:

Around 1917, the string band, in general, became known as a jazz band. This evolution of the stylistic character of dance bands can be seen and documented as a direct evolution from the string band of the later decades of the nineteenth century, to the jazz band in 1917. . . . The instrumentation gradually changed, the violin and flute being dropped, with the cornet, clarinet and trombone becoming the front line instruments. . . . The violinist was the leader of the string ensembles and we find some 27 violinists playing in New Orleans string/dance bands. The leaders included names such as A. J. Piron, Peter Bocage, Bud Scott etc.[13]

The fact that notable early jazz musicians started out on violin is further evidence of the instrument's general importance—and as a corollary, the importance of popular fiddle music—to early jazz. Examples of this trend include Tom Brown (trombone), Peter Bocage (trumpet), Freddie Keppard (trumpet), Lonnie Johnson (guitar), Bernard Addison (guitar and banjo, later with Fletcher Henderson), Henry "Red" Allen (trumpet) as well as his father, Meade "Lux" Lewis (piano), and Nick LaRocca (trumpet), the leader of the Original Dixieland Jazz Band who played with violinist Henry Young (in 1905) and with local string trios in New Orleans. (The German jazz historian Horst H. Lange examines the significance of the Original Dixieland Jazz Band to early jazz in his book *Als der Jazz begann 1916-1934: Die Anfänge des instrumentalen Jazz—Von der Original Dixieland Jazz Band bis Louis Armstrong*, published in 2000.[14])

Karl Koenig, who has collected string band arrangements, and with whom this author and other musicians performed them in Graz, Austria, in 2005, points in his publications to the significance of these large-format string bands in the emergence of jazz. However, since the bands mainly played arranged material, space for individual phrasing, variation, and improvisation must have been rather limited.

That possibility was much greater in the small string bands, particularly the string trios.[15] The musical structure of these small string bands was based on Scottish fiddle music, with the fiddle (later the violin) functioning as lead instrument and accompanied by banjo, guitar, or mandolin. Arrangements for the larger string and brass bands led to the composed passages in New Orleans jazz, which were usually arranged in three voices.

The playing practice—again descended from Scottish fiddle music—in the string trios, on the other hand, related to the origins of improvisation (both individual and collective), phrasing, and articulation.

In "Acorn Stomp" (cᴅ: *Times Ain't Like They Used to Be: Early American Rural Music, Classic Recordings of the 1920s and '30s*, vol. 3; Yazoo 2047, 1928, p 1999, ʟᴇ 13), played by the East Texas Serenaders, a string quintet consisting of violin, guitar, mandolin, tenor banjo, and cello, melodic-rhythmic structures derived from the Scotch snap can be discerned. Offbeat and generally "swinging" eighth-note phrasing—in some ways similar to ragtime—are prevalent, establishing a musical and developmental connection to the specific phrasing technique of traditional jazz.

This ("white") string band music, played by black musicians in identical or similar groups with an African aesthetic, developed a "dirty," "hot" intonation and was partly augmented by rifflike passages. A typical example is "Black Bayou" (Blind Pete, fiddle, and George Ryan, guitar; recorded by John A. Lomax in Little Rock, Arkansas, September 27, 1934; cᴅ: *Black Appalachia: String Bands, Songsters and Hoedowns*; Rounder Records 11661-1823-2, p & c 1999, ʟᴇ 14).

9

The typical phrasing and articulation of the "white" string trios is also relevant to blues interpretations and other musical forms played by "black" string trios. The blue notes and rifflike structures used here can also be found in traditional British folk music, as described in chapter 1. "Beaver Slide Rag" (Peg Leg Howell and Eddie Anthony; CD: *The Cornshucker's Frolic: Downhome Music and Entertainment from the American Countryside; Classic Recordings from the 1920s and 30s*, vol. 2; Yazoo 2046, p 1999, LE 15) offers one example.

In general, it can be concluded that black musicians working in this genre adopted the repertoire as well as the basic phrasing and articulation of the prevalent popular and dance music of the "white" small string bands, then modified it with elements of their African aesthetic.

If we consider all the relevant connections in music history, the following picture emerges of the musical properties of ensembles known as string bands: although these bands tended to be dominated by horns (mostly trumpet and trombone) and clarinet, the violinists were "classically" trained and led the bands to a great extent. However, since the Scottish fiddle tradition was the most practiced dance and popular music of the nineteenth century, it can be inferred that these classically trained violinists also possessed the swing feeling of the fiddlers, which they transferred to their own music. The Scottish-descended phrasing can also be heard in the small string bands.

The Role of Small String Bands in the Musical Development of the First Jazz Trumpeter, Buddy Bolden (1877–1931), and the Emergence of New Orleans Jazz

A quotation from Karl Koenig will serve as an introduction here:

> The Bolden Band was a string band. The violinist played the lead part in the band and was expected, and trained, to stomp off the band. As the violin could be relied on to stay with the straight lead or melody, the clarinet and cornet were released to play variations on the melody. In this way it was possible to have three lead voices in the band which were not playing exactly the same thing but were still fitting within the original melody. The recollections of men who actually played with the Bolden Band leave us in no doubt about two facts: it was a skilled music band and the regular personnel always included a violin player.[16]

The American jazz scholar Don Marquis, who works in New Orleans, offers numerous clues to Buddy Bolden's musical roots in his book *In Search of Buddy Bolden*. Bolden grew up partly in Irish and German neighborhoods in New Orleans; musical influences from these areas can be traced in his style.[17] Marquis also makes the following observations, fundamental to this theme: "Buddy Bolden developed his style in the small string band playing for dances and parties rather than apprenticing in parades . . . but he did not have a regular brass band. . . . The fact that very few people remember much about Bolden's street music career makes it seem a rather insignificant part of his musical development. . . . His efforts took the playing 'wide-open' on the cornet . . . playing in up-tempo or ragging the hymns, street songs, and dance tunes to create a musical sound that people were unfamiliar with"[18]—which points to the use of the original Scotch snap. This statement also suggests another important developmental connection between the music of the nineteenth-century American small string bands, the influence of Scottish fiddle music, and the musical conceptions of New Orleans jazz. The New Orleans banjo player Danny Barker, in his book *Buddy Bolden and the Last Days of Storyville*,[19] also tells the story of Bolden being the star attraction in a band with Buddy Bottley in New Orleans's Lincoln Park around 1890, where the (dance) repertoire consisted of schottisches, quadrilles, one-steps, and original blues pieces. This indicates on the one hand the dominance of the Northern European repertoire in this milieu, and on the other the commingling of the diverse musical styles relevant to this scene.

New Orleans was home to dozens of small string bands in the second half of the nineteenth century. One of the most popular was the band led by Charlie "Sweet Lovin" Galloway, who played rhythmically animated solos, similar to the Scottish music performed by string trios. Galloway's string band was also Buddy Bolden's first musical contact, with the exception of his teacher, Manuel Hall. Bolden spent a great deal of time with Galloway, as did other young musicians, and played in his band—a changing ensemble composed primarily of violin(s), cornet, clarinet, trombone, guitar or banjo, and double bass. Bolden came of age in Galloway's band and developed his own style, influenced by the leader's fiddle and mandolin solos. He also developed his own band, which initially was subject to frequent personnel changes, including Galloway on guitar. Bolden also tempted trombonist Frankie Dusen, clarinetist Frankie Lewis, and banjo player Lorenzo Staulz away from Galloway, acquiring their rhythmic drive and fire for his own group.

Donald M. Marquis has this to say about the situation:

Rags and blues had been played occasionally by the brass bands; now Bolden was playing them at smaller gatherings with his smaller band. His particular brand of ragtime or blues did not occur by accident. What other bands had been doing in the street parades ("ragging" the tunes, as indicated by Papa Jack Laine), Bolden began doing for a different audience—the dancers. The old string bands were overshadowed by Bolden's brassmen, and in this new arrangement the strings became part of the rhythm section. There was no one great influence on Bolden's cornet playing, no "king" to copy or dethrone. Buddy took musical bits from his background and environment and put them together in a way that utilized what he thought was best about the music, blending the parts with his own talent and personality. . . . Also by 1900 the makeup of the band was becoming solidified. In [trombone player Willy] Cornish's absence Bolden had tried using various trombone players including Ed Jones, James Philips, and Frankie Dusen, who at that time was young and inexperienced. When Cornish returned in 1899, Buddy had worked out his style. Cornish was a large man like Bolden and had the power to bring the brass into a more dominant role in the string band.[20]

The New Orleans bassist Pops Foster was, by his own account, mostly active playing dance music in string trios between 1902 and 1906.[21] Foster offers essential proof of the role of Irish-Scottish music—part of the regular dance repertoire of the small string bands and also of Cajun bands—in the development of New Orleans jazz in his autobiography, New Orleans Jazzman. Besides information about numerous significant violinists in New Orleans bands, Foster offers the following:[22]

> "There were a lot of string trios around playing street corners."
> "The band was usually a string trio. String trios would get a whole lot of jobs."
> "It was a lot more pleasure for me to play in the string trios than in the brass bands."[23]

Concerning the violin and violinists:

> "For a long time the violin was the top instrument around New Orleans."
> "The fiddler usually could read and taught the rest of the band the numbers, and played a whole lot of everything."[24]
> "Emile Bigard played violin in Kid Ory's band."
> "I played with Freddie Keppard before he left New Orleans" [in 1909 Jimmie Palao was playing violin].[25]

In addition to Bolden, other early jazz musicians, both black and white (including Original Dixieland Jazz Band trumpeter Nick LaRocca), also developed their styles in small string bands—another substantiation of the decisive causal relationship between string band practice, New Orleans jazz, and historical Dixieland. Danny Barker offers evidence that small string band music exerted an influence on syncopated jazz phrasing: "There were jazz bands of six, seven and eight pieces, but the string groups were the most popular because they were more rhythmic and spirited with the violin, guitar and mandolin, and a few also added

12

the accordion and the concertina."[26] This important statement refers once again to the basic, rhythmic fiddle technique of Scottish music as well as giving a nod, with the mention of the accordion, to the influence of Cajun music.

In light of the developments cited above, it can be reasonably concluded that the phrasing techniques of traditional jazz bands (triple eighth-note phrasing, use of the Scotch snap), from King Oliver to Louis Armstrong—for instance in "Cornet Chop Suey" (from the Louis Armstrong Hot Five, Chicago, February 26, 1926; CD: *Louis Armstrong: The Hot Fives*, vol. 1, CBS 4672782, p 1988, LE 16)— evoke the Irish-Scottish musical tradition, by way of the small string bands. The fact that Louis Armstrong's repertoire consists mainly of songs and ragtime-oriented pieces, with few blues recordings, is another pointer to the integrality, for both black and white bands, of primarily European-influenced dance music as a strong determinant in the development of jazz and swing. The recording "At the Jazz Band Ball" by Nick LaRocca and his Original Dixieland Jazz Band (New York City, September 3, 1917; CD: *Ragtime to Jazz 2, 1916–1922*; Timeless Records LC 5326, p & c 1997, LE 17), with its prominent use of the Scotch snap, underlines this conclusion.

The Emergence of Swing Rhythm Accompaniment in Folk, Popular Music, and Jazz

The general acceptance by jazz history of the importance of particular types of African music to the rhythmic component of jazz and music in the jazz idiom can be confirmed in as much as accompaniment structures in Latin and Central American music, and in Latin jazz, naturally evolved from African American musical practice. However, swing accompaniment (the ride cymbal pattern) and the related melodic-rhythmic swing feeling evident since the 1920s, especially since the advent of American folk and popular music (for example, both early and modern forms of country music), have their roots in the rhythmic melodies of Northern European folk music. The folk and popular music of the North American white populace, starting at the latest in the nineteenth century, as well as the triplet phrasing specific to jazz, are descended from Scottish, Irish, and Scandinavian folk music.

This theory began to develop with my experience as a pop musician in Stockholm at the end of the 1960s. On a visit to northern Sweden I became acquainted with the rural fiddle music of the region. The swing phrasing, similar to jazz, in this music can be found nowhere else, other than in and around Scottish-Irish folk music. Discussions with scholars of African studies, for example, provided no evidence of any comparable rhythmic phenomena in the music of Africa. The fact that the majority of early academic books on jazz history were written by jazz

13

what does that mean?!

researchers with an inherent bias toward African studies explains the emphasis placed on African music in the development of jazz and American popular music.

In addition to other U.S. immigrants from Ireland, Scotland, and Great Britain, Scandinavians settled in large numbers in the northern Midwest, establishing "Swedish communities," for example. The folk music of these Scandinavian immigrants is also part of the basis for North American folk music.

One example of the influence of Swedish folk music from the Dalarna region, with a typical two-beat accented on two and four, and triplet-based phrasing similar to swing, is the "Karl-Johann March" performed by the group Kurbits, whose seven violins embody a living folk music tradition (CD: *Folk-Music from Sweden*, ARC Music EUCD 1617, LE 18). The swing-rhythm accompaniment is integral to the multivoiced melodic-rhythmic structure of this music, and part of its authenticity.

This characteristic melodic/rhythmic model can also be found in solo fiddle music with chorded string accompaniment. The fiddle music of the Shetland Islands, off the northern coast of Scotland, follows the same template. Typical examples include "Three Reels from Unst," "Three Reels from Bressay," and "Two Herra Tunes for the Foula Reel" (CD: *Shetland Fiddle Music, Scottish Tradition*, vol. 4, 1973, LE 19). Numerous other recorded examples of this and all aspects of Scottish folk music are available in the wide-ranging Scottish Tradition series, released as CDTRAX 9004 on Greentrax Recordings, Edinburgh (Scotland).

A vital factor in the emergence of swing accompaniment rhythm is that the aforementioned melodic/rhythmic model is achieved by string instruments (guitar and/or banjo). Thus, the melodic rhythm and the accompanying rhythm merge into a single entity, coupled to the basic rhythmic pulse—the groove. This musical phenomenon attained a far-reaching significance in North American folk music, in the nineteenth century or earlier, and became the essential rhythmic foundation for the development of the following musical styles up to the present day:

1. American folk music: In American folk music we can recognize the Scottish-Irish fiddle practice already discussed. It is evident both in solos and accompaniment, as in the banjo accompaniment to "Two Italians/Red Bird" (CD: *The Music of Kentucky, Early American Rural Classics 1927-37*, vol. 2; Yazoo 2014, ibid., LE 20) and also in Swedish-derived folk music with banjo accompaniment, for example "The Romisch Lady" (ibid., LE 21). Both of these examples were recorded by Alan Lomax, who described the music as indigenous to America without referencing its European roots. The banjo accompaniment in these pieces features the swing rhythm that would later be associated with jazz.

These traditions can also be heard in the folk music of the Appalachian Mountains. Another characteristic of this region's music is the dulcimer, a string instrument providing swing accompaniment derived from Northern European melodic rhythms, as in "Amazing Grace." (LP: *Musica Strumentale degli Appalachi: Instrumental Music from the Southern Appalachians*; Albatros, USA Folk & Blues, VPA 8301, LE 22).

2. Hillbilly and country music: No forms of folk music were as prized as Scottish fiddle music and the rural fiddle tradition. They survived in the Appalachians into the twentieth century and, in combination with the banjo, formed the basis for hillbilly and country music (compare "Ned Went A-Fishin'," CD: *The Music of Kentucky*, vol. 1; Yazoo 2013, LE 23).

3. Minstrel shows—cakewalk: Many minstrel show tunes were taken from Scottish or Irish jigs and reels, based once again on the fiddle and its specific playing technique. The use of the same tunes in folk dance, in fiddle folk music, and as theater music in the nineteenth century underlines how supra-stylistic this music was. The further development of Irish-influenced fiddle music was also motivated by its use as cakewalk music in minstrel shows, mostly as accompaniment and comparable to the ride cymbal pattern that emerged later ("Coon from Tennessee," LP: *Blacks Whites and Blues*; CBS 52796, LE 24).

Many traditional jazz musicians, such as Lester Young's family, played in minstrel shows and were influenced by this tradition, transferring its rhythmic and melodic structures to jazz.

4. Honky-tonk and the Harlem piano style: Swing and the swinging accompaniment of the entertainment piano styles known as honky-tonk and Harlem style are, as evidenced by "Bar of Hanky Panky" (CD: *USA*, Sonia CD 77087, LE 25) also derived from the Northern European tradition.

5. Jazz: The swing accompaniment rhythm, played on both guitar and banjo, was *the* modern rhythm of American popular music in the nineteenth and early twentieth centuries, comparable to the dominance of rock rhythm in the 1960s. This basic rhythm, prevalent in white dance and popular music, was also played by black musicians; by reproducing the latest popular music, they were able to attract more work and thus advance their social status. For this reason, the swing accompaniment rhythm was not only used in the cakewalk as well as folk and country music, etc., but also became the model for the rhythm sections of swing bands, which originally played dance music. The swing rhythm was subsequently transferred to the hi-hat and the well-known jazz ride-cymbal pattern, adopted by virtually all jazz drummers with the exception of those playing Latin jazz, jazz/rock, or free jazz. In the later stages of development, drummers such as Elvin Jones, Tony Williams, and Jack DeJohnette extensively varied and modified the pattern.

When the Fletcher Henderson Orchestra—the first swing big band in jazz history—started up in 1923, rhythmic accompaniment was often provided solely by the banjo player, Charlie Dixon. The rhythm section gradually evolved with the occasional addition of a tuba player and, finally, of the drummer Kaiser Marshall. According to a statement by the American Armstrong biographer James Lincoln Collier in Graz in 2000, Kaiser Marshall was the first drummer to play the swing pattern on the hi-hat—around ten years before Count Basie's drummer Jo Jones. It would seem that Marshall, a relative latecomer to the Henderson rhythm section, adapted his playing to the existing banjo accompaniment, becoming (probably) the first drummer to introduce the ride cymbal pattern to jazz. "The Dicty Blues" (recorded August 9, 1923, CD: *The Fletcher Henderson Story*, vol. 1; Thesaurus of Classic Jazz, Columbia 57596, LE 26) is played by Henderson and his orchestra with only the banjo as rhythmic accompaniment; "Oh Baby" (recorded April 6, 1928, ibid., vol. 2, LE 27) features a complete rhythm section with Charlie Dixon on banjo, a tuba, and Kaiser Marshall on drums. The Fletcher Henderson Orchestra began as a dance band, as did many others, using popular "raggy" rhythms. Henderson himself came from a middle-class black family and grew up isolated from lower-income black society, in a milieu dominated by white (dance) music.

The banjo, playing the swing accompaniment rhythm, also took on most of the rhythmic duties in recordings made between 1922 and 1925 by the New Orleans Rhythm Kings, one of the first significant white jazz bands. The Rhythm Kings were pioneers in this respect, since black bands at the time were using accompaniments based more on quarter notes ("Bugle Call Blues," CD: *Dixieland to Swing: The Golden Collection*, vol. 1; Retro R2CD 4009, LE 28).

Bennie Moten's Kansas City Orchestra used banjo alongside tuba and drums as its rhythm section from its first recordings in 1923 until 1930. Eventually, as with most other bands of the period, the guitar supplanted the banjo. In the end, the march-influenced rhythmic drum pattern from New Orleans and Chicago remained only in the 4/4 guitar chording typical of, for example, the Count Basie Orchestra. The rhythm in Moten's band around 1928 was in a clear two-beat style, with the accents on two and four. The rhythmic patterns played on wood blocks may also be heard in earlier British folk music ("It's Hard to Laugh or Smile," LP: *Bennie Moten's Kansas City Orchestra*, vol. 2, 1928–1929; RCA 741078, Black & White, vol. 80, LE 29).

The banjo also played this original accompanying role in the swing orchestras of Duke Ellington and Louis Armstrong in the 1920s and '30s, as well as in Jelly Roll Morton's Red Hot Peppers ("Kansas City Stomp," 1929) and in Louis Armstrong's Hot Five in 1925 and '26, with Johnny St. Cyr playing the instrument. In "Gut Bucket Blues" (CD: *Louis Armstrong: The Hot Fives*, CBS 4608212, LE 30), for instance, there is a clear similarity to Irish banjo practice. The aforementioned swing accompaniment rhythm can be heard on "Oriental Strut" (ibid., LE 31).

6. The originally Northern European swing rhythm was "repatriated" into the European Alpine region from the 1950s onward by the brothers Vilko and Slavko Avsenik, with their ensemble the Original Oberkrainer in Slovenia. The Oberkrainer musicians were previously active in the Radio Big Band Ljubljana, and their jazz phrasing brought a subtle change to the Alpine polkas and waltzes composed or recomposed by Slavko Avsenik. The guitar accompaniment is often marked by the two-beat feeling familiar from swing and American popular music in the first half of the twentieth century, such as the fox-trot. The eighth-note phrasing on the accordion suggests Scottish fiddle phrasing (also that of Swiss folk music), closing the circle of the swing phenomenon from Northern Europe over to North America and then back to middle Europe ("Im Schweizer Hochland," CD: *Volkstümliche Melodien mit Slavko Avsenik und seinen Original Oberkrainern*; Activ Records AG, CD 5-2568, LE 32).

7. Funk and hip-hop: The swing and shuffle rhythms heard in folk banjo accompaniment are also, in double-time form, basic to funk and hip-hop. In this case, they appear as a triplet-based superimposition onto a basically straight quarter- and eighth-note rhythm. This simultaneous dualism of binary and ternary rhythmic schemes in a single meter and piece has existed in pop music at least since the advent of reggae. One example of fusing jazz and hip-hop is American jazz pianist Adam Holzmann's "Mad Cow Disease" (CD: *Adam Holzmann & Brave New World: The Big Picture*; Escapade Music 03653-2, LE 33). Another is "Got to Be Able to Know" by guitarist Jean Paul Bourelly, a musical successor to Jimi Hendrix (CD: *Jean Paul Bourelly and the Blue Wave Bandits: Saints & Sinners*; DIW 872, LE 34).

These more recent examples exhibit grooves that would not have been possible without the development of the traditional swing accompaniment rhythm described above. Evidence of this rhythm in countless traditional and modern musical styles, such as hip-hop jazz, confirms it as a globalizing phenomenon.

LIST OF LISTENING EXAMPLES

LE 1: "To Answer the Peacock," CD: *To Answer the Peacock: Music for the Scottish Fiddle*; Brian McNeil; FMS Records 2084, p & c 1998.

LE 2: "Comin' thro' the Rye," CD: *Songs of Scotland*; Marie McLaughlin, Malcolm Martineau, with Isobel Frayling-Cork; Hyperion CDA67106, c 1999.

LE 3: "The Fairy Reel," CD: *Shetland Fiddle Music*; Scottish Tradition Series, vol. 4, School of Scottish Studies: University of Edinburgh; Greentrax Recordings 9004, c & p 1993.

LE 4: "It's Time for Me to Rise Up," CD: *Music from the Western Isles*; Scottish Tradition Series, vol. 2; Greentrax Recordings CDTRAX 9002, c 1992.

LE 5: "Diddling & Mouth-Organ," CD: *Bothy Ballads, Music from the North-East*; Scottish Tradition Series, vol. 1; Greentrax Recordings CDTRAX 9001, c & p 1993.

LE 6: "One Day as I Roamed the Hills," CD: *Waulking Songs from Barra*; Scottish Tradition Series, vol. 3; Greentrax Recordings CDTRAX 9003, c & p 1993.

LE 7: "Boil the Breakfast Early," CD: *The Best of the Chieftains*; Columbia 4716662, p 1992, Sony Music.

LE 8: "Suite de l'Oust et du Lie," CD: *Pipes & Drums from Celtic Brittany: Bagadu du Moulin Vert*; ARC Music, EUCD 1508, p & c 1999.

LE 9: "A Coon Band Contest," Vess L. Ossman Banjo-Solo, July 19, 1900; CD: *Ragtime*, Jazz Tribune n 42, Ragtime (1900–1930), CD 1, RCA LC 0316, Compilation BMG France, p & c 1995.

LE 10: "Silence and Fun," Sousa's Band, New York, October 25, 1905; CD: *Ragtime*; CD 1, ibid.

LE 11: "Bull Frog Blues," the Six Brown Brothers, New York, June 19, 1916; CD: *Ragtime*; CD 2, ibid.

LE 12: "Lake Arthur Stomp," LP: *Musica dei Cajuns della Lousiana: Louisiana Cajun French Music*; Albatros, USA Folk & Blues.

LE 13: "Akorn Stomp," East Texas Serenaders, 1928; CD: *Times Ain't Like They Used to Be: Early American Rural Music, Classic Recordings of the 1920s and '30s*, vol. 3; Yazoo 2047, p 1999.

LE 14: "Black Bayou," Blind Pete (fiddle) and George Ryan (guitar), recorded by John A. Lomax in Little Rock, Arkansas, September 27, 1934; CD: *Black Appalachia: String Bands, Songsters and Hoedowns*; Rounder Records 11661-1823-2, p & c 1999.

LE 15: "Beaver Slide Rag," Peg Leg Howell and Eddie Anthony; CD: *The Cornshucker's Frolic: Downhome Music and Entertainment from the American Countryside; Classic Recordings from the 1920s and '30s*, vol. 2; Yazoo 2046, p 1999.

LE 16: "Cornet Chop Suey," Louis Armstrong Hot Fives, Chicago, February 26, 1926; CD: *Louis Armstrong: The Hot Fives*, vol. 1; CBS 4672782, p 1988.

LE 17: "At the Jazz Band Ball," Original Dixieland Jazz Band, CD: *Ragtime to Jazz 2, 1916–1922*; Timeless Records LC 5326, p & c 1997.

LE 18: "Karl-Johannmarschen," CD: *Folk-Music from Sweden*; ARC Music EUCD 1617.

LE 19: "Two Herra Tunes for the Foula Reel," CD: *Shetland Fiddle Music, Scottish Tradition*, vol. 4, 1973, Scottish Tradition Series; Greentrax Recordings CDTRAX 9004, Edinburgh (Scotland).

LE 20: "Two Italians/Red Bird," CD: *The Music of Kentucky, Early American Rural Classics, 1927-37*, vol. 2; Yazoo 2014.

LE 21: "The Romisch Lady," ibid.

LE 22: "Amazing Grace," LP: *Musica Strumentale degli Appalachi: Instrumental Music from the Southern Appalachians*; Albatros, USA Folk & Blues, VPA 8301.

LE 23: "Ned Went A-Fishin'," CD: *The Music of Kentucky*, vol. 1; Yazoo 2013.

LE 24: "Coon from Tennessee," LP: *Blacks Whites and Blues*; CBS 52796.

LE 25: "Bar of Hanky Panky," CD: *USA*; Sonia CD 77087.

LE 26: "The Dicty Blues," CD: *The Fletcher Henderson Story*, vol. 1, Thesaurus of Classic Jazz, Columbia 57596.

LE 27: "Oh Baby," ibid., vol. 2.

LE 28: "Bugle Call Blues," CD: *Dixieland to Swing: The Golden Collection*, vol. 1; Retro R2CD 4009.

LE 29: "It's Hard to Laugh or Smile," LP: *Bennie Moten's Kansas City Orchestra*, vol. 2, *1928–1929*; RCA 741078, Black & White, vol. 80.

LE 30: "Gut Bucket Blues," CD: *Louis Armstrong: The Hot Fives*; CBS 4608212.

LE 31: "Oriental Strut," ibid.

LE 32: "Im Schweizer Hochland," CD: *Volkstümliche Melodien mit Slavko Avsenik und seinen Original Oberkrainern*; Activ Records AG, CD 5-2568.

LE 33: "Mad Cow Disease," CD: *Adam Holzman & Brave New World: The Big Picture*; Escapade Music 03653-2.

LE 34: "Got to Be Able to Know," CD: *Jean Paul Bourelly and the Blue Wave Bandits Saints & Sinners*; DIW 872.

NOTES

1. See David Nichols, ed., *The Cambridge History of American Music* (Cambridge: Cambridge University Press, 1998).

2. See Franz Kerschbaumer, *Der Einfluss der iro-schottischen Musik auf die Entstehung des Jazz*, in *Jazzforschung/Jazz Research*, vol. 36, Akademische Druck- und Verlagsanstalt Graz/Austria 2004, pp. 97-106.

3. Peter Van der Merve, *Origins of the Popular Style: The Antecedents of Twentieth-Century Popular Music* (Oxford: Clarendon Press, 1992).

4. Karl Koenig, *Walking to the Gloryland: A History of the Cakewalk* (Running Springs, CA: Basin Street Press, 2000), p. 57.

5. Ibid., p. 23.

6. Giles Oakley, *The Devil's Music: A History of the Blues* (London: British Broadcasting Corp., 1976), pp. 29-30.

7. Pops See Foster, *The Autobiography of Pops Foster, New Orleans Jazzman, as Told to Tom Stoddard* (Berkeley: University of California Press, 1971), p. 7.

8. Karl Koenig, *The String Band: The Ancestor of the Jazz Band* (Running Springs, CA: Basin Street Press), p. 1.

9. Ibid., pp. 9-89.

10. Danny Barker, *Buddy Bolden and the Last Days of Storyville*, ed. Alyn Shipton (London: Cassell, Wellington House, 1998), p. 11.

11. Koenig, *String Band*, p. 111.

12. Ibid., pp. 4-93, 104-105.

13. Ibid., p. 2.

14. Horst H. Lange, *Als der Jazz begann 1916-1934: Die Anfänge des instrumentalen Jazz—Von der Original Dixieland Jazz Band bis Louis Armstrong* (Hildesheim, Zurich: Olms Presse, 2000).

15. See Koenig, *String Band*, pp. 94-95.

16. Koenig, *String Band*, p. 3.

17. See Donald M. Marquis, *In Search of Buddy Bolden: First Man of Jazz* (Baton Rouge: Louisiana State University Press, 1978), p. 22.

18. Ibid., pp. 42–43.

19. See Barker, *Buddy Bolden*, p. 8

20. Marquis, *In Search of Buddy Bolden*, pp. 47–48.

21. Foster, *Autobiography of Pops Foster*, p. 177.

22. Ibid., pp. 43–58.

23. Ibid., p. 18.

24. Ibid., p. 75.

25. Ibid., pp. 49–54.

26. Barker, *Buddy Bolden*, p. 12.

ADDITIONAL LITERATURE

Burman-Hall, Linda Carol. "Southern American Folk Fiddling: Context and Styles." Doctoral dissertation, Princeton University, 1974; Xerox University Microfilms, Ann Arbor, MI 45106.

Hardie, Daniel. *The Birth of Jazz: Reviving the Music of the Bolden Era*. New York: iUniverse Inc., 2007.

Harer, Ingeborg. "Afrikanisierungs- und Europäisierungstendenzen? Quellen zur Frühgeschichte des Ragtime." *Jazzforschung/Jazz Research* 39, Festschrift: Franz Kerschbaumer. Akademische Druck- und Verlagsanstalt Graz/Austria, 2007, pp. 171–84.

Nathan, Hans. *Dan Emmett and the Rise of Early Negro Minstrelsy*. Norman: University of Oklahoma Press, 1962.

Van Buerkle, Jack, and Danny Barker. *Bourbon Street Black: The New Orleans Black Jazzman*. London: Oxford University Press, 1973.

BRUCE BOYD RAEBURN

2 / BEYOND THE "SPANISH TINGE"
HISPANICS AND LATINOS IN EARLY
NEW ORLEANS JAZZ

D espite their relative absence as protagonists in most discussions of jazz
origins, musicians of Hispanic and Latino heritage contributed to the early
development of jazz in important ways. Their story is less about the transmission of European and African musical traits to the New World than it is
illustrative of how Old World traditions were transmuted into new forms
and practices that suited the New Orleans environment by musicians from various creolized communities, a cultural context pervaded by an African American
vernacular sensibility at the time jazz was coalescing. In this essay I will therefore
seek to move beyond the concept of "Spanish tinge" introduced by Jelly Roll
Morton in his Library of Congress interviews with Alan Lomax in 1938, a cate-
gorical imperative that has hitherto served as the alpha and omega of discussions
about Hispanic and Latino contributions to New Orleans jazz, by concentrating
on the musical actions of individuals in a regionally discrete environment, while
also offering perspective on how the term "Spanish tinge" has influenced jazz
history and historiography. Besides describing clave-based rhythms and related
musical practices,[1] and because Latinos often inhabited the penumbra between
white and black racial stereotypes, "Spanish tinge" could be used strategically by
New Orleans jazz musicians as a racial masquerade to thwart segregation when it
got in the way of their musical interests. Like Rudyard Kipling's proverbial "ele-
phant's trunk," the "Spanish tinge" can be stretched as needed, which has led
many of the scholars who study it to challenge the idea that jazz origins should
be explained by a "born in New Orleans" thesis without recourse to broader
perspectives.

I shall make my position on these issues clear from the outset: my belief is that
the proper locus for discussion of jazz origins *is* New Orleans and its immediate
hinterland, which does not eliminate the need to investigate pan-American antecedents to jazz or recognition of the affinities that existed within the circum-
Caribbean or Latin American cultural context. Yet dynamic models are necessary, and historical particularities must be respected, with due diligence given to
the role of human agency. One can agree with those "Spanish tinge" scholars
who eschew the standard theories of jazz origins that posit fusion of African and
European musical practices, simplistically assigning melody, harmony, and song

forms to Eurocentric conservatory and popular music traditions, and what Sam Floyd characterizes as "opposition" (call-and-response), rhythmic "overlap" (poly-rhythms), and antiphonal "indirection" (microtonal pitch bending) to Africa.[2] Thus, Place Congo in New Orleans becomes a repository of African continuity, a place where the bamboula, bongo, and calinda were danced within a ring, accompanied by drums, rattles, and stringed instruments reminiscent of Africa. But in exploring the cultural dynamics associated with Place Congo, Jerah Johnson emphasizes the vernacular transformation of such practices in New Orleans, the shifting of African into African American, which is similar to the strategy I want to employ in this essay.[3]

It is the blurring of ethnic boundaries and amateur and conservatory pedagogical traditions through an eclectic experimentation driven by creolized African American expressive modalities that interests me, which helps to explain how quotations from Italian operas that were performed at the French Opera House (and mimicked on the streets) are present in the recorded solos of Louis Armstrong in the 1920s and '30s, along with habanera rhythms denoting the influence of the "Spanish tinge" in recordings by King Oliver's Creole Jazz Band and others.[4] I believe that the essence of jazz resides in the expressive African American vernacular practices that transformed arias or habanera, including what Thomas Brothers identifies as "solo and cycle," but the various tools and raw materials that jazz musicians used were nevertheless contributed by many ethnicities.[5] On the functional level, New Orleans jazz represented an innovative vernacular approach to making music developed by an ethnically diverse community of skilled artisan and "blue collar" musicians to satisfy an equally diverse clientele in search of stimulating dance music. In order to properly understand the emergence of jazz, one must therefore examine the hybrid vernacular cultural systems that informed the regional market and how they were used by musicians to exchange ideas and generate work.

The New Orleans environment was particularly conducive to musical syncretism because of the coexistence of three systems of cultural production there: a process of creolization (including elements of *mestizaje*, a "fluidity of identity" rooted in the racial ambiguity intrinsic to creolized identities) deriving from the city's geographical proximity to Central America and the Caribbean ensconced clave and habanera in the city's variegated rhythmic "trick bag"; a trans-Atlantic cultural connection made New Orleans an early North American site of opera and *bals masqués*, in addition to European folk and popular music, such as Hungarian string bands that played "by ear" or the singer Jenny Lind; and from the watershed of the Mississippi River, an American vernacularism (driven primarily by African American practices) brought "alligator horse" ballads, minstrelsy, work songs, spirituals, and especially the blues into the mix.[6] The convergence of these discrete systems was unique to New Orleans, and jazz combined elements from all of them. Such systems were mutually reinforcing, and the source of the raw material mattered less than the vernacular process that transformed it. Explanations of the emergence of jazz that rely primarily on musicological concepts such as "Spanish tinge" do not adequately address how musicians of Latino and Hispanic heritage actively collaborated in the creation of New Orleans jazz. One must go beyond abstract concepts to discover who these people were and how they built a jazz culture in New Orleans through their relationships and associations, often in the face of social conventions that sought to inhibit such contact.

Given the prevailing Social Darwinist codes and attendant racism and anti-immigrant ethnocentrism present in the United States in the late nineteenth and early twentieth century, the degree to which Hispanics and Latinos interacted across the racial spectrum in New Orleans is notable. Demographic circumstances enabled connections across racial or ethnic boundaries, evident in ethnically diverse "crazy quilt" neighborhoods that stimulated cultural interaction and exchange. Tremé, the Seventh Ward, and especially the lower French Quarter had sizable Hispanic and Latino populations interspersed with Sicilians, Afro-French Creoles, and African Americans, despite the onus of segregation, because the settlement patterns predated the Jim Crow laws of the 1890s. Along with the uptown neighborhoods of Central City and the Irish Channel, and the West Bank community of Algiers, these "cultural estuaries" produced the vast majority of New Orleans jazz musicians in the early twentieth century. In these neighborhoods music pervaded the streets—via serenading, spasm bands, brass bands, and bandwagon "cutting contests"—so everyone within earshot could absorb musical innovations readily. Consequently, traditional elements that scholars have defined as "Spanish tinge," especially Afro-Latin habanera and clave rhythmic cells, Italian practices such as *solfeggio* and *bel canto*, and incipient African American ragtime and blues forms were quickly and widely disseminated, spreading to anyone who was receptive. One didn't have to be Hispanic, Latino, Italian American, or African American to respond to these practices or to use them, but it was the younger generation's inclination to rework this material into something new that accounted for the emergence of jazz.

"Crazy quilt" neighborhoods served as cultural wetlands because of the myriad of ethnic musical forms that coexisted in those environments and the ease of cross-fertilization that pertained there—everything was subject to reinvention. When the Afro-French pianist Jelly Roll Morton introduced the concept of "Spanish tinge" in his Library of Congress interviews with Alan Lomax in 1938, he talked about how New Orleans musicians "had their own way of doing":

In fact if you can't manage to put tinges of Spanish in your tunes, you will never be able to get the right seasoning, I call it, for jazz. . . . I heard a lot of Spanish tunes, and I tried to play them in correct tempo, but I personally didn't believe they were really perfected in the tempos. Now take "La Paloma," which I transformed in New Orleans style. You leave the left hand just the same. The difference comes in the right hand—in the syncopation, which gives it an entirely different color that really changes from red to blue.[7]

Morton "messed" with the tune to improve its musical and emotional content, retaining some essential features, while also customizing the rendition. He did the same with "Mamie's Blues," reconstructed from memory after hearing Mamie Desdoumes, an Afro-French pianist, playing the blues with a habanera rhythm in Central City, when he was a child visiting his godmother. This may have been a singular epiphany for Morton, but it is important to note that this practice was already commonplace in New Orleans when he first heard it. Among others, the Afro-Sicilian multi-instrumentalist Manuel Manetta, who lived in Algiers, also used habanera rhythms when he performed the blues on piano in Storyville.[8]

The creolized commingling of Afro-Latin rhythms with African American song forms was therefore widespread among so-called "downtown Frenchmen," even if they were women residing uptown in Central City or men living on the West Bank of the Mississippi River. The drummer Warren "Baby" Dodds commented on this proclivity, identifying it as a Creole trait, distinct from the way African Americans interpreted the blues uptown, but given the eclecticism intrinsic to jazz, the practice was bound to spread across ethnic boundaries.[9] Like Morton, New Orleans jazz musicians followed a functional imperative and sought to employ whatever musical ideas and tools would provide a competitive advantage with dance audiences and thus generate work. Over time, the habanera and clave spread among young musicians to the extent that it was needed, driven not only by the demands of a jazz-dancing public but also by the entourage that followed African American and Creole Mardi Gras Indian gangs who used *tresillo* as the ground rhythm for their chanting when roaming the streets on Mardi Gras and St. Joseph's Day, a tradition that has pre-jazz origins. In time, this rhythmic approach became the trademark of most brass band "second line" parades in the city as well, although it was increasingly applied to a repertoire that had little direct connection to Hispanic or Latin American sources.[10]

Musing on the ramifications of Morton's dictum to Lomax, John Storm Roberts concludes,

It is difficult to gauge the effect New Orleans's considerable Latin tinge had upon early jazz, but it may well be that much that has been labeled "creole" is either Cuban or syncretized with Cuban music. The rhythm of "Mo Pas

Lemme Ca," as played by clarinetist Albert Nicholas and other creole jazz musicians in the 1940s, is almost identical to the habanera rhythm, played fast and hot. While individual examples from a later period do not in any sense constitute proof, the available evidence does suggest that the Latin ingredients in early New Orleans jazz are more important than has been realized.[11]

In *The Latin Tinge* Roberts provides a balanced account of the Afro-Latin tendencies in North American music and discusses a process of variegated "absorption" in New Orleans, illustrated by the multiple uses to which W. H. Tyers's "Panama" (1911) was put by New Orleans bands:

> Tyers's original piano score used the habanera bass, and so did the orchestral arrangement played by the New Orleans society ragtime orchestra of Armand J. Piron.... "Panama" was widely played both as a rag and as a march. Most jazz groups dropped the habanera rhythm, but it can still be detected in a recording of the Olympia Brass Band of New Orleans. A long passage for marching drums, which is virtually identical to common conga patterns, leads to several final choruses in which the habanera and march-band rhythms are fused in an interesting demonstration of a halfway stage in the habanera's absorption.[12]

Theories advanced by the jazz critic Ernest Borneman in 1959 contrast sharply with Roberts's position. In two essays for *The Jazz Review* under the cumulative title "Creole Echoes," he argued that a "mature and developed form of Afro-Latin music similar to that of Martinique, Guadeloupe, Trinidad, and Santo Domingo" in mid-nineteenth-century New Orleans was the primary conduit for the development of jazz.[13] For Borneman, the proper dichotomy for discussion of jazz origins is European/African versus Asian/Arabic, with a "reunion of the African and European strains of Mediterranean music occurr[ing] during the Moorish conquest of Spain—a reunion which changed the structure of Spanish, Portuguese and Southern French music" prior to the colonization of the New World. "When slavery brought Africans once more into contact with Europeans," continues Borneman,

> the Africans recognized many familiar traits in the music of the Spanish, Portuguese and French settlers—but only a few familiar ones in the music of the other Europeans. Contrary to almost everything jazz critics have said, this familiarity was precisely in the field of harmony. While Anglo-Saxon music showed only harmonic similarities to African music, the French, Spanish and Portuguese settlers also showed similarities in the handling of rhythm and timbre. The slaves thus found it easier to assimilate the latter than the former, and this meant that Creole music had a head-start over the development of spirituals, blues and other forms of Anglo-African music.

Borneman concludes that

> jazz went tangent during the very years which, in recording history, appear to be the most fruitful ones—the years when the New Orleans jazzmen migrated to Chicago and were recorded there for the first time. It must have been during these very years that jazz lost its "Spanish tinge" and reduced itself to a series of improvisations in straight 2/4 and 4/4 time on Tin Pan Alley tunes. What got lost at that time was the essence of jazz: the African and Creole themes of the formative years, and the Creole manner of rhythmic accentuation.[14]

good

Although valuable for its insights, Borneman's account rests upon a myopic view of New Orleans culture, bereft of any grasp of the contradictions and ethnic diversity that existed within black, Creole, and white communities or of the power of the blues to inspire young musicians in the early twentieth century. In citing various recordings of Creole songs by New Orleans artists, he neglects to mention their predilection for diversifying repertoire, interspersing Creole material with blues and popular songs.[15] It would appear that the "Spanish tinge" was not so much lost by New Orleans jazz musicians as placed in perspective, which is what Borneman fails to do.

In "Jelly Roll Morton and the Spanish Tinge," Charles Hiroshi Garrett analyzes Morton's deployment of the "Spanish tinge" in his compositions and recordings in order to challenge "American exceptionalism" and the binary racial models embedded in such explanations of jazz origins, citing David Ake's work on reinterpreting Creole ethnicity.[16] As Garrett states, "Morton's incorporation of Latin and Caribbean musical influences implies that the international roots of jazz are more complex than the barebones equation involving Europe and Africa would suggest."[17] Claiming much more, John Szwed argues that Morton's "Spanish tinge" statements were intended as a call for a "pan-American comparative perspective" on jazz origins:

> What Jelly Roll saw as an enduring and integral part of American music, later commentators would dismiss as an imported craze from Mexico, say, or Cuba. The music that he thought called for a pan-American comparative perspective, these mid-century critics treated as an accidental and limited meeting of American and exotic forms. But in retrospect, it appears that Morton was correct. Those who ignored him erected a false evolutionary perspective that emphasized jazz as a radical break from the musical past, and by excluding the whole range of folk, ritual, and foreign musics from jazz history, all of the music of the United States was grossly oversimplified.[18]

Yet even a cursory reading of the Library of Congress commentary contradicts

26 this assertion, and as Szwed admits, Morton thought "Spanish tinge" came from

"Spanish people living in New Orleans."[19] One can also conceive, as Morton (and Lomax) certainly did, of New Orleans jazz as subsuming a "range of folk, ritual, and foreign music," while also constituting "a radical break from the past."[20]

Morton clearly desired to be seen as an innovator, and Garrett is particularly interested in his reworking of "Spanish tinge" elements into jazz, tracking varying degrees of *tresillo* and habanera in more than twenty Morton pieces. In Morton's piano rendition of his "New Orleans Blues" ("New Orleans Joys"), a *tresillo* bass line works against the blues-inflected treble figures before culminating in a 4/4 "out chorus," leading Garrett to conclude that

> such rhythmic flexibility . . . indicates both the dynamic improvisational possi-
> bilities and the perpetual tension produced by the collision of these different
> musical impulses. Indeed, because of the distinctive set of rhythmic patterns
> generated by improvising over a *tresillo* bass, it may be useful to characterize
> this aspect of the Spanish tinge not only by the presence of a specific rhythmic
> cell but also by its resulting polyrhythmic character. . . . To describe "New
> Orleans Blues" as failing to unify its disparate elements is not intended as a
> criticism; on the contrary, the piece may be heard as a sonic metaphor for
> cultural difference and conflict.[21]

Yet if "New Orleans Blues" is representative of an "ongoing musical tension" that Morton built into his compositions in the 1910s, which Garrett also interprets as a "foreshadowing of things to come" with Latin jazz fusions in the 1940s, one might still wonder if one composer's intent, even with Morton's proclivity for experimentation and variegation, is sufficient to explain the phenomenon without recourse to a more incisive environmental scan of the New Orleans scene in that period.

Garrett portrays Morton as a composer of masterworks who perfects a "Span-ish tinge"/blues/jazz symbiosis, observing that that "few early jazz musicians seem to have integrated Latin musical impulses to the same extent as Morton." Morton's "New Orleans Blues" (which Borneman describes as "based on a Cre-ole song that Jelly heard in 1902"[22]) employs a habanera motif throughout the piece until the final 4/4 "out chorus," a reversal of the more typical New Orleans practice of clave at the end; but as Garrett points out, there is a *tresillo* finale in "Jelly Roll Blues."[23] Genius theories notwithstanding, there may be utility in taking a closer look at how Morton and his contemporaries often put their com-positions together in a more prosaic way. The "pastiche/assemblage" method of constructing early blues and jazz repertoire from preexisting "floating folk strains" was already widespread when Morton first published "Jelly Roll Blues" in Chi-cago in 1915, as seen in the Arbreshe (Albanian-Sicilian) New Orleans composer

27

Anthony Maggio's "I Got the Blues" (1908), to which W. C. Handy's "Jogo Blues" (1913) and "Saint Louis Blues" (1914) bear striking similarities. In *Long Lost Blues*, Peter Muir's analysis of the structural correspondence of these compositions is compelling, but he is at a loss to explain the historical transmission of these kindred elements. Nevertheless, it is clear that all of these tunes derived from musical ideas that did not originate with the credited composers. The competing claims to authorship of "Tiger Rag" by Morton and Nick LaRocca raise similar issues, and neither version could be described as autodidactic composition.[24] According to LaRocca, "Tiger Rag" (1918) was a pastiche incorporating elements from "London Bridge Is Falling Down," "National Emblem March," and a "tango." In his Library of Congress interview, Morton dismissed LaRocca's claim, contending that he himself had reworked the song from a French quadrille. Given the contradictions that attended the organization and consolidation of the North American music industry in the early twentieth century, including the formation of ASCAP in 1914 to encourage the capitalization of all music as intellectual property, whatever the source, such disputes were commonplace.

Morton was in all probability reflecting common practices and ideas that were already pervading the New Orleans environment—a transmitter of a "Spanish tinge"/jazz/blues symbiosis, even if he helped to perfect it—working with "Spanish tinge" elements that may have been indigenous to New Orleans as early as the mid-eighteenth century.[25] The syncretism that Garrett alludes to was actually much broader, encompassing not only "Spanish tinge," blues, and jazz but also schottische, cakewalk, and ragtime permutations as well, all subject to an abiding penchant for experimentation and amalgamation among New Orleans musicians. Selections representing "post-Gottschalk exoticism" included in *Piano Music from New Orleans, 1851–1898*, compiled and with a preface by John H. Baron, illustrate this tendency. In his review of the compendium, J. Bunker Clark comments on the special features characteristic of the New Orleans environment: "William T. Francis . . . composed two Mexican dances that are reminiscent of Gottschalk's exoticism and pianistic virtuosity and arranged three others played at the 1885 World Cotton Exposition by the Mexican Military Band. Nearly all are characterized by the accompaniment and alternation of triple and duple rhythm best known in the 'Habañera' from Bizet's *Carmen*." Clark continues: "Historically, most important are a few pieces published near the end of the century that reveal themselves as immediate precursors of ragtime. The last Mexican piece arranged by Francis, composed by Señor Riderique, is close to a rag in its structure and cadences. One need only syncopate the right hand to complete the transition from 'Tempo di Schottische' to rag. Baron correctly identifies W. J. Voges' 'Pasquila: Medley' (first published in 1889, here in a 2d edition of 1895) as an early cakewalk, and most probably the first published—but not so identified—rag."

Clark concludes that "not many places in the United States show such cross-cultural currents."[26] As Lawrence Gushee argues in his interpretation of remarks made by W. T. Francis in 1890, the New Orleans music scene was indeed exceptional in the degree to which musical syncretism permeated its very *raison d'être*, especially in contrast to Boston and other northern cities, where music was regarded as a luxury for the wealthy. In New Orleans, the masses demanded a variety of new music and melody as necessary to existence—a means of coping with harsh realities—but they also expected innovations to suit their tastes, which included an innate "love of lyrical expressiveness in music" coupled with "rhythmic exoticism," especially "Caribbean or Mexican rhythms."[27] Morton's remarks on "seasoning" may, in fact, have been referring to something more inchoate than "Spanish tinge" as we now conceive it, adumbrating a broader sensibility that later became standardized in jazz discourse as "hot" (meaning exciting, expressive, and "from the heart"). W. J. Voges's annotations on "Pasquila" (1895) suggest exactly this interpretation. He indicates a tempo of *allegretto*, a bit more lively than the *andante* that is fairly typical of New Orleans jazz "second lines" (the proverbial "half fast" tempo), but the next marking is "Hot Stuff," revealing an aesthetic predilection very much in keeping with the vernacular tendencies that produced jazz in New Orleans in that period.[28]

Such localized tendencies had been marinating in the city's special blend of "habanera sauce" for many years. Louis Moreau Gottschalk's compositions reflecting his eclectic interest in Afro-French, Afro-Cuban, Puerto Rican, and Brazilian rhythms reveal the vast range of creolized music that was available in New Orleans by the mid-nineteenth century.[29] After the Civil War, Cuban and Mexican music had an even more pronounced effect on the city's musical imagination. The Cuban composer C. Maduell's "Two Cuban Dances" was published by Grunewald in 1883. Encarnacion Payen's Eighth Cavalry Band generated a mania for Mexican *danza* and Cuban *danzon* following performances at the World's Cotton and Industrial Exposition in 1884-85—a phenomenon promoted by music publisher Junius Hart—yet it was only one of numerous Mexican bands that visited New Orleans from 1884 to 1920, most of which were *orquestas típicas*, similar in instrumentation to jazz bands.[30] Payen's musicians engaged in various extracurricular activities in New Orleans.[31] One of Payen's saxophonists, Florencio Ramos, remained in the city. His composition "Dorados Ensueños" was published locally in 1885. Ramos went on to become a jazz musician and appears in a photograph of the Fischbein-Williams Syncopators at the LaVida Dance Hall in 1923. Emile "Stalebread" Lacoume, Buzzy Williams (from Birmingham, Alabama), Harold Peterson, and Charles Fischbein (a transplanted Romanian) were his bandmates.[32] (If anyone were to doubt the proclivity of New Orleans jazz musicians toward ethnic diversity, this band should be enough to quell such misgivings.) Yet ethnic identities were not always easy to decipher. Also at the World's Cotton Exposition was an Italian mandolin player, Carlo(s) Curti, who (along with his brothers) presented himself as Mexican, illustrating how convoluted ethnic representations could be.[33] The publication of Miss Amelia Cammack's "Echoes from Mexican and Cuban Shores" (1891), a refraction of Cuban and Mexican songs by a proper middle-class young lady, further attests to the pervasiveness of Afro-Latin music in fin de siècle New Orleans. Whether "Spanish tinge" rhythms would still have been viewed as "exotic" in late nineteenth-century New Orleans is therefore a matter of conjecture, so thoroughly were they ingrained there.

The question remains, who were the "Spanish people" that Morton was talking about in his exposition of "Spanish tinge" as an aspect of jazz origins in New Orleans? The possibilities are rife, because resident Hispanic and Latino populations in New Orleans were extremely diverse (including Iberian Spaniards and Portuguese, Canary Islanders, Filipinos, Mexicans, British Hondurans, Cubans, and Puerto Ricans), but it is not easy to track them. Some relative benchmarks on the proportions of black, Creole, Latino, Hispanic, and Sicilian (for comparative purposes) populations at the dawn of jazz are therefore in order. According to the U.S. Census in 1910, people of African heritage amounted to 90,000 (26 percent of a total population of 339,075; with 17 percent identified as "black" and 9 percent as "mulatto").[34] There were 21,000 Italian Americans in the New Orleans area (6 percent of the population), the vast majority of which were Sicilian.[35] Representation for Latinos and Hispanics is more difficult to ascertain. Totals for white foreign-born residents and natives with foreign-born parents from Cuba, Mexico, and Central America were 1,299 (slightly less than one-half of 1 percent) and for Spain the total was 1,799 (slightly more than one-half of 1 percent).[36] These figures do not account for Hispanics or Latinos who would have been considered "black" or "mulatto," nor does it account for natives of Hispanic or Latino descent who did not have foreign-born parents, so one assumes that such representation would be expanded accordingly, especially since so many photographs of early jazz bands (black, white, and Creole) include musicians with Hispanic surnames.[37] The Italian researcher Guido Festinese estimates that of the approximately one hundred musicians constituting the "first generation" of New Orleans jazz (those born before 1900), nearly a third had Italian surnames. Thomas Fiehrer finds about the same percentage to be "Creole" names, but places the number of Italians at one-sixth.[38] While they are submerged within these categorizations, Hispanic surnames nevertheless constitute a significant proportion of the total. Al Rose and Edmond Souchon's New Orleans Jazz: A Family Album lists twenty-four musicians with Hispanic or Latino surnames born before 1900, most of which

BRUCE BOYD RAEBURN

yes,

good question

30

would have been identified as Hispanic-heritage Creoles of color (Tios, Marreros, Santiagos, Dominguez, Toca, and Ysaguirre). The rest (Ramos, Abraham, Lopez, Nunez, Oramous, Ferrer, and Aquilera) were classified as white. That would put Hispanic and Latino musicians of various hues at about 24 percent of the "first generation," with musicians from these groups coming close to (or surpassing) the relative representation of Sicilians in early jazz bands, even though they comprised a much smaller percentage of the overall population.[39] Moreover, additional qualifications are necessary to make these "first generation" statistics meaningful: Festinese assumes that all Italian-derived surnames would indicate whites, but in some instances surnames such as Dominique, Manetta, and Cagnolatti denote Afro-Italian Creoles.[40]

The issue of racial ambiguity is significant. Jazz emerged at a time when racism and anti-immigrant ethnocentrism were ascendant in New Orleans, due largely to a backlash against the urban migration of freedmen from the rural hinterland after the Civil War and refugees fleeing economic dislocations in southern and eastern Europe. As the city's African American, Sicilian, and Jewish population swelled, Anglo-Protestant elites increasingly sought to define all of them as "non-white," a strategy that also held negative social and economic implications for the Creole population. While photographs of the earliest jazz bands show that Hispanics and Latinos were participating in the development of jazz from the outset and in substantial numbers, the strategies that enabled them to cross ethnic and racial boundaries in forming professional relationships are less evident. After the *Plessy v. Ferguson* Supreme Court decision in 1896, Creoles of color were defined as "black" under the law, which had a disastrous impact on the continuity of Creole language and culture, but Latinos were largely exempted and not specifically at risk unless they were very dark skinned. The existence of a racial penumbra based on popular perceptions of Hispanics as "white" and Latinos as possibly "black" or "white" thus benefited Afro-Creole musicians who sought to work with whites, even if they had no discernable Hispanic or Latino ethnic connection.

A case in point would be Jelly Roll Morton's recording session in July 1923 with the New Orleans Rhythm Kings for Gennett Records in Richmond, Indiana, where the state legislature was dominated by the Ku Klux Klan. Morton's racial identity was challenged when the band attempted to find accommodations for him at a hotel during the session, so the white trombonist George Brunies explained that Morton was "Latin American," backing up the assertion by pointing out the diamond inlay in Jelly's tooth, which was apparently accepted as sufficient proof.[41] The African American cornetist Lee Collins had a similar experience playing with a white band on Decatur Street in New Orleans several years later:

interesting
good
historical
grounding

I went with Sidney Arodin, a fine clarinet player and a fine man, in an all-white band. This was at a hole-in-the-wall on Decatur Street run by a Spanish pimp who was a swell dresser. This guy had about seven women working in his place. One of them was known as Sis, but for various reasons I can't call her real name. In those days there was a tough police captain named Smith. One night he came into this joint, so Sis warned me that if he asked any questions about me working in this white band I should tell him I was Spanish to avoid any trouble.[42]

A "Spanish tinge" racial masquerade thus became a way of dealing with racial prejudice for Creoles and African Americans who were sufficiently light skinned or brash enough to bluff white authorities.

In other cases, light-skinned Afro-Hispanics and Latinos found it easier to identify as Creole, even though that designation was eroding into an undifferentiated category of "black" under segregation. Rose Tio Wynn (daughter of Lorenzo Tio Jr.) stated that Roberto Ysaguirre, the British Honduran bassist in Armand Piron's band, "wasn't white or black—he was in the middle, like us."[43] The violinist James Palao lived in Algiers, worked in Storyville, and later traveled with William Manuel Johnson's Original Creole Band (the first band to take jazz beyond the city's regional hinterland, touring the Pantages vaudeville circuit from 1914 to 1918) and Joe Oliver's Creole Band in California in 1922, neither of which was led by a Creole. Due largely to the effects of segregation and modernism, in the early twentieth century Creole identity was dissolving as an ethnic marker of language and lifestyle and becoming an ethnically detached signifier designating exotic consumer goods with "class." In *Pioneers of Jazz*, Lawrence Gushee wonders "whether the name Palao is Spanish, Catalan, or Portuguese." He notes that "[Palao] nonetheless had printed in about 1924 a business card on which he called himself 'Creole Jimmy Palao.'"[44]

There is an image of Palao's earlier band circa 1900 that includes two obscure New Orleans musicians: Edward "Chico" Claiborne (trombone) and Louis Rodriguez (cornet). Besides their respective instruments, little is known about them. But their names are interesting, combining Anglo ("Claiborne"), Francophone ("Louis" rather than "Luis"), and Hispanic ("Chico") variants to create an American hybrid identity, similar to *mestizaje*. Hispanic ethnicity was often submerged within the creolized lifestyle of neighborhoods such as Tremé, the Seventh Ward, or Algiers, where francophone dialects tended to predominate, whatever the respective ethnic heritage. Other Creoles who appeared to be French had a submerged Hispanic heritage. Trombonist Edward "Kid" Ory, from LaPlace, Louisiana, became the most influential "black" jazz band leader in New Orleans after 1910. His father, Ozeme John Ory, was white, descended from Franco-

Alsatian immigrants who came to Louisiana in the mid-eighteenth century; his mother, Octavie Devezin, was Afro-Spanish and Native American. Ory was fully as much Hispanic as he was black, but he would have been classified as an octoroon under nineteenth-century social standards, and he spoke creolized French because that is what people spoke in LaPlace in the late nineteenth century. When he moved to New Orleans, he resided in Central City because he was a "country Creole" and therefore not rooted in any of the traditional Creole wards. Like Ory, who represented ethnic and racial diversity in a single individual, most New Orleans bands that were characterized as "black" under segregation were in truth quite ethnically diverse, which often meant several Hispanic or Latino members. In 1910 the Onward Brass Band, one of the preeminent marching bands in the city, was led by Emanuel (Manuel) Perez (of Cuban or Mexican ancestry)[45] and included the Afro-Latino clarinetist Lorenzo Tio Jr., whose grandfather Thomas Tio (of Spanish heritage) had fled New Orleans for Tampico in 1859 to escape the deteriorating racial climate prior to the Civil War. Lorenzo's father and his brother Louis, who were born in Mexico, returned to New Orleans in the 1880s, so many people assumed the family was Mexican, although they were originally from New Orleans.

The Tio family's experiences as musicians (all were clarinetists) and teachers reveals how Italians contributed to the education of Afro-Hispanic and Afro-French musicians in the nineteenth century. In *Music in New Orleans*, Henry Kmen recounts the arrival of Luigi Gabici from Havana in 1837. Gabici worked as a music publisher and educator in the 1840s and 1850s, instructing Creoles of color, such as Thomas Tio and the Afro-French violinists J. B. M. Doublet and Edmond Dédé. Tio's progeny, Lorenzo, Louis, and Lorenzo Jr., in turn taught numerous jazz musicians, including Barney Bigard, Jimmie Noone, Omer Simeon, Darnell Howard, and Albert Nicholas.[46] The Tios used *solfeggio* (as did Manuel Perez, Manuel Manetta, and Arnold Metoyer) because it was an effective introduction to performance techniques that did not necessarily require complete commitment to musical literacy.[47] As I have argued elsewhere, in New Orleans, "sight singing" was associated with "Italian masters" in the minds of many incipient jazz musicians, and the associations formed among Italians, Afro-Hispanics, and other Creoles in the mid-nineteenth century held important consequences for jazz. In time, the "Italian teacher–Creole student" paradigm would reverse itself, owing largely to the desire of young Sicilians to learn African American vernacular jazz techniques, such as when the Arbreshe banjoist Tony Schiro took lessons from his Afro-French neighbor Johnny St. Cyr in Tremé and the Afro-Hispanic banjoist John Marrero in the Seventh Ward.[48]

Hispanics and Latinos who were classified as "white" did not always appear to be so. The Franco-Hispanic mandolin player Joseph "Sou Sou" Oramous per-

hrm?

formed with the bands of Emile Lacoume and the Sonora Orchestra affiliated with "Papa" Jack Laine's circle of musicians.[49] In a photograph from 1906, Lacoume and Oramous (who appears to be rather dark skinned) are playing at a "blue collar" picnic at West End, and the demeanor of the audience leaves no doubt that these are working people out to have a good time with a "ratty" band. Creole and bourgeois propriety was giving way to a zeitgeist of relaxed informality promoted by young audiences seeking to fill their leisure time with ragtime, jazz, and the blues. Judging by their nearly ubiquitous presence in photographs of early New Orleans jazz bands, Latinos and Hispanics (no matter what their racial classification) played a significant role in developing improvisational "ear" music in New Orleans, usually via guitar, banjo, or bass. The guitarist Lorenzo Staulz worked with Buddy Bolden in 1906 and continued on for a decade after trumpeter Buddy Petit took over the band, which was renamed the Eagle after a favorite bar. Like Lacoume's bunch, the Eagle played "ratty" music for the underclass, and such bands always seemed to have guitar players (or mandolins), based on the popularity of string bands throughout New Orleans in the late nineteenth and early twentieth centuries. Such associations were time honored: as early as the mid-1820s, guitars were present in Irish coffeehouses in New Orleans (which served liquor), where observers noted how "the lower class amused themselves." One traveler—ostensibly to emphasize the déclassé nature of an establishment—specifically mentioned hearing a vocalist "singing in Spanish and playing a guitar."[50] Accordingly, one wonders if guitar should be viewed as a marker of Hispanic or "underclass" influence, or perhaps it was the Irish ethnic connection that was being targeted.

In New Orleans, jazz bands performed "ear music" based on "head arrangements" worked out by trial and error in rehearsal—this was the usual approach to developing repertoire. The objective was to blend the disparate tonal properties of a somewhat (but not always) standardized "front line" of cornet, clarinet, and trombone into a musical conversation, based loosely on concepts of polyphony and heterophony. The "rhythm section" of guitar, bass, and drums provided a big, syncopated beat and a consistent pulse for dancers, while the guitar also engaged in harmonic runs and filled short breaks within the ensemble. Cornet led most of the time and held responsibility for clear statement of the melody; the trombone sometimes covered bass parts, reinforced rhythms with "slurs" and "smears" (*glissandi*), and provided harmonic variations; and the clarinet played *obbligato*, often weaving around the interplay with arpeggiated "runs" corresponding to the melody line. Despite the mythology surrounding aspirations to "collective improvisation" among nonliterate jazz musicians, which were occasionally realized, most New Orleans jazz bands contained players of varying skill levels who memorized parts worked out in advance: "readers" who could introduce new material from scores to satisfy public demand (usually a cornet, violin, or piano player); "fakers" who could not read music but played expressively with a "hot" style; and "spellers" who could not sight-read notes but could extract the basic progression from sheet music and memorize it. In other words, almost all New Orleans jazz bands were blending conservatory and amateur practices, the specifics of which were dictated by the preferences of the band members and the functional requirements of the market. Because "pickup" bands made up of hastily recruited sidemen were fairly common, anyone who wanted to work regularly had to be familiar with a gradually evolving continuum of standard practices and repertoire, governed by a "survival of the fittest" formula best described by members of Sam Morgan's Jazz Band as "who fall down, stay down."[51]

Yet jazz was ultimately destined for elite status as art music, which required broad social approbation, given its underclass origins. Musicians responded accordingly, by catering to the expectations of various clienteles, especially the white "society" set. In the first decade of the twentieth century, the Superior Orchestra, including the Afro-French violinist Peter Bocage, African American cornetist Willie "Bunk" Johnson, and Afro-French clarinetist "Big Eye" Louis Nelson Delille (who later worked with Palao in the Creole Band), performed regularly for wealthy whites as well as black and Creole audiences, doing variations on rags and more polite versions of "hot" dance music according to audience preferences. The band's Afro-Hispanic bass player, Billy Marrero, lived on Spain Street in the Seventh Ward, but he worked all over town. Several of his sons (notably John, Simon, Lawrence, and Eddie—banjo and bass players) became jazz musicians and music teachers in the 1920s. Living nearby was Manuel Perez, whose Imperial Band also included James Palao. A few blocks away lived the white bandleader and entrepreneur Jack Laine, who was married to Blanche Nuñez (of Cuban ancestry). Pictured in a photograph of Laine's Reliance Band in 1910 is clarinetist Alcide "Yellow" Nunez, an Isleño (Canary Islander) from St. Bernard Parish.[52] Nunez went to Chicago in 1916 with the group that became the Original Dixieland Jazz Band but was replaced by Larry Shields (from Central City), Bolden's next-door neighbor, before the band made the first jazz recording in New York City in February 1917. Nunez's next band, the Louisiana Five, had numerous successful recordings in 1918–20, making him an early pioneer in jazz recording. Comparison of the membership of the Eagle, Superior, and Reliance bands shows how musicians of Hispanic and Latino heritage spanned the racial and class spectrum, fulfilling assignments in black, white, and Creole bands because they had the skills and flexibility that such work required.

A review of anecdotal information about how Hispanic and Latino jazz musicians acquired musical skills, and the trends embedded in those experiences, provides further insight into the means by which conservatory and amateur practices were being merged, as well as how ethnic music could serve as a threshold for aspiring jazz artists. Present in the Reliance photograph from 1910 is the tuba player Martin Abraham (better known as "Chink Martin," who is often identified as Filipino but claimed Mexican and Spanish parentage). Martin's first instrument was guitar, and his teacher, Francisco Quinones, a transplant from Spain, was the one who named him "Chinito," which Jack Laine translated as "Chink." Martin soon quit his formal musical studies because Quinones "wanted him to read music and to study piano, which was considered an instrument for sissies in those times." Nevertheless, he garnered a concept of "strict tempo" from Quinones, who would set the pace with a metronome, muffle it, and then remove the muffler with the expectation that the students would remain in time. In reminiscing about his lessons, Chink attributed his ability to memorize material and conform to "strict time" as a product of an inner, intuitive sense of how to play music, reinforced by practice: "It's got to come from under your heart; in other words, you got to have that feeling; if you haven't got that feeling, nothing happens."

Chink Martin grew up in the lower French Quarter at the intersection of Royal and Esplanade and remembered that "around 1907–08 the area . . . from Dumaine to Esplanade was populated mainly by Mexican and Spanish people." At age twelve he used guitar to accompany "Mexican and Spanish singers who would serenade their mothers or sweethearts or friends late at night," including renditions of "La Paloma," "La Golondrina," and a Puerto Rican song entitled "Cuba." By 1900 he was playing "Spanish style" (specifically paso doble, a lively march mimicking the movements of bullfights, danced as a one-step in 6/8 meter) for a "Mexican Band" consisting of "guitar, mandolin, violin, string bass, tuba, and sousaphone."[53] One can scarcely imagine a more thoroughly ethnic musical activity than this, but Martin quickly outgrew it, gravitating instead toward an African American vernacular sensibility through jazz. Drawing on both conservatory and amateur pedagogies as opportunity and inclination permitted, he learned to integrate what he learned from both approaches in order to satisfy the musical needs of his local ethnic community, while also positioning himself in a burgeoning citywide jazz market that became his pathway to the future.

Ultimately, Chink Martin switched to string bass and sousaphone because he could not find enough work as a guitarist, and his association with jazz bands seems to have coincided with the switch, reflecting changing times. He recalled that "white musicians were playing jazz as early as 1908 [or perhaps earlier]. . . . The [first] band [that he heard], which played what was then called ragtime, was called the High Rollers . . . [they] had about seven or eight members; some of them were: Johnny Fernandez, guitar; Willie Guitar [surname Guitard], string bass; 'Bullwinkle,' drums; Peter Dintrans, trumpet; Bill Gallaty, Sr., valve trombone and leader, and Johnny Pujol [actual surname Palliser], clarinet." Chink's approach to string bass was considered "strange in those times; all other bass players played only two beats per measure, which was the proper way for a bass in a ragtime band to play; I decided the sound was too empty, so I began playing four beats, and filling out the chord . . . playing that style two or three years after I began playing the bass."[54] Chink Martin's early experience emphasizes how "Spanish style" dance music (such as the habanera and paso doble) and serenading were basic components of the New Orleans music scene at the time that jazz was emerging, as well as illustrating the eagerness of young Latinos and Hispanics to abandon their traditional ethnic music in favor of jazz. Martin's hometown transition from two beats to the bar to a driving, percussive, and swinging "slap style" in 4/4 contradicts Ernest Borneman's contention that New Orleans jazz went "tangent" *after* it left town. Martin was not responding to ineluctable ethnic or musicological imperatives but instead to conditions within the local market. According to his testimony, he played that way because it "felt better" and because it satisfied the expectations of dancers looking for variety and excitement, which meant consistent employment. As a string bassist and sousaphone player, Chink Martin went on to an illustrious performing and recording career with the New Orleans Rhythm Kings (he was on the Morton sessions in Chicago and also recorded with the band back in New Orleans in 1925), Johnny Bayersdorffer, the Halfway House Orchestra, Johnny Miller's New Orleans Frolickers, Johnny Wiggs, Sharkey Bonano, Santo Pecora, and the Crawford-Ferguson Night Owls, amounting to more than six decades of jazz activity.

Despite the difference in respective backgrounds, the experience of the pianist, composer, arranger, and band leader Luis Carl Russell parallels Chink Martin's quite closely as far as the related issues of pedagogy and stylistic meandering are concerned. Russell was a transplanted Afro-Latino born at Careening Bay, Colombia, near Bocas del Toro—just before Panama achieved independence, which is why he is usually identified as Panamanian. His father, Alexander Russell, played the organ and led the church choir; Luis remembered him as "Mr. Music down there, and . . . one of the area's few music teachers." Luis was trained on violin, guitar, and trombone, but he ultimately chose piano as his primary instrument, the result of fortuitous circumstances: "When I was 15, I decided to concentrate on the piano because the local silent movie house always had a pianist. I got a chance to play for all the movies when the regular piano player, a man named Blackwood, took sick one night. He had a drummer and a horn player accompanying him, and when I took over, they took off in disgust. They didn't like my short pants. Well, I must have done a good job because Blackwood never did come back, and his two helpers came to me to ask for their jobs back."[55]

After his initial breakthrough into the profession, in 1918 Russell moved to Colon, on the Caribbean coast, where he performed for American soldiers and sailors with a six-piece band led by a clarinetist. Although he asserted that "Spanish-American music was the popular form in Panama," he used his association with American servicemen to gain exposure to North American popular music, including jazz: "'I'd ask the Americans for the names of the popular tunes in the United States and order the sheet music from the Feist publishing house in New York City. We used to have long rehearsals as I taught the American hit songs [such as LaRocca's "Tiger Rag"] to my band."[56] In 1919 he spent $3,000 won in a lottery to move to New Orleans with his mother and sister in order to become a jazz musician. His first assignment was with the Afro-French clarinetist Albert Nicholas and Manuel Manetta in Arnold Du Pass's band at the Cadillac Club, which led to work in a band led by Nicholas at Anderson's Annex in 1923. Nicholas's band was full of future jazz stars, with an Afro-French contingent including the drummer Paul Barbarin, cornetist Arnold Metoyer, and clarinetist Barney Bigard, along with the Afro-Hispanic banjoist Willie Santiago. In order to keep up with such a fast crowd, Russell sought instruction from an African American pianist, Steve Lewis, a stalwart of Armand Piron's orchestra, which included Roberto Ysaguirre and Lorenzo Tio Jr. Although Lewis did not read music, he was fluent in New Orleans–style vernacular jazz techniques and therefore a suitable teacher.[57]

Russell was a quick study and became so proficient in the New Orleans idiom that he assumed leadership of Nicholas's band when the clarinetist was called to Chicago by King Oliver to replace Buster Bailey in 1924, and by mid-1925, Russell, Nicholas, Bigard, and Barbarin had all joined Oliver's Dixie Syncopators in the Windy City. Russell became Oliver's "straw boss" and principal arranger, recording with the Syncopators and performing at the Plantation until March 1927. He pursued outside projects as well, including a recording session with Ada Brown in 1926, accompanied by an expanded version of the Chicago Hottentots (George Mitchell, Russell, Nicholas, Bigard, and Johnny St. Cyr). When Oliver moved to New York in 1927, Luis went with him but soon branched out on his own, joining George Howe's band at the Nest Club and taking it over a few months later. From that foundation, Russell built one of the most popular orchestras in Harlem, animated by a cadre of outstanding jazz players including Albert Nicholas, Louis Metcalf, J. C. Higginbotham, and Henry "Red" Allen, with "homeboys" George "Pops" Foster on bass and Paul Barbarin on drums. As a bandleader and arranger in the 1930s, Russell developed a big band swing style that drew heavily on his New Orleans roots while also successfully conforming to market trends requiring larger organizations showcasing soloists, a formula that thrilled dancers at the Saratoga Club, the Savoy Ballroom, and Connie's Inn. From 1935 to 1943, Russell's orchestra became Louis Armstrong's backing band of choice, an experience that proved to be a bit too taxing for the leader, and he retired from music in 1948 to become a chauffeur.

The experiences of Chink Martin and Luis Russell illustrate the myriad of ways in which amateur and conservatory musical practices were shuffled in the careers of New Orleans jazzmen, and how essentially parallel pedagogical paths could lead to contrasting stylistic preferences—Martin stayed true to a concept of traditional New Orleans style, while Russell sought to modernize it. In both cases, their respective contributions added substantially to the development of jazz as a vital and meaningful art form. In retrospect, it is clear that Martin and Russell were indebted to their "Spanish tinge" heritage, but in pursuing musical dreams in an era when American popular music came into its own and reached a creative zenith, they were bound to go beyond it.

Comprehensive coverage of the contributions of Hispanics and Latinos to early New Orleans jazz would require a fuller treatment than can be achieved in a short essay, and there are many other individuals whose stories would qualify them for inclusion in such an account. Ray Lopez, whose Spanish father was a cornet soloist at the French Opera House, was the cornet player with Tom Brown's Band from Dixieland, the second New Orleans jazz band to travel widely, in 1915.[58] His recollections of the difficulties attending the translation of New Orleans jazz into northern markets is essential reading for anyone interested in early jazz history.[59] The African American trumpeter Oscar Celestin's Original Tuxedo Jazz Orchestra, which played for white audiences on the Streckfus riverboats and at Tranchina's Restaurant at Spanish Fort, as well as for black audiences throughout the Gulf South region, in the 1920s, included two of Billy Marrero's sons, John (banjo) and Simon (bass), with Manuel Manetta on piano. The third son, Lawrence, became a star banjoist with Bunk Johnson during the New Orleans Revival of the 1940s, and later taught Bill Huntington, a white kid from Jefferson parish, how to play banjo in the traditional New Orleans style. Today Huntington is a "first call" modern jazz bassist in New Orleans.

In this essay, I have highlighted the careers of some Hispanic and Latino musicians whose names many jazz scholars will recognize, but there are others who remain anonymous, journeymen players who are also worthy of attention, such as the pianists Horace Diaz and Julius Chevez, the drummer Sal Gutierrez, the guitarist Alex Esposito, and the pianist, trombonist, and guitarist Bob "One-Leg" Aquilera. Whether famous or obscure, these musicians recognized the strength that ethnic diversity brings to American culture, and they availed themselves of the full range of tools that were at hand in New Orleans: *solfeggio* for beginners, habanera and clave for intensifying "out choruses" and rendering of the blues, and the blues itself, an expressive African American medium that spoke to them. They were blending amateur and conservatory traditions that had coexisted in the city since the colonial period, but in new ways, creating pathways to excellence, if not always to fame and financial reward. In transcending ethnic stereotypes and fashioning American vernacular identities for themselves through jazz, these musicians demonstrated the viability of New Orleans jazz as more than just "good dance music" and bequeathed to their hometown a new concept of cultural status that drew on the abilities of all its citizens. If for no other reason, this would be cause enough to recognize the contributions of Hispanic and Latino musicians to the development of New Orleans jazz, and to celebrate them.

Sure thing.

BRUCE BOYD RAEBURN

NOTES

1. For a full discussion of clave, a family of rhythmic patterns in 2/4 meter associated primarily with Cuban music, see Ned Sublette, *Cuba and Its Music: From the First Drums to the Mambo* (Chicago: Chicago Review Press, 2004), pp. 94-7, 166-71, and 342-43.

2. See, for example, Samuel A. Floyd Jr., "African Roots of Jazz," 7-16, and William H. Youngren, "European Roots of Jazz," 17-28, in *The Oxford Companion to Jazz*, ed. Bill Kirchner (New York: Oxford University Press, 2000).

3. Jerah Johnson, "New Orleans's Congo Square: An Urban Setting for Early African-American Culture Formation," *Louisiana History* 32/2 (Spring 1991), 117-57.

4. Joshua Berrett, "Louis Armstrong and Opera," *Musical Quarterly* 76/2 (Summer 1992), 216-41. Berrett identifies quotes from *Rigoletto* and *Pagliacci* in Armstrong's recorded solos in the 1920s-1930s, along with passages from *Cavalleria Rusticana* in performances with Erskine Tate. See also clave in the "out chorus" of "New Orleans Stomp," recorded by King Oliver's Creole Jazz Band in Chicago, October 16, 1923 (Columbia 13003-D). Dewey Jackson's Peacock Orchestra's June 22, 1926, recording of "She's Crying for Me" (Vocalion 1040/reissued on Origin OJL9), composed by the New Orleans trombonist Santo Pecora (later reworked by Jelly Roll Morton as "Georgia Swing"), illustrates the use of habanera by Jackson's band, which included New Orleanians Willie J. Humphrey on clarinet and George "Pops" Foster on bass. Humphrey and Foster were both African American with no Creole heritage.

5. Thomas Brothers, "Solo and Cycle in African-American Jazz," *Musical Quarterly* 78/3 (Autumn 1994), 479-509.

6. For a succinct theoretical perspective on creolization, see Roger D. Abrahams, with Nick Spitzer, John F. Szwed, and Robert Farris Thompson, *Blues for New Orleans: Mardi Gras and America's Creole Soul* (Philadelphia: University of Pennsylvania Press, 2006). See also Harry Shields, interview by William Russell, May 28, 1961, reel 1, pp. 1, 4, Hogan Jazz Archive, Tulane University (henceforth HJA). Clarinetist Harry Shields was the younger brother of Larry Shields, clarinetist with the Original Dixieland Jazz Band. When his mother, Emma Punèke, married his father, James Shields, in 1872, her brothers "played for her wedding . . . flute, violin, mandolin, two guitars, and bass . . . they played ragtime (or jazz) but could also play mazurkas and schottisches . . . none of the brothers could read

music" (p. 4). From his use of the term "jazz," one infers that Shields means that the string band musicians played "by ear."

7. John Storm Roberts, in *The Latin Tinge: The Impact of Latin American Music on the United States*, 2nd ed. (New York: Oxford University Press, 1999), quotations from p. 39.

8. *Jelly Roll Morton: The Library of Congress Recordings—Volume 7: Mamie's Blues*, Riverside RLP 9007 (1957); Manuel Manetta, interview by William Russell, Richard B. Allen, and Robert Campbell, March 28, 1957, reel 2, p. 5, HJA. Manetta plays a blues in habanera rhythm on the audiotape at this point in the transcript. A review of this interview indicates that, like Morton, Manetta had "Spanish tinge" tunes such as "La Paloma" and "Panama" in his songbook.

9. See Bill Russell, *New Orleans Style*, compiled and edited by Barry Martyn and Mike Hazeldine (New Orleans: Jazzology Press, 1994), pp. 23 and 124, and Larry Gara, *The Baby Dodds Story*, rev. ed. (Baton Rouge: Louisiana State University Press, 1959/1992), pp. 73-74. Despite later critics' desire to generalize, Dodds was referring to Creole pianists only.

10. Morton discusses "Tu Way Pocky-Way" on the Library of Congress recordings in 1938; *Jelly Roll Morton: The Library of Congress Recordings—Volume 11: Buddy Bolden's Legend*, Riverside RLP 9011 (1957). Sam Charters later documented the Mardi Gras Indian tradition in 1956, *The Music of New Orleans: The Music of the Streets/The Music of Mardi Gras, Volume 1*, Folkways FA2461 (1958). See also drummer Johnny Vidacovich's discussion of clave as the basic rhythm of "second line" parades in *New Orleans Drumming; Street Beats: Modern Applications* (DCI Music Video Productions, 1993).

11. Roberts, *Latin Tinge*, p. 38.

12. Ibid., p. 43. Roberts states: "A version of this [Piron's 'Panama'] on a limited-edition recording played by the New Leviathan Oriental Foxtrot Orchestra shows it to have been a somewhat lumpy hybrid, with the first note heavily emphasized by the tuba." See New Leviathan Oriental Foxtrot Orchestra, *An Oriental Extravaganza*, audiocassette of live performance (New Leviathan, 1972).

13. See Ernest Borneman, "Creole Echoes," *Jazz Review* 2/8 (September 1959), 13-15, quotation is from p. 14; and "Creole Echoes, Part II," *Jazz Review* 2/10 (November 1959), 26-27. For an alternative exposition of the differences between "Spanish tinge" and African American vernacular music, particularly with regard to "swing," see Ned Sublette, *Cuba and Its Music*, pp. 159-74.

14. Borneman, "Creole Echoes," *Jazz Review* 2/8 (September 1959), 14.

15. Borneman, "Creole Echoes, Part II," ibid., p. 27, in which he characterizes Bechet's Haitian Band recordings in 1938 as "the first deliberate reunion of jazz and Afro-Spanish folkmusic in history."

16. Charles Hiroshi Garrett, "Jelly Roll Morton and the Spanish Tinge," in *Struggling to Define a Nation: American Music and the Twentieth Century* (Berkeley: University of California Press, 2008), pp. 48-82. David Ake, *Jazz Cultures* (Berkeley: University of California Press, 2000), p. 14, calls for a reassessment of racial perspectives on jazz origins. Ake's work reinforces that of Thomas Fiehrer, who argues that jazz was a product of creolization in "From Quadrille to Stomp: The Creole Origins of Jazz," *Popular Music*

10/1 (January 1991), 21–38. Fiehrer's inclusion of Sicilians within the domain of "Creole" serves as a point of departure for perspectives contained in my essay.

17. Garrett, "Jelly Roll Morton and the Spanish Tinge," p. 50.

18. John Szwed, "Doctor Jazz: Appendix I—The Spanish Tinge," liner notes to *Jelly Roll Morton: The Complete Library of Congress Recordings by Alan Lomax*, Rounder 11661-1888-2 CD-al. (2005), pp. 33–36; quotations from p. 33. Szwed does not cite Borneman's work in the liner notes booklet, but he is clearly indebted to it. Yet if jazz was simply a continuation of Creole musical traditions, as Borneman, Fiehrer, and Szwed contend, then why did elder Creole musicians, most notably Louis "Papa" Tio, react so negatively to it? For Tio's antipathy to jazz brass bands, see also Natty Dominique, interview by William Russell, May 31, 1958, reel 1, track 1, p. 13, HJA, and Johnny St. Cyr, "Jazz as I Remember It; Part Two: Storyville Days," *Jazz Journal* 19/10 (October 1966), 22–24, especially p. 23.

19. Szwed, "Doctor Jazz," p. 20. Morton's other statements regarding the ethnic diversity present in New Orleans ("We had all nations in New Orleans. . . . We had Spanish, we had colored, we had white") bolsters this New Orleans–centric perspective. His discussion of "Spanish tinge" is about constituent elements that required *reinvention* in order to be suitable for jazz. The New Orleans–centric emphasis is clearly the most consistent narrative theme running through his testimony, and there is no actual mention of "pan-Americanism."

20. Morton saw jazz as a radical break—a new idiomatic playing style—and Lomax follows suit in describing jazz as "the first world musical language . . . invented in its capital here in New Orleans," a comment made in the "Jelly Roll Morton Symposium," untranscribed tape recording, May 7, 1982, HJA. Yet neither would have insisted that it was simply an act of spontaneous creation without antecedents. Morton did not pit "Spanish tinge" and American vernacular against each other but instead sought to reconcile them.

21. Garrett, "Jelly Roll Morton and the Spanish Tinge," pp. 59, 61, 62. Garrett speculates that Morton changed the title of this tune from "New Orleans Joys" to "New Orleans Blues" "for the sake of marketability" (p. 63). Another explanation would be that the purpose of the alternate titles was to allow the performer's mood to govern the emotional shading of the rendition, expanding the expressive range of the piece, rather than enhancing its commercial appeal.

22. Actually, Borneman's "Creole Echoes, Part II" provides a fairly substantial list of "Spanish tinge" recordings by New Orleans artists, including the Original Dixieland Jazz Band, Armand Piron's New Orleans Orchestra, Creole George Guesnon, Kid Ory, Wooden Joe Nicholas, Albert Nicholas, Omer Simeon, and others. See Borneman, "Creole Echoes, Part II," 26–27, for the list and for comments on "New Orleans Blues" as "the most famous case in point" of "Spanish tinge."

23. Garrett, "Jelly Roll Morton and the Spanish Tinge," p. 64. Garrett argues that Jelly Roll Morton was "staking out new territory for cross-rhythmic experimentation" in "New Orleans Blues," rather than referencing well-established Creole performance tropes, as Borneman's comment would seem to suggest. One must at least admit the possibility that Morton may have been drawing on the New Orleans environment in juxtaposing 4/4 meter with *tresillo*.

24. Peter C. Muir, *Long Lost Blues: Popular Blues in America, 1850-1920* (Urbana and Chicago: University of Illinois Press, 2010), especially pp. 86, 117-22. Muir also discusses the "Spanish tinge" influence on W. C. Handy and Jelly Roll Morton, stating that "Morton's claims about the importance of the 'Spanish tinge' are backed up by the testimony of other jazz musicians, such as the drummer Warren 'Baby' Dodds and pianist Willie 'The Lion' Smith, who both confirmed that it was in the earliest blues" (p. 122). In Dodds's case, however, the reference was specifically to Creole renditions of the blues and should not be stretched to encompass all early blues.

25. In *The World That Made New Orleans: From Spanish Silver to Congo Square* (Chicago: Lawrence Hill Books, 2008), Ned Sublette refers to the musical implications of a shift after 1763 from importation of Senegambian slaves with regional drum and stringed-instrument traditions under the French (pp. 58, 61-62, 68-69, 72-75) to Kongo slaves with discrete drumming traditions under the Spanish (pp. 106-7, 113-15, 116, 120-26). New Orleans differed from Cuba in the grafting of Kongo musical sensibilities onto Senegambian—a unique situation—while also situating Kongo as a threshold for clave. Particularly interesting is Governor Estevan Miró's use of the term *los tangos* to refer to "black dances" in 1786 (pp. 122-23).

26. See *Piano Music from New Orleans, 1851-1898*, compiled and with a preface by John H. Baron (New York: Da Capo Press, 1980) and the book review by J. Bunker Clark in *American Music* 4/1 (Winter 1983), 106-7.

27. Lawrence Gushee, "The Nineteenth-Century Origins of Jazz," *Black Music Research Journal* 14/1 (Spring 1994), 1-24, especially pp. 11-12.

28. W. J. Voges, "Pasquila," 2nd ed. (New Orleans: Published by W. J. Voges, 1895).

29. For information on Gottschalk, see S. Frederick Starr, *Louis Moreau Gottschalk* (Chicago: University of Illinois Press, 1995). See also Jack Stewart, "Cuban Influences on New Orleans Music," *Jazz Archivist* 13 (1998-99), 14-23.

30. See Jack Stewart, "The Mexican Band Legend: Myth, Reality, and Musical Impact; A Preliminary Investigation," *Jazz Archivist* 6/2 (December 1991), 1-14.

31. According to local legend, the famed Mexican composer Juventino Rosas performed "Sobre las Olas" ("Over the Waves") with the Mexican Military Band in New Orleans in 1884-85, yet this is probably apocryphal. Helmut Brenner, *Juventino Rosas: His Life, His Work, His Time* (Warren, MI: Harmonie Park Press, 2000) shows him to be at the Conservatorio Nacional de Música in Mexico City from January 1884 through March 1885, so it is not likely that he was in New Orleans during this period (pp. 12-17). Jack Stewart also challenges this assertion in "The Mexican Band Legend: Myth, Reality, and Musical Impact," pp. 1-3. However, "Over the Waves" was published in New Orleans barely a year after its initial publication by Wagner y Levien in Mexico in 1888. In a subsequent article Stewart places the earliest publication of "Over the Waves" in New Orleans in 1889: "The most important piece on the [World's Industrial and Cotton Centennial Exposition] program may have been the Mexican waltz *Sobre las Olas* (*Over the Waves*) by Juventino Rosas, in what might have been its first major public performance in the United States. It appears to have been published sometime around 1889 in New Orleans, by Junius Hart. The music itself bears no date, but an interpolation of the printing plate number puts it

between pieces published in 1888 and 1890, and a copy in a New Orleans depository bears a handwritten inscription dated 1889." See Jack Stewart, "The Mexican Band Legend— Part II," *Jazz Archivist* 9/1 (May 1994), 1–17, quote from p. 5. Sixty years later, this tune was still being featured by the jazz clarinetist George Lewis, even though it was a waltz.

32. See Al Rose and Edmond Souchon, *New Orleans Jazz: A Family Album*, rev. 3rd ed. (Baton Rouge: Louisiana State University Press, 1984), p. 246.

33. See Jean Dickson, "Carlos Curti: ¿compositor, director, rey del xilófono, camaleón? ¿Quién fue Carlos Curti? *Heterofonía* 140 (January–June 2009), 61–75. Ethnic or racial "cross dressing" was also employed by prostitutes in the Storyville District, 1897–1917, where white women identified as "Creole" or "Latina" to cash in on higher rates for exotic fare. Katy Coyle's preliminary research on this topic was presented at "Storyville, 1897–1917: Debunking the Myths," Satchmo Summer Fest, Old U.S. Mint, New Orleans, August 4, 2002; see also Alecia P. Long, *The Great Southern Babylon: Sex, Race, and Respectability in New Orleans, 1865–1920* (Baton Rouge: Louisiana State University Press, 2004), pp. 205, 218. Despite its definition as "black" after 1896, "Creole" remained a racially ambiguous hinge mask that could encompass black or white variations, and "Latino" followed suit. Of course, creolized blues rendered with habanera was the perfect musical accompaniment for such masquerades.

34. *Thirteenth Census of the United State: Abstract of the Census with Supplement for Louisiana, 1910*, p. 594, and Virginia R. Dominguez, *White by Definition: Social Classification in Creole Louisiana* (New Brunswick, NJ: Rutgers University Press, 1986), p. 116. Dominquez notes that distinction between "blacks" (58,782 or 17 percent) and "mulattos" (30,480 or 9 percent) does not adequately convey the diversity within the New Orleans creolized black community. On nineteenth-century racial fetish terminology and diversity within the black community, see Michael G. White, "The New Orleans Brass Band: A Cultural Tradition," pp. 69–96, in *The Triumph of the Soul: Cultural and Psychological Aspects of African American Music*, ed. Ferdinand Jones and Arthur C. Jones (Westport, CT: Praeger, 2001), especially pp. 70–73.

35. Ethelyn Orso, "Sicilian Immigration into Louisiana," in *A Refuge for All Ages: Immigration in Louisiana History*, ed. Carl A. Brasseaux, Louisiana Purchase Bicentennial Series in Louisiana History, vol. 10 (Lafayette: Center for Louisiana Studies, 1996), pp. 603–7 on Sicilian population and Arbreshe. See also *Thirteenth Census of the United States, 1910*, pp. 63, 586, and 592.

36. *Thirteenth Census of the United States, 1910*, p. 586. Lawrence Gushee notes that "the 1910 census marked a dramatic change from those of 1890 and 1900. While the overall total of male musicians and music teachers increased by a striking 33 percent, the number of African Americans doubled, thus forming 30 percent of the total." See Gushee, "Nineteenth-Century Origins," p. 7. This is the point at which black musicians cease to be "faceless," especially given the burgeoning of photographic documentation of Creole and African American bands in the period 1900–1910.

37. See photographs in Rose and Souchon, *New Orleans Jazz*, pp. 133–214, 241, 246, 258, 262, 267, 291, 285, 273, 301, 306, 308.

44   38. Guido Festinese, "Palermo–New Orleans, New Orleans–Palermo: Un doppio

cerchio nella storia del jazz," in *Contemporary Sicily, 1998,* conference program (New York: Edizioni La Centrale dell'Arte, 1998), 24–27, see 25–26; Fiehrer, "From Quadrille to Stomp," 32.

39. Rose and Souchon, *New Orleans Jazz,* pp. 1–132.

40. Dominique, interview, reel 1, track 1, p. 3, HJA. See Russell, *New Orleans Style,* pp. 140–41; Ernie Cagnolatti, interview by William Russell, Ralph Collins, and Harold Dejan, April 5, 1961, reel 1, pp. 1–5, reel 3, pp. 1–2, HJA; "Obsequies of the Late Ernie Joseph Cagnolatti, 1911–1983, Tuesday, April 12, 1983, Greater Asia Baptist Church," funeral program, persons vertical file: "Cagnolatti, Ernie," HJA.

41. See Rick Kennedy, *Jelly Roll, Bix, and Hoagy: Gennett Studios and the Birth of Recorded Jazz* (Bloomington: Indiana University Press, 1994), p. 74; Richard Sudhalter, *Lost Chords: White Musicians and Their Contribution to Jazz, 1915–1945* (New York: Oxford University Press, 1999), p. 44; and Donald M. Marquis, "Martin Abraham, Sr. 'Chink Martin,' Jazz Pioneer," *Second Line* 31 (Fall 1979), 28–37, in which Martin claims that Morton was passed off as "Cuban" (p. 33).

42. Lee Collins, *Oh, Didn't He Ramble: The Life Story of Lee Collins, as Told to Mary Collins,* ed. Frank J. Gillis and John W. Miner (Urbana: University of Illinois Press, 1974), p. 32.

43. Rose Tio Wynn and Corrine "Cookie" Gaspard, interview by Barry Martyn, July 20, 2003, New Orleans Jazz Commission Oral History Project, video 1 (of 2), HJA.

44. For this photo, see Rose and Souchon, *New Orleans Jazz,* p. 150. For quotation, see Lawrence Gushee, *Pioneers of Jazz: The Story of the Original Creole Band* (New York: Oxford University Press, 2005), p. 24.

45. Perez's ethnicity may not be as clear-cut as has previously been assumed. One theory is that his father was Cuban and mother Italian, but Jempi De Donder has also speculated about Perez's father being a Spanish immigrant, based on remarks made by Danny Barker: "His father and grandfather [were] Spanish and his mother colored." In personal conversation, Ned Sublette has suggested that the family might, in fact, be Mexican, from Veracruz, based on conversations with a distant relation in New York City. See Jempi De Donder, "Emanuel Perez," *Footnote* 17/6 (August/September 1986), 4–9, Jempi De Donder, "The Second Hundred Years," *New Orleans Music* 4/3 (September 1993), 14–15, and Daniel Vernhettes, "Manuel Perez, 1878–1947," *Jazz Puzzles* (October 2011), 55–70.

46. Henry A. Kmen, *Music in New Orleans: The Formative Years, 1791–1841* (Baton Rouge: Louisiana State University Press, 1966), pp. 151, 234, and Charles E. Kinzer, "The Tio Family and Its Role in the Creole-of-Color Musical Traditions of New Orleans," *Second Line* 43/3 (Summer 1991), 18–27. Kinzer notes that "Gabici was known to teach free-colored students, and the 1850 U.S. Census shows that he lived next door to two aspiring young musicians of that class" (19, 21).

47. See Kinzer, "Tio Family," p. 280. *Solfeggio* also appealed to students who could not at first afford instruments; see Tony Parenti and Tony Sbarbaro, interview by Richard B. Allen, June 29, 1959, reel 2, pp. 12–13, HJA.

48. Bruce Boyd Raeburn, "Stars of David and Sons of Sicily: Constellations beyond the Canon in Early New Orleans Jazz," *Jazz Perspectives* 3/2 (August 2009), 123–52.

49. Stewart, "Mexican Band Legend," especially p. 11.

50. As quoted in Earl F. Niehaus, *The Irish in New Orleans, 1800-1860* (Baton Rouge: Louisiana State University Press, 1965), pp. 6 and 164, which recounts the observations of Karl Bernhard, Duke of Saxe-Weimar-Eisenbach, in New Orleans, published in his travel memoirs, *Travels through North America during the Years 1825 and 1826*, 2 vols. (Philadelphia, 1828). For a photograph of the Eagle Band in 1916, see Rose and Souchon, *New Orleans Jazz*, p. 138. Although little is known about Staultz's ethnic heritage, he appears to be Latino, possibly Mexican, in this photograph.

51. For example, despite Peter Bocage's observation that the Armand Piron Orchestra "played strictly from music," he and his brother Charlie exhibited disparate skill levels, largely because their father—a shipbuilding carpenter with limited resources—favored Peter as the eldest with a formal musical education, while Charlie was left to pick up guitar "by head," describing himself as "self-taught . . . getting along mostly on talent . . . could read a little bit . . . could play anything I heard." See Charlie Bocage, interview by Richard B. Allen and Herb Friedwald, July 18, 1960, reel 1, p. 5, and reel 2, p. 14, HJA. Isaiah Morgan remembered that when playing at the Astoria Garden, his brother Sam would wait until the place was full and then "bring hard numbers such as 'Miss Trombone' and 'Sally Trombone' on the job," saying "who fall down, stay down" because the band "would not rehearse." Jim Robinson, the trombonist, who "could not read but could 'spell' a little," had no trouble with the trombone specialties because he had memorized them while working with Chris Kelly. See Isaiah Morgan, interview by William Russell and Richard B. Allen, December 1, 1958, reel 2, p. 7, HJA.

52. Rose and Souchon, *New Orleans Jazz*, p. 197.

53. All preceding quotations are from Chink Martin, interview by Richard B. Allen and William Russell, October 19, 1966, HJA, reel 1, pp. 1-3, reel 2, pp. 4-6; paso doble quotation is from Marquis, "Chink Martin," p. 29.

54. Chink Martin interview, reel 2, p. 6.

55. George Hoefer, "Luis Russell," *Down Beat* 29/28 (November 8, 1962), 43.

56. Ibid., 43. For characterization of preference for "Spanish-American music" in Panama, see Walter C. Allen, "Luis Russell," *Playback* no. 18 (June 1949), 5-7, especially p. 5.

57. Peter Bocage remembered that Steve Lewis could not read music at all. For comments on Lewis and composing/arranging for the Piron band, see Peter Bocage, January 29, 1959, reel 2, p. 32, HJA. Bocage also stated on another occasion that "he has played with all kinds of musicians and would adjust his style of playing to fit whatever band he played with, including bands of non-reading musicians," which succinctly describes the New Orleans aesthetic that Luis Russell wanted to acquire via Steve Lewis. See Peter Bocage, interview with Barry Martyn and Richard Knowles, February 6, 1962, reel 1, p. 8, HJA. For information on the Nicholas band at Anderson's Annex, see Barney Bigard, *With Louis and the Duke: The Autobiography of a Jazz Clarinetist*, ed. Barry Martyn (London: Macmillan, 1985), pp. 20-26.

58. Ray Lopez, interview by William Russell, August 30, 1958, reel 1, p. 1, HJA.

59. See Dick Holbrook, "Mister Jazz Himself—The Story of Ray Lopez," *Storyville* no. 64 (April-May 1976), 135-51.

MARTIN GUERPIN

3 / WHY DID ART MUSIC COMPOSERS PAY ATTENTION TO "JAZZ"?
THE IMPACT OF "JAZZ" ON THE FRENCH MUSICAL FIELD, 1908–1924

"Jazz" first arrived in France during the 1910s and had its first halcyon days during the 1920s.[1] The music corresponding to this term was mostly made of ragtimes, fox-trots, charlestons, and blues. Even if ragtime of 1908 is to be considered a pre-jazz genre, "jazz" will refer in this article to the kind of music that bore this name in France after the Great War. Associated with the modernity of the United States,[2] jazz burgeoned in Paris, mainly in Montparnasse and Montmartre, and had an important impact on the youth and artistic avant-garde.

If the presence of jazz in Paris has already been studied, most notably by Jeffrey H. Jackson[3] and Nancy Perloff,[4] its influence on art music composers[5] is still to be discussed. From Claude Debussy's *Golliwog's Cakewalk* (1908) to Maurice Ravel's *Sonata for Violin and Piano* (1927), the list of compositions using jazz is surprisingly long.[6]

Up to now, the corpus of art music compositions using jazz has never been systematically established.[7] However, five of its most representative elements are often quoted: besides *Golliwog's Cakewalk* and the 1927 *Sonata for Violin and Piano*, they are the *Ragtime du Paquebot* from the ballet *Parade* (1916–17), by Érik Satie; the "Ragtime" from *L'Histoire du soldat* (1917), by Igor Stravinsky; and *La Création du monde* (1923–24), by Darius Milhaud.

So far, two approaches have been applied to this corpus. Firstly, it is most often part of general studies about culture and society in interwar France, and epitomizes the vogue of this music in Paris. As a consequence, the aforementioned works are rarely taken into consideration out of this specific historical context, as compositions that deserve a musical analysis. This leads us to the second approach.

Only a few authors undertook such exclusive analytical study on a part of this corpus: Robert Rogers, Barbara Heyman, and most notably André Hodeir.[8] His analytical approach is organized around the concept of "authenticity" and focuses on what is common between original jazz music and art compositions using jazz. When pointing out differences between original ragtimes and the ones composed by Stravinsky, he speaks about "mistakes"[9] originating in a bad knowl-

yikes!

edge of jazz or in a reference to music that is not real jazz. Strictly focused on music, this analytical approach does not take cultural and aesthetic issues into account. Nor does it try to understand the very existence and the meaning of the corpus of art compositions drawing on jazz.

As interesting as they can be, these two different approaches tend to miss the point of view of the composers. Adopting a cultural and historical standpoint on those pieces, the former misses musical features that can be telling and very useful in understanding why composers based in Paris drew their inspiration from jazz. Speaking about "mistakes" and not taking into consideration any historical background, the latter also misunderstands what the Parisian composers really wanted to do.

That said, the stakes concerning the aforementioned works are double. First, the corpus of art music using jazz must be established and progressively completed so that one can better understand the weight of jazz in the field of art music during the 1910s and the 1920s. This research could help determine whether the composers who used jazz belonged to the same aesthetic milieux. Second, this corpus needs to be reexamined through a new prism that does not separate data drawn from analysis, history, and aesthetics.

My point is to show that the corpus of high music using jazz is far from monolithic. The sources, the composers' knowledge of jazz, and the degree of its integration in art music are very different from one composer to another and from one composition to another. Three of the most representative works from this corpus, *Golliwog's Cakewalk*, the *Ragtime du Paquebot*, and the "Fugue" from *La Création du monde*, encompass a period (1908-24) when the most important high music works using jazz were composed. Analysis of them thus can lead to a typology clearly underlining different approaches of the integration of jazz into art music. Nevertheless, beyond and despite this diversity, these works share a common aesthetic project observable through a comparison of the music with other sources, such as writings by the composers. In brief, the three compositions studied in this chapter are representative of the rest of the corpus, which seems to be part of a broader movement against Romanticism,[10] thanks to a use of neo-classical principles.

Another question can be raised concerning the expression of national identities in music. Composers who used jazz in their work did not want to imitate or emulate American music, but to exploit some of its connotations and some of its musical features. Interestingly enough, the corpus of art compositions conveying jazz was almost entirely composed at a moment when art music was in crisis. Such a book as Jean Cocteau's *Le Coq et l'arlequin*[11] is only the tip of the iceberg of intense debates about the definition of a music that would be properly French, rid of Romantic influences in general, and German ones in particular. How did

48

the use of a music clearly identified as coming from the United States help some composers to coin and promote a purely French art? *good question*

More generally, the role of the aforementioned corpus fully appears when contextualized into the history of the musical avant-garde in France. The stakes are the definition of new aesthetics during and after the Great War. It appears that jazz contributed to giving art music a new rhythmic energy and played a leading role in the promotion of new kinds of instrumentation. In this regard, the corpus of art music employing jazz evokes features of another avant-gardist movement: neoclassicism, in particular in the numerous debates around the definition of modernity in music after the Great War. *defined as an avant-garde movement, really?*

A Monolithic Corpus?
Debussy, Satie, and Milhaud in Front of Jazz

Employing jazz in art music is not only a matter of integration of syncopated rhythm and blue notes. Each composer made use of jazz in his own way, according to his knowledge of American music, and his musical and aesthetic preoccupations.

Debussy's Golliwog's Cakewalk: A Pastiche of Ragtime

Golliwog's Cakewalk is a part of *Children's Corner*, a collection of piano pieces composed by Debussy between 1906 and 1908 and dedicated to his daughter, Claude-Emma. The title refers to a popular character created by cartoonist and author Florence Kate Upton. Golliwog is black, with big red lips and unkempt hair. This kind and cheerful character was received in France as an epitome of the "bon nègre," a colonial version of the "bon sauvage." For Debussy, as for many of his contemporaries, ragtime, a music associated with entertainment and African American identity, and which he experienced during John Philip Sousa's concerts in Paris in 1900 and 1903, was the most efficient medium to illustrate this figure.

EXAMPLE 1: *Golliwog's Cakewalk*, bars 25–26 from a to b

TABLE 3.1A. Structure of *Golliwog's Cakewalk*

	Introduction	A		Transition
Bars	1–9	10–37		38–46
Number of bars	9 (4+1+4)	28		9
Analysis according to categories from ragtime	Introduction	Strain a	Strain b	Break
Bars	1–9	10–25	26–37	38–46
Number of bars	9	16	12	9
Tonal plan	Dominant of E-flat major	E-flat major		Dominant of E-flat major
Borrowings from ragtime	Homophony and syncopated rhythms, extensive use of the lowered sixth degree	"Oom-pah" pattern for the left hand and syncopated rhythm for the right hand		Homophony and syncopated rhythms, extensive use of the lowered sixth degree
Borrowings to other models				

Drawing from Formal and Structural Characteristics of Ragtime

From a formal standpoint, *Golliwog's Cakewalk* shares at least two common points with ragtime. First, Debussy uses juxtaposition and collage instead of techniques of organic development and continuity that are features of the Romantic music he employed in his own manner in some of his most famous works.[12] There is no organic transition between the different parts of the piece.[13] For example, *b* abruptly follows *a* (see table 3.1a). What is more, a brand-new musical idea comes almost by surprise after the half-close at bars 25 and 26 (example 1).

By the same token, the return of the introduction (bar 38) suddenly interrupts strain *b*. The impression of collage stems from the silence separating the two parts, from the harmonic gap and from the unexpected shift in pitch. As in ragtime, juxtaposition and collage give the piece a clear and easily understandable structure.

Golliwog's Cakewalk also owes a lot to ragtime in terms of structure. Table

B		Transition	A'		Coda
47–84		85–89	90–117		118–128
42		5	28		11
Strain c	Strain d	Transition	Strain a	Strain b' Coda	
47–62	63–84	85–89	90–105	106–117	118–128
16	22	5	16	12	11
G-flat major		Return to E-flat major	E-flat major		E-flat major
"Oom-pah" pattern shared by the two hands	–	Syncopated rhythm	Oom-pah" pattern for the left hand and syncopated rhythm for the right hand		–
Double pedal tonic-dominant	Quotation from the initial leitmotiv from *Tristan und Isolde* by Wagner	Progressive return of the fragmented term	–		Dissolution of the "oom-pah" pattern and homophonic phrase

[handwritten margin note: nice chart. well formatted]

3.1b illustrates the fact that the piece is built like a succession of independent musical ideas (*a, b, c,* and *d*), separated by interludes. Such an organization resembles the succession of *strains* in most of classical ragtimes like those by Scott Joplin. Another common point is the homophonic and homorhythmic introduction of the piece (bars 1 to 4). In this piece, the *breaks* are close to those of ragtimes.

[handwritten margin note: mmhmm (but Schumann did this too)]

As far as the bar structure is concerned, each phrase is divided into periods of four bars. This organization can be found in the introduction, but also in the construction of *a* (four groups of four bars, in which *a1* and *a2* are similar (see table 3.1b).

From the standpoint of tonal structure, the main modulation goes from E-flat major to G-flat major and occurs between *b* and *c*. This nonprepared and thus abrupt modulation, from the main tonality to the lowered third degree, can be found in some piano ragtimes. As with form, Debussy uses juxtaposition.

TABLE 3.1B. Detailed analysis of the first forty-five bars of *Golliwog's Cakewalk*

		Introduction		A				B		
Number of bars		17 (4+1+4)		16				12		
Subdivision	X	Silence	Y	a1	a2	a1	a3	b1	b2	b1
Number of bars	4	1	4	4	4	4	4	4	4	4

Obvious as they may be, these resemblances do not explain why *Golliwog's Cakewalk* sounds like a ragtime. The impression of pastiche originates in the rhythmic aspects of the piece.

Rhythmic Similarities

Debussy seems to have perfectly understood the main feature of ragtime: the "oom-pah" pattern consisting in syncopated figures played by the right hand "against" the left one. In example 2, the syncopated rhythm (mostly sixteenth-note/eighth-note/sixteenth-note figures) played by the almost mechanical right hand contrasts the regularity of the left hand (bass on the downbeat, chord on the upbeat), creating a polyrhythm.

In brief, Claude Debussy sticks closely to the musical model that he borrows. Nevertheless, it must be noticed that the composer does not want to compose a real ragtime.[14] He seems to play with the features of this genre, thus putting it at a distance.

Playing with Ragtime

The first bending of the rules of ragtime is to be found in the way Debussy seeks to break the regularity of some bar periods. For instance, before the end of the introduction, one bar of silence destroys the symmetrical four-four sequence. Likewise, the "impolite" and bursting interlude between *b* and *c* begins four bars before the expected end of *b*.

Whereas the strains of ragtime are usually repeated without variations (if we trust the scores), Debussy introduces subtle variations between repeated parts. In the first occurrence of *b2*, bars 30–33 are slightly different from their equivalent at bars 110–13, the first bar of which starts a semitone too high (on a B-natural) and comes back to the regular tonality after one measure (starting on a B-flat). This moment constitutes a real surprise.

Another infringement is to be found at *c*, where Debussy introduces a mocking ornamentation that generates slight dissonances, like the corrosive seconds from bars 47 to 52. Such a passage gives *Golliwog's Cakewalk* both an eccentric and joking tone.

EXAMPLE 2: *Golliwog's Cakewalk,* bars 10–13

EXAMPLE 3:
Ragtime du Paquebot, bar 1

TABLE 3.2. Structure of the *Ragtime du Paquebot*

	A		
Bars	1–24		
Number of bars	24		
Subdivision	a	b	a'
Bars	1–8	9–16	17–24
Number of bars	8	8	8
Tonal plan	C major	Dominant of C major and borrowing to A minor (bars 11–12)	C major
Remarks	Main theme (suspensive)	Game with the four-bar periods	Main theme conclusive

To sum up, Debussy clearly refers to ragtime, a musical genre whose features he seems to have perfectly identified. The infringements by the composer are all the more perceptible, in that ragtime is a tightly codified genre. From these departures, we can infer that instead of being a mere pastiche of ragtime, *Golliwog's Cakewalk* plays with ragtime. It is as if he was throwing a wrench into the mechanics of this genre. In another work referring to ragtime, the *Ragtime du Paquebot* from *Parade*, Satie adopts another approach.

Satie's Ragtime du Paquebot: *Sophisticated Jazz*

Composed in 1916, the ballet *Parade* is the result of a collaboration between Érik Satie, Jean Cocteau, and Pablo Picasso; Picasso designed the costumes and set for the premiere, which took place at the Théâtre du Châtelet on May 18, 1917. This avant-gardist creative team was completed by choreographer Léonide Massine and the Ballets Russes.

Strongly referring to the world of circus, *Parade* is conceived of as a show within a show. Three managers try to promote three routines in a big top. The reference to ragtime occurs in the second routine, "Petite Fille Américaine," where a little girl dances a two-step to the *Ragtime du Paquebot*.

This composition draws its inspiration from Irving Berlin's "That Mysterious Rag."[15] Satie must have read the score of this song, since he told his friend Valentine Cross in a letter dated October 25, 1916, "It's his ragtime." Still, the model from the repertory of Tin Pan Alley is not immediately recognizable. Yet the following analysis is meant to show that the model is well and truly present in

B			A'
25–36			37–44
12			8
c	d	d'	a'
25–28	29–32	33–36	37–44
4	4	4	8
Jamming (C major, borrowings to G minor and F major)	Borrowings to F major and A minor; preparation of the return to C major		C major
Progression and acceleration thanks to two rhythmic patterns			Main theme conclusive

the *Ragtime du Paquebot*, even if Satie's utilization of ragtime is different from Debussy's.

A Clear Evocation of Ragtime

As in *Golliwog's Cakewalk*, identifying musical features evoking ragtime is not difficult in *Ragtime du Paquebot*. Like Debussy, Satie arranges for orchestra the "oom-pah" pattern of ragtime. In the following example, the hierarchy between the upper part, bearing the melody, and the lower one, which brings the rhythmic foundation, is respected (see example 3). Similarly, Satie interpolates homophonic and homorhythmic passages that are reminiscent of the breaks in ragtime. As far as structure is concerned, table 3.2 shows that Satie punctiliously uses periods of four bars on which most ragtimes are built. In addition to this resemblance, Satie never makes use of techniques of development.

Instead, he resorts to juxtaposition of musical ideas. For example, the passage from A to B is abrupt (example 4).

Although A ends with an imperfect cadence, the music seems to come to a conclusion, mostly because of the iteration of the last chord after one rest. As a consequence, B sounds like a new beginning more than a logical continuation of A. Already in evidence in Debussy's *Golliwog's Cakewalk*, this abrupt handling of the form is also to be found inside the main parts of the *Ragtime du Paquebot*.

Numerous as the borrowings from ragtime may be, this piece is not really a pastiche. Satie's approach is not aimed at imitating orchestral ragtime, but at stylizing it. Granted, the glissando played by the trombones at bar 13 is reminiscent of the way this instrument was played in some pre-jazz orchestras, and is

EXAMPLE 4: *Ragtime du Paquebot*, bars 24-26

intentionally far from what was considered as good taste in art music (example 5). Yet in terms of orchestration, this element is almost the only one that evokes ragtime. One should wonder why Satie does not use any percussion in his *Ragtime*, whereas these instruments, which could be found in any jazz band, are used everywhere else in *Parade*.

Whatever the reason, Satie has conveyed enough features to make the reference to ragtime recognizable without composing a mere pastiche. This absence of percussion gives *Ragtime du Paquebot* more lightness. As a result, the work departs from the sound of pre-jazz bands, such as that of James Reese Europe, for instance. Whereas *Golliwog's Cakewalk* is almost a pastiche, the *Ragtime du Paquebot* is a *stylization* of the genre.

Putting Ragtime at a Distance

While maintaining a strong reference to ragtime through a strict regularity of almost all musical periods (invariably divided into groups of eight or four bars), Satie introduces discrepancies between the grouping of bars implied by the music and the subdivision expected in a regular ragtime.

While the subdivision of the eight bars of *b* (in part A) are supposed to follow a scheme in 4+4, Satie adopts a more complex one, in 2+2+3+1. He thus avoids the potential monotony of a music whose features are extremely regular. On a broader scale, the regularity of ragtime is respected at first sight, though perverted from the inside. Satie conveys musical characteristics clearly associated with ragtime, but transforms them into a more sophisticated music.

56

EXAMPLE 5:
Ragtime du Paquebot,
orchestral effect

nice

To keep to this idea of sophistication, the acknowledged quotation of Irving Berlin's "That Mysterious Rag" must be tackled. The most original trait of the *Ragtime du Paquebot* is indeed its use of preexisting music. Knowing about this borrowing, and then trying to identify it, can leave one with a strange impression. Granted, the music bears resemblance to "That Mysterious Rag," yet at the same time it is almost impossible to find the explanation for this likeness. Inventively, Satie does not refer to the theme of "That Mysterious Rag" but to the rhythm of its melody. In addition to that both inventive and odd process, the composer from Arcueil does not follow the structure of "That Mysterious Rag." More precisely, he turns it upside down: the beginning of the *Ragtime du Paquebot* uses the chorus of "That Mysterious Rag," while in the central part Satie exploits the verse. Table 3.3 displays the structure of Berlin's song, and table 3.4 sums up the borrowings from "That Mysterious Rag" made by Satie in his *Ragtime du Paquebot.*

The idea that the work is based only on the rhythm structure of "That Mysterious Rag" needs to be qualified. The melodies of the *Ragtime du Paquebot* are not created ex nihilo. To take only one example, the main theme of Satie's ragtime comes from the first eight bars of the chorus of "That Mysterious Rag." Though not harmonized in the same way, some passages show that Satie uses the first melodic pattern of his model: the second bar of the *Ragtime du Paquebot* is the same as the second one of "That Mysterious Rag," put in contrary motion. The same thing could be said about the eighth bar of the two pieces. Finally, their fourth bar is the same, apart from one interval.

With relation to rhythm and melody, the *Ragtime du Paquebot* is thus close to "That Mysterious Rag." This kinship is only attenuated by the inversion of the parts from one composition to the other, and by the modification of the dimensions of each part. The theme of the *Ragtime du Paquebot* owes to the melody of "That Mysterious Rag," but despite this proximity, Satie's music cannot be automatically linked to its model by the listener.

TABLE 3.3. Structure of "That Mysterious Rag" (Irving Berlin)

	Introduction	Prelude	Verse 1		Chorus		
Bars	1–8	9–10	11–26		27–50		
Number of bars	8	2	16		24		
Subdivision	C′	A′	A	B	C	D	C′
Bars	1–8	9–10	11–18	19–27	27–34	35–42	43–5
Number of bars	8	2	8	8	8	8	8
Tonal plan	C major	Dominant of A minor	Dominant of A minor and A minor (bar 17)	G major	C major	A minor and return to C major	C ma

Harmonic Sophistication

Harmony is the principal mean through which Satie distinguishes his composition from "That Mysterious Rag." In spite of the relatively simple modulations (to the relative minor and to the subdominant[16]) displayed in table 3.3, he employs more-sophisticated harmonic devices, absent from the ragtimes composed at the same time. Two examples can be singled out.

First, the bass lines of "That Mysterious Rag" are invariably composed of the root tonic of the chords or their bass in the case of an inversion. Satie's approach is slightly different. It consists in giving his bass lines a melodic quality. As a consequence, in some diatonic passages where the music is close to authentic ragtimes, the *Ragtime du Paquebot* sounds lighter, and harmonically more colorful. By the same token, it loses a bit of the energy and the straightforwardness of the characteristic oom-pah pattern.

In the very beginning of the *Ragtime du Paquebot*, when shifting from the first degree to the sixth (a shift used often in ragtime), Satie gives the cellos passing notes that provoke original sonorities, like the third inversion of a major seventh chord (when the bass hits the B), as well as a chord composed by two stacked-up perfect fourths (D–G–C). Fleeting as they may be, those sonorities, very rare if not nonexistent in jazz in those days, give the *Ragtime du Paquebot* a unique harmonic flavor.

The second harmonic feature that distinguishes *Paquebot* from regular ragtimes is the use of sophisticated harmonic surprises in certain passages of Satie's composition. At bar 26, Satie suggests a perfect cadence in C major thanks to an

Prelude	Verse 2		Chorus		
9–10	11–26		27–50		
2	16		24		
A′	A	B	C	D	C
9–10	11–18	18–27	27–34	35–42	43–50
2 (repeated ad lib.)	8	8	8	8	8
Dominant of A minor	Dominant of A minor and A minor (bar 17)	G major	C major	A minor and return to C major	C major

augmented sixth chord on the augmented fourth degree, followed by a dominant chord. This progression is perverted, as it were, by a winding melodic line of the first violins.

Instead of resolving this tension with a perfect chord on the first degree, the composer adds another dominant chord (third inversion of the dominant of G) at bar 27. The double basses and the cellos, which are given the equivalent of the characteristic writing of the left hand of piano ragtime, are given a tritone. To the surprise created by this deceptive cadence is added the dissonant sonority of the bass. In order to complicate this passage, Satie gives the first violins a sinuous melodic line, with strong appoggiaturas (B-natural and C-sharp at bar 26) and passing notes (B-flat at bar 27). Eventually, these two bars give the listener the impression of something both odd and jeering.[17] This kind of tone is perfectly appropriate to the almost surrealistic libretto of *Parade*.

All these analytical remarks pave the way for more general considerations about the *Ragtime du Paquebot*. It can be considered as a rewrite of Irving Berlin's "That Mysterious Rag." Satie's approach can be linked with Debussy's, insofar as both composers deal with quotation (ragtime in general in the latter's case, one particular ragtime in the former's). Nevertheless, the balance between resemblance and dissimilarity is not the same in these compositions, because they do not share the same objectives.

If the opening and closing parts of Debussy's *Golliwog's Cakewalk* stay close to ragtime,[18] the *Ragtime du Paquebot* is more loosely related to its model. All along his composition, Satie keeps using musical features of the genre that are always

TABLE 3.4. Satie's utilization of "That Mysterious Rag" in the *Ragtime du Paquebot*

	A	B	A'
Bars	1–24	25–36	37–44
Number of bars	24	12	8
Utilization of rhythmic sequence from "That Mysterious Rag"	Utilization of all the rhythmic sequence from the chorus	Utilization of all the rhythmic sequence of the verse from its fifth bar	Utilization of the rhythmic sequence of the last eight bars of the chorus
Utilization of melodic elements from "That Mysterious Rag"	Global modification of the melody, but some characteristic patterns are used	Modification of the melodic profile	Global modification of the melody, but some characteristic patterns are used

again — bit problematic

recognizable, yet produces a more refined and more sophisticated music. He gives the listener no more references to ragtime than what is necessary and essential to identify the musical genre. As to "That Mysterious Rag," it is not really quoted but subtly evoked. What is "Mysterious" is the *Ragtime du Paquebot* itself, because one has to decipher it if he wants to identify the source that Satie used as a framework for his composition.

To formalize the foregoing remarks, one of Gérard Genette's five categories of "transtextuality" can be applied. Transtextuality refers to "whatever links, openly or secretly, a text with another."[19] Debussy's and Satie's compositions can be related to what Genette calls "hypertextuality"—that is to say, a relation of imitation between two texts or between one text and one genre. This imitation is meant to be perceived. In Debussy's case, what is imitated is ragtime as a genre. This imitation is ludic. In Genette's terms, *Golliwog's Cakewalk* is then a pastiche. In Satie's case, it is not a genre but a composition that is imitated ("That Mysterious Rag"), even if Satie never seeks to write an authentic orchestral ragtime. Indeed, his imitation is full of personal inventions. Because of the presence of a creative imagination applied to a preexisting model, the *Ragtime du Paquebot* is not a pastiche, but what Genette calls a "*forgerie*."[20] The use of these technical terms is not the ultimate goal of analysis. It nonetheless helps to formalize efficiently the different ways of integrating jazz into art music.

In 1923, that is six years after the composition of *Parade*, Darius Milhaud gave birth to one of the most famous composition using jazz—*La Création du monde*. His approach differs quite considerably from Debussy's and Satie's.

EXAMPLE 6: *Ragtime du Paquebot*, bars 26–27

Milhaud's La Création du Monde: *Assimilating Jazz*

Contrary to Debussy and Satie, Milhaud learned about jazz not only through the prism of scores, but also through direct contacts with African American musicians,[21] and above all thanks to a stay in New York in 1922. His autobiography, *Ma vie heureuse*,[22] and an article entitled "L'évolution du jazz-band et de la musique des nègres d'Amérique du nord," published in 1923 in *Le Courrier Musical*,[23] are among the first thorough writings about jazz music by a composer. These texts are full of valuable information with regard to the opening fugue of *La Création du monde*. Some passages must be drawn attention to.

What struck Milhaud first was the instrumentation of jazz bands, mostly the dominance of the brasses, the saxophones, and the set of percussive instruments[24] played by one single musician: "In *Liza*, an operetta by the black American composer Maceo Pinkard (1897–1962), the orchestra is made of one flute, 61 one clarinet, two trumpets, one trombone, percussion played by one instrumentalist, a piano, a string quartet (the viola is replaced by an alto saxophone) and a double bass."[25] This list corresponds almost exactly to the instrumentation of *La Création du monde*. Second, during his trip to the United States, Milhaud had understood that the jazz music played in France was more rigidly interpreted than in America. Most important, he realized that jazz music performed in France was almost entirely written, whereas in the kind of jazz he heard in Harlem, "the space devoted to improvisation is more important. . . . Technically speaking, they [the musicians] are more at ease: each instrument has his own melodic line. . . . We are constantly in the presence of a disconcerting web of intermingled lines."[26] What strikes the composer are the new perspectives offered by the polyrhythms generated by the collective improvisation. Milhaud subsequently conceived a personal approach consisting in adapting the aforementioned characteristics to his musical language, in order to bring innovations into the field of art music. In this view, this last extract from his writings on jazz is telling: "what is to be done is offering the jazz bands a repertoire of instrumental chamber music, sonatas written for instruments that usually compose jazz bands."[27]

Milhaud's position was similar to that shared by many musical critics in the United States: ragtime was an interesting but primitive music that should be civilized by well-trained composers. In short, ragtime should be refined and adapted to art music. This view was clearly expressed by composer Charles Wakefield Cadman: "What is implied is that the beginnings of a healthy, red-corpuscle American music may be achieved by employing certain idealized and dignified forms of syncopation, coupled with a proper sense of balance and sanity in the creation of such music. [. . .] A few American composers have consciously or unconsciously cast certain large orchestral and chamber works in this pattern and have achieved a relative success. Why not experiment further?"[28]

Milhaud's remarks, like Cadman's, are almost programmatic, and can be used as guidelines to orientate the analysis of the fugue that opens *La Création du monde*. How does Milhaud integrate the features of jazz that he has identified into his own musical language?

A Fugue Built on a Blues Melody

Milhaud did not want to emulate a *fugue d'école*:[29] the different occurrences of his theme are not built on the tonic and the dominant. The iteration of the theme cannot be analyzed as a counterexposition or a reexposition. Nevertheless, the structure of this piece is patently inspired by the *fugue d'école*. Table 3.5 shows that a contrasting part precedes the return of the main theme. Considered through the prism of *fugue d'école*, this part can be heard as an episode. What is more, the introduction heard just before the fugue strongly brings to mind the diptych prelude-fugue.

What is remarkable here is that Milhaud applies some compositional techniques among the most representative of art music to a theme[30] reminiscent of blues. References to the blues can be found in the permanent ambiguity between the major and the minor thirds, in the heady repetition of a melodic motive,[31] and in the syncopated rhythm that closes it.

Whereas these elements refer to jazz, the way Milhaud builds his main theme also evokes art music. Its initial motif (an ascending and descending major second; ascending and descending minor third) seems to burgeon spontaneously (the second statement of the motif is lengthened and widened to the major third). Finally, the initial motif is transposed to the perfect fifth and reaches a climax before the tension decreases until the sixth bar of the theme.

Thorough and tedious as this motivic analysis may be, it shows that the theme of that fugue is built according to the principles of organic development, a technique strongly associated with art music. In other words, the way the theme is conceived can be heard as a metaphor of the process of creation.

Contrary to Debussy and Satie, Milhaud does not seek to put jazz into contrast with other genres. Nor does he want to build an effect of quotation, even if, as André Hodeir notices, the "countersubject contains the initial motif of the most famous jazz theme, *Saint Louis Blues*."[32] The reference is so slender that it can by no means be identified by the listener.

Instead of referring clearly to a genre or to a preexisting composition, Milhaud tries to merge musical traits of jazz with compositional techniques typical of art music. As a result, the fugue from *La Création du monde* cannot be clearly identified with art music or with jazz. The integration of jazz into art music is closer to "assimilation," since Milhaud seeks to blur the frontiers between the two genres. While Debussy's and Satie's approaches are a matter of *hypertextuality*, Milhaud's approach is closer to *intertextuality*, another category defined by Gérard Genette in *Palimpsestes*. One can speak of intertextuality when a text combines codes characteristic of other texts or other genres. Such a co-presence is not meant to be identified, which means that intertextuality has nothing to do with quotation. This combination can also be observed when it comes to rhythm.

An Original Use of Polyrhythm

Evoked by Milhaud in the aforementioned texts, the presence of the drums is another reference to jazz, as the syncopation created by the systematic use of the snare drum on the weak parts of the beat. What is noticeable is the pattern played by the bass drum, which does not indicate the strong or the weak beats. The periodicity created by type of bar chosen by Milhaud (4/4) is not the same as

TABLE 3.5. Structure of the "Fugue" from *La Création du monde*

	Intro.	Exposition				Episode 1
Bars	1–3	4–23				24–29
Number of bars	3	20				6
Subdivision	Intro.	Entry 1	Entry 2	Entry 3	Entry 4	Episode 1
Bars	1–3	4–8	9–13	14–18	19–23	24–29
Number of bars	3	5	5	5	5	6
Description	Rhythm section	Double bass	Trombone	Saxophone	Trumpet	–
Density of the polyrhythm (number of layers)	2	3				
Remarks	–	–	–	–	–	The double basses, cellos, and left hand of the piano stress the beats

the periodicity of the rhythmic pattern written for the bass drum (3+3+3+3+4 beats). Beginning at bar 3, the superimposition of this rhythmic pattern with the theme creates a two-layered polyrhythm.

The use of the drums draws a link between the fugue from the *Création du Monde* and jazz. But what Milhaud looks for is not only an exotic effect consisting of integrating African American sonorities into art music. He reemploys the drums so as to explore rhythmical combinations unknown by jazz music in the beginning of the 1920s.

All along the fugue, Milhaud progressively densifies this polyrhythm by adding new layers at the beginning of each part. Table 3.6 shows that the two-layer polyrhythm at the beginning of the piece becomes seven layers at the end. These layers can be heard and analyzed as autonomous lines allocated to instrumental groups. From bar 50 to bar 57, for instance, seven rhythmically independent lines can be distinguished: one for the double basses, the cellos, the drums, and the left hand of the piano, the second for the kettledrums, the third for the right hand of the piano, doubled by the horns and the bassoons, the fourth for the

"Contre-exposition"				Episode 2	"Re-exposition"		Coda
30–45				46–50	51–57		58–59
16				5	7		2
Entry 1	Entry 2	Entry 3	Entry 4	Episode 2	Entry 1	Entry 2	Coda
30–33	34–37	38–41	42–45	46–50	51–54	55–57	58–59
4	4	4	4	5	4	3	2
4 occurrences of the theme given to the clarinet (on A, C, G, D)				—	Violins (on D)		—
4				5	6 and 7		—
Acceleration produced by entries every 4 bars instead of 5; glissandi played by the trombone and the saxophone				The double basses, cellos, and left hand of the piano stress the beats; glissandi played by the trombone	Acceleration produced by a *stretto* (2 beats) between violins 1 and 2		—

trombones, the fifth and the sixth for the trumpets and the clarinets, and the last for the flutes.

This superimposition, in a moment when the dynamics are *ff*, when the beats are stressed by the first instrumental group, the glissandi played by the trombones (a feature borrowed by Milhaud from the jazz orchestras he had heard), results in an exuberant and almost cataclysmic music.

This passage is close to the spirit of collective, polyphonic improvisation in New Orleans jazz (even if it does not sound like such an improvisation), and can be linked with the above-mentioned "disconcerting web of intermingled lines"[33] heard by Milhaud in New York. Nuances can thus be heard in André Hodeir's somewhat disdainful assertion about this passage: "The resulting impression of disorder was certainly intentional, even if it seems that the author did not perfectly master the forces he was arousing."[34] In fact, it is as if Milhaud tried to reproduce the musical impression created by this kind of improvisation in the field of written music. Once again, his approach consists in elaborating on musical features directly drawn from jazz.

EXAMPLE 7: "Fugue" from *La Création du monde*, bars 1–10

As far as instrumentation and improvisation are concerned, these analytical remarks based on the fugue from *La Création du monde* correspond exactly with the written comments on jazz by Milhaud. What is more, the programmatic statement made by the young composer ("what is to be done is offering the jazz bands a repertoire of instrumental chamber music, sonatas written for the instruments that usually compose jazz bands"[35]) seems to be thoroughly applied in *La Création du monde*. Jazz is assimilated and merged into the field of art music.

Unlike Debussy and Satie, Milhaud does not employ jazz to generate a contrast with other musical genres whose connotations are extremely different. There is neither humor nor mockery in *La Création du monde*. If Satie's and Debussy's approaches have already been differentiated, Milhaud's can be considered as a third way to utilize jazz in high art music.

None of the three composers refer to the same music; none of the three use it in the same kind of work; none of the three combine jazz and art music in the same manner.

On the one hand, the analysis of three major works of the corpus of art music composition using jazz shows that each composer uses his own knowledge of jazz and integrates it in his own way to art music, from hypertextuality to intertex-

EXAMPLE 8: "Fugue" from *La Création du monde*, bars 48–51

tuality, from pastiche to assimilation, thus following his own musical preoccupations. Such a diversity does not mean that the corpus of art music using jazz lacks coherence. Nevertheless, it raises new questions. Is the use of jazz only a means to appear as a composer à la mode,[36] or does it mean anything deeper? Can this corpus be linked with aesthetical trends cutting new paths through the field of art music during the 1910s and the 1920s in France?

On the other hand, the three analyses reveal that the corpus of compositions using jazz is part of a broader movement rejecting the influence of Romanticism in general, and of Wagnerism in particular, and simultaneously promoting new values, mainly those of neoclassicism for the purpose of regenerating a so-called French music.

good questions

From Desacralization to Neoclassicism

Studying the corpus of high music using jazz immediately raises one question: which composers did take interest in jazz? Once this group is determined, is it possible to point out any coherent links among its members? At first sight, it seems difficult to gather such composers as Debussy, Satie, Stravinsky, Milhaud, and Ravel[37] into a single group. However, they all rejected (publicly at least) aesthetic conceptions that are the core of Romanticism in general, and Wagnerism in particular. As far as the utilization of jazz is concerned, the stakes are a double desacralization of Wagnerian imagination—specifically of the notion of the Sublime, and of a hierarchy of genres putting opera and symphonic music on a pedestal. One way or another, *Golliwog's Cakewalk*, the *Ragtime du Paquebot*, and the "Fugue" from *La Création du monde* deal with this double desacralization.

Debussy's Desacralization of the Wagnerian Imaginary

In *Golliwog's Cakewalk*, just before *d* (at bar 61) Debussy uses a melodic pattern which is immediately recognizable: the famous opening leitmotiv of *Tristan und Isolde* by Wagner[38] (example 9).

This quotation gives the apparently innocent *Golliwog's Cakewalk* an ironical tone. Indeed, at the beginning of the twentieth century, ragtime was perceived in France as a lowbrow music played in cabarets and music halls, both places where musical tastes were considered doubtful. This perception was shared by some American commentators like Arthur Weld.[39] Inserting in a ragtime a leitmotiv considered as the musical embodiment of love and pathos, as well as a summit of Romanticism in music, can be considered as a means to mock Wagnerism. Indeed, more than an homage, this game with the connotations of two very different musical genres is a way to desacralize what was considered to be sublime in Wagner's music.

Some hints reveal Debussy's intentions: each time the leitmotiv appears in the score, one can read the following indication: "avec une grande émotion."[40] Here, Debussy wants a clear contrast with the playful mood of *Golliwog's Cakewalk*. In addition, through repeated notes and appoggiaturas, the music itself seems to mock this Wagnerian quotation. According to Maurice Dumesnil, one of Debussy's favorite interpreters, the composer told him to "overplay" this passage. *Golliwog's Cakewalk* is thus much more than an example of exoticism in music. In this little composition, music comments on itself.

To come back to Genette's categories, this passage is different from the rest of *Golliwog's Cakewalk*. Debussy does not use pastiche, which is a process of imitation, but instead creates a parody, which is a process of transformation.[41] Wagnerian music jars with ragtime. Material borrowed from high art is introduced

EXAMPLE 9: *Golliwog's Cakewalk*

in a lowbrow context. The central part of *Golliwog's Cakewalk* is a perfect musical example of burlesque obtained by a clever and mocking use of musical genres. This iconoclastic utilization of the connotations of genres is also to be found in the global structure of Satie's *Parade*.

Satie: Desacralizing the Hierarchy of Genres

In *Parade*, the three routines[42] are framed by the exposition of a fugue in the "Prélude du rideau rouge," and by a reexposition of this fugue in the conclusive "Suite au prélude du rideau rouge." According to musicologist Ornella Volta, these two numbers are complementary: "The *Ragtime du Paquebot* was conceived as the exposition of a four-part Fugue . . . followed by a brief episode that gets stuck during three bars before suddenly stopping. After the three routines of *Parade* that form the core of the work appears the counterexposition of the Fugue that was exposed in the Prelude."[43] It is as if the parade was meant to replace this lacking part, which should have been a succession of episodes. The term "parade" corresponds to what Satie himself called "ornamental music" and "ambiance music, and it is no accident that Satie used these two expressions when evoking his three routines.

The overall organization of *Parade* gives much value to functional music, to which art music is most often only a curtain-raiser. The abovementioned centrality of the *Ragtime du Paquebot* is thus given a value at least equal to the value of art music. By the same token, Satie puts into question a canonic hierarchy of genres where art music, and especially the fugue, is at the top and popular modern music at the bottom. He goes further and turns this hierarchy upside down. Indeed, the chorale and the fugue are reduced to the role of curtain-raisers, which is usually the role of functional music.[44] On the contrary, the core of *Parade*, that is to say the part of the work where music is supposed to be heard for music's sake, consists only of entertainment music.

What is expressed through music under Debussy's pen and through structure in Satie's case is firmly stated by Milhaud in one of his articles.

Milhaud against the Wagnerian Fog and the Impressionist Mist

"L'évolution de la musique à Paris et à Vienne"[45] displays a more direct criticism of Wagnerism, associated with a relative coldness toward Debussyism. Milhaud's objections are leveled at musical aspects of these two trends and can be linked with the defense of French music against German influence:[46]

> Pessimism, the longing for seriousness, above all things, really created the musicians who founded the Schola Cantorum. They were naturally predisposed to receive favorably the tremendous influence that very nearly upset our national line of music. I mean Richard Wagner. I am not to censure Wagner. [. . .] He is and will always remain a formidable musician, and his enormous work was exactly appropriate. It is quite natural that before such a mighty power, many hesitated and fell. But, on the other hand, certain temperaments could not accept that form of thought. And in the face of this great clamor (where the noise of steel resounds in a foggy landscape) [. . .] the adorable subtlety of Debussy's writing (perfect in his case, because he possessed a wonderful sense of criticism and a sensitive nature) became the source of the movement called "Impressionism" which, combined with Rimsky's influence, led French music into a blind alley, where useless complications, the search for rare and delicate sonority instead of pure melody, caused a reaction. [. . .] After the blow of the Sacre du Printemps, Satie fully realized himself. He brought back music to simplicity and opened the path for the French musicians of the School "d'Après Guerre." He then gave us *Parade*, where the souvenir of music halls creates a new and attractive art.[47]

Later in this article, Milhaud evokes again this French school, mostly composed of the other members from the Groupe des Six. There follows an encomium of their quest of "clarity" and their "return to simplicity" that gives its identity back to French music.

As far as structure, harmony, and mood are concerned, these characteristics can be found in *Golliwog's Cakewalk*,[48] the *Ragtime du Paquebot*, and the "Fugue" from *La Création du monde*. All three compositions adopt a form in which the different parts are clearly separated. Even if they display some harmonic intricacies, they follow a relatively simple tonal plan and are based on a tonal language. What is more, none of these compositions conveys dark emotions. Rather they display gaiety and vitality, thanks, mostly, to rhythm.

These three examples from the corpus of high music compositions using jazz are in keeping with Milhaud's argumentation, and also with the famous defense of French music by Cocteau in *Le Coq et l'arlequin*. Cocteau, an adroit defender of the Groupe des Six, wished to promote a "French music from France"[49] that had to haul itself out of a Wagnerism and a musical impressionism that he considered to be its extension in France.[50] This quotation from *Le Coq et l'arlequin* underlines the community of ideas between Milhaud and Cocteau: "Simplicity must not be taken as a synonym of poverty or decline [...] simplicity that is a reaction against refinement is a matter of refinement."[51]

French music had to come back to its own characteristics: clarity and simplicity. To achieve this goal, it had to find new sources of inspiration in the rich and lively world of the everyday. For Cocteau, this world of the everyday meant popular music. By popular music, he was not referring to what we call "folk music," which had been used by Romantic composers, and by members of the Schola Cantorum. In *Le Coq et l'arlequin*, Cocteau gives some examples of what he means by "popular music": "As life, music-hall, circus, Negro American orchestras fertilize the artist. Using emotions conveyed by such shows is not making art from art. These shows are not art, they make us excited as do machines, animals, sceneries, and danger."[52]

Such a quotation deserves comment. For Debussy, as for Satie or Milhaud, the music played by "Negro American Orchestras"—what was generally called "jazz" in France at the beginning of the 1920s—was not considered art (that is, high music[53]), but was viewed as an interesting source, useful to distance their music from the aesthetics they wished to depart from. This source also appeared as a way to give music new possibilities of expression.

From now on, a paradox can be solved—jazz, a music exclusively associated with the United States at the beginning of the 1920s, was cited by Cocteau as a music capable of contributing to the regeneration of French music. French composers were less interested in the national connotations for which jazz was a vehicle, than in the new moods and the new musical ideas that could inspire French composers. Simplicity, rhythmic efficiency, vitality—the qualities of jazz heard by French composers and by Jean Cocteau at the beginning of the twentieth century—corresponded to the new orientations they wanted to give to their music, in order to distance it from Romanticism and Wagnerism in particular.

Parade by Satie was considered by Cocteau as the manifesto of the aesthetics he promoted because it avoided the principal sources of inspiration of the composers he condemned. *Parade* has nothing to do with the world of legends geographically and historically far away from everyday life, but draws from the world of circus.

Finally, what was targeted by Debussy, Satie, and Milhaud was the notion of the sublime, a key concept of Romanticism. Belonging to the everyday life, and to the world of entertainment, jazz stood as an efficient antidote against this category. Unlike Wagnerian music, the compositions analyzed here are short; they

refuse lengthy developments and poignant effects.[54] *Parade*, for instance, uses neither "pedals that melt the rhythm" nor "the stroke of strings." Their orchestration "does not use sauce."[55]

Furthermore, poetic and suggestive titles used by impressionist composers[56] are abandoned and give way to titles referring to the everyday life (*Golliwog's Cakewalk*, *Ragtime du Paquebot*) or to pure music (*Trois blues chantés* [1924] by Jean Wiéner, "Fox-trot" [1922] from *Épithalame* by Jean Roger-Ducasse). This aspect of the desacralization was also tackled by Cocteau: "One wonders why Satie rigs out his best works with funny titles. [. . .] These titles protect his work against listeners in the grip of Sublime and give the right to laugh to those who do not care about it. What is more, they can be explained by the abuse of mannered titles by Debussist composers."[57]

The characteristics of jazz that are present in art music compositions coincide with those of French music as described by Cocteau. The three compositions analyzed in this article display a simple architecture, an absence of development (replaced by juxtaposition), short dimensions, and very lively moods. All of them refuse pathos. Rhythms and a straightforwardness of harmony drawn from jazz contribute to give the art music compositions that use jazz the clarity evoked by Cocteau.

Are these examples of desacralization of art music and of the authorized hierarchy of genres mere iconoclastic provocations, typical of avant-gardism? It is true that these three pieces are more telling than the rest of the corpus of art compositions using jazz music. Nevertheless, they played a role in a broader movement that questioned a Romantic conception of music—neoclassicism. This statement paves the way for a reconsideration of the three works by taking into account the aesthetical evolutions that reshaped the field of art music during the first decades of the twentieth century. What do *Golliwog's Cakewalk*, the *Ragtime du Paquebot*, the "Fugue" from *La Création du monde* share with neoclassicism?

Proximity with Neoclassicism

Above all, these three compositions display a simple and clear conception of form, rid of the subtly intricate and lengthy forms used by the last Romantic composers. What is more, it can be noticed that the compositions that use jazz turn their back on two of the most representative genres of Romanticism: opera and pure symphonic music. Some of them are part of ballets, like the *Ragtime du Paquebot*, the "Fugue" from *La Création du monde*, but also Stravinsky's "Ragtime" from *L'Histoire du soldat*, and Ravel's "Foxtrot" from *L'enfant et les sortilèges*. Another group belongs to chamber music (*Golliwog's Cakewalk*, Ravel's

"Blues" from the *Sonata for Violin and Piano*, or the *Three Rag-Caprices for Chamber Orchestra* [1922] by Milhaud). Neoclassicist composers made an extensive use of these two genres.

Utilization of Simplified Forms

Though very close to ragtime, *Golliwog's Cakewalk* can be heard and analyzed from a broader standpoint. Table 3.6 shows that the succession of different parts mentioned at the beginning of this article is organized in a tripartite form: ABA', where A, B, and A' are clearly isolated by transitions.

By creating a formal ambiguity, Debussy exploits the rules of codified forms, which is one of the characteristic features of neoclassicism. This approach was also adopted by Serguéï Prokofiev in his *Symphonie classique*.[58] That is one reason why it can be said that in *Golliwog's Cakewalk*, ragtime is used in a neoclassical way.[59]

A similar neoclassical approach to ragtime can be found in Satie's *Ragtime du Paquebot*. Table 3.2 illustrates the fact that the structure using strains[60] and thus close to ragtime can also be seen as a more global ABA' form with almost no transition organically leading from one part to another.

On a broader scale, the organization of *Parade* reflects an architectural thought. The general structure of *Parade* shows that the "Ragtime" occupies the exact center of the work. (See Table 3.7.) "Petite Fille Américaine" is framed by the two other routines ("Prestidigitateur chinois" and "Acrobates") and by an introduction and a conclusion (the "Prélude du rideau rouge"). Besides, a closer look at the score shows that the *Ragtime du Paquebot* is also the center of "Petite fille américaine." Therefore, Satie's ragtime is given a central position and hence importance, at the core of a work whose construction is perfectly symmetrical and clear—in a word, classic.[61]

Neoclassic Aesthetics of "Salade"

What contributes to link the three compositions in question to neoclassicism is not only the mock attacks against a canonical hierarchy of genres, but also a perpetual blending of genres that belong to totally different spheres of music. Ragtime and opera coexist in *Golliwog's Cakewalk*, blues and fugue live together in *La Création du monde*. As for *Parade*, it juxtaposes ragtime, fugue, Chinese exoticism (that is America, Europe, and Asia), and even noises[62] in an almost cubist way. This kind of blending is to be found very frequently in the corpus of art music using jazz. The "Blues" by Ravel constitutes the second movement of a serious violin sonata. In Stravinsky's *L'Histoire du soldat*, the "Ragtime" is part of a dance suite also containing a tango and a waltz. One "Blues" and one "Foxtrot" by Bohuslav Martinů (1890–1959) belong to a cycle of eight preludes for

TABLE 3.6. The three parts of *Golliwog's Cakewalk*

	Introduction	A	Transition	B	Transition	A'	Coda
Bars	1-9	10-37	38-46	47-84	85-89	90-117	118-128
Number of bars	9 (4+1+4)	28	9	42	5	28	11

piano.[63] These works use styles that are geographically and historically rooted, to transform them into codes with which they play. In art music from the 1910s and the 1920s, jazz is used in a repertoire dominated by eclecticism, a key notion in neoclassicism, absent from another avant-gardistic movement, the Second Viennese School, which was more preoccupied by the purity of dodecaphonism and serialism.

Conclusion

In 1934, Darius Milhaud reviewed the first concert by Louis Armstrong in Paris. "Interesting as this virtuoso may be, a jazz concert is not possible anymore today. [. . .] It sounds too much old-fashioned to support without boredom [. . .] this tamed hurricane[,] though it brought so much relief to music in 1920, when it put an end to the last stupors of impressionist fireworks."[64]

According to Milhaud, jazz brought to high music the musical means to break with previous aesthetics. True, this role was played mostly from 1917 to 1924, when French art music was looking for new paths. However, in spite of Milhaud's personal opinion, many composers based in Paris kept using jazz in works, even if these works were less subversive for the field of art music than Milhaud's, Debussy's, and Satie's compositions during the 1910s and the beginning of the 1920s.

Golliwog's Cakewalk, the *Ragtime du Paquebot* from *Parade*, and the "Fugue" from *La Création du monde*, tell a lot about the integration of jazz and pre-jazz styles in art music. Debussy, Satie, and Milhaud experienced jazz in different ways. Debussy listened to John Philip Sousa in Paris in 1903 and, like Satie, probably read ragtime scores. Milhaud had the opportunity to listen to jazz in Harlem in 1923, a jazz that, according to his articles, was closer to New Orleans jazz than to ragtime. This diversity of sources partly explains the important differences displayed by the corpus of art music compositions employing jazz—only "partly" because these differences principally result from the kind of integration of jazz that the composers chose. *Golliwog's Cakewalk* is both a pastiche of ragtime and a parody of Wagner. The *Ragtime du Paquebot* is a *"forgerie,"* and the "Fugue" from *La Création du monde* assimilates jazz into a flagship genre of art music.

TABLE 3.7.

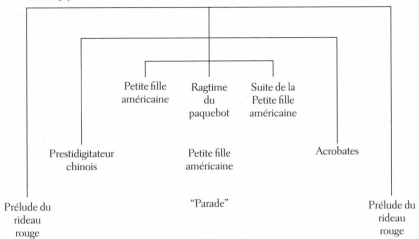

Petite fille américaine   Ragtime du paquebot   Suite de la Petite fille américaine

Prestidigitateur chinois   Petite fille américaine   Acrobates

Prélude du rideau rouge   "Parade"   Prélude du rideau rouge

Under this undeniable diversity are hidden deeper similarities that lie on an aesthetic level. The corpus of art music using jazz is part of a more global movement turning its back on Wagnerism and Debussyism and looking for new paths toward modernity, a modernity distinct from the Second Viennese School. In this regard, what Debussy, Satie, and Milhaud wrote (in words) corresponds to what they composed, as seen with Milhaud's articles.

What also unites composers who adopted jazz is an attempt to redefine French music. The notions brought to light are simplicity and clarity, and formal balance. In terms of music, these ideas correspond to the utilization of simpler forms understandable to the listener, to a language based on tonality, and to lively moods that avoid too much seriousness and too much pathos. All these characteristics correspond to the definition of neoclassicism, and can also be found in the jazz French composers heard. Therefore, it is no accident if most of the composers who made use of jazz were close to this movement.

This open attitude toward jazz was shared by only one group of French composers. Some of their colleagues, like Vincent d'Indy, Jean-Guy Ropartz, Joseph Canteloube,[65] Paul Dukas, or Florent Schmitt, also brought fundamental contributions to French music but sometimes openly despised jazz, and never used it. What distinguishes composers who adopted jazz from others is not only an inclination toward neoclassicism, but more generally toward avant-gardism.

Beyond neoclassicism, Milhaud was also keen on the idea that primitivism could renew art. At the end of the "Fugue," the rhythmical energy and the obsessive regularity of the beat of jazz reach a primitive dimension. At the same time this overflowing energy is contained by the mechanical aspect of the fugue,

75

taken as a genre, and by the rigor of the musical architecture created by Milhaud. From this association comes the original and unique impression that one can feel when listening to *La Création du monde*. On the one hand, modernity is tinged with primitivism. On the other hand, primitive energy is tinged with mechanism, a notion that became central in society and modern art after the Great War.

This triangular relation between jazz, primitivism, and mechanism helps explain why avant-gardist composers paid attention to this music. Mechanism was indeed a topic that fascinated a lot of musicians during the 1920s. Arthur Honegger composed his *Pacific 231* in 1923; George Antheil had his *Ballet mécanique* premièred in 1926. In the young USSR, Alexander Mossolov composed the famous *Iron Foundry*. Though not using jazz, these work are comparable with *La Création du monde* because the outburst of energy generated by the evocation of modern subjects (trains, machines, ironworks) is so powerful that it breaks all the rules of civilization dominated by temperance and moderation. Finally this overflowing of energy implied by modernity meets the overflowing of vitality usually associated with primitivism.

This same dialectic relation is exploited in *L'Inhumaine* (1924), a film by Marcel L'Herbier. A party takes place in famous singer Claire Lescot's modern house. Whereas its architecture is clearly inspired by geometrism and new technologies, the guests are entertained by an African American orchestra playing jazz. In this sequence, L'Herbier markedly contrasts the coldness and the self-control of the host with the energy spontaneously brought by the musicians.

In sum, not only did the characteristics of the jazz that French composers heard or read in scores fit the aesthetical project of neoclassic composers. These characteristics also attracted another branch of the avant-garde during the 1920s—a branch more interested in insufflating energy into music.

Granted, the corpus of art music compositions using jazz represents only a small fraction of the total production of music during the 1910s and the 1920s. Its importance must not be overemphasized. Nevertheless, a study of this corpus is important for two reasons. For one, it shows that the use of jazz in art music was not a mere ephemeral fashion; the part it played in the aesthetic debates that shook the French musical world in search of a new identity was not negligible. More generally, it can be viewed as a landmark, since it opened concerted reflection on the hierarchy between highbrow and lowbrow musical genres.

NOTES

1. In this chapter, I use the signification of "jazz" as conveyed by musical press and musicians in the second half of the 1910s and in the 1920s in France. Nowadays, many of the styles it once covered are not considered "jazz," most notably ragtime.

2. "In Paris, it [ragtime] is called "american music." Anonymous, "What Is American Music?" *Musical America* 3, February 1906. From this point forward, the term *jazz* appears without quotation marks.

3. Jackson, Jeffrey H., *Making Jazz French: Music and Modern Life in Interwar Paris* (Durham, NC: Duke University Press, 2003).

4. Perloff, Nancy, *Art and the Everyday: Popular Entertainment and the Circle of Érik Satie* (Oxford: Clarendon Press, 1991).

5. By "art music," I mean what we usually call "classical music."

6. A nondefinitive version of this corpus can be found at the end of this article.

7. Even if it has been sketched in 1935 by Robert Rogers. See Rogers, Robert, "Jazz Influence on French Music," *Musical Quarterly* 21, no. 1, January 1935, pp. 53-68.

8. Hodeir, André, *Hommes et problèmes du jazz*, Flammarion, Paris, 1954, réed. Parenthèses, Marseille, 1996, ch. 16. Hodeir, André, "L'influence du jazz sur la musique européenne," *Les Temps Modernes*, 9e année, no. 99, February 1954, pp. 1477-92.

9. Hodeir, André, *Hommes et problèmes du jazz*, p. 225.

10. The term "Romanticism" must be taken in a broad sense, as a musical tradition perpetuated at the end of the nineteenth century by composers like Wagner, or at the beginning of the twentieth century by Bruckner or Mahler.

11. Cocteau, Jean, *Le Coq et l'arlequin: Notes autour de la musique* (Paris: Stock Musique, préface de Georges Auric, 1979; first edition, Paris: Éd. de la Sirène, Collection des tracts, 1, 1918).

12. *Prélude pour l'après-midi d'un faune* (1892-94) or *La mer* (1903-5), for example.

13. Except between bars 85-88 that lead to the reexposition.

14. Some French musicians composed real ragtimes. To take only two examples, Gabriel Lordon published "A Jolly Cake Walk" in 1903. The same year, Roger de Beaumercy composed a "Cake Walk de salon." Unlike Claude Debussy, these composers scrupulously respected the rules of ragtime.

15. Composed in 1911, "That Mysterious Rag" was one of the first songs composed by Irving Berlin.

16. The most frequent modulations in classical ragtime.

17. This impression is reinforced by the fact that Satie doubles the basses at bar 26 with clarinets. In 1916, this orchestral device did not exist in orchestral ragtime.

18. Except for the contrasting B, which abandons the model of ragtime.

19. Genette, Gérard, *Palimpsestes: La littérature au second degré* (Paris: Seuil, coll. Essais, 1982), p. 7.

20. The choice of this term owes a lot to the signification of the English word "forgery."

21. Like the saxophonist Vance Lowry, who used to play at Le Boeuf sur le Toit.

22. Milhaud, Darius, *Ma vie heureuse* (Paris: Belfond, 1973).

23. *Le Courrier Musical* 25, no. 9, 1923, in Milhaud, Darius, *Notes sur la musique, textes réunis et présentés par Jeremy Drake* (Paris: Flammarion, coll. Harmoniques, 1982).

24. In all likelihood, Milhaud was evoking the drums, which French people also called "le jazz" in the 1920s.

25. Milhaud, Darius, "L'Évolution du jazz-band et de la musique des nègres d'Amérique du Nord", in *Notes sur la musique, textes réunis et présentés par Jeremy Drake* (Paris: Flammarion, coll. Harmoniques, 1982), p. 104.

26. Ibid., pp. 104–5.

27. Ibid., p. 102.

28. Cadman, Charles W., "Cadman on Ragtime," *Musical Courier*, 12 August 1914.

29. The *fugue d'école* is one of the most academic genres in art music.

30. In example 3.7, this theme is given to the double bass and the trombone.

31. This kind of repetition can be found, for example, in the verse of "Saint Louis Blues."

32. Hodeir, "L'influence du jazz," p. 1484.

33. Milhaud, Darius, "L'Évolution du jazz-band et de la musique des nègres d'Amérique du Nord", in *Notes sur la musique, textes réunis et présentés par Jeremy Drake* (Paris: Flammarion, coll. Harmoniques, 1982), p. 104.

34. Hodeir, "L'influence du jazz," p. 1487.

35. Milhaud, Ibid., p. 102.

36. One could say that this corpus is a new expression of exoticism in music after a period dominated in France by Hispanism and Orientalism.

37. To take the five names evoked in the introduction.

38. The Parisian premiere of this opera took place in 1904 and gave way to hot debates between admirers and fierce opponents of Wagnerism.

39. Weld, Arthur, "The Invasion of Vulgarity in Music," *Etude* 17, February 1899. "It cannot be denied that the lower types of rag-time—and the bulk of it—has done much to lower the musical taste and standard of all musical public, irrespective of color."

40. "With deep emotion."

41. "Imitation" and "transformation" are two central concepts in Genette's reflexion on hypertextuality.

42. "Prestidigitateur chinois," "Petite fille américaine," and "Acrobates."

43. Volta, Ornella, "*Parade*, une œuvre célèbre à découvrir," in *Parade* (score established by Gilbert Delor and Ornella Volta), Paris, Salabert, 1999, p. 18.

44. Like the genre of "overture," for instance, before it became a genre highly considered by composers like Beethoven or Berlioz in the beginning of the nineteenth century.

45. Milhaud, Darius, "L'évolution de la musique à Paris et à Vienne," *North American Review*, April 1923, pp. 544–54.

46. The aesthetic debate was influenced by the geopolitical situation opposing France and Germany before, during, and after the Great War.

47. Milhaud, "L'évolution de la musique."

48. In Milhaud's article, Debussy is considered as the model against which French music must be regenerated. Therefore, quoting *Golliwog's Cakewalk* seems like a paradox.

49. "Une musique française de France," in Cocteau, *Le Coq et l'arlequin*, p. 58.

50. A few years later, this link between Wagnerism and Debussyism is also established by Vincent d'Indy in *Richard Wagner* (Paris: Delagrave, 1930).

51. Cocteau, *Le Coq et l'arlequin*, p. 43.

52. Ibid., p. 63.

53. That is why Debussy contrasts a quotation from Wagner with ragtime.

54. Which does not mean that jazz cannot convey emotion. What is aimed at here is a certain category of emotions.

55. The three expressions between quotation marks are drawn from Cocteau's *Le Coq et l'arlequin*, p. 68.

56. To take only one example, Cocteau quotes "Les lunes descendant sur le temple qui fut" by Debussy. Here again, *Golliwog's Cakewalk* can be taken into account in the argumentation, because it is far different from works by Debussy considered as impressionist.

57. Cocteau, *Le Coq et l'arlequin*, p. 56.

58. This work, composed in 1916 and 1917 by Prokofiev, conveys all the rules extracted by his teachers from classical symphonies by Haydn and Mozart but displays obvious mistakes (committed jokingly on purpose), creating a comical effect.

59. This attitude toward references can be considered as neoclassical even if the author is conscious that neoclassicism is often considered to begin in 1917, with the *Symphonie classique*.

60. The line corresponding to "subdivision."

61. This kind of structure is a reference to neoclassicism.

62. In some passages of the works, a gun, a siren, and a typewriter are used.

63. Bohuslav Martinů (1890–1959) composed his *Eight Preludes for Piano* in 1929 during his long stay in Paris (1923–40). He played an important role in neoclassicism.

64. Milhaud, Darius, "Louis Armstrong et son jazz," *Le jour*, 11 November 1934.

65. And more generally the composers moving in Schola Cantorum circles.

BIBLIOGRAPHY

Anonymous. "What Is American Music?" *Musical America* 3, February 24, 1906.

Cadman, Charles W. "Cadman on 'Ragtime.'" *Musical Courier*, August 12, 1914.

Cocteau, Jean. *Le Coq et l'arlequin: Notes autour de la musique*. Paris, Stock Musique, préface de Georges Auric, 1979. First edition. Paris: Éd. de la Sirène, Collection des tracts, 1, 1918.

D'Indy, Vincent. *Richard Wagner*. Paris: Delagrave, 1930.

Genette, Gérard. *Palimpsestes: La littérature au second degré*. Paris: Seuil, coll. Essais, 1982.

Heyman, Barbara. "Stravinsky and Ragtime," *Musical Quarterly* 68, no. 4, October 1982, pp. 543–62.

Hodeir, André. *Hommes et problèmes du jazz*. Paris; Flammarion, 1954, rééd. Marseille: Parenthèses, 1996.

———. "L'influence du jazz sur la musique européenne." *Les Temps Modernes*, 9e année, no. 99, February 1954, pp. 1477–92.

Jackson, Jeffrey H. *Making Jazz French: Music and Modern Life in Interwar Paris*. Durham, NC: Duke University Press, 2003.

Milhaud, Darius. "L'évolution de la musique à Paris et à Vienne." *North American Review*, April 1923, pp. 544–54.

———. "Louis Armstrong et son jazz." *Le jour*, November 11, 1934.

———. *Ma vie heureuse*. Paris: Belfond, 1973.

———. *Notes sur la musique: Textes réunis et présentés par Jeremy Drake*. Paris: Flammarion, coll. Harmoniques, 1982.

Perloff, Nancy. *Art and the Everyday: Popular Entertainment and the Circle of Érik Satie*. Oxford: Clarendon Press, 1991.

Rogers, Robert. "Jazz Influence on French Music." *Musical Quarterly* 21, no. 1, January 1935, pp. 53–68.

Volta, Ornella. "*Parade*, une œuvre célèbre à découvrir." *Parade* (score established by Gilbert Delor and Ornella Volta). Paris: Salabert, 1999, p. xviii.

Weld, Arthur. "The Invasion of Vulgarity in Music." *Etude* 17, February 1899.

VINCENT COTRO

4 / VIOLIN AND BOWED STRINGS IN JAZZ
A FRENCH SCHOOL?

The first aim of this article is to discuss how much the use of the violin in jazz *really?*
has hitherto remained a typically European phenomenon. That means examining the close relationship between the violin—as well as bowed strings
in general, as opposed to, say, brass or reed instruments—and the European
influence on jazz, an influence forged by a long tradition of classical music.
We will then look at the contribution of French musicians, such as Stéphane
Grappelli and Jean-Luc Ponty, to this specifically European art and consider
whether there is a "French school" of jazz violin. The first of these issues needs
some qualification: while the "classical" heritage has heavily influenced notions
of violin playing in jazz, and continues to do so, there is also a different conception of the instrument, one that occurs within American as well as European jazz.
This alternative style of playing involves trying to adapt the violin to the requirements of a more specifically jazz-oriented approach. The same duality applies to
the question of a "French school," in as much as the French musicians who
appear in the history of jazz violin reflect these two different instrumental conceptions. The disparity in styles between Grappelli and Ponty, for example, is the
distance between the two approaches cited above. Although it is difficult, from a
strictly musical point of view, to make a substantial and consistent argument for a
French school of jazz violin, there is no doubt that a particular tradition of bowed
strings in jazz (including the violin, the cello, and string ensembles) has evolved
in France from the 1930s up to the present day. The main players in this trend, and
its current dynamics, will form the last part of this chapter.

The violin is notable for being one of the oldest instruments in jazz and one
that mostly stands for European classical culture and so-called serious music. We
should not forget, though, that instruments in the violin family are widely used in
European and American folk music (and can be found in various forms in the
Middle East and Asia). As such, they are a common feature of the American *yes.*
popular music that preceded jazz. Violins can be traced back to the origins of
jazz, from black string bands at the turn of the century, to ragtime orchestras and
the first New Orleans jazz bands.[1] The violin part in "Lou'siana Swing," recorded
by the Armand J. Piron Orchestra in 1924,[2] is even considered to be as important
as the horn parts (Piron himself was a very conventional violin player). A number
of violinists made their mark in early jazz recordings, among them Carroll Dick-
erson, Claude Williams, Darnell Howard (with W. C. Handy), Juice Wilson

(with Noble Sissle), and Edgar Sampson (with Charlie Johnson). However, Joe Venuti (1903–78) stands out in the history of jazz as the first real soloist on this instrument, recording as early as 1926 in duet with guitarist Eddie Lang or with his own orchestras (the New Yorkers, the Blue Four), as well as performing with Don Murray, Adrian Rollini, and the Dorsey Brothers.

After gaining traction as an improvising instrument in jazz, the violin mainly developed during the 1930s and 1940s from the individual contributions and experiences of Joe Venuti, Eddie South (1904–62), Stéphane Grappelli (1908–97), and Stuff Smith (1909–67). Virtually absent from bop and post-bop, the violin came back into favor as a jazz instrument during the 1960s, when a revival of sorts was led by performers associated with free jazz (Ornette Coleman, Leroy Jenkins) or fusion (Jean-Luc Ponty). A number of Americans (Billy Bang, Mark Feldman) and Europeans (Didier Lockwood, Michael Urbaniak . . .) took up the baton during the following decades. Although many other violinists are cited in these pages, the instrument's place in the general history of jazz appears undoubtedly diminished compared with the majority of wind instruments, the piano, the guitar, or even the bass.[3] At the same time, the role of Europe and European violinists seems particularly important throughout this history: French pioneer Michel Warlop (1911–47), the Danish Svend Asmussen (b. 1916), or, among the younger French generation, Dominique Pifarély (b. 1957) can be added to the already mentioned key figures (notably Grappelli and Ponty). Indications of this European influence can also be found in biographies of the most significant American jazz violinists. Thus, Joe Venuti was born in Italy, his parents having emigrated to America, while Venuti's future partner Eddie Lang was born in 1902 as Salvatore Massaro, becoming an American through the same circumstances.[4] Eddie South's biography, although it does not reveal any European lineage, tells of frequent or lengthy stays in Europe. This was thanks to privileged relationships with Grappelli and Django Reinhardt but also, as we will see below, so that South could improve his instrumental technique. As for Stuff Smith, he toured Europe with Jazz at the Philharmonic in 1957 and then settled in Copenhagen, Denmark, in 1965.

The long history and practice of the violin in Western "serious" music left a very distinct mark on that music, despite the instrument being used in all kinds of popular music. Can this be the reason why, compared with other instruments, the violin remained so specifically European as it further developed and acclimated within jazz? It is well known that almost all jazz instruments, with the notable exception of the drums, originated in Europe, where they had been more or less extensively used in the fields of Western serious and popular music. Whether self-taught or trained according to the various methods and techniques applicable to different styles or repertoires, early jazz musicians and their successors had to adapt, improve, or find their own technique using the instruments available to them. Inventing a new sound world from an existing instrumentarium is one of the key characteristics of jazz, and one of its main influences on the whole musical art of the twentieth century. In the jazz tradition, the instrument itself is of no specific interest beyond the player's ability to transform it or lift it out of routine use in a constant search for the most personal mode of expression. The highly individual instrumental technique of jazz musicians serves this purpose above all, as do the different kinds of mutes or other objects designed to modify sound or the wide range of vocal effects achievable with wind instruments (from a breath to a shout, from bent notes to vibrato). As Lucien Malson puts it, "It is in the way he breathes out, puts his lips against the mouthpiece, strikes the keyboard with his fingers, that the jazzman affirms an instrumental technique distinct from that of his associates in the European tradition."[5] This perennial feature of the instrumental conception in jazz applies only partly to the violin, though. When we listen to Stéphane Grappelli, Eddie South, Svend Asmussen, or, more recently, to Mark Feldman (b. 1955) or Regina Carter (b. 1966), what we are clearly hearing is an instrumental conception derived directly—in terms of tone, phrasing, or technique—from a (three or four) centuries-old tradition. The way the violin or the bow is held, the sound produced by alternating down-bows and up-bows—these basic requirements need not differ from one player to another. They are integrated into a body of common practice and guidance within the standard educational framework for classical violin. This kind of homogeneous approach in jazz is not seen with wind instruments such as the saxophone, trumpet, or trombone, nor even with string bass, piano, or guitar. The reasons for this particularity can be found, first of all, in the distinctive features of the instrument itself. The design of the violin, the fruit of a long and hardly progressive tradition, allows for few variations, as the aim is, whether in chamber music or an orchestra, that the sound should blend in with that of its fellow instruments. Moreover, the sound is produced through contact with the bow. This mediating tool drastically reduces the possibility of any direct physical intervention, and hence of individualizing the sound. Consider, by way of comparison, the various ways in which the clarinet or saxophone reed can be fitted to the instrument's beak, then gripped with the lips. Or think about the range of vibratory nuances available from a trumpet or trombone mouthpiece, not to mention the wider possibilities for wind players to distinguish themselves, or strive for a personal sound, by choosing their own equipment (the quality or harshness of the reed, for example).

There are other reasons why most jazz violinists play in a relatively standardized fashion. The majority of them are products of an academic apprenticeship, reputed to be among the most restrictive and normative in music. Particular attention is paid to the position of the head and body, the specific placing of each arm, hand, and finger, the way the bow is held and directed—all of them rigorously controlled.[6] In music schools and conservatoires, this process is nurtured through a corpus of studies, concertos and competition pieces, alongside a large repertoire of works composed mostly between the middle of the eighteenth and the middle of the twentieth century. It appears that only a tiny minority of jazz violinists define themselves as self-taught musicians; most of them received an academic apprenticeship. As such, the marginal status of the violin in the jazz tradition—which pushes its performers to the limits of their instruments in an effort to forge a unique sound—seems to derive from the particular characteristics of the instrument, combined with highly prescriptive teaching methods. Biographical evidence on a number of historical jazz violinists backs up this observation. Joe Venuti is supposed to have studied with Thaddeus Rich, an American violinist trained in Leipzig and Berlin before becoming concertmaster, then assistant director of the Philadelphia Orchestra.[7] Interviews are full of comments about Venuti's relationship with the classical repertoire.[8] Eddie South received an academic apprenticeship, first at the Conservatory of Chicago, then with Petrowitsch Bissing at the Chicago College of Music.[9] He traveled to Europe in 1928, deciding to stay until 1931 so that he could complete his technical studies with Firmin Touche at the Conservatoire de Paris,[10] then in Budapest.[11] Michel Warlop won the *Prix d'excellence* at the Lille and Paris conservatories.[12] In the same year of his first recordings with Django Reinhardt (1934), Warlop is said to have recorded classical duets with Leon Kartun.[13]

The son of two music teachers, Jean-Luc Ponty started playing the violin at five, then interrupted his scholarship to become a concert performer. He won the Premier prix at the Conservatoire de Paris shortly after he discovered jazz, in 1960.[14] Classical studies also feature in the early years of many contemporary jazz violinists: Michal Urbaniak practiced classical violin from the age of six, before obtaining (and refusing) a grant to study with David Oistrakh in Moscow.[15] Mark Feldman started violin at nine, then studied classical music with George Sweigert until he was seventeen.[16] Frenchmen Didier Lockwood and Dominique Pifarély served their apprenticeships at the École Normale de Musique and the Montreuil conservatoire respectively.[17] With these violinists and many others, the weight of the instrument's academic heritage has a deep influence on their stylistic identity. This is a compelling example of how jazz has preserved, throughout its evolution, a great number of aesthetic values peculiar to its multiple origins. These values and the European legacy can be heard clearly in the playing of the most important violinist in the history of jazz, Stéphane Grappelli, even though he appears to be one of the few self-taught musicians on this instrument.[18]

At the same time, these characteristics are a restraint on achieving full expression of the myriad sound qualities found in jazz, as noted above (individualiza-

84

tion, vocalization, transformation, or even corruption of sound). Doubtless this strong historical heritage explains the underrepresentation of violin in jazz. At the same time, it helps us to understand why many European or American jazz violinists also play saxophone (Frank Ottersen) or trumpet (Heinz Wehner, Ray Nance), or else add vocals to their performance (Svend Asmussen, Stuff Smith). The inadequacy of the violin in a jazz context seemed so obvious to Jean-Luc Ponty that he started out in jazz as a saxophonist and clarinetist, saving the violin exclusively for the classical repertoire: "He didn't even know there were jazz violinists."[19] In the same way, the Polish Michal Urbaniak (b. 1943) and Zbiegniew Seifert (1946–79) played both violin and saxophone (under the influence of Hank Mobley and John Coltrane), as if they wanted to compensate for the violin's narrow range of sound and expression (Urbaniak learned violin at the Music Academy of Warsaw, Seifert at the Frederic Chopin School of Kraków).

However, it would be inaccurate or overstating the case to regard jazz violin as exclusively dependent on, and emanating from, the European classical tradition. There is, indeed, another sensibility at work and a different conception of the violin, as illustrated and embodied by Stuff Smith. This approach moves resolutely away from the European classical tradition and closer to the sound conception developed in jazz by wind, keyboard, or percussion instruments. As is often mentioned, "Smith revolutionised the vocabulary of jazz violinists with his wild, biting attack, wide vibrato, unorthodox fingerings, and expressive intonation."[20] Although it is difficult to know the exact circumstances and conditions of Smith's apprenticeship in the violin, it seems to have been short and limited to his family circle.[21] While Smith's technical weaknesses (his intonation, for example) are sometimes commented on, he is regarded as the pioneer of a specific conception of jazz violin, where the music (jazz) clearly prevails over the instrument (violin). This conception tends to deviate from the inherited classical tradition and move closer to the various effects produced by reeds or brass. For that reason, Smith's sound has sometimes been described as "resonant" or "brassy." "While Eddie South has the range of a concert artist, Stuff Smith, on the contrary, seeks to change the very nature of his instrument, so as to achieve sounds like scraping or screeching, and thus approach the vocalisation specific to jazz."[22] Furthermore, Smith was one of the first musicians to play an amplified electric violin, back in 1936.[23] This highlights another drawback in the development of jazz violin up to the 1960s: lack of volume. Striving for a brassy sound, using expressive glissandos, playing double stops, or producing a jerky, unpredictable melodic flow—these are some of the distinctive qualities heard in Smith's playing, which is unlike Grappelli's style. (The difference is especially striking in their shared version of "How High the Moon": the two violinists teamed up for the *Stuff & Steff* album, recorded in Paris in June 1965.[24]) Although Stuff Smith, according to Matt Glaser, "completely reinvented the violin from a jazz standpoint,"[25] and even if we consider his impact on Jean-Luc Ponty (as discussed below), Smith's influence on jazz violinists should not be overstated, nor did his work erase all traces of the European classical tradition from jazz violin playing. Nevertheless, the second half of the 1960s and the following decade brought important technical innovations and new means of expression to jazz violin. On the one hand, increasing amplification and electrification gave the violin various options for withstanding, or even being heard above, the more aggressive sounds and rhythms of jazz fusion (Ponty, Seifert, Urbaniak, Jerry Goodman, Lockwood, Pierre Blanchard). Through the free jazz movement and its various modes of expression, on the other hand, the violin tried to escape both the clichés of "serious" playing and the standardization of "jazz" playing in the Grappelli-South mould. Moreover, the broader stylistic and geographical scope opened up by free jazz led the violin, as played by either virtuosos or self-taught musicians, to renew or reconcile with the instrument's popular, folk, and serious traditions (Ornette Coleman, Leroy Jenkins, Michael Sampson, Billy Bang).

Does this more recent expansion of the violin's scope in jazz fundamentally question the predominance of the "classical model" passed down by Venuti, South, and Grappelli? We don't believe so. While there are balancing factors, the European classical tradition continues to prevail in the most contemporary manifestations of violin in jazz (Mark Feldman, Mat Maneri).

Although it may be the best illustration of the tension between traditional Western conceptions (sounds, gestures, pedagogy) and the alternate practices invented by African American musicians through the twentieth century, the violin is certainly not the only instrument in jazz where playing and aesthetics express this conflict. While outside the scope of this chapter, it would be of great interest to discuss in the same context the piano, another hallowed instrument within the classical tradition. There is probably a better balance between the different gestures and models that coexist within, and blend into, jazz piano playing. Some of these refer to a more academic virtuosity (from Teddy Wilson to Keith Jarrett), while others are based on a percussive or fragmented style (Ellington, Monk, Taylor), thus suggesting and mapping out an alternate, more specifically jazz-oriented conception.

The role of France within the evolution and history of violin in jazz is important for two main reasons. First, as was discussed above, the European dimension (in a human as well as an aesthetical sense) has contributed in essential ways to the jazz identity of this instrument; second, one notes that, to a greater extent than with any other instrument, the history of violin in jazz is inescapably punctuated by a growing list of important French performers and/or leaders.[26] Thus, we must examine the constituent elements of this French contribution and ascertain if it is the product of a consistent and coherent chronological evolution. One must ask, if there is a lack of real stylistic filiation, does this evolution reflect at least some unity of conception, which could be personified by Stéphane Grappelli?[27] The question of a "French school" of violin is certainly nurtured and kept alive by the "story of Michel Warlop's violin,"[28] which tends to propagate like a founding legend:

> For his first recorded solo as a violinist on *Fit As a Fiddle*, in 1933, Grappelli didn't have his instrument with him in the studio, as he was a pianist at that time. So he borrowed Michel Warlop's. . . . Later, Warlop offered his violin (this one or another) to Stéphane, asking him to offer it, at his turn, to the ones he would judge worthy to own it. So was done, and Jean-Luc Ponty then Didier Lockwood became holders of the instrument.[29]

Beyond the purely symbolic aspect of this rite of passage, we also have to consider the national impact of the development of the violin in association with the guitar (Warlop, then Grappelli plus Reinhardt): this typical instrumentation became the basis for the conceptualization of a "French jazz" by the early actors in its development, anchored in the Hot Club de France:

> Talented musicians, with Django Reinhardt and Stéphane Grappelli emerging both as skillful and original improvisers; a surprising band: a string orchestra, playing jazz, no one ever saw that; these two factors may lead to a better reception of jazz in France, to increase the influence of the Hot Club de France. For with that band, a French jazz clearly attempts to establish itself.[30]

Moreover, the successful deployment of violin (the king of instruments in serious classical music) within jazz orchestras may also have helped to further the recognition of jazz as a credible musical activity in Europe during the 1930s. We can understand the following statements made by English bandleader and pianist Jack Hylton in 1932 accordingly:

> Many people think that classical music is the opposite of what can be heard from these "merchants of noise" also called jazz orchestras, and they base their judgment, above all, on the difference in instrumentation, presentation, atmosphere. While classical music is produced with basically serious, pigeonholed, well-known instruments, jazz sounds come from anything, cheap trumpets, roughly made without respecting any acoustic rules . . . However, it may be possible to find similarities between the classical music, respectable like an old lady of the past, and the syncopated, agitated rhythm flooding the current world in a whirl.[31]

Even though Stéphane Grappelli and Svend Asmussen are the two only European violinists to have gained international recognition as performers, early European jazz included a number of violinists, some of them also known as leaders: German Heinz Wehner (1910-44) and Helmut Zacharias (1920-2002), English Hugo Rignold (1905-76) and Bert Firman (1906-99), Belgian Eddie Tower [Emile Deltour] (1899-1956), Italian Pippo Barzizza (1902-94), Cesare Galli (1908-95) and Romero Alvaro (1908-?), or Norwegian Øivind Bergh (1909-87). Although scarce, the information available on recordings documenting these musician's styles[32] suggests the probable influence of Joe Venuti or of Grappelli and the Hot Club de France.

If we return to the question of a French school, the difficulty in establishing affiliation between these violinists lies in the fact that no significant performer stands in the halfway position between Grappelli's and Ponty's styles, that is, between the two antagonistic conceptions discussed above. To simplify, the Grappelli approach is tied to aesthetic values similar to Venuti's and South's, whereas Jean-Luc Ponty showed, very early in his career and with incomparably superior technical means, a certain influence from Stuff Smith. French critic and author Alain Gerber devoted a detailed study to Ponty[33] that assembles an inventory of characteristics that move Ponty away from any Grappelli heritage or influence: vocalization of sound, the search for a somewhat rough naivety, a phrasing based on dynamics rather than flexibility, a discontinuity suggested by the disjointed intervals or segmentation of phrases, and so on. A good example of these characters can be heard in the *Jazz Long Playing* album from 1964, prior to Ponty's electric period.[34] One can compare the first chorus of the violinist on "Satin Doll" with the first chorus by Grappelli on the same piece, recorded in the eponymous album in 1972.[35] Grappelli's improvisation sounds immediately and continuously tinged with liveliness, its construction based on flowing eights only interrupted with breathings. Most phrases consist of descending movements from accentuated bent notes in the upper register. In the Ponty version, after a surprising statement of the theme played pizzicato in octaves, the entrance of the improvised chorus sounds almost hesitant, flickering. The violinist alternates long sustained tones without any vibrato, a more animated and continuous section (à la Grappelli), then returning to a more jerky phrasing with frequent contrasts in playing modes (double stops, octaves). Gerber distinguishes between the violinistic jazz of Venuti, Grappelli, and South—that is, "violinists which express themselves in jazz"—and "jazzmen which express themselves on a violin . . . , which have always been disrespectful to the instrument in itself and tried to find despite it the phrasing, the accents and even the sound of the saxophones and the trumpets —traditional conductors of jazzity."[36] If there is no French violinist, as stated above, at the junction of Grappelli's and Ponty's distinctive conceptions, it is also

VINCENT COTRO

88

due to the obvious under-representation of violin in bebop (in Europe like in the United States), with the possible exception of the few recordings made by Dick Wetmore, Harry Lookofsky, and some others.[37] From a chronological perspective, Ponty's first recordings correspond to an eclipse in Grappelli's career, which was revived again at the end of the 1960s, after Ponty's discovery of rock, his collaboration with Frank Zappa, and his gravitation towards electronics.

The family ties between Jean-Luc Ponty and Didier Lockwood are much more plausible and lie in their shared interest for electro-acoustic devices, rock, and fusion, which influenced the first stage of Lockwood's development beginning in the middle of the 1970s. Lockwood remembers listening to his elder on the Frank Zappa *King Kong* album (1969): "I didn't even imagine it was possible to do that on a violin. Furthermore, the contribution of electricity completely changed the perspective on the instrument with regards to the sound. I began to work on these bases."[38] In the 1980s, Lockwood gradually came back to an acoustic (though amplified) conception of the violin. In "B Train Blues" (*Out of the Blue*, 1985), we are far away from the most impersonal fusion style of the early albums (*Fasten Seat Belts*, 1981). Even so, in spite of the choice of an acoustic sound, Lockwood remains attached to a vocal treatment and a constant search for sound distortion. Similarly, the initial statement of "Round about Midnight," from the same album, is full of glissandos or growling effects produced with the bow. Lastly, "Take Your Time" on *Live at The Olympia Hall* (1986) illustrates the shaping of an extremely delicate sound texture in the very high-pitched register. Though Lockwood's instrumental style is placed under the sign of a contemporary eclecticism, it may best be described as intermediary between the influence of Ponty (regarding sound, melody, and harmony) and that of Grappelli, which strengthened during the 1990s (*Tribute to Stéphane Grappelli*, 1999).

The case of Dominique Pifarély further illustrates and accentuates the complexity (and the hypothetical status) of the filiation between the major French jazz violinists. Classically trained and soon fascinated by both Grappelli's music and progressive rock, Pifarély discovered and absorbed the different possibilities offered to a young violinist by Ponty and Lockwood. Throughout his musical development, however, as well as in some interviews, Pifarély seems to be preoccupied by a double obsession: to escape from the growing temptation of imitation on one side, and to refuse the notion of entertainment traditionally attached to jazz on the other.[39]

Thus, a human and professional partnership was established early among Pifarély and several musicians sharing such conceptions, like pianist François Couturier, clarinetist Louis Sclavis, and bass player Didier Levallet, founder of the Swing Strings System. Moving away from both the canons of jazz and the traditions attached specifically to his instrument, Pifarély can be related from an aesthetical point of view to the new "French jazz" that developed during the 1980s and 1990s, exemplified by the Louis Sclavis-Dominique Pifarély Acoustic Quartet that included guitarist Marc Ducret and bassist Bruno Chevillon. His instrumental conception remains closely linked to the compositional process, his improvisations always strictly framed by the structures.[40] As for his work on sound, generally speaking it is much less influenced by Stuff Smith or Didier Lockwood than by his own performance and knowledge of Western classical and contemporary music, a convincing example of which is the use of harmonic sounds in the long introduction of "Poros," on the album *Poros*, performed in duet with François Couturier.[41] There is no doubt that we could isolate a number of features in the violin style of Pifarély that demonstrate typical influences of his predecessors. Even so, he remains largely independent from the corpus of traditions attached to the history of violin in jazz. To Jean-Luc Ponty, who "said and repeated that he wanted to be considered as a jazzman, not as a violinist,"[42] Dominique Pifarély would maybe answer, in substance, that he hopes to be considered neither as a jazzman, nor as a violinist, but as a musician in the fullest sense.

Finally, the establishment of a French school of jazz violin comes up against two main problems. On a purely quantitative level, the obvious underrepresentation of the instrument compels us to focus on a handful of individuals, performers who are clearly interrelated, instead of a large or representative sample. From a stylistic point of view, the diversity of historical and musical contexts requires us to consider three options: oppositions (Grappelli vs. Ponty), passing or lasting influences (Ponty and Lockwood), or eccentric positions (Pifarély). Anachronistic tendencies and the impact of nostalgia on jazz in the 1990s also played a part in "freezing" this tradition.

Yet even if it appears difficult to perceive a "school" of jazz violin (French or not), all of these violinists have kept alive a strong, but more or less conflicted, relationship with the classical tradition of their instrument, as discussed previously. In a country where a strong and renowned educational tradition has developed around this instrument, French violinists cannot escape this heritage, nor can they forget their own classical background. Moreover, they have to assume completely the tradition as it was established then passed on by Stéphane Grappelli. To play *with* or *against* him is possible; to play *without* him is not. Grappelli himself, as a pioneer in jazz violin, has never been compelled to assimilate, even less to transcend any influences: jazz models were rare, if not nonexistent, for a violinist. As a self-taught musician, he was spared the need or the desire to go beyond or to reject a teaching, a tradition, or a set of standards with which he was never directly confronted. In other words, Grappelli could invent his own academism in combining, with skill and talent, the jazz sensibility of Joe Venuti and the more classical virtuosity offered by Michel Warlop. He then founded a family whose cohesion is, in our opinion, symbolic (let us recall the ritual passing on of the Warlop's violin) more than real.

One can conclude that the tradition of the violin in jazz, embodied in the figure of Stéphane Grappelli especially, was represented more thoroughly and consistently in France than elsewhere. Ultimately, this French *tradition*, if there is no real *school*, spread out beyond the violin, extending to the cello and to string ensembles. Genuine cellists did not appear in jazz until the 1960s, this instrument being played until then by bass players (with the exceptions of Fred Katz with Chico Hamilton in 1955–58). These bass players, such as Oscar Pettiford, then Ron Carter and Red Mitchell, employed the cello to extend and diversify their sound potential. From the free jazz period on, use of the cello, like the violin, signified connection to the classical background and tradition, but it also became an unusual medium of sound exploration in the hands of such musicians as Irene Aebi, David Baker, Tristan Honsinger, and Ernst Rejseger. Although the instrument's use in jazz remains uncommon, France has a number of outstanding jazz cellists, among them the pioneer Jean-Charles Capon (b. 1936), Laurent Hoevenaers (b. 1957), Didier Petit (b. 1962), Alain Grange (b. 1966), and Vincent Courtois (b. 1968), who was undoubtedly the most active on the current French scene. These cellists share with the violinists an instrumental culture, largely based on the apprenticeship of the Western classical tradition. As far as we know, self-taught cellists are not only rare (compared with guitar and piano players) but cellists are also mostly trained in collectives like music schools or conservatories. For that reason, they are formed not only as individual performers or virtuosos but also with ensemble playing as a natural imperative. Hence, it is noticeable that a great number of French jazz orchestras feature violin(s) and cello(s) together, as well as string bass and/or guitar. The list of albums and ensembles below (including the date of creation and full instrumentation) illustrates what can probably be seen (and heard) as a French sound color:[43]

Abbreviations: soprano saxophone (ss); oboe (ob); flute (fl); violin (vln); viola (vla); guitar (g); organ (org); piano (p); string bass (b); drums (d); percussion (perc)

Confluence (1974): Jean-Charles Capon (cello), Christian Escoudé (g), Didier Levallet (b), Merzak Mouthana, Armand Lemal (perc), Jean Querlier (ob, fl)

Swing Strings System (1978): Dominique Pifarély, Pierre Aubert (vln), Jean-Charles Capon, Laurent Hoevenaers (cello), Lionel Benhamou (g), François Couturier (p), Didier Levallet (b), Manuel Denizet (d)

Texier/Capon/Lockwood (1979): Henri Texier (b), Jean-Charles Capon (cello), Didier Lockwood (vln)

91

Levallet/Marais/Pifarély (1980): Didier Levallet (b), Gérard Marais (g), Dominique Pifarély (vln)

Gulf Stream (1986): Pierre Blanchard, Zoltán Veres, Vincent Pagliarin (vln), Claire Fargier-Lagrange (vla), Dimos Goudaroulis (cello), Claude Mouton (b), Matthias Pizarro (p), Bob DeMeo (p)

Cello Fans (1989): Jean-Charles Capon, Vincent Courtois, Marc Steckar, Marie-Ange Martin (cello)

Sclavis-Pifarély Acoustic Quartet (1992): Louis Sclavis (cl, ss), Dominique Pifarély (vln), Marc Ducret (g), Bruno Chevillon (b)

Onztet de violon jazz (1994): Didier Lockwood (lead), Elisabeth Boudjema, Yves Garzuel, Régis Huby, Nicolas Krassik, Jean-Marc Ladet, Daniel John Martin, Jean-Luc Pino, Jean-Christophe Rouet, Debora Seffer, Patrick Tilleman, Gérard Vandenbroucke (vln), et al.

Archet Type (1995): Régis Huby, François Michaud (vln), Guillaume Roy (vla), Alain Grange (cello)

Courtois/Pifarély/Ducret (2001): Vincent Courtois (cello), Dominique Pifarély (vln), Marc Ducret (g)

Tchamitchian/Roy/Courtois (2006): Claude Tchamitchian (b), Guillaume Roy (vla), Vincent Courtois (cello)

Petit/Labarrière/Roy (2008): Didier Petit (cello), Hélène Labarrière (b), Guillaume Roy (vla).

We should add that many French performers have played with a string quartet (pianists René Urtreger or Michel Petrucciani, for instance[44]) or have routinely integrated bowed strings in their orchestra (Didier Levallet). Violinist Pierre Blanchard and cellist Hervé Derrien were members of the Martial Solal Orchestra as early as 1981. One might note as well the various string-related initiatives related to the teaching of jazz in France, like the Centre des Musiques Didier Lockwood (CMDL), founded in 2001. This particular initiative, and others in the same vein, definitely contribute to a real "French school" of bowed strings in jazz.

The question posed at the beginning of this article has received, as expected, a balanced answer: it is quite true that the violin as used by jazz musicians has retained, more than any other instruments, many qualities and features related to its long European history. These characteristics made its full assimilation into the specific sound culture developed by jazzmen more difficult. Beyond this explanation of the sporadic presence of the violin in jazz, we also tried to point out the crucial role of Europe and France, where most of the main performers lived or converged. If the concept of a French school of jazz violin remains debatable, the

almost overdone.

importance of Stéphane Grappelli as a founding and leading jazz figure in France and elsewhere is nevertheless assured. Lastly, we have addressed the particularly productive dynamics of bowed strings within recent French jazz groups. Some of the questions that have been raised will require research beyond the limits of this topic and this particular instrument, extending into the context of a general, transnational discussion about the making of jazz history. How shall we henceforth evaluate and define the notion of a school and what are the criteria for establishing continuity? Can the influence or filiation among different musicians be explained according to a given national identity, a given instrument, or even the combination of the two (like we have attempted here)? The utility of coordinating the general history of jazz and the corresponding history of a given instrument is particularly evident, yet we must not reduce the complex evolution of jazz, with its rich internal dynamics and synergies, merely to a body of instrumental transmission processes. The risk then would be to "instrumentalize"[45] the history of jazz, thus forgetting what Earl Hines's style owes to Armstrong, what Bud Powell's right hand owes to Bird, and what Jean-Luc Ponty's bow owes to the wind players. "He plays like Dizzy," Kenny Clarke is reported to have said.[46]

odd, somewhat abrupt endings, but ok.

NOTES

1. Glaser, Matt, et al., "Violin." "The degree to which such bands employed syncopation is not recorded, but it is known that New Orleans ensembles, among them the Big Four String Band, the Excelsior String Band, the Tio and Doublet String Band, and the Union String Band, played a repertory based on cakewalks and rags, and that for the most part they were led by violinists."

2. Ibid.

3. In *Das Grosse Jazzbuch* (Berendt, 1981), the chapter "Jazz instruments" is arranged in the following order: trumpet, trombone, clarinet, saxophones, flute, vibes, piano, organ (keyboards, synthesizer), guitar, bass, drums, percussion, *violin*, various instruments. It is easy to see where the violin, in this representative publication, ranks among other instruments in jazz.

4. In the outstanding documentary film *Play Your Own Thing—A Story of Jazz in Europe*, directed by Julian Benedikt (DVD Euro Arts, 2007), trumpet player Enrico Rava quotes these two examples, mentions Leon Roppolo's name, and concludes: "Jazz itself contains all the elements of my roots, of my culture." (This translation from the French, and the following, are from the author.)

5. Malson, Lucien, 1994, p. 14.

6. "The chin should not sit too far forward on the violin, it could prejudice the loose vibration and produce an inelegant effect." Virtuoso and teacher Jacques Thibaud, quoted in *Le petit Paganini* (Tours: Van De Velde, 1960), p. 9.

7. Rejaudry, 2001.

8. "We [Eddie Lang and myself] started at the beginning of the 1920s, playing the music

we liked, jazz, Mozart, Vivaldi, Scarlatti. . . . I love French harmonies: Couperin, Jacques Ibert, but my favorites remain Debussy and Ravel. What Debussy composed for the violin is wonderful": Joe Venuti interviewed by Gérard Rouy, *Jazz Magazine*, no. 236 (1975): 20.

9. Glaser and Grappelli, 1981.

10. Rejaudry, 2001, p. 21.

11. Barnett and Glaser, 1994.

12. Frank Ténot, in Carles, Comolli, and Clergeat, 1994, p. 1233.

13. Laplace, Michel, "Michel Warlop," *New Grove Dictionary of Jazz*, 2nd ed., 1994.

14. Philippe Baudoin et Christian Gauffre, in Carles, Comolli, and Clergeat, 1994, p. 945.

15. Kernfeld, Barry, "Michal Urbaniak," *New Grove Dictionary of Jazz*, 2nd ed., 1994.

16. Glaser, Matt, "A Question of Balance: Catching Up with Jazz Violinist Mark Feldman," *Strings* 21:3:142 (10/2006), pp. 66-67, 69.

17. Philippe Carles, in Carles, Comolli & Clergeat, 1994, p. 719 ; Rejaudry, 2001, p. 55.

18. "I learned . . . all alone. I never had any teacher, on any instrument": quoted by Michel Laverdure, "L'histoire de l'art chez Grappelli," *Jazz Magazine* (September 1983): 23.

19. Gerber, 1970, p. 45.

20. Barnett, Glaser, and Shipton, 1994. Considering particularly Smith's technique, but also Ray Nance's and others', the facility for producing microtones on violin, as with slide trombone, appears to be an important means for reaching this expressive intonation.

21. He performed as early as 1926 (age seventeen) as a dancer and violinist in "Aunt Jemima's Review." Glaser and Kernfeld, 1994.

22. Rejaudry, 2001, p. 41.

23. Ibid., p. 23.

24. *Stuff and Steff*, Barclay (F) XBLM110, reissued in the *Jazz in Paris* series (Universal). We discovered that Stuff Smith had also recorded this standard with Jean-Luc Ponty in December of the same year (issued on the Italian label Europa Jazz).

25. Matt Glaser, quoted in Eric Fine, 2009, p. 29. "But Stuff Smith completely reinvented the violin from a jazz standpoint, and that's unique because, prior to that, there really were only two ways to play the instrument: either in a folk, fiddling kind of way, or in a Western classical kind of way."

26. Stéphane Grappelli (1908–1997), Michel Warlop (1911–1947), Jean-Luc Ponty (1942), Didier Lockwood (1956), Pierre Blanchard (1956), Dominique Pifarély (1957). Composer and writer André Hodeir (1921) made a brief career as a jazz violinist under the name of Claude Laurence. Pierre Aubert, Hervé Cavelier, Bruno Girard, Régis Huby, Florin Niculescu, Jean-Luc Pino, Debora Seffer, Jean-Christophe Rouet and others represent the following generations.

27. One chapter in *Le jazz français: De 1900 à aujourd'hui* (Brierre, 2000) is called "Grappelli the Godfather."

28. Slightly younger than Grappelli, Warlop is considered to be the first French jazz violinist. He significantly influenced Grappelli, who started has a pianist.

29. Daniel Nevers, liner notes of *Stéphane Grappelli: The Quintessence (Paris-London 1933-1958)*, Frémeaux FA 281. Different sources corroborate this testimony, some of them

adding that Pierre Blanchard, Dominique Pifarély, and Hervé Cavelier received, in their turn, Michel Warlop's violin after 1984. See Brierre, 2000, p. 54; Berendt, 1986, p. 392, pierreblanchard.com. See also Didier Lockwood, in *Jazzman*, no. 123 (2006): 30.

30. Martin and Roueff, 2002, p. 53.

31. Jack Hylton, "Qu'est-ce que le jazz?" (1932), in Martin and Roueff, 2002, p. 306.

32. Hugo Rignold and Helmut Zacharias feature on the *Violon Jazz* (Frémeaux FA 052) anthology.

33. Gerber, 1970.

34. Recorded in 1964 (Paris) with Michel Portal (fl), Eddy Louiss (org), Gilbert Rovère or Guy Pedersen (b), and Daniel Humair (d), Philips 77810.

35. *Satin Doll*, 1972 (Paris) with Eddy Louiss (org), Marc Hemmeler (p), Jimmy Gourley (g), Guy Pedersen (b), and Kenny Clarke (d), Festival FLD596.

36. Gerber, 1970, p. 21.

37. Let us point out that one of the first recordings of bebop in France is due to a group set up by drummer Kenny Clarke on May 4, 1948. We can hear on it the violinist Claude Laurence (André Hodeir) playing his own composition, *Laurenzology* (*Be-Bop in Paris*, Vol.1: 1947-1950, CD EMI 780373-1, *Jazz Time* series no. 59, 1992). Fargeton, Pierre, "Le jazz comme œuvre composée: le cas d'André Hodeir," doctoral dissertation, Université de Saint-Etienne, 2006, pp. 43-44.

38. Lockwood quoted by Serge Loupien, *Jazz Magazine*, no. 281 (1979).

39. "Doux-amer Pifarély?", interview by Francis Marmande, *Jazz Magazine*, no. 380 (1989): 42.

40. This feature is also prominent in Louis Sclavis's performances.

41. *Poros*, ECM 1647.

42. Gerber, 1970, p. 21.

43. It is worthy of note that drums are absent in most of these bands, which is naturally reminiscent of the specificity of the Quintette du Hot Club de France (violin, guitar, two rhythm guitars, and bass).

44. See René Urtreger, *Serena*, with a string quartet led by Pierre Blanchard (Carlyne Music, 1990); Michel Petrucciani, *Marvellous*, with the Graffiti String Quartet (Dreyfus Jazz, 1993).

45. A term that also means, in French, to *use* in an excessive way.

46. J. E. Berendt in Gerber, 1970, p. 45.

BIBLIOGRAPHY

Berendt, Joachim Ernst. 1981. *Das Grosse Jazzbuch—Von New Orleans bis Jazz Rock*. Frankfurt am Main: Fischer Verlag.

———. 1992. *The Jazz Book: From Ragtime to Fusion and Beyond*. New York: Lawrence Hill and Co.

Carles, Philippe, Comolli Jean-Louis, and André Clergeat, eds. 1994. *Dictionnaire du jazz*. Paris: Robert Laffont.

Brierre, Jean-Dominique. 2000. *Le jazz français de 1900 à aujourd'hui*. Paris: Hors Collection.

Cotro, Vincent, 1999. *Chants libres - Le free jazz en France 1960-1975*. Paris: Outre Mesure.

Fine, Eric. 2009. "Up Jumped Stuff Smith: Tribute to a Jazz Violin Pioneer." *Strings* 24/2/173 (2009): 29-30.

Gerber, Alain. 1970. "Les inventives aventures de Jean-Luc Ponty." *Jazz Magazine*, no. 175 (1970): 18-23, 45-47.

Glaser, Matt, and Anthony Barnett. "South, Eddie." In *The New Grove Dictionary of Jazz*, 2nd ed. Ed. Barry Kernfeld. *Grove Music Online*, www.oxfordmusiconline.com (accessed October 1, 2010).

Glaser, Matt, and Stéphane Grappelli, 1981. *Jazz Violin*. New York: Oak Publications, 1981.

Glaser, Matt, and Barry Kernfeld, "Smith, Stuff." In *The New Grove Dictionary of Jazz*, 2nd ed. Ed. Barry Kernfeld. *Grove Music Online*, www.oxfordmusiconline.com (accessed October 1, 2010).

Glaser, Matt et al., "Violin." In *The New Grove Dictionary of Jazz*, 2nd ed. Ed. Barry Kernfeld. *Grove Music Online*, www.oxfordmusiconline.com (accessed October 1, 2010).

Kernfeld, Barry. "Urbaniak, Michal." In *The New Grove Dictionary of Jazz*, 2nd ed. Ed. Barry Kernfeld. *Grove Music Online*, www.oxfordmusiconline.com (accessed October 1, 2010).

Laplace, Michel. "Warlop, Michel." In *The New Grove Dictionary of Jazz*, 2nd ed. Ed. Barry Kernfeld. *Grove Music Online*, www.oxfordmusiconline.com (accessed October 1, 2010).

Lieberman, Julie Lyonn. 2002. "A Brief History of Jazz Violin." *American String Teacher* 52, no. 4 (2002): 78-85.

Martin, Denis-Constant, and Olivier Roueff. 2002. *La France du jazz*. Marseille: Parenthèses.

Malson, Lucien. 1994. *Histoire du jazz et de la musique afro-américaine*. Paris: Seuil.

Rejaudry, Richard. 2001. "L'intégration du violon dans le jazz: le cas de Dominique Pifarély." Master's thesis, Université de Tours, France (dir. Vincent Cotro).

Ténot, Frank. 1957. "Les dompteurs de violon ou du swing sur 4 cordes." *Jazz Magazine*, no. 27 (1957): 28-29.

Testoni, Giancarlo. 1966. "Venuti sur cordes." *Jazz Magazine*, no. 132 (1966).

Tournès, Ludovic. 1999. *New Orléans sur Seine—Histoire du jazz en France*. Paris: Fayard.

Selected Discography

Violon Jazz (Hollywood-Chicago-New York-Londres-Paris-Bruxelles-Berlin-Copenhague 1927-1944), Frémeaux FA052.

Stéphane Grappelli: The Quintessence (Paris-London 1933-1958), Frémeaux FA28.

Stéphane Grappelli. *Improvisations* [1956]. Universal 549 242-2 ("Jazz in Paris" no. 42).

Stéphane Grappelli. *I Hear Music* [1970]. RCA 74321192532.

Stéphane Grappelli & Michel Petrucciani. *Flamingo* [1995]. Dreyfus Jazz FDM 36580-2.

Jean-Luc Ponty. *Jazz Long Playing* [1964]. Universal 548 150-2 ("Jazz in Paris" no. 43).

Jean-Luc Ponty, Daniel Humair, and Eddy Louiss. *Humair/Louiss/Ponty, Vol. 1* [1968]. Dreyfus Jazz FDM 36509-9.

Jean-Luc Ponty, Daniel Humair, and Eddy Louiss. *Humair/Louiss/Ponty, Vol. 2* [1968]. Dreyfus Jazz FDM 36510-9.

Jean-Luc Ponty. *Le Voyage: The Jean-Luc Ponty Anthology.* Rhino R 1900693.

Didier Lockwood. *Live in Montreux* [1980]. Polydor 2473928.

Didier Lockwood. *Out of the Blue* [1985]. Gramavision 18-8504.

Didier Lockwood. *Tribute to Stéphane Grappelli* [1999]. Dreyfus Jazz FDM 36611.

Dominique Pifarély. *Oblique* [1993]. IDA Records 034.

Dominique Pifarély and François Couturier. *Poros* [1998]. ECM 1647.

Pierre Blanchard. *Music for String Quartet, Jazz Trio, Violin and Lee Konitz* [1986]. Sunnyside SSC1023D.

Pierre Blanchard. *Volutes* [1999]. Charlotte Productions CP 194.

Jean-Charles Capon. *Capophonie* [1997]. CC Productions CC 987621.

Vincent Courtois. *The Fitting Room* [2001]. ENJA 9411-2.

Didier Levallet. *Swing Strings System* [1979]. Frémeaux FA 449.

Henri Texier. *A cordes et à cris* [1979]. JMS 18649-2.

LUCA CERCHIARI

5 / SACRED, COUNTRY, URBAN TUNES:
THE EUROPEAN SONGBOOK
"GREENSLEEVES" TO "LES FEUILLES MORTES"
("AUTUMN LEAVES"), "GIGOLO" TO " 'O SOLE MIO"

"No Europe, no jazz," Norman Granz used to say in the sixties. Of course, he was referring to a collective economy of concerts, festivals, and record sales. Granz's roster of artists—from Ella Fitzgerald to Oscar Peterson, from Jazz at the Philharmonic to Stan Getz—used to have more success in the Old World than in the United States, especially during the summer.

But now we can vary the meaning of this statement. In fact, the development of musicological research has brought us to the conclusion that without European musics—and cultures—jazz itself would probably not exist.

It is not within the scope of this essay to analyze the forms of cultivated and ethnic European traditions inherited by African American music (for example, there is still work to be done on evaluating and illuminating the European origins of the American song form—something that might identify, say, European musical theater as so-far-underacknowledged common ground). I would rather focus here on the European jazz repertoire, and its different sources and fortunes. Repertoire in jazz is a topic in need of research: little has been written about it. What we all know more or less is that the core jazz repertoire belongs to three main categories: the African American blues form, the song form associated with Broadway theater, and the jazz originals (often referring the blues and the song form) written by Jelly Roll Morton, Fats Waller, Duke Ellington, Charlie Parker, Charles Mingus, Thelonious Monk, Wayne Shorter, and others. What these three categories, which make up a core repertoire of some seven hundred standards (a longer list of around a thousand tunes can be found on the American website www.jazzstandards.com), have in common is the relationship between a single composition and its "luck" in terms of interpretations.

The twentieth century can be divided in two in this respect: up to around 1950 there were few distinguished authors and many interpreters of jazz compositions; the opposite occurred in the second half of the century, with many authors and few interpreters of single compositions or songs (or whatever other definition applies). This reflects the European tradition of separating the composer and the interpreter. It implies that transmitting compositions through interpretation depends mostly on those compositions being written and published. Contrary to current beliefs, this is also partly true of jazz, especially if we consider the Broadway-related song form and its publishing counterpart, Tin Pan Alley. In all but a few cases, without a printed composition—the source of subsequent interpretations—jazz tunes would not exist. The published composition, and the associated legal deposit, always mark the beginning of the jazz repertoire's fortunes in terms of the number of interpretations that follow. But in the case of jazz and the so-called popular music of the twentieth century, which may use the same song form, the issue is complicated by the advent of recording techniques. Jazz was born, in fact, as published rather than recorded music. Even the first Victor shellacs of the Original Dixieland Jazz Band in 1917 were made because a German American publisher active in Chicago and New York—Walter Melrose—suggested that Victor should record some of its already published tunes, written by Nick LaRocca and friends. Over the years, though, records and phonographs became more popular than scores and printed music in terms of the available market and prevailing attitudes. The new recording media meant that interpreters on radio or film took on more importance than authors. This also explains why, in the second half of the last century, there have been many authors and compositions but few famous ones: what comes first is the recording and the interpreter, not the author and the publisher. Jazz developed against this background of historical change and evolution. Being at once a synthesis of oral and written traditions, it reflected this coexistence and the superimposition of different codes of transmission—also in the fortunes of its repertoire.

So why did musicians choose to play or sing a particular composition? Partly due to economic or professional pressures (namely, the interests of publishers, record and radio producers, and managers) but mainly because they liked it. And how does a musician get to know, or learn, a particular tune? Either through visual means, because the musician acquires and plays a published composition; or by ear, because he or she hears it being played by other musicians, either on record or live. The story of the jazz repertoire and its interpretation has, in essence, to do with elaborations of recorded tunes, even if many of the tunes that form the repertoire are available in their original printed form. As previously mentioned, though, the practice of reading a score or a printed composition, which was the norm in the nineteenth century, changed in the twentieth century. Recordings defined a new culture of musical transmission, characterized by scholar Walter Ong as a "secondary oral tradition." This implied a paradox. Jazz developed variations and improvisations on a songbook whose printed originals were mostly unknown to jazz musicians. Those musicians chose to play certain tunes because they had heard them from other musicians or previous recordings. If you compare the printed originals of certain Broadway songs—which, by the way, have seldom been recorded—with the jazz versions, you may find significant differences: parts of the original form, such as the verse, are cut out or forgotten (see the later discussion of "Autumn Leaves"); there are changes to the melodic contour, the rhythm, the chord progression, and so on. Jazz brought new sounds (horns, reeds, strings) and rhythms to melodies that were conceived for voice and piano, in the European parlor tradition. Moreover, jazz often recast and re-created these songs, giving them a new meaning or meanings.

This also happened to the European side of the jazz repertoire, which is broader than one might imagine. I have found many European tunes that achieved a certain distinction in the story of jazz interpretation. They fall into four main categories:

1. Lyrics and tunes related to the Bible, the European Reformation, and their assimilation into in the African American repertoire of spirituals, psalms, hymns, and even blues. Three surviving examples in the jazz repertoire are "Just a Closer Walk with Thee" (ascribed to Kenneth Morris, who heard it from a Kansas City religious choir led by William H. Hurse, which had picked it up from oral sources related to the nineteenth-century camp-meeting phenomenon; it has been re-corded by various New Orleans jazzmen, including George Lewis and the Dirty Dozen Brass Band, by bluesmen such as Sonny Terry and Brownie McGhee, and by guitar player and singer Sister Rosetta Tharpe); "Doxology" (recorded by singer Joe Williams); and "Count Your Blessings" (recorded by saxophone play-ers such as Gene Ammons and Sonny Rollins).

2. Ethnic secular tunes, transmitted orally or through published transcriptions. Some examples are "Greensleeves," "Danny Boy (Londonderry Air)," "Auld Lang Syne," "Chevy Chase," "Loch Lomond," "Barbara Allen," and "Billy Boy (My Boy Willie)." These were inherited from the British Isles as far back as the Middle Ages and Renaissance, ranging from ethno-musical originals to rewritten or transcribed versions, as often occurred in the second half of the nineteenth century as a consequence of Romaticism.[1] In fact, the tunes also survived thanks to their circulation in printed anthologies of English, Scottish, and Irish music, easily available nowadays and including songs like "Scarborough Fair," which was recorded in the sixties by American pop-folk singers such as Simon and Garfunkel. Since 1955, "Greensleeves" has been recorded at least two hundred times by famous jazz musicians, ranging from Kenny Burrell to John Coltrane, from Jimmy Smith to George Shearing, and from Oscar Peterson to Coleman Hawkins. There are versions of "Danny Boy" by Art Tatum, Sarah Vaughan, Bill Evans, and others; of "Auld Lang Syne" by Don Redman; "Loch Lomond" by Maxine Sullivan; "Barbara Allen" by Doris Day; and of "Billy Boy" by Red Garland, Oscar Peterson, Ahmad Jamal, and other pianists.

3. Urban popular songs, written and published in the twentieth century. This

category obviously has more tunes. Every major European country has contributed to the repertoire, from the French "Mon Homme" (which became "My Man": remember the Ella Fitzgerald and Peggy Lee versions, but especially Billie Holiday's unrivaled interpretation?), "La vie en rose" and "C'est si bon" (recorded by Billie Holiday and by Louis Armstrong, who has been one of the main "pickers" of European melodies), or alternatively "Ménilmontant," "Au clair de la lune," and "Clopin clopant," to the Swedish "Ack Värmeland, du sköna" ("Dear Old Stockholm"—distinguished versions by Stan Getz, Miles Davis, John Coltrane); from the Spanish "La Paloma" (listen to Charlie Parker's interpretation), to the Hungarian "Szomorú vasárnap" ("Gloomy Sunday"—again, wonderfully recorded by Billie Holiday); and the Russian "Ochi chyornye" ("Dark Eyes"— Dizzy Gillespie, Charlie Ventura, Slam Stewart). Three very famous jazz standards come from European authors: "Autumn Leaves," which is the American version (lyrics by Johnny Mercer) of "Les feuilles mortes," by French writers Jacques Prévert and Joseph Kosma, and the equally well known "Cherokee" and "These Foolish Things." "Cherokee" was composed in 1938 by English writer and bandleader Ray Noble, who was responsible for other notable standards such as "The Very Thought of You," "The Touch of Your Lips," "Mad about the Boy," and "I Hadn't Anyone Till You."[2] "These Foolish Things" also comes from England: writers Jack Strachey, Harry Link, and Eric Maschewitz worked in musical theater in London, European counterparts of the American musical comedy artists.[3] It is likely the American circulation of these songs was also a result of music publishing and discographical relations between England and the United States; some tunes were probably heard in England, and then exported to America, by New World musicians touring in the United Kingdom.

4. (More or less standard) jazz compositions by European jazz musicians. It is worth noting that Chuck Sher—the well-known Californian publisher of the *Real Book*—has produced another anthology of jazz tunes, called *European Real Book*[4] and including over one hundred titles. Once again, the pieces are transcribed from recordings. The best-known names in this strange anthology are, besides gypsy guitar player and "father" of European jazz Django Reinhardt, French pianist Michel Petrucciani; Belgian guitarist Philip Catherine; British pianists George Shearing, Victor Feldman, and John Taylor; Belgian singer and composer David Linx; German pianist and arranger Claus Ogerman; Swiss saxophonist George Robert; Canadian but UK-based trumpet player Kenny Wheeler; Swedish guitarist Ulf Wakenius; Italian trumpet player Enrico Rava; Italian pianist Enrico Pieranunzi; Austrian born keyboardist Joe Zawinul (author of quasi-standards such as "In a Silent Way"); and many others. At the same time, the European "presence" is particularly marked among the first two generations of the so-called Broadway/Tin Pan Alley songwriters. Some of these musicians were

born in Europe, then their families emigrated to the United States; some were born in the United States or arrived there at a very young age. It is a long list that includes, notably, the Russians Irving Berlin and Vernon Duke; the Polish Bronislau Kaper; the Hungarian Jean Schwartz; the German Gus Kahn; the Austrian Frederick Loewe; the Swiss Al Dubin; the Italian Vincent Rose (who is this man, whose family arrived in the United States from Palermo, Sicily? The composer of very successful American tunes such as "Whispering," and "Blueberry Hill"); the English Jule Styne (whose melodies were often sung by Frank Sinatra); the Irish Victor Herbert; and so on. Even some of the first American jazz interpreters were European, as in the case of Russians Al Jolson and Sophie Tucker.[5] The roster of American composers with Jewish roots is also particularly significant: it includes not only George Gershwin, or other members of the Tin Pan Alley/Broadway community, but also German composer Kurt Weill, who was already familiar with jazz from his home country when he emigrated to the United States (jazz influenced some aspects of Brecht/Weill's famous *Die Dreigroschenoper/Threepenny Opera*—for the première, in Berlin, a jazz band was expressly hired and presented onstage), and who wrote songs that would become Broadway (or "off-Broadway") and jazz classics, from "Die Moritat von Mackie Messer" ("Mack the Knife"—sung and played with enormous success, among many others, by Louis Armstrong, expressly chosen by Columbia Records producer George Avakian, in the mid-fifties) to "September Song." Some other Kurt Weill songs also became quite significant, and frequently played, jazz standards ("Bilbao Song," lyrics by Bertolt Brecht; "My Ship," lyrics by Ira Gershwin; "Alabama Song"; "Lost in the Stars"; and the beautiful "Speak Low").

This article will focus on some of the British, French, and Italian titles that belong to the categories of ethnic and urban tunes. In some cases, as often happens with music, the two "sonic languages" (oral and written) are mixed together.

Great Britain

The most famous and the most recorded tune in the first category may be "Greensleeves," which is also the most "transatlantic" of them all. The words and music of "Greensleeves" originated in Renaissance England. The song then survived and flourished in Europe as well as the American colonies. Its lyrics changed in a parallel version that appeared at the end of the nineteenth century—English composer William Chatterton Dix's "What Child Is This"; the melody is the same but the lyrics are inspired by a biblical passage. The song was rediscovered in the twentieth century, becoming even more popular thanks to the cinema and a number of jazz interpretations. Today, "Greensleeves" is still a reference piece for music teachers in the United Kingdom. An orchestral version (*Fantasia on Green-sleeves*), written in 1934 by English composer Ralph Vaughan Williams, is regularly performed in concert halls.

The history of this song is at once that of its oral and written sources, of its almost pendular swings between oral and written forms, of its transformations, and of its popular reception. Of course, it is also the history of the song's varied and sometimes wonderful interpretations in the realm of recorded African American music. What other tunes have survived for five hundred years? It is surprising to learn that, though the original melody is that of a popular dance tune, the lyrics first appear in published form in September 1580, although no copy from that date has been found. The lyrics were printed in 1584 (London) as part of the anthology *A Handful of Pleasant Delites*, published by Richard Jones and compiled by Clement Robinson and others. The melody, without words, first appeared in published form—under the title of "Greensleeves"—in 1652, when it was included in *A Booke of New Lessons for the Cithern and Gittern* (London). As James Fuld points out, "although today the ballad is sung slowly and soulfully, the Shakespearian reference and its inclusion in (publisher John Playford's) *The Dancing Master*, commencing with the 7th edition in 1686, London, state that it was originally a vigorous dance tune."[6] American musicologist Charles Hamm specifies that the melody of "Greensleeves" first occurs in the fourth, not the seventh, edition of John Playford's anthology.[7]

A key point about the tune, and its subsequent interpretations, is the apparent disparity and/or ambiguity between its original, ethnic character—from what we know, vigorous and dancing—and, at the opposite extreme, its contemporary rendering: that of—a final quotation here from James Fuld's *The Book of World Famous Music*"—a ballad sung slowly and soulfully." Without any aural documentation of the melody in its original form, we have to rely on speculation (although in the first American printed version, "Greensleeves" is transcribed in joyful and quite fast 6/8 time). Nonetheless, this may throw light on some of the strangest, most beautiful jazz versions of the tune. If the ethnic origins of "Greensleeves" and its musical peculiarities can only be inferred indirectly, from secondary sources, the printed versions make clear that the song and its rhythmic setting are slow, and its lyrical meaning that of a love song filled with sadness. Some jazz versions of the tune, such as those by John Coltrane and Eric Dolphy, have actually managed to synthesize in a contemporary way (and with unexpected theoretical implications) these two apparently antithetical conceptions of the song, the folk dance and the slow, sad, soulful ballad, as well as being the version everybody knows, or at least most people recall.

Even the story of the "Greensleeves" lyrics, like the music, involves a degree of anonymity. If the melody originally comes from the oral tradition, the words were first printed separately in the version by Richard Jones in 1584, described as "A New Courtly Sonnet of the Lady Green Sleeves." This was to be rendered to the tune of "Greensleeves," which suggests there were earlier versions, preceding even the aforementioned publication of the lyrics in 1580—which is also attributed to Richard Jones.

"Greensleeves" emerged in a period—the sixteenth and seventeenth centuries—in which the flowering of publishing techniques and activities enabled traditional lyrics and tunes that had been handed down orally to be transcribed and printed. In turn, the circulation of printed lyrics and music led to new variations, both oral and written. A sort of intermediary between the printed form and oral transmission was the so-called broadside ballad. It is possible that some of the versions of "Greensleeves," whose music is otherwise referred to as "a new Northern dittie of the *Lady Greensleeves*,"[8] also belonged to this category. Or, more precisely, that the oral form, the broadside ballad, and the modern printed version, as well as the very many variations and improvisations on these blueprints that make up the tune's jazz history, are of equal weight in the changing life and transformations of both the song and its lyrics, which were almost certainly adapted to a preexisting tune. On the other hand, referring to the English cultural milieu, this is the period in which William Shakespeare (1564–1616) came to prominence. Curiously enough, one version of the "Greensleeves" lyrics is attributed to Shakespeare himself.

As lutist Desmond Dupré points out in the liner notes to his CD *Shakespeare Songs* (Harmonia Mundi France), "Shakespeare's audience ranged from the highest nobles to the lowest commoners: between them they knew a great variety of music ranging from the complex fancies for a consort of viols to the bawdiest folk songs. A tune like *Walsingham* was known to all and served as the basis of many compositions. . . . Instrumental music was used to place the mood of many settings or to accompany a tender love scene. . . . Perhaps the most beautiful music in the plays is set to Shakespeare's own lyrics."

It is possible, therefore, that Shakespeare wrote his own lyrics to a popular tune like "Greensleeves" and used it as a dramatic device in his dramas and plays. He certainly quotes it twice in the *Merry Wives of Windsor* (around 1600). John Falstaff, speaking to Mistress Ford, says, "Let it thunder to the tune of Greensleeves" (act 5, scene 5), while earlier (act 2, scene 1) Mistress Ford has the line: "But they do no more adhere and keep place together than the Hundredth Psalm to the tune of Green-sleeves." Even Shakespeare's dramatic language is based on a mixture of oral and written elements: his actors used to improvise parts of the plots, while it appears Shakespeare had nothing to do with the printing of his plays. The first sixteen editions were published without his approval, being un-

authorized transcriptions made during live performances. Are these textual os-
cillations and amendments not, by the way, in the nature of jazz music?

[handwritten margin note: oh, nice!]

In any case, these are the original words to the song, or at least the best-known
printed version:

Alas my love you do me wrong
To cast me off discourteously
And I have loved you so long
Delighting in your company

Greensleeves was all my joy
Greensleeves was my delight
Greensleeves was my heart of gold
And who but my Lady Greensleeves

I have been ready at your hand
To grant whatever you would crave
I have both waged life and land
Your love and goodwill for to have

I bought three petticoats of the best
The cloth so fine as fine might be
I gave thee jewels from my chest
And this cost I spent on thee
Well I will pray to God on high
That thou my constancy mayst see
For I am still thy lover true
Come once again and love me

How did the English Renaissance—the Tudor period—interpret this song?
Desmond Dupré recorded "Greensleeves" with singer (countertenor) Alfred
Deller for the aforementioned Harmonia Mundi France CD *Shakespeare Songs
and Consort Music*. Dupré is a renowned Renaissance lute virtuoso, and hence
this recording (1969) is a good example of how the tune might have been played
and sung in the early sixteenth century. The Dupré-Deller version illustrates

[handwritten margin note: oh really?]

how—if this actually happened—the song changed in terms of its rhythm and
other features. It is actually a slow and soulful ballad, whose melodic sadness,
already expressed in the first interval (a minor third), occurs again just two bars
later, where another minor third—this time a descending one—perfectly matches
the words "(you do) me wrong." "Greensleeves" is, in fact, the story of a lost love:
the lady for whom the male character of the song has done so much, both in

terms of emotional commitment and gifts, has "cast him off discourteously" (is that a courtly act?).

The melancholy character of these parts of the tune—whose semantic interdependence with the lyrics is quite evident: consider also that the melody, in the second half of the four bars, is descending, a precise correlative for the concept of sentimental abandonment—is somewhat reinforced by Alfred Deller's falsetto-style vocal. The lute part played by Dupré is almost certainly taken from Williams Ballet's *Lute Book*, which today can be found in the New York Public Library. This is, if not the only, surely one of the few recorded examples of this (almost) original version of the tune, and certainly a good one for appreciating the chords underlying the melody, whether as symbols or written according to the typical Renaissance system of tablature. Songs for voice and lute accompaniment (airs, rounds, madrigals) are typical of the English music of this period. Its best-known composers are John Dowland, William Byrd, Thomas Morley, and Thomas Ravenscroft (later a popular author in the American colonies). Ravenscroft also became famous for his *Pammelia* (1609), *Deuteromelia* (1611), and *Melismata* (1619), three collections of popular songs. These songs were originally played by ballad mongers, minstrels, waits, violin players, and other dance musicians. As scholar Gustave Reese points out in his *Music in the Renaissance*, "these musicians, as well as tailors and others, used to sing these repertories of catches and ballads. A huge number of ballad texts were printed of broadside sheets, with the indication 'to be sung on the air of . . .' a very famous ballad, like *Greensleeves*."[9] For which particular instrument was the tune originally conceived, or, at least, on which instrument was it played? It is likely to have been the violin, one of the favorite instruments in the popular (and dance) tradition. A folk-violin version of "Greensleeves," already turning up in America, is cited by Hamm[10] in Howe's *Musician's Omnibus* (1861). From these elements we can infer that the melody had a double life, surviving through, and being interpreted by, both cultivated and folk musicians—first on the violin, then the lute, then on the violin again, certainly on the virginal, and so on. This, by the way, is what happens with many melodies and tunes, as it does with different forms of spoken and written languages. The oral and the written, the aural and the visual, are coexisting traditions in music. It is also true, though, that through the principles of adaptation, transformation, and transcription, oral versions of a particular lyric become written versions, and vice versa.

Besides the folk-violin version printed in *The Musician's Omnibus*, the American life of "Greensleeves" has been a varied and interesting one. The ballad has been through some significant transformations. As already noted, at the end of the nineteenth century, composer William Chatterton Dix wrote a new lyric, called "What Child Is This?" re-creating the song as a kind of Christmas carol for children. A new edition of "Greensleeves" was published in 1951 and became a hit. In 1962, under the title "Home in the Meadow," the secular tune was on the soundtrack for the film *How the West Was Won*. And in 1955 singer Peggy Lee started a very long and fruitful series of jazz interpretations.

Among the highlights of this cycle can be counted saxophonist John Coltrane's version (with a musical arrangement by Eric Dolphy, Impulse 1961), and those by organ virtuoso Jimmy Smith (Verve 1965) and classical/electric guitarist Kenny Burrell (musical arrangement by Gil Evans, Verve 1965). There are other recordings by well-known jazz players such as Coleman Hawkins (Prestige 1958), Oscar Peterson (MPS 1970 and Concord 1977, although under the title of "What Child Is This?"), Wes Montgomery (A&M 1971), Paul Desmond (Finesse Records 1971), George Shearing (MPS 1975), and others.

The three excellent jazz re-creations of the ancient tune mentioned above are all very different. How did Coltrane, Burrell, and Smith come to know the song, and what gave them the idea of recording new versions? Their sources were either the new edition published in 1951 or the jazz and pop recordings that followed— also, probably, the soundtrack of *How the West Was Won*.

Kenny Burrell's version is a masterpiece of aesthetic beauty, enhanced by the excellent quality of the sound recording, which was engineered by Rudy van Gelder. Burrell was a self-taught guitar player who, in the 1950s, studied classical guitar at Wayne State University in Detroit. It was probably during this period that he found a guitar transcription of "Greensleeves" (guitar versions of the tune remain easily available today) and decided to include it in his repertoire. Burrell's jazz interpretation of "Greensleeves" is actually a tribute to both classical guitar and electric guitar, which jazz started to incorporate in the 1930s and developed with stylistic contributions from Charlie Christian, Billy Bauer, Barney Kessel, Jim Hall, Wes Montgomery, and Burrell himself, as well as other soloists and virtuosi from the period 1940 to 1970, before the eruption of jazz-rock and fusion styles. In the first part of his recording, Burrell plays the melody alone, in an elegant classical, *arpeggiato* fashion. After a brief pause, a much faster jazz rhythm starts up, punctuated by Gil Evans's harmonically sophisticated arrangement for brass and reeds. Burrell's guitar flows in a dynamic, swinging series of phrases. More specifically, because Evans's arrangement is in AA'BC form (eight bars each), while, in its printed English traditional version, "Greensleeves" is in binary AABB form, Burrell first plays an introduction on classical guitar, running through the B, C, A, and then A' sections of the arrangement, followed by the other eight bars on the dominant pedal. Then comes the exposition: Burrell plays the whole AA'BC sequence, while Evans's arrangement counterpoints him in B. Following the theme, Burrell, shifting to electric guitar, improvises on sections A, A', B, and C. During the second improvised chorus the band is arranged in A. In the third and last chorus the band plays in A and A′, rather than B and C, while Burrell finally restates the theme, although only its A and A′ sections. In the coda you can hear a quotation from the famous E-minor *bourrée* by Johann Sebastian Bach.

Jimmy Smith's quartet version (electric organ, guitar, bass, drums) appears to be the furthest removed from the other interpretations. Smith quotes the melody briefly, and then literally flows on the organ keyboard, producing a very fast, swinging, brilliant, rhythmic-ritual, sometimes African-style sound exploration. The cyclical appearance of the melody, quoted three or four times in all, is subsumed in an almost endless improvisation. The time signature is 6/8. In the introduction, Smith plays a Dorian vamp on two chords, D and E. The theme is then stated in sections A and A′; an eight-bar riff follows, before the quartet completes the (B and C sections of) the exposition. The organ and guitar improvisations follow the same scheme, although in the end Smith improvises only on the riff, with continual shifts and delays in time—a feature that lends a hypnotic mood to this strange and exciting interpretation.

Recorded four years before Jimmy Smith's, John Coltrane's version of "Greensleeves," with the now classic arrangement by Eric Dolphy, is found on the renowned Impulse recording *Africa/Brass*. This, in my opinion, is the most interesting and personal re-creation of the song. Coltrane takes an almost endless, vibrating, energetic, abstract solo on his soprano sax. Dolphy dresses it in a sometimes complex, sometimes deliberately straightforward score for two reeds, four French horns, one trumpet, one trombone, one euphonium, and a tuba. The group is completed by a rhythm section that includes two basses (Art Davis and Reggie Workman), a drummer (Elvin Jones), and Alfred McCoy Tyner at the piano (at the time, this was also Coltrane's backing band, a marvelously efficient rhythm section). The very refined, original arrangements by Dolphy here are largely inspired by the idea of reinterpreting African culture and sounds in a modern style (the *reinterpretation* of African cultural traits was a concept fundamental to anthropologist Melville Herskovits's theoretical assumptions during the 1940s, especially with regard to African American culture and its relationship with European culture in the United States and the Americas). *Africa Brass*'s version of "Greensleeves" is an opportunity to hear a number of times the typical African, and later African American, call-and-response pattern. Here, though, as in other contemporary jazz of the period 1955–61, the musicians are also drawn—on another level—by modality (Miles Davis, John Coltrane, George Russell, Bill Evans are just a few of the musicians who took this path). A certain number of jazz compositions, and a larger number of jazz improvisations, refer to the ancient European modes, which are different, and somewhat more complex (in terms of their intervals) formulations of the modern European major-minor scales—both the Medieval-Renaissance modes and the even older ethnic modes.

In fact, "Greensleeves" in its folk origins is likely to have been a Dorian melody (even one with Aeolian elements at the start—section A—and later in the *Passamezzo antico* chordal progression). Statistically, the English folk music of the Renaissance preferred Dorian, Mixolydian, Ionian, and sometimes Aeolian modes. Once transcribed and published, in a period marked by the emergence of the tonal system, the old (Aeolian and Dorian) "Greensleeves" became a tonally minor tune, one that was printed in E minor or other transposed keys, depending on the chosen instruments.

Why did jazz musicians such as Miles Davis and John Coltrane so often choose the Dorian mode in the late fifties and sixties? Probably because the Dorian mode includes degrees (flat third and flat seventh) typical of the African American blues scale. The B melody of "Greensleeves" is Dorian; its major sixth is another degree typical of the blues scale. Thus it could be argued that modal Renaissance Europe and jazz—among the most representative expressions of contemporary African American culture—are linked. Is this cultural phenomenon subconscious or intentional? Probably both.

The modal reinterpretation, in Coltrane and Dolphy's jazz version of "Greensleeves," is not the only example of this practice. As James Fuld has pointed out, the English versions of the tune vary from the older, rhythmic folk-dance feel to the newer style of a courtly, slow, sad, and soulful ballad—on the one hand, the brilliant viol version people could dance to; on the other, a modern rewriting for lute with melancholy lyrics, interpreted vocally in an adolescent fashion that matched the theatrical conventions of Shakespeare's time. The song's change of mood possibly relates to the transition between the Middle Ages and the Renaissance, as well as the shift from country to court, from dance to chamber music, from modality to tonality, and from melody to melody plus harmony (harmonizing a preexisting tune generally involves slowing down the tempo to set appropriate chords).

The Coltrane-Dolphy version of "Greensleeves," whether by intuition or conscious choice, is the only jazz interpretation that synthesizes both of those two worlds. Coltrane's solos are seductively sad and full of nostalgia, not unlike the voice of the man who, in the song's lyrics, has been cast off discourteously. But in the background Dolphy's brass arrangement is propulsively energetic, supported by Elvin Jones's polyrhythmic drumming, which is at once immense and refined. So while Coltrane sweeps, the other musicians dance. And the contrast between the two approaches resolves in a contemporary masterpiece, a rare example of jazz demonstrating Herskovits's anthropological theory of reinterpretation: together, Coltrane and Dolphy have reinterpreted some specifically African American traits using a very old English folk tune.

The French section of the American jazz songbook includes a tune that ranks eleventh in the special chart established by American website jazzstandards.com: "Autumn Leaves." This song became famous in jazz from the fifties onward, thanks to interpretations by masters such as Erroll Garner, Miles Davis, Nat King Cole, Sarah Vaughan, Bill Evans, Stéphane Grappelli, and many others. It was written by the Hungarian-French composer Joseph Kosma (who came to Paris in 1933 and started writing music for ballets, light operas, and films, working with directors Jean Renoir and Marcel Carné) and the French poet and writer Jacques Prévert. The legal deposit of the composition occurred in 1945, under the title "Les feuilles mortes"; it was then published in 1947 by Enoch & Cie. Prévert had just come back to Paris, after the war, to resume his regular career as poet, theater writer, and scriptwriter. In Paris he wrote the script for the renowned film *Les enfants du paradis* with director Carné. Here are Prévert's lyrics:

> Oh! je voudrais tant que tu te souviennes
> Des jours heureux où nous étions amis
> En ce temps-là la vie était plus belle,
> Et le soleil plus brûlant qu'aujourd'hui
> Les feuilles mortes se ramassent à la pelle
> Tu vois, je n'ai pas oublié . . .
> Les feuilles mortes se ramassent à la pelle,
> Les souvenirs et les regrets aussi
> Et le vent du nord les emporte
> Dans la nuit froide de l'Oubli.
> Tu vois, je n'ai pas oublié
> La chanson que tu me chantais.
>
> C'est une chanson qui nous ressemble
> Toi, tu m'aimais et je t'aimais
> Et nous vivions tous deux ensemble
> Toi qui m'aimais, moi qui t'aimais
> Mais la vie sépare ceux qui s'aiment
> Tout doucement, sans faire de bruit
> Et la mer efface sur le sable
> Les pas des amants désunis.
>
> Les feuilles mortes se ramassent à la pelle,
> Les souvenirs et les regrets aussi
> Mais mon amour silencieux et fidèle

Sourit toujours et remercie la vie
Je t'aimais tant, tu étais si jolie,
Comment veux-tu que je t'Oublie?
En ce temps-là, la vie était plus belle
Et le soleil plus brûlant qu'aujourd'hui
Tu étais ma plus douce amie
Mais je n'ai que faire des regrets
Et la chanson que tu chantais
Toujours, toujours je l'entendrai!

The song was originally expected to be used in a ballet by Roland Petit, *Le rendez-vous*. Then Carné discovered and liked it, thinking Marlene Dietrich could sing it in his film *Les portes de la nuit*. But the film's main players changed: Dietrich and Jean Gabin left the production when their personal relationship broke down, and were replaced by Yves Montand and Nathalie Nattier. Montand (Ivo Livi), would become the song's most famous interpreter: his recording on shellac (Columbia 1949), with Bob Castella's Orchestra, sold one million copy in five years. Montand became world famous, and started proposing the song in French. The 1949 Montand interpretation is fully mature: perfect pitch, beautiful sound, vibrato; his voice—with a typical French use of the consonant "r"—draws out the phrases, while in the background we hear as counterpoints a piano, a pizzicato bass, and brief orchestral passages. Female singers Cora Vaucaire (Pathé-Marconi 1947) and Juliette Gréco (Philips 1951, with the André Grassi Orchestra) have recorded other significant early versions of the tune. Gréco's interpretation is like an introduction to her contralto voice: a hot, dark, theatrical performance, although her melodic phrasing lets her down. Jujube, as Gréco was known in Paris, became a sort of symbol of French existentialism, the philosophical and cultural movement led by Jean-Paul Sartre—which, by the way, was also open to jazz (Sartre and his partner Simone de Beauvoir had listened to Miles Davis, in a New York club, as early as 1947). Sartre, who regarded Gréco as the young muse of the movement, suggested she should pursue a career as a singer, while Gréco had instead started dancing. She would subsequently become famous both as an actress and a singer. In encouraging Gréco to sing, Sartre had in mind a sort of mini-revolution in French "light music" and the related song repertoire. He disliked and criticized most of the current song lyrics, and wanted Gréco to develop a new, cultivated, intellectual style of song, based on contemporary poetry. He also introduced Gréco to Joseph Kosma, who had worked with German theater writer and director Bertolt Brecht. Gréco developed her musical skills in parallel with pianist Jean Wiéner, who had been a major figure in the Parisian music scene of the twenties, when jazz became fashionable and appreciated by musicians and audiences alike. Kosma wrote the music for several songs, including some with lyrics by contemporary poets and writers: Sartre ("Rue des blancs manteaux"), Robert Desnos ("La fourmi") and Raymond Queneau ("Si tu m'imagines"). But Gréco had a special affinity for Jacques Prévert, and she sang and then recorded, among others, his lyrics for "À la belle étoile" and "Je suis comme je suis." By that time, Prévert was already famous in France. In the thirties he had started his career working with André Breton and Raymond Queneau, who were then part of the Surrealist movement. Prévert was subsequently recognized, in his parallel career as screenwriter, for his contributions to films such as *Quai des brumes* and *Le jour se lève*. In 1938 he went to Hollywood, where he lived for a year. Prévert became well known as a poet in 1946, when his published anthology *Paroles* turned into a bestseller. Besides Juliette Gréco, other singers who would record his lyrics included Florelle, Marianne Oswald, Edith Piaf, and Jacques les Frères. But with Gréco, Prévert became world-famous for his song "Les feuilles mortes," with music by Joseph Kosma. Gréco first recorded "Les feuilles mortes" in 1949. In the same year she met Miles Davis in Paris, when the young trumpet player was invited to perform at an international jazz festival organized in the French capital by critic and discographer Charles Delaunay. Gréco and Davis, as we know, had a brief but very intense love affair. The relationship would continue for the rest of their lives, although they would actually meet again on only a few occasions, in France (where Gréco put Davis in touch with the film director Louis Malle, in 1958) and in the United States (where she went to make some films). We do not know, from Davis's autobiography[11] and Bertrand Dicale's biography of Gréco,[12] whether Davis started playing "Les feuilles mortes" because he had heard it in Paris, sung by Gréco or anyone else.

In musical terms, Kosma's chorus uses a simple, repeated motif (three notes ascending in a major-second interval, plus a fourth note on the upper fifth), while the verse—at the start—is based on triplets, which remind us of the song's dance origins. The sadness of this part of the melody is enhanced by the use of the E minor key, while the tune's main key is G major. The E minor key returns at the end of the song, after a chromatically descending chord progression. Prévert's lyrics describe in simple and touching language the memory of a lost love. The theme seems to fit the emotional implications of the Davis-Gréco affair in Paris: while at the time (May 1949) Jean-Paul Sartre had suggested to Davis that he should marry Gréco, Davis—already a husband and a father—left Gréco to return to the United States. Drummer Kenny Clarke, on the other hand, having arrived in Paris with the musicians who would perform at Charles Delaunay's international jazz festival (Davis, Erroll Garner, Sidney Bechet, Charlie Parker, Tadd Dameron, and others), then decided to live in France.

A few months later began the American history of the Kosma-Prévert song. In

1950 the well-known songwriter (and composer) Johnny Mercer wrote the English lyrics for "Autumn Leaves," published in New York by Ardore Music. Jazz musicians liked the "new" song, and within a few years it had been recorded by Joe Venuti, Artie Shaw, Stan Kenton, and Stan Getz. The popular-music pianist and arranger Roger Williams then recorded (Kapp 116) an orchestral version that was a chartbuster for six months in 1955. In 1952 Mercer, who wrote well-known standards such as "Jeepers Creepers," "Skylark," "That Old Black Magic," and "Blues in the Night," founded a new Californian record label, called Capitol, in association with Buddy DeSylva and Glenn Wallichs. Capitol was closely affiliated with the cinema: DeSylva was at that time president of Paramount; Mercer, following his long commitment to Broadway, was already an established Hollywood songwriter. Mercer's lyrics for "Autumn Leaves" were suggested by Michael Golden, who had heard one of the most successful French recorded versions of the song, by Edith Piaf. The first American voice chosen to sing "Autumn Leaves" on the Capitol label—by Mercer himself—was Jo Stafford. Then came Bing Crosby, Nat King Cole, Paul Weston, and Frank Sinatra. Cole's version was particularly successful as, like Yves Montand's, it was used in a film (*Autumn Leaves*, Columbia 1956, directed by Robert Aldrich, with Joan Crawford and Cliff Robertson the main players). Nat King Cole's "Autumn Leaves" first appeared on his LP *Nat King Cole Sings for Two in Love* (Capitol T-420, 1955, with orchestral arrangements by Nelson Riddle). Cole sang it with typically immaculate diction (listen to his pronunciation of vowels and consonants such as "e" and "o," "d" and "t," reinforced by Mercer's lyrics) and his trademark liquid, crooning vocal style. As often happens, the fortunes of a jazz standard are related to the cinema, specifically to the film in which the song first appeared. This is an international "media" topic that calls for further specialist research.

Here are Mercer's lyrics for "Autumn Leaves":

The falling leaves drift by the window
The autumn leaves of red and gold
I see your lips, the summer's kisses
The sunburned hands I used to hold

Since you went away the days grow long
And soon I'll hear old winter's song
But I miss you most of all, my darling
When autumn leaves start to fall

Compared with Prévert's original, Mercer's version is much shorter. The main reason is that the form of American songwriting had changed since its Broadway-related origins. In fact, the verse—so often used in songs conceived for musical comedies—was later removed, making the chorus the sole focus of the song. There were also discographical considerations: 78 rpm and 45 rpm records last two or three minutes per side, more or less the same time as a chorus. From 1920 to 1940, verses used to be written to "prepare," in narrative terms, the stories developed in the choruses. Then things changed. There is another difference between Kosma/Prévert's and Kosma/Mercer's versions of "Autumn Leaves." It's at the beginning of the song: the key words of the original version (*C'est-une-chan/son*) only come at bar 13, while Mercer uses the three notes, e-f-sharp-g-(c), corresponding to the syllables *The-fal-ling* (*leaves*), to introduce bar 1 (singer Cora Vaucaire commented that the French "asymmetry" of the song was something like "a body without a foot").

Here are some of Philip Furia's very interesting comments on Johnny Mercer's new English lyrics:[13]

Instinctively he must have known that French, a Romance language, was rich in rhyme; there are fifty-one rhymes for *amour* in French, including such evocative rhymes as *toujours*. By contrast, English, a Germanic language, has far fewer words that rhyme; there are only five rhymes for *love*—*above, dove, glove, shove*, and *of*—only the first two of which really lend themselves to romantic parlance. The real poetry in English, moreover, lies in its hard accents and harsh consonants. The earliest poetry in English employed not rhyme but alliteration ("Bitter breast cares have I abided") and Shakespeare laced his unrhymed iambic verse with crabbed consonants ("I had rather hear a brazen candlestick turned on a dry wheel grate"). Even modern advertising slogans employ the rough accents and alliteration at the poetic heart of the language: when better cars are built, Buick will build them. Johnny Mercer's English lyric used only three rhymes, relying instead on alliteration consonants in what could be described as a lyrical "Concerto in T and D":

The falling leaves drift by the window,
The autumn leaves of red and gold
I see your lips, in summer's kisses,
The sunburned hands I used to hold.

With the paucity of rhymes, those harsh *t* and *d* sounds underscore a loss at once personal and universal.

Later there would be other successful popular interpretations of "Autumn Leaves," and the song would be used on the soundtrack of other films, such as *Hey Boy! Hey Girl!* (1959, directed by David Lowell Rich), where it was sung by Louis Prima and Keely Smith. Around the mid-fifties, the song became a jazz standard. Since "Les feuilles mortes" / "Autumn Leaves" was conceived for piano and voice, its jazz interpretations came both from piano players and from instrumentalists who, in the typical jazz tradition, adapted to the saxophone, trumpet, or violin the original vocal line.

The first really successful jazz interpretation of "Autumn Leaves" was by Erroll Garner on *Concert by the Sea* (Columbia CL 883, recorded live at Carmel, California, 1955, with Eddie Calhoun, bass, and Denzil Best, drums): a wonderful record, in spite of the poor recording quality and piano, which is almost out of tune. Garner's style, in the fifties, was very original: he had a marvelous sound, a unique rhythmic feel (in 4/4, the piano interacting with the plucked bass and the brushed drums), and a very personal harmonic approach, which often implied block chords. Garner's keyboard style could also be described as "orchestral": he regularly used octaves, tremolos, and arpeggios (which, in the case of "Autumn Leaves," he probably took from Roger Williams's version). He also was a master at balancing accelerandos and rallentandos, at developing the "sonic narrative" of a composition, and at improvisation. Garner's "orchestral" concept of the keyboard somehow fit the orchestral features of "Les feuilles mortes" / "Autumn Leaves"; in fact, in his 1955 version of the song, Garner's orchestral approach recalls Bob Castella's string arrangements in Yves Montand's French recording for Columbia in 1949.

Duke Ellington's 1957 interpretation of "Autumn Leaves" (on his LP *Ellington Indigos*, Columbia CS 8053) ranked among the best, in terms of creativity. One of the most original features of this version was the use both of Prévert's lyrics, in French (although limited to the chorus), and of Mercer's, sung by Ozzie Bailey. But Ellington's orchestral arrangement is equally impressive. On the one hand, the tentative bass line (Jimmy Woode's) and the low, "gray" sound of the brass develop a suspended, meditative, theatrical mood, which may evoke an autumnal atmosphere. On the other hand, there's a typically jazzy feature to this unique recording: Ray Nance's violin, which literally flows, in melodic terms, with some oriental flavors, and counterpoints Ozzie Bailey's vocal line—or is, alternatively, superimposed on it. Ellington plays piano with his characteristic unadorned touch, whose textures at times suggest French impressionism. His keyboard part opens and closes the interpretation.

The Bill Evans version of "Autumn Leaves" (on his LP *Portrait in Jazz*, Riverside RLP 12-315, 1959) is among the most famous, and the best, of those undertaken by a trio of piano, bass, and drums. An inexperienced listener would probably have difficulty following how Evans develops, in melodic terms, Kosma's tune. The pianist was at the time tapping into the new trends in contemporary jazz. African American music was developing an avant-garde style that would suggest different linguistic and aesthetic paradigms. Evans introduced a kind of revision of the traditional roles within the piano-bass-drums trio: the bass started to develop a parithetical dialogue with the piano (a technique that would have been called "interplay") and to be heard as a solo, "singing" voice, with the piano in the background. This was something rather different from the traditional theme–solo piano–theme progression. In his 1959 version of "Autumn Leaves" (with Scott LaFaro on bass and Paul Motian on drums), Evans reveals the theme in a quiet, classical way, with quite a mainstream feel. But then the rhythm drops out to leave room for the aforementioned piano-bass interplay (with Motian *tacet*). The drums return in the final reprise of the theme, where Evans shows his personal mastery of piano innovations and techniques (extended chords, chord inversions). In essence, Kosma's theme appears to be subsumed by Evans to his personal revision of functions within the piano trio, and in his search for a dissolution of conventional song form—although Evans's achievements are different from those of the contemporary free-jazz style.[14]

Who better than Miles Davis to have captured, in jazz, the deep feeling of sadness and nostalgia expressed by the French authors of "Les feuilles mortes" / "Autumn Leaves"? Our first thought may be that his choice of Kosma's tune was related to his Parisian affair with Juliette Gréco. Instead, it is more likely Davis decided to record "Autumn Leaves" after hearing pianist Ahmad Jamal's version of the classic song (Epic 1955). Davis always cited Jamal (and Frank Sinatra, in fact) as one of his major influences. Davis's first take on "Autumn Leaves" appeared on Cannonball Adderley's album *Somethin' Else* (Blue Note BLP 1595, 1958), and the song featured regularly in his own repertoire until 1966. At first, Adderley's version does not sound memorable, with its arranged riff for piano (Hank Jones), saxophone, and trumpet. But when Davis starts to improvise, the mood changes completely. His muted trumpet helps the music develop in a linear motivic progression, with brilliant rhythmic counterpoints from Sam Jones on the bass and Art Blakey on drums. Davis manages to render, in a bluesy, minor-key style, the sadness of "Autumn Leaves," the story of lovers who were separated by life. Following the trumpeter's chorus, there are interesting solos from Cannonball Adderley on alto saxophone and Wynton Kelly (indispensable as ever) on piano. One of the very best performances of "Autumn Leaves" by Davis is on his *Miles Davis in Europe* album (Columbia Col PC8983), recorded live in 1963 at the French Antibes Juan-les-Pins Jazz Festival. This was Davis's introduction to a European audience of his new quintet with Herbie Hancock at the piano, George Coleman on tenor saxophone, Ron Carter on bass, and Tony Williams on drums. This combo, especially when Wayne Shorter replaced Coleman a little later, would become one of the turning points of Davis's career. "Autumn Leaves"—which would also be played at concerts in Berlin and Paris, and later on in Chicago—is presented in a long, diffuse version, allowing each soloist to express himself fully for several minutes. We can appreciate Davis's

extended, melodically free lines, Coleman's strong phrases on the tenor saxophone, and Hancock's matchless piano playing, able to blend tradition and the
avant-garde, the blues and a cultivated European sensibility.

Paradoxically, there are few jazz vocal versions of "Autumn Leaves" (Mel
Tormé, Helen Merrill, Sheila Jordan, Patricia Barber, Karrin Allyson—the last of
these presenting the song both in French and English, as if she had heard Duke
Ellington's version). A surprising interpretation comes from Sarah Vaughan on
her Pablo album *Crazy and Mixed Up* (Pablo Today PBL 6011, 1982). Sassy offers a
scat-vocal, bebop version of the Kosma-Mercer masterpiece, backed up by the
brilliant, rapid harmonic changes of Joe Pass on electric guitar and Roland
Hanna on piano, and by the equally brilliant rhythmic skills of Andy Simpkins on
bass and Harold Jones on drums. The song here is transformed into a completely
new entity.

Finally, there are some interpretations of "Autumn Leaves" proposed by European jazzmen or by "Americans in Europe." Among the European musicians we
may quote the versions of Bireli Lagrene, Jacky Terrasson, Stéphane Grappelli,
Toots Thielemans, Ferenc Snetberger, and Thomas Clausen, while saxophone
player Ben Webster, one of the most famous "Americans in Europe" in the sixties
(he lived first in Copenhagen, and then in Amsterdam from 1964 until his death in
1972) made of "Autumn Leaves" one of the signature tunes of his final years. He
recorded it with Euro-American rhythm sections, approaching the tune in different ways. His Black Lion version (recorded in Copenhagen with Niels-Henning
Ørsted Pedersen on bass, Alex Riel on drums, and Kenny Drew on piano; Black
Lion BLC D760151, 1965) is slow and romantic, while his later Spotlite interpretation (recorded in Paris with George Arvanitas on piano, Jacky Samson on bass,
and Charles Saudrais on drums; Spotlite LP 9, 1972) is, on the contrary, a brillant,
swinging, up-tempo one, with some remarkable solos by the French Arvanitas.

Italy

The Italian contribution to the jazz repertoire includes a dozen titles. The most
popular of them ("Nel blu dipinto di blue / Volare," "E se domani," "Non
dimenticar," "Senza fine," "Odio l'estate") were written in the fifties and sixties,
and they attracted renowned American jazzmen like Louis Armstrong, Nat King
Cole, Oscar Peterson, Wes Montgomery, and Chet Baker as interpreters. In the
nineties Pat Metheny was influenced by Ennio Morricone, the celebrated Italian
composer of film music (the same happened with saxophone player John Zorn,
who played some compositions by Morricone in his 1985 album *The Big Gundown*), and recorded some tunes of his (and one of his son Andrea Morricone),
taken from the soundtrack of the film *Nuovo Cinema Paradiso*.[15]

Two other songs, belonging to the earlier part of the last century, became very successful in the United States: "Gigolo" and "'O sole mio." The first, the most interesting in its implications for the jazz repertoire, was composed by Leonello Casucci. A piano player and composer from Tuscany, Casucci was playing with his group in Germany in 1929. One of his tunes, part of a musical show, was published by Wiener Boheme Verlag in Berlin and Vienna under the title "Schöner Gigolo, armer Gigolo" with lyrics by Julius Brammer. In 1930, the sixteen-bar song was published in Italy by Curci as "Gigolò" (lyrics by Enrico Frati). It was then recorded by singer Daniele Serra on Italian Gramophone in a typical bel canto style, with a rigid marching rhythm.[16]

"Schöner Gigolo, armer Gigolo" was first recorded in Germany by Dajos Béla, Richard Tauber, the Weintraub Syncopators, and others. Then it traveled to the United States. With English lyrics by Irving Caesar, the tune—renamed "Just a Gigolo"—was a big hit, thanks to its inclusion in a Betty Boop cartoon and especially to the 78 rpm vocal recordings by Louis Armstrong on Okeh in 1930[17] and by Bing Crosby on Victor in 1931.[18] Satchmo also improvised a brilliant trumpet variation on the melody, shifting its rigid European rhythm to a syncopated one, and transforming the melancholy mood of the composition and the emphasis of the bel canto interpretations into a new, joyous performance.

Other notable interpretations of the tune, with completely different approaches, have come from Art Tatum, Bud Powell, Django Reinhardt, Thelonious Monk, and Louis Prima.

The lyrics of "Gigolo" present a poetic vision of social collapse in Austria after World War I, represented by a former hussar who remembers himself in his uniform. Now he has to get by as a dancer or by entertaining women for money. The English version sets the action in a Paris café, where a local character tells his sad story. The bittersweet effect of the harmonic progression highlights the mixed emotions of the song.

Thelonious Monk's interpretation of "Gigolo" / "Just a Gigolo" on Prestige Records (1954)[19] is particularly impressive, and very personal. His percussive, surreal, puppetlike keyboard approach perfectly matches the low-down, "bluesy" feeling—and the lyrics—of this European tune.

The mood of "Gigolo" / "Just a Gigolo," in fact, is not only bitter but also positive. Following the lead of Louis Armstrong—who, as mentioned above, offered a smiling, sunny interpretation of the gigolo's sexual role in 1930—trumpet player and singer Louis Prima recorded in 1956 for the Capitol label[20] (with singer Keely Smith and Prima's group called the Witnesses) a danceable version of the song whose sense is miles away from the original but which, with its typical Las Vegas feeling, is a little masterpiece of contemporary entertainment.

118   The traditional image of Italy is conveyed through notions such as love, the

sun, the sea, pasta, and Mediterranean mandolins. These are, in a sense, classic—albeit stereotypical—symbols of Neapolitan culture. The image is mirrored by a number of songs, of which "'O sole mio" (lyrics by Giovanni Capurro, music by Eduardo di Capua, published by Bideri in 1898) is the perfect synthesis. It became a worldwide hit, thanks also to the Victor recording by tenor Enrico Caruso in Camden, New Jersey, in 1916. Along with the Caruso vocal style, this and similar tunes served as a model for some of the New Orleans fathers of jazz, including King Oliver, Louis Armstrong, and Sidney Bechet. In his autobiography, Bechet cites the Neapolitan tenor as an influence on his typical saxophone vibrato.

As with "Gigolo," jazz history has produced completely different, even polar versions of this old Italian tune. The following are two contrasting examples. The first is by Lee Konitz,[21] who approaches the melody with his unique vitreous, liquid alto saxophone sound, while Stefano Battaglia, at the piano, offers an accompaniment that deliberately recalls the style and symbolic tone of French impressionism. The feeling is of another sun (a northern one) and another sea, as Battaglia suggests by quoting Maurice Ravel's famous composition *La mer*.

Again, as in the case of "Just a Gigolo," the freedom and creativity associated with jazz interpretation can result in a radically different take on "'O sole mio." That is what happens with the second version, by Spike Jones, who recorded the Italian tune for RCA, in 1949, with his group the City Slickers[22] under the title of "Charlestonio mio." A Californian drummer and vaudeville actor, Jones was a popular musician and bandleader who specialized in satirical arrangements of popular songs (one of his best-known records was *Murdering the Classics*). Ballads and classical works given the Jones treatment would be punctuated with gunshots, whistles, cowbells, and ridiculous vocals. As in this case: in the adapted English lyrics, the words /'O sole mio (my sun)/ are followed by the parodic reply /'O sole *you* (*your* sun)/; meanwhile, an incredible up-tempo yet capable Dixieland-like arrangement of the Neapolitan song, in the performing style of Ward Kimball's Firehouse Five Plus Two, features "serious" solos played on the clarinet and the muted trombone, but punctuated and "embellished" by the futuristic sounds of horns and whistles, and turning into a demented, machine-like, collective Charleston.

Pianist Bruno Martino and lyricist Bruno Brighetti are the authors of "Odio l'estate," a song composed and published in 1960 that became an Italian hit in 1961. It was later translated into English as "Summer." Martino was a successful pianist, songwriter, and singer in Italy during the sixties and seventies, appearing in several television shows. He had previous experience abroad, though, through a long-term association with drummer Ole Jorgensen in Denmark. During his Danish years Martino became well known as an entertainer who could mix modern pop songs with a jazz feeling and a modest propensity for improvisation on the keyboard. This was also the case with "Odio l'estate." It is not exactly a masterpiece in melodic terms, but the song was conceived and subsequently recorded by Martino, for the Italian RCA in 1960,[23] with an African American rhythm that illustrates how transatlantic exchanges are a recurrent feature of contemporary music, including jazz and its European sources. A book dedicated to "Odio l'estate" was recently published in Italy.[24]

The prince of Brazilian bossa nova, singer João Gilberto, probably came to know Martino's "Odio l'estate" through the RCA recording. He then offered his own, wonderful interpretation of the song on Warner Bros., 1977.[25] Gilberto's version of the tune is a perfect example of synthesizing European, North American, and South American musical elements. The lyrics are Italian, and thus European. The marvelous slow-tempo orchestral arrangement by German American composer and conductor Claus Ogerman draws on French impressionism in its use of the strings but also of the flute, which became a typical feature of contemporary Brazilian orchestral music. Gilberto's voice, with its smooth, soft, low timbre, is Brazilian but somehow also recalls Martino's vocal interpretation in the middle to low register. In semiotic terms, Gilberto seems more attracted by the sound than the sense of the lyrics: his articulation of the vowels and consonants makes them vibrate, creating a circular feeling of suspension. Gilberto's idea of summer is beautifully static, in a typically Brazilian way, in contrast to the original dynamic, but slightly superficial, interpretation of this "seasonal" love story. The rhythm is Brazilian, but the use of drums with brushes is in the postbebop modern jazz tradition: in fact, the drummer is the African American Grady Tate.

"Odio l'estate," or "Summer," became a jazz standard, especially after João Gilberto recorded the song. It has been being played by, among others, Gábor Szabó (Mercury 1977), Chet Baker (Red Records 1983), Monty Alexander (Concord 1985, 2000, and 2004), Bobby Hutcherson (Jazz Records 1986), Shirley Horn (Verve 1987, 1992, and 1999), Toots Thielemans (Concord 1988), Joe Pass (Pablo 1988), Doug Raney (Steeplechase 1994), Grover Washington (Columbia 1994), Mark Murphy (Jive Music 1995), Billy Higgins (Red Records 1995), Meredith D'Ambrosio (Vocal Jazz 1995), Dave Liebman (Arkadia 1997), Ray Brown (Telarc 1997 and 1998), Bireli Lagrene (Dreyfus 2000), John Pizzarelli (Telarc 2004), Bobby Durham (Island 2005), Don Grusin (Bad Dog Music 2005), Lynne Arriale (Teb 2006), Chris Botti (Columbia 2007), Eliane Elias (Blue Note 2008), and Guitars Unlimited with Niels-Henning Ørsted Pedersen (Universal 2009).

A particularly meaningful jazz interpretation of this summer song is Michel Petrucciani's live performance for Blue Note in Metz in November 1991, with Steve Logan on bass and Victor Jones on drums.[26] "Odio l'estate" occurs at the beginning and end of this version, but with a whole different world in between. The French pianist of Italian origin offers a unique balance of poetry and musical science. His melodic approach is lyrical, his ability to alternate sound and silence masterly, his skill at building long, sequential, almost architectural improvised phrases with his right hand is breathtaking. Petrucciani flows on the keyboard, building crescendos toward unprecedented dramatic climaxes. He references Keith Jarrett's "singing" lines in the always floating "Standards Trio" with Gary Peacock and Jack DeJohnette, and finally abandons himself to the ecstasy of resonant overtones and an intense spirit of vibration.

NOTES

1. Some of these transcribed folk songs may be found in three Dover Publications sources: *One Hundred English Folksongs*, edited by Cecil Sharp (New York: Dover 1975); *Seventy Scottish Songs*, selected and arranged by Helen Hopekirk (New York: Dover 1992), and *Popular Irish Songs*, edited by Florence Leniston (New York: Dover 1992). Recorded jazz versions of some of the tunes are included on the CD *Jazz & European Songs*, vol. 2, Saga 066 476-2 (2003).

2. Alec Wilder, *American Popular Song: The Great Innovators, 1900-1950* (New York: Oxford University Press, 1972/R 1990), pp. 424-27.

3. A different category, which cannot be addressed here since it does not involve popular song forms, is arrangements of classical European compositions played by jazz groups and orchestras, such as swing bands. See Manfred Straka's detailed article "Komposition der abendlandischen Kunstmusik im Repertoire von Swing-Ensemble," in *Jazzforschung/Jazzresearch* 36 (Graz: Adeva 2004), pp. 29-49. Giacomo Puccini, one of the major contemporary composers of Italian opera, and renowned for his refined, subtle melodic invention, has recently caught the inspiration of some jazz musicians, including Italian trumpet player Enrico Rava. He has recorded some of Puccini's most famous arias, from the operas *Tosca*, *La fanciulla del West*, *Gianni Schicchi*, and *Madama Butterfly*, on his CDs *Rava l'Opera va* (Label Bleu LBLC 6559 HM83, 1993) and *Italian Ballads* (Venus TKCV 35002, 1996). Going back to the early days of jazz in New Orleans, Giuseppe Verdi and Gaetano Donizetti's compositions often influenced some of the major jazz players of the first generation, starting with Jelly Roll Morton. See Gunther Schuller, *Early Jazz: Its Roots and Musical Development* (New York: Oxford University Press, 1968), pp. 146-49. An overview of the complex and fascinating influences of classical music (composers and interpreters) on jazz, and vice versa, can be found in my essay "Intorno al jazz. Musiche transatlantiche: Africa, Europa, America" (Milan: Bompiani, 2007), pp. 259-62, 382-83, 412-13.

4. *The European Real Book* (Petaluma, CA: Chuck Sher, 2005).

5. Philippe Baudoin, *Une chronologie du jazz* (Paris: Outre Mesure, 2005), p. 30.

6. James Fuld, *The Book of World Famous Music: Classical, Popular and Folk* (New York: Dover, 1961), p. 259.

7. Charles Hamm, *Music in the New World* (New York: Norton, 1983), p. 94.

8. Gustave Reese, *Music in the Renaissance* (New York: Norton, 1959), p. 877.

9. James Fuld, *The Book of World Famous Music: Classical, Popular and Folk* (New York: Dover, 1961), p. 258.

10. Hamm, *Music in the New World*, p. 84.

11. Miles Davis with Quincy Troupe, *The Autobiography* (New York: Simon & Schuster 1989/R 2005).

12. Bertrand Dicale, *Juliette Gréco: Les vies d'une chanteuse* (Paris: Lattes 2001).

13. Philip Furia, *Skylark: The Life and Times of Johnny Mercer* (New York: St. Martin's Press, 2003), pp. 176-77.

14. Bill Evans, during his career, has been the jazz interpreter of several compositions of French musician, pianist, and big-band leader Michel Legrand (1932), whose general artistic contribution falls among pop music, film music, and jazz. Legrand's June 1958 Columbia/Philips LP *Legrand Jazz*, recorded in New York, included in fact such famous jazzmen as Miles Davis, John Coltrane, Ben Webster, Phil Woods, and Evans. This discographical experience led to a musical friendship with Miles Davis (who would record Legrand's tune "Once upon a Summertime" in his album *Quiet Nights*, CBS CK 65693), and especially with Evans, who has recorded Legrand's tunes "I Will Say Goodbye" (*I Will Say Goodbye*, OJC CD 761-2), "You Must Believe in Spring" (*You Must Believe in Spring*, Rhino 812273719-2), "Noelle's Theme" (*The Last Waltz*, Milestone 8MCD 4430-2), "Orson's Theme" (*I Will Say Goodbye*, OJC CD 761-2), "Why Did I Choose You" (*From Left to Right*, Verve 557451-2), "What Are You Doing the Rest of Your Life?" (*Blue in Green*, Milestone MCD 9185-2), "Summer of '42" (*Montreux III*, OJC 20 644-2). Legrand's music has been recorded by several other jazz musicians, including Oscar Peterson, Sarah Vaughan, Chet Baker, Blossom Dearie, Freddie Cole, Joe Pass, Toots Thielemans, Laura Fygi, Woody Herman, Charlie Haden, Kenny Burrell, and Shirley Horn.

15. See John Zorn, *The Big Gundown: John Zorn Plays the Music of Ennio Morricone*, LP Nonesuch 979139-1, recorded in 1984 and 1985. The album has been reissued in CD with the same title but with the addition of six melodies in 2000 (Tzadik TZ 7328). Pat Metheny recorded the Morricone compositions from the film *Cinema Paradiso* in his 1996 CD *Beyond the Missouri Sky*, Verve 537130-2.

16. Its CD reprint is *Daniele Serra cantante*, Fonit Cetra CDFO 3616.

17. Its CD reprint is *Louis Armstrong Sings*, Sony Music-Columbia 488613-2.

18. Its CD reprint is *Bing Crosby: It's Easy to Remember*, Proper P1233.

19. Its CD reprint is *Thelonious Monk*, Prestige / Original Jazz Classics OJCC10-010-2.

20. Its CD reprint is Louis Prima, *Collectors Series*, Capitol CDP 7 94072 2.

21. Lee Konitz, *A Night in Italy: Canzoni italiane in jazz*, Musica Jazz MJCD 1117 (1997).

22. Its CD reprint is in *Jazz & European Songs*, vol. 1, Saga 066475-2.

23. Its CD reprint is in Bruno Martino, *I grandi successi originali*, BMG Ricordi 743211820412-2.

24. Paola De Simone, *Odio l'estate: Bruno Martino e il più famoso standard jazz italiano* (Rome: Donzelli 2010).

25. Its CD reprint is in João Gilberto, *Amoroso*, Warner Bros. 2.3053.

26. *Michel Petrucciani: Live*, Blue Note CDP 0777 7 80589 2 2.

6 / ACROSS EUROPE
IMPROVISATION AS A REAL AND METAPHORICAL JOURNEY

"March of the pilgrims singing their evening prayer"
The long line of those who want to see
Travels around the world
Little ants looking for beauty.
Eyes like coins that shine
To support this overflowing
Economy of the visible.
It looks like an ex voto, instead it is a pay per view,
The "pay and see" of new pilgrims
that are looking for the sanctuaries of difference
and that while looking for them erase them

Cruel paradox of love for traveling:
Midas and Tantalus suffering from the same torture!

VALERIO MAGRELLI

Sad word, tourists

VALERY LARBAUD

European Jazz and the Myth of the Journey ~~really earlier, eh?~~

ince its beginning in the thirties of the last century, jazz has been experienced in Europe as a turning point, the ultimate exile, the conquest of a new "citizenship of the world," as something searching for the instinct, spontaneity, and energy that are free at last and that stand as the symbol for Africa, black America, and to an extent also for white America.

You cannot play jazz remaining European. Just like our emigrants traveled to America a few decades ago, jazz music gives the myth of "the American dream" a cultural meaning, and it does it in a moment when Europe is trying to turn over a new leaf during and after fascism.

Gianni Coscia, the accordionist, told me a joke they used to make in Italy in the fifties. When you heard someone play good jazz in Milan they said: "It feels like we're over there," where the mythic "over there" was represented by America at the time. This is a revealing joke.

yuck

In those years jazz fans felt like outcasts, distant from their own communities. You wanted to be part of a bigger, cosmopolitan community, the "jazz community," as it was and is still called by many jazzmen. This feeling of non-belonging was doomed to create problems especially during fascism; that is the reason why fascism always looked on jazz music with distrust and even tried to stop its diffusion. Nowadays things have changed.

Traveling abroad has now become an ordinary thing for Europeans; traveling abroad no longer is a turning point in one's life, as it was in the fifties. In many cases it is American jazz (and African and Asian jazz) that looks on Europe as a potential source of renewal and not only because of the higher fees it offers.

The Europe they are looking on is not only that of classical music, which has been an inspiration for American jazz since the thirties. It was so inspiring that it led to the birth of the Third Stream jazz in the fifties; the Third Stream jazz is a no-man's-land between jazz and classical music. One of the examples of this kind of music is represented by Uri Caine, who successfully combined Mahler and the klezmer sound, but who wasn't as successful with Mozart's or Beethoven's music.

yes

Nowadays many American jazzmen look on Europe as the home of a freer and more unconventional jazz, which leads at times to a funny exchange between European jazzmen who look on an America that no longer exists and American jazzmen who look on a Europe that does not exist yet. This is evidence that European jazz, even if it no longer feels inferior to American jazz, is still deeply influenced by the concept of journey.

interesting! although hindered by issues of style

European Jazz simply transformed the journey from a life-changing experience and turning point to a kaleidoscope of events and experiences. Europe still considers itself as the starting point but not as the final destination. If we want to understand ourselves and the world we live in, we have to free ourselves from the idea that "old Europe matters."

You have to travel, see and experience many things, despite what an "old Europe" member, Robert Musil, maintained: "Having too many experiences is a prerogative of fools." But since actual traveling is now underrated, you travel with your imagination, and not just in one country like Emilio Salgari did, but you easily and freely go from one place to the other re-creating, revisiting, and remaking things.

America is no longer the myth. The myth is the world, which is only partly globalized. Jazz music is no longer experienced as a language with its own specific rules, but it goes back to its primordial and "American" being as a "music of the borders" that can cross and erase musical, political, race, and music borders. Nothing new, some may say.

but not gender, eh.

Improvisation based on set harmonic structures, on the bebop and modal syntax, on a kind of harmony based on the dominant seventh, on the triplet rhythm of swing, was criticized, and it was anticipated by the "free" revolution of the sixties. Yet this is something new: it is not about breaking the rules of harmony or the implosion of melody or freedom from rhythm, but it is about the use of codes, syntax, and grammars that were once considered incompatible with jazz music and that are now suddenly accepted.

It is not the alleged freedom of the "free," but the encounter between traditions and languages that has always existed in jazz (think of Art Blakey, Abdul Malik, Randy Weston, and their relationship with Africa, Dizzy Gillespie's Afro-Cuban Jazz, the ambitions of the late Coltrane toward a universal music) that now becomes almost compulsory for a jazzman who wants to be "cool."

It is not the end of jazz music, as many maintained in the past; it is a debate on the idea of jazz based on the concept of "swing" or based on the concept of freedom. These concepts are still valid if we consider them in a wider sense than Joachim Ernst Berendt does.

The swing as propulsive energy, and the freedom as the ability that only improvisation has to explode languages, to give them life, putting them in relationship with the body-instrument of the musician, are what still make us prefer jazz to any other kind of music.

But the question is: what kind of jazz? In the following pages we will try to analyze the development of a new possible un-definition of jazz, examining the most meaningful experiments of "European" jazz in the last few years. In this analysis, we will be guided by the concept of journey, intended as the exploration of borders as well as the search for the roots, but we have to be aware of the risks that curiosity and fascination for the exotic can always have.

The Imagined Journey

A critical investigation into the concept of journey in European jazz is strictly connected with the ECM experience, where for the very first time the question of jazz and its relationship with other kinds of music was solved by creating a new and unique sound. Manfred Eicher chose this sound for most of his records because it is so evocative and full of reflection, and it is also ideal because it leads to pure, measured, slightly melancholic melodies that are the trademark of the ECM label.

Melody plays such an essential role for the very first time; no jazzmen had ever "dared" so much. Jazzmen used to take commercial songs to attract people and then completely renew them from the inside.

Yet right when melody triumphs, it loses its appeal and substance, and it becomes abstract, weak, impersonal, and not only because of the sound. The musicians whom Manfred Eicher chose for his melodic revolution, from Jan Garbarek to Charlie Haden, from Egberto Gismonti to Kenny Wheeler, from Dino Saluzzi to Misha Alperin, from Keith Jarrett to Anouar Brahem, take the colors and the flavors of "other" kinds of music, from Brazilian music (Gismonti) to Argentinian folklore (Saluzzi), from Arab (Brahem, Jon Balke) to Russian Orthodox music (Alperin, Vassilis Tsabroupulos) from English folklore (John Surman) to a Nordic one (Garbarek, Terje Rypdal). Except that the original music rarely emerges in a clear and explicit way.

More often melody floats above its roots and becomes universal, a melody that belongs to us all.

In his musical anthropology studies, Kurt Sachs emphasized how there are some anthropological characteristics in music that belong to all people and to all ethnic groups. The ECM project aims at proving this theory, focusing on melody and not on rhythm.

Elementary melodic cells based on pure intervals (the fifth, the eighth) and on catchy modes are the heart of melodies that hardly are self-revealing and that do not tell anything about their social, historical, and psychological origins but that are metaphysical in the sense that they go beyond the substance and aim at an unknown "beyond."

In some cases melody has an ambiguous fascination, that of a no-man's-land that is not inhabited but that reminds of a past human presence.

In other cases the music sounds spineless, deprived of rhythm and energy, and has a general effect of cold abstraction. As a matter of fact, an element of this music that you can often find in ECM "products" is a certain stillness.

The fact that this music has exotic and non-European elements that are not part of the jazz tradition might be misleading.

The promised journey is evoked, imagined, dreamed of, but never really made. The real journey is telling a story, is a story that unfolds.

ECM music never moves significantly, and you are immediately aware that it is the final destination; it is like when you travel with a travel agency where everything is planned out. In the same way, it does not matter if the atmosphere of the music is not real or is too artificial and "planned out."

What really matters is to reach the consumers, to persuade them that they are facing something different and distant from them.

The unknown they are looking for (otherwise they wouldn't have left in the first place) must be suggested, but they must not be led there on a difficult and risky path. Everything is organized and studied in a way that they are not led far from what they are and which brings them back to their ordinary lives feeling proud of having met a fascinating and mysterious "beyond" that cannot really (thank God for that!) change their lives.

126

This incomplete journey, one that is evoked but not really made, is the characteristic of many ethno-jazz experiments, not only by the ECM label.

That is why some extraordinary "ethnic" musicians, who could tell us a story and take their music to unexpected and original solutions, are often used as an element of color to give music a taste of exoticism and nothing more than that.

Not managing or not wanting to make this element a true moment of change and yet not wanting to abandon it, the music only floats around it, and it resolves in being extremely still. Some may argue: what about improvisation? Shouldn't its presence in ethno-jazz guarantee freedom, unpredictability, and adventure?

In spite of this, improvisation is often shy, influenced by the theme and by strict chord structures.

Most instruments used in ethno-jazz, like the oud, the kora, the kalimba, the bouzouki, the launeddas (a popular Sardinian direct-breath polyphonic instrument), the duduk, the shakuhachi, the ney, and the bandoneon, are perfect for a diatonic-modal improvisation.

But this is not a good reason to improvise only with elementary harmonic chords and common modes. This is a regression from the models of improvisation (modal, atonal, polytonal) that have been used since the sixties; and instead of trying to create an exchange among different styles, genres, and music cultures, from which everyone could benefit, the musicians adapt to the needs of the weakest or to those less used to improvising in a non-idiomatic way. In a word: music goes back. What really matters are the instruments and the musicians that go onstage, that is, the image, and not the music they could really play.

Back to the Roots

This is obviously not always true. Many ECM records fortunately have a different purpose: that of going back to the roots, of finding in the musicians' own musical past the reasons and the motivation to carry on with their experiments with improvisation and jazz music.

This is what happens when extraordinary improvisers, instead of relishing a tasteless exoticism, openly challenge their origins and their music in a risky and unpredictable process.

The journey, intended as "sending yourself to the others and the others to yourself" (Marc Augé) and not as the evocation of indeterminate and other atmospheres, plays again the main role.

It is interesting to consider the theory by the French philosopher and anthropologist Marc Augé about how the concept of journey would be threatened in our times by the realm of evidence and the tyranny of the present. When Augé speaks about the "tyranny of the present," he refers especially to the supremacy of images; but music can be an image (or music-image) when instead of telling a story it gives us a persistent, obsessive, somehow conceited representation.

This is what happens in many ECM products (and the term "products" wants to emphasize all that is prepackaged and stereotyped about them) where, despite the idea of journey being constantly evoked, nothing ever happens.

The image in music confounds itself with the image on the cover of the CD, which therefore plays an essential role, and it is as if the image crystallized the music in an eternal present. But there are musicians that represent an exception, and with whom not everything is defined in advance. The great English saxophonist and clarinetist John Surman, for instance.

In many of his projects, like the SOS trio in the seventies (with Mike Osborne and Alan Skidmore) and the duo with the double-bass player Barre Phillips, Surman is influenced by the jigs of Nordic folklore. He is also influenced by the compositions of John Dowland and by the English Renaissance, like in the beautiful "In Darkness Let Me Dwell" with singer John Potter. Listening to Surman's music, it is easy to understand how he tries to draw inspiration from these models and not only color. The melody is disconnected from traditional jazz syntax and from the kind of modal jazz that is common Surman's music.

Nothing is taken for granted, and there is no mannerism in his music; it is clear to see that those themes really belong to him, as much as they do not have to be quoted but destroyed and rebuilt. His music tells a story, and it is the story of a journey through a tradition without which Surman couldn't exist and would lose his identity.

We could say the same thing about another extraordinary English musician, trombonist Annie Whitehead, who combines English folk songs and jazz in her CD *Northern Lights*. There are other examples among some of the European jazz musicians of the last decade: Spanish pianist Diego Amador, who uses the rhythmic liberty of flamenco in a jazz context, Armenian pianist Tigran Hamasyan, who uses Armenian tradition, Portuguese couple Maria João and Mário Laginha, who can go back to the Brazilian, Mozambican, Capo Verdian rhythmic roots of Portuguese music maintaining the melody of fado and a remarkable variety of harmonies.

The French-Spanish-Portuguese pianist Jean-Marie Machado, who with his ensemble combines bandlike sounds and French popular traditions together with Baroque dances and Andalusian traditional music, the Greek trumpet player Pantelis Stoikos, who with the unprecedented sound of his trumpet and caval alternates Balkanic rhythms and very lively free jazz, which are deeply rooted in the rhythms and sounds of his country.

The case of Sardinian trumpet player Paolo Fresu is extremely significant. For many years Fresu has devoted himself to a passionate "recovery" (a word he says he doesn't like because "what is lost is lost and instead what is left with me, was given to me by Sardinia and by my folks, and is therefore not lost") of traditional Sardinian music in a "mixed" musical context, made of jazz musicians and ethnic musicians that are not only Sardinian, but African, Breton, and Vietnamese.

The successful result of this project is the soundtrack for the documentary film by Gianfranco Cabiddu, *Sonos e Memoria* (Sounds and Memory), a sort of sample of instruments and styles of today's and yesterday's Sardinia. Monody, sacred and profane polyphony, dance, jazz, improvised music are performed both with traditional instruments (voices, launeddas, accordion) and classical instruments (cello), with typical jazz instruments (trumpet, drums, double bass) and other musics' typical instruments (mandola, tabla, multi effects), with lyrics in the three main dialects of the Sardinian language (Logudorese, Campidanese, Gallurese).

But Fresu participated in other projects, like "Ethno Grafie" in cooperation with the ISRE (Sardinian Ethnographic Institute), where he rewrote traditional music and played it with other musicians who are distant from Sardinia, like singer David Linx, who performs "Ninna Nanna Pitzinnu" with Elena Ledda and singer and oud player Dhafer Youssef, who plays in the choir Su Concoru of Santulussurgiu (a village in Sardinia). He also worked on projects with Breton musicians ("Condaghes," with singer Erik Marchand and guitarist Jack Pellen), with Senegalese musicians, the Macedon Koçani Orkestar, and Moroccan musicians of the Gnawa group.

Leaving aside the world projects, which are at times a bit forced, the undoubted success of Fresu's Sardinian projects is due to his Sardinian origins, and if we consider that Fresu has always looked with suspicion on ethno-jazz, this success is really surprising. His success is also due to his feeling part of a tradition and especially to the cooperation with extraordinary musicians who do not "fake" like some jazzmen do sometimes, but who are the real and passionate supporters of that tradition.

This is why Fresu acts more like a "tailor" and a supervisor rather than a musician in *Sonos and Memoria*. You can only hear his trumpet a few times, careful as he is not to exaggerate with jazz phrasing that, considering his Davisian influence, might be out of place (the same does not go for the extraordinary pianist and accordionist Antonello Salis, whose jazz has a deep melodic-popular vocation). In many cases respecting means listening and creating measured and cautious approaches. And it is in this respectful combination of projects and genres rather than in a risky and tumultuous journey to one's own roots that lies the difference between Fresu's approach and Salis's and the abovementioned musicians' approaches to combining jazz and popular tradition.

The Impossible Journey and the Phantasmagoria

There is another way followed by European free musicians, despite the fact that nowadays free jazz seems to be going through a crisis. It is neither the journey, be it real or imaginary, to "other" cultures and countries, nor the search for one's own roots in a near or far past. It is the ambitious and somewhat crazy project to combine different kinds of music and contrasting genres in an unthought-of and free way, aiming at creating a vortex, a phantasmagoria that can go beyond the idea itself of musical development.

The project draws inspiration from bands such as the Liberation Orchestra of Charlie Haden, Carla Bley, Charles Mingus (who was one of the first musicians to introduce an ever-changing jazz), and Frank Zappa, and finds its original expression in the European free jazz of the last thirty years.

It varies from "ethnical" projects that we examined before because it doesn't aim at going beyond the differences with a superior synthesis or a generic exoticism, but rather at comparing them and then seeing what really happens. Among its members, who are nearly all still active, are the Dutch Misha Mengelberg, Han Bennink, and Willem Breuker with Kollektief, the French Michel Portal, Louis Sclavis, and Martial Solal, the Swiss Sylvie Courvoisier, the English Keith Tippet and Maggie Nichols, the Italian Gianluigi Trovesi and Antonello Salis, the Polish Ursula Dudziak, and the Russian Vyacheslav Ganelin, Vladimir Chekasin, Vladimir Tarasov, Anatoly Vapirov, and Vyacheslav Guyvoronsky.

The Russians, in particular, who were discovered in the eighties by Leo Records, are still surprisingly fresh and full of energy. Their jazz is so caught between tradition and avant-garde that many "free" improvisations are done on old standards or folk songs, and it is truly beyond genres. Unfortunately, Russian jazz no longer has that genuine liveliness and follows the mainstream model (like Marsalis) or loses itself with ultra-refined exercises (Misha Alperin).

The main characteristic of the abovementioned musicians is the patchwork, the "broken" speech, the succession of contrasting musical moments and genres, a kind of improvisation that is best expressed in free jazz and in particular with Ornette Coleman and Paul Bley, even if some elements like quoting and sudden changes have always belonged to jazz.

We have two different types of free. The first type is schizophrenic, as it is based on short phrases, fragments of themes, musical moments that are almost always interrupted and disconnected. The unity of the subject, in which jazz—just like the philosophy of the last century—never believed in, is now lost, and it is as if improvisation broke into different speeches that at times interact and at times completely ignore each other. This is the antiphonal model, the question-answer, used in the oldest kind of jazz; but a question is not always followed by an answer, or it may be that there is a series of unanswered questions or that the answer may not always be pertinent to the question.

The other type of free is the propulsive-energetic one. The phrase itself doesn't matter, nor does the connection between the phrases. Improvisation at the beginning gives a direction, suggests an atmosphere, then goes into it with the most intense rhythm possible, often in an obsessive and repetitive way. Time is almost suspended; the duration of the improvisation can seem, for those who aren't used to it, excessive, like in the latest Coltrane. You are not worried about the "form," but despite this, improvisation is structured in real time, as Ekkehard Jost noted about the solos of Cecil Taylor.

These two types of improvisation can never (or almost never) be found in their pure state. Yet this distinction is useful, and it suggests the existence in free jazz of two ideas of journey: one "external," neurotic, constantly longing for new ideas, that reminds us of mass tourism but also of TV and online channel surfing—and despite this, to avoid chaos and confusion, it implies a logic of its own ("organized" journeys!); and an "internal" one, that is difficult, obsessive, similar to a random exploration of the abyss.

In European free jazz the first kind of journey prevailed, together with an idea of improvisation that, for its rapid changes, makes me think of the phantasmagoria but also of cabaret, with its constant and funny changes of scenes. That is why the Misha Mengelberg–Han Bennink duo or the female trio Les Diaboliques (Irène Schweizer, Maggie Nichols, Joëlle Léandre) include several visual and spectacular elements in their performances.

This kind of jazz resembles cabaret in the "staging," the constant change, the lightness and irony. There is a piece by Sylvie Courvoisier's quintet in the record *Sauvagerie courtoise* called *La Petite fille au ballon rouge* that well explains it. It is a short suite in three movements introduced by a simple march in band style of the soprano sax, repeated many times in a frantic acceleration and accompanied by the trombone played in tuba style. The second movement (the most representative one) starts with a pointillist improvisation of piano and drums followed by quotes of very popular and kitsch themes of the sax soprano and the trombone, but all of it happens in the "absence of tempo." With a dissonant chord, the piano signals the end. A short funeral march comes in in a Mediterranean style. Then again, the march of the beginning, this time in a minor key. Followed then by a "montuno" of the piano Cuban style, interrupted by different stops, taken by other instruments and free at last to evolve. But also the Latin choice is not definitive. When the opening march comes back under the triumphing Cuban rhythm, it is slightly different, and there is even an Arabic reference of the soprano sax. In this phase the music appears undecided between the two grooves, the free and the Latin one.

The movement ends with a perfect unison of the Latin rhythm. In the third movement, the final one, the march of the beginning comes back but with a harmonic base of the piano that is undone and impressionistic. At the end it evolves toward a new classicism "à la Satie" in a gradual movement toward silence.

The above description, with all the limits that a description without audio can have, gives us an example of the elements of phantasmagoria and of "craziness" that are characteristic of the kind of improvisation we are dealing with. The musical atmospheres that unfold are kept together by the opening march and by the distribution of roles where the piano plays the predominant role. But the music freely switches from the band-popular to the atonal free, from Cuban style to neoclassicism Satie style, from tango to collective improvisation in Dixieland style. There are no planned changes, distributed according to a determined temporal order, as in classical suites.

Everything is left to chance and to the free interaction among musicians, without forgetting that the "wild" idea (well represented by the title of Courvoisier's *Sauvagerie courtoise*) of a very rapid combination of contrasting musical genres and atmospheres implies, like all "free" music, a sense of the form that is more developed than the so-called idiomatic jazz.

The prevalent idea is that seriousness and irony and risk and control can all coexist in this improvisation; this has not always been true in historical "free." This sort of musical postmodernism is very common in France, the country of the *esprit de finesse* and home of the literary postmodernism current. The Dutch pianist Misha Mengelberg, who is a sort of Buster Keaton of the keyboards, and the French-Algerian pianist Martial Solal, with his unpredictable piano solos as well as with his arrangements (think of the Decaband), are probably the most representative examples in jazz. Solal, despite being an excellent composer, moves often from the older and more obsolete "standards"; he breaks them down and deconstructs them in fragments, and then he rebuilds them starting from the fragments themselves.

The resulting reconstruction is unrecognizable as the "standard," yet it cannot be defined as completely new, because the fragments it is made up of belong to the old "standard." It is what happens in Cubism (take Picasso or Bacon), where the new figure is made up of pieces in an apparent random order, while using old elements like eyes, mouth, nose, hair, etc.

This process of decomposition is not new in jazz. It originates from the "broken speech" of boppers, and before that in some of the greatest piano solos (think of Art Tatum), which for the first time broke the narrative continuity of improvisation.

This is a fundamental characteristic of the style of Thelonious Monk, Ornette

Coleman, and Paul Bley. But with them the music, interrupted at the crucial point, restarted more or less from the same point, similar to a stutter, similar to the inability of speaking of some characters of Samuel Beckett.

It is not only about the end of every finished speech. It is about the ability to make several speeches and languages coexist, which might coexist if fragmented and reduced to their simplest elements, but which are invincible if they manage to keep part of their nature.

The only element that can keep them together is irony, of which the musicians make abundant use.

It is not the clowning of the black heir of the minstrel shows that tries to conquer the white audience, and it is not the joke of the virtuous jazzman that using quotations shows his ability to adapt to any material, but it is the desperate irony of those who no longer have a unique language and are surrounded by a tangle of languages and whose only chance is to reproduce that confusion.

Quotation and irony become the only means of survival in a universe that is too complicated to be summarized in a unique speech or language. But in this way improvisation loses seriousness; it becomes a mere game. Even the metaphor of the journey cannot express any longer the idea of an improvisation that collects its material here and there, in a casual way, without trying to mark a path and find a direction.

The idea of the journey starts to lose importance when the journey itself loses its seriousness, its drama. Setting off for a journey should imply the acceptance of a bet, it should mean leaving the certain for the uncertain, and cannot be separated from the idea that from that very moment our life might change. It cannot be separated from a certain heroic atmosphere. But what happens to the idea of journey in this style of improvisation?

This idea of journey is not so different from the virtual journey we experience daily online or with video games. And together with the idea of journey, the idea of improvisation loses its value too, because it has a sense only if it tries to mark a path, to give a form to what is unpredictable.

"A workshop of human potential" (P. Auster)

We talked about a virtual, immediate, and phantasmagorical journey through different kinds of music that can take place thanks to a world that tends to abolish clashes, barriers, and even "the idea itself of opposition" (M. Perniola). Yet the real journey is not abandoned.

Apart from those who feel the need to make their jazz more attractive by giving it that undetermined and mysterious color that only exoticism can give and those who go back to the roots of their musical origins, there are also many European and American jazzmen who "travel" only to try themselves and find new ideas to help their music and their creativity.

The Norwegian jazzman Jan Garbarek, one of the first in Europe to collaborate with musicians from non-Western countries and traditions, worked mainly with musicians from the East such as Ravi Shankar, Trilok Gurtu, Shaukat Hussein, Anouar Brahem, Ustad Fateh Ali Khan, and Tigran Mansurian. His example was followed by many other Scandinavian musicians, such as pianist Bobo Stenson and his cooperation with Turkish drummer Okay Temiz (former member of the Don Cherry trio) and more recently by drummer Helge Andreas Norbakken, in cooperation with nyatiti soloist (nyatiti is a sort of Indian lyre) Ayoub Ogada.

Other more recent examples are the cooperation between Joachim Kühn (piano) and Lebanese Abu Khalil (oud) that led to the beautiful CD *Journey to the Center of an Egg*, with Jarrod Cadwin (drums); that between the polyinstrumentist Michel Portal and the Indian dancer, choreographer, and musician Raghunat Mamet; between the Polish vocalist and experimenter Ursula Dudziak and the Turkish guitarist Erkan Ogur; between the trio of the Dutch saxophonist Yuri Honing and the Lebanese singer Rima Kcheich—and many, many more.

A different case is represented by Guido Manusardi, who during his stay in Romania between 1967 and 1974 created a peculiar mix between jazz and Romanian musical folklore and was in this sense a real forerunner. The question is: why do the abovementioned musicians and many more, who often have a definite and anticonventional identity, risk their identity and look for a possible coexistence with strong personalities that belong to different musical worlds?

Money is not a good reason, for often the results of these works are not successful and arouse many critics against them. Think of the incredible fiascos of a star like Jan Garbarek, when he played with Ravi Shankar, or his experiment with Gregorian chant (Hilliard Ensemble).

Perhaps it is about "finding new sources of inspiration." But what does that really mean? Is it that these musicians have exhausted their creativity and need to come into contact with something from the "outside"?

This sort of "mechanical" approach to creativity does not take into consideration the psychology of the artist who is experiencing a block, who usually holds on to beliefs rather than risk losing his own identity. This is what happened to Bill Evans in the last few years of his life.

Instead, when a jazzman can totally master his own expressive abilities, that is when he feels the urge to come in contact with the outside, with the journey intended as a "challenge," as American jazzmen are used to calling it (and now European jazzmen too). There is no jazz without a challenge. The jazzman (or at least the ideal jazzman) does not rely on what is certain, but constantly tries to break his own rules. He is free by definition.

When a jazzman stops experimenting and therefore surprising his audience, then "jazz is over," as Steve Lacy said.

In our globalized world with its tangle of cultures and musical genres, there no longer is a "high" or "low" music, artistic or commercial music, foreign and local music. Therefore the challenge for a jazzman is to come in contact with other kinds of music, often chosen at random, as well as with other forms of art (dance, cinema, theater . . .), with new softwares that can generate music in real time (think of George Lewis experiments), and so on. Without this exchange, a jazzman is lost. But yet once again words are misleading, and the term "exchange" seems to be too generic. What does "exchange" mean? In this context it can mean either clash, opposition, or trying to find a mediation, a way to communicate (not the notorious "contamination"!).

Here are two examples that can better explain this: When pianist Joachim Kühn cooperates with oud player Abu Khalil, they both play in their own and independent way. Kühn gives intense improvisations reminiscent of an Arab world, and that is the only concession he makes to his Lebanese fellow, because other than that, when he plays he sounds like part of a normal jazz trio. When the protagonist is Abu Khalil, the music regains its typical Arab mood. The extraordinary percussionist Jarrod Cagwin has the task of mediating between the two with moments of "solo drums." In the case of another "ethnic" player like Argentinean bandoneonist Dino Saluzzi, it is his fellow musicians' music that changes and reveals its hidden potential.

The same happens to pianist Wolfgang Dauner or trumpet player Enrico Rava, with double-bass player Anders Jormin or cellist Anja Lechner, who is, by the way, a jazz musician only in a certain sense.

Despite the fusion that originates in this case from jazz and Argentinean folklore (mostly due to Saluzzi's personality and leadership), the experiment seems to be better than those situations when jazz and ethnic music cannot find a common field. In any case, the exchange we are analyzing is creative and fruitful.

In the first case, coming in contact with musicians with different traditions and background, the jazzman is forced to show the essence of his own style and his own personality.

In the second case, thanks to the influence of a new language, he is encouraged to find the hidden potential in his own language. In both situations, the myth, the metaphor of the journey, reveals itself: the chance not to lose yourself but to find yourself again. Those who travel are always changed by the experience. Seeing the beyond allows us to see ourselves and our own world in a

Who? a woman?

different light. Everything happens like in José Saramago's tale "O Conto da ilha desconhecida," where the unknown island is the unknown place from which we can look at ourselves in a completely new light.

Any trip that is deprived of this subversive potential has no meaning and does not serve any purpose; it is the trip, as Magrelli says in the poem that opens this essay, of "the new pilgrims that are looking for the sanctuaries of difference and that while looking for them erase them." This is sad. *oh*

My Own Experience

This is why I would like to conclude my essay writing about my own experience as a jazzman. I traveled a lot with my music, and in different moments of my life I had the opportunity to play with some of the greatest contemporary jazzmen (Steve Swallow, Barre Phillips, Bill Elgart, Lew Soloff, Ralph Alessi, John Hebert, Jeff Hirshfield, among others) but also with musicians much more distant from my ethnic and cultural background (Olivier Manoury, Custodio Castelo, Alexandra, Polina Runovskaya, Mamadi Kaba).

Everything started back in 1989 when, having fallen in love with Astor Piazzolla's Argentinean tango (I didn't know at the time that Argentineans do not consider his music real tango), I wrote my first compositions influenced by tango, and I looked for a bandoneonist or an accordionist who could play them. In Italy at the time there were no bandoneonists, so I tried to contact Piazzolla himself (I succeeded, but unfortunately he passed away shortly afterward). Eventually saxophonist Giulio Visibelli introduced me to Gianni Coscia. Coscia was looking for a new "sound" for his accordion at the time; his sound was rooted in Piedmont musical folklore (as you can hear in his CD *La Briscola*). That is how my first band of jazz-tango was born—the New Latin Ensemble, with Coscia, Visibelli, and Maurizio Dehò, a klezmer violinist who, among other things, founded the Theatre Orchestra of actor-singer Moni Ovadia—and I released the CD *Pianure* (Splasch, 1990), which was well received by critics on a national and international level.

The themes I wrote were reminiscent of Piazzolla's style—though they were probably more articulated and harmonically complex than his—but the room I gave to improvisation, and the sound of the band with its curious mix of jazz-folk-tango-klezmer, made our music very original.

There were cadences for the piano reminiscent of Pablo Ziegler, but there were also moments of collective improvisation where the union of the jazz phrasing of Visibelli's soprano sax, the diatonic-melodic style of Coscia's accordion, and the klezmer ghosts of Dehò's violin gave birth to a sound that no one had ever heard before. Being the first jazzman in Italy who tried something of this

ARRIGO CAPPELLETTI

kind, I could have been satisfied with myself, but the sound of the accordion, so sweet and melancholic, did not satisfy me. I was looking for a sharper and more dramatic sound, the sound of the bandoneon.

So I set off and eventually found the bandoneonist I was looking for in Paris in the fall of 1990, Olivier Manoury. I cooperated with Manoury very often between 1991 and 1995; we released the CD *Transformations*, produced by Silex (Paris, 1993) for a jazz trio (Pintori, Fioravanti, and me) and bandoneon. This band was very different from the New Latin Ensemble and showed my desire to go back to my favorite band, the jazz trio, and simply add a bandoneon. But with Manoury being more of a tango player than a jazzman, the risk we ran was that the combination of the two languages, tango and jazz, would be disappointing. Today, after almost twenty years, I realize how the New Latin Ensemble project, with its search for a collective sound, was more far more advanced than this project. But I did not realize that at the time, being so in love with the sound of the bandoneon, and my cooperation with Manoury went on for a few more years until 1995, when in a last attempt to recreate the old New Latin Ensemble I put together a sextet with some new young Italian jazzmen (Bebo Ferra playing the guitar, Andrea Dulbecco the vibraphone, Salvatore Majore the double bass, Roberto Dani the drums), Manoury, and me.

There is still a recording of this band that was never released; listening to it you can easily understand how my passion for tango had already decreased, and I was more interested in other Latin rhythms, in a few jazz standards, and in free improvisation. At the time I had other interests. I had started writing songs, mainly with words of the Mexican poet Octavio Paz, and I had given them to a new trio with singer Gioconda Cilio and my old friend Gianni Coscia and his accordion. This experiment gave birth in 1998 to another relevant "ethnic" turning point of my musical career. I was invited together with my friend Gianni Coscia to the Expo in Lisbon in September 1998. I started learning Portuguese and composing a series of lieder, mainly with Fernando Pessoa's texts.

These lieder were easier and catchier than those written on Paz's texts, inspired in a way by fado, whose simple rhythm in 2/4 I often used, but they always moved outside the structure of the classical song (verse + chorus, or chorus + bridge) and on complex harmonic structures that at times did not have a tonal center. My purpose, very ambitious indeed, was to have them sung by a fado singer, maybe using other fado musicians to give the music, so different from traditional fado, its taste and colors. I was particularly fond of the sound of the Portuguese guitar.

So there I was in Lisbon in September 1998 looking for a fado singer to give her my songs just in time for the concert with Coscia at the end of the month for the

Expo 98. I eventually found a very famous Portuguese fado singer, Alexandra, and with guitarist Jorge Fernando, Portuguese guitarist (*guitarra*) Custodio Castelo, and Italian bandoneonist Daniele Di Bonaventura, whom I had just discovered (together with guitarist Flavio Minardo and cellist Davide Zaccaria during the mixing in the studio), we recorded in spring 1999 in Lisbon the CD *Terras do risco*, which would be released two years later as an audiobook for Amiata of Florence. In that CD there are ten songs I wrote on texts by Portuguese poets Fernando Pessoa, Teresa Rita Lopes, Mário de Sá-Carneiro, and Eugénio de Andrade. Listening to that CD today, I am still amazed at how the three basic instruments—piano, bandoneon, and Portuguese guitar—sound so good together. The idea was that the three instruments played together accompanying the voice, a project of collective improvisation that was meant to be also in instrumental parts and which gave the music a strong chamber music touch. Undoubtedly the absence of the double bass, which had always been present in my model, the band of tango, might be surprising, but it allowed the pianist's left hand (my hand) the full freedom to "lead" the music, without ruining the rhythm.

Another original element of the CD is the presence of two voices, a male one (Jorge Fernando) and a female one (Alexandra), that represent the two different souls of fado, the sweet and melodic one and the more dramatic (and cathartic) one; and even if the female voice prevails, the vocal polyphony enriches the dynamic and timbre range. This project represented the natural consequence of my tango project, but also the breaking point. Using the texts of Pessoa, the poet of multiplicity, allowed the music to have sudden changes—changes in direction and the free element of improvisation. It is not by chance that many improvisations do not move on preestablished harmonic structures but on the unpredictable interaction among the instruments rather than on a solo. The concept is that music is both in improvisation and in themes like a "magic box" where anything can happen, even if the general magical, solitary, and dreamlike atmosphere remains the same.

But obviously things have moved on from there. After the recording I did not leave my "lands of risk" (from the novel *The Lands of Risk* by Agustina Bessa Luis), and I reproposed my projects several times, with different voices, Maria Anadon, Ana Moura, and lately the great singer from Trieste, Alessandra Franco. With her, my faithful Custodio Castelo playing the Portuguese guitar, and accordionist Fausto Beccalossi, thus always starting from my songs inspired by fado, my music changed and was free to move among different influences and echoes that range from Kurt Weill to free jazz, from tango and fado to African music and to musical folklore from Trieste.

I felt increasingly attracted by an idea of improvisation that I would define as "free-world improvisation," where elements coming from different kinds of mu-

ARRIGO CAPPELLETTI

138

sic combine in an unpredictable way but following a precise narrative line and without falling in the ironic and full-of-quotes postmodernism.

Even if I am still devoted to both Portuguese fado and Argentinean tango, I now feel free from their rules and their style. I go wherever the music and the musicians I play with lead me, paying attention not to lose the thread of the story.

I can do it because I know that what I have loved and have acquired by now will sooner or later reemerge in my music, telling a part of my story. Because the story of my "ethnic" turning points is not limited to tango and fado and will probably continue long after this essay. Quem sabe?

While I was still promoting my jazz-fado project (that is how I used to call it), in 2002 some personal reasons took me to Russia, and that is where I started playing music with a Russian singer-actress, Polina Runovskaya. Polina did not know jazz music.

She knew popular Russian romances, some Jewish melodies, and she loved to improvise in a non-idiomatic way. We did our first concerts in a club in Saint Petersburg, with her singing what she wanted and me playing along without knowing the harmonies of the songs, inventing them on the spot. Then Polina heard my Portuguese songs and other songs in French on a text by Mara Cantoni; she translated them into Russian and sang them during our concerts. The result? Amazing. She really blew my mind when I first heard my fado-mazurka "Amo tracinho te" in Alexandra's version sung by Polina Runovskaya. This version was included in 2002 in the CD dedicated to Portugal that was released in the collection *Music from the World* by Fratelli Fabbri publishers.

It sounded like a popular Russian romance! This feeling helped me rediscover the song, draw new inspiration from it, and find new ways of improvising.

There is fortunately a recording of my cooperation with Polina: our concert with Giulio Visibelli (soprano sax and duduk) in April 2003 for the event "The Voices of Jazz" at the Auditorium in Milan. Despite an exaggerated Polina at times during the concert (she always sang, even during Visibelli's solos), it is amazing that Visibelli and I, without rehearsing, could fit so easily in the musical world of a singer so distant from jazz and from our own musical background.

In the past, always with Giulio Visibelli, my partner in "ethnic investigations," we lived a similar experience with African griot Mamadi Kaba, from the Republic of Guinea. But Mamadi's songs were too organized and predictable to let us move freely within them, or maybe at the time (in the eighties) we were not brave enough for it. That was my very first contact with ethnic music, and it was not successful, maybe due to a lack of love (that we felt for African modalism and that Mamadi felt for jazz music).

What conclusions can we draw from this short story? The undoubted success of my experiments with Argentinean tango, with Portuguese fado, with popular

Russian romances is not a coincidence. Maybe it could have worked with other kinds of music too. This I will find out in the future, if I come across other kinds of music that intrigue me like Puccini's, Sephardic melodies, and flamenco.

But I know for a fact that my music will hardly benefit from an exchange with country music, for example, or with the music from Northeast Brazil, or West African music.

There have already been examples of similar exchanges with brilliant results. Think of Keith Jarrett, Hermeto Pascoal, Randy Weston and his experiments with the Highlife of West Africa. But it is a different story for me.

Jazz music plays a fundamental role in my musical background, but there are many other elements, both inside and outside music, that contributed to create my musical tastes and tendencies: going for long walks with my father in the mountains; listening to Puccini's operas as a child; my grandfather's music (he was a composer); the choruses of the alpini that I used to listen to when I was a child; the passion of my parents' family for any kind of narrative, be it oral or written.

This does not mean that everything is clear to me by now. There comes a time in life when we start to understand what is for us and what isn't. Coming into contact with new and unknown worlds—not necessarily musical worlds—allows us to get to know ourselves better, triggering our positive and negative reactions.

I would have never thoroughly understood my passion for melody without my passion for Neapolitan songs and for tango and fado.

And I would have never grown my interest in investigating tonality without my passion for Hindemith, Schulhoff, Poulenc, and, within the jazz field, the undetermined and mysterious chords of Paul Bley—rather than the clusters of Cecil Taylor. But who I really am I will find out at the end of my life, or I will never find out completely. And yet, in any case, there is still time for that.

II

JAZZ MEETS
EUROPE

RAINER E. LOTZ

7 / CROSS-CULTURAL LINKS
BLACK MINSTRELS, CAKEWALKS, AND RAGTIME

The prehistory of jazz dates back to the nineteenth century, and thus to a time when there were few documents of recorded sound and apparently little tangible evidence to support discussions on the origins and evolution of these musical developments. It is widely accepted that jazz has black roots. It seems that jazz appeared out of nowhere, and within a very short time spread *←not really.* around the world, with occasional visits to Europe. This article discusses some aspects of how Europeans were first exposed to African American performers and performances, and whether there has been any cross-fertilization between those Americans and Europeans, and perhaps with other music cultures.

Early European Writers on Jazz and Blues

Most of the early authors of books on jazz, as well as the compilers of blues and jazz discographies, were Europeans who had few or no firsthand impressions of New Orleans or Chicago, of Sedalia, Missouri, or Clarksdale, Mississippi.[1] Their major contact with the music was through the recordings available in Europe from the 1920s,[2] although there were some visiting musicians. A review of record catalogues shows that the number of available recordings was extremely limited.[3]

In Britain and Germany (home of the major record companies), and therefore across the rest of Europe, American "jazz" was represented almost exclusively by now mostly forgotten white performers such as Ed Kirkeby, Vincent Lopez, Mike Markel, Harry Reser, Ben Selvin, Sam Lanin, and Paul Whiteman. Authentic hot performances by black bands were as rare as hens' teeth and could not have achieved broad distribution.[4]

The situation was even more drastic with the blues. Before the Second World War, American companies had released some 7,000 double-sided blues and gospel records involving around 1,200 artists. (If recordings for the Library of Congress are included, the estimated total would be around 22,000 titles.) Only about fifty of these were available to record buyers in Europe over a period of twenty years, almost all of them released in Britain and nowhere else.[5] Travelers and sailors brought back discs but in insignificant quantities—although sometimes they had a wide audience.

Today we take it for granted that, for all practical purposes, just about any jazz or blues recording is readily available for research. That is not least due to the efforts of Johnny Parth, an Austrian, who realized his dream of releasing and maintaining permanently in print a complete catalogue of all historical blues and gospel recordings by black American performers.[6]

During the 1920s the situation was dramatically different. Those early writers and record collectors were mostly unaware of areas of musical tradition that are now underrepresented or not represented at all on record, or which antedate the 1920s and 1930s. When the European commentators were writing, technologies such as cylinders, player pianos, and musical boxes were at best vaguely remembered by a past generation in Europe.[7] The prehistory of jazz, blues, and cross-cultural links tended to disappear from history.

RAINER E. LOTZ

German Musicians and American Audiences from the 1870s up to the First World War

At the time, vast stretches of Germany were extremely poor. Poverty and over-population in marginal agricultural hinterlands left ambitious people with few choices: become a priest; join the military; start a cottage industry; survive through itinerant activities; or emigrate. Many villagers became itinerant musicians, earning their living abroad—mainly in Britain and the United States. Whole areas of Germany became known as the "musicians' belts" (*Musikantenland*), borne out by the heraldic images on the little townships' coats of arms.[8]

The Palatinate (Pfalz) is in the remote southwestern region of Germany. The following statistics are from the tiny village of Hohenöllen, which even today has fewer than four hundred inhabitants. A hundred years ago, around three hundred people from the village worked as itinerant musicians, roughly a quarter of them in the United States.

It is only logical to assume that these musicians had to deliver whatever the public demanded. As professional musicians they had to be capable of reading music and playing by sight, and their repertoire had to include ragtime, cakewalks, two-steps, and any other fashionable American dance tunes, many of them with Afro-American influences. There is proof of this, as some of the local history museums maintain the original collections of part books.

Four percent may appear a small proportion at first sight, but the statistics cover four decades, and cakewalks, two-steps, and their like were not introduced until around the turn of the century.

Itinerant professional German musicians employed in the United States played rags and cakewalks written by both white and black composers—and played to both white and black audiences—during the 1890s. A photograph shows musicians from Jettenbach, which today has fewer than nine hundred inhabitants. These musicians apparently performed for prison inmates, although there

Coat of arms of Hohenöllen, Pfalz.
Courtesy Gemeinde Hohenöllen, Doris Huber

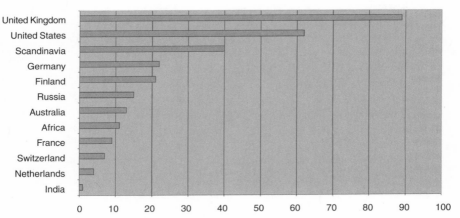

German itinerant musicians from Hohenöllen, Pfalz, 1831–1921. *Source: Westricher Heimatblätter*

is no information on the back of the photo about the circumstances under which it was taken. The Jettenbach coat of arms once again features a lyre as a symbol of music and musicianship.

The tradition of working abroad as musician was revived, although on a much smaller scale, after the war. An interesting photograph announces "Bill Henri and His Headliners" on the backdrop, but the band leader is one Heinrich Jacob from Mackenbach, a tiny township in Germany. Although it had then only a few hundred inhabitants, it may be known to many Americans today, as it is just a few hundred meters from the U.S. Airforce headquarters in Europe, the airbase at Ramstein. The Mackenbach coat of arms displays the telltale lyre again. Heinrich Jacob had worked as a musician in America between 1914 and 1920, and he returned in 1922 as a permanent immigrant. He formed another orchestra and

Breakdown of 5.929 pieces noted in part books of itinerant musicians from the western Palatinate (Westpfalz, Germany) between 1870 and 1914

Genre: Name	Number	(%)	(%)	Total (%)
1. European ballroom dances of the 19th Century				
Marches	1.394	23,5		
Waltzes	1.139	19,2		
Polkas	381	6,4		
Rheinländer	196	3,3		
Galops	136	2,3		
Schottisches	103	1,7		
Mazurkas	79	1,3		
Ländler	44	0,7		
Polonaises	22	0,4		
Gavottes	13	0,2	59,1	
2. American fashionable dances / Ragtime related				
Two Steps	162	2,7		
Quick Steps	33	0,6		
Cake Walks	26	0,4		
One Steps	19	0,3		
Barn Dances	16	0,3	4,3	
3. National dances (Tango, Reel, Krakowiak, Csárdás, Hornpipe, etc)				
Total	31	0,5		
			0,5	
4. Songs and Ballads (treasury of songs)				
Folk songs, hymns	1.228	20,7		
Potpourris, selections	246	4,1		
			24,9	
5. Operatic and concert				
Character pieces	242	4,1		
Potpourris, selections	178	3,0		
Ouvertures	114	1,9		
Lancers, Quadrilles	75	1,3		
Fantasies	28	0,5		
Oratories	24	0,4		
			11,1	
				100,0

Analysis of part books of German itinerant musicians from Hohenöllen, 1870–1914.
Source: Westricher Heimatblätter

Coat of arms of Jettenbach, Pfalz.
Courtesy Gemeinde Jettenbach,
Frank Naumann

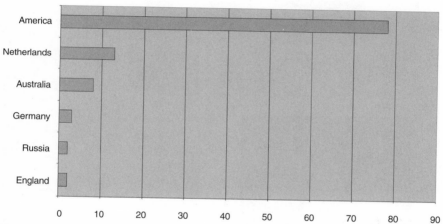

German itinerant musicians from Jettenbach, 1905. *Source: Westricher Heimatblätter*

toured from his home in Hoboken, New Jersey, where his brother Otto lived. As a vocalist he employed none other than a young Frank Sinatra, in one of Sinatra's early professional engagements. (The Mackenbach museum dates the photo as 1932, but it may have been taken as late as 1938).

Mechanical Music and Sheet Music

Those German musicians who did not leave their villages earned their living as home workers. In mountain areas such as the Schwarzwald (Black Forest), Erzgebirge, and other poor neighborhoods, they spent winters manufacturing mechanical musical instruments for export.[9] (The Swiss made toys and clocks.) These people arranged and manufactured authentic syncopated cakewalks and ragtime for hundreds of piano rolls and metal-disc music boxes, mainly for export.

Kapelle Backes from Jettenbach, Pfalz, playing for prison inmates (around 1900). *Courtesy Musikantenland-Museum Burg Lichtenberg*

Coat of arms of Mackenbach, Pfalz. *Courtesy Gemeinde Mackenbach, Volker Halfmann*

really?

The details printed on the discs (they had no labels) were often in German, English, and Russian.

"The Brooklyn Cake Walk" (1899) must be the most popular cakewalk of all time: it was recorded more often than any other cakewalk and yet was virtually unknown in the United States under that title. This serves as a striking example of cross-cultural linkage: "The Brooklyn Cake Walk" takes its name from a formerly Dutch district of New York; it was written by a British composer, was dedicated to an Australian music hall act ("The Permans"), and became very popular in Germany when topical lyrics were added referring to a widely publicized fraud

Kapellmeister Heinrich "Bill Henri" Jacob, from Mackenbach, performing with singer
Frank Sinatra (1935). *Courtesy Musikantenland-Museum Burg Lichtenberg*

Kalliope musical box metal disc:
"Von Hamburg nach Kiel" (1907).
Collection Lotz

scandal. (The German sheet music cover nonetheless depicts stereotypical
American plantation scenes.) Everybody knew, sang, and whistled the tune in
Germany to the words of "Schorsch'l ach kauf mir doch ein Automobil," or "Von
Hamburg nach Kiel." In the United States, the melody was known as "Dream of
a Rarebit Fiend."

Another German-made metal disc features a cakewalk composed in 1895 by
the black comedian Bert Williams, who was born in the Bahamas and raised in
California. The piece was dedicated to the greatest of all cakewalk dancers, Dora
Dean, who toured Europe for decades and had her portrait painted in oils in
Germany. The "Dora Dean Cakewalk" has never been recorded under that   149

name—not on piano rolls, cylinders, flat shellac discs, nor vinyl microgroove LPs—since the time it was composed well over a century ago.

In 1896—a year after Bert Williams saw his original composition reproduced in print—one Charley Sydney O'Brien published "Ma Angeline," which was a note-for-note, word-for-word steal, except that the reference to "Dora Dean" was replaced by "Ma Angeline" (which still rhymes). The music was recorded under that name by an unnamed orchestra in that same year, 1896. Williams went to court, where the judges decided that his song had indeed been stolen, but that his original composition was not entitled to protection by copyright because of its alleged indecency and obscenity: the original printed sheet music referred to Dora Dean as "the Hottest Thing You Ever Seen." Williams complied by re-printing the song with new words: "Dora Dean, the Sweetest Gal you ever seen."

Scott Joplin composed his masterpiece "The Entertainer" in 1902. It was never recorded under that title on cylinder or shellac disc, but a contemporary music-box metal disc survives—playing in the slow tempo that Joplin prescribed. There are an impressive number of cakewalks and "coon songs" on German-made metal discs, but in contrast to disc recordings very few are currently available on CDs for further analysis.[10] In Memphis, Tennessee, in 1928, Nap Hayes and Mat-thew Prater (under the name the Blue Boys) recorded a guitar/mandolin duet

entitled "Easy Winner" on Okeh 45314. This is not the Scott Joplin composition of that name but an improvisation loosely based on Joplin's "The Entertainer."

It can be said that Europeans knew how to perform for live audiences music written by black American composers as well as American dance tunes with Afro-American influences.[11] They also knew how to arrange this music for mechanical players (notably pianos and musical boxes) before the end of the nineteenth century. By the time the pioneering writers got interested in blues and jazz, memories had faded, and many important tunes had not been recorded, although they had been widely distributed in middle-class households both as sheet music and on mechanical media.

The Etymology of "Rag" Time

For more than one hundred years, historians, musicologists, etymologists, and performers speculated about the musical and etymological origins of "rag" and "ragtime," until Karl Gert zur Heide, a German researcher, suggested a plausible solution to the riddle (he published it in 2005[12]). Zur Heide looked into a statement by rag pioneer Will Marion Cook, who attended the Columbian World Exposition held in Chicago in 1893.

Among the popular attractions at the Midway Plaisance amusement alley were the "Street in Cairo" and other stands featuring Oriental music and belly dances—or, as Will Marion Cook described it, "the peculiar music of the 'muscle dance.'" Belly dances had been performed in tent shows and carnivals and similar settings in the United States for decades. But on this occasion, and following considerable publicity, twenty-seven million Americans visited the Chicago event within six months. That was the equivalent of about half the U.S. adult population. One of the visitors was Will Marion Cook, and he wrote: "It is worthy of note that after that time the popularity of the "rag" grew with astonishing rapidity and became general among negro pianists."[13]

There are some photographs showing the "oriental" performers witnessed by Cook.[14] Zur Heide suggests that the performances must have been announced under their Arabic name, "raqs" (meaning dance). He presents evidence of an "oriental" origin for rag the rhythm, rag the dance, and rag the word, which derives from the Arabic word for dance as it was adopted by American musicians.

Although ragtime is without doubt American music, it displays striking similarities to "raqs" in terms of the asymmetrical accentuation of the melody, while some dances from the ragtime era follow the patterns of Oriental dances, later also known in the United States as the "hoochie-coochie." An Edison film from 1896 shows the same dancer, Fatima, who had performed in Chicago. For public viewing the censors added grids obscuring her bosom and belly. Fatima is also known to have taken part in a 1904 ragtime competition in St. Louis.

The Chicago exposition ended in late 1893. Although there is controversy over what was the first published ragtime song, it seems to have been Irving Jones's "Possumala Dance" from 1894. Other candidates include "La Pas Ma La" by Ernest Hogan (1895) or Max Hoffmann's arrangement of Hogan's "All Coons Look Alike to Me" (1896). The earliest ragtime was thus published only months after the Columbian World Exposition had closed.[15]

Chicago Midway Plaisance "Das Arabische Orchester" (1893). *Collection Lotz*

Etymologies of the US vernacular word *rag*

a) in standard encyclopedias (e.g. Grove*):*
                    [??]   [??]
Engl. *ragged time* > *rag(-)time* (style of music) > *rag* (musical trademark)
b) on historical principles (e.g. Oxford English Dictionary*):*
??? US slang *rag* "(a special kind of) dance" > US coll. *rag* (musical trademark)
     > *rag + time* = *rag(-)time* (special rhythm) > *ragtime* (style of music)
c) Karl Gert zur Heide's solution (first discovered in February 2001⁺):
Arab. *raqṣ* = رقص "dance" > US slang *rag* "(a special kind of) dance" > US coll. *rag*
     (musical trademark)
> *rag + time* = *rag(-)time* (special rhythm) > *ragtime* (style of music)

   [??] + a-historical (i.e. no evidence for this sequence in contemporary sources)
   ⁺ first published by zur Heide in his essay "Chicago, 1893 (Part 2)", *Doctor Jazz Magazine* (NL),
No. 188 (March 2005), p. 13

The etymology of "rag". *Courtesy Karl Gert zur Heide, Bremen, 2009*

Pioneer African American Vocalists and Musicians in Recorded Music

RAINER E. LOTZ

For around one hundred years, historians regarded cylinders and discs recorded by black Americans as "lost sounds." Over the past years they have been rediscovered; some have been transferred to CD and accessible to researchers.[16] One pioneering recording artist was May C. Hyers. She recorded some fifty cylinders for the Kansas City Talking Machine Company in 1898. Her repertoire ranged from opera and patriotic songs to minstrelsy items and so-called coon songs such as "Hot Coon from Memphis."[17]

We cannot be sure these songs were recorded, as the evidence is only that they were advertised in catalogues.[18] In those days, recordings could not be easily duplicated, and individual cylinders were made to order. Thus the catalogue may represent Hyers's potential repertoire. On the other hand, one cylinder has survived among the many advertised by the Louisiana Phonograph Company for Bebe Vasnier—and these date to 1891.[19]

May C. Hyers toured with Sam Hyers, father of the then famous Hyers Sisters, Anna Madah and Emma Louise. Contemporary Louisiana Phonograph Company flyers suggested that May was another sister. In fact, she was the sisters' stepmother—May was the second wife of Sam Hyers. In 2007 the present writer met and interviewed May C. Hyers's great-great-granddaughter in Georgetown, Washington, DC. She explained that the family had moved only a few years previously and that much of what was in their old house had to be discarded. She had saved some theatrical poster photographs—one shows May C. Hyers with her daughter Bohee (named after the black banjo virtuosos and recording artists). If there had been any cylinders in the old house, she would probably not have recognized what they were if she had seen them. I was just a few years too late.[20]

African Americans in Europe from the Nineteenth Century

In June 1879 the *Daily Nevada State Journal* reported from Reno: "This is positively the last appearance of the Hyer [sic] Sisters previous to their European tour." This tour may not have taken place, but the Hyers Sisters were in Britain as members of Callender's Coloured Minstrels from April to September 1894. There were strong socioeconomic motives for African Americans to visit Europe. Although slavery had been abolished in the United States in 1865 through the Thirteenth Amendment to the U.S. Constitution, the Ku Klux Klan was founded only two years later. After the Reconstruction era, legally enforced discrimination reached such levels that the 1890s were remembered as the "Terrible Nineties," when lynchings were announced in newspapers so that white people could at-

May C. Hyers (kneeling) and daughter Bohee Hyers, theater photo (n.d.). *Courtesy Adrienne Wheeler*

tend as if they were going to a picnic or some other form of entertainment, and photographs were sold as souvenirs.[21]

The survival strategies of African Americans were not that different from those of their counterparts in Germany: migration to America's northern states, where they faced comparatively less discrimination and better job opportunities; filling employment niches that were not easily available to whites; and, finally, emigration overseas. While poor German musicians migrated to the United States, African American musicians and song-and-dance artists migrated to Europe, and to Germany.

An impressive number pursued their livelihood overseas—including instrumentalists and bands, musical clowns and dancers, singers and theatrical performers, minstrels and eccentric acts. *Der Artist*, a German weekly publication for touring artists, includes references to more than one hundred black performers in Germany during 1896.[22]

Some blacks arrived as members of larger troupes such as Callender's Minstrels or William Foote's forty-strong African Character Concert Company, which arrived in Hamburg in 1891. When the troupe broke up, many of the members remained in Europe and can be traced all over the continent and even to Asia, from Spain to Siberia. The year 1897 saw John W. Isham's "Octoroons" in

Foote's African American Character Concerts, Frankfurt am Main, poster (1891). *Collection Lotz*

England. Once again, many members of the company stayed in Europe. Another large company, totaling eighty-one, took the black revue "In Dahomey" to London in 1903. Again, some remained in Europe or returned there shortly afterward.[23]

In Europe, discrimination was never as dangerous as it was in the United States. Quite a few African Americans married Europeans, and it was far from rare for them to appear onstage as "Black & White" racially mixed duets. This would have been almost impossible in the United States. John Hammond (a white man) caused a sensation when he organized his first Carnegie Hall jazz concert, featuring black and white performers on the New York stage, in the late 1930s. In Europe that was a common sight three or four decades before the Carnegie Hall event.

Racially mixed couple performing onstage in Europe—Dixy Davis and Yambo (about 1907). *Collection Lotz*

African American Recordings in Europe

Considering the vast number of African Americans who toured Europe, it is not surprising that some of them cut cylinders and discs there. The first were probably the African Canadian banjoist brothers James and George Bohee. The black population in Saint John, New Brunswick, had its origins in the Caribbean and the United States, and by 1859 the Bohee family had moved to Boston. The city was the center of banjo manufacturing, and the brothers took up that instrument. Around 1876, the Bohee brothers started their own, racially mixed Bohee Minstrels, which also included composer James Bland. After touring with various minstrel companies and also the Hyers Sisters, they too set sail for Europe.

In July 1880, the Bohee brothers opened with a minstrel company at Her Majesty's Theatre in London. When the troupe returned to the United States a couple of years later, the Bohees stayed in England. By 1890 they had become a

London institution, and members of royalty were among their pupils. As well as singing, tenor George Bohee danced to his brother's banjo and played banjo duets with him (George also played piano). James supplied banjo solos.

The Bohee brothers kept in contact with America, and it seems that May C. Hyers's daughter Bohee was named after them. The Bohees catered to a white European audience, and "Home Sweet Home" and "A Boy's Best Friend Is His Mother" are examples of the sentimental compositions that made them famous. But their repertoire consisted not only of sentimental songs, but included anti-slavery protest material, cakewalks, and minstrel songs. Sometime between 1890 and 1892 the Bohee brothers recorded banjo duets in London on Edison wax cylinders. They may have been the first African Americans to do so, and may even have antedated Vasnier. These recordings are known only from a report of their being played in Australia;[24] it is impossible to assess their musical character. George Bohee recorded at least another eleven banjo solos for the Edison Bell Supply Company in Liverpool during 1898, but the titles (including "Darky's Dream" and "Darky's Awakening") are known only from catalogues.[25]

The Bohees may have been the first, but the most-recorded American in Europe, black or white, was the African American Pete George Hampton.[26] As a teenage member of a banjo-playing vocal quartet, Pete Hampton appeared in medicine shows. During the 1890s he toured with prominent minstrel troupes. He then became associated with Bert Williams and George Walker. By 1900, Hampton was on the roster of the Sons of Ham Company, and a couple of years later he was part of In Dahomey (1902). Williams and Walker took this revue to England in 1903. Hampton fell in love with Laura Bowman, who was also with the In Dahomey revue; they were together until Hampton died back in the United States in 1916.

The company toured successfully in the United Kingdom. It was accepted socially, and Hampton became a member of the Free Masons Grand Lodge of Scotland. After the tour ended in 1904, Hampton and Bowman continued their career in Europe, until the outbreak of the World War forced them to return to the United States. Having grown up with the African American minstrel tradition, Hampton was an above-average comedian, actor, singer, instrumentalist, dancer, and composer. He played a five-string banjo and the harmonica. Among the tunes credited to him is "Lindy, Lindy, Sweet as Sugar Cane," with lyrics by Laura Bowman. The couple sold this song to Charles Johnson and Dora Dean. Hampton's talents were widely recognized: within a few years he had made not only a movie but well over a hundred and fifty cylinders and discs.

Like many of his fellow song-and-dance artists and the Bohee brothers before him, Hampton relied heavily on "coon songs" written by white composers, but he performed them in a distinctively black style. His performance of his own

Pete Hampton pictorial cylinder box (1904).
Collection Lotz

composition "Dat Mouth Organ Coon" (he recorded it for four different companies in 1904) is the first "black harmonica" record. After an interesting ragtime piano introduction, Hampton sings a few stanzas of a typical ragtime song, then suddenly he speeds up. Right in the middle of the performance, Hampton abruptly changes the tempo. He switches to harmonica—hence the song's title— and quotes from "The Last Rose of Summer." Hampton's specialty was playing the harmonica through his nose, but on this cylinder, after stating the melody, he performs at such a breakneck speed that it is hard to believe. He bends the melody, adds blue notes, produces all sorts of strange sounds that must have made Ireland's national poet Thomas Moore—who wrote "The Last Rose of Summer"—turn in his grave, and composer Friedrich von Flotow as well. Hampton also adds shouts and vocal interjections, something blues singers would do on record decades later. It is an astounding performance.

Other visiting African Americans made recordings in Europe as well.[27] Among these were the Black Troubadours, an all-male vocal quartet. They were an offshoot of the Jubilee Singers and performed in formal attire.

To attract the attention of their German audiences, some entertainers dressed up as Alpine farmers. Among them were the Four Black Diamonds (who did not record until 1921) and "The Black Nightingale," Arabella Fields.

Fields was one of several women to make records at this time. Her first recording for the Anker label was in Berlin in 1907; reissued many times, her twenty-year-old original records were listed in a 1928 catalogue. In this respect, the only 159

The 4 Black Diamonds as Tyroleans, poster (1909). *Collection Lotz*

dudes.

goodness,
some !
women.

artist comparable to Fields is Enrico Caruso, whose acoustic pre-1914 recordings were available well into the 1920s era of electric recording.

Another black female recording artist was Belle Davis. She was born in Chicago and first came to Europe as a member of Isham's Oriental America troupe in 1897. She stayed in Europe, where she toured with black children and recorded as Belle Davis and her Piccaninnies from 1902, as well as making silent films.

Then there was Laura Bowman, another veteran of the *In Dahomey* revue who was one of the Darktown Entertainers—the others being her husband Pete Hampton, and Fred Douglas and Will Garland.

Theodore Walton Wilson (b. 1879) was from Philadelphia, and his wife Lavina (b. 1878) from New Orleans. Like Hampton and Bowman, both had been with the *In Dahomey* company in 1903. In 1906 the Wilsons recorded at least three duets, and Mrs. Wilson at least another five solo titles, by some of the most prominent contemporary black composers: Tim Brymn, Will Marion Cook, Alex Rogers, and James Vaughn. They recorded for Globos, an obscure record company based in Hanover, Germany.

Among the titles recorded were numbers from In Dahomey: "Why Adam Sinned" was Aida Overton Walker's specialty, while "When the Moon Shines" was a featured duet for Williams and Walker. No copies of any Wilson discs have been found. If they surface, though, we will have the only recorded examples of these tunes, since Aida Overton Walker never recorded herself, while Williams

160

Arabella Fields as an Alpine cowgirl, advertisement (1910). *Collection Lotz*

and Walker never recorded "When the Moon Shines." We know very little about Wilson and Wilson, although they spent half a decade in Europe, touring widely, from Liverpool to Zwickau in Saxony. The Wilsons are a good example of the hundreds of pioneers in their respective fields of entertainment who remain unrecognized. They returned to New York from Boulogne, France, in 1909.

African American performers were among the pioneers of recorded music, not only in the United States, but also in Europe.

African Americans and Sound Films in Europe

Some history books claim that the first sound film was *The Jazz Singer*, featuring Al Jolson in blackface, in the late 1920s. But in fact, sound movies had been a common form of entertainment in music halls and variety theaters before the First World War. In Germany alone, well over a thousand sound movies were made, and perhaps even two thousand. Sometimes the film was shot, and matching sounds were recorded on discs afterward, or alternatively a commercial recording was used and a suitable film made afterward. The novelty wore off after a few years, and due to the imperfect technology, nobody bothered to preserve either the films or the discs. The situation today is that some of the films lack soundtracks, while the matching films are missing for some of the discs; but in most cases neither has survived. A search is now on to locate those artifacts and to match surviving discs to their film counterparts.

European sound films featured black vaudeville acts. In Germany alone, between ten and twenty films included black dancers, entertainers, minstrel troupes, and musicians. The black minstrel veteran Will Garland and his Negro Operetta Troupe recorded a couple of sound films in Berlin in 1910. After the war, in 1925, they recorded spirituals on disc.

There are two films featuring Arabella Fields (1907). And there are several films with Josephine Morcashani (1908). Morcashani often toured with someone billed as a Native American Sioux, who seems to have been of African descent. Morcashani was advertised as a Creole female baritone. Contacts with her family, including her grandson and great-grandson, revealed that she was the British-born daughter of a black American. Neither her films nor the discs that went with them have been found.

Another group that made at least two sound films was the Georgia Piccaninnies. Again, the films are presumed to be lost, but a double-sided thirty-centimeter-in-diameter film disc, recorded in Berlin in 1907, survives. The sound quality may appear poor, but the recording engineers did a remarkable job nevertheless. Remember, at the time engineers had to record through an open horn. It was quite difficult to capture the sound of an individual singer or instrumental soloist. But in this case they had to capture a rousing performance that was normally performed onstage. The engineers (from the Gramophone Company, working on commission for the Messter-Film Company) had to cope not only with an entire orchestra but also with a troupe of several lead singers, a responding chorus, and step dancers, all of them used to moving around onstage: "Get your partners for this ragtime dance."

In addition to films with sound, a number of silent films were made in Europe. Pete Hampton was filmed in Britain in 1906, then again in 1908. In Paris, the stage performance at the Nouveau Cirque in 1903 involved both black and white cakewalk dancers. Among the black performers were the siblings Rudy and Fredy Walker, and Charles Gregory. Three short takes featuring Belle Davis and her Piccaninnies were filmed by Pathé, presumably in Germany.

Most sources maintain that the "march king" John Philip Sousa introduced the cakewalk to Europe in 1900.[28] But long before Sousa performed in Europe, German musicians were playing original American dance tunes, including cakewalks, for the Americans, both live and as mechanical music. And long before Sousa's arrival, African Americans were performing buck, sand, and tap dances, as well as cakewalks, often to banjo accompaniment.

A long time before Josephine Baker reached the shores of Europe, hundreds of black vaudevillians toured all over the continent, as well as across Northern Africa, the Balkans, and east into Siberia. Their mobility was astounding even by today's standards. No passports were needed (except for Russia);[29] they traveled the theater circuits, whose programs changed weekly or every fortnight. The

RAINER E. LOTZ

162

cleverly managed circuits provided steady employment. Many African Americans chose to stay, and some left entertainment to pursue other professions.

Continental European audiences were not free of prejudices and stereotypes. People of African descent were certainly often disregarded and despised as a racial minority in the Old World. Nevertheless, racially mixed stage acts—often involving husband-and-wife teams—were common and seem to have been socially acceptable.

Black performers—singers, dancers, and musicians—had to provide what the mainly urban, white, lower- and middle-class audiences expected. All blacks traveling overseas had to bear in mind that they were performing for exclusively white audiences. Their niche in vaudeville entertainment was threefold: in addition to their exotic appearance and eccentric performances, they represented the recently enslaved blacks of America whose spirituals had been performed in many European countries from the 1870s onward. (My book *Black People: Entertainers of African Descent in Europe and Germany* [Bonn: Birgit Lotz Verlag, 1997] quotes contemporary German reviews and comments at length.[30])

Exotic these performers were, on account of their dark skin and different facial features, while eccentricity was achieved by posing as knockabout clowns and introducing African American elements into dancing, singing, and the playing of instruments—even though many, if not most, of the performers might have had no affinity with African American musical traditions. They had to provide a carefully balanced selection of popular tunes and Tin Pan Alley "coon songs," spiced with both European—recognizable to their audiences—and black elements.

Just how continental European audiences reacted to black performance styles we shall probably never know. Although, in contrast to Britain, the language barrier seems to have been something of a problem on the European continent, there was nonetheless ever-increasing demand for what was then advertised often as "nigger song and dance" until the First World War. After that, black U.S. song-and-dance shows, then jazz, gave Europeans different angles on black American entertainment and changed the picture dramatically.

These performances left a legacy of recordings and moving pictures, as well as postcards, publicity shots, and illustrated publicity items. Thanks to their rediscovery, we now have a much better understanding of this period than we did some years ago. As a result, we shall have to amend the blues, gospel, country, music hall, and ragtime discographies, reconsider this black strand of European urban entertainment onstage and in song, dance, humor, music, and comedy, and rewrite some chapters of black-music research literature.

1. Carl Gregor Herzog zu Mecklenburg, *International Jazz Bibliography: Jazz Books from 1919 to 1968* (Strasbourg & Baden-Baden: H. Heinz, 1969. Band 49 Collection d'études musicologiques / Sammlung musikwissenschaftlicher Abhandlungen).

2. Serious collectors were certainly able to import direct or through specialist dealers such as Levy's in Britain, or Alberti in Germany.

3. Rainer E. Lotz, "Black Music prior to the First World War." In Neil Wynn (ed.), *Cross the Water Blues* (Jackson: University Press of Mississippi, 2007), p. 67.

4. Brian A. L. Rust, *Jazz and Ragtime Records, 1897–1942* (Denver: Mainspring Press, 4th ed., 2002). Horst H. Lange, *Die deutsche 78er-Discographie der Hot-Dance und Jazz-Musik 1903–1958* (Berlin: Panther Verlag, 3rd ed., 1992).

5. Robert M. W. Dixon, John Godrich, and Howard Rye, *Blues and Gospel Records, 1890–1943* (Oxford: Oxford University Press, 4th ed., 1997).

6. Document Records, www.document-records.com, attempts to maintain a complete catalogue of all historical blues and gospel recordings by black performers only. The reissue situation with respect to vaudeville and white blues is still unsatisfactory.

7. Rainer E. Lotz, *German Ragtime and Prehistory of Jazz*, vol. 1, *The Sound Documents* (London: Storyville, 1985). Rainer E. Lotz, "Foolishness Rag; Ragtime in Europa—neue Gedanken zu alten Tonträgern." In *Jazzforschung/Jazzresearch* 21, 1989: 97–135.

8. Landkreis Kusel (ed.), *Westpfälzer Musikantentum* (Kusel: Westricher Heimatblätter. Nachdruck der Nr.2 des Jahrgangs 15, Juni 1984). Fremdenverkehrszweckverband Landkreis Kusel (ed.), *Pfälzer Bergland–Kuseler Musikantenland* (Kusel: Sonderdruck aus ‚Pfalz am Rhein' der Jahrgänge 1981, 1986, 1987 und 1988). Paul Engel, *Das Westpfälzer Wandermusikantentum im Lichte musikwissenschaftlicher Untersuchung*. Sonderdruck aus: Zum Beispiel—Der Landkreis Kusel, 1985). These publications are the source for most of the statistics shown below.

9. Q. David Bowers, *Encylopedia of Automatic Musical Instruments* (New York: Vestal Press, 1972).

10. Rainer E. Lotz, *Black People: Entertainers of African Descent in Europe and Germany* (Bonn: Birgit Lotz Verlag, 1997; with CD). Horst Bergmeier and Rainer E. Lotz, *Der Jazz in Deutschland. Vol. 1. Vom Cake Walk zum Jazz* (Hambergen: Bear Family, 2008; with three CDs).

11. A very popular cakewalk seems to have been "At a Georgia Camp Meeting," written by Frederick Allen "Kerry" Mills.

12. Karl Gert zur Heide, "Chicago, 1893, Part 2," *Doctor Jazz* (Hilversum), no.188 (2005): 6–16.

13. Doug Seroff and Lynn Abbott, "Black Music in the White City." In *78 Quarterly* 9 (Key West), n.d.: 105–17.

14. Peacock Publishing Co. (ed.), *Die verschwundene weiße Stadt: Eine Sammlung photographischer Aufnahmen auf der Columbischen Welt-Ausstellung* (Chicago: Peacock Publishing Co., 1893)

15. Trebor Jay Tichenor, *Ragtime Rarities* (New York: Dover, 1975), vii. Chris Ware, *The Ragtime Ephemeralist* 1 (Chicago, 1998): 45.

Doug Seroff & Lynn Abbott, "The Origins of Ragtime." In *78 Quarterly* 10 (Key West), n.d.: 121–43. David A. Jasen and Gene Jones, *That American Rag* (New York: Schirmer, 2000), 32, 45–46. Karl Gert zur Heide, "Saint Louis, 1904, Part 1." *Doctor Jazz* (Hilversum), no.185 (2004).

16. Tim Brooks, *Lost Sounds: Blacks and the Birth of the Recording Industry, 1891–1922*, edited by Richard Martin and Meagan Hennessy (St. Joseph, IL: Archeophone ARCH1005, double CD, 2005). The team of Horst Bergmeier, Jeffrey Green, Rainer Lotz, Howard Rye, and Christian Zwarg intends to document and reissue many recordings made by people of African descent in Europe: *Black Europe* is scheduled for publication by Bear Family Records in 2012.

17. Turn-of-the-century "coon songs" presented a racist and stereotyped image of African Americans to the melodious strains of ragtime music. They are discussed in detail in Lynn Abbott and Doug Seroff's *Ragged but Right: Black Traveling Shows, Coon Songs, and the Dark Pathway to Blues and Jazz* (Jackson: University Press of Mississippi, 2007).

18. I am indebted to collectors Randy Stehle and Quentin Riggs, who shared facsimile copies of the catalogues they found.

19. Brooks, *Lost Sounds*.

20. I am indebted to Adrienne Wheeler, who invited researcher Jeffrey Green and this author to a family gathering to discuss the Hyers Sisters in 2007.

21. In spite of all this discrimination, the literacy rate improved from 5 percent in 1865 to 50 percent in 1900: those educated blacks became potential competitors to poor whites.

22. *Der Artist—Central-Organ der Circus, Variété-Bühnen, reisenden Kapellen und Ensembles*. Vol. 4 (Düsseldorf, 1896). The chief editor in 1896 was Hermann Waldemar Otto ("signor Saltarino").

23. Jeffrey Green, "*In Dahomey* in London in 1903." In *Black Perspective in Music* 11, no. 1 (Cambria Heights, NY) Spring 1983: 22–40. Jeffrey Green, *Black Edwardians* (London: Frank Cass, 1998).

24. In the mid-1890s, a Professor Douglas Archibald introduced the Edison phonograph to Australia. He was reported in the press to have used the cylinder recording of a banjo duet by the Bohee Minstrels for demonstration purposes (*West Australian* [Perth], Wednesday, August 19, 1891, p. 5).

25. Rainer E. Lotz, "The Bohee Brothers (1844–1897/1856–1926?): Were These Afro-Canadians the Best Banjoists Ever?" In *78 Quarterly* 1, no. 7 (Key West) 1992: 97–111.

26. The white banjoist Vess Ossman (b. 1868 in Hudson, NY) recorded more titles in total, but far fewer in Europe than Hampton. Rainer E. Lotz, "Pete Hampton, Laura Bowman & the Darktown Aristocrats in Europe, 1904–1912: A Preliminary Bio-Discography." In *International Discographer* 1, no.1, (Canberra) 1992: 1–13. Uli Heier and Rainer E. Lotz, *The Banjo on Record: A Bio-Discography* (Westport, CT: Greenwood Press, 1993).

27. Lotz, *Black People*. Lotz, "Black Women Recording Pioneers." In *IAJRC* [*International Association of Jazz Record Collectors*] *Journal* 40, no. 2 (Naperville, IL), May 2007: 32–41.

28. He was certainly well received as leader of the official American orchestra at the 1900 Paris World Exposition. However, Sousa had an apparent aversion to African Ameri-

can influences in his music; he hardly understood what a cakewalk was, he did not compose any, and he did not normally perform cakewalks unless audiences explicitly demanded them. He avoided ragtime and later confessed to hating jazz. John Philip Sousa, *Marching Along: Recollections of Men, Women and Music, etc.* (Boston: Hale, Cushman & Flint, 1928). James Robert Smart, *The Sousa Band: A Discography* (Washington, DC: Library of Congress, 1970).

29. Before the First World War, only Brazil, Venezuela, Turkey, and Russia required visitors to show a passport, although U.S. citizens could carry a passport for the purpose of identification. Martin Lloyd, *The Passport: The History of Man's Most Traveled Document* (Derby, PA: Diane Publishing, 2003).

30. Lotz, *Black People.*

8 / BENNY CARTER IN BRITAIN, 1936–1937

blegh.

enny Carter's residency in Europe between 1935 and 1938 has been summarized in the seminal text on his life (Berger et al., 2002) and in an
invaluable article by Howard Rye in the "Visiting Firemen" series for
Storyville (Rye, 1981). Carter's visit began with nine months in France as a
sideman in Willie Lewis's band and ended with a period of just over a year
as a bandleader in Holland; but at the core of his time in Europe was a year,
beginning in March 1936, in which he was primarily resident in London. Rather
than providing another survey of his European activities, my focus in this chapter
will be this period, which was formative both for Carter and for British jazz. I
argue that study of Carter's time in Britain is important not only for those who
wish to gain a comprehensive picture of his life and work, but also, due to the
length of his residency and the breadth of activities in which he was involved, for
understanding the nature of transatlantic relations and the development of British jazz performance in the interwar period.

Carter had been preceded in Britain by Coleman Hawkins, his colleague from
Fletcher Henderson's band, who had performed with Jack Hylton's groups during 1934 (and returned in 1939). Although, as Rye points out, "there was no time in
which both were professionally active in Britain at the same time," other musicians have recalled the former bandmates jamming together at the Nest club in
London—both Hawkins and Carter moved fairly fluidly around Europe (Rye,
1981b). Carter's arrival in Europe coincided with a time of significant change for
jazz in Britain. Restrictions on American musicians working in Britain had arisen
as a result of tensions between the British Musicians' Union, the American Federation of Musicians, and their respective governments from the late 1920s. Although restrictions were supported by the Musicians' Union with the idea that
British jobs were being safeguarded, these were initially applied flexibly in recognition of the contribution that American musicians could make to British popular
music by introducing new ideas and educating musicians (Parsonage, 2005:220).
However, as the result of a long and complicated series of actions and reactions by
the British and American governments under pressure from the unions, American
bands were prohibited from performing publicly in Britain from 1935 unless as an
integral part of a stage show. This was an expensive prospect for producers, as the
American band would appear on the stage while a British band was retained in the
pit. This led to a tendency for visits from individual American musicians, who
could also only appear onstage, in effect as variety "acts" (Parsonage, 2005:252–55).

interesting

As these individuals were regularly backed by British musicians, their visits were arguably more deeply influential on British jazz than those of complete bands. These policies persisted for the next twenty years, at which point a system of transatlantic exchange began to bring American bands to Britain again.

Interest in and knowledge of jazz in Britain had developed apace, in parallel with the increasingly restrictive policies on American musicians, as a result of the availability of American jazz recordings and associated criticism, particularly in British periodicals such as *Melody Maker* and *Rhythm* (from 1926 and 1927 respectively). High-profile live performances from musicians such as Duke Ellington and Louis Armstrong in the early 1930s brought jazz to public attention as an African American art form, and its particular qualities began to become better understood (Parsonage, 2005:65–67). By the mid-1930s a specific audience for jazz was well supported by a national network of Rhythm Clubs, which relied mainly on records and informal performances of local musicians to provide fans with their fix of jazz. These activities responded to and fueled the distinction between "hot" jazz and swing and "sweet" dance music.

Encountering Carter

The interest in jazz alongside the governmental restrictions on American musicians resulted in a situation in which demand for jazz outstripped supply in Britain. This led to some of the most dedicated jazz aficionados visiting America to experience for themselves the latest innovations in the music. Bass player, composer, and journalist Patrick "Spike" Hughes, who wrote opinionated record reviews for *Melody Maker* under the pseudonym "Mike," recalled that his discovery of African American jazz performance, initially on record, threw the prevailing British dance music, and even jazz played by white Americans, which had dominated the British experience of jazz recordings, into relief: "The Negro's music achieved a degree of personal expression rarely found in that of his white colleagues; it had a directness, a suggestion of personal experience translated into terms of music which began to raise jazz from the status of a musical accomplishment to that of an art" (Hughes, 1951:146)

On Hughes's initial visit to America in 1933, under the auspices of John Hammond, *Melody Maker*'s first American correspondent,[1] the first band he heard was Carter's:

We drove straight to a large, cold room where a young Negro called Benny Carter was in the middle of rehearsing a fourteen-piece band. Nobody noticed John or me as we entered the room; the band was in full cry and making what was quite a stupendous noise to my inexperienced European ears. I had heard

CATHERINE TACKLEY PARSONAGE

Negro bands on gramophone records . . . [but] Benny Carter's band was producing a sound which I had never realised existed. (Hughes, 1951:222).

Carter ran through one of Hughes's compositions, "Six Bells Stampede," asking him with his customary attention to detail, "Was the tempo right? Should the crescendo rise to fortissimo or only to forte behind the trombone solo?" (Hughes, 1951:223). Hughes quickly realized that he wanted to take the opportunity to make recordings with black musicians while he was in New York. Carter's band provided a nucleus of musicians for Hughes to use in three sessions in which he recorded fourteen titles. Hughes's attitude to jazz composition changed in this period, as he moved away from his previous rather simplistic emulation of its African American roots: "Once I had set foot on American soil all suggestion of Negro music vanished from the titles of my work . . . once I had trodden on the side-walks of Harlem, . . . I became almost obstinately European in my choice of titles" (Hughes, 1951:271).

Instead, Hughes began to draw on his own cultural background in compositions such as the "pseudo-Irish" "Donegal Cradle Song," which was much more successful than his attempts to incorporate African American elements into his work. "At the first session, when we recorded four titles, I included only two works of my own; at the following two sessions I gave the band nothing but my own music to play, and paradoxically the players were more at home with it than ever they were with my arrangements of standard tunes which they already knew" (Hughes, 1951:267).

In addition to previous reviews of Carter's own recordings (he did not record as a leader from the end of 1934 until he came to Britain), Carter's work with Hughes and associated reports in *Melody Maker* undoubtedly played a significant part in ensuring that British jazz fans were familiar with Benny Carter before his arrival in Europe.

The BBC Dance Orchestra

Until the mid-1930s, British jazz fans were unlikely to find their preferred style of music on the British Broadcasting Corporation's radio service.[2] From its inception in 1923 under the leadership of Sir John Reith, the BBC had pursued a policy of providing entertainment that it considered acceptable for public consumption, which usually did not extend to jazz. Instead, the BBC presented "dance music," which was tightly controlled through careful selection of bands broadcasting from upper-class London venues such as the Savoy Hotel and also through a succession of "house" bands. Dance music was managed within the BBC's Variety Department, rather than alongside classical music in the Music Department, indicative of the perception of the former as lowbrow and functional and the latter as highbrow and autonomous.

In 1932 Henry Hall was appointed leader of the BBC Dance Orchestra, having been responsible previously for bands in a chain of hotels owned by the London, Midlands and Scottish Railway. Hall's strengths that had made him attractive to the BBC were outlined in a memo reporting a meeting that took place at the time of the termination of his contract: "[Hall] said that he had always regarded himself more as an executive than as an artist and was, in fact, more interested in executive work. . . . He said that although he conducted the LMS bands, including the Gleneagles one, he was in executive charge of 30 and that the executive side appealed to him immensely" (BBC Written Archives Centre Contributors 910 Hall, Henry, File II 1936–39, 15 July 1937). In addition to Hall's ability as a leader, his perceived lack of interest in artistic matters would allow the BBC to continue to shape the Dance Orchestra in accordance with their evolving policies. Initially, the change of leader allowed for a significant reformulation of the Dance Orchestra, the intention being to create a "Paul Whiteman orchestra" (BBCWAC R29/13 Orch. Gen. BBC Dance Orchestra 1932–33, 11 March 1937) with "a *sweet* soft sound for a change" (BBCWAC Contributors 910 Hall, Henry, File 1a, 13 January 1932; emphasis in original). Henry Hall recalled that "A complete contrast to the style of [Hall's predecessor] Jack Payne's band was wanted: the emphasis was to be on melody," with violins, reduced brass, and even, unusually, an oboe (Hall, 1955:87). Although this instrumentation was "not intended to make impossible thereby the playing of "hot" orchestrations" (BBCWAC R29/13 Orch. Gen. BBC Dance Orchestra 1932–33, 2 June 1932), the views of prominent members of the BBC's executive on jazz remained unequivocal:

There is practically no really "hot" music broadcast (by which is implied definitely "negroid" music of the Ellington-Armstrong type), though Henry Hall does include from time to time clever arrangements of tunes which cannot, however, be said to fall within the category of "hot" music. I consider we are justified in including these on the grounds that, with the inevitable repetition of popular songs, an orchestral leader does right to make them as interesting, musically, as possible—and to meet the need of a very large body of enthusiasts who are interested in the development of so-called jazz songs. By far the greater proportion of Hall's programmes consist of bright English comedy numbers and straight sentimental tunes. . . . I really think we are trying to meet a variety of tastes in the best possible way, and I can assure you there is no sympathy with what I would again term the "negroid" type of music.[3]

A review of dance music broadcasting in late 1935/early 1936 led to the decision to enlarge Henry Hall's band into a twenty-one-piece group, which enabled him to "feature five or even six violins when required, while he can also call upon a five-piece sax section . . . [and a] a six-piece brass team" (*Melody Maker*, 7 March 1936:1). The idea behind this was to allow the band to perform a wider range of repertoire, not necessarily just contemporary dance music, presented in thematic programs (such as "Fascinating Rhythm," which illustrated different dance styles) thereby fulfilling the requirements of variety entertainment (*Melody Maker*, 7 March 1936:9). This made "special arrangements" a necessity, and *Melody Maker* noted that "an important step towards the fulfilment of these plans will be the appointment of two extra arrangers who will work exclusively for Henry Hall on the preparation of material for the BBC Dance Orchestra" (*Melody Maker*, 4 January 1936:1). Around the same time, young jazz-loving BBC employees such as Leslie Perowne and Charles Chilton encouraged the Corporation to develop specific programs that would address the growing public awareness of and interest in jazz and swing. As well as educative programs based on records, this led to the increase in outside broadcasts from British and European bands and eventually, from 1937, a remarkable series of transatlantic relays from America.

The idea of Leonard Feather, a precocious British jazz writer who was then only in his early twenties, to engage Carter as an arranger for the BBC Dance Orchestra was an opportunistic and innovative approach to partially circumventing the recently instituted restrictions on American musicians. As Feather himself put it, Carter "would not be permitted to play in England, but what could stop him from entering the country as an arranger? And why not, say, with some firmly established group such as Henry Hall's BBC Dance Orchestra?" (1986:32). Feather had not encountered Carter in person because by the time Feather made his first visit to the States in 1935, Carter was already in France with Willie Lewis's band. However, he had heard him on broadcasts from France and would have been familiar with his recordings as well (Feather, 1986:32). Importantly, under the terms of his contract, Henry Hall had a free rein as to the musicians and arrangers he employed and did not need to seek BBC approval to either appoint or dismiss them (contract in BBCWAC Contributors 910 Hall, Henry File 1a File 1a 1931–33). Therefore, Feather only had to get Hall to agree to employ Carter, rather than negotiate with the BBC directly. He recalled that Hall "seemed receptive" to the idea, which was hardly an overenthusiastic response (Feather, 1986: 32). Hall had visited America twice since beginning his tenure with the BBC, but his attention was apparently focused on music publishers and "show bands" such as the Casa Loma Orchestra (see Hall, 1955). Similarly, Hall's autobiography devotes a single sentence to his employment of Carter, which is presented as just a small part of his overall quest for novelty and perhaps also publicity: "I was criticized a little for bringing in the American coloured swing musician, Benny

Carter, but he gave the band a 'new note' which was invaluable for variety during the course of finding nine programmes a week" (1955:144).

Feather "wrote to Carter and received, promptly, an expression of interest" (1986:32). Similarly to when he decided to join Lewis in France and eventually to leave Britain in 1937, Carter demonstrated a decisive attitude toward opportunities to further his career. He recalled that in 1936 he "was eager to visit England and to meet Feather, whose work I had read and admired in *Melody Maker* and other music publications" (Carter in Feather, 1976:17). Although Carter had sat in occasionally with the Quintette du Hot Club de France during his time in Paris and wrote arrangements for Lewis's band, Feather's offer must have been enticing since, after having led and formed his own bands, Carter was now a sideman playing music that he described as "mainly melodies as written, with a little jazz occasionally" and obviously lacked the same degree of artistic autonomy as earlier in his career (Berger et al., 2002:144). Having secured the necessary work permit, Carter arrived in Britain on Wednesday, 18 March 1936, apparently inquiring immediately about the instrumentation of the BBC Dance Orchestra and proceeding to the BBC studios in Maida Vale to meet "Hall and the boys" (*Melody Maker*, 21 March 1936:11). On the Friday of the following week, Carter made "his BBC Bow" in a lunchtime broadcast where he spoke briefly to the audience, and the orchestra played five of his arrangements (*Melody Maker*, 11 April 1936:5).

Carter's arrival was also opportune for the BBC, which recently had been subject to some criticism from *Melody Maker*, firstly for withholding details of the new dance music policy from the press so that these could be released in the *Radio Times*, the BBC's own magazine, and secondly for instituting "half-hearted" reforms that contributed little to the variety and quality of broadcast dance music (*Melody Maker*, 7 March 1936:1, 8). Carter's input would allow some of the criticisms of the new dance music policy to be addressed. Feather was also undoubtedly well aware of the changes being made at the BBC, possibly with insider knowledge, as he began writing in the *Radio Times* around this time. Feather must have realized that Carter would be invaluable to the reformed Dance Orchestra within a BBC that had begun to recognize swing as a growing and significant trend that could be incorporated into their popular music programming, manifest in the changes to the Dance Orchestra's instrumentation. Carter's band in the early thirties is described by Berger as "a very well-rehearsed and polished unit that played with a tight but relaxed collective swing," indicating that Carter's approach would be compatible with the BBC Dance Orchestra, which was under constant pressure to set the standard for broadcast dance music, particularly the new swing genre, through the consistency and quality of its performances (Berger et al., 2002:109). Carter's arrangements demanded individual solos, which presented a challenge for many of the musicians (*Melody Maker* noted that "One or two of the boys [in the BBC Dance Orchestra] have wisely consented to have Benny write solos out for them" [11 April 1936:5]). However, Carter's trademark, technically difficult ensemble passages, particularly for the saxophone section, played to the strengths of the band, many of whom were classically trained musicians. This may have been what Hall meant by Carter's "new note." Carter was not officially permitted to play on or conduct BBC broadcasts but rehearsed his own arrangements from the outset. Trombonist Dicky Wells recalled the rigor of Carter's rehearsals: "All [Carter] would ask you to do was play the notes—nothing extra. If you accidentally played a wrong note, he'd stop the band and ask you what note you played. 'The one on the paper,' you'd answer. 'You'd better look again,' he'd say" (quoted in Dance, 2001:135).

Russell Procope recalled that as a leader, Carter was "easy-going . . . dignified, calm and confident, with no affectations or showbiz flash," so not dissimilar to Henry Hall. Just as Hall was reluctant to appear on the stage (although he was to build his post-BBC career in variety), Carter's focus was on the music to the extent that Berger suggests that his reluctance to be a showman compromised the success of his early career (2002:106).

Berger also notes that "Professionally, Carter worked easily and comfortably with white musicians even when racial mixing was rare. In the early 1930s he led a recording band of white and black sidemen." He certainly commanded the respect of the white musicians in the BBC Dance Orchestra (2002:8). It is tempting to view Carter's work with this group as a progressive step, given the attitudes to jazz as black music in evidence at the BBC only a few years previously. However, it is important to remember that the BBC was not employing Carter directly, and moreover, many of Henry Hall's regular listeners would have been unaware of Carter's identity, since as an arranger his input was largely anonymous (Hughes invited *Melody Maker* readers to try to identify which items on the BBC Dance Orchestra's broadcasts were Carter arrangements [*Melody Maker*, 16 May 1936: 4]). Feather noted that Carter's contribution was "the most important change of all in the band [and] has been virtually overlooked," and outside the BBC his performances and recordings, as we shall see, were aimed specifically at jazz fans (Feather, 1936a:13). When Carter eventually had the chance to play, unadvertised, on a broadcast, this leading American jazz musician was heard by Hall's vast audience only within the confines of his "Waltzing the Blues" (for further discussion of this number see below) on a program called *The Everlasting Waltz*, described as "a welter of old-fashioned waltzes and comedy waltz songs" (*Melody Maker*, 17 October 1936:14).

Carter wrote a large number of arrangements, estimated variously between thirty-six and fifty, for the BBC Dance Orchestra during his time in Britain, but even so, this was a small fraction of the arrangements commissioned by the band over the period of his involvement (Berger, 2002:146; Rye, 1981a:87). Indeed, Hall included Carter in a list of no fewer than ten arrangers that he was using "as we approached 1937" (1955:144). However, Carter's approach to leadership and performance had an undeniable impact on the BBC Dance Orchestra, even after only a month, as Spike Hughes described in *Melody Maker*:

> Last Saddy [Saturday] nite, I happened to hear, for the first time, Hall's band playing a tune of Benny's. . . . It wasn't Benny Carter's Band I heard, but it was a band that had obviously been directed by Benny at some stage of rehearsal. That is one of the great assets of the BBC Band. It is amazingly adaptable. If it has an arrangement to play, it plays it as the arranger wants. If the arranger doesn't know what he wants, you can hear that in the playing at once. Benny always knows what he wants. And what I heard was something rather extraordinary last Saddy nite. Just before Benny's tune, it had played some other arranger's "pop." When Benny's tune came around, the whole character of that band changed. The brass playing had an edge on it that I have never heard in any British brass section. The boys were playing brass instruments; the sound that came out of them had bite, brilliance and clean attack. I attribute those three very pleasant minutes of music to two things: the aforesaid adaptability of the band, and Benny Carter's own personality. The greater a band's adaptability, the more easily it is able to reflect its conductor's personality. Obviously. Benny, for the purposes of his tune, was the band's conductor. And he has a very strong personality as a conductor. (Hughes, 1936a:7)

nice quote

Swing Music Concert

The only advertised public performance given by Carter in Britain was a concert on Sunday, 10 January 1937, at the London Hippodrome, sponsored by *Melody Maker*. When notifying the readership, the publication noted the tradition in London of such events, which had previously provided musicians such as Duke Ellington the opportunity to play for a knowledgeable audience in an atmosphere more akin to the presentation of classical music. These concerts were staged ostensibly to offer educational opportunities for British musicians, in order to ensure that the necessary permits would be granted. Similarly, Carter's concert was intended to be "a show which will be both educational and entertaining to a specialised audience." Beyond this, the emphasis in the initial publicity was not that this was a rare opportunity to hear Carter play in public, but instead to demonstrate "that British dance musicians are nowadays not behind their American contemporaries in the ability to play swing music." In this context, Carter is

emphasis is education is intriguing

portrayed primarily as an educator who "has proved on his Vocalion records that he can get better results out of English musicians in this branch of the art than any other musician in the country." The announcement cited Fred Elizalde's concert with his Anglo-American band at the Shepherd's Bush Pavilion in 1929, which had allowed British musicians such as the young trumpeter Norman Payne to shine alongside American stars of the caliber of Adrian Rollini (Parsonage, 2005: 216), concluding optimistically: "This will be the first concert of English swing music ever to be given, and the press will be invited to hear for themselves what our fellows can do about it. The whole occasion will be another landmark in the progress of dance music, and all present will live to look back upon it as an event of historical importance" (14 November 1936:1).

Carter's relatively low profile during his time in Britain may have led to the decision to incorporate other "acts" (a compere/comedian, a "straight" saxophone soloist, and Hylton's vocal group, the Swingtette) into the concert to make it more appealing to the general public. However, it is clear Carter would be the main draw for the most devoted jazz fans, as explained by Feather in a vivid metaphor in his report of the concert:

> Of the sixteen hundred swing fans at Sunday's concert, at least half must have been feeling like Tantalus at the banquet of the Gods. That poor sufferer, you may remember, had the choicest of fruits placed just out of his reach, and in his starvation was tortured by the sight of them. For a year the jazz fraternity of England has had Benny Carter in its midst, but never until last Sunday was an opportunity afforded to everyone to feast on the musical delicacies he had to offer. So, when the curtain went up to reveal the broadly smiling, fast-moving figure with a baton, leading thirteen musicians through the familiar strains of "Blues in my Heart," these hundreds of Tantaluses were unfettered and their saviour prepared to entertain them in the flesh. (Feather, 1937:11)

Judging from contemporary reports, the concert was well received. The inclusion of a jam session in response to audience requests was a distinctive feature, which anticipated Benny Goodman's famous Carnegie Hall concert almost exactly a year later, and served to prove the jazz credentials of the British musicians as spontaneous improvisers: "Everyone in the audience seemingly yelling a request for this tune and that player . . . Benny Carter deafened but plainly amused . . . soloists tearing off their choruses, but not allowed to finish before another vociferous outbreak of nominations from the auditorium . . . grand fun" (*Melody Maker*, 16 January 1937:1, ellipses in original).

Rhythm Clubs and Nightclubs

The scarcity of opportunities to hear Carter live in Britain meant that there was particular interest among British jazz fans in the performances he gave in semiprivate Rhythm Clubs and nightclubs. These were necessarily unadvertised, since Carter was supposedly prohibited from performing in Britain. Rhythm Clubs were formed in the 1930s initially to provide opportunities for British jazz enthusiasts to share their collections of rare records, but a standard format evolved for meetings whereby a "record recital" was often followed by a live, often informal, musical performance by the members, sometimes joined by visiting professionals. In May 1935 there were ninety clubs in existence in the United Kingdom under the auspices of an umbrella organization, the British Federation of Rhythm Clubs, and two publications, *Swing Music* and *Hot News and Rhythm Record Review*, had been launched. As well as a source of information and recreation for members, the Rhythm Clubs acted as a "pressure group" that attempted to influence record companies and the BBC (Parsonage, 2005:72).

Soon after his arrival in Britain, No.1 Rhythm Club took the opportunity to invite Carter to a meeting as guest of honor, and in return Carter "put over a show on alto which more than fulfilled the high expectations of his many admirers. A record crowd of two hundred and thirty-two turned up to enjoy his wonderful playing" (*Melody Maker*, 11 April 1936:10).[4] Although Carter's attendance at the No. 1 Club was sometimes advertised in advance, his playing was never mentioned specifically, presumably to avoid attracting the attention of the authorities—who, however, did not act on the retrospective reports of occasional and apparently spontaneous performances: "In addition to excellent record recitals by H. Livick and Leonard Feather, there was a grand surprise at Monday's meeting of the No. 1 Rhythm Club in the unheralded appearance of a magnificent busking trio consisting of Benny Carter (piano), Jeff Aldam (trombone) and Bill Morter (drums)" (*Melody Maker*, 16 May 1936:10).

Whereas Rhythm Club news was included in each edition of *Melody Maker*, there was no regular reporting of the informal performances that regularly took place in London's nightclubs. Although the extent of Carter's participation in this scene is unclear, two articles by Feather do provide some indicative detail. In *Melody Maker* in October 1936, Feather suggests that Carter performed in nightclubs reasonably regularly: "Because he has so little opportunity to play over here, some of his nights are spent at the little Soho resorts, where he can sit in with the band. The places hardly correspond with his idea of Paradise, but at least they give him the chance to keep in practice" (Feather, 1936b:2).

Nightclubs, mainly situated in the West End of London and particularly in Soho's compact grid of streets, had long provided formative opportunities for

British musicians to interact with visiting American musicians, free from the musical, social, and legal restrictions that governed their regular places of work. Criminal activity of all types was rife in the underworld of London, and it is unlikely that musicians contravening the terms of their work permits by "sitting in" informally would have concerned many of the proprietors. Although such activities had been occurring for many years, the lack of general public awareness is shown through Feather's explanation of the "jam session" in which he reports Carter was involved:

> One night in London's miniature Harlem, the Shim-Sham Club (run by Ike Hatch), there was a "jam session" that will live long in the memory of every musician who was there. A "jam session" is an informal gathering of musicians, playing improvised jazz, not for money, but because they like to play. Not a note of written music is used on these busman's holidays. On this occasion Carter played sensationally on several instruments, while the band that had assembled with him comprised one member from each of six famous groups, including Bert Ambrose's, Roy Fox's, Harry Roy's and Lew Stone's. (Feather, 1936a:13)

African American and black British musicians and entertainers had a constant presence in London's club scene at this time. Although the numbers of American musicians visiting Britain dwindled due to the governmental restrictions, imported shows with all-black casts remained popular. Black British musicians were often recruited to provide the musical entertainment in clubs, such as the Nest, Jigs, and the Bag O'Nails, which provided after-hours hangouts for these visitors. These venues were also popular with leading British dance band musicians, who had relatively few opportunities to play jazz in their day-to-day employment. African American singer Ike Hatch seized the opportunity to develop a club for American performers that would also attract an interactive "audience" of curious white Britons, opening the Shim-Sham Club in February 1935. The club was subject to frequent undercover police observations for illegal sales of alcohol, which culminated in a raid in July 1935, but then continued to operate more or less as before, temporarily changing its name to the Rainbow Roof. Records of the police observations consistently noted the racial mix in the club and in the band, which varied in size, obviously according to who was sitting in (National Archives: Public Records Office MEPO 2/4494). It seems likely that Carter's performance in the Shim-Sham as described by Feather was not an isolated event, especially given that Carter often worked closely in the recording studio with many of Britain's leading jazz musicians, who were the stalwarts of this scene.

Recording

Other than his work with the BBC Dance Orchestra, Carter's most regular and prolific musical activity during his time in Britain was recording. Similarly to the Rhythm Clubs and nightclubs, recording had often provided performance opportunities for visiting musicians outside their main employment in Britain, sometimes under pseudonyms if they were bound to a particular employer by an exclusivity contract (Parsonage, 2005:202). A further similarity was that recording with American visitors presented important learning opportunities for British musicians who were employed as sidemen, the main difference being that recording work was paid. Feather was once again instrumental in arranging opportunities for Carter, as he recalled: "Carter's arrival coincided with a plan in which I had become involved to start a new label in England, reviving the long-familiar Vocalion label, to issue some of the recordings by Teddy Wilson, Billie Holiday, Artie Shaw and others that had been in short supply in the UK" (Feather, 1986:32).

Carter led a total of seven[5] recording sessions for Vocalion during his time in Britain, with groups varying in size from a quintet to a full swing band (six brass, four saxophones, and rhythm). Feather explained that there were no restrictions on Carter's recording in Britain provided that he "gave work to English musicians," and accordingly practically all the musicians that worked with Carter were British (several commentators noted that many were from Scotland) (Feather, 1986:33). The band at Carter's first British session, which took place on 15 April 1936, consisted of players from the leading dance orchestras, including Bert Ambrose, Sidney Lipton, Lew Stone, and Al Collins, with the addition of some freelancers. Writing in *Swing Music*, Carter reflected on the session:

> I should like to emphasise how pleasantly surprised I was by the work of the English boys in my first session over here. The Rhythm section really did exactly what was required; the brass were splendid; Max Goldberg is a great lead man, and Duncan Whyte and Tommy McQuater both did some swell solo work. Andy McDevitt on clarinet is, in my opinion, one of the very best in this country, and I particularly liked the tenor work of Buddy Featherstonhaugh. Who said British musicians can't swing, anyway? (Carter, 1936:71)

Carter is rather unenthusiastic about the rhythm section here, and perhaps it is no surprise that completely different personnel were used in this section after Carter's first two sessions in April 1936. Although the personnel of Carter's recording groups were not maintained with complete consistency over the course of the seven sessions, the members of this original rhythm section were not used again. Certainly, strong rhythm section players were particularly vital for Carter to make successful small group recordings. The recording sessions did not use members of the BBC Dance Orchestra, with the exception of George Elrick, who took over on the drums for the June sessions. This may have been a result of lack of availability, contractual restrictions, or the lack of improvisational ability. The list of Carter's arrangements for the BBC Dance Orchestra compiled by Rye (1981a) indicates that there was only minor overlap in repertoire with his Vocalion recordings; for example, his first British record (Vocalion S4) featured "Swingin' at Maida Vale" and was also among the first of Carter's arrangements to be broadcast in Britain. Where repertoire was duplicated, it was not the case that Carter's solos were simply omitted from the BBC Dance Orchestra's performances. When *Melody Maker*'s "Detector" compared the broadcast version of "Nightfall" with the recently released recording, the reviewer noted that it was "quite different from the recorded arrangement, with a heavier and less appropriate first chorus, a vocal by the three girls, and then some beautiful all-out brass stuff in sharp contrast to the subdued clarinet that follows" (16 May 1936:4). This strongly suggests that Carter made specific arrangements for broadcasting and recording even when the same numbers were used.

Although Carter's abilities on alto and tenor saxophones, clarinet, trumpet, and piano (as well as the occasional vocal) would have provided plenty of interest and variety in the solos, the Vocalion sides also featured many solos from the British musicians, noted approvingly by *Rhythm* magazine:

> Other stars, making their first recordings over here, have been given individual solo billing to which they have become quite unaccustomed. Hawkins, whom we had known as a member of Fletcher Henderson's Band, became a soloist with accompaniment. Admittedly in such cases as his, this was permissible. But with Benny Carter it might have been easy to fall into the trap of providing him with this same setting—of focusing the entire limelight on him and undervaluing his importance as a leader and arranger relative to his importance as a soloist. That is why we should appreciate the fact that Vocalion provided Benny with a full band, of which he instantly became a member. The difference between "Benny Carter with Orchestra" and "Benny Carter and His Orchestra" is a vast and important one. (*Rhythm*, June 1936:26)

The British Vocalion label drew most of its releases from the ARC and Brunswick catalogues, therefore two numbers from Carter's first British session were released alongside performances from Taft Jordan (including Teddy Wilson), Benny Goodman, and Wingy Manone in the first batch of records in the "Swing Series" (Rye, 2011b; *Melody Maker*, 4 April:1). Therefore, it was important for Carter to work with the best British musicians that were available, especially since these recordings were for the British market, but also to educate and develop the band to produce work of a comparable standard to that of the American bands that were on the label.

An overview of Carter's work with large ensembles on sessions in April and June 1936 and January 1937 is indicative of the way he worked with British musicians to produce a noticeable impact on both solo and ensemble performance. On the first two sessions in April 1936, with thirteen-piece and nine-piece groups respectively, relatively simple arrangements are used, including two based on the twelve-bar blues form, "Big Ben Blues" and "Swingin' the Blues." The former was put together in the studio, where apparently Carter "speedily wrote out an ensemble chorus for the finale; a few rhythmic figures were arranged to accompany the solos, and within thirty minutes the record was made" (*Melody Maker*, 18 April 1936:1). On the first number recorded, "Swingin' at Maida Vale," saxophones are scored in unison rather than Carter's customary close harmony, and the solos by the British musicians are restricted to eight-bar bridge sections. On the second session later in the month, sidemen Buddy Featherstonhaugh (tenor saxophone) and Andy McDevitt (clarinet) perform tentative-sounding complete choruses on the standard "When Day Is Done" and Leonard Feather's "I've Got Two Lips." Either Tommy McQuater or Duncan Whyte appears somewhat more confident on trumpet on the latter. In June, when a thirteen-piece group was assembled once again, the arrangements of numbers such as "Scandal in A Flat" and "Accent on Swing" are noticeably more complex, with homophonic sections for the saxophones, different muting effects in the brass, passages for a three-piece trombone section, and full chorus solos, including from new pianist Billy Munn, at faster tempi over more-complex harmonies. Carter's final British session involved a group of the same size, and began with another attempt at the up-tempo "Gin and Jive" from the June session, not only with a different sequence of solos at a faster speed, but with an introduction and new passages in the arrangement, demonstrating how Carter challenged himself as well as the musicians with whom he was working. Other arrangements from this session, such as "Nagasaki," are once again faster, with more-complex ensemble writing, especially for the saxophones, yet the band produces a superlative performance.

Carter's facility on many instruments allowed him to exert a direct and wide influence on the solo playing of the British musicians. On Feather's "I Got Two Lips" from the late April 1936 session, a trumpeter, either McQuater or Whyte, imitates the Armstrong-esque climax of Carter's trumpet solo on the previous number. Ultimately, a disagreement between Carter and the ever-present Feather about the arrangement of "There's a Small Hotel" in the final session provided the opportunity for wholesale imitation, which evidences the impact of Carter's playing on the British musicians, as Feather recalled:

Benny and I disagreed a little on this date; I didn't dig him as a ballad singer and wanted him to play the melody on alto. We finally cut two takes, one with his vocal and one with an alto solo, and released both. But the alto version fooled a lot of people; it wasn't Benny playing. He didn't want to play this number and assigned the chorus to the late Freddy Gardner, who did a remarkable job of making people think it was Benny. (Feather, 1951:18)

Carter's three small group sessions in June and October 1936 encompass an eclectic selection of repertoire: Carter originals, recent popular songs by George Gershwin, Alexander Hill, and British composer Vivian Ellis, standards such as "Poor Butterfly," "Royal Garden Blues," and "Tiger Rag," and, rather incongruously, "Jingle Bells." Carter and the rhythm section backed American-born singer Elisabeth Welch throughout the second session, and the trumpeter Tommy McQuater joined the group for an instrumental third session. It is the first session, however, that is of particular interest.

"Waltzing the Blues"

Feather recalled that "In a country as thoroughly starved of authentic jazz as England, every move by Carter made a *Melody Maker* headline and even leaked into the general press" (1986:33). However, it was the first small group session, on 20 June 1936, that resulted in a record (Vocalion S19) that attracted more press coverage than any of Carter's other activities in Britain. On this occasion the group incorporated two further American musicians: pianist Gene Rodgers, who was on tour in a variety act with dancing trumpeter Frank Radcliffe, and Bernard Addison, performing in London with the Mills Brothers (Rye, 1981a and 2011a). Welch was featured on a Carter original, "When Lights Are Low," and the two instrumental numbers—Carter's original composition "Waltzing the Blues," backed by the New Orleans standard "Tiger Rag"—were released as a coupling in September 1936.

Aside from the inclusion of his composition "I've Got Two Lips" in Carter's broadcast and studio repertoire, "Waltzing the Blues" is the clearest manifestation of Leonard Feather's omnipresent influence on Carter's European activities. Back in 1933, Feather had written a letter to the editor of *Melody Maker* asking why there was no jazz in waltz time, to which the printed editorial reply was that this was "like asking for a blue piece of red chalk" (cited in *Melody Maker*, 12 September 1936:6). Another correspondent then wrote a "hot chorus" for the popular standard "Tiger Rag" in three-time, called the "Three Legged Tiger." Three years later, when Feather "suggested to Benny that we try a blues in waltz time, he took to the concept immediately" (1986:33). Whether by coincidence or design, in August, *Melody Maker* printed a letter entitled "Waltzes wanted" from a "Chas A J Wild" asking, in not dissimilar terms from Feather's 1933 letter, "When will firms publish a few waltz numbers?" (29 August 1936:10). Carter's record was announced on the front page of the next issue under the heading "Hot Waltzes! Benny Carter Starts Something." Before most readers would have been able to hear the record, the article suggested that "it may cause considerable controversy among dancers," continuing, "Whether it will lead to further recordings of hot waltzes, or result in bands attempting them in ballrooms, is a much more open question than whether this record will cause an argument" (5 September 1936:1). It is important to bear in mind that "Waltzing the Blues" consists of a relatively straightforward succession of solo choruses over a twenty-four-bar blues progression in 3/4 time. Nevertheless, the idea of fusing an established European dance form with modern, "hot," American blues, encapsulated clearly in the title, was always likely to generate interest. Although Feather stated retrospectively that he had not intended to trigger a controversy with "Waltzing the Blues," the coverage of the release suggests that there may have been attempts to exploit the concept as an opportunity for publicity (1986:34).

Rather like the discourse surrounding Gershwin's *Rhapsody in Blue* in Britain in the 1920s, which was perceived to have mediated between highbrow (classical) and lowbrow (jazz), "Waltzing the Blues" provided the backdrop against which current debates on popular music could be played out (Parsonage, 2005:50ff.). In the 1930s, *Melody Maker* and *Rhythm* each had separate critics to review hot jazz and dance music records. In the case of "Waltzing the Blues," *Melody Maker* grouped four assessments together in a single feature, thereby highlighting that the piece could not be categorized easily in these terms. For the hot record critics, who fundamentally adhered to the idea of jazz as a progressive art form, "Waltzing the Blues" seemed to represent a new way forward for jazz and, in particular, offered insight into the nature of swing, the current preoccupation: "What the record really proves to me is that a larger proportion than I realised of the character of swing music is indebted to melodic rather than rhythmic invention." The commercial critics agreed, finding it inadequate as a dance record but assessing it as "one of the most agreeable records ever produced" "from the listening angle" and a "fine example of classy jazz" (*Melody Maker*, 12 September 1936:6–7). However, in the following weeks these initial opinions were reversed, as the idea was found to be not as novel as it had first appeared, and it was considered possible to dance to it after all: "All this business about waltzing the blues isn't so new as it sounds. . . . [About ten years ago] the dancing teachers were interested in the waltzing-the-blues idea, and if I remember rightly they soon fitted a sequence of steps to it and demonstrated the dance at their annual fiesta" (*Melody Maker*, 19 September 1936:10).

Hughes similarly pointed out that it was perfectly possible to waltz to "Waltzing the Blues," but that fundamentally "blues in 3/4 doesn't SWING!" (1936b:5). For Hughes and others, the whole idea of the waltz-blues fusion was profoundly unsatisfactory:

"You can, if you like, graft the melodic line of the blues on to the rhythm of the waltz. But the result is about as beautiful as the cross between a horse and a donkey known as the mule. Mules, you must remember, are sterile and barren (according to sex). Waltzing the Blues is an idea that has a much prospect of posterity as a mule" (Hughes, 1936b:5).

"On the whole, I think that my objection to this record is based on the unnaturalness of the crossbreeding. Waltz swing is one thing; Jazz swing is another. They are like sister and brother to each other. Individually they are both healthy forms of expression, but their marriage must be unhealthy" (Ballard and Hibbs, 1936:92).

"The fact of the matter is that I heartily disapprove of both Waltzing the Blues and Tiger Rag. The former I find affected, 'clever' in the most odious sense of the term, and utterly lacking in motion or warmth. In monkeying with the structure of the blues, Benny robbed them of all form and directness. After all, the blues is essentially simple folk music, far too pure for defilement at the hands of sophisticates" (Hammond, 1936:13).

At the very least, the record appears to be a deliberate attempt to achieve sales by referencing popular trends. In the issue of *Melody Maker* in which the record was reviewed, a representative from the publisher Francis, Day and Hunter responded to Chas A J Wild's letter, noting that although bandleaders preferred "hot rhythm numbers," the waltz remained popular with the public and was coming back strongly into favor in America (5 September 1936:8). In the world of dance, the introduction of swing and associated dance had provoked the development of strict-tempo dance music to which it was easy to dance standardized steps. But at the same time, the *Dancing Times* continued to recommend a range of new releases for dancers, including some of Carter's Vocalion sides. In November 1936, Alex Moore wrote that "Waltzing the Blues" had a "very interesting rhythm" (Moore, 1936:253). In the same issue of the magazine, Victor Silvester contributed an article on "New Variations in the Waltz," describing "some of the more popular variations which have come into vogue" (Silvester, 1936b:162). Previously, at the time when test pressings of "Waltzing the Blues" were circulating, Silvester had written more extensively on "The New Viennese Waltz": "Owing to the increasing number of quick Waltzes which are played in the majority of ballrooms to-day, the Ballroom Committee of the Imperial Society of Teachers of Dancing thought that the time had arrived for something to be done about it" (Silvester, 1936a:600). Silvester's article indicates the existence of a recent innovation in waltz dancing in response to quicker tempi, yet there was a need for guidance as "ninety-nine people out of a hundred do the steps which have come to be known as the Old-fashioned Waltz." He then provides details of steps for which "the ideal tempo is 56 bars per minute, but all the figures described below can be adapted to any Waltz that is played at a tempo that is quicker than 44 bars per minute." Moore's recommendation of "Waltzing the Blues" indicates that the tempo is 46 bars per minute, thereby aligning it with a contemporary trend in popular dance.

With the possible commercial motives behind the record in mind, the B-side of "Waltzing the Blues," the New Orleans standard "Tiger Rag," is also worthy of consideration. The choice of this number provides an additional link with the circumstances of Feather's original letter. In addition, it references the Original Dixieland Jazz Band, which had played a leading role in popularizing jazz in Britain during their visit in 1919-20. The ODJB had reformed in autumn 1936 and rerecorded some of their best-known numbers, including "Tiger Rag." The timing of the release of Carter's version, recorded in June, may have been a happy coincidence. However, Henry Hall had asked Carter to prepare an arrangement of this piece for the BBC Dance Orchestra over the summer, and likewise the British dance band leader Jack Hylton recorded a version in August, suggesting that there may have been some knowledge of the reunion.

Conclusion

Despite the concession of allowing Carter to give a public concert, the governmental restrictions on American musicians remained firmly in place, and in March 1937 Carter left England to take up residence in Holland, just as Hawkins had done in 1935: "The Ministry of Labour, unbending in its attitude against granting permits to Americans to play in this country, has denied him several opportunities of forming and directing a British band for stage work—so he has packed his bags and sadly left us. The responsibility belongs to President Weber, of the American Federation of Musicians, who refuses all reciprocity with England" (*Melody Maker*, 20 March 1937:1). Notably, Carter recorded in Paris with Hawkins, Django Reinhardt, and Stéphane Grappelli just over a month later.

This article makes an explicit link between Carter's departure and the restrictions that had profoundly influenced his activities throughout his time in Britain. Indeed, there is a sense that Carter's visit had been used to explore the boundaries and strength of the recently introduced regulations. Even before Carter arrived, *Melody Maker* reported that "Benny Carter May Become Orchestrator to Henry Hall" only if the application for a work permit was successful, which may have been intended to put pressure upon the authorities (22 February 1936:1).

Feather had ensured that Carter's arranging and recording work was as high profile as possible, which allowed him and others to constantly highlight the lack of opportunities for Carter to perform. This was expressed initially as optimism, then longing, and finally exasperation:

"It is to be hoped that we shall have a chance to hear him on reeds and trumpet" (*Melody Maker*, 21 March 1936:11).

"If only Benny had been able to play himself" (*Melody Maker*, 11 April 1936:5).

"Naturally, what the [BBC] band is really waiting for is the day when Benny will be able to take part himself in playing these arrangements. He is known equally well as an alto saxophonist, trumpet player, and clarinettist, but at present has no permit to do permanent work as an instrumentalist" (Feather, 1936a:13).

"When Benny gets back to London next week, someone should really fix him up with an English broadcast of this sort [a performance with Kai Ewans's Orchestra had been broadcast on Danish radio]. It's disgraceful that two weeks in Copenhagen should have yielded more radio work for him than five months in London, though this is certainly not due to any lack of effort on Henry Hall's part" (*Melody Maker*, 26 September 1936:6).

Despite this, Carter's visit had a more profound influence on British musicians than if he had been part of a discrete performing unit. The importance of this was recognized from the outset by contemporary commentators, who, whether discussing Carter's work with the BBC, in the recording studio, concert hall, Rhythm Clubs, or nightclubs, cast him as an educator of British musicians:

"The longer Benny stays here, the better it will be for British dance music" (*Melody Maker*, 11 April 1936:5).

"[His first Vocalion recordings] proved to be a revelation of what can be achieved by a British band under inspired guidance" (*Melody Maker*, 25 April 1936:11).

Similarly, Feather identified retrospectively that "the dual importance of Carter's presence, for me, was that I learned more about music from him, quite informally, than I had from any other musician, and that, assigned to supervise his recordings, I enjoyed my baptism as an A&R man (known nowadays by the more pretentious title of producer)" (1986:33).

Feather's personal investment and influence upon Carter's visit as a way of critiquing government policy and yet at the same time developing British jazz should not be underestimated. If there was no flexibility in the regulations that restricted the visits of American jazz musicians (jazz in Britain), then the future of jazz in Britain would have to lie with British musicians (British jazz). Feather used Carter to fundamentally influence the output of British broadcasting and recording industries by working directly with the musicians themselves, thus trying to ensure that change would be more likely to be sustainable in the long term.

Carter returned to London in May to recruit several British musicians for his band at the Scheveningen Palais de Danse, creating what Feather termed "the first interracial and international jazz orchestra." Feather continued his involvement, producing two recording sessions with the band in Holland, the second of which incorporated Coleman Hawkins (Feather, 1986:35). After Carter finally returned to New York in May 1938, Feather recorded jazz versions of British folk songs in London, which represented a clear articulation of a British jazz aesthetic, but recalled that these had little impact. Ultimately, having tried to advance both jazz in Britain and British jazz through his work with Carter, with some success, it had become clear to Feather "that Britain was a musical blind alley and America represented the only way out" (1986:38). He took up permanent residence in 1939 and eventually became an American citizen.

NOTES

1. In this capacity Hammond had brought Carter to the attention of British jazz fans as early as 1932 (see Hammond 1932:631).

2. The bbc was the British Broadcasting *Company* until 1927.

3. R. H. Eckersley, bbcwac R19/585/1 Entertainment: Jazz 1933–1946, File 1, 7 December 1933.

4. The clubs were numbered in order of their foundation; No. 1 met in the West End of London. Carter is also known to have performed at Rhythm Clubs in South London, Brighton, and twice at Southend-on-Sea (both on the south coast) (Rye, 1981a).

5. One of these sessions, in June 1936, was specifically for the purpose of backing Elisabeth Welch.

BIBLIOGRAPHY

BBC Written Archives Centre; Contributors 910 Hall, Henry; File 1a 1931–33, File II 1936–39.

BBC Written Archives Centre; R29/13 Orch. Gen. BBC Dance Orchestra, 1932–33.

BBC Written Archives Centre; R19/585/1 Entertainment: Jazz 1933–46, File 1.

National Archives, the MEPO 2/4494, "Shim Sham or Rainbow Roof Unregistered Clubs: Bottle Parties and Sale of Liquor out of Hours 1935–1938."

Ballard, Eric A. C., and Leonard Hibbs. 1936. "Some Recent Records Reviewed." *Swing Music*, Autumn 1936, pp. 90–92.

Berger, Morroe, Edward Berger, and James Patrick. 2002. *Benny Carter: A Life in American Music*, vol. 1. Lanham, MD: Scarecrow.

Carter, Benny. 1936. "My Nine Lives Alto Soprano Composer Tenor Clarinet Trumpet Arranger Vocalist Piano." *Swing Music*, February/March 1936, pp. 55, 71.

Dance, Stanley. 2001. *The World of Swing: An Oral History of Big Band Jazz.* Da Capo.

Feather, Leonard. 1936a. "Tempo di Jazz." *Radio Times*, 24 April 1936, p. 13.

———. 1936b. "Bennett L. Carter Esq.: An Answer to the Fan's Craving for 'The Inside Stuff.'" *Melody Maker*, 31 October 1936, p. 2.

———. 1937. "1600 Fans' Night Out—Leonard Feather Analyses the BC Concert and Gives Full Marks to Benny, His Men and the Audience." *Melody Maker*, 16 January 1937, p. 11.

———. 1951. *Down Beat*, 18 May 1951, p. 18.

———. 1976. *The Pleasures of Jass.* Horizon.

———. 1986. *The Jazz Years: Earwitness to an Era.* Quartet Books.

Hall, Henry. 1955. *Here's to the Next Time.* London, Odhams Press.

Hammond, John. 1932. "Benny Carter, London Bound." *Melody Maker*, August 1932, p. 631

Hammond, John. 1936. "Tampering with the Blues." *Rhythm*, November 1936, p. 13.

Hughes, Spike [as "Mike"]. 1936a. "The Admirable Amalgamation of Henry Hall and Benny Carter: Hot Records Reviewed." *Melody Maker*, 2 May 1936, pp. 7, 6.

———. 1936b. "What's It All About?—Demands Mike, Back from Holiday and Confronted with Benny Carter's Disc of 'Waltzing the Blues.'" *Melody Maker*, 3 October 1936, p. 5.

———. [Spike]. 1951. *Second Movement—Continuing an Autobiography.* London: Museum Press.

Moore, Alex. 1936. "Records for Dancers." *Dancing Times*, November 1936, pp. 251-53.

Parsonage, Catherine. 2005. *The Evolution of Jazz in Britain, 1880-1935.* Aldershot: Ashgate.

Rye, Howard. 1981a. "Visiting Firemen 4: Benny Carter." *Storyville* 93, February/March 1981, pp. 84-87.

———. 1981b. "Visiting Firemen 5: Coleman Hawkins." *Storyville* 97, October/November 1981, pp. 14-25.

———. 2011a. "Rodgers, Gene." *The New Grove Dictionary of Jazz*, 2nd ed., ed. Barry Kernfeld. Grove Music Online. Oxford Music Online, www.oxfordmusiconline.com (accessed February 1, 2011).

———. 2011b. "Vocalion (ii)." *The New Grove Dictionary of Jazz*, 2nd ed., ed. Barry Kernfeld. Grove Music Online. Oxford Music Online, www.oxfordmusiconline.com (accessed January 31, 2011).

Silvester, Victor. 1936a. "The New Viennese Waltz." *Dancing Times*, September 1936, pp. 600-603.

———. 1936b. "New Variations in the Waltz." *Dancing Times*, November 1936, pp. 162-63.

Melody Maker

"Larger Band, Greater Shows," 4 January 1936, p. 1.

"Benny Carter May Become Orchestrator to Henry Hall," 22 February 1936, p. 1.

"BBC Explodes Its Dance Music Reforms: Damp Squib Disclosures," 7 March 1936, pp. 1, 9.

"Half-hearted Radio Reforms," 7 March 1936, p. 8.

"Benny Carter at Last Here," 21 March 1936, p. 11.

"Benny Carter into His Stride," 4 April 1936, p. 1.

"Benny Carter Makes His BBC Bow," 11 April 1936, p. 5.

"Rhythm Club News," 11 April 1936, p. 10.

"Rhythm Club News," 25 April 1936, p. 11.

"Benny Carter—Tenor Sax!" 18 April 1936, p. 1.

"Benny Goodman's 'Commercial,'" 16 May 1936, p. 4.

"News from the Rhythm Clubs," 16 May 1936, p. 10.

"Letters," 29 August 1936, p. 10.

"Hot Waltzes! Benny Carter Starts Something," 5 September 1936, p. 1.

"Letters," 5 September 1936, p. 8.

"Benny Carter's Hot Waltz Record," 12 September 1936, pp. 6, 7.

"The Busker Gossips," 19 September 1936, p. 10.

"Benny Carter's Broadcasts as Piano Soloist: BBC Misses a Chance Which Dutch
    Station Takes," 26 September 1936, p. 6.

"Carter's Radio Waltz," 17 October 1936, p. 14.

"Sunday Swing-Music Concert for 'M.M' Readers—Benny Carter to Direct All British
    Star Combination." 14 November 1936, p. 1.

"All about the Historic Swing Concert," 16 January 1937, p. 1.

"No Scope Here for Benny Carter! He Leaves London for Holland," 20 March 1937, p. 1.

Rhythm
"Benny Carter's British Band," June 1936, pp. 26-27.

Discography
Benny Carter in Chronology, 1933-1936, Chronological Classics Complete Jazz Series
    530.
Benny Carter in Chronology, 1936, Chronological Classics Complete Jazz Series 541.
Benny Carter in Chronology, 1937-1939, Chronological Classics Complete Jazz Series
    552.
Leonard Feather in Chronology, 1937-1945, Chronological Classics Complete Jazz Series
    901.

9 / "A NEW REASON FOR LIVING"
DUKE ELLINGTON IN FRANCE

n the long and storied career of Duke Ellington, who was born in 1899 and died in 1974, no nation save his own played as significant role as did France. Ellington enjoyed a long and rich association with France, especially its City of Light, spanning forty years. He performed in Paris and twenty-six other French cities, playing nearly one hundred concerts, as well as making radio, television, and film appearances.

During his band's three-year residency at Harlem's Cotton Club, from late 1927 to early 1931, Ellington honed his compositional abilities and showmanship and achieved international attention through recordings and radio broadcasts. In February 1931, he embarked upon nearly ceaseless touring for the rest of his life. Despite the hectic pace, he nearly always found time to compose every day, even if just a few measures on the back of an envelope. (A testament to his productivity is the trove of 100,000 pages of unpublished music that he composed for his orchestra, now preserved at the Smithsonian Institution's National Museum of American History.) By the early 1930s, he had developed a singular compositional style, by creating his own harmonic rules and eliciting unusual tone colors from the distinctive voices of his gifted instrumentalists such as trumpeter Cootie Williams, alto saxophonist Johnny Hodges, and trombonist Joe "Tricky Sam" Nanton. As a result of his originality and his players' individuality, his band sounded unlike any other.

France had proved hospitable to jazz beginning in early 1918, when U.S. Army lieutenant James Reese Europe's band took the country by storm.[1] In 1918 or 1919, the American drummer Louis Mitchell took his band to Paris and remained there for a decade; in 1922 his became the first black jazz band to record in Europe. Jazz was, as John Szwed put it, "'the shock to the system the French had been waiting for': modern, energetic, exotic."[2] The clarinetist/saxophonist Sidney Bechet had performed in Europe in 1919, and lived and performed in France during the latter 1920s. But visits from top-tier American jazz musicians to Europe were rare.

Ellington's first appearance in France was in 1933, during the lowest point in the Great Depression. Ellington's manager, Irving Mills, always seeking new opportunities for his artists—Ellington, Cab Calloway, Mills's Blue Rhythm Band, the Mills Brothers—traveled to Europe in November 1932.[3] The result was a European tour by the Ellington orchestra in the summer of 1933, sponsored by the British bandleader Jack Hylton. The dancer Bessie Dudley, best known for the shake, was part of the act. The Ellingtonians left New York on the SS *Olympic* on June 2, arrived in Southampton on June 9, and embarked upon a fifty-five-day tour of Great Britain, Holland, and France.[4]

After a triumphant tour[5] of England, the band left Britain on July 24, 1933, for a short tour of the continent. Ellington had been scheduled to play a week at the Rex, a deluxe movie theater in Paris, but when management resisted and then refused to pay the $6,000 fee that Mills asked, the engagement fell through. Nevertheless, Ellington's orchestra triumphed in three concerts in Paris at the 3,000-seat Salle Pleyel, on its way to becoming the leading concert hall in Paris, on July 27 and 29 and August 1, 1933. The audience, as one writer commented, included "young girls with platinum wigs, adolescents with shiny, plastered hair. . . . Some wore only a sleeveless shirt and golf pants. Africans with ebony faces. Dancers form fashionable cabarets. Movie stars. Artists from the extreme edge of the avant-garde. And above all the socialites with a passion for Americanism drunk with negromania."[6] Ellington wowed the audience. "It was perhaps the most riotous scene of joy ever witnessed within the four walls of this building," exclaimed the African American writer J. A. Rogers in the New York City newspaper the *Amsterdam News*.[7] Rogers asserted that "apart from the waltz and tango, the European orchestras cannot play good dance music—that is, the jazzy, peppy kind. They simply haven't got the feeling for it. The Duke Ellington concerts . . . have shown that the European public is . . . eager for properly played jazz."[8]

The twenty-one-year-old writer and co-founder of the Hot Club of France, Hugues Panassié, had met Ellington's band at the train station, and anxiously asked Ellington if the bandleader would be allowed to play "as he wished or if any 'commercial' concessions had been imposed on him" by Hylton. "Duke replied that he would play as he intended."[9] At the first two concerts, Panassié was struck by how much better the band sounded in person than on record and the variety of Ellington's arrangements.

What struck me strongly was the discovery that the arrangements themselves sometimes differed from those used on the records. I understood that some had been done over, improved, enriched over the years by new ideas that came to Duke or his men. For others, I realized with astonishment at the second concert, several quite different arrangements existed which Duke used alternatively—sometimes one, sometimes another. Thus the *Mood Indigo* of the first concert scarcely resembled that of the second, where the melody was stated *pianissimo* by an extraordinary brass sextet.[10]

"Each of the musicians, noted Panassié, "carried himself onstage in a quite different manner, according to his temperament. . . . Among the brass, [trom-

190

bonist] Tricky Sam [Nanton] and [trumpeter] Cootie [Williams] made a real show."[11] The first half of the evening was a musical concert, evidently focused on the band's instrumental numbers, and the second half included several black dancers, notably Bill Bailey, and "the singer and 'comedienne' Ivie Anderson." Panassié bemoaned the audience's laughter during Nanton's and Williams's solos—very possibly the laughter was in response to then-novel wah-wah and other effects created by the brass players' creative use of mutes.[12]

After the second evening's concert, the band repaired to Bricktop's, a cabaret in the Rue Pigalle, to hear a local band. Alto saxophonist Johnny Hodges and other Ellington musicians wanted to jam, but were deterred by tour organizer Jack Hylton, who insisted the band members play only in the concert venue or face a fifty-dollar fine.[13]

In Paris, Ellington's band members were startled at how seriously their European fans treated their music—memorizing solos from records that the players themselves had forgotten. "This was respect and knowledge of a kind they seldom encountered at home," Mercer Ellington, Duke's son, wrote later, "at least from white folks. The affection and admiration they received more than balanced whatever prejudice and surviving ignorance on racial matters that they met."[14]

Ellington's concerts generated considerable verbiage from Parisian critics and became a kind of test case for those arguing about categorizing jazz musicians as either "hot" or "straight." Some felt that Louis Armstrong was a genuine "hot" player and doubted Ellington was. His concerts prompted writers to complain about "*snobbisme du hot*" of some critics and fans, to argue about true French music vs. true *musique nègre*, and to debate other such issues of interest primarily to intellectuals.[15] If Ellington was aware of any of these controversies, his thoughts went undocumented.

What was the significance of this tour? Ellington had proven himself in the world's centers of cosmopolitan culture. During this tour, Ellington's music and, as Mercer Ellington has written, his "composure, wit, and innate dignity had 'commanded respect'—to use a phrase he always liked—in the two most sophisticated capitals of the world, London and Paris."[16] Despite some negative reactions, he was now hailed by some as "probably the first composer of real character to come out of America."[17]

The tour had several effects on Ellington, one fundamentally commercial, the other more substantive. The orchestra's smashing success was seized on by Mills and his staff in their subsequent publicizing of Ellington—now they called him "internationally famous"—and no doubt increased Ellington's commercial viability and public stature. Ellington recalled, "The entire first European tour in 1933 was tremendous uplift for all our spirits."[18] Like his men, Ellington returned from Europe more seasoned and somewhat changed. "The main thing I got in Europe was *spirit*," he said. "That kind of thing gives you courage to go on. If they think I'm *that* important, then maybe I have kinda said something, maybe our music does mean something."[19]

But it wasn't just the adulation he received, it was the way his music and performances were treated. In the United States, Ellington was booked to play dances, stage shows, and theatrical performances—almost never concerts. But this European tour was different—primarily stage shows and concerts. The experience stimulated his ambitions in his career as a serious composer. In 1935, he would tell interviewer Frank Marshall Davis, "A musician should have both Europe and America."[20] "These United States are better for dance stuff," Davis wrote, "but for concerts he'll take the other side of the Atlantic. It seems Europeans, because of a different cultural background, have a general understanding and appreciation of art not found on these shores."[21] Put simply, the bandleader in Ellington liked America, while the composer in him preferred Europe.

Before Ellington and longtime manager Irving Mills parted company in 1939, Mills arranged a return to Europe for the orchestra, and the maestro, who had long wanted to replay the continent, went along with the plans. Mills arranged with the Reuter & Reuter agency of London and A & M Dandelot in Paris a thirty-four-day tour consisting of twenty-eight concerts, each booked at $1,000.[22]

The threat of war was everywhere by 1939; no one knew what would come next. The band left amid not only war jitters but controversy in the press about the British musicians' union's ban that prevented American musicians from performing in the United Kingdom. The orchestra set sail from New York on March 23, on the French ocean liner *Champlain*, with Ellington, thirteen instrumentalists, and singer Ivie Anderson. When the party landed in Le Havre seven days later, according to *Down Beat* magazine, "hundreds of jitterbugs stomped and shouted at the dock."[23] Cornetist Rex Stewart recalled the scene and feeling: "There were a lot of people from all over France to meet us, members of the various 'hot clubs,' both fans and musicians, who all greeted us with such absolute adoration and genuine joy that for the first time in my life I had the feeling of being accepted as an artist, a gentleman and a member of the human race."[24]

Upon arriving in Paris, the band was met at the train station by a "big contingent of jazz buffs and oh, so many pretty girls," Stewart recalled. "For the first time in my life I realized the tremendous scope of this music and the general acceptance throughout the world from a cultural standpoint."[25] Again in Europe, Ellington and the orchestra were taken seriously as artists. The most significant aspect of his 1939 tour was that it gave Ellington a chance to perform almost exclusively for listeners. With the exception of one stage show, these were *concerts*—his most extensive concert circuit since his first European tour of 1933.

After holding a press conference in Paris, the orchestra played two concerts to packed houses at the new Théâtre National de Chaillot, one of the largest concert halls in Paris. As were Ellington's 1933 concerts at the Salle Pleyel, these performances, outside the normal circuit of music hall and nightclubs, were seen as confirmation that jazz deserved to be treated as a serious art.[26] Because Ellington was not going to be able to perform in England, a number of his British fans went to Paris, and both concerts were sold out.[27]

At each session the musicians performed about thirty-eight numbers, according to press reports, for 2,800 enthusiastic listeners. "We were accorded an uproarious reception," Ellington wrote, "and were forced to play innumerable encores."[28] The reviews were glowing. The Paris newspaper *Le Figaro* marveled: "By what orchestral imagination does one arrive at strange fluted sound effects, atmospheric vibrations with powerful humor!"[29] *Variety*'s Paris correspondent reported that Ellington and his orchestra "wowed the Parisians."[30] Ellington was feted by musicians and nightclub proprietors alike. His music was hailed by Jacques-Henry Lévesque, a Paris critic, as "related to the rhythm of the atom" and as revealing "the very secret of the cosmos."[31] The poet Blaise Cendrars was ecstatic: "Such music is not only a new art form but a new reason for living."[32] When Ellington moved on, he left a lasting legacy in Paris: thousands of old and new fans and greater interest in his recordings.

While in Paris, Ellington's cornetist led a small-group recording session, as Rex Stewart and his Feetwarmers, for Swing Records.[33] The quartet consisted of Stewart, Ellington's clarinetist Barney Bigard, Ellington's bassist Billy Taylor, and the great Gypsy guitarist Django Reinhardt. They recorded five tunes: "Montmartre," "Low Cotton," "Finesse," "I Know That You Know," and "Solid Old Man."[34] In his book *The Swing Era*, Gunther Schuller waxes rhapsodic about this group of sides, calling them "among the all-time gems of small group jazz, virtually in a class by itself . . . masterpieces of chamber jazz . . . amongst the finest achievements of jazz."[35] "They are gemstones of jazz that should be heard by every appreciator of good music—of whatever ideological persuasion."[36]

Ellington had several encounters with Reinhardt, who would, in later years, tour the United States with the maestro. When the Hot Club of Paris opened a new headquarters, Reinhardt was one of the performers, and in the audience were Ellington and his manager, Irving Mills. Reinhardt was hoping that Mills would book him for a U.S. tour, but nothing came of the contact.[37] One evening, Ellington went to hear Reinhardt's quintet perform at a tiny cabaret, and was invited to join in. He "sat in" with the band for fifteen minutes, an event that, in the words of Reinhardt biographer Michael Dregni, "quickly entered the rich annals of the quintet's folklore."[38]

"After our very successful European jaunt," recalled Rex Stewart, "the band started hitting on all cylinders like a wonderful musical juggernaut."[39] Indeed, many experts consider the next three years or so the peak of Ellington's entire musical career: he hired the powerhouse tenor saxophonist Ben Webster and the virtuosic bassist Jimmie Blanton, who helped the band develop new facets and facility; hired Billy Strayhorn, who quickly proved his value as a composer-arranger; and switched to Victor Records, which gave him, for the first time, the freedom to record the material he chose. The band, blessed with considerable stability of personnel and buoyed by its European accolades, would make one masterwork recording after another.

The World War II years created serious problems for American bands, including Ellington's: difficulty in touring, challenges in making recordings due to a 1942–44 ban by the U.S. musicians' union, and turnover of personnel. The war negated any possibility of Ellington performing on the continent, and made his records more difficult to secure overseas. His admirers in France would have to wait nine years between his last visit and his next. In 1947, cornetist Rex Stewart, having left Ellington, found upon visiting Paris that the French "had been craving our music all during the long war. Incidentally, next to nylon hose the most valued export which was sneaked past the German noses was American jazz discs."[40]

In 1948, the American musicians' union dictated another ban on making records, which would last all year. Then, when the strike was over, Ellington's record label, Columbia, in no hurry because pop singers now dominated the record market, took another eight months before returning him to the studio. Thus Ellington was out of commercial recording studios until September 1949—an unprecedented period of twenty months. During his hiatus, Ellington accepted an offer to return to scenes of triumph and to tour Europe—England, Paris, Antwerp, Brussels, Geneva, and Zurich—for six weeks in June and July 1948. The British musicians' union refused to allow his band to join him, so he took only the quadruple-threat Ray Nance and the coloratura soprano Kay Davis, and they played as a "variety" act. Nance was a sensation, for he played trumpet and violin, sang, danced, and clowned, and stole the show at each performance. The band was accompanied by a trio of British musicians on guitar, bass, and drums.

At the Salle Pleyel, the audience was expecting Ellington's full orchestra, and when the curtain went up, reported Ernest Borneman, gave "a great gasp of disappointment at finding a trio on the stage. But within 20 minutes, Duke has captured them."[41] Borneman continued:

> Building on the mood he has established, he brings out Nance for two comedy numbers, *Squeeze Me, but Don't Tease Me* and *Just A-Settin' and A-Rockin'*, both of them brilliantly done by one of the great comedians of our day. With the audience screaming for more, Duke goes into the last number on the program, *Take the A-Train*, and leaves the stage.

There is so much of an uproar that the curtain is up again, within seconds, and with carefully calculated showmanship, Duke gives them a whole third act of five numbers, some of the best in the program—*Mood Indigo, C-Jam Blues, Body and Soul* (with Ray's extraordinary stomach ache parody of the bop vocalists), *Turnip or Tulip*, and *Honeysuckle Rose*—a most generous series of encores.[42]

Even without his regular band, Ellington was energized by his return to Europe. "I wanted to get back to Europe for a while," he told Borneman. "It's good for the morale. It gives you the kind of adjustment of mind you need in this business. Over there [in the United States] you get too used to the *Hit Parade*. You know it means nothing, and yet after a while, you start paying attention. That's bad for your music."[43]

The late 1940s were difficult for Ellington, who was facing a decline in the ballroom and nightclub business for big bands, falling sales of jazz records generally (complicated by a confusing war of phonograph record speeds, when consumers faced three different formats—33⅓ rpm, 45 rpm, and 78 rpm), reduced recording opportunities for himself, resulting financial pressures, and continued problems with the stability of his personnel. In the midst of these tough times, Ellington took action. With his entire band, he returned to the fans who had earlier rejuvenated him and undertook the first European trip for the whole orchestra in eleven years. After arriving at Le Havre on April 4, 1950, the Ellington orchestra played seventy-four concerts in seventy-seven days in France, Belgium, Holland, Switzerland, Italy, Denmark, Sweden, and West Germany, returning to the United States on June 30.

Ellington was booked to give five concerts at Paris's Théâtre National du Palais de Chaillot. The promoter, Jules Borkon, issued a handsome program booklet. But there was trouble at the opening concert—the audience was unhappy with the selection of pieces. The Paris concert, according to *Der Spiegel*, was a "sensational disaster" during which the band was almost booed off the stage.[44] *Melody Maker* magazine reported the audience "almost gave vocalist Kay Davis 'the bird.' After 'Lush Life,' interrupted by shouts and whistles, she ran off the stage.... The audience wanted more of the old Ellington jazz."[45] Except for "Creole Love Call," which dated from 1928, evidently Ellington's entire repertory was his recent material. Since he and his orchestra had not performed in Paris for eleven years, there was a time lag, and his fans were not ready for the *new* Ellington—they wanted the old, familiar Ellington. According to some people who attended these concerts, "it was mainly members of the Hot Club de France who created the uproar. They were very organized and liked to do that sort of thing in concerts even with jazzmen they liked if they didn't play exactly what they wanted to hear."[46]

A letter from the concert promoter, found in the Duke Ellington Collection at the Smithsonian Institution's National Museum of American History, sheds light on the matter. Borkon complained that Ellington's road manager Al Celley refused to allow enough light onstage so the audience could properly see. Borkon saw it as a psychological mistake not to cut short Kay Davis's song when the public showed its dissatisfaction. "We should never allow ourselves to go against the public's whishes [*sic*] as it is the thing of greatest importance. The audience was dissatified [*sic*] as well because the programme was too short." Borkon complained "This experience is going to cost me too much. . . . The unfortunate evening of yesterday was not my fault at all."[47] This letter is one of the very few truly negative documents in the entire 200,000 pages that make up the Duke Ellington Collection; considering that Ellington liked to project a very positive public image, its survival is surprising.

Though not all the audiences were happy with Ellington's selection of tunes, the concert tour (as in 1933 and 1939) gave him inspiration, and now, on the return voyage, he wrote an important fourteen-minute work, which had been commissioned by Arturo Toscanini for the NBC Symphony Orchestra (though never performed by them) and which came to be called *Harlem*.

Ellington weathered difficult seas in the early 1950s: his leading player, Johnny Hodges, bolted the band in March 1951, taking with him several other top musicians—trombonist Lawrence Brown and drummer Sonny Greer; altogether the three had seventy years with the band. Ellington bided his time until Hodges returned to the fold in 1955; then the maestro led his band into a big comeback after a sensational performance at the 1956 Newport Jazz Festival, which coincided with *Time* magazine's placement of Ellington on its front cover. From 1956 to the end of his life would mark the second great arc of his career, as he and collaborator Billy Strayhorn increasingly wrote extended works—"suites" they called them—that took full advantage of the longer playing time of the long-playing record. During this period when rock 'n' roll had siphoned off most young listeners, Ellington increasingly turned abroad for bookings.

In October and November 1958, the Ellington orchestra returned to Europe for nearly fifty days of concerts in thirty cities in England, Scotland, France, Belgium, Holland, Sweden, Norway, Denmark, Germany, Austria, Switzerland, and Italy. The concerts were critically well received.[48] The second of two concerts on October 29 at the Alhambra theater in Paris was recorded by Radio Europe and issued on record and later on CD.[49] The band returned to Europe for a five-week tour, including, in September 1959, three concerts in Paris.[50]

In 1960, Ellington received a film commission, to write the music for the United Artists production *Paris Blues*. Filmed in the City of Light at the Studios de Boulogne, this motion picture starred Paul Newman and Sidney Poitier as expatriate American jazzmen, Joanne Woodward and Diahann Carroll as their girlfriends, and Louis Armstrong in a cameo appearance as trumpeter "Wild Man" Moore.[51] For *Paris Blues*, Ellington composed in Hollywood during November and December 1960, then flew to Paris for three weeks, during which he composed and performed a little while the band had a holiday.[52] The score that he and Strayhorn created incorporated several evergreens—"Mood Indigo," "Take the 'A' Train," "Sophisticated Lady," and a new version of "Unclothed Woman"—as well as a number of new tunes: "Amour Gypsy," "Autumnal Suite," "Big Bash," "Nite," "Paris Stairs," "Battle Royal," "Wild Man Moore,"[53] and the title tune "Paris Blues." The score was recorded by three different ensembles: a group of studio musicians in California, a mix of American expats and French musicians in Paris, "and some final material by a studio band including current Ellingtonians and alumni in New York."[54]

Though the jazz press found the movie's story disappointing, it applauded Ellington's music, especially the underscore of background music, which was nominated for an Academy Award.

Recalling his stint in Paris, Ellington later wrote, "It was the closest thing to a vacation I'd ever been able to think about."[55] He enjoyed his time in Paris in part because he was feted at parties, given by notables such as actors Newman and Woodward, the record and film producer Eddie Barclay, and the French composer Georges Auric. And Ellington socialized with actress Ingrid Bergman, author James Jones, singer-actor Yves Montand, poet-screenwriter Jacques Prévert, and other luminaries.[56] While in Paris, Ellington was invited to perform at a midnight Mass, and played *Come Sunday*, presaging by four years the major composition he would write, *Concert of Sacred Music*. *Paris Match* publicized the visit, in December, of Ellington and Armstrong with a large photo, spread over two pages, showing the pair waving from the balcony of their hotel to a band of musicians jamming in the street, and a crowd of well-wishers that included butchers, creamers, and other working people—seeming to testify to the two musicians' popularity among ordinary Parisians.[57]

While in Paris, Ellington was commissioned to compose a musical score for a revival by the Théâtre National Populaire of *Turcaret*, a comedy by Alain-René Lesage from 1709. The score consisted of interludes, mostly briefer than thirty seconds, heard between the dialogue, recorded by a band under Ellington's direction and reproduced during the play by a tape recorder. According to the *New York Times*, "Ellington composed it after reading hurriedly through a translation of the play."[58] *Paris Blues* and *Turcaret* were among the very few times that Ellington composed for an ensemble other than his own orchestra.

"I enjoyed writing the music for *Paris Blues*," he said in 1961. "I still keep writing and think I must be just about getting my second wind. Have written more in the last two years than for ten years previously."[59] In fact, Ellington and Strayhorn were in the midst of a composing streak that yielded, in addition to *Paris Blues*, such extended works as *Toot Suite* (1958); *Idiom '59*, *The Queen's Suite*, the film score *Anatomy of a Murder*, new music for *Jump for Joy* (all 1959); *Suite Thursday*, and reimaginings of Tchaikovsky's *Nutcracker Suite* and Grieg's *Peer Gynt Suite* (all 1960).

In March 18, 1961, Paris was treated to a rare concert by six Ellingtonians (without Ellington): alto saxophonist Johnny Hodges, trumpeter Ray Nance, baritone saxophonist Harry Carney, trombonist Lawrence Brown, bassist Aaron Bell, drummer Sam Woodyard, with Al Williams brought in to play piano.[60]

In 1962, inspired by his sojourns in Paris, Ellington recorded the album *Midnight in Paris*, with thirteen tracks evoking the City of Light. In addition to Ellington compositions "Guitar Amour" and "Paris Blues" from the film *Paris Blues*, the album included Strayhorn's "Midnight in Paris" and ten standards associated with Paris such as Edith Piaf's "No Regrets" and Charles Trenet's "Speak to Me of Love." Strayhorn had a special relationship with the City of Light that went all the way back to the imagined Paris of his youth, when, still a Pittsburgh teenager, he penned the fatalist, sophisticated-beyond-his-years torch song "Lush Life," with its memorable line, "A week in Paris will ease the bite of it."[61] Strayhorn spent stretches of time in Paris, and had a long romantic relationship with the expatriate African American pianist Aaron Bridgers. In 1970, Ellington would recall, "Strayhorn loved Paris, and it was one of his favorite places."[62]

The year 1963 would see Ellington travel abroad more than he would in any other year—a total of 174 days, almost half the year. In January 1963, the Ellington orchestra traveled to Europe for its second-longest foreign tour to date, under the auspices of the American producer Norman Granz: sixty-one days in Western Europe, including ten days of recording sessions in Paris, Stockholm, Hamburg, and Milan, and television programs in London and Stockholm.[63] The band played three concerts at Paris's Olympia Theater, which were recorded and issued in the United States as *Duke Ellington's Greatest Hits* (Reprise) and *The Great Paris Concert* (Atlantic), showing Ellington in especially fine form as a band pianist.[64] According to the *New York Times*, "The audiences overflowed into the aisles. The reception could hardly have been warmer."[65] Reviewing another concert during this tour, the *Sunday Times* of London wrote, "Last night the band lived up to the highest Ellington standard—that is, the highest standard ever reached by any large jazz band."[66]

Also, with symphony and opera orchestras of Paris, Hamburg, Stockholm, and Milan, the Ellington band made an album called *The Symphonic Ellington* that finally realized his dream to record *Night Creature*, his composition from 1955, which Capitol and Columbia had been unwilling to record because of the costs of hiring more than one hundred musicians to play music out of Ellington's "category," which, everyone knew, was jazz.

In Paris, Ellington recorded a Reprise album titled *Duke Ellington's Violin Session*, featuring his rhythm section and his violinist Ray Nance, along with the French violinist Stéphane Grappelli and the Swedish violinist Sven Asmussen—a singular recording in the Ellington oeuvre. And on March 24, 1963, Ellington produced two albums featuring exiled South African musicians: singer Sathima Bea Benjamin's *A Morning in Paris* and pianist Dollar Brand's *Duke Ellington Presents the Dollar Brand Trio*, thereby helping two gifted musicians early in their careers, making a statement of endorsement, and perhaps lodging an indirect protest against the apartheid policies of their native country.[67]

Despite a terrible winter, the concerts of the 1963 tour were thronged and the newspapers full of flowing praise. This trip may rank as the most successful foreign tour of Ellington's life. The trip was not without its downside, however. Ellington, now sixty-three years old, contracted pneumonia and spent five days at the American Hospital in the smart Paris suburb of Neuilly. This illness underscores what a demanding, even grueling schedule he found himself having to keep. When he was thirty, and touring in the United States, he would often "sit down" for a one-, two-, or even three-week engagement at a theater or nightclub. But now, with changing musical demographics and economics, in order to keep the band together, he had to keep up a killing pace, consisting—whether in the United States or abroad—of long strings of one-nighters, each in a different city, with rarely a day off.

In January and February 1966, Ellington made another tour of Europe. In Paris, he and Ella Fitzgerald performed several sell-out concerts at the Salle Pleyel.[68] Ellington was invited to reopen a newly restored thirteenth-century château at Goutelas-en-Forêt.[69] He was very moved by the coming together of Catholics, communists, and other disparate groups to lovingly restore the thirteenth-century building, by his nighttime welcome as he proceeded through a corridor of fifty children holding torches, and by the superb quality of the Steinway grand brought in for the occasion. He played a piano concert and dedicated a performance of his *New World A-Comin'* to his newfound friends, stating, "The title refers to a future place, on earth, at sea, or in the air, where there will be no war, no greed, no categorization, and where love is unconditional, and where there is no pronoun good enough for God."[70] His deeply felt experience at Goutelas led him to compose the *Goutelas Suite*, which was premièred at Lincoln Center, in New York City, on April 16, 1971, recorded on April 27, 1971, in New York, and issued by Pablo on *The Ellington Suites*. Of the four movements, the long, slow "Something," with its sumptuous harmonies, is the highlight.

Another French milestone was achieved in July 1966, when promoter Norman

Granz arranged for Ellington and another of his recording artists, Ella Fitzgerald, to jointly perform at the seventh annual Antibes Jazz Festival in Juan-les-Pins. Mike Hennessey wrote in *Down Beat*: "*Take the A Train* had growling Cootie Williams, and *Diminuendo and Crescendo in Blue* brought Gonsalves back to solo, but the evening really belonged to altoist Johnny Hodges, whose *Passion Flower* and *Things Ain't What They Used to Be* were musical art.... Four concerts by the best band in the world, three by the best singer in the world—perhaps it is a little churlish to ask more of a festival."[71] Two of the concerts were telecast by French national television (Office de Radiodiffusion-Télévision Française or ORTF). All the concerts were recorded and filmed; subsequently an hour-long film premièred in the United States on National Educational Television,[72] titled *Duke Ellington at the Côte D'Azur*.[73] The film contains the only complete filmed performance of the Ellington-Strayhorn suite on Shakespearean themes, *Such Sweet Thunder*, and of the new composition *La Plus Belle Africaine*. Tension, however, arose between Ellington and Granz, and their relationship would soon be over.[74]

Back home in the United States, Ellington's European travels were a source of pride for the African American press. From Paris, Ollie Stewart reported in the Washington, D.C., *Afro American* that although there was a general strike in France, "It didn't stop the faithful from finding a way to get to Pleyel to hear" Ellington and Fitzgerald. "Matter of fact," Stewart continued, "whenever the word gets out that Duke and Ella are coming to town as a package deal, nothing short of war can stop them from playing to a packed house. The two names are magic that the French can't resist."[75]

In October 1969, the band went to Europe, under the auspices of George Wein, founder of the Newport Jazz Festival and of Festival Productions, for a seventieth birthday tour. The trip was grueling—thirty-two cities in just thirty-five days, often requiring two performances in one day—but a big success. While in Paris, the Ellington orchestra performed at Salle Pleyel for the Fifth Paris Jazz Festival,[76] as well as a concert of Sacred Music at the Église Saint-Sulpice,[77] which was attended by five thousand people and taped for later telecast by ORTF. Though the church had a ban on applauding, the audience, according to the *New York Times*, "clapped for every number and stomped toward the end."[78] As in the United States, the novelty of fusing jazz with sacred music created a stir. One Parisian newspaper headline quoted the Saint-Sulpice vicar as worrying, "And if they start to dance?"[79]

In Paris on November 20, there was a large, belated birthday party at L'Alcazar,[80] one of the city's most famous cabarets, attended by such notables as Maurice Chevalier (with whom Ellington had first worked with in New York City in 1930) and Salvador Dali. According to a UPI wire-service story, "Highlight of the show—apart from an hour of swinging sounds from the Ellington band—was a 10-foot wide cake, from which popped three nude dancers." The concert was taped and later broadcast by ORTF as *Les 70 Ans de Duke Ellington*. The French were not shy about expressing their admiration for Ellington. Among the 200,000 items in the Duke Ellington Collection at the Smithsonian is a souvenir from Parisian fans who created a commemorative cigar band bearing his likeness, and a copy of an Ellington commemorative edition, on special durable paper, produced by *Le Figaro*.[81]

By 1970, Ellington had lost his two greatest musicians: Billy Strayhorn had died in 1967, and Hodges in 1970. But Ellington soldiered on. He continued to perform "live" and to make recordings both for a growing private stockpile and for issue by record companies, but he was without a long-term association with a major record label. In the summer of 1970, Ellington, now seventy-one, again toured Europe under George Wein, from June 28 to August 1. The impresario paid Ellington $94,500 for the tour—about $560,000 in 2011 dollars. In addition to this sum, Wein also provided all air and ground transportation.[82]

A novelty of the trip was a concert in the town of Menton, on the French-Italian border, during which the Ellington band performed on the bridge straddling the frontier, playing for audiences in two countries. The French audience paid in francs, and the Italians in lire. At the piano, Ellington's right hand was in Italy, and his left in France![83] In Paris, one of the highlights was a solo piano concert he taped for ORTF. In fact, I consider this tape one of the most remarkable film or video recordings Ellington ever made. He is alone in the television studio, playing and speaking directly to *you* and *you*—members of the unseen audience at home. His intimacy is palpable, his musicianship extraordinary, his charm polished to a high luster. In September 1971, again under Wein, the orchestra made an extensive tour of Europe, including six concerts in France. However, with the loss of some of his stars, frequent turnover in personnel, and the aging of other players, Ellington increasingly was carrying the show with his public personality and stage presence, now honed to a fine level of smoothness, cliché, and charisma. After 1971, he made a number of recordings but was glimpsing few new musical horizons.

On July 8, 1973, President Georges Pompidou and the government of France gave Ellington its highest recognition. At the French Consulate in New York City, Jacques Kosciusko-Morizet, ambassador of France, presented Ellington with France's most prestigious award, the Legion of Honor.[84] No American composer had ever been so widely honored, nationally and internationally, as Duke Ellington.

From October through December 1973, the orchestra performed in Europe, with a brief side trip to Ethiopia and Zambia for the U.S. State Department. His last performance in France was for a concert in Brest. That was November 15; just over six months later, he was dead from lung cancer. *yipes - oddly phrased*

What was the significance of France to Ellington? It was psychological, social, and musical. As did Strayhorn, Ellington loved France. He once told an interviewer, "You don't visit France as a tourist, once in your life. You have to kiss this country at least once a year."[85] More so than anywhere else in Europe, France conveyed, especially for black Americans, a sense of freedom, or at least far more freedom and dignity than they were accorded in their homeland in the pre-civil rights era. Especially during the 1930s tours, France gave Ellington and his gifted musicians a great deal of validation, encouragement, and musical inspiration. "Europe is a very different world from this one," Ellington told his first biographer, Barry Ulanov. "You can go anywhere and talk to anybody and do anything you like. It's hard to believe. When you've eaten hot dogs all your life and you're suddenly offered caviar it's hard to believe it's true."[86] France also provided opportunities for Ellington to make significant recordings and television broadcasts and inspired three long-form works—the score to *Paris Blues*, the score for *Turcaret*, and the *Goutelas Suite*.

What was the significance of Ellington to France? In the 1930s, Ellington demonstrated to the French, with firsthand authority and considerable style and eloquence, the enormous artistic power in orchestrated jazz; he set an example for composing with unusual tone colors and individual harmonies; and he created high standards for native French musicians to try to match. He also validated, inspired, and influenced French musicians such as the pianists Raymond Fol, Claude Bolling, and Aaron Bridgers.[87]

During the forty years spanning Ellington's performances in France, jazz enjoyed breathtaking growth and development: increasing influence on culture, rising respect and prominence, and unfolding possibilities as a compositional pursuit. More than anyone else, Ellington helped bring jazz to this significant position in his native country, as well as in France. *really?*

THE ITINERARY OF DUKE ELLINGTON IN FRANCE

Year	Date	City	Event/Venue	Recording or Broadcast
1933	July 27	Paris	Concert, Salle Pleyel	
	July 29	Paris	Same	
	August 1	Paris	Same	
	August 3	Le Havre	Departs on the *Majestic* for New York	
1939	March 30	Le Havre	Arrives on the *Champlain*	
	April 1	Paris	Press conference by Duke Ellington (hereafter DE)	
	April 3	Paris	Concert, Palais de Chaillot	

Year	Date	City	Event/Venue	Recording or Broadcast
	April 4	Paris	Same	
	April 5	Paris	Recording session by Rex Stewart and His Feetwarmers (including Django Reinhardt)	Recorded for Swing
1948	July 19	Le Havre?	Ellington, Kay Davis, Ray Nance cross the English Channel, take train to Paris	
	July 20	Paris	Concert, Salle Pleyel (sextet)	
	July 21	Paris	DE attends a cocktail party in his honor given by Présence Africaine magazine	
	July 30	Paris	Passes through Paris on way to board Queen Elizabeth in Cherbourg	
1950	April 4	Le Havre	Arrival on Île de France	
	April 5	Le Havre	Concert, Cinéma Normandy	
	April 6	Rouen	Concert	
	April 11	Lille	Two concerts, L'Opéra	
	April 12–16	Paris	Five concerts, Théâtre National du Palais de Chaillot	
	April 14	Paris	Recording session by Harold Baker and Johnny Hodges (with Don Byas and Raymond Fol)	Recorded for Swing
	April 15	Paris	Recording sessions by Johnny Hodges and Nelson Williams	Recorded for Vogue and Mood
	April 17	Lyon	Concert	
	April 18	Strasbourg	Concert, Palais des Fêtes	
	April 19	Nancy	Two concerts, Grand Théâtre	
	April 20	Paris	Recording session by Johnny Hodges and his Orchestra	Recorded for Vogue
	April 26	Roubaix	Concert, Cinéma Le Colisée	
	June 20	Paris	Two concerts, Salle Wagram	
	June 20	Paris	Recording session by Johnny Hodges and His Orchestra	Recorded for Vogue
1958	October 28	Paris	Two concerts, Palais de Chaillot	
	October 29	Paris	Two concerts, Alhambra theater	The second (evening) concert recorded by Radio Europe and issued, in part, by Pablo (PACD-5313-2) and RTE (710707)
	October 30	Paris	Cat Anderson (and a group of Ellington band members) record with Georges Arvanitas	Recorded for French Columbia
	November 20	Paris	Concert, Salle Pleyel[a]	Telecast by RTF and issued on Magic DAWE39 and DAWE40
1959	September 20	Paris	Two concerts, Salle Pleyel[b]	Released by BYG on YX2035 and YX2036
	September 21	Paris	Concert, Salle Pleyel	
1960	December 8	LA-Paris	DE flies to Paris	

Year	Date	City	Event/Venue	Recording or Broadca...
	December 9	Paris	Party in DE's honor hosted by Paul Newman	
	December 14–15	Paris	Recording session, Barclay Studios	*For film* Paris Blues
	December 17	Paris	Television broadcast, RTF Studios	*Telecast by RTF*
	December 24	Paris	DE performs at a Midnight Mass	
	December 25	Paris	DE appears on Jean Sablon show	*Telecast by RTF*
	December 29	Paris	DE records, Barclay Studios	*Recorded for Barclay*
	December 29–30	Paris	DE conducts recording, *Turcaret*	*Issued by Azure as CA3...*
1961	March [n.d.]	Paris	DE records "Blues No. 23"	*Issued on Storyville 101-8399*
	March 7	Paris	DE joins Billy Strayhorn to work on *Paris Blues*	
	March 18	Paris	Johnny Hodges and five other Ellington musicians perform two concerts, Olympia theater	*Recorded by Verve but unissued*
	May [n.d.]	Paris	Strayhorn records LP *The Peaceful Side*[c]	*Recorded for United Artists (UAJ-14010)*
1963	January 28	Paris	DE and orchestra fly to Paris	
	January 29–30	Paris	Duke Ellington Orchestra (hereafter DEO) records *Night Creature* with the Paris Symphony, Salle Wagram[d]	*Recorded for Reprise (R6097)*
	January 31	Paris	DEO records *Harlem* and third movement of *Night Creature*[e]	
	February 1	Paris	Concert at Olympia theater; issued in U.S. as *Great Paris Concert* (Atlantic) and *Ellington's Greatest Hits* (Reprise)	*Recorded for Atlantic (DS-2-304) and Reprise (R6234)*
	February 2	Paris	Two concerts, Olympia theater	*Issued as Azure CA11 and CA12*
	February 22	Paris	DE records w/ violinists Stéphane Grappelli, Ray Nance, and Sven Asmussen for *Duke Ellington's Jazz Violin Session*	*Recorded for Atlantic (SD-1688)*
	February 23	Paris	Two concerts, Olympia theater	*Issued in part on Atlant... SD2-304 and Reprise R6234*
	February 24	Paris	DE supervises recording session of Sathima Bea Benjamin, at Studio Hoche, issued as *A Morning in Paris*	*Issued as Enja ENJ-9309-2 and Repris...*
	February 24	Paris	DE supervises recording session of Dollar Brand, at Studio Hoche, released as *Duke Ellington Presents the Dollar Brand Trio*	*Issued as Reprise R6111*

Year	Date	City	Event/Venue	Recording or Broadcast
	February 28	Paris	DE records with Alice Babs, issued as *Serenade to Sweden*	*Recorded for Reprise (RS5024)*
	March 1	Paris	Same	*Same*
	March 5-11	Paris	DE is hospitalized for viral pneumonia, American Hospital	
	March 15	Paris	Ellington departs for NYC	
1964	March 16	Paris	Two concerts	
	March 17	Marseille	Two concerts	
	March 18	Lyon	Two concerts	
	March 19	Roubaix	Two concerts	
	March 20	Paris	Recording session by Cat Anderson and the Ellington All Stars	*Recorded for French Columbia*
	March 20	Paris	Two concerts, Théâtre des Champs Élysées[f]	
	March 21	Paris	DE appears on the Jack Diéval show[g]	*Telecast by ORTF*
	March 21	Paris	Two concerts, Théâtre des Champs Élysées[h]	
	March 23	Limoges	Concert, Théâtre Municipal	
1965	January 26	Paris	Concert, Cinéma Paramount	
	January 27	Bourges	Concert	
	January 28	Lyon	Concert	
	January 29	Paris	Concerts, Théâtre des Champs Élysées[i]	*Recorded for RTE[j]*
	January 30	Paris	Same[k]	*Issued as Jazz Club JC124*
	January 31	Paris	Same (early-morning concert)	*Issued as RTE Europe 1*
1966	January 29	Paris	DEO and Ella Fitzgerald concert, Salle Pleyel[l]	
	February 11	Paris	DEO and Ella Fitzgerald, two concerts, Salle Pleyel	*Recorded*
	February 24	Goutelas-en-Forêt	DE plays a solo piano concert at this restored medieval castle	*Issued as Jean B. Piazzano JBP91*
	February 25	Château de Cousan	DE visits as a tourist, in the Massif Central, lunches in Montbrizon	
	February 26	Lyon	DE flies from Lyon to Paris to NYC	
	July 26	Juan-les-Pins	Concert, 7th Annual Antibes Jazz Festival	*Filmed for NET; recorded for Verve (issued as V-4072-2 and 314-539033-2)*
	July 27	St-Paul-de-Vence	DE meets Joan Miró and plays the piano, Fondation Maeght	*Filmed for NET; recording issued by Pablo (as PACD2308-247-2)*

Year	Date	City	Event/Venue	Recording or Broadcast
	July 27–29	Juan-les-Pins	Concert with Ella Fitzgerald, 7th Annual Antibes Jazz Festival	*Filmed for NET; recorded for Verve (issued as V-8701 and V-8702-2); July 27–28 telecast by ORTF*
1967	January 31	Paris	Two concerts with Ella Fitzgerald, Salle Pleyel[m]	*First concert issued, in part, on Azure CA2*
	February 1	Paris	Same	
	February 2	Caen	Same, except at Maison de la Culture	
	February 3	Nancy	Same, except at Cinéma Royal	
	February 21	Reims	Concert[n]	
	March 10	Paris	Concert, Théâtre des Champs Élysées	*Issued as Pablo PACD-5304-2 and Azure CA29*
	March 10	Paris	Ellington records three piano solos	*Issued on Azure CA29*
1969	November 1	Paris	Two concerts, Salle Pleyel[o]	*First concert issued on Jazz Music Yesterday 1011-2; second concert issued on BYG (F)YX-6031*
	November 16	Paris	Concert of Sacred Music, Église St-Sulpice[p]	*Taped by ORTF for broadcast later*
	November 17	Paris	Paul Gonsalves recording session	*Issued on Riviera*
	November 17	Lyon	Concert	
	November 18	Nancy	Concert, Salle Victor Poirel	
	November 19	Bordeaux	Concert, Alhambra theater	
	November 20	Paris	DEO performs for dinner party, L'Alcazar, to celebrate DE's 70th year	*Taped by ORTF: Les 70 Ans de Duke Ellington; issued in part as Sarpe Top Jazz SJ1024*
	November 21	Grenoble	Concert	
1970	June 29	Lille	Concert	
	July 1	Paris	DE prepares for a TV appearance	
	July 2	Paris	DE videotapes a piano recital, with no audience, ORTF Studios[q]	*Taped by ORTF for later broadcast; issued as the Jazz Collection JCD05*
	July 4	Paris	DE films and records *Bienvenue Chez Guy Béart*, ORTF Studios[r]	*Taped by ORTF for later broadcast (Aug. 7, 1973)*
	July 4	Provins	Concert	*Recorded*
	July 5	Toulon	Concert	
	July 6	Paris	Recording session for Paul Gonsalves et al.	*Recorded for Blue Star*
	July 25	Orange	Concert, Théâtre Antique[s]	*Recorded*

Year	Date	City	Event/Venue	Recording or Broadcast
	July 26	Orange	Concert of Sacred Music, Théâtre Antique	Recorded
	July 27	Orange	A rare day off for the band	
	July 28	St.-Tropez	Concert, La Citadelle	Recorded
	July 31	Menton	Concert	
971	October 18	Roubaix	Concert, Cinéma Le Colisée	
	October 26	Lyon	Concert	
	October 27	Bordeaux	Concert, Alhambra theater[t]	
	October 28	Paris	Two concerts, Théâtre National Populaire, Palais Chaillot	
	November 13	Strasbourg	Concert	
973	January 3	Paris	Performance with Stéphane Grappelli on Michel Legrand show[u]	Taped by ORTF for later broadcast (June 6)
	January 4	Paris	Performance with Stéphane Grappelli on his 65th birthday	Taped for ORTF for later broadcast (March 27)
	November 12	Sochaux	Concert	
	November 13	Besançon	Concert	
	November 14	Paris	Concert, Palais des Sports[v]	Recorded
	November 15	Brest	Concert	

NOTES

Full citations for books noted below may be found in the main chapter notes, beginning on page 208.

a. The repertory for this concert is listed in Ken Vail, *Duke's Diary, Part 2*, p. 134 (hereafter *DDP2*).

b. Repertory is listed in *DDP2*, p. 148.

c. For details on the recording of this recording, see Hajdu, *Lush Life*, pp. 211–14.

d. Though Ellington recorded all movements of *Night Creature* in Paris, only the first movement was issued. The Ellington orchestra rerecorded the second and third movements in Stockholm. The three movements were issued on Reprise Records.

e. Claude Carrière, e-mail message to the author, August 3, 2011.

f. Repertory is listed in *DDP2*, p. 238.

g. Repertory is listed in *DDP2*, p. 238.

h. Madeleine Gautier, "Sur les récents concerts Duke Ellington," *Bulletin du hot club de France*, April 1964. In DEPS.

i. Repertory listed in *DDP2*, p. 257.

j. Issued as RTE 71043/434, with notes by Claude Carrière.

k. Repertory listed in *DDP2*, p. 257.

l. Repertory listed in *DDP2*, p. 279.

m. Stewart, "Report from Europe"; for the repertory, see *DDP2*, p. 306.

n. Jean-Pierre Binchet, "La tournée du grand Duke," *Jazz*, March 1967, pp. 18–24. In DEPS.

o. Repertory listed in *DDP2*, p. 366.

p. The concert's repertory is listed in *DDP2*, p. 368.

q. Repertory listed in Vaile, *DDP2*, p. 381.

r. A discussion of this film is included in Stratemann, *Day by Day and Film by Film*, pp. 603–4.

s. Hugues Panassié, "Duke Ellington au Théâtre Antique d'Orange," *Bulletin du hot club de France*, September 1970. In DEPS.

t. The concert was reviewed by Madeleine Gautier, *Bulletin du hot club de France*, November 1971, pp. 3–4. In DEPS.

u. Repertory listed in *DDP2*, p. 405.

v. Repertory listed in *DDP2*, p. 444.

NOTES

The author wishes to thank Philippe Baudoin, Claude Carrière, and Isabelle Marquis, all of Paris, for their kind and generous help reviewing the manuscript and locating French source materials. Thanks also to Salomone Baquis for his research assistance. Portions of this chapter appeared previously in *Nottingham French Studies* 43, no. 1 (Spring 2004), pp. 7–18.

1. Of the beginnings of the jazz scene in Paris, violinist Stéphane Grappelli stated, "However jazz was defined (and to the confused general public it was almost anything that wasn't a waltz) it was obviously a hit." Geoffrey Smith, *Stéphane Grappelli* (London: Pavilion Books, 1987), p. 24. The French public was not alone in their confusion about the true nature of jazz. "Until the 1940s," writes Cyril Moshkow, "the very word 'jazz' for Eastern Europeans meant a certain type of band rather than a style of music (a band that, unlike a traditional brass band, included saxophones, a drum set, and, in many cases, violins and accordions along with the brass). Any modern danceable music, even with a strong influence from local folkloric traditions, was called 'jazz' if it was played by a 'jazz band.'" Cyril Moshkow, "Jazz in Eastern Europe," in *Discover Jazz*, ed. John Edward Hasse and Tad Lathrop (Upper Saddle River, NJ: Pearson, 2011), p. 309.

2. Kevin Whitehead, "Jazz Worldwide," in Hasse and Lathrop, *Discover Jazz*, p. 290. Szwed's quotation is from John F. Szwed, *Space Is the Place: The Life and Times of Sun Ra* (New York: Pantheon, 1997), p. 287.

3. "Mills Abroad to Sell for Mills and Duke," *Chicago Defender*, January 8, 1933, p. 5.

4. Besides taking the Ellington orchestra to Paris, the tour, by some accounts, included a special concert at the Casino de Deauville in the famous seaside resort. See Edgar A. Wiggins, "'Won't You Come Back?' Is Paris' Plea to Ellington," *Chicago Defender*, August 19, 1933, p. 5.

5. The Ellington orchestra opened its visit to England with a two-week engagement at London's Palladium. A description of those performances, which undoubtedly included many of the same tunes played in Paris, was published in *Melody Maker*, June 17, 1933, pp. 1–2, and reprinted in Mark Tucker, ed., *The Duke Ellington Reader* (New York: Oxford University Press, 1993), pp. 75–78.

6. Henry Malherbe, "À la salle Pleyel: Duke Ellington et son orchestra," *Temps*, August 2, 1933. As quoted in Jeffrey H. Jackson, *Making Jazz French: Music and Modern Life in Interwar Paris* (Durham, NC: Duke University Press, 2003), p. 157.

7. J. A. Rogers, "Duke Ellington," *Amsterdam News* (New York), August 9, 1933, in Duke Ellington Publicity Scrapbooks (hereafter DEPS), Series 8 (Scrapbooks), Duke Ellington Collection (DEC), Archives Center, National Museum of American History, Smithsonian Institution, Washington, DC.

8. J. A. Rogers, "The Duke's Success Encourages Musicians," *Amsterdam News*, August 16, 1933, in DEPS. For a different perspective on the concert, see Stéphane Mougin, "Après Duke Ellington," *Jazz-Tango Dancing*, September 1933, p. 3. Mougin complains that French jazz musicians were getting short shrift vis-à-vis the American ones.

9. Hugues Panassié, "Duke Ellington at the Salle Pleyel," translated by Stanley Dance, in Tucker, *Duke Ellington Reader*, p. 82.

10. Ibid., p. 84.

11. Ibid.

12. Ibid., p. 85.

13. Ibid., p. 87.

14. Mercer Ellington with Stanley Dance, *Duke Ellington in Person: An Intimate Memoir* (Boston: Houghton Mifflin; London: Hutchinson, 1978. Reprint: New York: Da Capo, 1979), p. 61.

15. Matthew F. Jordan, *Le Jazz: Jazz and French Cultural Identity* (Urbana: University of Illinois Press, 2010), pp. 151–58.

16. Ibid.

17. *London Sunday Referee*, quoted in unidentified article, *New York American*, August 7, 1933, in DEPS.

18. Duke Ellington, "Ellington on Career Highlights," in Tucker, *Duke Ellington Reader*, p. 266.

19. Barry Ulanov, *Duke Ellington* (New York: Creative Age Press, 1946. London: Musicians Press, 1947. Reprint. New York: Da Capo, 1975), p. 151.

20. Frank Marshall Davis, "Duke Ellington, 'Just Plain Folks,' Likes Drinks, Cards and Movies," *Afro-American*, February 9, 1935, p. 9.

21. Ibid.

22. Klaus Stratemann, *Duke Ellington: Day by Day and Film by Film* (Copenhagen: JazzMedia, 1992), p. 158.

23. Onah L. Spencer, "French J-Bugs in Wild Welcome for Ellington," *Down Beat*, May 1939, p. 9.

24. Rex Stewart, *Boy Meets Horn*, ed. by Claire P. Gordon (Ann Arbor: University of Michigan Press, 1991), p. 182.

25. Ibid., p. 183.

26. Colin Nettelbeck, *Dancing with DeBeauvoir: Jazz and the French* (Carlton, Victoria, Australia: University of Melbourne Press, 2004), p. 47.

27. Stratemann, *Duke Ellington*, p. 158.

28. "Ellington Gave Concert in Bomb-Proof Hall! Crowd Rioted in Holland; Nazis Tossed Valet into Jail, Reveals Duke's Diary," *Metronome*, June 1939, pp. 10, 35.

29. "Concerts et Recitals: Le langage du jazz—style nègre et style blanc les familiers du piano et du chant," *Le Figaro* (Paris), April 7, 1939. Translation by Monique Steiner.

30. Hugo Speck, "Ellington Bd. Whams Paris," *Variety*, April 19, 1939, p. 48.

31. Richard O. Boyer, "The Hot Bach," in Tucker, *Duke Ellington Reader*, p. 215.

32. Ibid.

33. Stewart describes the recording session in *Boy Meets Horn*, pp. 185–86 and 190–91.

34. When these sides were released in the United States in the early 1940s, on the HRS label, they bore the name of Rex Stewart's Big Four, and several titles were changed: "Montmartre" became "Django's Jump," "Finesse" was changed to "Night Wind," and "Solid Old Man" to "Solid Rock."

35. Gunther Schuller, *The Swing Era: The Development of Jazz, 1930–1945* (New York: Oxford University Press, 1989), p. 834.

36. Ibid., p. 840.

37. Michael Dregni, *Django: The Life and Music of a Gypsy Legend* (New York: Oxford University Press, 2004), p. 149.

38. William A. Shack, *Harlem in Montmartre: A Paris Jazz Story between the Great Wars* (Berkeley: University of California Press, 2001), p. 31. See also Charles Delaunay, *Django Reinhardt*, trans. Michael James (New York: Da Capo Press, 1981), p. 62.

39. Stewart, *Boy Meets Horn*, p. 189.

40. Ibid., pp. 215–16.

41. Ernest Borneman, "Diary—68 Hours without Sleep: The Duke in Paris—Part I," *Down Beat*, August 25, 1948, pp. 6–7.

42. Ibid., p. 7.

43. Ernest Borneman, "Diary—68 Hours without Sleep: The Duke in Paris—Part II," *Down Beat*, September 8, 1948, as quoted in Harvey Cohen, *Duke Ellington's America* (Chicago: University of Chicago Press, 2010), p. 247.

44. *Der Spiegel*, June 11, 1950, p. 4, as cited in Stratemann, *Duke Ellington*, p. 322n.

45. "Mixed Reception for Duke Ellington's Paris Opening: Kay Davis Silenced," *Melody Maker*, April 15, 1950, p. 1, in the DEPS. The assertion that it was after "Lush Life" that Kay Davis was booed is contradicted by the recollection of jazz connoisseur Jean Portier, who attended three of the five 1950 concerts at the Palais de Chaillot, and who further related to the Ellington expert Claude Carrière that Ellington "tried to explain to the people what he was doing, a text translated on stage by Charles Delaunay. At that time the audience was much more reactive than now." Claude Carrière, e-mail message to the author, April 29, 2011.

46. Philippe Baudoin, e-mail message to the author, April 28, 2011.

47. Borkon to Ellington, April 13, 1950, in the DEC, Series 3 (Business Records).

48. Ellington's 1958 Parisian concerts generated considerable publicity, before, during, and after. The following are drawn from the DEPS: E. C., "Un événement musical: Duke Ellington et son orchestra donneront quatre concerts à Paris les 28 et 29 Octobre," *Le Parisien Libéré*, October 22, 1958. François Mallet, "Jazz: Duke Ellington en France," *Expresse* (Paris), October 23, 1958. "Duke Ellington, à Chaillot, ce Soir avec un concerto-surprise: Shakespeare en jazz," *L'Aurore* (Paris), October 28, 1958. Mowgli Jospin, "Du Jazz aux 'feuilles mortes' Duke Ellington: Heir à Chaillot," *Le Figaro* (Paris), October 29, 1958. Philidor, "Duke Ellington au Palais de Chaillot," *Le Monde* (Paris), October 30, 1958. Hugues Panassié, "Duke Ellington joue de son orchestra comme d'un instrument," *Paris Presse*, October 30, 1958. Philippe Roussel, "Jazz: Duke Ellington au Palais de Chaillot," *Amites Françaises*, November 1958. "Les Lundis du Jazz: Libres opinions après les concerts

Duke Ellington," *Combat* (Paris), November 3, 1958. "Bienvenue Duke Ellington," *Arts* (Paris), November 4, 1958. "Duke Ellington, aristocrate du jazz," *Le Lorrain Metz*, November 8, 1958. "Le courrier du jazz: 'Duke': Un grand-père qui est un jeune chef," *Yvonne Républicaine* (Auxerre), November 15, 1958. A. N., "Les Adieux à Paris de Duke Ellington," *Les Lettres Françaises* (Paris), November 27, 1958. "Les Concert dit d'adieu de Duke Ellington," *La Discographe Française*, December 1, 1958. Art Buchwald, "'What Is Jazz?' Ellington Asks," *Intelligencer* (Wheeling, WV), November 17, 1958.

49. The record was released as two LPs, RTE 710582/583, with notes by the Ellington specialist Claude Carrière. The repertory for Ellington's Salle Pleyel concert of November 20, 1958, is listed in Ken Vail, *Duke's Diary, Part Two: The Life of Duke Ellington, 1950-1974* (Lanham, MD: Scarecrow Press, 2002), p. 134; hereafter DDP2.

50. The repertory for Ellington's two Salle Pleyel concerts on September 20, 1959, is listed in ibid., p. 148.

51. Both Ellington and Armstrong were honored by the French Academy of Jazz with awards. "Louie, Duke Both Honored aboard Boat," *Amsterdam News* (New York), January 14, 1961, in DEPS. Also, the International Jazz Club awarded its Grand Prix for the recording Ellington made with his star alto saxophonist, Johnny Hodges, under the title *Back to Back*, issued in the United States on the Verve label and in France on the Barclay label. See "International Jazz Club Prix 1960," Duke Ellington Collection, Series 11 (Publicity), box 1, folder 25.

52. For a discussion of the filming of *Paris Blues*, see David Hajdu, *Lush Life: A Biography of Billy Strayhorn* (New York: Farrar, Straus and Giroux, 1996), pp. 208-11.

53. Louis Armstrong filmed "Battle Royal" and "Wild Man Moore" with a French studio orchestra, in Paris, December 14-15, 1960. The session was supervised by Ellington, but he did not perform on these two numbers. See the Jazz Discography, Tom Lord, www.lordisco.com, under Louis Armstrong.

54. Eddie Lambert, *Duke Ellington: A Listener's Guide*, Studies in Jazz, No. 26 (Lanham, MD: Scarecrow Press, and Institute of Jazz Studies, 1999), p. 224. For a detailed discussion of Ellington and the music for *Paris Blues*, see Stratemann, *Duke Ellington*, pp. 429-40.

55. Stratemann, *Duke Ellington*, p. 441.

56. Ibid.

57. "Aubade pour le duc et le roi du jazz," *Paris Match*, n.d. [probably December 1960 or January 1961], p. 44.

58. "Paris Play Uses Jazz," *New York Times*, January 15, 1961, in DEPS.

59. Sinclair Traill, "Paris Blues," *Metronome*, April 1961, p. 17, in DEPS. Traill reports on a visit with Ellington and Armstrong, both staying at the Hotel Tremoille, during the filming of *Paris Blues*.

60. H. P. [Hugues Panassié], "Les Concerts Johnny Hodges," *Bulletin du hot club de France*, no. 107, April 1961, p. 38, in DEPS.

61. Hajdu, *Lush Life*, pp. 34-35.

62. Cohen, *Duke Ellington's America*, p. 522. For more on Strayhorn in Paris, see Hajdu, *Lush Life*, pp. 111-14 and 142-45.

63. No records survive of how much Ellington was paid for his concerts in France, but a contract in the Duke Ellington Collection reveals that for his concerts in Sweden, Denmark, Norway, and Finland, the orchestra was paid $2,000, in U.S. funds, per working day, plus transportation. Duke Ellington Collection, Series 3 (Business Records), box 4, folder 3.

64. The complete repertory for the Ellington orchestra's concerts of February 1, 2, and 23 is listed in Vail, *Duke's Diary*, p. 214.

65. Robert Alden, "Duke Ellington Cheered in Paris," *New York Times*, February 4, 1963. The same quotation is in Harold Lundstrom, "The Solid Beat," *Deseret News-Telegram* (Salt Lake City), February 6, 1963, in DEPS.

66. "Duke Ellington Draws Raves during 6-Week European Tour," *Daily Defender* (Chicago), March 6, 1963, in DEPS. The Paris concerts were reviewed by Madeleine Gautier, "Duke Ellington à Paris (1ᵉʳ et 2 Février 63)," *Bulletin du hot club de France*, February 1963, pp. 4-5, in DEPS.

67. After converting to Islam in the late 1960s, Brand changed his name to Abdullah Ibrahim.

68. "Duke & Ella Conquer Paris," *Cash Box*, February 12, 1966. "Ella & Duke's Near-SRO at Paris' Salle Playel [*sic*]; Slate 2 More Concerts," *Variety*, February 9, 1966. Both articles in DEPS.

69. Colette H. Dupin, "Au château de Goutelas-en-Forez; Devant cent cinquante privilégiés le 'Duke' a joué Ellington," *Le Progrès* (Grenoble), February 27, 1966, in DEPS.

70. Edward Kennedy Ellington, *Music Is My Mistress* (Garden City, NY: Doubleday, 1973), p. 342. He discusses his time in Goutelas on pp. 340-44.

71. Mike Hennessey, "International Jazz Festival, Antibes—Juan-les-Pins, France," *Down Beat*, September 22, 1966, p. 33.

72. NET was the direct predecessor of PBS, the Public Broadcasting System.

73. See Stratemann, *Duke Ellington*, pp. 539-42, for a detailed discussion of *Duke Ellington at the Côte d'Azur*.

74. Tad Hershorn, *Norman Granz: The Man Who Used Jazz for Justice* (Berkeley: University of California Press, 2011), pp. 316-19.

75. Ollie Stewart, "Report from Europe," *Afro-American* (Washington, DC), February 21, 1967, in DEPS.

76. "Duke Ellington et son orchestra au 5e Festival de jazz de Paris," *Québec Le Soleil*, 4 November 1969, in DEPS.

77. Michael Perrin, "Duke Ellington à Saint-Sulpice," *Jazz*, December 1969, p. 4. R. G. Caumnat, "Duke Ellington monstre sacré du jazz," *Le Progrès* (Grenoble), November 20, 1969, in DEPS.

78. "5,000 Fill Paris Church to Hear Duke Ellington," *New York Times*, November 18, 1969, in DEPS.

79. "'Et s'ils se mettent à danser?' s'inquietait le vicaire de Saint-Suplice devant les fans de Duke Ellington," [unknown Paris newspaper], November 18, 1969. Copy of the article in the possession of Philippe Baudoin, Paris.

80. "Aux 70 ans de Duke Ellington le gâteau est venu du plafon," *France Soir*, November 22, 1969. Odile Grand, "Pour fêter les 70 ans de Duke: Nixon au piano sur l'écran de

l'Alcazar," *L'Aurore* (Paris), November 21, 1969. Edgar Schneider, "Le Tout-Paris s'est attendri sur papa 'Duke,'" *Paris-Press-l'Intransigeant*, November 22, 1969. "Duke Ellington Feted in France for Birthday," *Philadelphia Daily News*, November 25, 1969. All articles in DEPS.

81. A copy is preserved in the Duke Ellington Collection, Archives Center, National Museum of American History, Smithsonian Institution.

82. A copy of the contract between Wein's Festival Productions and Ellington, dated June 19, 1970, is part of 3 (Business Records), Duke Ellington Collection, Archives Center, National Museum of American History, Smithsonian Institution.

83. Ollie Stewart, "Ellington Shows on France-Italy Border," *Afro-American* (Washington, DC), July 21, 1970. "Duke Plays in France, Italy," *Jet*, August 20, 1970. Both articles in DEPS.

84. "Duke Ellington Is Awarded France's Legion of Honor," *New York Times*, July 9, 1973. Ellington performed part of his *The Shepherd (Who Watches Over the Night Flock)*, as documented by news service film. See Stratemann, *Duke Ellington*, p. 656.

85. As quoted from an April 1950 interview in a French newspaper, translated by Philippe Baudoin in an e-mail to the author, April 28, 2011. The original text is: "La France ça ne se visite pas en touriste une fois dans sa vie. Cela doit s'embrasser au moins une fois par an."

86. Ulanov, *Duke Ellington*, p. 217.

87. Fol performed as guest soloist with Ellington in 1969 and leader in 1974. Among Bolling's chief influences as pianist is Duke Ellington. Bolling made the first unabridged version of Ellington's *Black, Brown, and Beige* in 1989, and on March 22, 1996, he led a performance of Ellington's *A Drum Is a Woman* in Paris.

BIBLIOGRAPHY

Duke Ellington Collection. Archives Center, National Museum of American History, Smithsonian Institution, Washington, DC.

Hasse, John Edward. *Beyond Category: The Life and Genius of Duke Ellington*. New York: Simon & Schuster, 1993. Reprint, with revisions, New York: Da Capo, 1995.

Lord, Tom. The Jazz Discography, www.lordisco.com (accessed July 15, 2011).

Stratemann, Klaus. *Duke Ellington: Day by Day and Film by Film*. Copenhagen: JazzMedia, 1992.

Timner, W. E. *Ellingtonia: The Recorded Music of Duke Ellington and His Sidemen*. 4th ed. Studies in Jazz, No. 7. Lanham, MD: Scarecrow Press, 1996.

Vail, Ken. *Duke's Diary, Part 1: The Life of Duke Ellington, 1927–1950*. Lanham, MD: Scarecrow Press, 2002.

———. *Duke's Diary, Part 2: The Life of Duke Ellington, 1950–1974*. Lanham, MD: Scarecrow Press, 2002.

Van de Leur, Walter. *Something to Live For: The Music of Billy Strayhorn*. New York: Oxford University Press, 2002.

10 / COOL JAZZ IN EUROPE

Cool jazz, which is strongly related aesthetically and in its sonic ideals to European art music, was welcomed, copied, and interpreted avidly in Europe itself—although the intensity of that interest varied from country to country. In general, the following characteristics emerged:

Compositions and arrangements were often written in two voices, mostly in the manner of the Gerry Mulligan Quartet, occasionally contrapuntally or in a fugue or canon. The techniques of Gil Evans, a broadly orchestrated style mixing reeds and brass in dissonant voicings, were less imitated.

Trumpeters modeled their tone and phrasing on the introverted style of Miles Davis and Chet Baker. There was a similar trend among trombonists, for whom J. J. Johnson's smooth tone and clear phrasing became a comparable influence.

By contrast, many clarinetists favored the passionate style of Buddy DeFranco, with its wide intervals and forays into the highest register of the instrument.

For alto and tenor saxophonists, Lee Konitz and Warne Marsh were the key influences: many musicians emulated their thin, restrained tone with few overtones, their long legato solo lines and occasional use of a fragile terminal vibrato on longer-held notes. The "Four Brothers" style of playing, especially that of Stan Getz and that of the West Coast alto saxophonists (Art Pepper, a. o.), was also popular. Gerry Mulligan was the exemplar for most baritone saxophonists, although some gravitated more toward the Konitz-Marsh school.

The vibraphone was particularly popular in cool jazz, appearing as it did in three leading ensembles: the Red Norvo Trio, the George Shearing Quintet, and the Modern Jazz Quartet. As a result, the instrument exerted a proportionate influence on European musicians.

Pianists played in the Lennie Tristano style, employing long, swung, legato phrases and complex chains of eighth-note triplets, rising and falling in dynamic intensity with accented climaxes in the "upper extensions" of the chords, or sparse, distinctly laid-back single-note lines or block chords.

Guitarists imitated cool jazz players such as Billy Bauer, Tal Farlow, and Jimmy Raney.

Bassists persisted in the bebop style; the advances of Charles Mingus and other more modern practitioners had not found any European disciples yet.

For drummers, the rule was a subtle and understated style of accompaniment in the manner of Denzil Best and Shelly Manne.

Inquiries into the nature of cool jazz in individual areas of Europe have been limited to the years 1949-57. After 1957, a large number of former cool jazz musicians migrated to other styles, particularly hard bop and mainstream jazz. (The following text is occasionally supplemented by selected "listening examples"—LE 1, LE 2, etc.—keyed to a discography at the end of the article.)

England

One of the most important and successful cool jazz musicians, George Shearing, was born in England. With the help of Leonard Feather, he emigrated in 1949 to the United States, where he started his famous quintet and worked from that point onward. As such, Shearing was absent from the British music scene during the cool jazz period. Two other English musicians, pianist Ronnie Ball and bassist Peter Ind, studied with Lennie Tristano and became significant members of the Tristano/Lee Konitz/Warne Marsh school.

Johnny Dankworth, who led the Johnny Dankworth Seven from 1950 onward, composed and arranged for his group, using voicings that mixed brass and reeds in the style of Gil Evans. Examples of Dankworth's style include "Seven Not Out," recorded on July 29, 1950,[1] and his homage to Bix Beiderbecke, "Leon Bismarck" (LE 1).

While Dankworth's alto saxophone style hewed close to the Charlie Parker tradition, trumpeter Jimmy Deuchar showed the influence not only of Fats Navarro but of Miles Davis's restrained, laid-back soloing, as can be heard on "Strictly Confidential" (LE 2), again arranged in the Gil Evans manner. The tenor saxophonist, Don Rendell, also played in a "cool" style, his laid-back rhythmic approach and soft, supple phrasing reminiscent of the style of his role model, Stan Getz.

At the end of 1953, Dankworth formed a big band in which his use of the Gil Evans–style mixed voicing technique virtually disappeared, although the linear two-voice section writing can still occasionally be heard, as in "The Jerky Thing" and "Melbourne Marathon."[2] "Somerset Morn" (LE 3) features a combo known as the Laurie Monk Quartet, including Dankworth on alto saxophone and a trombonist, bassist, and drummer from his big band. For this tune, Dankworth composed a linear melody in two voices, in the style of Gerry Mulligan, for the band. He then solos with a smooth tone, no vibrato and few overtones, a style reminiscent of West Coast saxophonists such as Art Pepper.

From 1954 onward, Don Rendell performed mainly with groups of his own. His playing gradually developed a more-robust style recalling the Four Brothers school. Ronnie Ross, a student of Rendell's, was by his own account influenced by his teacher as well as by Lester Young and Gerry Mulligan. The latter influence is audible on the piece "Thames Walk,"[3] recorded by Rendell's quintet and arranged in the two-voice linear Mulligan style, as well as on "Cool Sparks" (LE 4). Ross also participated in John Lewis's[4] Third Stream composition "European Windows" in 1958.

Ronnie Scott, a prominent British tenor saxophone player, since 1951 with his own quartet, occasionally also improvised in the Konitz/Marsh manner, as on "Have You Met Miss Jones?"[5] When playing with larger ensembles he preferred playing in the bebop manner.

Ted Heath's ensemble, in addition to its more traditional big band arrangements, played pieces arranged in a two-voice linear style. One example is "Late Night Final," recorded on July 21, 1955, and arranged in the manner of the Stan Kenton band of the time, with Heath's star soloist, Don Lusher, playing a Frank Rosolino–style solo. Another example is "After You've Gone," recorded on the same date.[6] The contrapuntal voice leading is particularly impressive on the piece "Procession" (LE 5), composed by Bill Russo and performed on May 5, 1956, at New York's Carnegie Hall.

Vic Ash was England's leading clarinetist in the modern style during this period and a member of the Melody Maker All Stars from 1952 to 1954. His improvising on "Doxy" (LE 6) reflects the Buddy DeFranco approach described above, with large intervallic leaps into the highest register of the instrument.

Belgium and France

Belgium produced two important exponents of the cool jazz style during the period under review: the guitarist René Thomas and the saxophonist Bobby Jaspar. However, both men quickly joined the French jazz scene and thus can be considered along with their counterparts in that country. Thomas started out playing in the style of Django Reinhardt but soon became one of many guitarists in the Jimmy Raney/Tal Farlow tradition. He favored rapid phrases, generally with a somewhat laid-back offbeat and an impressively original melodic sense, for example on "How About You?" (LE 7).

Bobby Jaspar, who by his own account was influenced by Stan Getz's style on pieces such as "Early Autumn," as well as by Warne Marsh, started playing with French musicians in 1951. Another member of the French scene at the time was the American guitarist Jimmy Gourley, who also moved to Paris in 1951 and was also heavily influenced by the Raney style. Both musicians can be heard, playing in manner typical of the time, on "Milestone No. 2" (LE 8). In 1954 Jaspar played in an ensemble led by the pianist Bernard Peiffer. His solo on "There's a Small Hotel" shows the continuing influence of Getz and Marsh.[7]

André Hodeir, who had studied in Paris under luminaries such as Olivier Messiaen and had been educated in serial music, formed his Jazz Groupe de Paris in 1954, an ensemble that garnered a great deal of respect in the music world at large. The nonet played compositions by Hodeir such as "Cross Criss" (LE 9), composed and arranged very much in the Gil Evans style of pieces like "Boplicity," with broad, mixed voicings in a relaxed legato flow. The solo work in the Jazz Groupe de Paris is also reminiscent of Miles Davis's band at the time: the trumpeter, Jean Liesse, plays in Davis's restrained, laid-back style, while Bobby Jaspar's fast Warne Marsh–style legato runs are again in evidence. These two soloists, as well as bassist Pierre Michelot, are underpinned by a gently dissonant tapestry of sound. In 1956 Hodeir dedicated his piece "Evanescence" to Gil Evans, taking Evans's "Moondreams" as a model.[8]

Claude Bolling is a multifaceted composer, arranger, pianist, and bandleader who also wrote pieces in which the cool jazz influence can be detected. "Show Me a Rose" and "Gee Lee,"[9] for example, are written and arranged for a Gerry Mulligan–style pianoless quartet with trumpet and baritone saxophone. Bolling's septet composition "The Jockey" (LE 10) features canonic voice leading in the theme. Pianist Martial Solal improvises in his well-known virtuoso style, with a somewhat laid-back rhythmic feeling. The versatile trumpeter Roger Guérin achieves the desired "cool" sound through use of a mute, while tenor saxophonist Jean-Claude Fohrenbach's playing references Stan Getz.

Born in Algeria, Martial Solal moved to Paris in 1950 and has been based there since. Like his hero, Art Tatum, Solal developed a very high level of technique and was comfortable in several different styles. In a cool jazz setting he reined in his impressive technical skill somewhat, playing with a more laid-back rhythmic feeling and flirting with the modern harmony of the Lennie Tristano school. On "Tenderly" (LE 11), there are also hints of laying back behind the rhythm from vibraphonist Fats Sadi.

Solal's leanings toward cool jazz became more pronounced in later years, especially starting in 1968, when he undertook frequent European tours in partnership with Lee Konitz.

Bernard Peiffer, like Solal a technically proficient, versatile musician not tied to a particular style, seems to have been influenced by the Baroque stylings prevalent in cool jazz in his composition "Prelude, Fugue and Trio" on "Lullaby of Birdland." The fugue section of this piece is particularly interesting (LE 12).

Italy

The tenor saxophonist Gianni Basso was influenced by Stan Getz and other West Coast saxophonists in the early 1950s. This influence can be heard on "Ain't Misbehavin'" (LE 13), where Basso plays with a soft tone, a subtle vibrato, and a laid-back rhythmic feel.

In 1955 Basso formed the Sestetto Italiano with the trumpeter Oscar Valdambrini, whose tone and melodic sense owed much to Art Farmer. In 1958 the sextet became a quintet; the resulting Basso-Valdambrini Quintet was one of the best-known Italian jazz ensembles until around 1962. On "Come Out, Wherever You Are" (LE 14), the group can be heard improvising simultaneously in the Mulligan-inspired two-voice linear style. In the intervening five years, Basso's tone had grown somewhat more robust, reflecting a Sonny Rollins influence.

The accordionist Gorni Kramer recorded a jazz fugue on March 9, 1954, written on the popular Italian song "In cerca di te." The piece is through-composed, with no space for an improvised solo.[10]

Spain and Portugal

During the Fascist dictatorship in Spain, which lasted from 1939 to 1975, jazz was condemned as a symbol of capitalism and Western decadence and was practically forbidden. As a result Spanish jazz musicians, such as Tete Montoliu, were forced to emigrate.[11] In Portugal, also under a Fascist regime in the years following World War II, the situation was much the same.

Sweden

Ake "Stan" Hasselgard, the only clarinetist ever to be co-featured by Benny Goodman, and who unfortunately was killed in an accident on November 23, 1948, in the United States, can be estimated as one of the first well-known Swedish cool jazz musician. His 1947 two-chorus blues solo on "Swedish Pastry" (LE 15) (dedicated to him by composer Barney Kessel) shows the clarinetist improvising in a manner similar to that of the Tristano school, with a rather restrained tone, long legato phrasing, and frequent use of altered chords.

Like Denmark, Sweden had also escaped the Nazi prohibition on playing jazz, and thus had a functioning jazz scene in the forties, with a relative wealth of educated musicians, among whom the cool jazz influence became evident around 1949 or 1950. Since Sweden boasted few steady bands in the early fifties, the scene was more collective, with a large group of musicians playing in different combinations under a changing nominal leadership. Accordingly, an overview of the musicians, arranged by instrument, will be provided first, followed by the listening examples in chronological order.

Rolf Ericson was certainly the most prominent Swedish trumpeter of this period. From 1947 to 1950, he worked in the United States in the big bands of Charlie Barnet, Woody Herman, and Elliot Lawrence, returning to Sweden in 1950 with a quintet led by Charlie Parker. Ericson stayed in Europe for several years after that, contributing to the cool jazz movement. His native versatility and technical proficiency allowed him to adapt to the new music, playing with a restrained tone and often with a mute. Other trumpeters on the Swedish cool jazz scene included Leppe Sundewall, Bengt-Arne Wallin, and Reine Wenliden.

The solid tone and adept rhythmic feel of trombonist Ake Persson, who died in a car crash at the age of forty-two, made him the dominant Swedish personality on that instrument. His phrasing places him stylistically between J. J. Johnson and Frank Rosolino.

The playing of clarinetist Putte Wickman, who was also widely admired by his U.S. peers, owed much to that of Buddy DeFranco; however, his tone is somewhat softer and richer in overtones than DeFranco's—similar to the sound of saxophonist Arne Domnerus on that musician's occasional clarinet performances, such as "Side Car."[12] Another notable clarinet soloist was Carl-Erik Lindgren.

Domnerus was the dominant alto saxophonist in Sweden during the 1940s and 1950s. His "Favourite Group" was still playing in the bebop style in 1949 but gradually metamorphosed into a cool jazz ensemble. Domnerus's alto style went through a similar transformation: in the forties he played in the style of his earlier model, Benny Carter, but changed his approach under the influence of Lee Konitz, improvising from then on with a smooth tone in lively legato phrases.

Among the tenor saxophonists, Hacke Björksten played in a style similar to that of Warne Marsh in tone and phrasing.[13] Rolf Blomquist, Bjarne Nerem,[14] and Carl-Henrik Norin, on the other hand, hewed closer to the Stan Getz/Four Brothers school.[15]

Baritone saxophonist Lars Gullin played a central role in Swedish cool jazz. No other Swedish musician at the time received as much recognition as Gullin did, both at home and abroad. In 1954, for example, he became the first European musician to win the "New Star" award on his instrument in the *Down Beat* magazine critics' poll. Gullin had played alto since 1949, switching to baritone in 1951; his tone may have been closer to that of Stan Getz than Gerry Mulligan. He also claimed Lee Konitz and the Miles Davis band as influences. Gullin contributed many compositions to jazz: one of the best known and most beloved is the ballad "Danny's Dream,"[16] dedicated to his son. Gullin often arranged in the two-voice linear Mulligan vein[17] but also partly in the style of Gil Evans, with broad, mixed voicings.[18] One of the high points of his career must also have been a January 1956 concert tour of Germany with Lee Konitz and Hans Koller's New Stars, during which Gullin was able to measure himself against his idol, Konitz, in two concerts. The two musicians, both playing baritone sax, improvised together over the changes to "All the Things You Are."[19]

In the 1960s Gullin concentrated on his work as a composer. He died untimely in 1976, at the age of forty-eight.

As with the saxophonists, the Swedish cool jazz piano scene was dominated by a single personality: Bengt Hallberg, also a fine composer and arranger, who had played with Stan Getz on his 1950 quartet tour of Sweden and whose sparse single-note phrasing and laid-back offbeats quickly found favor with the listening public. It was during the first studio session of this Getz quartet that a Swedish folk song, "Ack Värmeland, du sköna," was recorded; it subsequently became a much-loved standard under the title "Dear Old Stockholm."[20] The aforementioned characteristics of Hallberg's style were blended, however, with elements of Lennie Tristano's, which Hallberg could reproduce at will.[21] Two other noteworthy Swedish exponents of the Tristano school were Reinhold Svensson, like Tristano and George Shearing a blind pianist who also played with his quintet in the style of the Shearing group,[22] and Gunnar Svensson, who made a name for himself as the composer of music for numerous films—and is also the uncle of pianist Esbjörn Svensson.

Two guitarists, Sten Carlberg and Rolf Berg, were improvisers in the Bauer-Raney-Farlow mold, while Simon Brehm and Georg Riedel stood out among the Swedish bassists as melodic soloists.[23] A large number of drummers accompanied these and other Swedish musicians in the prescribed subtle manner.

At this point we turn to the previously mentioned listening examples of Swedish cool jazz, arranged in chronological order:

The first example, from the spring of 1950, is "Chloe" (LE 16). It demonstrates the early piano style of Bengt Hallberg in sparkling single-note lines, integrating the harmonic lessons of the Tristano school.

The next example, "Miles Away" (LE 17), is a composition by Rolf Ericson arranged in the Gil Evans style. The theme is rendered with a smooth, restrained tone in broadly voiced mixed chords; Ericson and Arne Domnerus play solos.

Reinhold Svensson improvises in the Tristano vein on "Fine and Dandy" (LE 18), but the most noticeable characteristic here is the use of frequent runs to the high-end notes of extended chords.

Lars Gullin composed "Dorica" (LE 19) using the harmonies of "All the Things You Are," other than in the final four bars; Gunnar Svensson once again plays a solo in the Tristano style.

Gullin arranged the standard "Liza" (LE 20) for a four-part wind group with French horn, in the mixed-voice style of his role model, Gil Evans.

Lennie Tristano and Lee Konitz composed the piece "Ablution," again using the much-loved changes of "All the Things You Are." In addition to Gullin, on the recording of this composition made on September 9, 1952 (LE 21), Bengt Hallberg can be heard once more delivering his sparse, accented single-note lines with a laid-back feel and an audible Tristano influence.

In a pianoless quartet based on the Mulligan template, Lars Gullin performs his composition "Holiday for Piano" (LE 22) over the harmonic structure of "Fine and Dandy," with trombonist Ake Persson in the two-voiced linear style. Persson's technical proficiency is evident in his distinctive melodies, offset by Gullin's sonorous baritone saxophone.

On the occasion of a Stan Kenton Orchestra tour of Sweden, Gullin organized a recording session with soloists from the band, including his idol, Lee Konitz. The composition "Dedicated to Lee" (LE 23) is based on "Fine and Dandy" again, and the Konitz influence can easily be heard in the melodies of Gullin's two solo choruses.

The following example shows once again the influence of the Baroque on cool jazz. This influence was perhaps less prevalent in Sweden than in Germany, for example. However, Bengt Hallberg's contrapuntal arrangement of "All the Things You Are" (LE 24)—particularly well suited to this treatment due to its harmonic movement down the circle of fifths—illustrates that the Baroque was very much part of the picture.

"Whiskey Sour" (LE 25), again from Bengt Hallberg, showcases not only the profound musicianship of Ake Persson and Lars Gullin but also the moving, smooth-toned soloing of alto saxophonist Arne Domnerus.

The final example in this cross-section of Swedish cool jazz is "Primula veris" (LE 26). It highlights Putte Wickman's clarinet playing, somewhat softer than that of Buddy DeFranco and very fluent.

Although a trend toward hard bop and mainstream jazz can be observed in other European countries from around 1957 onward, the jazz musicians of Sweden stayed true to the "cool school" for quite a bit longer.

Czechoslovakia

Czech and Slovak jazz musicians had to struggle against the prejudices of their political leaders from the end of the Second World War into the mid-1950s. West Coast jazz helped to alleviate this problem, as Lubomir Doruzka writes:

> This was the time of West Coast jazz; the tendency of that music to take European forms as role models made it seem hardly provocative at all. Clean intonation without "growls" or "honks," restrained means of expression, three-

or four-voice imitative passages with canonic or even contrapuntal voice lead-ing—all this supported the idea that jazz had become cultivated, that it was moving closer and closer to the noble European ideal. West Coast tunes com-prised another third [Dixieland being the first third] of Gustav Brom's program—the rest was pop music, without which the big band, even at that time, couldn't have survived. Karel Krautgartner tried to cultivate his own style but there was no doubt that his roots lay in West Coast jazz. Cultivation and the new values in jazz music became the most important arguments of jazz apologists.[24]

Gustav Brom had a technically proficient trumpeter in Jaromir Hnilicka, who played with a smooth tone and reserved phrasing.[25] In Karel Krautgartner's band, the leader himself and Jan Konopasek, on alto and baritone saxophone respec-tively, were the outstanding soloists in the new style.

Poland

In Poland in the early 1950s there was some sustained jazz activity despite the problems with the communist regime. Krzysztof Komeda had serious difficulties with the Polish government due to his championing of jazz music. These were resolved only after Komeda met with great success at the first Polish jazz festival, held in Sopot in 1956. Among other pieces, he performed his own "Memory of Bach," in which he adapted various motifs from Bach's music.[26] Jazz later began to flourish in Poland, and in the 1960s Polish artists even toured the United States.

Hungary

The most successful Hungarian cool jazz musician was undoubtedly the guitarist Attila Zoller, who early after the war escaped to Austria. From 1948 on he worked in Austria and Germany—Zoller made his first recording in Austria with Vera Auer in 1950, though not in the cool style;[27] from 1954, he worked a great deal with Jutta Hipp and Albert Mangelsdorff. As such, Zoller's career will be dis-cussed in the context of the German jazz scene.

Otherwise there was no cool jazz activity in Hungary. The jazz musicians there—as the ones in Russia and other countries with communist governments—suffered from the political pressure on jazz as being American and capitalistic.

Germany

As in Sweden, cool jazz was welcomed in Germany and played by a number of
ensembles, with the difference that the use of Baroque devices was particularly

popular. One of the first groups in Germany to play in the "cool" style was the Johannes Rediske Quintett, resident from 1951 onward in the Berlin club Badewanne. The group often played its themes in the "Shearing style," the unison melodies performed by clarinetist Lothar Noack and Rediske's guitar over block chords from pianist Alexander Spychalski. On "Pick Yourself Up" (LE 27) this ensemble approach is preceded by a contrapuntal introduction. The guitar solo is similar to the style of Jimmy Raney or Chuck Wayne; the pianist, in addition to block chords in the Shearing manner, plays single-note lines with a rhythmically laid-back feel.

Pianist Michael Naura also drew on Shearing's arranging techniques in his own 1955 quintet featuring the vibraphonist Wolfgang Schlüter—for example, on Naura's original composition "Micha's Dilemma."[28]

Hans Koller was born and raised in Vienna, attending the city's music academy. In 1947, after serving in the German armed forces and a period as an American prisoner of war, Koller returned to the Austrian capital and played for a time in the Hot Club Vienna, as well as in the Horst Winter orchestra. In 1951 Koller was engaged by Freddie Brocksieper and moved to Munich; from that time on he was mainly active in Germany. Although Koller's playing with Winter and Brocksieper in 1950 and 1951 was still characterized by a robust, voluminous tone and a Coleman Hawkins–like vibrato,[29] his tone and phrasing soon changed completely under the influence of Stan Getz and especially Lee Konitz. He began to play with a more fragile tone in long, connected lines, as can be heard on recordings from 1952 with a quartet including the pianist Jutta Hipp. Hipp had taken a kind of correspondence course, studying by letter with Lennie Tristano, and she soloed in the pianist's style.[30] In 1953 Koller added trombonist Albert Mangelsdorff to the group, which he now called the Hans Koller New Jazz Stars and which became one of the best-known bands in European cool jazz.

Asked about his stylistic lineage, Mangelsdorff replied: "It was naturally the Lennie Tristano school at that time—but as a soloist, Lee Konitz impressed me most. It was this improbable balance in his playing."[31] Mangelsdorff delivered cool and intellectual solos with a subtle tone, a fine melodic sense, and astounding technique, such as "Indian Summer" from May of 1953.[32]

The themes of some pieces, such as "Flamingo" and "All the Things You Are," were in a two-voice linear form.[33] This was also the case with "Sound Koller" (LE 28), a Koller original based on the changes of "Out of Nowhere." Koller's solo on this piece is very much in the Lee Konitz/Warne Marsh style. Mangelsdorff plays in the aforementioned subtle, melodic, carefully considered fashion. Jutta Hipp shows clear characteristics of the Lennie Tristano school, with laid-back rhythm, complex altered chords, and fast runs into the upper reaches of both the piano and the harmony.

In 1954 Jutta Hipp left the ensemble and founded her own group (see below). In her place, Koller hired the Viennese musicologist Dr. Roland Kovac, who improvised contrapuntally (as on his composition "Feuerwehr"[34]) as well as in the Tristano style. Most importantly, Kovac became the main composer and arranger for the group; his ambitious compositions enriched the repertoire. Some of his pieces were canonic, such as "Iris,"[35] some two-voice linear, such as "3 x 2" and "For Gerry."[36] Mangelsdorff, who also left the group, was replaced by baritone saxophonist Willi Sanner, whose tone and phrasing were reminiscent of Lars Gullin's. "Porsche" (LE 29) is a composition by Kovac's, using "Fine and Dandy" as a harmonic basis. The theme is in unison, composed in long, swung lines in the style of the Tristano school. Echoes of Tristano can also be heard in Kovac's piano solo, while Koller improvises once again in the Konitz mold. Johnny Fischer also contributes a melodious bass solo.

Kovac's "Little Concert," on which both Koller and Sanner play solos in their typical styles, as previously described, was also recorded during this period.[37]

In January 1956 Koller led his New Stars, with Lee Konitz and Lars Gullin as guest soloists, on the aforementioned tour of Germany. Kovac composed his piece "Variations No. 8 from 'Passacaglia'" for this tour. The opening is in the form of a fugue, followed by contrapuntal, through-composed melodies. Later in 1956 the New Stars's personnel changed once again; Albert Mangelsdorff returned and stayed until 1958, replacing the baritone saxophonist, while Koller engaged the Hungarian guitarist Attila Zoller to fill the pianist's slot. As is evident on "Serpentinen" (LE 30), the theme to which is arranged in the two-voice linear style, Zoller's playing is animatedly arpeggiated, somewhat in the style of Jimmy Raney, with interesting melodic turns. Mangelsdorff begins his solo with Zoller's concluding motif, as usual delivering an elegantly structured, melodic improvisation. Koller has by this point departed somewhat from the Konitz school and tends now—and ever more markedly after 1957—toward more spirited soloing à la Zoot Sims.

As has already been mentioned, Koller's playing from 1957 onward began to lean more and more toward the mainstream, although the New Stars with Mangelsdorff continued to perform until 1958. Mangelsdorff himself played in 1957 with two West Coast luminaries, Bud Shank and Bob Cooper, and in 1958 he assumed leadership of the newly founded Hessischer Rundfunk radio network.

Jutta Hipp, the Leipzig-born, Tristano-style pianist, formed her own ensemble in 1954 after leaving the Koller band. It featured Emil Mangelsdorff and Joki Freund on alto and tenor saxophones respectively. Both musicians were heavily influenced by Konitz and Marsh, much as Hipp's writing and playing were influenced by Tristano—all easily recognizable on "Variations" (LE 31), a Hipp arrangement based on "Fine and Dandy."

On the piece "What's New?" recorded on the same day,[38] Hipp begins her solo contrapuntally, switching later to Tristano-style phrasing. This phrasing can also be heard clearly on Hipp's own composition "Two Oranges," written on the base of the changes of "Lover Man."[39]

In 1955 Hipp also played with both Lars Gullin and Attila Zoller, before moving to New York at the invitation of Leonard Feather. She played there in a trio at the Hickory House (two LPS are taken from these performances[40]), at the Newport Jazz Festival, and on a recording date with Zoot Sims.[41] Thereafter, Hipp gave up music as a profession.

Rolf Kühn also grew up in Leipzig, where he appeared in 1949 as a clarinet soloist with Kurt Henkel's band. In 1952 Kühn emigrated to West Germany, where he performed with Werner Müller and the RIAS Dance Orchestra as well as with the Walter Dobschinsky Orchestra, quickly making a name for himself as a technically proficient clarinet soloist in the Buddy DeFranco style. In 1954, at the German Jazz Festival in Frankfurt, Kühn played in the illustrious company of pianist Paul Kuhn, guitarist Johannes Rediske, and bassist Hans Last. The bassist would later become famous as a composer, arranger, and bandleader under the name of James Last. Kühn's solo on "September Song" (LE 32) shows his technically impressive, DeFranco-like qualities, often using wide intervals across the whole range of the clarinet.

Kühn played many more noteworthy "cool" solos; he is particularly outstanding on "Sweet Georgia Brown" from 1953.[42] He was also successful overseas: 1956 found him working with American musicians, and in 1957 he led a quartet that performed at the Newport Jazz Festival and toured with the "Birdland Stars."

From 1947 onward, one of Germany's most prominent bands was that of Kurt Edelhagen. Besides popular and dance music, the group played challenging jazz pieces similar to those of the Stan Kenton Orchestra. Edelhagen's big-band music includes few hints of cool jazz, but the recordings of a smaller combo from the same band, known as the Kurt Edelhagen All Stars, are more emphatically influenced by the cool movement. The group consisted of Rolf Schneebiegl (trumpet), Otto Bredl (trombone), Franz von Klenck (alto saxophone), Paul Martin (tenor saxophone), Helmut Reinhardt (baritone saxophone), a variety of pianists, and Bobby Schmidt (drums). On "Cherokee," recorded in 1952,[43] Schneebiegl can be heard soloing in the Miles Davis style, the saxophonists in the manner of Konitz and Marsh, and pianist Heinz Kiessling in the Tristano vein. "There's a Small Hotel,"[44] "The Lady Is a Tramp,"[45] and "Sonny Boy"[46] are further examples of the influence of cool / West Coast jazz on arrangements and soloing.

On "The Continental" (LE 32), the arrangement evokes Gerry Mulligan, with a low countermelody. Baritone saxophonist Helmut Reinhardt's playing also echoes that of his role model, whereas von Klenck's alto saxophone is now more reminiscent of West Coast exponents such as Art Pepper than of Konitz. Rolf Schneebiegl's soloing style is similar to that of Shorty Rogers.

Bandleader Erwin Lehn was also obliged on a regular basis to play popular music. Like Edelhagen, Lehn was blessed with several good soloists, including trumpeter Horst Fischer, saxophonists Werner Baumgart and Gerry Weinkopf, and pianist Horst Jankowski. At Frankfurt's German Jazz Festival in 1955, Lehn presented his big band playing pieces in the cool style, such as the canonically structured "Cool Street" and "E.V.G.," with a two-voice linear melody.[47] A combo was formed from this band as well, in 1957: the Horst Jankowski Sextett, featuring Weinkopf on flute, Baumgart on oboe, bassoonist Fritz Dautel, and Jankowski on piano and cembalo—the instrumentation reflecting Europe's musical past—accompanied by bass and drums. The band played music strongly influenced by the Baroque, such as "Humoreske in Blues" (LE 34)—a "blues in Baroque," with composer Gerry Weinkopf as the main soloist.

Wolfgang Lauth also introduced his newly formed quartet to a wider audience at the 1955 German Jazz Festival in Frankfurt. His performance of chamber-style pieces, including contrapuntal and canonic sections owing much to John Lewis and the Modern Jazz Quartet (for example "Cool March" and "Cafe Souvenir"[48]), found favor with German audiences. Lauth continued in this vein with mostly original pieces such as "Goofy," "Cool Cave," and "Lauthentic," over the harmonies of "Just You, Just Me."[49] At the 1956 German Jazz Festival he opened his set with "French Fries" (LE 35), a hard-swinging, fugato-composed original. Worthy of note is the solo from guitarist Werner Pöhlert: animated and rhythmically somewhat laid back in the style of Jimmy Raney and Tal Farlow.

In 1957 Lauth replaced Pöhlert with vibraphonist Fritz Hartschuh, making the group's instrumentation, in line with its penchant for contrapuntal composition, identical to that of the much-loved Modern Jazz Quartet. On "Schwetzinger Original" (LE 36) Hartschuh plays with a fairly hard attack but otherwise much like Milt Jackson. Lauth uses clearly delineated phrases with a laid-back offbeat. Other, similar pieces from this period include "Malu" and "Sunday Picnic."[50]

As with Lauth's ensemble, the New Jazz Group Hannover made its debut in front of a large audience at the 1955 German Jazz Festival. The group's alto saxophonist, Bernd Rabe, impressed listeners with his Konitz-style improvising, notably on "Lover Man" (LE 37).

In August of that year, American trombonist Bill Russo recorded a few numbers with the band; Rabe impresses once again in a similar fashion, for example on "Night in Tunisia."[51]

Helmut Brandt, a baritone saxophonist in the Gerry Mulligan style, formed a band in 1955 basically modeled on Mulligan's quartet, although it included a pianist. This had the effect of thickening the compositions' harmonics compared with the Mulligan band. The trumpeter, Conny Jackel, played—in a manner similar to Chet Baker's—melodious phrases with a restrained tone. On "11 x 50 Kilometer" (LE 38), an original composition, Brandt impresses with a clearly structured, logically developed solo with well-timed climaxes.

Austria

Hans Koller, the Viennese saxophonist discussed above, worked occasionally in the early 1950s with Austrian cool jazz musicians, who went by the name of the Austrian All Stars.[52] Of particular note in this ensemble was alto saxophonist Hans Salomon, whose tone and phrasing were reminiscent of those of Lee Konitz and a number of West Coast saxophonists. The other members of the group were Karl Drewo, at the time clearly influenced by the Konitz/Marsh school, and the pianist Joe Zawinul, who was then mostly playing striking single-note solos with a generally laid-back rhythmic feel but making occasional forays into Lennie Tristano–style harmonic and melodic territory. The two saxophonists can be heard in characteristic form on "There's a Small Hotel" (LE 39), while Zawinul's Tristano-oriented soloing style is evident on "The Way You Look Tonight" (LE 40).

Friedrich Gulda was often featured with the Austrian All Stars and composed for them as well, including "Cool-Da" (LE 41). This piece is a twelve-bar blues, arranged in two and three voices and partly canonic; Karl Drewo plays a tenor saxophone solo. Gulda composed two similar pieces—linear, with two or three voices and canonic tendencies—for his concert at New York's Birdland in June 1956: "Quintet" and "Introvert."[53] Gulda surprised the American audience by not sounding like a European classical pianist. Rather, the hallmarks of his playing were a sharp attack, bebop-like single-note phrasing, a broad range, and laid-back, "cool"-influenced rhythms, as on "All the Things You Are" (LE 42).

Perhaps one of the best proofs of cool jazz's—and especially Lee Konitz's—influence on European musicians during the 1950s is the well-known Viennese Dixieland clarinetist Fatty George, who made no bones about occasionally picking up the alto saxophone (an instrument he seldom played) and improvising in the Konitz style. "I Never Knew" (LE 43) is such an instance, as well as featuring a Mangelsdorff-inspired, coolly restrained trombone solo of Willi Meerwald.

Graz was also home to a group of young musicians playing in the cool style, led by the pianist Fridl Althaller. The arrangements, often inspired by the West Coast jazz of the time, were mostly written by drummer Friedrich Waidacher. The soloists, also appearing on "Cool Me Madam" (LE 45), included Friedrich Körner, a trumpeter and great admirer of Shorty Rogers; Erich Kleinschuster, a trombonist in the J. J. Johnson mold; and tenor saxophonist Heinz Hönig, remi-

niscent of Stan Getz in both phrasing and tone. This example is a rather dense
Waidacher arrangement in four voices with canonic touches.

Conclusion

As we have seen, cool jazz was a major influence on the playing of European
ensembles and musicians from 1950 to 1957. The most intensive utilization of the
cool style occurred between 1952 and 1956; after 1957, personal playing styles,
repertoires, and arrangements in Europe turned more to mainstream jazz and
hard bop. European cool jazz was concentrated geographically in England,
France, Belgium, and Austria but figured most prominently in Sweden and Germany. Germany also exhibited the strongest tendencies to incorporate older
European art-music techniques and styles, particularly those of the Baroque era.
Jazz and jazz musicians suffered in countries ruled by communist or fascist dic-
tatorships, both of which regarded jazz as too Western and libertarian. These
regimes dismissed, opposed, or even banned the music, making impossible all
but the most limited development in the direction of cool jazz. European countries other than those mentioned above did not show any remarkable cool jazz
activities in these years.

LISTENING EXAMPLES

*Abbreviations: Trumpet (tp); trombone (tb); French horn (frhn); clarinet (cl); soprano
saxophone (ss); alto saxophone (as); tenor saxophone (ts); baritone saxophone (bs);
drums (dm); piano (p); vibraphone (vib); guitar (g); bass (b); composer (comp);
conductor (cond); excerpt (Exc.)*

LE 1: "Leon Bismarck," Exc. 0:00–1:06, Esquire 317. Johnny Dankworth Seven: Jimmy
Deuchar (tp), Eddie Harvey (tb), Johnny Dankworth (as), Don Rendell (ts), Bill
LeSage (p), Eric Dawson (b), Tony Kinsey (dm), July 12, 1951, London.

LE 2: "Strictly Confidential," Exc. 0:00–1:36, Esquire 317. Johnny Dankworth Seven:
Eddie Blair (tp), Eddie Harvey (tb), Johnny Dankworth (as), Don Rendell (ts), Bill
LeSage (p), Eric Dawson (b), Eddie Taylor (dm), Frank Holder (bongo), Nov. 8, 1951,
London.

LE 3: "Somerset Morn," Exc. 0:00–1:50, Vocalion CDNJT 5303. Laurie Monk Quartet:
Laurie Monk (tb), Johnny Dankworth (as), Eric Dawson (b), Kenny Clare (dm), Sept.
4, 1957, London.

LE 4: "Cool Sparks," Exc. 0:00–2:02, Jasmine JASCD 613. Don Rendell Quintet: Don
Rendell (ts), Ronnie Ross (bs), Damian Robinson (p), Sammy Stokes (b), Benny
Goodman (dm), May 16, 1955, London.

LE 5: "Procession," Exc. 0:00–1:12, Limelight 820 950-2. Ted Heath and His Music:
Bobby Pratt, Bert Ezard, Duncan Campbell, Eddie Blair (tp), Wally Smith, Don
Lusher, Jimmy Coombes, Ric Kennedy (tb), Ronnie Chamberlain (ss,as), Les Gilbert

(as), Henry Mackenzie (cl,ts), Red Price (ts), Ken Kiddier (bs), Frank Horrox (p), Johnny Hawksworth (b), Ronnie Verrell (dm), Ted Heath (cond), May 1, 1956, New York, Carnegie Hall.

LE 6: "Doxy," Exc. 0:35–1:08, Jasmine JASCD 614. Vic Ash Quartet: Vic Ash (cl), Terry Shannon (p), Pete Eldersfield (b), Benny Goodman (dm), Feb. 18, 1956, London, Royal Festival Hall.

LE 7: "How About You," Exc. 0:00–1:58, Gitanes 549400-2. René Thomas Quintet: René Urtreger (p), René Thomas (g), Benoit Quersin or Jean-Marie Ingrand (b), Jean-Louis Viale (dm), April 17, 1954, Paris.

LE 8: "Milestone No. 2," Exc. 1:07–1:49, Harmonia Mundi PJC 222008. Orchestre Henri Renaud: Sandy Mosse, Bobby Jaspar (ts), Henri Renaud (p), Jimmy Gourley (g), Pierre Michelot (b), Pierre Lemarchand (dm), May/June 1951, Paris.

LE 9: "Cross Criss," Vogue 74321610202. Le Jazz Groupe de Paris: Jean Liesse, Buzz Gardner (tp), Nat Peck (tb), Jean Aldegon (as), Bobby Jaspar (ts), Fats Sadi (vib), Armand Migiani (p), Pierre Michelot (b), Jacques David (dm), André Hodeir (comp,cond), Dec. 13, 1954, Paris.

LE 10: "The Jockey," Exc. 0:00–1:27, DRG Records SL 5201. Claude Bolling et son orchestre: Roger Guerin (tp), Jean-Claude Fohrenbach, Pierre Gossez (ts), Martial Solal (p), Victor Apicella (g), Pierre Michelot (b), Christian Garros (dm), May 28, 1956, Paris.

LE 11: "Tenderly," Exc. 0:00–1:28, Vogue 74321115142. Sadi–Solal Quartet: Fats Sadi (vib), Martial Solal (p), Jean-Marie Ingrand (b), Jean-Louis Viale (dm), Jan. 9, 1956, Paris.

LE 12: "Prelude, Fugue and Trio on 'Lullaby of Birdland,'" Exc. 1:16–2:12, Brunswick 10168 EPB. Bernard Peiffer Trio: Bernard Peiffer (p), Ernie Furtado (b), Johnny Cresci (dm), July 10, 1957, New York.

LE 13: "Ain't Misbehavin'," Exc. 0:00–2:04, Musica Jazz MJCD 1111. Gianni Basso Quartet: Gianni Basso (ts), Vittorio Paltrinieri (p), Al King (b), Rodolfo Bonetto (dm), May 20, 1954, Milan.

LE 14: "Come Out, Wherever You Are," Exc 1:32–2:08, Musica Jazz MJCD 1111. Basso-Valdambrini Quintet: Oscar Valdambrini (tp), Gianni Basso (ts), Renato Sellani (p), Giorgio Azzolini (b), Gianno Cazzola (dm), June 9-10, 1959, Milan.

LE 15: "Swedish Pastry," Exc. 0:43–1:18, Capitol CR-8803. Stan Hasselgard and His All Star Six: Stan Hasselgard (cl), Red Norvo (vib), Arnold Ross (p), Barney Kessel (g), Rollo Garberg (b), Frank Bode (dm), Dec. 18, 1947, Los Angeles.

LE 16: "Chloe," Exc. 1:18–1:58, Dragon DRCD 358. Arne Domnerus Favourite Group: Leppe Sundevall (tp), Arne Domnerus (as), Ulf Linde (vib), Bengt Hallberg (p), Gunnar Almstedt (b), Anders Burman (dm), March 3, 1950, Stockholm.

LE 17: "Miles Away," Exc. 0:53–1:58, Dragon DRCD 394. Rolf Ericson med Reinhold Svenssons Orkester: Rolf Ericson (tp), George Vernon (tb), Arne Domnerus (as), Gösta Theselius (ts), Lars Gullin (bs), Reinhold Svensson (p), Simon Brehm (b), Sven Bollhem (dm), Sept. 19, 1950, Stockholm.

LE 18: "Fine and Dandy," Exc. 1:32–2:32, 1950, Dragon DRCD 394. Jam Session at Karlaplan: Rolf Ericson (tp), Carl-Erik Lindgren (cl), Carl-Henrik Norin (ts),

Reinhold Svensson (p), Lasse Karlsson (g), Leppe Sundevall (b), Jack Norén (dm), Olle Helander (master of ceremonies), late Sept./early Oct. 1950, Stockholm, Karlaplans-Studion.

LE 19: "Dorica," Exc. 2:02–2:46, Dragon DRCD 380. Lars Gullin Quintet: Rolf Ericson (tp), Lars Gullin (bs), Gunnar Svensson (p), Yngve Akerberg (b), Jack Norén (dm), Jan. 19, 1952, Stockholm.

LE 20: "Liza," Exc. 0:00–1:09, Dragon DRCD 380. Lars Gullin Cool Sounders: Weine Renliden (tp), Ake Björkman (frhn), Carl-Erik Lindgren (ts), Lars Gullin (bs), Gunnar Svensson (p), Yngve Akerberg (b), Jack Norén (dm), May 15, 1952, Stockholm.

LE 21: "Ablution," Exc. 0:32–1:58, Dragon DRCD 405. Bengt Hallberg Sextet: Rolf Ericson (tp), Lars Gullin (bs), Ulf Linde (vib), Bengt Hallberg (p), Gunnar Almstedt (b), Jack Norén (dm), Sept. 12, 1952, Stockholm.

LE 22: "Holiday for Piano," Exc. 0:00–2:03, Dragon DRCD 395. Lars Gullin Quartet: Ake Persson (tb), Lars Gullin (bs), Simon Brehm (b), Jack Norén (dm), Feb. 12, 1953, Stockholm.

LE 23: "Dedicated to Lee" (orig. take 1), Exc. 0:00–1:58, Dragon DRCD 234. Lars Gullin and His American All Stars: Conte Candoli (tp), Frank Rosolino (tb), Lee Konitz (as), Zoot Sims (ts), Lars Gullin (bs), Don Bagley (b), Stan Levey (dm), Aug. 25, 1953, Stockholm.

LE 24: "All the Things You Are," Exc. 1:05–2:08, Caprice CAP 22042. Bengt Hallberg Quartet: Bengt Hallberg (p), Herbert Katz (g), Erik Lindström (b), Risto Vanari (dm), Oct. 20, 1953, Helsinki.

LE 25: "Whiskey Sour," Exc. 1:16–3:08, Dragon DRCD 402. Bengt Hallberg and His Swedish All Stars: Ake Persson (tb), Arne Domnerus (as), Lars Gullin (bs), Bengt Hallberg (p), Simon Brehm (b), William Schiöpffe (dm), Nov. 9, 1953, Stockholm.

LE 26: "Primula veris," Exc. 1:52–2:33, Dragon DRCD 401. Lars Gullin Septet: Ake Persson (tb), Putte Wickman (cl), Bjarne Nerem (ts), Lars Gullin (bs), Bengt Hallberg (p), Georg Riedel (b), Robert Edman (dm), June 3, 1954, Stockholm.

LE 27: "Pick Yourself Up," Exc. 0:00–1:54, Bear Family BCD 16172 AH. Johannes Rediske Quintett: Lothar Noack (cl), Alexander Spychalski (p), Johannes Rediske (g), Manfred Behrendt (b), Joe Glaser (dm), Jan. 30, 1952, Berlin.

LE 28: "Sound Koller," Exc. 0:00–2:21, Decca DL 8229. Hans Koller Quintet: Albert Mangelsdorff (tb), Hans Koller (ts), Jutta Hipp (p), Shorty Roeder (b), Rudi Sehring (dm), June 21, 1953, Baden-Baden.

LE 29: "Porsche," RST 91562-2. Hans Koller New Jazz Stars: Hans Koller (ts), Willi Sanner (bs), Roland Kovac (p), Johnny Fischer (b), Rudi Sehring (dm), Oct. 25, 1955, Vienna.

LE 30: "Serpentinen," Exc. 0:00–3:34, Jazztone J 1038. Hans Koller New Jazz Stars: Albert Mangelsdorff (tb), Hans Koller (ts), Attila Zoller (g), Johnny Fischer (b), Rudi Sehring (dm), June 29, 1956, Frankfurt/M.

LE 31: "Variations," Fresh Sound FSR-CD 421. Jutta Hipp Quintet: Emil Mangelsdorff (as), Joki Freund (ts), Jutta Hipp (p), Hans Kresse (b), Karl Sanner (dm), April 24, 1954, Frankfurt/M.

LE 32: "September Song," Exc. 0:31–1:48, Bear Family BCD 15430-1. Rolf Kühn All Stars: Rolf Kühn (cl), Paul Kuhn (p), Johannes Rediske (g), Hans "James" Last (b), Teddy Paris (dm), June 5, 1954, Frankfurt/M.

LE 33: "The Continental," Exc. 0:00–1:50, Koch 323 981. Kurt Edelhagen und die All Stars: Rolf Schneebiegl (tp), Otto Bredl (tb), Franz von Klenck (as), Paul Martin, Bubi Aderholt (ts), Helmut Reinhardt (bs), Werner Drexler (p), Werner Schultze (b), Bobby Schmidt (dm), Kurt Edelhagen (cond), 1954, Baden-Baden

LE 34: "Humoreske in Blues," Teldec 6.22563. Horst Jankowski Sextett: Gerry Weinkopf (flute), Werner Baumgart (oboe), Fritz Dautel (bassoon), Horst Jankowski (cembalo), Peter Witte (b), Hermann Mutschler (dm), Nov. 8, 1957, Stuttgart.

LE 35: "French Fries," Exc. 0:00–1:14, Bear Family BCD 15717 AH. Wolfgang Lauth Quartet: Wolfgang Lauth (p), Werner Pöhlert (g), Hans Kresse (b), Joe Hackbarth (dm), May 21, 1956, Frankfurt/M., German Jazz Festival.

LE 36: "Schwetzinger Original," Bear Family BCD 15942 AH. Wolfgang Lauth Quartet: Fritz Hartschuh (vib), Wolfgang Lauth (p), Wolfgang Wagner (b), Joe Hackbarth (dm), July 18, 1957, Berlin.

LE 37: "Lover Man," Exc. 0:00–2:18, Bear Family BCD 15430-8. New Jazz Group Hannover: Bernd Rabe (as), Gerd Mann (p), Heinz Kitschenberg (g), Eberhard Pommerenke (b), Helmut Perschke (dm), May 28–30, 1955, Frankfurt/M. German Jazz Festival.

LE 38: "11 x 50 Kilometer," Exc. 0:00–2:25, Jazztone J 1038. Helmut Brandt Combo: Conny Jackel (tp), Helmut Brandt (bs), Ludwig Ebert (p), Klaus Gernhuber (b), Hans-Dieter Taubert (dm), June 29–30, 1956, Frankfurt/M.

LE 39: "There's a Small Hotel," Exc. 0:00–1:22, RST-91549. Austria(n) All Stars: Hans Salomon (as), Karl Drewo (ts), Joe Zawinul (p), Rudolf Hansen (b), Victor Plasil (dm), Oct. 18, 1954, Vienna.

LE 40: "The Way You Look Tonight," Exc. 0:53–1:33, RST-91549. Austria(n) All Stars: Same, same date.

LE 41: "Cool-Da," Exc. 0:29–1:50, RST-91527. Friedrich Gulda und die Austrian All Stars: Dick Murphy (tp), Hans Salomon (as), Karl Drewo (ts), Friedrich Gulda (p), Rudolf Hansen (b), Victor Plasil (dm), spring 1955, Vienna.

LE 42: "All the Things You Are," Exc. 5:09–6:20, Decca 06024-984-7128. Friedrich Gulda and His Sextet: Idrees Sulieman (tp), Jimmy Cleveland (tb), Phil Woods (as), Seldon Powell (ts), Friedrich Gulda (p), Aaron Bell (b), Nick Stabulas (dm), June 29, 1956, New York, Birdland.

LE 43: "I Never Knew," Exc. 0:00–1:38, Columbia DW 5357. Fatty George and His Two Sounds Band: Willi Meerwald (tb), Fatty George (as), Bill Grah (vib,p), Heinz Grah (b), Bob Blumenhoven (dm), Nov. 10, 1954, Cologne.

LE 44: "Cool Me Madam," Radio broadcast. Fridl Althaller und seine Solisten: Friedrich Körner (tp), Erich Kleinschuster (tb), Heinz Hönig (ts), Walter Kühn (bs), Fridl Althaller (p), Gerhard Trötscher (b), Friedrich Waidacher (dm), March 16, 1956, Graz.

1. Johnny Dankworth Seven, "Seven Not Out," rec. July 29, 1950, Esquire 317.

2. Johnny Dankworth and His Orchestra, "The Jerky Thing," rec. Jan. 21, 1954, and "Melbourne Marathon," rec. Dec. 19, 1956, both IAJRC 39.

3. Don Rendell Quintet, "Thames Walk," rec. Feb. 22, 1955, Jasmine JASC 613.

4. John Lewis and members of the Stuttgart Symphony Orchestra, "European Windows," rec. Feb. 20-21, 1958, RCA LPM 1742.

5. Ronnie Scott Quartet, "Have You Met Miss Jones?" rec. Feb. 28, 1951, Properbox 131.

6. Ted Heath and His Orchestra, "Late Night Final" and "After You've Gone," rec. Aug. 21, 1955, Vocalion CDLK 4203.

7. Bernard Peiffer et son Saint-Germain-des-Prés Orchestre, "There's a Small Hotel," rec. Jan. 14, 1954, Gitanes 013042-2.

8. Le Jazz Groupe de Paris Evanescence, rec. June 26, 1956, Savoy MG 12113. André Hodeir writes in the liner notes: "A dedication to the great arranger Gil Evans, whose famous 'Moondreams' hovers here in the background . . ."

9. Claude Bolling et son orchestre, "Show Me a Rose" and "Gee Lee," rec. May 29, 1956, DRG Records SL 5201.

10. Orchestra Gorni Kramer, "In cera di te," rec. March 9, 1954, Twilight Music TWI CD AS 06 26.

11. According to Christa Bruckner-Haring, in her presentation "Jazz Research in Spain" at the 9th Jazz Research Congress, "Jazz and Jazz Research in Europe," on May 17, 2009, in Graz.

12. Bengt Hallberg and His Swedish All Stars, "Side Car," rec. Nov. 9, 1953, Dragon DRCD 402.

13. Lee Konitz in Sweden, "Sax of a Kind," rec. Nov. 19, 1951, Dragon DRLP 18.

14. Lars Gullin Septet, "Galium verum," rec. June 10, 1954, Dragon DRCD 401.

15. Lars Gullin Septet, "How About You," rec. April 23, 1956, Dragon DRCD 401.

16. Lars Gullin Quartet, "Danny's Dream," rec. April 25, 1955, Dragon DRCD 224.

17. Lars Gullin Quartet, "She's Funny That Way," rec. Feb. 12, 1953, Dragon DRCD 395; Lars Gullin Quintet, "The Front," rec. March 31, 1953, Vogue 74321610232; and Lars Gullin Octet, "Fedja," rec. May 31, 1956, Dragon DRCD 224.

18. Compare Lars Gullin Cool Sounders, "Liza," LE 20.

19. Lee Konitz and Lars Gullin with Hans Koller's New Jazz Stars, "En Rodage," rec. Jan. 17, 1956, and "Ablution," rec. Jan. 21, 1956, both Moon MCD 057-2.

20. Compare Stan Getz Quartet "Night and Day" and "Ack Värmeland, du sköna," both rec. March 23, 1951, WEA 9031-77577-2.

21. Also compare Lee Konitz in Sweden "Sax of a Kind," rec. Nov. 19, 1951, Dragon DRLP 18.

22. Reinhold Svensson Quintet, "Tasty Pastry," rec. Sept. 10, 1952, Prestige LP155.

23. The typical styles of Rolf Berg und Georg Riedel can be heard on the Lars Gullin Quartet's "Jump for Fan," rec. Nov. 5, 1953; "Be Careful" and "Igloo," both rec. May 25, 1954; and "Lars Meets Jeff," rec. Jan. 26, 1955, all Dragon DRCD 396.

24. Lubomir Doruzka: "Jazz in der Tschechoslowakei 1945 bis 1993," in *Jazz in Europa: Darmstädter Beiträge zur Jazzforschung*, vol. 3 (Darmstadt: Publ. Wolfram Knauer, 1993), 134-35.

25. Compare Gustav Brom mit seinen Solisten, "Cool and Crazy (Short Stop)," rec. March 7, 1957, Amiga LP 850023.

26. Krzysztof Komeda, "Memory of Bach," rec. August 1956, Power Bros. PB 00157.

27. Vera Auer und ihre Solisten, "Meine Augen sagen ja," rec. Spring 1950, Harmona 17081.

28. Michael Naura Quintett, "Micha's Dilemma," rec. July 31, 1955, Bear Family BCD 16911-9.

29. Compare Horst Winter und sein Orchester, "Ray's Idea," rec. Nov. 8, 1950, RST 91766, and Freddie Brocksieper All Stars, "Come Back to Sorrento," rec. May 1951, Bear Family BCD 16277.

30. Compare Hans Koller Quartett, "Hans Is Hip," rec. May 20, 1952, Savoy SJL 1202.

31. Martin Kunzler, *Jazz-Lexikon*. Reinbek bei Hamburg, 1988: 790-93.

32. Hans Koller New Jazz Stars, "Indian Summer," rec. May 1953, Vogue 74321610232.

33. Hans Koller New Jazz Stars, "Flamingo" and "All the Things You Are," both rec. May 1953, Vogue 74321610232.

34. Hans Koller Quintet, "Feuerwehr," rec. Dec. 15, 1954, RST-91562-2.

35. Hans Koller New Jazz Stars, "Iris," rec. May 30, 1955, 1955, Bear Family BCD 15430.

36. Hans Koller New Jazz Stars, "3 x 2" and "For Gerry," both rec. Oct. 25, 1955, RST-91562-2.

37. Hans Koller New Jazz Stars, "Little Concert," rec. Autumn 1955, RST-91562-2.

38. Jutta Hipp Quintet, "What's New?" rec. April 24 1954, Fresh Sound FSR-CD 421.

39. Jutta Hipp Quintet, "Two Oranges," rec. April 13, 1954, L+R Rec. LR 41.006.

40. Jutta Hipp Trio, "At Hickory House, Vol. 1 & 2," Blue Note TOCD-1515 and 1516.

41. Jutta Hipp Quintet, "Jutta Hipp with Zoot Sims," Blue Note CDP 7243-8-52439-2-9.

42. Rolf Kühn Combo, "Sweet Georgia Brown," rec. May 19, 1953, Polydor 45508 LPH.

43. Kurt Edelhagen und die All Stars, "Cherokee," rec. July 1952, Koch 323 981.

44. Kurt Edelhagen und die All Stars, "There's a Small Hotel," rec. June 13, 1953, Koch 323 981.

45. Kurt Edelhagen und die All Stars, "The Lady Is a Tramp," rec. Feb. 1954, Koch 323 981.

46. Kurt Edelhagen und die All Stars, "Sonny Boy," rec. July 24, 1954, Koch 323 981.

47. Erwin Lehn und sein Südfunk Tanzorchester, "Cool Street" and "E.V.G.," both rec. May 29, 1955, Bear Family BCD 15430-7.

48. Wolfgang Lauth Quartet, "Cool March" and "Cafe Souvenir," both rec. May 30, 1955, Bear Family BCD 15430-6.

49. Wolfgang Lauth Quartet, "Goofy," "Cool Cave," and "Lauthentic," all rec. May 1, 1956, Bear Family BCD 15717 AH.

50. Wolfgang Lauth Quartet, "Malu" and "Sunday Picnic," both rec. Oct. 14/15, 1957, Bear Family BCD 15942 AH.

51. Bill Russo, New Jazz Group Hannover, "Night in Tunisia," rec. Aug. 24, 1955, Brunswick 10.032 EPB.

52. For example, Hans Koller Quartett/Sextett, "Zero," "These," "M.S.K.," and "Koller's Idea," rec. Sept. 16, 1954, RST-91562-2.

53. Friedrich Gulda and His Sextet, "Quintet" and "Introvert," rec. June 28, 1956, Decca 06024-984-7128.

11 / ORCHESTRAL THOUGHTS: JAZZ COMPOSITION IN EUROPE AND AMERICA
AN INTERVIEW WITH COMPOSER-DIRECTOR GIORGIO GASLINI

Prologue

Dearest readers,

Before addressing the questions of music critic Davide Ielmini, I must satisfy the request put to me to present a brief autobiography.

We will begin not on the Ark of Noah, but in the city of Milan, the moral and creative capital of Italy, where I was born, emitting shrill and surreal sounds, on the twenty-second of October 1929. My father was a writer, a journalist, and anthropologist *ante litteram* [ahead of his time], who specialized in African culture and costumes.

At the age of six, at my request, I began to study classical piano. I also began to improvise by myself. Someone told me later that this is called jazz!

During the war (1940–45), a jazz big band close to the city of Lecco made me their conductor. I was twelve years old. While continuing to practice piano, I performed a few concerts with them in the area. It was my professional debut. I was later invited by the National Radio of Italy to broadcast a weekly concert of jazz piano duos. I was about seventeen and was beginning to be nationally recognized.

In 1948, I released the first of three albums for His Master's Voice (today known as EMI). These were very possibly the first albums ever produced in the history of Italian jazz. At this time I was known as the premier pianist of big band jazz in Italy. It was a great experience for me. Working with this orchestra [Orchestra del Momento] I got to know and perform the best-known American orchestral songs.

Edgard Varèse then introduced me to the music of Stan Kenton, and I developed a passion for contemporary music that was greater than my love of classical music. I abandoned everything and enrolled into the prestigious Giuseppe Verdi Conservatory of Music in Milan. I studied more than ten hours per day and obtained five diplomas.

During the 1950s, I dedicated myself to composing pieces for orchestra and directing symphonies. Then in 1957, I felt the strong urge to reunite the two principal musical experiences of my life: the music of the 1900s and jazz.

For an International Festival (San Remo, 1957), I composed and directed a song written for eight performers titled "Time and Relation." This piece was the first example of an organic synthesis between the "progressive" language of jazz and the dodecaphonic technique of Arnold Schoenberg. It made a big splash in Italy and internationally. "Time and Relation" signaled the beginning of a new way to do jazz in a more European style.

After the great director Michelangelo Antonioni heard "Time and Relation," he brought me, along with my quartet, onto the set of his film *The Night*, and asked me to compose the soundtrack for it. The critics awarded the soundtrack the national Silver Ribbon prize, and suddenly the doors to composing for cinema and working with famous directors were opened to me.

The 1960s were the predominant period in Italy of our quartet concerts. Our discs became internationally recognized. I continued to publish new discs for Soul Note and to compose symphonic music. The invitations from abroad began to pour in.

In 1976 and 1977, I was invited to the New Orleans Festival in America and then to the jazz festivals in Houston and Chicago. I also did a tour from California to the Public Theater in New York City. I received invitations from over fifty other nations, where I held solo piano concerts and performances with my groups. I also received invitations to compose three symphonic ballets for the great Italian theaters: La Scala in Milan, Teatro Massimo in Palermo, and the Teatro dell'Opera in Rome.

I continued working to unite both symphonic and jazz music, arriving at a concept of a style of "total music."

In 1972, I was invited to the Saint Cecilia Conservatory of Music in Rome to teach the first official course on Italian jazz music. In 1978–79, I did the same at Giuseppe Verdi Conservatory of Music in Milan. These two teaching opportunities paved the way for jazz instruction to be included in the curriculum of all Italian conservatories and to be officially recognized by the Ministry of Instruction. Today in Italy there are many active jazz departments in the conservatories.

In these years I published three books: *The Technique and Art of Jazz* (Ricordi), *Total Music* (Feltrinelli), and *The Time of the Total Musician* (Baldini Castoldi Dalai).

In the 1970s and 1980s I was very busy bringing music and my philosophy to new environments, such as factories, psychiatric hospitals, prisons, piazzas, schools, universities. It was a wonderful experience of both music and life. In

that same period I had the privilege to personally meet many great artists, including Duke Ellington, Stan Kenton, Oscar Peterson, John Coltrane, Don Cherry, Cecil Taylor, Steve Lacy, and Lenny Tristano. I produced three albums of duets with Roswell Rudd, Eddie Gomez, Anthony Braxton, and I became a friend of Max Roach and Ornette Coleman. I also met the main players in the new music scene of the late 1990s, including John Cage.

I had a special encounter with Maestro Leonard Bernstein, who asked me to assist with all his rehearsals at La Scala.

I continued to publish my compositions, first with the editor Vienna Universal and today with Suvini Zerboni Italiana, and to release new albums. Over one hundred of these albums have received critic's awards.

My work continues. In 2002 the president of the republic, Carlo Azeglio Ciampi, awarded me the gold medal for an artistic career with great cultural merit. In 2010, the mayor of Milan conferred upon me the city's greatest honor for artists, the Ambrogino d'Oro. And still today, I find myself with the same passion and dedication to what started me as a boy.

But now I don't want to take more of your attention. In the course of the next long interview, you can learn much more.

I thank you for your kind attention. In closing, permit me to pronounce that now-historic phrase with which my beloved Duke Ellington hailed his listeners: "I love you madly!"

Your Giorgio Gaslini

Jazz, Europe, and Giorgio Gaslini

A fetishistic culture of structure and accusations of following a purely and exclusively aesthetic language: the avant-gardes of twentieth-century high-culture music refused tradition as an expression of a path turned back on itself. In 1957 you composed "Tempo e relazione" (Time and Relation); the Darmstadt school was founded in 1949: where does Gaslini place himself in the post-Webern vanguard of the school?

At the end of the forties I entered the Giuseppe Verdi Conservatory in Milan, where I obtained five diplomas (composition, orchestral direction, piano, vocal polyphony, band orchestration). At the same time, I was active in orchestral direction and composition for the new music of the second half of the twentieth century. Around 1950, together with Luciano Berio, I met the chief protagonists of the Darmstadt school: Karlheinz Stockhausen, Pierre Boulez, John Cage, and the great Bruno Maderna, but also Franco Donatoni, Niccolò Castiglioni, Giacomo Manzoni, and many others. We exchanged experiences and refined our aesthetic positions.

The jazz experience (which they had missed out on) and the new music experience made me realize I had to achieve a synthesis of these two components. I resolved that difficult and anguished period by composing, in 1957, "Tempo e relazione," the first example of an organic work of synthesis between the language of progressive jazz and the technique of twelve-tone music.

International schools, in their romantic conception, were in the midst of a crisis. We witnessed a first, deep split between composer and audience. The wind of musical reform was blowing hard. When did you start on the path toward what you call "total music"?

"Tempo e relazione" had been performed in concert and a live recording made. This was subsequently broadcast in the USA, where I was invited to perform. At the same time, it was heard by famous film director Michelangelo Antonioni, who asked me to compose the soundtrack of his movie *La notte* [*The Night*].

This soundtrack of mine, recorded with my quartet on the movie set, won the Nastro d'Argento award (a kind of Oscar) and introduced me to the cinema and the jazz concert seasons. Finally I had found my own musical orientation, so I started down the path of "total music" that I am still on today.

My advanced music sought to communicate with listeners, overcoming firmly but naturally that "split" you mentioned between composer and audience; this I owed to jazz.

"Tempo e relazione" also marked a creative turning point for Italian jazz and was considered the start of European experimental jazz.

What do you mean by "total music," and when and how did you get the inspiration for a new style on your compositional path?

Before answering this question, I think we need to go back to concert activities and discography, both in the jazz and contemporary-classical fields, in 1960 and beyond:

JAZZ

From the beginning of 1960 and during all the decade from 1960 to 1970, my new quartet was a linchpin of the Italian national scene. It included the talented saxophonist Gianni Bedori, a close colleague for many years; the powerful double-bass player Bruno Crovetto; and the intellectual of percussion, Franco Tonani.

Some key albums remain as a record of this collaboration:

1 *Oltre* (Over), winner of the critics' award "Top Jazz Arrigo Polillo"
2 *Dall'alba all'alba* (From Sunrise to Sunrise)
3 *Africa*
4 *La stagione incantata* (The Enchanted Season)

From the same period is the album *New Feelings* (1965), recorded with leading international avant-garde artists Don Cherry, Steve Lacy, Gato Barbieri, J.-F. Jenny-Clark, Kent Carter, Aldo Romano, Enrico Rava, Gianni Bedori, and Franco Tonani. It was the first European album to earn five stars from the critics at American *Down Beat*.

From 1969 is the album *Newport in Milan*, a live recording from a concert at Teatro Lirico di Milano [a Milan theater famous for opera performances], where artists such as the Miles Davis Quintet and the Cecil Taylor Trio played in addition to my big band.

CONTEMPORARY MUSIC

1 Composing the symphonic ballet *Drakon*, commissioned and performed by
   Teatro Massimo di Palermo and by Teatro dell'Opera di Roma [Rome's
   opera house]

2 Composing the symphonic ballet *Contagio* (Contagion), commissioned and
   performed by Teatro alla Scala di Milano [La Scala Theater in Milan]

3 The 1964 album *Gaslini, Composizioni Cameristiche* (Gaslini's Chamber
   Compositions), with a presentation speech by the Nobel Prize–winning poet
   Salvatore Quasimodo

All of this activity is indeed the testimony of an "absolute" musician in action.

Around the middle of the 1970s, the publisher Feltrinelli asked me to write the book *Musica totale* (*Total Music*), in which I briefly expounded on the creative and aesthetic principles of this new direction. The book was widely read across the Italian musical spectrum. I didn't intend to make a proclamation or proselytize; the book was principally a testimony of my personal creative and operative path through a music open to many experiences, to different cultures, to many languages from different places of origin, to folk music.

In short, the concept of "total music" is that the musician subject to its principles is 360 degrees open-minded about music.

The second crucial point is to start again with listening, that is, the basis of communication with people in the places where they listen to music, where they live, where they work, or where they study.

The third point is refusing to restrict oneself to just one form of radical technique (usually post-Webern) and thus being open to the free use of all known compositional techniques, or those not yet explored.

The fourth point is to avoid quotation in favor of creating original themes in the desired style.

The musician is "freed" from scales, trends, or models that deviate from the true primitive significance and role of music—something that "came from people for people," not from professionals for the professionals, and therefore denies the split between composer and audience.

The "absolute musician" is a musician of synthesis, a "syncretic" musician— exactly the opposite of an eclectic and diffuse musician.

The ideas for "total music" and the "Manifesto di musica totale" originated in 1964 from a striking vision I had, written on impulse on a paper napkin while I was alone at a restaurant in Milan. They took shape during the following fifteen years.

What did you mean to show with the "total music" concept? Was it a way of accentuating the divide between cold aestheticism, musical revolution, and the listeners' collective conscience, or was it a simple experiment, to be consolidated and acknowledged over time?

With the idea of "total music"? None of those things.

I wrote the manifesto and the book just to pin down and make clear to myself the significance of what I had done and of what I was doing and planning to do with my music. It's a sort of personal confession, a private matter.

I couldn't have imagined that, from the very beginning, it would have aroused such keen interest, and how much influence it would have later exercised not only on many musicians but also on critics, concert promoters, and not least on the teaching courses of several Italian music institutes.

This influence can be seen in the official introduction of jazz as a study subject at all the Italian conservatories, something I started with the pilot chairs entrusted to me first in Rome [1972] at Saint Cecilia's Conservatory and later in Milan at Giuseppe Verdi's Conservatory.

Against tradition or based on tradition—or possibly establishing another tradition?

I repeat, I didn't want, nor do I want, to establish anything. It was just about communicating artistically and giving some keys to interpretation and knowledge. Certainly, determined coherence and following a nonconformist path in life and art can also provide the basis for a new tradition. In any case, only the value of the work and the fullness of time can confirm this.

"Tempo e relazione" is once again the first example of a "fusion" between advanced jazz and the twelve-tone technique. What were your sources of inspiration?

It would be very restrictive to consider a composition solely from the point of view of the musical technique used. Unfortunately, until now this is the way the critics have treated "Time and Relation."

240   Wrapped around a composition is a set of visionary meanings, of emotional

poetics both suffering and joyous, of environments, of relationships with one's profound ego, with the subjectivity, the nature and the colors of life, with civil and personal zeal.

"Time and Relation" reflects my human condition during that period, in 1957. I went through a phase of deep loneliness, because I loved jazz, with all its energy and powers of communication, but I also studied and lived the twentieth century's "high culture" music.

I found myself at a crossroads, facing a dilemma I could not solve. I said to myself: either you work this problem out or you give up music forever! I launched myself into the task of forging a synthesis between these two treasured cultures. That is exactly what happened: "Time and Relation" reflects all of this.

It includes three expressive phases: the first, with its headlong rush, its swing feeling achieved through the lines and polyphonies of the twelve-tone series; the second, with its lento canon movement that reflects a longing concealed by Apollonian serenity (I remember being inspired by the dark charm of some metropolitan suburbs); the third, with the final movements expressing irony and mental exploration, suspending the rhythmic beat and only at the end resuming the vitality of the opening.

All of this is "Time and Relation": a combination of technique and feelings.

Jazz undeniably influenced twentieth-century music: the French impressionists, as well as those in Russia (Shostakovich, Prokofiev, Kabalevsky) and Czechoslovakia (Schulhoff, Martinů, Haba). . . . What is your debt to them?

Certainly, from Ravel onward, composers in the first half of the twentieth century were fascinated by the sounds, the polyphonies, the rhythms of jazz. Some of them (don't forget Igor Stravinsky's *Ebony Concerto*) tried to use and reproduce certain aspects of jazz language in their chamber or symphonic works.

I have had good relationships with important composers such as Gian Francesco Malipiero, Goffredo Petrassi, Bruno Maderna, and Luigi Dallapiccola. They all had a real respect for jazz music, and particularly a strong admiration for Duke Ellington and his music. By contrast, composers in the second half of the twentieth century kept their distance from jazz and were very prejudiced against it. The hasty opinions expressed by the philosopher [Theodor] Adorno in his writings had a drastic influence on them. It was a generational catastrophe!

We know that the language and the style of jazz originated from the suffering and passion of African Americans. Everything in jazz is humanity and lyrical-dramatic poetry. I believe this music can't be imitated, or transferred to different contexts, by drawing superficially on a few of its external characteristics.

It may be that certain aspects of jazz, such as its communicative energy and intrinsic pathos, influenced the music of some composers outside jazz. But few of them—perhaps only Bernstein—have understood the true character and spirit of the blues.

On the one hand you seem to look toward the Viennese school, still a point of reference; on the other, toward the national influences that pulsated throughout Europe, tracing a direct line from Weill's Weimar Republic to Gershwin's African Latin rhythmic inflections. What doubts, uncertainties, and confirmations did you encounter on your journey?

I loved and studied George Gershwin's music, and on a few occasions I directed an orchestra interpreting all of his symphonic works. Gershwin's stylistic synthesis is admirable and unrepeatable.

Schoenberg and Gershwin were good friends and sincerely admired each other's work.

Gershwin himself welcomed Kurt Weill with friendship and esteem when Weill arrived in New York, and helped him to enter the musical world of Broadway.

On several occasions I had the opportunity to conduct Weill's *Threepenny Opera* (with Bertolt Brecht's lyrics), and I listened to Weill's other work, both before and after that masterpiece.

These experiences have been significant for me, so it has been very important to assimilate the great lesson of the Vienna school, which is something more than just an influence.

I remember Picasso saying: "To copy others is necessary, but to copy oneself is pathetic."

Music "from the inside," rationalized and radicalized, yet integrated into a medium where the vanguard does not renounce emotional communication. In terms of your art, could we ever speak of a linguistic and emotional compromise between African American scales and European scales?

The creation of a musical work, as far as I am concerned, has a mysterious genesis. Sometimes a composition arises all of a sudden in my mind, like a visual image and sonic perception. In these cases, I try to write it down straightaway, so that the intuition does not escape me.

Most of the time a composition involves a long, slow phase of "interiority" that can last for months or years, then it suddenly emerges and takes shape "from the inside" on the page. At other times the composition can develop from an initial point in the writing—a sound, a series of intervals, a confrontation between harmony and rhythm, an orchestral tone. Progressively, it goes deep into the ego, into inwardness, striving to communicate emotions and ideas; then I put it down on paper.

I generally go through all of this with a 360-degree mind-set—also in terms of using familiar scales or inventing new ones based on the relationships of intervals within the sounds.

The choice of new or recognizable materials depends on the nature of the work, with functional clarity and without compromises, as this tendency must always prevail over the formal synthesis.

Let's try to be methodical: in 1963 comes Oltre (Beyond), for jazz quartet—can you confirm this? With it you get close to the twelve-tone technique—which, to avoid any misunderstanding, must not be confused with Schoenberg's twelve-tone system. Serialism could embrace the tonal approach. What distinguished you from high-culture composers?

what?

The album *Oltre* was released in 1963 by His Master's Voice, today known as EMI. In 1964 it received the Critics' Award as the year's best Italian album. After *Tempo e relazione* [1957] and the soundtrack for Antonioni's film *La notte* [1960], *Oltre* [1963] opened a new chapter in my artistic development.

In this suite, comprising eight separate pieces, I used a free twelve-tone technique, not bound to the limitations of the dodecaphonic system. Its character is deeply operatic, and at the same time it is jazz, with a marked inclination toward a European style. I think this is the difference between my compositions and the "refined" musical tendencies of those other composers.

The genesis of this suite was really strange: I had formed my new quartet and had trained my soloists to improvise freely on "serial material." I validated the music through direct listening. As I remember, in 1962 I had obtained a small space for a few weeks in Milan. I invited about ten people each week, as a sort of "listening sample" to check the music before the album was recorded and the suite performed in front of an audience. During these sessions we played one piece from the suite, asking the people invited to voice their emotional responses and considerations. Over the weeks that followed, we continued in this vein with all the other pieces in the suite. We came out of that experience reinforced and reassured, after which we recorded the album.

So began a decade of intense concert activity, during which the quartet presented this new music to a wide audience. The album was reviewed internationally and was the precursor to invitations from abroad a few years later.

The line of demarcation between European and African American music is weak, almost evanescent. And yet in your chamber music and symphonic repertoire— but also in your soundtracks for the cinema, such as La notte—we can hear a subtle distinction. Can you explain this?

oh ?
dally.

The jazz pieces composed from 1960 onward all lean toward Europe. The point is that, in these works, the European cultural component is never exhibited. 243

It is a completely natural fact, a light coloring of the musical language. Only very careful listening can reveal this stylistic aspect, which is intrinsic to music. I don't mind it being evanescent for some listeners. But in the context of symphonic and chamber music, that is a different matter.

For example, you only have to listen to my *Blue Symphony* to recognize clearly the multiple use of blues motifs, while the extensive themes reflect the mood of the African American spiritual.

In my other chamber works, the contribution of jazz relates mainly to the rhythmic energy and the phrasing. The music for cinema is another matter entirely; it is not "pure music," in the sense of free from other considerations, but "applied music" linked to the character of the story, to the scenes filmed, the actors, the emotional shifts, the historical context, the costumes, to what happens in the film.

Antonioni's masterpiece *La notte* is set initially in Milan, so the music is a little abstract, almost industrial, evoking an atmosphere of suspension. The second part is given over entirely to a big party, with toasts and dancing, held in the renowned writer's [Marcello Mastroianni] honor. We interpreted the whole party through our playing, like four actors on a set. I therefore composed some functional music, pulsating jazz that was accessible but sometimes ironic and allusive.

At the end, when the guests have all left, the true story emerges of the main couple [Mastroianni and Jeanne Moreau]. We hear "Blues all'alba" (Blues at Dawn), the last piece played by the quartet as the party ends, which later transitions into "Lettura della lettera" (Reading of the Letter), a love letter not recognized by the protagonists. It's this episode that brings out the couple's "noncommunication" problem. The music of "Lettura della lettera" is no longer a functional element of the party but becomes an active player in the dramaturgy of the scene.

The end of the film conveys their drama with "Ti amo" (I Love You) and "No, non t'amo più" (No, I Don't Love You Anymore), closing with a desperate last embrace, at the edge of impossibility and with no words left. At this point the quartet's music, just for one decisive minute, becomes the protagonist in that tense silence, while the camera leaves the couple and soars toward the white misty dawn.

The theme of "Finale" here is based entirely on a series of twelve harmonized sounds, while the melodic line ascends, sustained by the pulsating and fragmented rhythm section.

So, serial jazz was perfectly attuned to the story's ending. And that's how jazz accompanied and interacted with the dramatic structure of the film.

You once said: "In the distant future, all music will be one, there will be no predominance of one kind or another, but a synthesis of the true values of every

musical style will be achieved in an [e pluribus] 'unum.'" Are you still convinced of that?

Everybody knows that at the end of the nineteenth century the tonal system was over. With the dawn of the twentieth century, the twelve-note system, the dodecaphony, emerged as a new musical system that would later transform and spread in other directions.

Today the "refined" composers adopt various "atonal" harmonic systems, different types of scales, or they create their own personal systems.

It's true, in 1975 I made the statement you mention, in my book *Musica Totale (Total Music)*. I wanted to underline the need for a general methodology that applies both to musicians and authors, a mutual basic code, taking into account all forms of known music—a "unum," a unifying system, a new working method. I adopted this "unum" in my symphonic and chamber pieces.

With jazz it is a different story. It is common knowledge that the modal, tonal, and blues scales have been the harmonic basis for all jazz musicians. From 1960, Ornette Coleman proposed a "harmolodic" approach, a very interesting theory bound to Coleman's artistic personality and to his use of a monophonic instrument, the saxophone. Later on, the "free jazz" movement paved the way for different monophonic and polyphonic combinations.

Personally, when it comes to writing and improvisation I prefer to think in terms of "atonality," "polytonality," "polymodality," free "serialism" and, where necessary, "tonal" chords, all combined and sequenced in new ways.

In conclusion, there is a "total" method in our jazz as well. ok.

With Nuovi sentimenti (New Feelings), in 1966, you dealt with free jazz, probably as a point of contact between African modality and the compositional misalignment of the avant-garde. Since the fifties, free jazz and European experimental music have seemed, at times, to be two faces of the same coin. How did you regard free jazz at that time: as a purely American medium or as an assimilation of European musical culture by the United States?

To answer your question properly, I need to give you a detailed account of the incredible story of making this album!

Don Cherry read a very enthusiastic article about me that was published in London. He called me, and we arranged a meeting, which occurred shortly afterward when he played a concert in Italy. We met in Milan, with the intention of recording an album together.

Some more time passed before I received another call from Don Cherry, informing me that on Saturday of that particular week, he and his friends would be free and ready to record the album with me. He would come with Steve Lacy,

Gato Barbieri, Ken Karter, J.-F. Jenny-Clark, and Aldo Romano. I arranged a session with them in Milan, the next Saturday at 2 p.m.

I immediately summoned my quartet, adding a young Enrico Rava, who was keen to participate. In total there were ten soloists, a star cast of the best musicians in the international jazz avant-garde!

I remember it was Thursday. . . . Immediately three problems arose: (a) funding; (b) availability of the recording studio; (c) the music.

I rushed to speak with EMI's management and managed to obtain a reasonable amount of money, enough to pay nine musicians. I decided to compose, direct, and play "for free," avoiding any further economic difficulties. The whole studio was placed at my disposal, from 2 p.m. to midnight on that fateful Saturday, and "not a minute later"!

I accepted the challenge. I had only the Friday left to write the score and parts for the suite "New Feelings." I worked throughout the day and night, copying all ten parts in freehand on Saturday morning, right up to a few minutes before the start of the recording.

At 2 p.m. we were all lined up, and the music was ready to play. We started to rehearse and immediately felt this fantastic mutual understanding and complicity. By midnight the recording of "New Feelings" was completed, not a minute later!

I had a group of ten extraordinary musicians of different origins—American, Latin American, European, Italian—but all united by a common "elective affinity."

This was the basis for the composition of the suite: I used a "serial" line that recurs throughout the composition, as well as other tonal and atonal interventions. I conceived the music as a sort of text interpreted by the actors in a theatrical company. It therefore called for a gestural "direction," which it received.

There was no difficulty in uniting and arranging these forces in the field, nor was there any discrepancy between the European and American experience of free jazz.

"Composition tending towards objectivity": that's what you wrote about "Jazz Makrokosmos," featured on the album Newport in Milan in 1969. But your jazz often arises from a severed relationship between the objective and the subjective. Is it more structured or unstructured?

The album *Newport in Milan* consists of the pieces that we played at the Teatro Lirico di Milano during the European tour of the Newport Festival in 1969. The concert was opened by the Miles Davis Quintet, followed by Cecil Taylor's Trio and our big band.

246   I composed "Jazz Makrokosmos" with the idea of a work similar to a futuristic

architecture, with solid foundations and a fanciful elevation. I thought about a rational structure, a shape/object, an edifice inhabited by prestigious musicians and instrumental sections.

Actually in "Jazz Makrokosmos" you will not find the intimacy with the ego-protagonist, but rather a harmonious whole, strong and clear, that presents itself to the listener. In that sense, the structure is objective, not subjective.

On other occasions, certain compositions of mine came out of express-ing subjectivity. It all depends on the initial idea, whether a piece is more inti-mate or objective. They are different creative moments that belong to the same author.

In spite of everything, it seems that in jazz and symphonic music (let's use those definitions for the sake of convenience) you had traced a line that could not be crossed: I'm thinking of Busoni's or Maderna's arbitrariness, where the chamber or symphonic parts are left to the discretion of the musical director and the individual musicians; or of Morton Feldman's compositions, where the interpreter is the supreme arranger of the sounds. Apart from the improvised passages entrusted to individual instrumentalists, but always prefixed by ordered notation, you seem to prefer a written score. Why is that?

I'll give you some examples:

If I have at my disposal a certain number of musicians trained in free improvisa-tion, then the "written" parts will consist of brief divisions, intervals between the collective and individual improvisations, a minor "input" to maintain the musical form, like a "path." It's a kind of surreal tale with just a few necessary stations, from which you can start again straightaway.

If instead I have at my disposal a small group comprising musicians who have been collaborating with me for several years, then I conceive the compositions *ad personam,* trying to put the soloists in the optimal context to draw out their latent talent. I know every one of them, and I know how they can achieve the utmost level of expression.

The written score is necessary so that, in the end, a true composition emerges. But it needs to be balanced and not overshadowing the free sections.

In symphonic music or in "contemporary" chamber music, composers have sometimes, and especially in the sixties, included brief sequences with little direction, entrusted to the soloist. They are not improvisations but rather extem-poraneous interventions, guided by certain signals from the composer.

The difference is that true improvisation, as found in jazz, has always been about telling a story. The same goes for deeply structured pieces and for ones that are more free and unstructured. Jazz has always been highly pragmatic. It is about doing things "with what there is and for what there is."

In your concept of "total music," how important is the space given to so-called fundamental elements and to decorative elements—the accidental and the variable? Can structure itself be regarded as musical content?

The structure of an "open" composition, one shaped by the idea of "total music," is purely the work of the composer. It is the composer who "builds" the formal structure of the work and inhabits it with harmonic, melodic, rhythmic, and tonal events, dictated by compositional techniques and the composer's own fantasies.

The concept of "musical content" has been a matter of interpretation since the late nineteenth century (see Eduard Hanslich's famous essay "On the Musically Beautiful," and Igor Stravinsky's "The Musical Poetic"). Personally, I like to think that music has the power to mirror and arouse in the human mind a mixture of images, ideas, reflections, emotions, impulses to action and feelings.

All music has an evocative power, "total" music as well.

In "Reportage da l'Isola di Utopia" (Report from Utopia Island) from 1973, you incorporate into your musical art the concept of pop art, which shapes the "Pop Tale." At this point, it would be interesting to know how much the pictorial currents of the nineteenth century influenced you on your sonic path.

Certainly! You have to know that painting, with its masterpieces over the past centuries and especially the aesthetic currents of the nineteenth century, has always been my passion. Nineteenth-century painting, in particular, has often inspired both my jazz and "contemporary" music.

I find there is a close connection between music and the other arts, especially with painting and architecture—also "pop art" in the case cited in your question.

Your music never becomes fragile or elusive; on the contrary, it's characterized by an insistent rhythm, almost percussive, and density of sound. Sometimes it's in the fullness of the instrumentation, sometimes in the details between fading and compression: Blue Symphony (2005) is a typical example of this, with the ambiguity of the writing serving as an emotional tool. Do you pursue a cinematic technique?

Music for the cinema is applied music, subject to rules dictated by the film's narrative. On the contrary, *Blue Symphony* is pure music: the writing is not "ambiguous" but "multiple"—in other words, it articulates "multimodal" blues scales and, without referring to anything specific, re-creates the harmonic and thematic mood appropriate to the African American spiritual.

The lento movement is a humble homage to the renowned "Adagietto" from Gustav Mahler's Symphony No. 5, but this too is interspersed with allusive and diverting musical ideas that, later on, combine again in the adagio theme.

Does all of this reflect emotions? . . . I shall leave the answer to the listener. Undoubtedly there are a variety of different expressive and evocative levels.

Boulez asserts that in serial music "there isn't a preconceived scale, there aren't preconceived forms, that are general structures into which a particular thought enters." You don't seem to share this view entirely, or am I mistaken?

Pierre Boulez's statement is correct if it refers to strict use of the serial technique. The technique used in "Tempo e Relazione" is rigorously serial as well.

Nevertheless, in certain works during the second half of the twentieth century, some composers applied that system more freely, less radically. Sometimes "serial" superior melodic lines were used, but they were freely harmonized.

Today, all of this belongs to the recent past. There is now more freedom in composing.

To quote Lévi-Strauss, we risk attaining a form of expression in which we have "the word without the language." Do you find that absurd?

The reconstruction of a musical "language" of universal value has been the general trend during the second half of the twentieth century. How to create a clear and compelling alternative to the centuries-old "mythical figure" of the tonal system?

A new radicalism, then. With the concept of "total music," there is a shift, toward a different kind of open radicalism, with a broad-minded, 360-degree perspective on the musical forms of the past, present, and future. This is a new language with new words—therefore, "syncretism" rather than extreme "radicalism."

And yet you succeeded in the aim of "homogenizing" the "circular" scale into a "heptaphonic" scale, sometimes playing, in basic intervals, with themes constructed on "remnants" of notes. It is as though the music wanted to conceal itself, once again, from an inspiration that draws on the blues, song grammar, and twentieth-century historical precedents. Could we, in your case, speak of many languages and many words?

Yes, that is right: many languages and many words in the infinite pulsation of the composer's unifying fantasy.

"Moto velocetto perpetuo" and "Interno intorno" (both composed in 2006), "Porter's Portrait" (2001), "Adiantum" (a concert for piano and orchestra, composed in 1993, that owes much to Gershwin)—they are all driven in some way by a marked communicative instinct. You are one of the few artists in contemporary music who, in the course of their research, have attracted an ever larger and more heterogeneous audience. How do you explain this?

I wouldn't want to conduct my own exegesis; let's leave that to the professionals.

The famous saying, "The audience is always right," sounds like a truism but, unfortunately or fortunately, it's mostly true. The audience of listeners, even if sometimes it doesn't "understand," nonetheless can perceive whether a musical offering strikes those universal notes of emotion and feelings (not sentimentalism). For the same reason, audiences the world over were touched and moved watching Charlie Chaplin's films!

Music can retreat into its own speculative world, or it can be strongly "afferent"—that is, passionate and communicative.

This second instinct is the mainspring to a choral response of participation, one that is sometimes even overwhelming or unpredictable. It's like the shoot that springs up from the seed thrown into a furrow in the ground.

"Alabama Suite" (2002) involves the transfiguration of archaic African American elements such as spirituals, work songs, and tunes for children at play. This process, in its construction, recalls Bartók's Romanian folk dances, but also Chopin's mazurkas and Dvorak's Slavonic dances. Will the musical models of the past always be a point of reference?

But of course they will!

I was looking for those folk themes that are at the basis of "Alabama Suite," and I found them in New Orleans during the mid-seventies, when I was officially invited for two years in succession [1976 and 1977] to take part in the New Orleans Jazz Festival.

It has been and still is a piano transcription much listened to and remembered internationally. How could we ever forget the folk-dance components and chants in the masterpieces of Bartók, Chopin, and Dvořák? They will live forever in our subconscious memory, making history.

In "Canti di Lotta" ("Fight Chants," from the album Cantos, *released in 2000), you talk about the "fight as a constant human condition, but also the fight against lack of freedom in the artist's mind, against the limits, mental addiction, shortness of breath." What should the contemporary composer do to start breathing again?*

Your introduction is correct. In my opinion, the answer is to free yourself from everything in order to find yourself, and to breathe the new air of freedom in artistic creation, which comes from the depths of the ego and not from the super-neurotic and conditioned ego.

"Planets Promenade Suite" (2002) is another example of fluid, enthralling music, liberated from any certainty, yet at the same time interacting with the listener on

a course rich with polyharmony, polyphony, and monody. What do you think would add more to your maturation as a composer, speaking in terms of syncretism?

Again your introduction is real and correct.

The sea of music is actually an infinite ocean. There is always something new to learn, to assimilate, to experiment with. Maturity and syncretism are not firm, static points but stations on a long and patient journey. The rest is a gift that comes goodness knows when and from goodness knows where.

yipes

On your last two CDs of "refined" music—and I don't mean to say jazz is less refined, but the distinction has to be made in terms of common understanding— released in 2010 (Gaslini Sinfonico and Piano Sonata Décollage e A.), *you reversed the perspectives that were the basis for the works mentioned up until now. Yet the question arises all the same: does jazz end where contemporary music begins? Is jazz regarded as contemporary music, or can we get rid of these distinctions, at last, and speak of total music?*

Whether we focus on the three cycles of your "Piano Sonata Décollage e A." or on your "Silver Concerto" for baritone sax and orchestra, it seems that your mode of action reveals itself particularly in the piano pieces, which are reminiscent of Copland's, Barber's, and Ives's complex compositions. All three, incidentally, are United States citizens. Is it by chance?

Then we have the "Elizabethan Suite," for transverse flute.

To conclude, these two last chapters in your creative history do not deny your passion for amusement in music. John Cage occasionally composed by throwing dice: do you like playing with dice?

You refer to the two CDs just released: *Gaslini Sinfonico* [label Velut Luna (2010)] and *Composizioni Pianistiche* [label Bottega Discantica (2010)]. We must not lose sight of the concept of "total music," that is, the concept of a composer who, remaining true to himself, can use in his work writing techniques of different origins, but who can also delve into bygone languages and bring them close to the present day.

That's the case with these two CDs of "pure" classic-modern music. They are not explicitly jazz. Nevertheless, my lifelong experience and practice of jazz enter indirectly into the writing. None of the pieces on the two CDs, whether they are symphonic or chamber music, directly adopt jazz, but they make use of it for some characteristic elements: the use of percussion, for example (see "Sinfonia Breve"), or sometimes the nature of the phrasing ("Silver Concert"), the strong rhythmic beat ("Ritual"), or a certain improvisational mood (see the three-piano sonata "Décollage").

ok

But jazz is not the only influence; there is another explicit source: the pictorial art of the twentieth century (see "Peintres au café Sonnant"), or even the marvelous fount of the sixteenth-, seventeenth-century music, by composers such as Thomas Morley and John Dowland (see the "Elizabethan Suite").

The only pure jazz piece is "Interlude—Piano Improvisation" [by Bottega Discantica].

I am very fond of the composers you have mentioned. Copland's wonderful music has various origins and characteristics, although little in the way of jazz influence. Barber's beautiful music has a strong serious-classical imprint, remote from jazz. Ives is the composer I love more and feel is very close to my own attitude. His music is full of America, spirituals and folk melodies, but we can't say it's full of jazz.

Finally, John Cage, whom I had the pleasure to know very well. His music is "aleatory," his work highly original and revolutionary, but it has little or nothing to do with jazz.

There remains the idea of "amusement," and I am happy if in my work "the child that (very seriously) plays, enjoying himself" comes through, because I haven't yet silenced the child inside me. I hope that it will always be so.

To conclude, do you think that the definition "total music" sums up all of the work you have produced over a sixty-year career?

The helm of my ship has always pointed toward a "total" vision of music. To date, it seems to me this course, even if it has ranged from calm sea to rough seas, has been a coherent one. I really hope so.

In any case, let's leave the "word" to the musical works; they can speak better than us.

In conclusion, I wish to express my sincerest gratitude. And I want to extend that gratitude both to you, my excellent interviewer, and to all the readers of this courageous, necessary and important book.

Let the music be . . .

12 / THE NEW ORLEANS REVIVAL IN BRITAIN AND FRANCE

Background to the Revival

At the end of the 1930s, a movement began in the United States that looked back fondly at the jazz of the 1920s and sought to revive it in various ways. On the one hand there were record producers, such as George Avakian, who set out, although he was still a sophomore at Yale, to produce discs for Decca that re-created the sounds of pioneers in Chicago, New York, and Kansas City. In the event, he only made the Chicago set, leaving other producers to go on and make the others in subsequent years. However, between August 1939 and January 1940 he recorded the bands of Eddie Condon, Jimmy McPartland, and George Wettling, playing in the style of a decade and a half earlier. The twelve sides they cut were compiled into one of the first—if not *the* first—ever jazz "albums" (*Chicago Jazz*, Decca A 121). Its six 78 rpm discs were packaged together with a booklet containing Avakian's notes about the Chicagoan style. "I was inspired by the recordings Milt Gabler made at Commodore," said Avakian. "But I thought to myself, 'Gee, why don't they play the way they did ten years or so earlier?' So I said to Eddie Condon, one of the things I want to do is put in the old Chicago flares. Everybody jump in on the last two bars of a chorus and give a springboard to the next soloist. Or give a big roar into the last chorus and then drop down on the middle eight, that sort of thing. So they were delighted to do it."[1] Following the success of this project, Avakian went on to produce reissues for Columbia of the best of its 1920s jazz catalogue.

On the other hand, at almost the same time, the Chicagoan cornetist Muggsy Spanier, himself a pioneer of 1920s jazz, but latterly a swing band player with Ted Lewis's orchestra and then Ben Pollack's band, formed a band "to play the kind of music I used to play with Tesch and the old Chicago gang."[2] In 1938, Spanier had slowly recovered from a perforated ulcer and horrendous complications, and this near-death experience made him resolve to play the music he loved to the exclusion of more recent styles. His Ragtime Band was formed in April 1939. He built its repertoire not only around the music he had witnessed in 1920s Chicago, by King Oliver, Louis Armstrong, and Jelly Roll Morton, but also by drawing on pre-1920 recordings by the Original Dixieland Jazz Band (which had briefly reformed in 1936 to be filmed and recorded). Spanier's actual Ragtime Band lasted barely a year, but it was to be hugely influential on the revival that followed.

He was to continue to work in similar settings at Nick's Club in Greenwich Village, and in Bob Crosby's Dixieland-orientated groups. Spanier (like Eddie Condon, as demonstrated on Milt Gabler's recordings of both men for the Commodore label) saw his work more as part of a continuous tradition than a revival.

Meanwhile, on the West Coast in San Francisco, within twelve months of Spanier's debut, the trumpeter Lu Watters formed his first seven-piece band at the Mark Twain Hotel to play a repertoire that was similarly drawn from earlier models.[3] This group was the precursor of his Yerba Buena Jazz Band, the principal Californian revivalist ensemble. In their different ways Avakian as an external producer who dictated a set of aesthetic values to his musicians, and Watters and Spanier creating a similar impetus as players of the music themselves, were to be the two paradigms for the jazz revival of traditional styles in the years that followed. This was at first the case in the United States, although there the movement gradually lost its initial momentum, but it became particularly true of Europe, where such initiatives lasted well into the 1960s and beyond.

In American jazz historiography, the work of Avakian, Spanier, and Watters is generally seen as the launch of the revival of interest in traditional jazz.[4] However, a year before their efforts got under way, a couple of European pioneers had arrived in the United States with similar, and in some ways more ambitious, ideas that reinforce the paradigm of the revival being simultaneously initiated by producers and musicians. One was the British guitarist Vic Lewis, and the other the French author, critic, and record collector Hugues Panassié. Both were to become pivotal figures in launching a revival of traditional jazz styles in Europe, following their endeavors in America.

Panassié's efforts have become better known over time, but Lewis's were equally significant. The son of a London jeweler, Lewis was an avid record collector, and he eschewed his father's occupation to become a guitarist. In 1938 his swing quartet won a radio talent contest. That same October his parents bought him a passage to New York on the *Queen Mary*, and he spent six weeks in the city, sitting in with Joe Marsala, Eddie Condon, and Sidney Bechet.[5] He intended to put together a band of the best players in the traditional style to record with him, and consequently Lewis made twelve discs in New York with an interracial group, mostly featuring the veteran New Orleans drummer Zutty Singleton. The front line of Bobby Hackett (cornet) and Joe Marsala (clarinet) catches the mood of informal New Orleans small groups to perfection, buoyed by Singleton's excellent drumming and the guitars of Lewis and Condon. A second permutation involved Pee Wee Russell, Brad Gowans, Bernie Billings, and Ernie Caceres alongside Hackett. Apart from a jokey "Tiger Rag," this session includes several pieces that would become cornerstones of the traditional jazz revival in Europe, such as "That's a Plenty," "Muskrat Ramble," and "Basin Street Blues." Following Lewis's experience in making these discs, after his return to Britain he went on to make a set of comparable traditional jazz records with a band that he co-led during World War II with the drummer Jack Parnell. In 1944 this band's records were selling as many as 50,000 copies apiece, suggesting that there was a ready public for boisterous Dixieland, even at the height of the big band era.[6]

When Panassié arrived in the United States in late 1938, he avoided the living tradition of Chicagoan jazzmen who had learned their trade in the 1920s from New Orleans pioneers, in other words the kind of musician with whom both Avakian and Lewis had worked. Instead he tried to connect directly to an earlier period from African American jazz history by seeking out two actual originators of the music from Louisiana. These were the trumpeter Tommy Ladnier, a veteran of Fletcher Henderson and Sam Wooding's bands, and the clarinetist and soprano saxophonist Sidney Bechet. At the start of the 1930s, Bechet and Ladnier together had cut some splendid examples of New Orleans–style jazz, and Panassié hoped to rekindle some of the spirit of those earlier discs. He put six hundred dollars of his own money into financing the sessions at RCA, where the young Artists and Repertoire man Steve Sholes was detailed to produce them.[7]

By December 1938, Ladnier was in the early stages of a terminal illness, and his playing was a shadow of its former self, although Bechet was still in the prime of his musical life. Their recordings for Panassié, such as "Royal Garden Blues" and the plaintive "If You See Me Comin'," are among the very first discs consciously produced as part of a "revival." In seeking to reunite instrumentalists of Morton and Bechet's generation whose work he already knew from record, Panassié initiated another aspect of the revival, the search for "authenticity." The term crops up frequently in Panassié's colleague Mezz Mezzrow's book *Really the Blues*, in which he refers to the style of music played on these recordings as "the authentic blues."[8] Mezzrow acted as a talent scout for the French producer, and also played clarinet ad tenor saxophone on the sessions. The older, and ultimately the more obscure, the musicians involved were, the more it was possible to claim that their output was "authentic" and untouched by fashion. Panassié's recordings, and his books such as *Le jazz hot* (English translation 1936) followed by the subsequent publication in America during 1939 of the book *Jazzmen* by Charles E. Smith and Frederic Ramsey Jr., triggered what would gradually become a movement to record legendary players who had never before been heard on disc.

In the United States, Heywood Hale Broun (later to become a well-known sports reporter) stole a march on his competitors by assembling a band in New Orleans in August 1940 led by the trumpeter Kid Rena, and including the clarinetist Alphonse Picou. It was the first time most of these players had recorded, including Albert Glenny, the bassist associated with the legendary "founder" of jazz Buddy Bolden. This element of revivalism was continued avidly by the record collector, violinist, and avant-garde composer Bill Russell, who wrote two chapters of *Jazzmen* and who interviewed, befriended and struck up correspondence with many jazz pioneers. As a result of his and his colleagues' work, many New Orleans players came to be recorded, most notably Bunk Johnson and George Lewis. Their output, principally for Russell's American Music record label, was profoundly to influence the New Orleans revival in Europe. Although, consistent with the search for authenticity, it was sometimes hailed as a style of jazz that harked back to the days before jazzmen migrated to Chicago in the 1920s, it would be more accurate to regard Russell's records as reflecting the contemporary folk music of New Orleans jazz players in the 1940s.[9]

The Revival in Great Britain

The New Orleans revival took hold in Britain slightly earlier than in most other European countries. However, the chronology is difficult to trace, because World War II disrupted the musical scene as effectively as it disrupted every other aspect of normal life. Vic Lewis, in the wake of his visit to America, attempted to build on his efforts in New York, but the outbreak of the war in 1939 threw him into a different musical environment. Lewis joined the Royal Air Force, and as well as working in the RAF Central Band, he played in a service swing group led by the tenor saxophonist Buddy Featherstonhaugh. However, he wanted to return to the Chicago-style jazz he had played in the States and eventually did so in 1944, as mentioned above, with Jack Parnell, who was a drummer in the same RAF band. In parallel with Lewis's activities, the bass saxophonist Harry Gold, a man who had witnessed the dawn of jazz in Britain when his father took him to see the Original Dixieland Jazz Band at the Hammersmith Palais in 1919, organized his Pieces of Eight as a Dixieland group, also in 1944. Turned down for military service because of problems with his feet, Gold played for many of the leading wartime dance and swing orchestras, but like Lewis, he felt that there was a ready audience for "rehearsed traditional jazz in the dixieland style."[10]

Gold made his everyday living turning out stock arrangements for BBC dance orchestras, and leading small bands on the BBC's Caribbean service. Although he liked traditional jazz, his decision to specialize in it was not driven solely by enthusiasm. It was, he thought, a potentially marketable avenue for his talents that was different from the swing music of the day. Likewise, Lewis was a versatile musician, who contributed to both Featherstonhaugh's band and the BBC Radio Rhythm Club Sextet, playing contemporary swing, while believing that his own ambitions to play traditional jazz would be more commercially successful. Both

Lewis and Gold achieved a following for a more traditional type of jazz at the very height of the vogue for large swing orchestras.

Yet their popularity was greatest among the general public. By contrast, serious fans of 1920s New Orleans and Chicago records were wont to dismiss the efforts of professional musicians like Lewis and Gold. These enthusiasts sought the same kind of authenticity that Panassié had been trying to find in the United States, and they discovered it in the unlikely figure of the diminutive Londoner George Webb, and his Dixielanders.

This group of amateur musicians had been formed in 1942 in the southeast London suburb of Bexley Heath, where it played a weekly session at the Red Barn public house, opposite Barnehurst railway station, a thirty-minute ride from the city center. It attracted a large crowd, many traveling from a considerable distance, and the critic Charles Wilford wrote: "Before the formation of this band, I am sure no English jazz-fan believed it possible for an English band to capture so closely the spirit of a New Orleans band of the early twenties."[11]

It was this attempt to "go back to the roots," to ignore the latest trends in dance music, and to pursue the purism of the 1920s style, that set Webb and his musicians apart from Lewis and Gold. Their aims were not entirely dissimilar, but the Webb band's fans believed that it was untainted by commercialism or by the prevailing swing style. After making privately produced records in 1944, the band began recording for Decca on May 5, 1945, and the same year it began broadcasting on Denis Preston's BBC program *Radio Rhythm Club*. (Preston was to go on to become a highly influential record producer in the jazz revival, although he would also be a significant force in the development and documentation of British modern jazz, starting with George Shearing's 1948 London sessions with Jack Fallon and Norman Burns.)[12] The George Webb Dixielanders' repertoire was uncompromisingly based on 1920s Chicago, with pieces such as Jelly Roll Morton's "Black Bottom Stomp," Artie Mathews's "Weary Blues," and Mamie Smith's "Jenny's Ball" among its recordings. Indeed some dated from even earlier, such as Abe Holzmann's 1899 rag "Smoky Mokes" and W. C. Handy's 1919 "Hesitating Blues." Reg Rigden and Owen Bryce emulated the Armstrong/Oliver two-cornet lead of the Creole Jazz Band of 1923, and the clarinetist, the Canadian-born cartoonist Wally Fawkes, played in a style that had absorbed much from Johnny Dodds and Sidney Bechet.

By 1948 Webb's two cornetists had given way to the sole trumpet of the young Humphrey Lyttelton, and that same year he effectively took over the band. A fine instrumentalist, who at that stage played in the manner of early Louis Armstrong, Lyttelton put much of the band's success down to not "so much what we played as what we stood for."[13]

In February 1948, Lyttelton played in a specially assembled British band (led by the multi-instrumentalist Derek Neville) that was invited to the world's first international jazz festival in Nice, France, organized by Hugues Panassié. Although American traditional jazz was represented there by Louis Armstrong's recently formed All Stars, and a band led by Mezz Mezzrow that included a mixture of New Orleans veterans and young revivalists such as the soprano saxophonist and clarinetist Bob Wilber, Lyttelton's ensemble crossed over several stylistic boundaries, and could hardly be described as revivalist. However, the festival experience brought him into direct contact with several founding fathers of jazz for the first time. More important for his role in the British revival was the record session he made with Sidney Bechet in London on November 13, 1949, and a public concert that they played together the same evening at the Winter Garden theater.

Since the mid-1930s, after the triumphal visits of Louis Armstrong, Duke Ellington and Cab Calloway, Britain had instituted an almost total ban on American jazz musicians performing in the country, as the Musicians' Union and the Ministry of Labour colluded to "protect British jobs." After the ban was imposed, Benny Carter worked in Britain as an arranger for the BBC, Fats Waller toured as a solo act in variety, and Coleman Hawkins managed to work as a soloist with Jack Hylton, but these were rare exceptions, as was the visit of Teddy Hill's New York orchestra which played in the United Kingdom in 1937 as part of a revue. After World War II, other Americans, including Duke Ellington and Benny Goodman, worked with local backing groups on the variety circuit, and a few isolated visitors like Jimmy McPartland and Johnny Mince were guests on privately recorded jam sessions. When Lyttelton flouted the ban to play with Bechet (he feigned ignorance, and went along with the organizer's plan that Bechet was "on holiday"), he publicly allied himself with what many enthusiasts saw as one of the founding fathers of jazz. In the 1920s, Bechet had been deported from Europe, but he had overcome the resultant consular difficulties, arriving in France to make it his home the previous month. As documented in the next section, he had a profound effect on French revivalism, but the totemic importance of his appearance in Britain cannot be overstated.

Bechet's biographer John Chilton described him being perceived at the time as "the music's patron saint."[14] Lyttelton offered a more penetrating analysis in respect of Bechet's influence on younger revivalists. He wrote: "Of all the great American masters, Sidney Bechet seems to have realised most the nature and significance of the New Orleans revival and his responsibilities towards the young musicians engaged in it. . . . He has made it his business to advise and train those with whom he has come in contact."[15].

Following his concert and recordings with Bechet, Lyttelton led what was to become a commercially successful band, nevertheless playing firmly within the revivalist style, until he moved toward the looser swing of Kansas City in the mid-1950s. He ran a successful jazz club in Leicester Square, in central London, taking over from the Australian band led by Graeme Bell, which had introduced to British audiences the idea of dancing to traditional jazz in 1947, after touring (and recording) in Czechoslovakia en route from Melbourne to London. In due course, Bell and Lyttelton brought together musicians from both their bands to form a larger group, the Bell-Lyttelton Jazz Nine. "It was never our intention to 'recreate' anything," wrote Lyttelton, but he went on to point out that they "had in mind the sort of music made by the Luis Russell band in the late twenties. This was music directly derived from the New Orleans idiom, but with simple arranged passages replacing the improvised ensemble."[16] On pieces such as Bell's "Take a Note from the South," recorded in November 1951, the band lacks the energetic drive and confidence of Russell's band, but it is clearly emulating such large 1920s bands. When Lyttelton introduced a transcription of an actual Russell composition, "Jersey Lightning," into a club set by his regular band, he received protests and letters of complaint that he "should stick to jazz" and leave "dance music" to such popular leaders of the time as Victor Silvester.

Lyttelton was always catholic in his enthusiasms, and in experimenting beyond the narrow format of the revivalist jazz band of clarinet, trumpet, trombone, plus rhythm section, he endangered the very enthusiasm for "authenticity" that had endeared him and Webb to the New Orleans jazz fraternity in the first place. Ironically, his experiments with Afro-Caribbean musicians in London, in the so-called "Paseo" Jazz Band, with the West Indian clarinetist Freddie Grant and his colleagues, were lively and surprisingly authentic explorations of New Orleans's Creole heritage. But his regular audience knew nothing about the subtler nuances of Louisiana's musical patrimony. It was not until 1976 when the Meters and the Wild Tchoupitoulas began exploring the Mardi Gras Indian and the Creole island repertoires that this music was bought back to public attention, but Lyttelton was playing pieces like "Mam'selle Josephine" and Jelly Roll Morton's "King Porter Stomp" in 1952 with plenty of Creole cross-rhythms played by the guitarist Fitzroy Coleman, and percussionists Donaldo, George Roberts, Brylo Ford, and George Walker. "The public wanted a certain type of music from me," Lyttelton recalled, "[but] I felt the urge to do something different."[17] He dropped the trombone from his band, substituting the alto saxophonist Bruce Turner, and gradually moved into 1930s "jump band" music, before forming a nine-piece band that encompassed the Kansas City style so effectively that he toured with the likes of Big Joe Turner, Jimmy Rushing, and Buck Clayton.

The vacuum in satisfying the audience hunger for authentic New Orleans jazz was filled by a former merchant seaman, the trumpeter Ken Colyer. In 1948, Colyer's ship, the *Port Sydney*, had docked in New York, and he had heard the bands of Eddie Condon and Muggsy Spanier at first hand. "The sensation I got from hearing Wild Bill [Davison] for the first time was a sort of numb joy that such a man lived and played," he recalled. "If this is Chicago jazz I told myself, then it is better than expected and not far from the New Orleans pattern and sound."[18]

Colyer was well aware of the sound of New Orleans jazz, as he had become an avid record collector before he joined the Merchant Navy. On his return to Britain in 1949, Colyer and his brother Bill formed a band to play music along the lines of Bill Russell's American Music discs by Bunk Johnson and George Lewis. The Crane River Jazz Band began playing regularly in March 1949 and focused on ensemble playing rather than solos. "We were," remembered Colyer, "a bunch of roughnecks playing a purposely primitive music."[19]

This is borne out by the band's recording from 1950, at the Royal Festival Hall, of "I'm Travellin'," which veers from chaos to moments of plaintive beauty, not least in Colyer's singing lead trumpet part, emerging clearly over the gruffer second trumpet of Sonny Morris. The Crane River band took on a symbolic importance greater than its actual artistic achievements, as a band that sought "authenticity" and played without compromise. However, Colyer's most electrifying playing from his early years was in a short-lived group led by the brothers Keith and Ian Christie, who had both been regular members of the Humphrey Lyttelton band. The Christie Brothers Stompers made several recordings, but its March 1951 recording of "Weary Blues" shows both an awareness of Wooden Joe Nicholas's version of the same piece (under the title "Shake It and Break It") for American Music and of the Kid Ory band's approach to ensemble playing. There is a relaxed ebb and flow between the instruments, a tight ensemble sound, and a driving rhythm section propelled by bassist Mickey Ashman and drummer George Hopkinson from Lyttelton's band, and pianist Pat Hawes and banjoist Ben Marshall from the Crane River group.

The ambitions of Keith Christie and Ken Colyer were different, and as Christie moved inexorably toward modern jazz (he would eventually become a trombonist with Johnny Dankworth's band), Colyer rejoined the Merchant Navy with the intention of working his passage to New Orleans, and hearing for himself the music of the men Bill Russell had been recording since the early 1940s. He arrived in late November 1952 on a twenty-nine-day shore pass. For almost a month Colyer met, sat in, and finally recorded with a cross-section of African American jazz musicians in the Crescent City. Although he was to be arrested under the McCarran-Walters Act and deported for overstaying his permitted time, he absorbed more about the practical business of playing the music of New Orleans than any European had hitherto done.

When he returned to Britain in 1953 to lead a co-operative band put together by

Chris Barber and Monty Sunshine, Colyer was perceived as bringing something akin to Moses's stone tablets to the local revivalists. Indeed the effects of his experience were immediately obvious in his band's music. Although the rhythm section was somewhat lightweight and tidy compared to Billy Huntington, Albert Glenny, and Albert Jiles, with whom he had recorded in America, the interplay between Colyer's trumpet, Barber's trombone, and Sunshine's clarinet had much of the spontaneous collective fluidity that Colyer had experienced while sitting in with George Lewis or Percy Humphrey. This applied equally to reinterpretations of old pieces such as Freddie Keppard's "Stockyard Strut" as it did to the band's "Isle of Capri," based on Lewis's arrangement, which was itself based on the popular 1935 record by Wingy Manone.

"Ken is still the best three piece front line lead I have ever played with," recalled Barber in 2009, "and that includes Sidney De Paris and Doc Cheatham."[20] The band's first album for Decca, *New Orleans to London*, was well received. It also led to some misconceptions, including the singer and critic George Melly's oft-quoted assertion that Colyer "sounded and intended to sound like an old man who had never left New Orleans when they closed Storyville."[21] Indeed the language used in the press of the time to describe Colyer is not unlike that which the Swiss conductor Ernest Ansermet used to describe Sidney Bechet in 1919, in that he "can say nothing of his art, save that he follows his 'own way,' and then one thinks that his 'own way' may be the highway the world will rush along tomorrow."[22] Colyer might have been as inarticulate as the young Bechet in conversation, but his letters reveal a man who thought deeply about his music, and in particular his desire to capture the spirit of the bands he had encountered in America. The American banjo player Bill Huntington, who recorded with Colyer in New Orleans, wrote: "I think Ken felt that it was the real music. I think he felt like the African-American musicians . . . that the music had more potency, it had more strength, it had more feeling."[23] To Colyer, then, the force that drove his playing in 1953 was the feeling that he was playing the music of the day, that he was bringing to Europe the very excitement and energy he had felt himself in contemporary New Orleans. This was evident in everything that survives of his first band's work, including a set of pieces recorded in Denmark at the very start of the band's life, and a recently discovered set of concert recordings from the Royal Festival Hall.[24]

The Colyer band's Danish visit in the spring of 1953 was to prove very influential on local players there, notably the trombonist Arne Bue Jensen (known as Papa Bue), who formed his own New Orleans Jazz Band in 1956. Two years later it became the Viking Jazz Band, which celebrated its golden jubilee in 2008.

However, back in the spring of 1954, before Decca could record a sequel to the first full album by the Ken Colyer Jazzmen, the band and Colyer went their

separate ways. According to Barber this was because Bill Colyer wished to replace the rhythm section with something "more authentic." The result was that
Barber took over what had been Colyer's band, and Colyer recruited the first of a
succession of replacement lineups, with Bernard (soon to be known as "Acker")
Bilk on clarinet.

Barber's band, with its new trumpeter Pat Halcox in place, through a canny
choice of music, strong presentation, and astute management, became popular
and successful. Its 1954–55 repertoire spanned New Orleans marches ("Over in
the Gloryland"); hymns ("We Shall Walk through the Streets of the City"); and
rags ("Panama"); Ellingtonian compositions ("Black and Tan Fantasy," "Shout
'em Aunt Tillie"); 1920s big band pieces ("Tight Like That," "Papa De Da Da");
and Louis Armstrong's current hit "Skokiaan." When the Irish blues singer Ot-
tilie Patterson joined the band on January 1, 1955, the classic blues repertoire of
Bessie Smith was added to the mix. This variety of material, the band's professional delivery, and exposure through radio, records, and touring quickly made it
the most commercially successful revivalist group, yet for many fans it retained
the tinge of authenticity acquired during the year with Colyer at the helm. In
1956, Barber began focusing his efforts on extensive touring, as well as Sunday
concerts in large municipal auditoriums (many of which were recorded), and in
1957 the band decided to focus exclusively on concerts and overseas touring,
restricting its club work to the Marquee in London, which Barber ran with his
business partner Harold Pendleton. By 1959, twenty-nine weeks a year were spent
abroad in Europe and in the United States, where Barber was billed as "the man
who took trad back to America."[25]

As a result, Barber's group, with its piano-less rhythm section, became one of
the most influential and widely imitated bands in the history of the traditional
revival anywhere in the world.

Meanwhile, Colyer's band matured into an ensemble that helped him to
channel his experience of playing New Orleans jazz through a collection of like-
minded individuals, and in due course he settled into a lineup with the clarinetist
Ian Wheeler and trombonist Mac Duncan. This group took on a collective
personality as musically distinctive as Barber's. Although Colyer attracted an
audience that identified with his purist and somewhat curmudgeonly ideas about
how the music should sound, he was in some ways more like Barber than he
would care to admit. Colyer toured in Britain and Europe with George Lewis in
1957 and 1959, whereas Barber brought over blues artists such as Sonny Terry and
Brownie McGhee. In both instances, the idea was to present authentic performances by African Americans to European audiences. Writers at the time presented the first Lewis tour with Colyer as "undoubtedly the most important event
of recent trad times."[26]

Some members of the press who had little sympathy for traditional jazz went along with Leonard Feather's phrase that Lewis was "superannuated and mediocre,"[27] yet audiences loved the frail clarinetist. His biographer, Dorothy Tait, described the crowd at the Free Trade Hall in Manchester "surging to its feet in a spontaneous cheering tribute."[28] Colyer's band accompanied Lewis for the majority of his concerts in Britain in 1957, and played as the supporting act to Lewis's entire New Orleans group in 1959. Lewis also made guest appearances with the Chris Barber band.

In addition to Barber, several of the musicians who had played with Colyer went on to lead their own bands, which to a greater or lesser degree maintained his view of New Orleans jazz. Most notably Colyer's former clarinetists Acker Bilk and Monty Sunshine capitalized on the short-lived vogue for "trad," as the pop press called traditional jazz, at the start of the 1960s. Ironically, their respective hit records, Bilk's "Stranger on the Shore," a television theme tune for clarinet and strings, and Sunshine's cloying, prettified solo version of Sidney Bechet's "Petite Fleur"—which he recorded with Barber's rhythm section—were the antithesis of polyphonic traditional jazz. It was Denis Preston who was responsible for producing many of Bilk's most populist sessions (which amid the string chorales and Somerset songs included one outstanding and musically satisfying collaboration with Stan Tracey's big band on a set of Ellingtonian material). Preston also produced records by many other traditional jazz musicians, including the lightweight fare of Terry Lightfoot and Ken Sims, but also the finest work of the clarinetist Sandy Brown, who moved under Preston's aegis from a narrowly focused Johnny Dodds–style revivalist to a wide-ranging, idiosyncratic, original musician with a flair for Ghanian hi-life music in such pieces as "Everybody Loves Saturday Night," and "African Queen."

At the very time that Bilk's and Sunshine's groups were most popular with the general public, British New Orleans fans started to turn their attention to the work of two musicians whose concept was even more "purist" and "authentic" than Colyer's, the trumpeter Keith Smith and the drummer Barry Martyn. They were friends who in 1958 organized one of the first New Orleans–style marching bands in Europe, the New Teao Brass Band, which (like Ken Colyer's contemporaneous Omega Brass Band) emulated the recordings of Bunk Johnson's Brass Band from the 1940s.

Martyn was one of the editors of a short-lived magazine, called *Eureka*, founded in 1960 and devoted to New Orleans jazz. It published pictures and essays concerning the Crescent City's musicians that went into layers of detail far beyond the George Lewis circle of players, describing brass bands, obscure dance halls, and legendary figures who no longer played. When Martyn first arrived in New Orleans in December 1960, he was already steeped in the city's musical heritage to a degree that far outstripped Colyer's knowledge of almost a decade earlier.

In February 1961 he recorded the first session for his Mono ("Music of New Orleans") label, by Kid Sheik's Swingsters, a traditional New Orleans band with Harold Dejan on alto saxophone and Alex Bigard on drums, playing a gutsier, rawer version of the music than English listeners had become accustomed to from the Johnson/Lewis records, or the homegrown Colyer/Barber music derived from them. Martyn happened to be in the city when Bill Grauer and Herb Friedwald produced their "Living Legends" series of recordings for the Riverside label, which Martyn immediately realized was "the most significant set of recordings since Bill Russell's American Music series."[29]

As a result, a new set of influences, those of the Riverside discs, including such musicians as Louis Cottrell, Sweet Emma Barrett, Jim Robinson, Billie and DeDe Pierce, and those of Martyn's Mono series, began to affect European players. Martyn formed his own Ragtime Band in Britain to play this music, and trumpeters Cuff Billett, Clive Blackmore, and Dan Pawson, reed players Bill Greenow and Sammy Rimington, trombonist Pete Dyer, and pianist Graham Patterson were among the circle of musicians who worked with him. As the 1960s progressed, Martyn returned to New Orleans to record with local musicians, and also organized British tours for such New Orleans players as Kid Thomas, Kid Sheik, Louis Nelson, Captain John Handy, and Emanuel Paul. They played and recorded with his band, just as George Lewis had done with Colyer, thereby presenting a new level of "authenticity" to European audiences.

Smith also brought over visiting American soloists to play with his Climax Jazz Band, but in 1966 he risked what little capital he had to bring a complete American band to Europe. "It wasn't a totally out and out New Orleans band," recalled Smith, "because we had Jimmy Archey and Darnell Howard, but I make no excuses for that. We also had Pops Foster, Cie Frazier, Alton Purnell, and Kid Howard should have made the trip . . . but due to illness we signed Alvin Alcorn."[30] Particularly having gone through the tortuous process of arranging union exchanges and work permits, Smith was disappointed by the size of his British audiences for this band, but in Germany, Scandinavia, and Switzerland, where the tour was promoted by Horst Lippmann and Fritz Rau, there were sizable audiences, with a hunger to hear a genuine ensemble of traditional jazz veterans.

Martyn went on to lead a comparable band, the Legends of Jazz, in the United States in the 1970s, and Smith subsequently toured several package shows in Europe, including, from 1981, "The Wonderful World of Louis Armstrong," in which he led a reunited version of the All Stars, with Peanuts Hucko, Big Chief Russell Moore, Dick Cary, Arvell Shaw, and Barrett Deems.

Just as Colyer's bands spawned a second generation of bandleaders and influential revivalists, so, too, did those of Martyn and Smith. Notably the clarinetist Sammy Rimington (who also played with Colyer) became the European embodiment of George Lewis, although he also played fiery alto saxophone in the style of Captain John Handy. Rimington spent time in the United States playing with bands in Connecticut and New Orleans, but from the late 1960s he has led a distinguished series of groups in Europe that have come as close as any to the style of music played at Preservation Hall in New Orleans, founded in June 1961 to present the kinds of players sought out by Colyer, Smith, and Martyn.

From the 1960s, Dan Pawson led his Artesian Hall Stompers in Birmingham in the English midlands, recreating a more fundamental type of music, namely the kind of New Orleans dance hall session that had been recorded in the years following Colyer's visit by enthusiasts such as Leonard Brackett, Lord Richard Ekins, and Grayson Mills in places such as the Dew Drop Inn, Kohlman's Tavern, Luthjen's, the Moulin Rouge, and the Paddock Lounge. These sessions appeared on such specialist labels as Arhoolie, Center, Icon, Jazzology, LaCroix, Mono, 504, and 77. In the late 1980s, Pawson occasionally led bands of New Orleans veterans in Europe, notably a July 1989 tour built around the Ascona Festival in Ticino, Switzerland, with Louis Nelson, Pud Brown, Danny Barker, and Chester Zardis in the lineup.

As restrictions on American musicians playing in Britain were gradually lifted from the 1970s onward, audiences were at last able to hear more authentic New Orleans–style playing firsthand. The London-based trombonist Mike Casimir brought in Louis Nelson, Kid Thomas, Paul Barnes, and Alvin Alcorn in the 1970s to play with his New Iberia Stompers. Martyn toured frequently with the former George Lewis band pianist Alton Purnell, who also played and recorded with Keith Smith. Rimington brought over a succession of interesting and unusual players, from the tenor saxophonist Sammy Lee to the younger-generation trumpeters John and Wendell Brunious. The drummer Trevor Richards, who had studied with Zutty Singleton, played in both Britain and Germany with a wide variety of players, including the clarinetist Herbie Hall and the drummer Freddie Kohlman. In the 1990s, Richards toured widely in Europe with larger ensembles under the rubric "Legends of the Swing Era," but there was a strong New Orleans flavor in these bands, with such experienced revivalists as Doc Cheatham, Franz Jackson, Red Richards, and Truck Parham among the personnel.

Ken Colyer led bands until shortly before his death in 1988, also guesting with various New Orleans–inflected package shows run by the Australian trombonist Max Collie. Although Chris Barber's band has encompassed a huge stylistic range, from electric blues to Balkan dances, and (from the late 1990s) has functioned as an Ellingtonian big band, in 2011 his repertoire still includes plenty of New Orleans revivalist material. His group continues to be a role model for other bands in Britain, Holland, and Germany.

The Revival in France

Following the liberation of Paris from German occupation in late August 1944, it was not long before jazz, which had been officially frowned upon by the Nazis, began to be heard legitimately again in the French capital. The occupying Germans had turned a blind eye to their regime's opposition to the music in some respects, and the gypsy guitarist Django Reinhardt continued to lead a swing band in the city for much of the war, but other forms of jazz remained secret, semi-underground enthusiasms. After the liberation, the Potomac Club, close to the Bastille, was a Red Cross club for "Negro soldiers," but black American bands played there both for soldiery and Parisian fans alike, as was the case at the Left Bank Club, formerly an all-white venue, where integrated jam sessions took place. There were similar sessions at the Salon Pélissier in Marseilles, where the town's Hot Club was re-formed. Hugues Panassié reported that the plethora of black talent in these bands made Marseilles temporarily the "new jazz capital of France."[31] Once the troops withdrew following VE Day in 1945, however, it was down to local French musicians to regroup after the war, and once again establish a national jazz scene for concerts, clubs, and tours, which was mainly focused on Paris.

In 1944, swing was the prevailing musical language in French jazz, although it was not long before the arrival of the 1945 bebop records of Charlie and Dizzy Gillespie provoked a critical schism between those prepared to embrace such modern jazz and those whom the French musician and critic Boris Vian described as "the intolerant fanatical defenders of New Orleans jazz to the exclusion of all others."[32] The liberal-minded Charles Delaunay, who had done much to champion Django Reinhardt before the war, spearheaded a new movement that endorsed bebop enthusiastically. Panassié, however, sided with the "fanatical defenders" described by Vian. In general, the turf war between traditionalists advocating the values of Armstrong, Morton, and Oliver, and modernists keener on Gillespie and Parker, somewhat overlooked the American revival involving Bunk Johnson and George Lewis. Indeed the historian Gérard Conte wrote: "As a whole, French critics failed to understand the importance of this revival, and came to the conclusion a little too rapidly that this music was little more than a maladroit copy of the 1920s New Orleans style." Instead, the battle was joined against modernists by traditionalists on the basis of original 1920s recordings representing "the true jazz."[33]

interesting

The divide between critics was reflected by the policy of Parisian clubs. Whereas most prewar clubs had presented the lingua franca of swing, the Caveau de la Huchette and the Tabou now turned their attention to the new music. Meanwhile, in May 1946 a young clarinetist named Claude Luter opened a New Orleans jazz club at 5 Rue des Carmes, in the basement of the Hotel Lorientais, run by Madame Perrodot, who as the establishment's name suggests came from the Brittany town of Lorient.[34] This Club Lorientais, in an arched stone cellar with a dirt floor, briefly became the capital of the traditionalist movement, and the band played there at nine every night, as well as playing for student matinees on Thursdays, Saturdays, and Sundays at five. The band's first records from March 1947 reveal a group in thrall to the sounds of King Oliver, Johnny Dodds, and Jelly Roll Morton. The band perfected this style as the year went on until fire regulations forced the Lorientais to close, and the band transferred first to the Kentucky Club, then to the Kent, and finally in January 1949 to the Vieux Colombier in Saint-Germain-Des-Près.

Whereas in England George Webb was in thrall to the music of Oliver and Morton, Luter was above all influenced by Sidney Bechet. In the magazine *Jazz Hot*, Luter (just twenty-four years old) wrote a critical appraisal of the clarinet playing of Johnny Dodds, Jimmie Noone, Mezz Mezzrow, and Bechet. He concluded: "The personality of Bechet is extraordinary. Above all, this is because in the ensembles it is he who takes on the cornet part in the last choruses, and wipes everybody out. He's a musician who possesses a great power of attack, and an awesome punch. It is he who possesses the greatest swing of these four clarinetists, and his vibrato is of a formidable vehemence."[35]

Luter's admiration for Bechet gradually became noticeable in his recordings, starting with "Wild Cat Blues," from February 1948, in which he shed his extremely passable imitation of Johnny Dodds for his new idol. By the end of the year, on a quartet version of his own composition "Riz à la Creole," the transformation was complete. Luter's enthusiasm for all things Bechet was shared—despite his modernist leanings—by Delaunay. He not only outdid his rival Panassié by bringing the veteran soprano saxophonist to play in Paris at the city's first jazz festival alongside other Americans in May 1949, during which Bechet's playing was favorably compared to his fellow guest Charlie Parker, but lured him back that autumn on a more permanent basis, just prior to the aforementioned trip to England. As Andy Fry has pointed out, Bechet and Delaunay then colluded to cement Bechet's status as the father figure of French jazz. They played on his "authenticity" as surely as Colyer subsequently exploited that of George Lewis, but also stressed Bechet's French-speaking Creole roots, and emphasized his earlier "successes" in France, thereby creating in the public imagination a "feigned familiarity" with him.[36]

Significant

267

Luter's band, which was to become Bechet's main accompanying group, was somewhat pedestrian in comparison with Lyttelton's. However, the recordings it made with Bechet on October 14, 1949, produced a hit record, "Les Oignons," based on a Creole nursery song, and featuring a simplistic verse and chorus structure punctuated by silent breaks. It soon became de rigueur for audiences, whether listening to the song being played live or on a jukebox, to shout "Oignons!" in the silences, such responses creating a feeling of listener participation as vital as that precipitated by Cab Calloway's chants of "Hi de ho!" in the 1930s. The record would sell over a million copies during the course of the next decade and underpinned Bechet's remarkable Indian summer as a performer until his death in May 1959. His popularity in France was unmatched in traditional jazz, and in 1955 a vastly oversubscribed concert at the Olympia in Paris led to injuries and unrest as riot police were called in to quell the thousands of fans unable to get in to hear his music.

Bechet recorded frequently with Luter's band, a larger and less wieldy ensemble than his own latter-day American bands, which he led on his occasional returns to New York or Chicago. By contrast to Bechet's U.S. sessions with Wild Bill Davison or Jonah Jones, Luter favored the two-trumpet front line style of Lu Watters and Bob Scobey, and his band had a big, solid sound with little opportunity for delicacy or subtlety. The same was true of Bechet's other regular French accompanists, the similar-sized ensemble of the clarinetist André Reweliotty, and the house band of the Métro Jazz club (later renamed the Trois Mailletz) led by the saxophonist Michel Attenoux. However, the French recordings included plenty of local source material, or pieces from Bechet's earlier career suitably adapted and given francophone titles. Hence "Au clair de la lune," "Ce mossieu qui parle," "Le loup, le biche et le chevalier," "Moulin à café," "Promenade aux Champs-Élysées," and many other such songs became the backbone of his repertoire.

The consequence of Bechet's presence in France was to engender a generation of reed players who adopted his broad tone on both clarinet and soprano saxophone, and his domineering approach to the three-piece front line. Luter and Reweliotty were the first in a sequence of musicians that also included Olivier Franc, Jacques Gauthé, Daniel Huck, and Alain Marquet, all of whom continued to keep elements of Bechet's style alive in the decades following his death.

Bechet was not the only New Orleans musician to live and work in France. Unlike Britain, there was no Musicians' Union agreement to prevent Americans playing in the country, and so from the late 1940s onward a steady trickle of traditional jazz stars came into the country. Most influential after Bechet were the Louis Armstrong All Stars, even though they were only short-term visitors. Following their appearance at Nice in 1948, they played at the Salle Pleyel in Paris in November the following year. Boris Vian singled out a glorious Armstrong solo on "Muskrat Ramble" as the highlight, describing it as a return to Armstrong's "good old days," backed by "the accompaniment of Earl Hines and the consistent support of Cozy Cole, whose precision and dependability is unbeatable."[37]

It took until the mid-1950s for the Armstrong All Stars to be allowed to play in Britain, but by that time their visits to France had already spawned many bands that adopted elements of their style, although the most notable among them was still to emerge. This was the band of Irakli de Davrichewy. In 1958, while still a teenager, Davrichewy formed his New Orleans Ambassadors, also featuring his brother Sandrik on piano or guitar, which uncannily echoed the sound of the All Stars.

Two years after Armstrong's second visit to France with the All Stars, his colleague from the Nice festival Mezz Mezzrow returned in 1951 with an international band that contained the New Orleans veterans Lee Collins on trumpet and Zutty Singleton on drums. Although Collins was not in the best of health, he blew lustily in the Armstrong manner, recording with the band for Vogue. "The tone was pretty hot and big," wrote British critic Max Jones of Collins's Salle Pleyel appearance with Mezzrow. "[He had] a kind of crackling vibrato on the long notes that I had noticed with Armstrong and Bechet when hearing them in person. The feeling was right, too, and there was the dragged timing and off-the-beat swing of Armstrong's blues playing. Lee Collins was like Louis not in a piecemeal fashion, but in an organic musical way."[38]

Mezzrow had recruited local players to complete his lineup, and both tenorist Guy Lafitte and pianist André Persiany were to go on to be significant figures in French jazz. Persiany, who had made a brief foray into bebop, would make several influential recordings with Bechet, among others. He had already appeared on disc in 1949 with the swing trumpeters Bill Coleman (a longtime Paris resident) and Buck Clayton, playing a loose fusion of swing and Dixieland. This style was even more prevalent on Clayton's return to France in 1953, where he worked with another of Mezzrow's Franco-American bands. "My dixieland training came in handy, because Mezz liked a lot of dixieland," recalled Clayton, who had spent the intervening years working off and on with the New Orleans clarinetist Tony Parenti.[39] On the 1953 Mezzrow records, bassists Pierre Michelot and Georges Hadjo alternated in the lineup alongside Mezz, Clayton, Gene Sedric, and Kansas Fields, but Clayton remained in France for much of 1953, after Mezzrow returned home, and his recordings that fall with Persiany are more swing-oriented than revivalist. However, Persiany's other traditional jazz recordings from the period included sessions with the New Orleans clarinetist Albert Nicholas in 1954.

269

Nicholas had settled in Paris in 1953, and he remained there until 1968, ultimately replacing Bechet as the major influence on the city's New Orleans–style players. Even before his arrival, there is evidence from recordings of his style influencing local players. For example, Guy Lafitte produced a couple of choruses on "Muskrat Ramble" in a Salle Pleyel concert in October 1952 with Bill Coleman that capture exactly Nicholas's burbling lower chalumeau register and his incisive, decorative playing in the instrument's upper range. From those who learned from Nicholas after his arrival, in particular Marc Richard should be singled out. Richard began his career as a trumpeter in the 1960s with the Parisian band Les haricots rouges, but soon settled on clarinet and alto saxophone as his main instruments. The two men recorded once together with the Jazz-O-Maniacs at the Hamburg "Hot Jazz Meeting" in 1968. Subsequently, although much of his attention has gone to the Paris Swing Orchestra, Richard's clarinet playing in his New Orleans Quartet, which he led into the 2000s, shows the strong influence of Nicholas's delicate Creole filigree style.

Although Bill Coleman had made his name before World War II in the United States as a swing and big band trumpeter, perhaps best remembered now for his excellent recordings for Fats Waller, it was evident that by 1952 he was including a fair amount of traditional jazz in his performances in France. The aforementioned "Muskrat Ramble," with parade drumming from Zutty Singleton and some more-than-adequate tailgate trombone from Count Basie's onetime star Dicky Wells, shows an intuitive understanding of the New Orleans small group style, even if it seems that Coleman based his own solos firmly on the record of the 1947 Boston Symphony Hall Concert by Louis Armstrong. At the end of 1952, Wells returned home, and the clarinetist and saxophonist Benny Waters joined in his place with Coleman.

Although Waters had recorded with King Oliver, he was always more of a swing musician than a New Orleans stylist, but alongside Coleman he produced some creditable traditional jazz recordings in France in October 1953, and the band's versions of "St. Louis Blues" and "Royal Garden Blues" were to give Parisian listeners a taste of authentic-sounding New Orleans polyphony, played by a band that included several American jazzmen, among them the drummer Wallace Bishop, who had replaced Singleton. Waters went on to record with the Guadeloupe-born trombonist Al Lirvat in 1955. Lirvat had composed the beguine "Touloulou" in the 1930s, which had become a standard of the genre, and his band played a mixture of robust New Orleans jazz and the beguines, meringues, and Creole songs of the French Antilles. To the customers of the Cigale bar in the Pigalle area of Paris where Lirvat played, this Caribbean-tinged music was "not the kind of jazz that the public wanted," recalled Waters.[40]

Benny Waters himself returned to playing small group swing there until the late 1960s, with the trumpeter Jack Butler replacing Lirvat. Nevertheless, Lirvat's fusion of jazz with the traditional music of the French Caribbean was as vibrant as Humphrey Lyttelton's recordings with Freddie Grant's band. The exploration of Creole rhythm and melody in conjunction with traditional jazz would be carried on in France not only by Lirvat, but by a new band of young players, Les haricots rouges. As well as playing traditional jazz and Caribbean music at the highest level, the band also specialized in comic routines that depended on excellent comedic timing, and an element of acrobatic agility. To their general audience, their exuberance, bonhomie, and comic flair conceal their considerable achievements as France's best traditional jazz band.

Beneath the humor, Les haricots rouges, formed in 1963 by the clarinetist Gérard Tarquin, became the principal French jazz band to espouse the 1940s New Orleans style of Johnson and Lewis, thereby launching what might be regarded as the "second revival" in France. In its early days, the band's trombonist was the classical conductor and flutist Daniel Barda, who subsequently founded the long-running traditional jazz quartet Paris Washboard, whose alumni include Alain Marquet and the pianists Louis Mazetier and Christian Azzi (an ex-Luter sideman who was formerly Bechet's principal pianist in France). Barda was replaced by Larry Weston and later Denis Carterre with Les haricots rouges, and their original trumpeter Marc Richard was replaced by several musicians over the years, including Patrick Geoffroy, "Boss" Querand, Jean Dufour, Patrick Artero, and Pierre Jean.

In the 1970s, the band toured and recorded with Alton Purnell and Louis Nelson, and it welcomed Sam Lee as a guest in 1982 and 1988. On several of these occasions, the personnel included the Belgian pianist and banjoist Walter De Troch, one of his country's most versatile musicians in the New Orleans style, who played over the years with several Belgian groups, including the Cotton City Jazz Band, the Fondy Riverside Bullet Band, and Rudy Bailliu's Society Serenaders.

One particularly unusual project involving musicians from Les haricots rouges and their circle was the Anachronic Jazz Band, formed by Marc Richard and the pianist and jazz historian Philippe Baudoin in 1976, and lasting for four years. It tried the experiment of playing a repertoire drawn from bebop and post-bop in the style and instrumentation of a classic jazz band of the 1920s. With Patrick Artero, trumpet, Daniel Barda, trombone, and Richard, clarinet, plus occasional additional reed players such as Daniel Huck, the band recorded such pieces as "Anthropology," "Bernie's Tuine," "Giant Steps," and "Round Midnight," replete with tuba and banjo. Artero's virtuosic lead, and the robust and inventive trombone of Barda, gave the band a strong and distinctive attack, and despite its

So then from what definition of New Orleans jazz? is this a

use of chord sequences far more complex than the average New Orleans repertoire, the results that can be heard on the band's eponymous recording (Open 02,
1976) are extremely convincing.

Although Paris has remained the center of French traditional jazz, and is the
home of Association Française des Amateurs de Jazz Nouvelle Orléans, there
have been other areas of France where traditional jazz has a strong foothold.
Nîmes in the southerly département of Gard is the home of the Hot Antic Jazz
Band, founded in 1979 by the trumpeter Michel Bastide. Its members specialize
in doubling on several instruments, which was a skill particularly displayed by the
band's reed soloist from 1979 to 1989, Jean-François Bonnel. He mastered a range
of classic jazz styles on clarinet and saxophones, and his and his fellow band
members' instrumental virtuosity marked the group out from most other revivalists. Although the band's stage clothes with colorful dungarees and fedoras had
much in common with the apparel of Les haricots rouges, this similarly conceals
serious musical intent—its music-making has been consistently intense and sym-
pathetic to 1920s ensemble jazz. The Hot Antic players were appropriate accompanists to the pioneer trumpeter Jabbo Smith, who toured and recorded with the
group in 1982, reviving many of Smith's original compositions, and recording
some of them for the first time.

In the 1980s, another major center for traditional jazz was Mâcon, whose
active local traditional jazz society presented concerts by most of Europe's leading New Orleans–style jazz bands, as well as American guests. Montaubon
hosted a festival along traditional lines run by the Hot Club of France, from the
1980s, but this has largely lost its revivalist content in the twenty-first century.
More recently, Bayonne and Périgueux have hosted long-running traditional jazz
festivals, and the international festival at Marciac has a considerable focus on the
Crescent City, owing to its long-running connection to Wynton Marsalis.

of course

The inescapable conclusion, however, is that a music that had thousands of
fans clogging the streets of Paris, and mobbing its hero Sidney Bechet in the
1950s, is now a minority taste. Just as Chris Barber has continued to keep New
Orleans jazz alive for British audiences for over five decades, albeit wrapped in a
larger band format, and often financed by ventures with pop musicians such as
Van Morrison or Mark Knopfler, New Orleans jazz in France has depended on a
small coterie of players to keep it going. The days of a jazz club in every town are
long gone, and so too are the final vestiges of the schism between followers of
Panassié and those of Delaunay. Instead, it is down to musicians who have a
similar track record to Barber, Irakli, Les haricots rouges, the Hot Antic, and Paris
Washboard, to preserve the legacy of Bechet, Nicholas, and the other New
Orleans masters who sought to pass on their music at first hand.

decent conclusion

272

1. Author's interview with George Avakian, February 24, 1999.

2. Bert Whyatt, *Muggsy Spanier: The Lonesome Road* (New Orleans: Jazzology Press, 1995), p. 41.

3. John Buchanan, *Emperor Norton's Hunch: The Story of Lu Watters' Yerba Buena Jazz Band* (Middle Dural, NSW, Australia: Hambledon Productions, 1996), p. 31.

4. James Lincoln Collier, "The Dixieland Revival," in *The Making of Jazz* (London: Macmillan, 1981), p. 280. Ted Gioia, "The Fragmentation of Jazz Styles," in *The History of Jazz* (New York: Oxford, 1997), p. 277.

5. Michael Pointon, "Vic Lewis New York Jazzmen" (liner notes to Upbeat URCD 192, 2003).

6. Clarrie Hanley, "Vic Lewis and Jack Parnell's Jazzmen: Singin' the Blues" (liner notes to Upbeat URCD 163, 2001).

7. Sholes' life reads like History Lesson in A and R," *Billboard*, March 20, 1961, p.4.

8. Mezz Mezzrow and Bernard Wolfe, "Appendix 3: A Note on the Panassié Recordings" in *Really the Blues* (London: Jazz Book Club, 1959), p. 361.

9. Alyn Shipton, *A New History of Jazz*, 2nd ed. (New York: Continuum, 2007), p. 455.

10. Harry Gold, *Gold Doubloons and Pieces of Eight* (London: Northway, 2000), p. 120.

11. Wilford quoted in Humphrey Lyttelton, *I Play as I Please* (London: Macgibbon and Kee, 1954), p. 123.

12. George Shearing with Alyn Shipton, *Lullaby of Birdland* (New York: Continuum, 2004), p. 106.

13. Lyttelton, *I Play as I Please*, p. 125.

14. John Chilton, *Sidney Bechet: The Wizard of Jazz* (London: Macmillan, 1987), p. 228.

15. Lyttelton, *I Play as I Please*, p. 177.

16. Humphrey Lyttelton, *Second Chorus* (London: Macgibbon and Kee, 1958), p. 94.

17. Ibid.

18. Mike Pointon and Ray Smith, *Goin' Home: The Uncompromising Life and Music of Ken Colyer* (London: Ken Colyer Trust, 2010), p. 56.

19. Ibid., p. 75.

20. Chris Barber interviewed by Alyn Shipton, BBC Radio 3, October 10, 2009.

21. George Melly, *Owning Up* (Harmondsworth: Penguin, 1970), p. 46.

22. Ernest Ansermet, "Sur un orchestre nègre," in *La revue romande*, October 5, 1919, trans. Walter Schaap.

23. Pointon and Smith, *Goin' Home*, p. 146.

24. Ken Colyer, *The Lost 1954 Royal Festival Hall Tapes* [Upbeat URCD 198, 2004].

25. Brian Matthew, *Trad Mad* (London: Consul, 1962) (caption in plate section following p. 33).

26. Ivan Berg and Ian Youmans, *Trad* (London: Foulsham, 1962), p. 32.

27. Jim Godbolt, *A History of Jazz in Britain, 1950-1970* (London: Quartet, 1989), p. 216

28. Jay Allison Stuart (Dorothy Tait), *Call Him George* (London: Jazz Book Club, 1963), p. 248.

29. Barry Martyn and Mick Burns, *Walking with Legends: Barry Martyn's New Orleans Jazz Odyssey* (Baton Rouge: Louisiana State University Press, 2007), p. 40.

30. Terry Dash, "Keith Smith," *Footnote* 16., no. 6, August/September 1985, p. 9.

31. William A. Shack, *Harlem in Montmartre* (Berkeley: University of California Press, 2001), p. 128.

32. Boris Vian (trans. Mike Zwerin), *Round about Close to Midnight: The Jazz Writings of Boris Vian* (London: Quartet, 1988), p. 58.

33. Gérard Conte, "Revival" (trans. A. Shipton), in Philippe Carles, André Clergeat, and Jean-Louis Comolli, *Dictionaire du jazz* (Paris: Goffin, 1988), p. 858.

34. Jean-Pierre Daubresse, "Claude Luter et les Lorientais" (liner note to Memories CD ME 13-14-15, 2011); Rosemary Wakeman, "Street noises: celebrating the Liberation of Paris in music and dance," in Alexander Cowan and Jill Steward, *The City and the Senses— Urban Culture Since 1500* (Aldershot, UK: Ashgate, 2007). p. 234.

35. Claude Luter, "Quatre clarinettistes" (trans. A. Shipton), *Jazz Hot*, November 1948.

36. Andy Fry, "Remembrance of Jazz Past: Sidney Bechet in France," in Jane Fulcher (ed.), *The New Cultural History of Music* (New York: Oxford, 2011), p. 307.

37. Vian, *Round about Close to Midnight*, p. 104.

38. Max Jones, *Talking Jazz* (London: Macmillan, 1987), p. 100.

39. Buck Clayton, with Nancy Miller Elliott, *Buck Clayton's Jazz World* (London: Macmillan, 1986), p. 146.

40. Benny Waters, *The Key to a Jazzy Life* (Toulouse: Les Arts Graphiques, 1985), p. 72.

EKKEHARD JOST

13 / THE EUROPEAN JAZZ AVANT-GARDE OF THE LATE 1960S AND EARLY 1970S
WHERE DID EMANCIPATION LEAD?

decentink [handwritten]

W riting jazz history—as with any other kind of historiography—necessitates a reliance on documentation. What cannot be verified by written sources or recordings will either fall into oblivion or be consigned to mythology. Something recalled by a contemporary may be rather vague, whether glorified by nostalgia or distorted by failing memory: Did Buddy Bolden really play that loud? What exactly happened when bebop was "invented" at Minton's Playhouse? Was the Swiss saxophonist Werner "Barbu" Lüdi really an unrecognized pioneer of free jazz in Germany, or did someone else in Wanne-Eickel, Itzehoe, or wherever start it earlier? Is it true that, from as early as 1957, the "Reform Art Unit" in Vienna were playing a form of music that, as they have claimed, omitted all conventional principles of musical creation[1]—and, if so, how important was that in the development of avant-garde jazz in Europe?

In general, our presumptions about history imply that any event not publicized will not be accepted as part of history. Almost from the very start, jazz has been publicized through the mass media: articles in magazines, radio broadcasts, and—most important—recordings. Anyone or anything not documented through any of these media channels was almost automatically eliminated from the process of historical reflection. As regrettable as this may seem, it is a fact we cannot overlook. [handwritten margin: *historiography*]

If we accept that statements made about music that has long since faded away—especially music for which no written scores exist and large portions of which cannot be pinned down by scores—are necessarily filtered by memory and saturated with personal preferences that cannot be controlled a posteriori, we soon realize that the gap between past and present needs to be bridged by analyzing significant documents from the past—in our case, mainly recordings. Recorded musical documents (records, broadcasts, etc.) are, however, subject to the mechanics of selection. This is an important truth, especially if we want to address the earliest phase of European free jazz. Usually, record companies are profit-oriented and mostly interested in recordings with potential for quick profit. Since few people in the record business believed European free jazz would become a commercial success, documentation of the music was initially sparse. A more complete picture of what went on at the time only began to emerge as musical cooperatives such as FMP, INCUS, and ICP started to make their own recordings—that is, when an increasing number of musicians turned to recording the music themselves.

In addition to these objective, formal restrictions, there are subjective factors to consider. In the earliest years of free jazz in Europe, I observed the music's development with my own eyes and ears, particularly in West Germany and West Berlin. I regularly attended the "Free Music Workshops" at the Academy of Arts in Berlin and the "Total Music Meetings" in the Quartier Latin, but I could neither listen to the sessions held at the Little Theatre Club in London nor experience the Free Jazz Workshop de Lyon or the Lille Jazz Action. I was generally aware of the self-recordings by musicians in my own country but knew less about those in Scandinavia or Great Britain. Therefore, my personal view of the way free jazz developed in Europe could be considered "ethnocentric," and if I place more emphasis on one event or another, it may be due to my own geographical location.

Yet another limitation on plotting this history is subjective but in a more general sense: listening to records as an objective documentation of music does not mean this alone enables able us to write history objectively. Anyone claiming an ability to describe objective facts without letting even a tinge of personal opinion intrude is inevitably caught in a kind of naive positivism. The act of selection itself—what an author chooses to write about—is based on the author's own opinion, what he or she thinks is or is not worth writing about, and thus depends on the author's own valuations. As such, I cannot conceal from the reader that my approach to analyzing the structural elements of free jazz in Europe is embedded in my own subjective experiences. All this, of course, is quite normal and not very new. But in view of the dogmatic aesthetics established in jazz literature, I feel it may be necessary to emphasize this point.

The history of jazz in Europe up to the middle of the 1960s is marked by a common effort among European musicians to imitate creative developments in the United States. The changing aesthetics of African American music, the development of new structural patterns, and a gradual expansion of musical material were—usually with a more or less significant time lapse—readily absorbed by European musicians: the closest possible imitation of the American original became a measure of musical quality. However, this lack of confidence about their own creative capacity was likely not the only factor that made European musicians produce legions of plagiarists and imitators. The expectations of audiences and jazz critics aggravated this situation. To them, the prophet was esteemed in his own country only when interpreting the message sent by the American gods. The extent to which this European system of critical assessment hewed to U.S.-

centric standards, even up until the end of the 1960s, is illustrated by the following cover copy written by Joachim Ernst Berendt in 1969: "It is my opinion that, in Tchicai, Europe has a European-born black musician whose standard is equal to the great American innovators of the new jazz"[2]—lucky Europe!

Toward the middle of the 1960s, there was a gradual change in the way European musicians related to their American models. The development of American jazz itself may have caused this, but it could also have been a change in the way European musicians perceived themselves. *yes*

The evolution of free jazz in the United States during the late 1950s and early 1960s was obviously the most radical departure in this music since the "bebop revolution" of the 1940s. Among the most pronounced characteristics of free jazz, as performed by Ornette Coleman and Cecil Taylor with their groups around 1969, was the way certain fundamental rules of jazz improvisation were ignored. Formal standards accepted since the beginnings of jazz, and never questioned, were suddenly no longer the norm: adhering to a fundamental rhythm (playing "time"), the principles of tonality and functional harmony, and the predominance of melodic continuity. On the one hand, free jazz abided by the basic emotional qualities of traditional Afro-American music and even stressed its inherent rhythmical intensity. On the other hand, free jazz in its formal aspects and tonal structures gradually came closer to resembling structural patterns developed within composed avant-garde music during the previous fifty years.

A number of jazz musicians in Europe who played modern jazz in all its forms during the 1960s began—with a time lag of some years—to catch up with the developments introduced by American free jazz musicians around 1965. Like their American models, they broke with the routine of harmonic-metrical schemes, dissolved the beat into an irregular series of accents, and concentrated on musical sound rather than improvisations oriented toward melodic lines. At the same time, though, they began to drift away from the direct influence of American musicians. The European players created their own means of expression and structural patterns, making these the focus of their musical activities. Thus, toward the end of the decade, a specifically European type of free jazz found its way to audiences. *interesting!*

What were the reasons for this unexpected emancipation? At least two factors are worth mentioning, one inherent in the music itself and the other as a sort of ideological or, if you will, political factor. In terms of the music, the arrival of free jazz meant European musicians were for the first time in jazz history confronted with a *style* that was no longer clearly defined, that had ceased to be a system of relatively limited norms. Instead they faced a variety of individual and group styles, one hardly comparable to the next. The distinctions between the structural patterns established by individual musicians such as Taylor, Coleman, or Coltrane outweighed what they had in common—a characteristic certainly not appli-

277

cable to Gillespie, Parker, or Powell. Consequently, developing a unique style within this conglomerate of individual styles called free jazz was obviously easier than ever before.

The second cause for change had much to do with the social and political atmosphere among young people during the late 1960s. The students' movement in Germany and France had reached a climax in 1968, and numerous young musicians sympathized with it. Above all, two essential features of this movement might have influenced the self-perception of the young free jazz contingent: a distaste for any kind of authority, and an underlying anti-Americanism that was intensified by the cruel consequences of the Vietnam War. For the first time since World War II, the role of the United States as international "lodestar" had been thoroughly questioned. And, since jazz musicians do not live outside society but are part of it, it seems quite natural that these tendencies shaped their self-perception and—in a mediated way—their music.

The separation of European free jazz from its American models was not an event with a fixed date, but rather a process. Although recordings document a certain stage in that process, they do not represent the process itself; rather, they may be considered provisional outcomes of a development whose beginning and ending remain for the moment hidden from the listener. The shorter the time interval between such provisional outcomes in a series of events, the clearer becomes the view of the whole process. Unfortunately, very few of these provisional documentations covering the early stages of European free jazz exist. The few recordings that do exist, however, testify to three essential stages in the early part of this developing emancipation.

1. An initial and still hesitant approach to disengaging from the patterns of bebop/post-bop, as evident on the LP *Heartplants* by the Gunter Hampel Quintet, recorded in January 1965.

2. An increasing trend toward the "Europeanization" of musical expression, together with an attempt to unite all the available creative capacities, as in the music of the Globe Unity Orchestra, recorded in December 1966.

3. A first attempt at multiplying individual and group approaches, as in the recordings of ensembles led by Peter Brötzmann, Manfred Schoof, Joachim Kühn, and Wolfgang Dauner in the year 1967.

The 1965 version of the Gunter Hampel Quintet comprised musicians whose range of experience was crucially influenced by modern mainstream jazz. Besides Hampel himself, the group consisted of Manfred Schoof (trumpet), Alexander von Schlippenbach (piano), Buschi Niebergall (bass), and Pierre Courbois (drums). *Heartplants*, the only LP recorded by this group, presents free jazz as music involving harmonically and metrically "free" interaction in one piece only, *Iron Perception* by Schlippenbach. All the other pieces are influenced by various

278

styles of modern jazz, representing far less a synthesis than a parallel investigation of diverse creative principles, including modal structures as initiated by Coltrane/ Davis during the *Milestones* era (*Heartplants* and *Our Chant*) as well as free tonal lines à la George Russell (*No Arrows*) and even sections that recall the smooth sound-aesthetics of the Modern Jazz Quartet (*Without Me*). Although all of this is sporadically blended with more or less extensive free jazz eruptions, one could hardly call it a truly original style. The significance of *Heartplants* was certainly not—as the LP's producer Berendt noted in his "Fenster aus Jazz"[3]—"the first German—and European—free jazz record which revealed to a large audience that a new European jazz was born." Rather, the recording marked a first tentative step in a gradual process of detachment, the notion *detachment* referring less to American jazz itself than to its traditional procedures for making music.

Unlike *Heartplants*, the first recording by the Globe Unity Orchestra roughly two years later breaks with tradition more radically—not only in terms of its departure from traditional schemes of form and sound but primarily in its dismissal of the guardian relationship between American and European jazz. The Globe Unity Orchestra was founded in 1966. It owed its existence to the radio station RIAS Berlin's having asked Alexander von Schlippenbach to write a composition for the Berlin Jazz Festival that year. Schlippenbach managed to construct a compositional framework that accommodated a large number of free jazz players and allowed for structural variety without falling back on big-band clichés, while still—despite a high level of formal organization—leaving enough space for individual creative exertion and spontaneous interactions between all the participants. The nucleus of the Globe Unity Orchestra was members of the Manfred Schoof Quintet and the Peter Brötzmann Trio. Also contributing were five horn players and, in an overdubbed performance, vibraphonist Karl Berger.

Schlippenbach wrote two very distinctive compositions for the orchestra's Berlin performance and the recordings that followed: *Globe Unity* and *Sun*. The former is marked by an intensive rhythmic power play, with the corresponding parts for solos and the collective ensemble organized by scalar material, clusters or tonally undefined chords. The basic conception shows certain affinities with Coltrane's *Ascension*, although a direct influence is unlikely (call-and-response patterns are a common organizing principle in orchestral free jazz). Still, a comparison with *Ascension* is quite instructive, as it reveals certain essential characteristics of free jazz produced in Europe—already discernible in that early phase of the music's existence. The basic rhythmic stance of *Globe Unity* is, compared with that of *Ascension*, more hectic, nervous, at times more violent. The improvisations by the horns concentrate more on sound and energy than on melodic continuity; they are so antimelodic that not even the "screamers" in *Ascension* (Pharoah Sanders and Archie Shepp) can match them.

Even more impressive than the approach to composition and improvisation in *Globe Unity* is the systematic exploration of sound in *Sun*. This recording is looser in its musical structure than *Globe Unity*, more contemplative in its emotional substance, and more focused on color than energy. The instrumentation emphasizes "little instruments," as the Art Ensemble of Chicago later dubbed them—rattles, triangles, lotus flutes, flexaphones, etc., all of which play a prominent role. However, there is also a differentiated approach to sound structures in the way the horns are played, particularly the trumpet solos by Claude Deron and Manfred Schoof. Both of these solos involve distortion and undefined pitch (generated by the technique of half-valving, that is, depressing the valves halfway).

When the Globe Unity Orchestra's first recording was presented to the public, it met with strong resentment and was widely misunderstood. There were newspaper headlines like "Odd men playing jokes at the Philharmonic Hall," describing "a blend of jazz and contemporary art music." Neither of these quotes says much for the perceptiveness of contemporary jazz critics.[4] In any case, press resentment of the music and its classification as part of the hybrid Third Stream movement meant that public performances by the Globe Unity Orchestra remained rare. Only in 1972 did the ensemble begin to perform on a regular basis, gradually stabilizing its musical language. This in no way diminishes the standing of the first Globe Unity Orchestra within the historical development of original European free jazz. It heralded the advent of a musical paradigm that could do without predetermined patterns. And it helped clarify the growing potential of European musicians, both within and outside Globe Unity, to bring this paradigm to life.

Already in 1967, the energies unleashed by the Globe Unity Orchestra in 1966 were being taken up in a number of recordings that also represented a certain stylistic demarcation on the European free scene: *Transfiguration* by the ensemble led by brothers Rolf and Joachim Kühn; *Free Action* by Wolfgang Dauner; a recording by the Manfred Schoof Sextet for the "serious" avant-garde label Wergo; and *For Adolphe Sax* by the Peter Brötzmann Trio.

The common denominator in all of these four recordings is their firm rejection of most of the established norms in modern mainstream jazz. Nevertheless, the consequences of that rejection were unique to each of these groups and the musicians involved.

The Kühn brothers mostly used structural patterns already developed within traditional styles, but they transposed them to the context of free interaction, without questioning fundamental musical values such as swing, linear melodic invention, and "workmanship" in the traditional sense.

Brötzmann's *For Adolphe Sax* is the most radical break with the same values. He consciously avoided tonal centers, discernible melodic lines, or themes. Only occasionally can a developmental process be detected in this music, a process with an end in sight; instead, there is an almost breathless series of brief episodes of contrasting temperament, in which the extrovert phases by far outweigh periods of calm and poise. At these points, Brötzmann's music could be called "destructive"—not meant disparagingly, but rather indicating the destruction of an experience that has become dear and familiar to the listener, an experience particular not only to jazz but to music in general.

Compared with *For Adolphe Sax*, Wolfgang Dauner's *Free Action* seems almost conventional. Unlike Brötzmann's largely monochromatic music with its sustained high emotional intensity, Dauner's conception could be described as "polychromatic." His pieces include carefully preplanned formal development, and focus on structural and instrumental variety. Spontaneity and emotion are rationally controlled; technical virtuosity, in the traditional sense, remains important.

The Manfred Schoof Sextet's recording made in December 1967 serves almost as a mediator between Brötzmann's emotionalism and Dauner's constructivism. In many respects, the music of Schoof and Schlippenbach is a transformation of the experiences gained with the Globe Unity Orchestra (there is a clear affinity with *Sun* and *Glockenbär*), while it consistently pursues the developments introduced by the Hampel Quintet (*Heartplants*). The music of this group is polychromatic also, with a wide range of expressive patterns and organizational principles. But in contrast to *Heartplants*, recorded three years earlier, the various styles do not coexist without relating to one another; instead they form a convincing synthesis. Free-bop linearity (as in Schlippenbach's *Grains*), percussive sound improvisation, energy-packed ensemble parts, modal improvisations and reflections on Monk are woven into an original mode of expression, one that has overcome the past without ignoring it.

The diversity of approaches manifested by the recordings of 1967 narrowed somewhat during the years that followed. The Kühn brothers disappeared from the free jazz scene and worked in more lucrative fields (one in jazz rock, the other mostly in popular music). Wolfgang Dauner's sense of adventure obviously prevented him from focusing on just one aspect of the relevant musical spectrum.

The mainstream of West German free jazz after 1968 was represented mainly by the various followers of Brötzmann and Schlippenbach. There was a growing tendency toward working in large ensembles, while the scene became increasingly international, bringing in mainly British and Dutch musicians. In an interview with Didier Pennequin, Brötzmann stated: "In retrospect, 1968 was the year of large ensembles, where we met with friends to play like crazy."[5]

The sound of these large ensembles is documented by a number of recordings under different leaders, but with some of the same personnel: Brötzmann's *Machine Gun* (March 1966), Schlippenbach's *Living Music* (April 1969), Schoof's

European Echoes (June 1969), and two excerpts from the Brötzmann ensemble's performances at the Holy Hill Festival in Heidelberg (July 1989) and at the Jazz Festival in Frankfurt (March 1970).

While the details vary, all these recordings have one thing in common: a single-minded intent to destroy established aesthetic standards. As Peter Kowald commented in an interview in 1972: "It was the *kaputt-playing time*. The main objective was truly and thoroughly to tear apart the old values, to omit any harmony and melody. And the result wasn't just boring, because it was played with such high energy. . . . In a way, the period of *kaputt-playing* made anything 'playable,' equally playable, which is possible in music. . . . Then, for the first time, it became clear that our generation could well do without the musical influence of most Americans."[6]

The question remains: what were the concrete musical outcomes of that period of "kaputt playing," a period Kowald and others consider to have been a transitional phase? In the context of the recordings mentioned above, some general characteristics may be noted:

1. Composition is usually kept to a minimum; by and large, the music operates without thematic material, while presenting rifflike attacks and interjections, at times directed only in their movement (upward-downward). Moreover, there is a tendency to use distorted thematic quotations, or tags—as in Brötzmann's "Lolla-palooza," where the national anthems of Germany and Britain were intertwined in a deliberately chaotic manner.

2. Definite pitch as the stable element of musical organization is abandoned in favor of unstable sound patterns. A structural distinction is achieved mainly through collective variations in the density and volume of the sound.

3. Developmental processes are drawn, somewhat inevitably, toward an extreme where individual musical events cannot be strictly identified as such, but combine into a diffuse and intense totality. Sometimes, this tendency is supported by extremely homogeneous and low-pitched instrumentation, as was frequently employed by the Brötzmann ensembles (in 1970, for example, Brötzmann played in Frankfurt with four trombones and three tenor saxophones).

4. In general, the attitude toward time can be described as restless. Even when the density and intensity recede and the structures open up, the basic time (not necessarily played but felt) remains hectic. In fact, at this stage of development there is something akin to standard time, probably for physiological reasons: a majority of recordings show an identical rhythmic-metric basis, with q = 240 to 270. This, however, means that a four-four bar approximately corresponds to the human pulse. It also means that the kind of free jazz we are dealing with here is much more body-related than is generally assumed. (Anyone doubting this theory of pulsation as a common rhythmical basis should take their own measurement).

5. One point touching on this music's reception, rather than its structural characteristics, is the problem of instrumental technique. Talking to friends and neighbors, I gathered that many listeners—especially those well acquainted with traditional jazz—wonder, in view of the dense and difficult musical structures characteristic of this period, whether the musicians making all that noise onstage simply cannot play; whether they really have mastered their instruments or are just getting their rocks off. It seems relatively easy to dub this music "kaputt playing," as Kowald did in his interview, yet it isn't that simple. In fact, most of the musicians working in the ensembles of Brötzmann, Schlippenbach, and Schoof had developed individual techniques that enabled them not only to demolish conventions but to develop—in a constructive way—new, personal techniques. Anyone arguing that Evan Parker's nuances of sound production or Brötzmann's overblown harmonics have nothing to do with technique, or that Dudek's and Skidmore's almost classical virtuosity are the sole acceptable definition of the term, is simply revealing his or her own narrow conception of technique.

Unlike technology in an industrial context, "technique" in music also means the ability to do exactly what you want to do. Brötzmann—of course—expressed this more pointedly: "I'm not what you would call a 'good technician.' To me, technique as taught by conservatories is bullshit. To make a music like ours, you have to develop your own technique first and then make your own music. The objective of our music is not to play 'right' or 'wrong.' That doesn't mean a thing. What really counts is to know what one is playing."[7]

During the early part of the 1970s, the monochromatic or "kaputt-playing" phase of the large ensembles was nearing its end. In Brötzmann's and Schlippen-bach's small groups—with their opposing conceptions—transparency began to prevail over sonic diffusion. The Globe Unity Orchestra resumed its activities and found a new identity. In England and the Netherlands, more and more original—one might even say national—creative principles emerged and solid-ified; throughout the West German provinces musical initiatives began to stir, in revolt against not only the American hegemony but the predominance of the Wuppertal-Berlin axis as well.

An ensemble of vital importance to the further development of European free jazz was the Trio Brötzmann-Hove-Bennink, formed in the summer of 1970. Here, the three musicians' very distinct temperaments guaranteed a structural clash: the Dutch percussionist Han Bennink had already worked with a number of prominent American musicians of the swing and hard bop eras before venturing into free music in 1967. He drew on these experiences, transforming them into a special kind of percussion technique that embraced both swing and drive, yet paradoxically questioned these values—surprising the listener with sudden erup-tions and sonic escapades in the "happening" style, as if to demolish his own sense of swing. An essential quality of Bennink's musical conception was his intense awareness of sound. This conception was realized not only in the way Bennink used his massive arsenal of sonic tools but in the fact that the mere quantity of instruments was just one of many possibilities. As Bennink put it: "There is a chance that one day I might use only a thousand matchsticks to play."[8]

The Belgian pianist Fred van Hove was the antithesis to the extroverted Bennink in many respects—a musician who said the chimes of Antwerp had influenced him more than Cecil Taylor.[9] Van Hove very rarely displayed eruptive emotion and power; he had a more contemplative attitude, with a strong tendency toward crankiness, especially when he countered Brötzmann's atonal screams and Bennink's violent drum attacks with soft arpeggios and serene, reflective major chords. While van Hove is often sidelined or dominated by his two fellow musicians in the turbulent trio context, his solo LP recorded for FMP in 1977 is a marvelous introduction to his own conception. Van Hove does not aim to impress with his virtuosity, as do many other pianists when left to their own devices. He prefers to surprise, to create tension, stimulate reflection, or simply to tease. His *Klompenouvertüre* starts with a clattering sound like wooden shoes, suggesting Flemish local color. It is as if Van Hove is consciously, purposely using a dilettante's technique; it sounds like someone looking for something without finding it. This way of playing the piano has little or nothing to do with Afro-American music—and it doesn't want to. In contrast to Schlippenbach, there is no rhythmic fluency, but rather a sort of cheerful stumbling, tinted with despair.

In the course of the unpredictable interaction that became the trio's main formative principle, there was a gradual change in the way Brötzmann played the saxophone. While overblowing (playing multiphonics) with an undefined pitch remained his favored mode of expression, Brötzmann's improvisations became less noise-oriented. At times he would establish thematic relationships, paraphrase Ben Webster's "erotic" ballads, quote fragments of polkas or other popular songs and grind them through the mill of his fantasies.

In the trio's subsequent work (Albert Mangelsdorff joined the band for a brief period in 1971), certain characteristics began to emerge that became a trademark of their music. I shall try to outline some of these in the following.

1. Unlike in the "kaputt-playing" phase, with its extensive dense and homogeneous collective improvisations (sometimes lasting for hours on end), there was now a tendency toward "small" forms. Many of the trio's "pieces" were like miniatures, each incorporating certain emotional characteristics, special instrumentation, movement, etc. This is particularly marked in *Tschüs* (FMP 0230), Brötzmann's and Bennink's duo recording *Ein halber Hund kann nicht pinkeln* (FMP 0420), and in *Schwarzwaldfahrt* (FMP 0440).

2. The following years saw an increasing multi-instrumentalism, extending the

range of sounds in general and bringing in new, often unorthodox instrumental combinations. At the same time, the considerable instrumental variety was a way of overcoming personal technical clichés.

3. The sense of a theatrical musical event permeated the ensemble, with diverse emphases. The group began to move. The inclusion of space as a prime factor in this theater effect had acoustic consequences of its own. One example: in "Claptrap" from the LP *Tschüs*, a duo for clarinets, Brötzmann plays close to the microphone while Bennink walks around while playing. In the same way, space and distance constitute significant means of formal expression on *Schwarzwaldfahrt*, an open-air recording that begs the question of whether a record is the right medium for communicating this kind of musical theater.

4. As a corollary to the development of musical theater, there is an increasing trend toward musical gags and use of the human voice, often resulting in bits of nonsense and bizarre jokes—for example, Brötzmann on *Schwarzwaldfahrt*: "But here I feel much too cold—and so do my clarinets."

Compared with the stylistic meanderings of the Brötzmann-Hove-Bennink trio, the work of Alexander von Schlippenbach's group during the following years (with Evan Parker, saxophone, Peter Kowald, bass, and Paul Lovens, percussion) took a relatively straight course in developing a specific identity. This does not mean there were no changes, but the changes that did occur were more about details, more in the delicate musical structures than on the surface. This Schlippenbach Quartet, and the later trio (without Kowald), consequently played music that was athematic and energetic and made no concessions to fashion—a world of its own. Although Schlippenbach's piano technique is in some ways reminiscent of Cecil Taylor's (an affinity with Monk is also highly apparent), his ensemble conception cannot be compared with Taylor's. Briefly put, this ensemble was more "democratic." Instead of a "master" dominating the entire musical process and steering it in a particular—that is, his own—direction, this process developed from within the ensemble, with each contributor taking a turn.

Evan Parker played an extremely important role in this music. In my view, his absolute lack of compromise has made him one of the most impressive free jazz saxophonists ever. In his book on contemporary jazz in Great Britain, trumpeter Ian Carr gives a vivid description of Parker's style, one I consider very accurate. Here is an excerpt:

Parker explores the technical range of tenor and soprano saxophone to their possible limits; he uses harmonics so high that they are on bat frequencies; he sustains tensions for long periods, and plays extremely unusual melodic shapes; he also splits up notes into their component parts—the harmonics that form one normal saxophone note. The resultant effect is possibly something

The European Jazz Avant-Garde

like (if it could be done) putting one bar of music under a very powerful microscope or stethoscope. What we see or experience is still music, but we are aware of the fibres of it, the component parts, the usually concealed physics, in extreme close up. But the continuity with the jazz tradition is there . . . it is in the energy and intensity both of the feeling and of the way they are expressed. . . . His style appears to be wild and abandoned, but it is, in fact, extremely disciplined and controlled.[10]

The existence of a large jazz orchestra has always depended on economic as well as musical factors. As with the swing bands, free jazz orchestras often pay for their survival with show-business compromises and a life on the road, especially since their musical direction does not necessarily coincide with the preferences of a mass audience. As a result, free jazz orchestras are quite rare, particularly those existing on the basis of constant cooperation. That sort of cooperation, though, is needed to ensure continuous musical development. During the 1970s the Globe Unity Orchestra was the only group of its kind to achieve such continuity. Neither the London Jazz Composers Orchestra nor the French Celestrial Communication Orchestra launched by Alan Silva managed at the time to offer anything more than sporadic performances with changing personnel.

The Globe Unity Orchestra's "comeback" was a workshop organized by Peter Kowald and supported by the Wuppertal City Council in 1973. The orchestra was able to rehearse for four days in a row, presenting the results of its work at a final concert. During the workshop a certain dualistic conception emerged, which on the one hand emphasized a completely free form of collective improvisation. On the other hand—and as if to offer up a contrasting scheme—the program also included composed pieces, sometimes of an ironically conventional stamp: for example, Schlippenbach's adaptation of Jelly Roll Morton's "Wolverine Blues," his own composition "Bavarian Calypso," or an arrangement of Gordon Jenkins's "Good Bye" by Willem Breuker. These "songs" could be presented without any improvisation. They may have been designed to provide expressive links to an unprepared audience, establishing connections with their own musical experience and offering moments of relaxation between freely improvised sets that demanded close attention.

In contrast with the "kaputt-playing" phase of the 1960s, the total improvisations of the Globe Unity Orchestra from 1973 onward were marked by a development toward open structures. It might be equally important that a fortissimo was recognized as such only when preceded by a quiet passage or that each player's personal style became audible only when the collective ensemble did not obscure it with a noisy power play. The individual means of expression shown by the Globe Unity musicians, who all worked in various other ensembles, was perhaps the most vital element in the diverse musical spectrum created by the orchestra. The kind of uniform aesthetic that represented the sonic ideal for the traditional big bands in their section work did not fit the Globe Unity view of reality. Instead, the orchestra made room for the distinct musical temperaments of each individual musician while maintaining its collective purpose, as a joint statement. That produced variety, friction, and tension. (To understand fully what I mean, the reader should try to bear in mind the expressive contrasts between saxophonists such as Peter Brötzmann, Rüdiger Carl, Evan Parker, and Gerd Dudek, or between trombonists such as Paul Rutherford, Albert Mangelsdorff. and Günter Christmann.)

That German ensembles like those of Brötzmann and Schlippenbach or the Globe Unity Orchestra played on the front lines of free jazz, were well known to European audiences, and were considered representative of contemporary "Teutonic" jazz (in the words of *Melody Maker*) abroad, should not conceal another fact: that at the time there was a much wider range of musical activity taking place; the variety of individual and ensemble approaches substantially exceeded the assumptions made in this article so far.

One of the most consistent ensembles in terms of straightforward development had been, for quite some time, that of the Frankfurt-born trombonist Albert Mangelsdorff. Mangelsdorff was a veteran of the German jazz scene. His style embodied the imitational period of jazz in Europe, ranging from swing to cool jazz to hard bop, yet Mangelsdorff mastered all of these without ever becoming a disciple himself. Always preferring evolution to revolution, he came to free music relatively late. When Mangelsdorff did embrace it, though, it was with an absolute mastery of the new material that was lacking in many of the hotheads from the "kaputt-playing" epoch. In many respects, Mangelsdorff's career and his position in European jazz was comparable to that of John Coltrane in the United States. Both passed through the various stages of jazz history without ever bowing fully to one opportune trend or another; both had their own direction and became a "father figure" of sorts, both musically and personally, for the next generation. It was not by chance that Mangelsdorff was elected the first president of the German Jazz Musicians' Union (UDJ) in 1973; choosing him was almost an imperative.

The quintet that Mangelsdorff put together at the beginning of the 1970s, while also collaborating with Brötzmann-Hove-Bennink, played a type of music that was deeply rooted in the jazz tradition. It swung in a free and specific manner, while seldom abandoning the development of melodic and thematic variety in favor of sound and energy. Mangelsdorff's linear style contributed much to the group sound, but it was equally indebted to his saxophone players, Heinz Sauer and Gerd Dudek—the former rough and bluesy, the latter tending toward Coltrane's extended modality.

Starting in 1972, Mangelsdorff focused on working as a soloist. Much has been said and written about his chord-playing technique, so I can spare you the details here. However, the following comment by Mangelsdorff about the relationship between solo and ensemble playing is interesting: "A musician physically exhausts himself much more in a solo because it is more demanding than playing with an ensemble. But full emotional exhaustion only happens when you play with others. . . . Even though the soloist may play freely, everything he lets out is still somehow under his control. It is a music completely different from that played in a group. The group provides another sort of outlet or eruption."[11]

Two other remarkable ensembles were formed at the periphery of the German jazz scene (or was it just the periphery of my own vision, oriented to Berlin and Wuppertal?) at the end of the 1960s. Their creative principles tended more toward a productive take on the American tradition than a destruction of it. The Modern Jazz Quintet Karlsruhe and the Free Jazz Group Wiesbaden both consisted of musicians who earned their livelihood mostly in bourgeois or middle-class professions. It may well be that their "amateur" status was responsible for the relatively indifferent public response to their music and their neglect by the media. (It becomes clear at this point just how inadequate a description the traditional notion of an "amateur"—including that of a "dilettante"—can sometimes be.)

Unlike the mainly athematic music played by groups associated with the FMP label, thematic material and structural planning played an important part in the conception of the Modern Jazz Quintet Karlsruhe and its successor ensemble, Fourmenonly. These groups offer distinct pieces contrasting in sonic color, degree of density, rhythmical intensity, and—accordingly—emotional affect. Power play is used sparingly or as a means of achieving structural contrast. In general, the structural developments are less flat; they are (to extend the metaphor) more "craggy," leaving a lot of time for solo contributions by the individual musicians. The compositions of flugelhorn player Herbert Joos, at the time one of the most significant composers of contemporary jazz in Germany, were a decisive factor in the range of music played by the Karlsruhe group. Joos was an outstanding innovator, with a marked capacity for timbre and instrumentation, as evidenced in his works *Eight Science Fiction Stories* and *The Philosophy of the Flugelhorn*. Typical of his compositional style were his slow movements with deep homophonic pitches, suggesting the cool aesthetics of the Miles Davis Capitol Orchestra transposed into contemporary jazz.

The sound-conscious constructivism of the Karlsruhe-based ensemble was in contrast to the more extrovert "let's go" mentality of the Free Jazz Group Wiesbaden. The two main "actors" in this group, trumpet player Michael Sell and saxophonist Dieter Scherf, transformed their technical experience of playing hard bop into the free jazz context with remarkable vigor. Generally, they organized their collective energies into a set of motifs (that is, in reactive order) that ended in freely swinging solos. Technique in the traditional sense was of considerable importance in their playing. All things considered, this was not "European" free jazz from the "kaputt-playing" period, nor did it have to do with the breakaway from that phase. It was much more a successful adaptation of American models.

Making a definite statement on the earliest phase of free music played in the German Democratic Republic on the basis of the few records I knew at the time seems a little bold. If anything can be said about this period, it will constitute a judgment on certain trends. The ensemble of saxophonist Ernst Ludwig Petrowsky (*Just for Fun*, April 1973) and the Gumpert-Sommer-Hering Trio (*The Old Song*, July 1973) played music similar to that of the FMP-oriented groups. They tended toward power play and distortion of sound structures, radically questioning the relevance of aesthetic principles applied in traditional jazz, and preferring noise to linear development. The basic rhythm was hectic, full of tension, and not particularly fluent. On the latter recording, percussionist Günter Sommer played in an intensely sound-conscious style, following in the footsteps of Han Bennink and Paul Lovens. The music documented on a recording from March 1974 (*Auf der Elbe schwimmt ein rosa Krokodil*) shows the Petrowsky quartet leaning more toward open structures, at times even reintroducing melodic balance and thematic material. Whether this reflected a developmental process or was just another facet of their musical spectrum is uncertain. I am also unsure whether the clearly audible affinities between the aesthetic concepts of Gumpert and Petrowsky on the one hand, and those of musicians such as Brötzmann and Schlippenbach on the other, stemmed from direct influences or whether these concepts developed independently.

So-called "national styles" are very common in the history of Western art music. Even though the cultural internationalism promoted by the media during the twentieth century smoothed out most distinctions, it is still possible to detect certain national characteristics in the field of contemporary music, This has nothing to do with nationalism or chauvinism in any political sense but is shaped by the different historical development of nations—including, of course, their cultural history.

During the sixties, no one would have bothered to ask whether such diverse national tendencies prevailed in jazz. Jazz was considered a global musical language, a notion propagated assiduously by the Voice of America and the American State Department, which employed the term "world language" with an ideological tinge. That term not only upheld the international and worldwide significance of American culture but also drew a veil over the cultural deprivation of Afro-American musicians—although, as we all know, jazz was mostly about *their* language and *their* musical expression. At festivals in the 1970s, one would occasionally see black American free jazz musicians leave the concert hall shaking their heads during sets by their European colleagues. They did so not because they thought the musicians onstage were incompetent but because they could not identify or sympathize with their music. With the advent of free playing, jazz had clearly lost the quality of a generally accepted binding force, the world's musical language.

This relatively crude suggestion of a break between European and American jazz aesthetics was also true—perhaps to a lesser degree—of certain regional performance trends in contemporary European jazz. For example, it was customary for musicians and listeners to speak in terms of "the Dutch" or "the English" (or "the Wuppertalers"), meaning not just the geographical classification of musicians or ensembles but a certain approach to music. (The drummer I worked with in the 1970s sometimes used to say, "Let's play British!")

As with all clichés and stereotypes, those used in music fall short because they are simplifications; however, they do have some roots in reality, or at least a view of reality. I do not personally believe there is a form of free jazz that is specifically Dutch, English, or German, nor do I believe in *the* Dutchman, *the* Englishman, *the* German—or *the* worker, *the* professor (Karl Marx did not even want to believe there was *the* capitalist). However, it became evident in the course of the 1970s that some free jazz idioms had evolved with divergent characteristics, reflecting different social conditions or, to a much greater extent, the different ways in which musicians reacted to those conditions. I will not attempt to reduce the cause and effect of this interaction to a common denominator using some sort of crass Marxist "representation theory" (*Widerspiegelungstheorie*), but I will try to describe some of the musical consequences. Certain generalizations are, of course, inevitable. One of the most significant hothouses of the British jazz avant-garde in the mid-1960s was the Little Theatre Club in London, started by the percussionist John Stevens. It was a kind of musical workshop, where—without any regard for an audience, which was rather limited anyway—musicians experimented with an intensity and consistency almost unprecedented in jazz history, with the possible exception of the Monroe and Minton sessions in New York at the beginning of the bebop era.

The Little Theatre Club was the geographical focal point for the groups involved in this constantly changing personal experimentation. In musical terms they centered on the Spontaneous Music Ensemble (SME), founded by Stevens and saxophonist Trevor Watts. This was an ensemble that included almost every musician in the London avant-garde circle at some point, for longer or shorter periods. Among the many contributors were trumpeters Kenny Wheeler and Ian

Carr, saxophonists Trevor Watts and Evan Parker, trombonist Paul Rutherford, guitarist Derek Bailey, bassists Ron Matthewson, Dave Holland, Barry Guy, and Johnny Dyani, drummers Eddie Prévost, Paul Lytton, Tony Oxley, and Alan Jackson, and singers Maggie Nichols and Julie Tippetts.

A growing sense of community among the musicians who collaborated with the SME on an informal basis finally led to a foundation with a strong political and social emphasis, the Musician's Co-Op. The most important function of this institution for the musicians involved was, as Evan Parker put it, "to run their own business."

During its experimental phase, the music of British free jazz players moved toward a level of abstraction that not only questioned the relevance of melody and harmony but went as far as to make them taboo. Noise structures were no longer simply an alternative to melodic phrases but became the vital basis of this music; British musicians produced live what *musique concrète* had only fabricated via tape collages. Traditional characteristics of specific instruments were ignored or even turned on their head: while saxophonists produced percussive, noisy rhythm patterns, percussionists developed a quasi-melodic way of playing and explored sound spectra never before heard; bassists delivered twittering falsettos, and guitarists such as Derek Bailey invented the most astonishing sounds without all the devices usually found only in electronic music studios with their arsenals of technical equipment.

A characteristic feature of British free jazz was the widespread use of female vocalists. This may have been due to the particular status of vocal music in British culture, a phenomenon that can be traced back to early Baroque music or even beyond. To delineate these historical roots may appear somewhat daring, but it is a striking fact that nowhere else in the world was the female vocal potential in free jazz as rich as it was in England: Christine Jeffrey, Maggie Nichols, Julie Tippetts, and Norma Winstone are just a few examples.

An important role within the British school of sonic experimentation was played by a group called Music Improvisation Company (MIC), founded in 1968 with Evan Parker on tenor and soprano saxophones, Derek Bailey on guitar, Jamie Muir on drums, and Hugh Davis on electronics. The essence of the MIC's work resided in the concept of non-idiomatic music, as formulated by guitarist Derek Bailey. This was a freely improvised music, independent of all existing musical languages, that would follow exclusively the individual techniques and preferences of the players.

Of course, this idea is probably illusory. Although the mere avoidance of any idiomatically fixed means of creation may well result in a music that sits outside all previously existing idiomatic systems (it could also, as with John Cage, lead into the realm of chance), the practical results of the MIC's work make it quite clear that this music, termed as non-idiomatic, can easily be identified as a particular and unmistakable form of musical creation—in other words, as a musical idiom. *Style*, under certain preconditions, may be established through the forceful avoidance of any associations with existing musical languages. One of the most important preconditions is that the improviser acts as a conscious ego, refusing to follow only the generative energy of chance: this was clearly the case with the members of the MIC.

In describing the group's conceptual framework, it seems easier to identify features the MIC *lacked* rather than those it possessed: no tonality, no repetition, no melodic continuity, no periodicity, no system. On the other hand, there was one immediately obvious feature: the emancipation of noise as an independent means of creation—"noise" meaning sound with a dense structure of nonharmonic frequencies, the amplitudes and phases of which are subject to random change.

The most efficient noise producer in the group was Hugh Davies, who did not have a jazz background like the other players but came out of the school of Stockhausen. With his electronics, Davies brought a vast repertory of noise to the music: static sounds such as buzzing or humming, pulsating sounds such as crackling and clapping, variable noise like gliding frequency bands, etc. Guitarist Bailey also used his instrument to produce irregular sound structures by rubbing the strings with his fingers or other devices and working with variable string tension. Evan Parker found a number of ways to produce nonharmonic or percussive sounds on his saxophone. Thus, the conscious manipulation of noise was one dominant feature of the MIC's work.

The other was interaction. Since any written score or even verbal arrangement was taboo, the group relied exclusively on spontaneous actions and reactions among the four players. These interactions converged most of the time. Although both Davies and Bailey spoke of a tendency toward "mutual subversion," meaning one player might force a clash with another through nonparticipation or counteraction, these situations occurred only rarely—or at least in the group's recordings. This type of understanding should not be confused with harmony and linear development: the overall sonic structure of the group's music was usually dissonant and discontinuous.

All in all, free jazz from Great Britain followed a basic emotional pattern that tended to favor ecstasy over asceticism, leaning stylistically more toward Western academic avant-garde music but not reaching a point where the joy of playing music was lost. Moreover, there were other streams within contemporary British free jazz—again showing how inadequate clichés really are—that drew their inspiration and emotional power mainly from Afro-American music. This suggested that the period of imitation in European jazz had not yet entirely faded out.

Was there a French school of free jazz, as there seems to have been a German, British, and Dutch school? It is hard to say: during the 1970s, the domination of the French jazz scene by American musicians was much more pronounced than in any other European country. However, there was at least one musician in France who embodied what might be called the French spirit in new jazz in an outstanding way.

The multi-instrumental reed player Michel Portal was (and is) an exceptional musician. Many listeners have praised him as a brilliant interpreter of Mozart's Clarinet Concerto; others know him as a sonic experimenter who worked his way through Stockhausen's intuitive music as well as Pierre Boulez's *Domaines*. Then there are those who saw him in the band accompanying Edith Piaf for the staging of *Shéhérazade*, and those who consider him one of the most important improvisers in European contemporary jazz.

A musical chameleon? Although Portal's work was highly proficient in all these areas, his main interest—his love—has always been jazz. As Portal put it: "Jazz, for me, really offers the only possibility to be free, to float, to dream."[12] In 1966 he was a member of the first French free jazz group, led by pianist François Tusques. He worked with German pianist Joachim Kühn in 1969 and with English baritone saxophonist John Surman in 1970. In 1972 Portal appeared with his own group at the Châteauvallon jazz festival; the concert was recorded and produced under the title *No, No, but It May Be!* by the small French label Chant du Monde. It is, I believe, one of the most stimulating recordings of European free jazz from the 1970s.

A cursory listening reveals a music as far removed from American free jazz as it is from the diverse regional branches of the European avant-garde. The initial impression is of something raw and rough-hewn, with sound complexes resembling square tones and rudimentary melodic contours more like signals than songs. There is no trace of French elegance and refinement; in fact, the core creative dimensions of this music are to be found neither in melody nor harmony, but in rhythm and sound. That is, the group's structural and formal efforts are expressed essentially through a conscious stratification and alignment of sound and rhythm, rather than in sequences of melodic invention or harmonic twists.

Among the most important preconditions for the success of this endeavor seems to be a distinct and collectively adapted sense of the importance of time and economy of material. In both respects the musicians, notwithstanding their drive toward ecstasy, display some quasi-bourgeois virtues: they are patient; they do not jump hectically from one event to another but take their time, so that processes and situations can evolve gradually. They maintain their concentration over long periods in exposing or modifying a rather narrowly defined repertory of sound structures, in pursuing certain forms of groundwork, certain patterns or variations of intervallic combinations or phrases. All in all, this ensemble was a collective enterprise of acute sensibility, which unfortunately never received the acclaim it deserved.

"All music is political; our improvised music is political, it is a continuation of our political ideas and actions. The fact that we have strictly defined our political position has made our music stronger than ever, at least as strong as the music played by Afro-American musicians."[13] This statement by pianist Misha Mengelberg is more than a personal credo; it is symptomatic of the position taken by numerous other musicians on the Dutch free jazz scene. This does not mean that musicians of other countries failed to notice the political situation around them. But the musical consequences, the conclusions drawn by the Dutch musicians from their political existence, were more evident. This was most explicit in the work of two groups whose similarities stemmed much less from their music (their "style") than from their political-artistic attitudes.

The spontaneous duo music of Misha Mengelberg and Han Bennink aimed primarily to abrogate all valid tools of aesthetic evaluation, all a priori principles. Among the targets of this quest were standards such as concert-hall performance techniques, reverence for material values, and respect for the inherent character of anything that seemed to occur as a matter of course. One example of their subversions would be Bennink's repeated attempts to saw the legs off Steinway pianos—not only a good way to get up the noses of house stewards but also a means of provoking an audience for whom the big black object onstage still stood for artistic seriousness (like the tuxedos of orchestra musicians).

The essential structural framework within Mengelberg's and Bennink's actionist conception was certain types of collage. They paraphrased jazz tradition (Monk!), broke it down and warped it, interspersing their distortions with rhythmical patterns on the steel drum or slit drum. Combining what seemingly could not be combined became a principle of their music. Like the Belgian pianist Fred van Hove, Misha Mengelberg constantly challenged the relevance of conventional piano technique (which he certainly mastered). He would stumble, search, and find—a cigarette! The duo's music only appeared to be easy to listen to; its manifestly "happening" character concealed a high degree of concentration and reflection. Says Mengelberg: "What counts for me more than sound and the instrument is construction. Not the harmonies or the themes, but the fact that I know at which moment I produce this sound and no other."[14]

Although it might have been similar in its political ambitions, in its external manifestation the concept of Willem Breuker and his Kollektief seemed the diametric opposite of the Mengelberg-Bennink approach. Abiding by the words of the Dadaist Marcel Janco, who spoke of a "rebirth of popular art as social art," Breuker integrated into his early output not only the music of Hanns Eisler and

Kurt Weill but also his youth in and around Amsterdam's working-class district, experiences marked by the sounds of steam organs, chimes, brass bands, and mandolin orchestras. Breuker's Kollektief, although it consisted of outstanding free jazz players such as pianist Leo Cuypers, trombonist Willem van Manen, and bassist Arjen Gorter, was not a free jazz orchestra like Globe Unity but rather an extremely well organized musical theater group whose vitality—often teetering on the edge of chaos—could make you forget the constant presence of composer (or director) Breuker guiding the action.

While there are numerous recordings of the Kollektief's music, and although the ensemble could often be heard in concert situations, their essential frame of reference was musical theater. Their concert performances often presented "extracts" from previous theater productions, and inevitably their political message often had to remain hidden.

Outstanding examples of the Breuker Kollektief's theatrical productions were *Oltre Tomba*, where the Dutch musical-political situation of the 1960s was parodied as a gathering of troubadours in the Middle Ages; *Kain en Abel*, which dramatized the social difficulties faced by avant-garde musicians; and *Het paard van Troje gaat met vakantie, ofwel de huisvestingsperikelen van de Nederlandse jazz-musicus* (The Trojan horse goes on vacation, or the housing problems of Dutch jazz musicians).

One might reasonably wonder what all this had to do with new European free jazz. First, the structural patterns of free jazz—at times exaggerated to the point of parody—played a significant, albeit not dominant, role in the Kollektief's music (non-jazz musicians, for example, could not have played this music). Secondly, the Breuker-Kollektief's conception, like that of Mengelberg and Bennink, signaled very pointedly the consequences of a change in the self-perception of European jazz musicians: playing music "for the people" without having to submit to the manipulative aesthetics of the hit parade (as such, a replacement or substitute for folk music) and thwarting this kind of manipulation through parody and irony. That Breuker's music was extremely amusing (and his musical theater even more so) should not disguise the fact that humor as a means of revealing a socially institutionalized lack of humor is a matter of eminent seriousness.

Is there a conclusion to be drawn? Did the oft-cited emancipation of European jazz really take place? And if so, what were the characteristics that made this specifically European jazz different from that of Afro-American provenance? At least one truth should have emerged from the preceding reflections: *the* European free jazz, in the sense of a compact totality, strictly distinguished from other forms of jazz by its musical characteristics, never existed. Instead, the contemporary jazz scene in Europe was distinguished by a stylistic pluralism more pronounced than ever before, and even more so than the various techniques and styles of American free jazz centered on New York. Nevertheless, the mere existence of stylistic variety per se denotes at least some degree of emancipation—and not the emancipation of European musicians en bloc but primarily of each individual musician.

The decision to stop playing "like Coltrane," "like Taylor," or "like Shepp," to learn to stand on their own feet, was not a collective but a personal decision for the individual musicians. The fact that collective patterns of problem solving developed in the course of this process was almost inevitable, especially since jazz was, and is, based on ensemble music, on interaction. In looking for these collective patterns, one must start by attempting to generalize and define the differences between European and Afro-American free jazz aesthetics. Most of the relevant components have already been mentioned in this article. Are there any others?

- The isolation of sound and noise parameters from the melodic or harmonic context is, in principle, a procedure essential to all—or nearly all—free jazz. But while in the United States improvisation with sound and without any melodic implications has always remained a secondary creative principle in free jazz, numerous ensembles in Europe have concentrated on precisely this conscious manipulation of sound. Accordingly, some fundamentally new instrumental techniques were developed: the expanded role and sensitive treatment of percussion instruments in the hands of musicians such as Paul Lytton, Paul Lovens, Han Bennink, or Pierre Favre; the atomization of sound by saxophonists like Evan Parker or Peter Brötzmann; the thoroughly unorthodox guitar techniques of Derek Bailey or Hans Reichel; and, above all, the giant steps taken by trombone players such as Albert Mangelsdorff, Radu Malfatti, Paul Rutherford, or Conny Bauer.
- I have considered the basic rhythmic pattern of European free jazz players in the context of the so-called "kaputt-playing" phase. All in all, I think free rhythm in Europe seemed to point less to continuity than to contrast—more nervous than relaxed at slow tempi, and more hectic than forward-driving at faster tempi.
- During the early phases of American free jazz, collective improvisation played a significant part in the music. In time, however, this form of group improvisation was muted in favor of the old dualism of soloist and accompanist. In Europe, however, collective improvisation between equal partners has remained the dominant organizing principle, something that may stem from elements not inherent to the music but outside it; whereas in the United States, with relatively few exceptions, the star system of leader and sidemen never really disappeared (on posters and in New York newspaper advertise-

ments, one would often search in vain for the names of the musicians backing the announced "main attraction"), European ensembles worked predominantly in cooperative groups, with equal pay and publicity for all concerned.

• While in American free jazz (and not just behind its back), a quite marked retrospective tendency was already noticeable by the early 1980s and bebop (freebop?) flourished through all the musical permutations, these tendencies had, at least at the time, not yet surfaced in Europe. The all-embracing global phase of stylistic regression came later.

NOTES

1. Cover text of LP *R.A.U.* *1005*.

2: Joachim Ernst Berendt, Liner notes to John Tchicai—*Afrodisiaca*, MPS 15249. Tchicai is a Danish-born saxophonist of Danish and Congolese descent, who also plays several other instruments.

3. Joachim Ernst Berendt, *Ein Fenster aus Jazz*, Frankfurt 1977, 222.

4. The first quote comes from a headline in the daily *Berliner Zeitung*, the second from *Die Welt*. I found both in J. E. Berendt's liner notes for the LP *Globe Unity*, SABA 15109.

5. Didier Pennequin, "Allemagne—Pays-Bas" (interviews with Peter Brötzmann, Han Bennink, and Misha Mengelberg), *Jazz Magazine* 220 (March 1974), 19-21.

6. Dirk Fröse, "Freiheit wovon-Freiheit wozu: Peter Kowald Quintett," *Jazz Podium* 12/1972, 22-25.

7. Pennequin, "Allemagne—Pays-Bas."

8. Quoted from Werner Panke, *Jazz Podium* 4/1972.

9. Gérard Rouy, "Belgique: Fred van Hove," *Jazz Magazine* 220 (March 1974), 24.

10. Ian Carr, *Music Outside: Contemporary Jazz in Britain* (London: Latimer, 1973), 8.

11. "Zwischen Solo und Ensemble," Albert Mangelsdorff (interview), *Jazz Podium* 2/1977, 10-13.

12. Philippe Carles and Francis Marmande, "Michel Portal ou la parole au present," interview, *Jazz Magazine* 329 (April 1973), 33.

13. Pennequin, "Allemagne—Pays-Bas," 19-21.

14. Ibid.

III

THE CIRCULATION
OF EUROJAZZLAND

To Karl Koenig

14 / DID EUROPE "DISCOVER" JAZZ?

Just asking. Am I missed? After fifteen years of expatriatism, I miss the Afro-American swing of New York streets. It had been central in my life. It may have triumphed throughout the world but it gets into French heads, not under their skin. It has not triumphed in France.

MIKE ZWERIN, *Swing under the Nazis: Jazz as a Metaphor for Freedom*

One of the most commonly accepted notions about the relationship between Europe and jazz is that the Europeans had recognized jazz as an important music right at the outset, while the Americans had dismissed it as a minor form of entertainment, not worth taking seriously, let alone studying. This idea derives partly from the belief that the issues of race and racism account for this disparity: with racism far less virulent in Europe, people were better able to recognize a black contribution. However, the preliminary results of the large-scale research project in which I am engaged, examining early commentaries on jazz and pre-jazz, encourage me to believe that this claim is largely unfounded, or at least needs to be substantially revised and reformulated. To discuss this question, we need first to distinguish between two phases in the reception of jazz: pre-jazz and jazz. I have chosen to set the dividing line somewhere around the end of the 1910s.

The Pre-Jazz Reception

Before considering what the initial response to jazz was—both within and outside the United States—we should ask whether there was any reception for pre-jazz music, that is, for Negro spirituals, ragtime, blues, and what was sometimes known as folklore. The answer is clearly that there was a significant reception.

As early as 1856, articles were published addressing the music of slaves (Anonymous 1856a, b, and c). In 1863, the very year of the Emancipation Proclamation, the *Continental Monthly* published an article by H. G. Spaulding that included song transcriptions with words and music (Spaulding 1863). From this moment on, writings on this topic became more and more frequent. After the famous *Slave Songs of the United States* (Allen, Ware, and McKim 1867), which included some transcriptions of African American songs, other collections of Negro spirituals appeared (Fenner, Rathburn 1874; Barton 1898, 1899a, 1899b), extending as far as *St. Helena Island Spirituals, Recorded and Transcribed at Penn Normal, Industrial and Agricultural School, St. Helena Island, Beaufort County,*

South Carolina (Ballanta-Taylor 1925) and both *The Book of American Negro Spirituals* and *The Second Book of Negro Spirituals* (Johnson and Johnson 1925 and 1926).

Next were pieces on ragtime, apparently starting with the *Ragtime Instructor* by Ben Harney in 1897 (Harney 1897). In 1899 two articles were published under the same simple title "Ragtime" (Anonymous 1899a, Crozat Converse 1899). We should note that in the same year an article appeared, the title of which showed a grasp of what would become one of the first descriptions of jazz: "Syncopated Music" (Anonymous 1899b). The frequency of articles on ragtime reached a peak around the middle of the 1910s.

Writings about the blues emerged later, as the music itself was not well known at this time in the 1910s. One of the very first printed instances of the word used to designate the music apparently dates from 1915 and in fact happens to be a very early article on jazz. Both kinds of music are explicitly linked in the title: "Blues Is Jazz and Jazz Is Blues" (Seagrove 1915). Dorothy Scarborough would publish her "The 'Blues' as Folk-Songs" the following year (Scarborough 1916). In 1926, Abbe Niles provided an extended analysis of the blues in his introduction to the anthology by W. C. Handy (Handy 1926).

What do these pre-jazz texts say? Here is an extract from one of the earlier examples, "Under the Palmetto," published in the *Continental Monthly* in 1863 (Spaulding 1863):

> The words of the shout songs are a singular medley of things sacred and profane, and are the natural outgrowth of the imperfect and fragmentary knowledge of the Scriptures which the Negroes have picked up. The substitution for these crude productions of appropriate hymns, would remove from the shout that which is now the chief objection to it in intelligent minds, and would make of the dance, to which the Negroes are so much attached, a useful auxiliary in their religious culture. The tunes to which these songs are sung, are some of them weird and wild—"barbaric madrigals"—while others are sweet and impressive melodies. The most striking of their barbaric airs it would be impossible to write out, but many of their more common melodies are easily caught upon being heard a few times. This music of the Negro shout opens a new and rich field of melody—a mine in which there is much rough quartz, but also many veins of sparkling ore.[1]

We can regard this as a fairly accurate description, given the mentality and manner of speech of the time. Note also that there is an early indication of the problems of musical transcription. Then comes the question of the object itself and its representation:

302

A tinge of sadness pervades all their melodies, which bear as little resemblance to the popular melodies of the day as twilight to noonday. The joyous, merry strains which have been associated in the minds of many with the Southern Negro, are never heard on the Sea Islands. Indeed, by most of the Negroes, such songs as *Uncle Ned* and *O Susanna* ["Oh! Susanna"] are considered as highly improper.[2]

Here we have the suggestion that some products of minstrelsy or of "coon songs" should not be mistaken for what appeared to be an authentic expression of African Americans at the time.

Finally, on a Negro minstrelsy show he had attended, Spaulding states:

As an imitation of our Northern minstrelsy given by a band of uneducated Negro musicians, the performance was a wonderful success. Yet the general impression left upon the mind of the hearer was far from pleasing. One could not help feeling that a people, whose very natures are attuned to harmony, are capable of something better than even the most perfect imitation of those who have so grossly caricatured their race.[3]

If we consider that Spaulding was writing only a few months after the Emancipation Proclamation, it is hard not to be impressed by what at least seems to be an accurate approach to the music, far removed from the cliché of an inevitably negative or paternalist view of a minority forever denied its rights.

Ragtime was initially assimilated into syncopation, and the two terms were regarded as equivalent. Some authors (Crozat Converse 1899, Anonymous 1899) immediately insisted that syncopation was a long-established concept in Western art music. Many authors have, for this reason, denied the value of ragtime, treating it as a silly repetition of a musical feature, syncopation, that had supposedly been used since time immemorial by much more clever and inspired composers in Western art music:

What objection lies against ragtime music? [F. W. Root]: "It is a repetition of the same thing, that's all. There is nothing else in the world the matter with it. As I said, if it were not a good thing the masters would not have used it." . . . [Prof. Emil Lebling]: "The song from *Carmen*, 'Love is a wild bird,' is one of the best examples of ragtime in modern music. In the overture to *Don Juan*, by Mozart, and in some compositions of Bach we have good examples of syncopation. Ragtime is simply having its day. It will be forgotten as a craze in a few years."[4]

The verdict returned in 1901:

303

In conclusion, it is evident that none of the so-called ragtime songs or dances is, in any sense, new or original, but that they are adaptations and perversions of the czardas, the habanera and the southern plantation song. Also, that unusual rhythmic combinations and syncopations have been used so extensively by high-class composers that it is not possible for coon song composers to invent anything along these lines.[5]

Others saw this music as having some value, but only as entertainment:

> To most people music is not a serious matter. It is amusement and relaxation. It drives away the blues, and makes happy thrills run all over our system. It is refining and has a natural tendency to elevate mankind. But the people do not want to be educated all the time. They have not asked anybody to change their natures. They know what they want. Their great desire with music is to be pleased—to forget for a time that there is anything in this world but sunshine and laughter, and birds and flowers and purling brooks. And they find all those things in the homely and catchy pieces that quicken the heartbeats and make the nerves tingle with delight; yes, in ragtime, bubbling, frothing, sparkling; as light as a summer breeze and as sweet as woman's kiss. Ragtime is here to stay. It's the people's music. It's children's delight.[6]

But others recognized something other than an obsessive and vain repetition of music for entertainment, whatever its value. In 1901, Charles Reginald Sherlock, writing in *Cosmopolitan*, mapped out a history of black entertainment going back to 1830, Thomas D. Rice, and the birth of the eponymous Jim Crow, in order to place the arrival of ragtime in a lineage of African American expression. And he did so in a manner that verged on the sarcastic or at least the negative:

> All sorts of efforts were made to get out of the old ruts, but not until the specialty known as the "song and dance" was developed did the Negro minstrels reach a milestone.... It set the performers who went with the tide singing love-songs, and not a few of them were skilfully written and beautifully scored. Unusual chances were afforded men who had vocal gifts. Of these, perhaps Billy Emerson was the foremost. His singing of a waltz like *Love among the Roses* was a grateful reminder to old theater-goers of the good times in minstrelsy when *Old Folks at Home, Massa's in the Cold, Cold Ground, Way Down Upon the S'wanee river, Oh, Susanna, Don't you Cry for Me*, and other songs as tuneful and plaintive, were made to suggest the melody of the wind soughing in the canebrake. It can be said of the older minstrels that they did not often believe the name they took. They could sing.[7]

Sherlock's attitude undoubtedly reflects a thoroughly historical perspective. He continues in the same vein:

It began to look as if the Negro delineator, like Uncle Ned, would have to "hang up the fiddle and the bow," for minstrelsy was of a truth on its last legs. Not a theater in New York was devoted to it, where once it held high revel. And yet the Negro can never wholly lose his place on the American stage. Even where the old-time darkey has not been preserved, his melodies are sung and his steps are executed by the vaudeville artists or the ballad singer, and even the Irish comedian often tells a "coon" joke. There are, moreover, but few light operas or plays which can afford to ignore the darkey lullaby of ragtime, and it is safe to say that while the Negro may be slighted for a time he has left a lasting impress on the American stage. . . . Even, the ragtime, that decidedly unique development of harmonies, is a child by adoption of the stage. As for the cake-walk, it had been a waiters' diversion in hundreds of hotels long before it was subjected to the glare of the footlights, and introduced into ballrooms to relieve the monotony of the Virginia reel.[8]

Then comes what we can regard as a real analysis and understanding, both of the function and origins of the music. For example, from Gustav Kühl in 1902:[9]

The continuous re-appearance and succession of accentuations on the wrong parts of the bar and unnatural syncopations imparts somewhat of a rhythmic compulsion to the body which is nothing short of irresistible and which makes itself felt even before the ears have discerned the time of rhythmic value of the various parts of the bar. . . . There can be little doubt that "ragtime" is a genuine creation of Negro blood. . . . Naturally the old rhythm has changed in the course of time, just as the melodies, the instruments and the entire life of the colored people has changed. One idea prevalent is, that ragtime has been de-veloped out of the Czardas of the Gypsy, the Spanish Sarabande, the Cuban Habanera, and that it was greatly influenced, in singing at least, by that pecu-liar grace note in the Scotch Folks tunes, known as the "Scotch Snap." But such comparisons can only be applied to the products of the "professional ragtime composers" and to their products known as "raggers." The original ragtime of the South is something entirely different and proclaims its orig-inality and passion through means of its fascinating effectiveness. Now it has spread over all North America. . . . But on the other hand, there is no magic connected with it. As its name implies, ragtime is no special style of composi-tion, but merely a rhythm. Every melody can be transformed into ragtime, providing we tear its rhythm to tatters. It is primarily based upon the principle of syncopation. . . . Therefore, as already mentioned, there is no magic con-nected with it, although a European will never succeed to produce anything near to genuine ragtime.[10]

Writings about the blues appeared somewhat later, simply because the music itself did. But we know that the idea of the blues, both as a sociological and musical construct, had existed prior to this. Use of the word to denote a state of mind can be traced as far back as 1807. Since the blues as music probably emerged before the end of the nineteenth century (there are some mentions, for example, of "Joe Turner's Blues"), the first evidence in terms of publishing and recording dates from the 1910s—notably the songs "Oh, You Beautiful Doll," published in 1911 (this had a twelve-bar verse but was not called a blues), "The Dallas Blues," "The Baby Seals Blues," and W. C. Handy's "Memphis Blues," "Saint Louis Blues," and "Yellow Dog Blues," all of which were published in 1912.[11] The recordings came later.

It is worth noting also that the phenomenon was much better understood than one would have guessed, not only in its sociological and cultural aspects, but also in its musical aspects. In the first article on jazz, with its pointed title "Blues Is Jazz and Jazz Is Blues" (1915), one can read this description of the blue note by an imaginary black performer:

> "A blue note is a sour note," he explained.
> "It's a discord—a harmonic discord. The blues are never written into music, but are interpolated by the piano player or other players. They aren't new. They are just reborn into popularity. They started in the south half a century ago and are the interpolations of darkies originally. The trade name for them is 'jazz.'"[12]

This is, I think, a fairly accurate description, encompassing in just a few words the musical, cultural, and historical aspects of the form.

In my opinion, the early great text about the blues is the extensive introduction to the W. C. Handy anthology written by Abbe Niles in 1926. He surveys many aspects of the then new music (most of them, I think), covering both music and lyrics. On the latter subject, for example, he comments:

> What makes the typical words, as well as the music, striking—what has caught the attention of white song writers who were indifferent to the musical devices by which it was expressed—is an unconscious philosophy between the lines, of making a little mirth of one's troubles while one dwells on them; of choosing as the reaction to disaster, laughter instead of tears; instead of sodden despondency, an attractively unexpected mood, exuberant and fantastic, native, not virtuously forced, finding a gusto in its self-expression.[13]

This is part of a broader and very inspired reflection on the lyrics of the blues, notably related to the three-line form. More generally, it ties together the literary and the musical:

The structural peculiarities of the blues tunes may be the result of those of the stanza, more likely the reverse is the case, but suffice it to say that the blues architecture is admirably adapted to impromptu song and versification alike. Just as the stanza had three lines instead of the two or four normal to simple verse, so the voice would sing (always in two-four or common time) twelve instead of the normal eight or sixteen bars to the strain, each line being complete in four bars of the air. As each line usually expressed a thought which, with a period after it, would still make sense, so the air with the last syllable of each line would return to the keynote or the tonic third or fifth, so that the whole presented a period of three semi-independent phrases—three wing-clipped hops (separated, as will be shown by noticeable intervals) instead of one sustained flight—with successive bizarre effects of internal finality and of final incompleteness. Where one expects the melody to stop it resumes; just as one is waiting for a fourth, and final, phrase, it stops, and instinct calls for a repetition.[14]

Turning to the blue note, Niles is very much preoccupied with justifying the makings of his mentor, W. C. Handy. But this does not stop him from offering another insightful train of thought about the phenomenon itself, its reception, and some of the misunderstandings around it:

Writing down his tunes with the memory of how the Negroes had sung, Handy was first met by the problem of perpetuating the typical treatment of the tonic third—the slur of the voices, whatever the song. This aberration he chose to represent by the frequent introduction of the minor third into melodies which (however melancholy their undercurrent) exhibited a prevailing major. It might divide a beat between itself and the major third, appear (more nearly as in the originals) as a grace-note to the major, or here and there entirely replace the major; Handy's interpolated minor third, appearing thus as signifying a change of mode followed by a re-exchange, and appearing nearly as often as the melody reaches the third at all, caught and holds popular attention as have none of the structural peculiarities which alone distinguished the folk-blues from all other negro song. It has acquired a name of its own: "the blue note." The more of such notes, the "meaner" the blues. Its occasional use furnishes the work of most of the white writers with its only claim (from the historical standpoint) to such titles as "The _____ Blues," while from the standpoint of the folklorist "Rhapsody in Blue" presents a neat contradiction in terms. It is, in short, a method consciously chosen by W. C. Handy to represent a characteristic vocal treatment of songs *in general* that had impressed him, which has become to most observers the earmark of the blues.[15]

307

What do we find on the European front? I would not claim to be able to trace all of the European writings on pre-jazz. But for some obvious cultural, sociological, historical, and geographical reasons, there are far fewer of them. We can say with some confidence that they are very rare.[16] What about early jazz, then? I shall talk mainly about French texts, for the sole (and wrong) reason that they are the ones I know the best.

After Jean Cocteau and his famous expression "tame disaster,"[17] used to describe a music that he thought was jazz (actually a musical called *Laisse-les tomber* [Forget Them], with Gaby Deslys, Harry Pilcer, and Murray Pilcer's American Sherbo Band, which opened at the Casino de Paris in late 1918), the first real piece of writing about jazz in French is the famous "Sur un orchestre nègre" (About a Negro Orchestra) by Swiss conductor Ernest Ansermet, published in *La Revue Romande* in 1919. The last paragraph of this piece has been reproduced many times, probably due to its visionary dual conclusion, addressing both a particular musician and the future of the music itself:

> There is in the Southern Syncopated Orchestra an extraordinary clarinet virtuoso who is, so it seems, the first of his race to have composed perfectly formed blues on the clarinet. I've heard two of them which he elaborated at great length. They are admirable equally for their richness of invention, their force of accent, and their daring novelty and unexpected turns. These solos already show the germ of a new style. Their form is gripping, abrupt, harsh, with a brusque and pitiless ending like that of Bach's Second Brandenburg concerto. I wish to set down the name of this artist of genius; as for myself, I shall never forget it—it is Sidney Bechet. When one has tried so often to find in the past one of those figures to whom we owe the creation of our art as we know it today—those men of the 17th and 18th centuries, for example, who wrote the expressive works of dance airs which cleared the way for Haydn and Mozart—what a moving thing it is to meet this black, fat boy with white teeth and narrow forehead, who is very glad one likes what he does, but can say nothing of his art, except that he follows his "own way"—and then one considers that perhaps his "own way" is the highway along which the whole world will swing tomorrow.[18]

But it is a pity there are no more references to the rest of this eight-page article, which shows a remarkable understanding of music heard on only a few occasions, that of Will Marion Cook's Southern Syncopated Orchestra, featuring Sidney Bechet, at the People's Palace in London during the summer of 1919. Not

the least astonishing thing about it is that the whole piece consists solely of impressions of a few performances. It evidences a great acuity of perception, both aurally and conceptually, as well as an authentic knowledge of some American popular music forms.[19]

At the start of the article, Ansermet gives a fairly accurate description of what ragtime is and how it was performed in Europe, "with the one-steps, two-steps, foxtrots, and all the American dances or songs to which the subtitle of ragtime is applied."[20] He also notes that, with Debussy, Stravinsky, and Ravel, ragtime is about to seep into art music, a subject that he of course knows very well. Ansermet then identifies the compositions he heard that night—mentioning that the musicians generally played without a written score—and concludes with the following statement: "Thus all, or almost, all of the music of the Southern Syncopated Orchestra is of an origin foreign to these Negroes. How can that be? It is because Negro music is not material, it is spirit."[21]

Ansermet thus anticipates what will be the hobbyhorse of many authors during the 1920s and the 1930s (among them Robert Goffin and Hugues Panassié): when considering this music, the emphasis should be not on the compositions but on the way they are played. He then moves on to his interpretation of syncopation, as it is played by African American performers:

> The desire to give certain syllables a particular recoil, or a prolonged resonance, in other words an expressive concern, seems to have determined in Negro singing the anticipation or delay afforded them by part of the rhythmic unit. This is the birth of syncopation. All "traditional" Negro songs are strewn with syncopations, realized by the voice as the body's movement taps out a regular rhythm. Then, as far as profane music is concerned—the Anglo-Saxon "ballad," or banal forms of dances that have reached *Dixie-land*, the land of plantations—Negroes appropriate them in the same way, and that is the birth of the *rag*. But it is not enough to say that Negro music consists of the habit of "syncopating" any musical material. We have seen that syncopation itself was merely the effect of an expressive need, the manifestation in the rhythmic field of a particular taste, in a single word, of a racial genius.[22]

Here, where so many commentators (see above) had seen in ragtime nothing more than a banal use of syncopation, and therefore a mere repetition of what Western art music had been doing since at least Johann Sebastian Bach, Ansermet makes the obvious point about the use of syncopation, yet immediately notes that it is not a simple case of borrowing a well-known musical feature, but is on the contrary the result of a very particular expressive need and of the way it is put into music, which makes all the difference. And he does not hesitate to attribute this aspect to "racial genius"—what we would today describe as a unique cultural manifestation.

On the blues scale and blue notes:

In the melodic order, although his familiarization with our scales has erased in him the memory of the African modes, an old instinct urges the Negro to seek his pleasure outside the orthodox intervals: he realizes neither major nor minor thirds or false seconds, and often stumbles by instinct on the natural harmonic sounds of a given note; then again, no written music can give an idea of his playing.[23] *ha*

Even if a contemporary commentator would probably shy away from attributing this to instinct, the important thing, for me, is the clear view presented of how the scalar system works. Note as well a foretaste (which we also find in some very early writings on Negro spirituals[24]) of the nowadays still passionate debate about musical transcription and its limitations.

Finally, Ansermet returns to his previous acknowledgment of the preference for performance over composition, introducing in the process an important distinction between the written and the fixed: "The importance of the composer in the creation of the work is strongly balanced by the action of tradition, represented by the performer. While the work can be written, it is not *fixed*, and it is fully realized only in performance."[25]

ok In the end, considering whether this music could turn from oral tradition to composition (another keen debate at the time), Ansermet's conclusion is without ambiguity: "Maybe someday a Glinka of Negro Music will appear. But I tend to think that it is in the *Blues* that the racial genius manifests itself with the greatest force."[26]

Then comes the final paragraph quoted above, with its well-known look into the future.

This piece has sometimes been criticized on the basis of displaying a familiar paternalism toward African Americans.[27] This assertion seems to me a mere anachronism. Accustomed to reading a lot of French texts from this period, I would say this one makes average use of a vocabulary that would not be used anymore today, but had no pejorative meaning at the time.[28] As far as the global vision of African Americans is concerned, the collective acuity of these numerous subtle observations largely balances some representations that appear problematic to our twenty-first-century understanding, but which were not so at the time.[29] I would go further and say this text appears to be a turning point in the history of jazz commentary, since it establishes a setting for many of the ideas that would be developed in the ensuing decades. But Ansermet was just a bystander. He was not so interested in jazz, and as far as I know, he would never write about this music again.[30]

What comes next? Not much until the fertile year of 1926, when the first books about jazz appear, along with some major articles: in France *Le jazz* by André

Schaeffner and André Coeuroy;[31] in Germany *Das Jazz-Buch* by Alfred Baresel;[32] in the United States *So This Is Jazz* by Henry Osgood[33] and *Jazz* by Paul
Whiteman;[34] plus articles by Don Knowlton ("The Anatomy of Jazz"[35]), Abbe
Niles ("Blue Notes"[36] and the introduction to W. C. Handy's *Blues: An Anthology*[37]), Irwing Schwerké ("Le jazz est mort! Vive le jazz"[38]), and Aaron Copland
("Jazz Structure and Influence in Modern Music"[39]). And the following year saw,
among others, Bernhard Egg's *Jazz Fremdwörterbuch*,[40] Paul Bernhard's *Jazz,
eine Musikalische Zeitfrage*,[41] and Arthur Hoérée's *Le jazz*.[42] I will not comment
on all these texts, of course, but will focus on Schaeffner's *Le jazz*, Baresel's *Das
Jazz-Buch*, and Hoérée's *Le jazz*, as examples of what appears to me a strong
tendency among European writings.

André Schaeffner was a major French anthropologist at the time, a renowned
Africanist, onetime director of the Musée de l'Homme in Paris, inventor of a new
instrument classification system in 1936, and author of many studies on twentieth-
century composers. First, in *Le jazz*, he acknowledges the organic link between
kinds of music originating in Africa:

> Music from the Negroes of Africa and America, whatever it may be, places
> directly back before us a properly *elementary* art, linked much more to the
> conditions of its native soil than to any other, suggesting for that matter some-
> thing vegetable, as much in the making and the timber of its instruments as in
> the boldness of its offshoots and in a longevity whose chants bear the mark,
> even in their supple way, of participating indistinctly in any expression, be it of
> joy or sadness. From the violent musics of Africa to the singing of plantation
> workers from the West Indies or Louisiana, and from *spirituals* finally to jazz, it
> is only ever about one musical fact, with strangely little variation: a legacy of
> expressions kept to the minimum, of an even disturbing simplicity, and that will
> have been enough to conquer three continents.[43]

As a result of this acknowledged African lineage, Schaeffner comes to the
same conclusion as Ansermet: the important thing is the way the music is played
and not the original material:

> We have before us a type of music whose whole character and originality lay in
> a few technical practices linked to a problem of race, and in whatever this
> problem had to offer in more physiological terms. Even when blacks borrowed
> melodies and instruments from whites, they still played music that was authen-
> tically negro, as evidenced by the small catechumenates of *fang* country who
> poured their canticles in the modal system of their ancestors. Such ease with
> borrowing lies not only in the Negro's capacity to imprint what he touches with
> a properly Negro character, but in that gift he possesses of always considering a

musical expression in isolation of what it could convey. The liberties that negro music takes with white music are proportionate to the liberties that music takes with itself.[44]

The explanation of the blue note (the expression is not used here) is quite accurate as well, even if the formulation is somewhat tortuous:

> Would those diminished seventh chords that we always find in Afro-American songs, in the *blues*, in jazz harmony, take their origins from the ambiguous character of the dominant of the major mode? And what about those quarter tones perceived by Father Trille: would not jazz later rehabilitate their use, always, admittedly, within the strict frame of diatonism, as Darius Milhaud noted? For this interval has, according to Milhaud, "a uniquely expressive character, and is linked to diatonic harmony in the same way as chromaticism is regarded as a bridging note in the middle of a diatonic scale and one that has no relation to the quarter tone system now under consideration in Central Europe, based on the multiplication by two of the twelve notes in the scale, and linked to atonal harmony."[45]

The argument here is that the specificity of the African American treatment of the scale lies in tweaking the diatonic scale a few degrees, rather than replacing the scale itself. The tension in the playing of some degrees (the third one, mainly) produces, at the end of the process, a scale of sorts—if we need to consider the phenomenon in such a way—and not a change of scale that would lead to different degrees. It is about a different treatment of the scale and not a new scale. This belief in maintaining diatonism in jazz, in preference to an explanation focused on the choice of different scales or modes—which seems to me quite accurate—is further emphasized, but again in a somewhat obtuse manner:

> Jazz contributed to a more definitive break with the hieratism of asiatic modes, although its diatonism had sometimes been regarded as suspect, pretension the premise that can recognize many traces of pentatonic scales in Congo and in *spirituals*, where fourth and seventh degrees are omitted: these defective scales, which one finds in Scottish music as well as in Wagner and Debussy, never jeopardized diatonism, nor do they explain the frequency of plagal cadences and the number of dominant chords in the harmonies of *spirituals*.[46]

With *Le jazz*, Schaeffner thus provides a very insightful reflection that declares once and for all the relationship between African music and jazz. What he is really more interested in, though, is African music, and not so much jazz itself, which is used here as a medium for discussing Schaeffner's real specialist field and interest: African music. The fact that among the very few musicians quoted anywhere in the book are Roland Hayes of the Fisk University Quintet and Paul Whiteman ("At the present time, the most complete jazz band is that of Paul Whiteman. It comprises twenty-three performers using *thirty-six* instruments. One understands here the main difference from our traditional orchestras: every musician is a *soloist* and has to play several instruments in succession"[47]) gives us an indication of Schaeffner's (and, of course, many others') lack of contact with jazz music at the time, and finally, of the lack of interest shown by some authors in really finding out about the true subject of their research.

Though we can view Schaeffner as having largely missed the point of jazz due to his lack of interest in it, on another level Baresel's *Das Jazz-Buch* and Hoérée's *Le jazz* each show—on opposite sides of the Rhine, but in an identical manner—a fundamental misunderstanding of the object itself.

In the second edition of *Das Jazz-Buch* (*Das Neue Jazz-Buch*), published in 1929, the first chapter—"Geschichte des Jazz"—relates the history of jazz, relying in part, the author says, on Paul Whiteman's book *Jazz* (published in 1926). Jazz is said to have begun around 1915. Besides a lot of European composers, which musicians and bands are cited? The Brown Orchestra, Bert Kelly, Jubilee Singers, Paul Whiteman, Vincent Lopez. The body of the book then consists of musical analyses, although examples are singled out, not on any recordings but in dances (one-step, tango, boston, waltz, fox-trot, shimmy, charleston, black-bottom), in tunes such as "Valencia" and "Carolina Blues," in a fox-trot by Irving Berlin, in the piano technique of Zez Confrey or a German author (*Instruktive Jazzetüden*), and in the "jazz-opera" (its composer did not call it that) *Jonny Spielt Auf*, by Ernst Krenek.[48]

Very similar in its intentions but less extensive is *Le jazz* by Arthur Hoérée, published in 1927. Hoérée, a composer, teacher, and critic, is very much focused in this article on the fox-trot, although he first states: "It would seem, *a priori*, that the musical history of jazz is linked to the choreographic history of foxtrot, which remains the characteristic dance of jazz today. This parallelism seems to me unreliable for more than one reason."[49] However, it very quickly appears that the heart of the matter lies, for this author, somewhere in this area:

> The evolution of jazz and the music of the foxtrot . . . was particularly sensitive between 1918 and 1922, when the foxtrot, completely free of ascendants, achieves perfection in scoring, a highly balanced form, great rhythmic richness, and finally that unique style distinguishing it from anything that came before. Four years have been enough for this genre to flower, a genre whose exceptionally homogeneous language exposes the apathetic writings of many a sterile researcher and creates in a few bars the most peculiar feeling, as beyond suspicion as could ever be found, and where boundless human sadness con-

nects with an ancestral dance frenzy. Few have understood the deep modifications that jazz was subject to, and which transformed ordinary foxtrots from 1917 into the 1922 compositions that enchant us and which, while probably equalled since, have not been surpassed.[50]

This does not seem, in the author's mind, to contradict the statement made immediately afterward: "Jazz is, for the most part, characterized by its rhythmic elements of specifically Negro origin. Thus it is music, instruments, dances, in a word the musical tradition of Negroes, that we will need to study: above all that of Negroes from Africa, who had been shipped to America."[51]

Hoérée seems to have no idea that the music of the "Negroes from Africa, who had been shipped to America," was more likely to be found in, for example, Negro spirituals, some forms of ragtime, or the blues instead of in fox-trots. The answer comes one page later:

Contrary to the common conception, I do not view jazz as an essentially Negro expression, but as the Negro interpretation of an art of the white race and of European origin. However, some American musicians happen to crystallize its various elements to great effect. An examination of the first foxtrots allows me to make this hypothesis. . . . As a matter of fact, the Negro tinge ("staggered" rhythms, choral effect, melancholy) that we appreciate in today's jazz expressions does not appear in foxtrots between 1915 and 1917 and even in 1918. It rises in proportion to the evolution of the genre and achieves its complete seduction when the elements of European origin (sinuous contours of counter-melodies, logically developed form, harmonic subtlety) markedly dominate the jazz language.[52]

The blues itself is described as a "slow by-product of the foxtrot that takes its name from a Negro slang expression corresponding to our word '*cafard*.'"[53]

Few musicians' names are cited in this piece, other than Belgian pianist Jean Doucet, Billy Arnold, and the inevitable Paul Whiteman.[54] The author confesses in his introduction that he "could, through much reading, some listening, a few personal experiences with a Negro banjo player [probably Vance Lowry] who would accept [him] as a voluntary reader of novelties from America, and keyboard at hand, assimilate this very singular jazz approach, analyze its mechanism, and acquire a modest competence in it."[55] Clearly, Hoérée did not hear what we would consider today a more representative form of jazz before writing his article, but mainly focuses on written music instead of performed music, be it live or recorded, even though a great many jazz records were available in France in 1927.

What could he have heard? We know that the Original Dixieland Jazz Band was in London in 1919 but did not visit France. It is difficult to know if the records

314

that the band cut in 1917 were available in France, but they probably were not for quite some time.[56] Therefore, it would be unfair to reproach our authors for not being aware of this music. But then what about Louis Mitchell, for example? This African American player had been in Europe with Irene and Vernon Castle prior to World War I and spent extended periods in Paris during the 1920s.[57] He was a prominent Parisian figure, playing at the Casino de Paris and managing his own restaurant in Montmartre. His all African American band cut at least fifty tracks (such as "The Montmartre Rag," "Une femme qui passe," or "Sing 'Em Blues") between January 1922 and July 1923, recorded in Paris for Pathé, and these were obviously distributed in France. When we hear these records, we might notice the fact that this music is quite close to what the Original Dixieland Jazz Band, or even King Oliver or Kid Ory, were playing at the time. Actually, we would surely categorize it as hot jazz. How could people who claimed to be interested in jazz in Paris let it go unnoticed? The only plausible answer might be that they were looking in another direction, obviously preferring written sheet music to live or recorded music.

I would finally like to add a most amazing case from Czechoslovakia. Emil František Burian was born in 1904, and in February 1928 he published a book entitled—once again—*Jazz*. This son of a famous opera singer had graduated from the Prague Conservatory in 1927; he was something of a cultural activist—a composer, musician, writer, musicologist, theater director, playwright (and much more). His book, written between 1925 and 1927, reveals a tremendous knowledge of music and musicians. Not only does he quote Palestrina, Bach, Handel, Beethoven, Chopin, Berlioz, Puccini, Wagner, Strauss, Rimsky-Korsakov, Mahler, Scriabin, Debussy, Schoenberg, Stravinsky, Hindemith, and Berg, but he also talks about his fellow Czech composers (including Smetana, Janáček, Ostrčil, Hába, Martinů, Schulhoff, and Ježek), and demonstrates a solid knowledge of both contemporary French composers (Auric, Satie, Milhaud, Honegger, Poulenc, Taillefere, Durey, and even the less famous Henri Cliquet-Pleyel), and the Americans (Henry Cowell, Georges Antheil, Louis Gruenberg, Emerson Whithorne, John Alden Carpenter), as well as others (including Leonid Polovinkin, Wilhelm Grosz, Ernst Krenek, and Ivan Wyschnegradsky). Moreover, he knows the French cultural scene fairly well: Jean Wiéner and Clément Doucet, Jean Cocteau, Man Ray, Fernand Léger, Pablo Picasso, Ernest Ansermet. Burian also quotes a variety of American popular musicians (George Gershwin, Jerome Kern, Ferde Grofé, Rudolf Friml [a Czech expatriate], Arthur Lange, Zez Confrey, Charlie Chaplin, Art Hickman, the Revelers, Ted Lewis, Ben Bernie), and had read many of the most recent authors writings about popular music. These articles appeared in German (by Alfred Baresel, Paul Bernhard, Frank Thiess, and Oskar Bie, writing about popular music in *Die Musik* and *Musikbaltter des Anbruch*), and in French (André Schaeffner, André Coeuroy, Jean Cocteau, Maurice Delafosse). He had also read many American authors writing about Negro spirituals and folk songs (including W. O. Odum, H. F. Krehbiel, Hugo Frey, James Weldon Johnson, J. A. Cox, Harry Burleigh, and H. W. Looncis). He also quotes Alain Locke's *The New Negro* and W. C. Handy's *Blues Anthology*. And, of course, Paul Whiteman's *Jazz*. And we have only scratched the surface, since the book's bibliography mentions a vast array of music education literature by Rube Bloom, Zez Confrey, Jimmy Dorsey, Miff Mole, Sam Perry, Joe Pettis, and others, mostly about the well-known and widespread models of the time. These amazing lists demonstrate from a man still in his early twenties an outstanding voracity and capacity to digest intellectual food and instantly integrate it into a personal discourse. Most of the books cited above were published between 1924 and 1927; astonishingly, Burian writes *Jazz* between 1925 and 1927, and publishes it in 1928!

At least one question is raised. How could all these books have been available to him? We know that Burian traveled in Europe with his vocal group, the Voiceband, modeled on the Revelers (and perhaps its German version, the Comedian Harmonists). He was notably in Siena, Italy, but not before 1928. He apparently did not leave Czechoslovakia prior to 1929, and he worked alternately between Prague and Brno. We also know that he met his friend Bohuslav Martinů when Martinů returned from Paris, where he had been living for a while. Perhaps Martinů had books and musical scores in his trunk that he could share? In any case, Burian most likely received by mail most of these documents cited in his book.

What about the book itself? Divided in four main chapters ("Jazz," "Syncopation," "New Instruments," and "Craft Orchestration"), just as was Schaeffner's *Jazz* (and perhaps due to its influence), it acknowledges the black character and African origins of jazz. But it is obviously intended to show—just as Roger Pryor Dodge or Goffin had done—that this new music represents a revolutionary stage with the potential to transform an aging Western art music tradition from within. Burian first quotes Karl Teige:

> Music, just like theatre, cannot keep up with the times and with other arts. Concerts and chamber seances are really the putrefying water of a carp pond . . . the revival of music . . . is arising from external and worldly impulses. Although dead in the concert hall, music continues to live out in the world. Passionate for the real live thing . . . will not be afraid, nor disdain instruments and interpreters thus far regarded as taboo, Jazz![58]

Then he states: "We are on the verge of a new era. The contrivances of past eras have been used up . . . we are searching for new means of expression. New techniques are based on new discoveries . . . a revolution in notes has begun and is in its most active phase."[59] Following the very well-documented bibliography on pages 180 to 182, there is a discography citing some of Paul Whiteman's tracks on His Master's Voice. It is very likely that this is the only recorded music heard by Burian; all the other music had likely been read (as had been the case with Arthur Hoérée) or perhaps played by musically literate friends and associates. We could hardly reproach the author for not knowing, in 1927 Czechoslovakia, of the recordings by the Original Dixieland Jazz Band, King Oliver, Fletcher Henderson, Duke Ellington, or Louis Armstrong. But the fact remains that he did not know them. Since Burian was exceptionally well documented, the question that arises now is: was it materially impossible for him to hear this music through recordings, or was he uninterested in doing so because his research was focused elsewhere? Pavel Eisner, reviewing the book at the time of its release, wrote: "[Burian] fights for the future of jazz, believes therein, and thinks that jazz is also the way to get something to happen in the world of classical music."[60] The whole problem is in this "also." "Also" or "only"?

Finally, I would say that a first generation of observers—French at least, but probably from some other European countries as well—from the very birth of the music onward, loved to love jazz without much caring to go beyond what jazz immediately seems to be. Some made honest attempts to understand it (Schaeffner, Milhaud to some extent, Hoérée mostly, and Baresel in Germany), while others were more dilettantish (for example Cocteau, who in some ways inaugurated a literary jazz tradition whose most flamboyant representative today is Alain Gerber). Most of them got bored with jazz at some point. Darius Milhaud—who declared in 1924 that "it is necessary to hear a serious jazz band such as Billy Arnold's or Paul Whiteman's . . . [where] nothing is left to chance, everything is balance and proportion, revealing the touch of the true musician, the perfect master of all the possibilities of each instrument"[61]—would finally express the fleeting nature of this passion with another statement in 1927: "Already, the influence of jazz has passed, like a beneficial storm after which one rediscovers a pure sky, a surer weather. Little by little, a reborn classicism is replacing the broken parts of syncopation."[62]

Finally, another famous French composer, Georges Auric, a friend of Milhaud's, made the same point in a book of memoirs published in 1979, focusing on the poor quality of what was heard and sometimes played, and the general attitude toward this so-called jazz, in a much crueler way:

I have since learnt to know well and to judge as it deserves the admirable "jazz" performed, in those far-off times, by black Americans we knew nothing about, not even their names. But the imminent "tame disaster," so far from the rue de

Clichy and its Casino, would not be too long in coming. Aside from the excellent piano playing of [Jean] Wiéner, there were, to start with, the "fantasies" of our poet.[63] Then appeared—mercifully brief but badly "tamed" as well as, on this occasion, "catastrophic"—the "Parisian Jazz." Here, honesty becomes a necessity! Could a few young men who really made an effort—and they did work hard—take the liberty of playing the drums, smashing cymbals, hitting a piano, making a violin screech, on the fringes of a few dance tunes under the sign of a "different" jazz? Yes, a "Parisian Jazz." The culprits, and how easy it is for me to denounce them here: Cocteau of course, Darius Milhaud (what would Paul Claudel think?), and myself who, obviously, left no one proud of this adventure![64]

Second Generation

The way was then opened for another generation of commentators from a completely different background, such as Robert Goffin and Hugues Panassié. None of them were musicians, nor did they even know anything about musical technique, be it art music or jazz, but they would nevertheless demonstrate a much better appreciation and knowledge of the subject at hand.

Goffin, a Belgian lawyer and poet, published, as early as 1932, *Aux frontières du jazz*[65] (On the Frontiers of Jazz), two years before Panassié, a Frenchman of independent means, produced his famous *Le jazz hot*,[66] which was translated and published with some success in the United States in 1936 as *Hot Jazz: The Guide to Swing Music*.

Explaining his need to start writing a jazz history (even if he does not call it that), Goffin, in his characteristic highly lyrical style, admits to (and romanticizes) the fact that at the time, he knew jazz mainly through recordings (he would cross the Atlantic in 1941 and stay in the United States until 1945):

> The days irretrievably fly by. I struggle to look back and prepare myself, 1920–1930: there are now ten years of popular tunes waiting to be translated. I am alone with all my memories, which balk when I play any record on my Columbia. Tunes born in Harlem, the Negroes' paradise, or in any American ghetto, will die in the small Brabançon[67] valley in which I live and where frightened tourists listen. Louis Armstrong, Hawkins, Jimmy Dorsey, Adrian Rollini and you, Joe Venuti, who have definitely domesticated the violin, it is high time I proclaim to everyone your pure creative genius and, if the law gives me a little time, I will not fail to do so.[68]

But this very generous statement is immediately followed by another declaring the author's legitimacy, which he refuses in quite an aggressive manner (somewhat justified in light of some of the texts we looked at previously) to recognize in most of his contemporary commentators:

> In Europe we are but a scant few who can talk about it calmly; a few I know well, for whom jazz has been a daily need that ten years were not enough to satisfy; there are probably some others I'd like to know and then I'd be happy. I deny to a fairly large number of ignoramuses the right to talk about things they know only through experience. They saw in jazz only a musical façade that they failed to layer onto the African past; they did not feel what had to be felt. Only their mind expressed itself, because they left their heart imprisoned in pre-war music.[69]

Goffin was wrong to emphasize that the African origins of jazz had previously been unrecognized (Ansermet, Schaeffner, Hoérée, and others had fully acknowledged this), but he was right in the sense that the music identified as jazz was not precisely one of African (or African American) descent, and in most cases was neither played nor composed by black musicians. But we can locate in his comments the main themes that Goffin (and Panassié to some extent) would revisit throughout the '30s and the '40s: jazz music should be taken in through the heart, not the mind, and jazz commentary should be reserved for experts who knew the real, authentic music, who truly cared about it and did not use it as an instrument to argue about other subjects. And, most of all, they should feel all of its human content, as if living it from the inside, something Goffin expressed in a very romantic manner:

> There is a very weighty history of jazz that starts with the pages Coeuroy and Schaeffner wrote on the subject.[70] Jazz starts where their book ends. It has the Edenic innocence of days we have not lived; it is as naive as the Negro slaves' singing in the Southern plantation, it is the expression of an oppressed people without a fatherland and the cry of deliverance for Negroes and Jews, instilled with their inexhaustible loneliness and devastating depression.[71]

Panassié, writing two years later, shows his agreement with Goffin's vision first by respectfully but firmly stating his opinion of Schaeffner's *Le jazz* as an interesting book rendered irrelevant by the author's ignorance:

> It is however curious to think that the French lacked information on the main elements of jazz for so many years. Indeed, Coeuroy and Schaeffner wrote a book entitled *Le jazz*, devoting it to the—incidentally interesting—study of this music's distant origins, but paying no attention to its definitive form.[72]

Panassié then goes on to acknowledge the work of his fellow writer Robert Goffin, but immediately distances himself by relegating his colleague to a subjective position while he, Panassié, claims to have an objective, and therefore superior, one:

Robert Goffin, in his excellent book *Aux Frontières du Jazz*, concerned himself on the contrary with the present form of jazz. We do not consider these new pages useless, though, because Robert Goffin was mostly engaged in describing jazz through his own impressions, in a fairly subjective way, whereas here, we propose to give you, in a strictly objective analysis, the essential information required to know exactly what real jazz consists of, and especially *hot* jazz. We have left out the question of the origins of jazz, because despite its interest, it is not directly situated within the scope of our topic, since our only goals are to give you a precise notion of what jazz is in its definitive form, and to try to dispel the regrettable misunderstanding that has lasted for so long. There can actually be no more fateful mistake in relation to an art form: *imagining that one knows it by seeing it from completely the wrong angle*. We hope that by considering it from a more genuine perspective, the music's detractors will see their objections fall apart. What we insistently ask of the reader is to become liberated from any legitimate prejudices you may have conceived up until now, to examine without bias these arguments, which are not ours but rather a loyal translation of those of the great jazz musicians. In short, to listen to this cause as if it had never been heard before.[73]

Of course, it is not without irony that one notices that perhaps the most biased author of all, the one riddled with prejudices, the one who is about to reveal himself as the most intolerant of all jazz writers, should require—apparently in all sincerity—objectivity, lack of prejudice, and a serene observation of a reality that would ask only to be viewed as it is out there in the real world. We may notice, too, how easily he relegates the necessity of knowing the history of origins—we might even say the very history of this music—that extends no further than a few decades back. What we retain from this kind of statement is that Hugues Panassié simply but firmly is establishing his own legitimacy, his ultimate legitimacy, since even Robert Goffin, in his view, is less of an expert than he is.

The problem is that both of them are actually true experts, but relative experts. Neither of them knows musical theory (Panassié did learn some clarinet with Christian Wagner but admits he did not get very far). We will see that Panassié has a very approximate view of the origins of jazz. Last but not least, he indisputably knew some jazz recordings very well, but came across the real, live music only through American expatriates or non-American musicians, or when American musicians came to France, such as Duke Ellington in 1933, or Louis Armstrong and Cab Calloway in 1934.

These considerations are not a basis for arguing that Goffin and Panassié are not important authors within jazz commentary. They obviously are, and they initiated important ideas about the history and theory of the music. Take Raymond F. Kennedy, for example:

If not the first, then, certainly the most influential attempt at understanding jazz improvisation and the catalyst for subsequent studies, was by the French critic Hugues Panassié. In his 1934 book, translated and made available to the English-speaking world in 1936 as *Hot Jazz*, he discusses—in often difficult-to-decipher prose—what he feels are the most characteristic features of the "hot style" of jazz (a designation Panassié uses to distinguish it from the commercial jazz of such bands led by Paul Whiteman and Jack Hylton, which was widely regarded at the time as jazz).[74]

And one page later:

This mention of the role of memory in jazz improvisation is probably Panassié's most extraordinary observation—one that strikes at the very heart of the myths about jazz improvisation. It has been picked up and corroborated by others in subsequent studies.[75]

We can easily agree with these observations. The point here is not to deny these authors the legitimacy of their place in the history of jazz commentary, but to put in perspective their contribution and its importance. They are major authors, but not the first, and they are not without certain partial positions. They have their strengths and weaknesses, as with any point of view, the weaknesses being particularly evident in Panassié's perception of early jazz history. And both have the disadvantage of all European (or non-American) writers, that they were not where the real action was. This is particularly embarrassing when they themselves proclaim the importance of expertise and put themselves in the position of absolute experts, which they are obviously not.

There was in the United States at least one forerunner to achieving a proper understanding of jazz music and musicians: Roger Pryor Dodge, who, quite like Ernest Ansermet, was a bystander, since, as far as I know, he wrote relatively few articles about jazz, but his first two are major accomplishments that precede Goffin and Panassié and tackle some aspects ignored by the French-speaking duo.

Born in 1898, Dodge was initially a salon dancer before he encountered the Russian ballets and Nijinsky in 1916. He then decided to leave for Paris to study classical dance, returned to New York in 1921 and joined the ballet of the Metropolitan Opera. He attended the second performance of Gershwin's *Rhapsody in Blue* in 1924. Shocked by the press reports for what he considered to be a misunderstanding of the nature of real jazz, Dodge wrote, apparently in 1925, an article called "Jazz Contra Whiteman," which was not published until 1929 in London, rechristened as *Negro Jazz*.[76] There one reads:

> The word "jazz" is being used too loosely and too indiscriminately by persons who have little perception of the true nature of the embryonic form now developing amongst us. It is no wonder that critics are unable to agree when no two of them are discussing the same thing. The word "jazz" as it is currently used seems to cover both true jazz and popular music in general. It covers Paul Whiteman, George Gershwin, and Irving Berlin, none of whom I consider as belonging to the ranks of jazz at all; but if these men are not exponents of jazz, who is? And what is jazz?[77]

The author gives his answer a little further on:

> To my mind the creative playing found in *low-down* jazz is establishing a stronger form than any that has arisen for centuries. It is a musical form produced by the primitive innate musical instinct of the Negro and of those lower members of the white race who have not yet lost their feeling for the primitive. It is appreciated not only by these primitives but by those who can participate in the enjoyment of a stern school and can appreciate its vitality while it is still in the process of development. It is disliked by those who know it only in its diluted form and who, often under the impression that they are defending it, desire to bring about its fusion or confusion with the windbag symphony or the trick programme-closing rhapsody. There is no important similarity between the orchestras of Paul Whiteman, Jack Hylton, etc., and such organizations as Ted Lewis and His Band, Fletcher Henderson, and His Orchestra, Mound City Blue Blowers, King Oliver's Jazz Band, Thomas Morris and His Seven Hot Babies, Red Nichols and His Five Pennies, Duke Ellington and His Orchestra, Louis Armstrong and His Hot Five, and Jimmy O'Bryant's Famous Original Washboard Band.[78]

Not only was Dodge on the right track, but one also cannot help but be impressed—whether it was written in 1925 or 1929—by the list of musicians, including King Oliver, Fletcher Henderson, Duke Ellington, and Louis Armstrong, none of whom were composers of fox-trots.

After this major article, Dodge published another, also significant, in 1934. In "Harpsichords and Jazz Trumpets"[79] can be found transcriptions of several solos by Bubber Miley on different takes of Duke Ellington's "Black and Tan Fantasy." Let us note in passing that Dodge was—as were some early transcribers of Negro spirituals—clearly conscious of the limitations of transcription. He clarifies this precisely in the context of jazz:

Contrary to the modern academician and similar to the early composers, jazz musicians give forth a folk utterance, impossible to notate adequately. For even if every little rest, 64th note, slide, trill, mute, blast, and rhythmic accent is approximately notated and handed back to them, it is impossible to get them to read it.[80]

This transcription is followed by what we must undeniably call a musical analysis of the recording, probably one of the very first of its kind. This analysis is fascinating in many respects. Dodge does not provide an explicit theoretical framework for improvised solos and their analysis, but he actually uses certain notions that will later be formalized by other authors. For example, in this passage:

> As I have said, Negro improvisations are either on the melody or on the harmony, and it would appear that Miley paid no attention to the melody, so far removed are his variations; but by playing certain parts of the theme, then the corresponding part in any one of the hot solos, you will find that many times he did have the theme in mind.[81]

This quote takes into account reception and conscious intention: the listener might not have noticed that the head melody was present in the improvisation, but close examination shows that the performer was clearly conscious of making reference to it.

Leaving that subject behind, the author then proceeds with general considerations on the evolution of jazz and its reception. At the conclusion, we find a certain skepticism toward the existing commentary of the time, alternately positive and negative. The argument finally leads to an impassioned call for analysis:

> Of the many American writings on jazz, both pro and con, few are knowledgeably critical, none of any instructive value. There are magazines and articles in Europe with an attitude towards jazz as serious music, that we haven't approached. And there is Prunières,[82] the one important critic, to my knowledge, who has an appreciation of the improvised solo in jazz. The American criticisms on the subject seem confusedly to hover around on the one hand, the spirit of America, the brave tempo of modern life, absence of sentimentalism, the importance of syncopation and the good old Virginia cornfields; and on the other hand, the monotonous beat, the unmusical noises, the jaded Harlem Negro, alcoholism, and sexual debauch. These solos in the Black and Tan Fantasy may not have the significance I attribute to them but they could at least be a premise for criticism. As notated music it certainly is not just noise, squawks, and monotonous rhythm: nor do vague favourable praises seem appropriate. Such solos as I have printed demand musical investigation.[83]

This contribution is substantial.[84] Not only did Dodge warn as early as 1925 that jazz was to be found not only in George Gershwin or Paul Whiteman, but he also set essential marks for the foundations of technical analysis that were adapted to jazz from 1934. He therefore paved the way for a musicology of jazz whose foundations Winthrop Sargeant would clarify for the most part in his 1938 *Jazz: Hot and Hybrid*, and which a collection of musicologists would broaden after World War II, starting with André Hodeir and Gunther Schuller, who were subsequently followed by many others.

As important as some of their commentaries may have been, I believe the French-speaking writers on jazz cannot be regarded as forerunners, with the flamboyant exception of Ernest Ansermet. And on major topics such as the history and pre-history of jazz, Panassié at least is a long way from the knowledge of the main American commentators. It is highly embarrassing to quote this page from *Le jazz hot*, wherein Panassié naively reveals his complete lack of knowledge in this field:

We don't know exactly what the origins of the hot style, nor the origins of jazz music itself, are. The French trumpet player Ray Binder, under the title "History of jazz," published a few articles on the subject, briefly summing up the most likely hypothesis about these origins. First, the distant source of jazz music: "Once upon a time there was a country where chained-up Negroes worked as slaves for nasty New Orleans ship-owners. This country, located in the southeast of the United States, has the Mississipi[85] as its main arterial route. At the time, confining the river was of great importance, as it was always threatening the neighboring cotton fields. Blacks imported from Africa were employed for this work. These Negroes where intensely unhappy: most of them pushed stakes into the ground and, to help each other, they did the job in *rhythm*, a rhythm that obviously had to be slow and steady. Their laments inevitably became songs in rhythm and it seems natural to see in this the origin of 'sung blues.' Negroes don't forget easily, and a few years later the black slave, now a free citizen, would teach his children the painful songs of his ancestors— *Saint Louis Blues, Memphis Blues, New Orleans Blues*, etc—while scratching an old banjo. Here is the national repertory that any American Negro knows and reveres, just as much as we revere our old French songs." Binder then recounts how, during the early part of our century, around the year 1903, some poor wretches put together street bands in New Orleans featuring cornet, clarinet, banjo, drums and trombone, playing old-time Negro themes. These street bands quickly became popular and were soon copied by numerous black and white musicians. This was the origin of the first jazz bands, which gained early success in America, mainly as dance orchestras for ragtime, blues, cake-walk.[86]

We should not forget that Panassié was at the time very young (twenty-two years old when his book was published) and that he lived in France, far not only from the music itself but also from other magazines and books on the subject; these, of course, did not travel quickly in those early days. However, it is impossible to ignore how incomplete his knowledge was, at least in terms of the origins of jazz. It is clear Panassié was forced to rely on a series of articles by another French author and probably did not read anything else. Not only does he take for granted a story that was highly problematic—even in 1934—about the sudden birth of jazz in 1903, but he is obviously ignorant of the provenance of "Saint Louis Blues" and "Memphis Blues," composed by W. C. Handy in 1909-12 and 1917 respectively and as such in no way the "painful songs of [the freed black slave's] ancestors."

Let us now compare Panassié's assertions with the simple diagram (below) that appeared in Winthrop Sargeant's *Jazz: Hot and Hybrid*,[87] published only four years later (1938).

This diagram could be used today in a jazz history class with only a few modifications. There is no comparison with the meager, nebulous, and anecdotal overview imparted by Panassié. Besides history, Sargeant addresses issues of aesthetics, rhythm, melody, scalar structure, blues, harmony, African influence, and form, referencing musicians such as Louis Armstrong, Benny Goodman, Benny Carter, Fletcher Henderson, Duke Ellington, the Mound City Blue Blowers, the Mitchell Christian Singers, Frankie Trumbauer, Bix Beiderbecke, and Bessie Smith. This is, for me, another turning point in the history of jazz commentary: the start of what we would now call a musicological approach to the music. Sargeant himself conveyed this very simply in his introduction to the book:

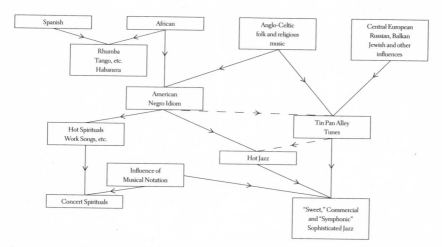

Jazz origins and influences. Winthrop Sargeant, *Jazz: Hot and Hybrid*. New York: Da Capo, 1975, p. 45.

The particular field that *Jazz: Hot and Hybrid* sets out to explore however, has, as far as I am aware, remained almost exclusively its own. It is not primarily a critical or a biographical or a historical book. Its purpose is descriptive. What evaluation it contains is limited mainly to the consideration of jazz as a type of art compared with other types of art. Its task has been to define jazz, to analyse its musical anatomy, to trace its origins and influences, to indicate the features that distinguish it from other kinds of music and that give it its unique place in the music of the world.[88]

With this apparently modest agenda, the book actually calls for a less passionate and polemical approach in favor of an approach that would focus primarily on the music itself, in its various aspects, which is nothing less than a highly ambitious program.

The enormous gap between the two authors—Panassié and Sargeant—is perhaps exemplified by these two simple facts: (1) jazz music was not only born on one side of the Atlantic but, in the 1920s and 1930s, still lived and developed there, and (2) what we would describe as a tradition of criticism started somewhere around the middle of nineteenth century on the same side of the Atlantic and did not exist (or was far less developed) on the other side.

A Revision of the Canon?

One question has been left latent up to this point: should the jazz canon of the '20s and '30s, hardly defended and in some way imposed by some of the authors discussed here, giving priority to "authentic" hot jazz over the straight or symphonic jazz as embodied by Paul Whiteman and George Gershwin, be revised today?

John Howland very recently published a really interesting book that takes a fresh approach to early jazz and its reception. This is not the place to explore the question of reevaluating this music and the position of Paul Whiteman.[89] It suffices to say that I agree with the author when he states:

> Beyond the formal evidence that Ellington might have adapted a generic formal model from the forgotten concert works of the Whiteman camp, there is also significant biographical evidence of Ellington-Whiteman connections. This evidence does not mean that Ellington did not draw more abstract compositional inspiration from African American peers—and friends—like James P. Johnson and William Grant Still. He very likely did to some level, but I have found few obvious signs of formal modeling, or even biographical evidence linking Ellington's extended jazz works to the concert works of these two individuals.[90]

Therefore, I would like to propose a slightly different perspective, albeit very close to Howland's. He uses large categories such as "concert jazz" or "modern American music" to which Paul Whiteman, Duke Ellington, or James P. Johnson could be linked at some stages of their work and under some conditions. This is very much about the modalities of historical perspective. One way of evading the classic alternatives such as diachrony/synchrony or music/culture is to think about the historical totality as a braid that tangles up a multitude of threads, made up of as many partial and local histories as have their own degree of autonomy. These threads can be properly musical: instruments (a history of the piano, of drums, trumpet, etc.), orchestral templates (a history of the trio, the quintet, the big band, etc.), musical parameters (a history of rhythm, harmony, melody, form, sound), musical practice (a history of improvisation, arranging, composing, etc.). These threads may be based on a common identity, (a history of black musicians, white musicians, female musicians, etc.), a shared geography (a history of jazz in Europe, in New Orleans, New York, London, Africa, etc.), a social network (a history of jazz places, the jazz economy, jazz sociability), and many other criteria. Some musicians will appear simultaneously or successively in one or more threads of the braid, some will be decisive in one thread or another, some completely absent from those threads. None of them will appear in all of these partial histories.[91]

It seems to me that for the question at hand, we can single out four of these threads. So, we have a history of scoring, a history of improvisation, a history of small bands, and a history of large bands. John Howland reproaches some of the critics of the 1930s—Roger Pryor Dodge, Hugues Panassié, Frederic Ramsey Jr., and Charles Edward Smith (we could add Robert Goffin) for having "constructed" a myth of hot jazz, created through improvisation in small bands, as opposed to sweet, commercial jazz, using scoring for large bands: the former being "authentic," the latter "unauthentic." It is easy to fall in with this perceived duality of good and evil (often associated with the fundamental dichotomy of black/white). It seems obvious to me that there is a tradition of scoring in jazz, probably starting with the fanfares of late nineteenth century, with John Philip Sousa and James Reese Europe, and tracing a line through Jelly Roll Morton, Duke Ellington, Paul Whiteman, Fletcher Henderson, Benny Goodman, Count Basie, Cab Calloway, Dizzy Gillespie, Stan Kenton, Woody Herman, Jimmy Giuffre, Charles Mingus, Gil Evans, George Russell, John Zorn, Maria Schneider, John Hollenbeck, Avishai Cohen, etc. And of course, there is no need to mention the most prestigious jazz musicians who define the fundamental, core tradition of improvisation, some of whom are in the list above. Both traditions, both threads, include black and white musicians and have the same legitimacy.

To be fair, though, one can understand that there was a serious risk with the early reception of jazz (during the late 1910s and 1920s) that only one side—the 327 scored, large-ensemble thread, if you want to look at it that way—would alone have been acknowledged as representing jazz, the whole of jazz.[92] A strong shift was needed to throw light on what could have remained obscure, such as the music played by small bands in New Orleans, Chicago, and a few other places. And as is often the case in these circumstances, it had to be done in a very isolated, partisan way—the issue, moreover, sometimes was muddied by other paradigmatic threads such as black/white, inauthentic/authentic, etc. But it is easier to denounce these "constructs" once time has passed and history has revealed some direction and balancing factors. As confusing as they may have been, the positions of Dodge, Goffin, Panassié, Charles Edward Smith, and Frederic Ramsey Jr. should still, in my opinion, be considered of capital importance.

About Racism

I would like to conclude with one last reflection. Among the most significant arguments for the desired better reception and understanding of jazz in Europe and by Europeans is the issue of racism. Racism would have been less virulent in Europe than in the United States, with two consequences, the first relating to the ideological frameworks around ways of thinking, the second to everyday life. The first point is that white Americans would have found it impossible to consider the creations of African Americans objectively because of ideological barriers of which they were unconscious. This may have some relevance on a general level, but obviously not as far as individuals are concerned. The few examples quoted at the beginning of this article—and dozen of others could be cited—show clearly that some commentators, at least after the abolitionist movement, could go beyond existing prejudices and consider work by black artists in a benevolent way.

As far as everyday racism is concerned, the difference is manifest, and many accounts confirm it. Among others, two direct African American witnesses, Gene Bullard and Ada "Bricktop" Smith, have reported it. Bullard came first to Scotland, then England, before landing in Paris in 1913, where he would stay until World War II. About London and England, his biographer, Craig Lloyd writes:

> According to a London correspondent, whose feature story appeared in a number of U.S. newspapers, among them the *Dawson (Ga.) News* of September 16, 1908, thousands of American Negroes had entered England "in the last year or two and thousands more are coming." The first arrivals, the story continued, were "artists and athletes who realizing that they suffered in England but few of the disabilities attached to their race in the United States" had written to friends to join them. Citing figures made available by the U.S. Embassy in London, the story reported that there were "five thousand Ameri-

can negroes in England and four thousand had come within the past year." The same source noted that a "Negro quarter" had developed in the Soho district of London, where two restaurants "were offering fried chicken, sweet corn and other delicacies dear to the negroe's heart."[93]

This fact does not hide its opposite side: some forms of racism still existed in England of that time. *but of course!*

The British Boxing Board of Control was racist in those years, refusing to recognize colored fighters as British champions in any weight class, even when they defeated white champions. English racial politics also led to a ruling by Home Secretary Winston Churchill that cancelled a scheduled fight of Jack Johnson. In spite of these disabilities, Bullard and his fraternity of expatriate boxers found England a hospitable place to live and work—a circumstance that testifies again to the oppressive racial situation existing in the United States at that time; the BBC's policy of "white only" champions and the anti-Jack Johnson spirit reflected elite British opinion—Anglican church and Governmental leaders concerned about the impact of a black British champion on imperial politics—rather than the broadly based prejudice that obtained in America.[94]

Lloyd finally speaks of a "relative racial liberalism" in England, which appears as an appropriately moderate expression.

For the African American entertainers in minstrelsy, performing in England meant a chance to make a decent living without the feeling that haunted some of their counterparts on American stages: that they were reinforcing stereotypes used to justify the American racial caste system. Furthermore, outside the English theater, black entertainers were usually treated as respectfully as they had been onstage. In those few cases where such a performer was insulted in the street, he could literally strike back, as Charles Hart, principal comedian in "Come Over Here," did. Instead of the threat of the lynch mob, Hart, who had toured in Europe as early as 1904, and his wife had the law on their side in London. The election of John R. Archer, of black West Indian ancestry, in 1914 *really?* as mayor of Battersea, one of London's boroughs, suggests the relative racial liberalism that existed in the British capital in these years.[95]

About France, Bullard himself went one step beyond the positive appreciation:

Bullard's boxing fraternity also included white American fighters such as [heavyweight Blink] McCluskey. Indeed, he [Bullard] fell in love with Paris not only because of its beauty and the friendliness of its inhabitants but also because "it seemed to me that French democracy influenced the minds of both black and white Americans there and helped us all act like brothers as near as possible."[96]

We find a similar version of a "relative racial liberalism" in Ada "Bricktop" Smith's view, a globally positive appreciation balanced by some restrictions. Bricktop, as she was usually called, arrived in Paris in 1924 and would stay, as Bullard did, until World War II.[97]

There was very little racial discrimination in Paris. In fact, there was a strong pro-Negro prejudice. There had been a lot of colored soldiers in Europe during the war, and the Parisians welcomed colored Americans as heroes. Also, of course, the Parisians identified the new jazz with Negroes. If there had been a lot of average white Americans around, *they* might have influenced the Parisians, but there weren't. White Americans in Paris who were not rich and sophisticated and well traveled were pretty rare. Anyway, the Americans didn't mix much with the Parisians. However, just across the Channel, things were very different—maybe because of the way things were across the Atlantic, in America.[98]

After coming back in 1950, she acknowledged a noticeable change.

There were other sad things about post-war Paris. There was a lot of resentment toward Americans—YANKEE GO HOME signs all over the place. At the same time, the Parisians had started picking up some distinctly American attitudes toward Negroes. It started with the American soldiers, I'm told. I never saw them in Paris. When I was there, World War I was over and World War II hadn't reached Paris. People who stayed there through World War II, though, told me that the minute the American soldiers came to France, you could just feel the prejudice in the streets. The white American soldier brought it. After the war more and more Americans—average Americans, not the quality of Cole [Porter] and his crowd—started coming, and they made it even worse. I remember hearing a French prostitute call somebody a nigger. I walked over to her and said, "Where in the world did you get that from?" she pointed to a white musician. "He told me. He told me in U.S. you don't treat them the same. *You* know, Bricktop." I said, "Don't you ever . . ." I should have knocked her down, because she became one of the biggest nigger-haters I've ever known. And all this because of a white American. Big Brother to Europe?[99]

But obviously, black American musicians felt better in Europe, where the climate was much more relaxed. We all know Louis Armstrong's recollections of being welcomed with a triumphal reception right there on the platform of a Parisian railway station. But these assumptions should be qualified. For one thing, this kind of enthusiasm, with its somewhat childish aspects, has to be taken positively for what it was—an authentic recognition of talent, be it black or otherwise—but we might also consider the element of exoticism, whereby the stranger from far away is more likely to get this sort of admiring reception. Secondly, we should note that relatively few musicians—albeit still a significant number, even if we take into account only those who had the opportunity to come to Europe—chose to stay there. Probably one of the main reasons was expressed by Miles Davis in his autobiography. On the one hand, he states:

Paris was where I understood that all white people weren't the same, that some weren't prejudiced and others were. I had kind of known this after I met Gil Evans and some other people, but I really came to know it in Paris. It was an important thing for me to know and it made me conscious of what was happening around me politically. I started noticing things that I hadn't noticed before, political stuff—what was really happening to black people. I knew about that stuff before on account of growing up around my father. But I was so much into music that I didn't really pay any attention to it. Only when it hit me right in my face did I do something about it."[100]

Some pages later, though, Davis says:

And while I didn't love being in America all the time, I never thought about moving over to Paris. I really loved Paris, but I loved it to visit, because I didn't think the music could or would happen for me over there. Plus, the musicians who moved over there seemed to me to lose something, an energy, an edge, that living in the States gave them. I don't know, but I think it has something to do with being surrounded by a culture that you know, that you can feel, that you come out of. If I lived in Paris, I couldn't just go and hear some great blues, or people like Monk and Trane and Duke and Satchmo every night, like I could in New York. And although there were good, classically trained musicians in Paris, they still didn't hear the music like an American musician did. I couldn't live in Paris for all those reasons.[101]

There was undoubtedly racism in the United States, but some kind of musical intensity too. And we should not forget there was also racism on this side of the Atlantic—in France, for example. Consider this astonishing and horrifying account by Al Lirvat, a black trombonist from the West Indies who spent most of his career in metropolitan France between the 1940s and the 1990s. During World War II, Lirvat was in Paris under the German occupation. This is what he has to say when Michael Zwerin asks him about this period:

I knew many German musicians and jazz fans who had been in Paris before the war. They spoke French, now they were back as soldiers. We drank together in the cafes. We had French passports. Nobody tried to send us to the camps. I felt no racism. I never knew anybody who had any trouble for being black. I remember a cafe with a sign in the window, "No Jews or Niggers," but that was the French who did that. The French were much more racist against blacks than the Germans.[102]

On another hand, racism probably had less of a presence in the press and among commentators during the 1920s. But it would be unwise to deduce that it did not exist and could not be virulent. Consider this assertion by a renowned French writer, published in *La Revue Musicale* in 1931:

> Jazz is, cynically speaking, the orchestra of bullies with non-opposable thumbs and still prehensile feet from the forest of Voodoo. It is all excess, and by that stage, more than monotonous: the ape is left alone, without lifestyle, without discipline, fallen in the whole undergrowth of instinct, showing his naked flesh in every leap, while the flesh of his heart is even more obscene. These slaves should be suppressed.[103]

well, that is worse.

Conclusion

This kind of extreme manifestation was fortunately rare and should not blind us to the genuine cultural differences between the two continents, which include the issue of racism. But however much less virulent racism may have been in France, for example, as far as the reception of jazz is concerned, I believe this aspect was largely offset by an obvious cultural and geographical distinction: the music was mainly not in these countries but in the United States. That means most of the commentators, whether they are named Panassié or Goffin, who made that transatlantic journey were far from the music itself and from its context.[104] As a result, a long tradition of commentary on jazz had been established in United States before jazz itself even existed there, a tradition based on the study of Negro spirituals and black popular music, ragtime and blues, to which American observers could refer while Europeans had to start from scratch. Scott De-Veaux made a kind of similar assessment some twenty years ago:

> For Panassié, the history of jazz was necessarily abstract, a narrative to be deduced from the evidence of recordings and supported by shadowy speculation. In America, by contrast, that history was more concrete. Although still remote, it could be traced in the urban topography of New Orleans and Chicago, in the memory of those who listened to it, and, above all, in the direct testimony of those who created it.[105]

Before closing, I would like to make my point very clear. My attempt is not to redefine a whole relation between Europe and the United States in the early days of jazz and its commentary. I did not talk about Alfredo Casella and Fernando

Liuzzi in Italy,[106] Robert William Sigismund Mendl in England,[107] Paul Bernhard and Bernhard Egg in Germany. I did not evoke what appears to have been
the first jazz class in the world, opened by Mátyás Seiber at the Hoch Conservatory in Frankfurt, nor many other texts and events of which I have little knowledge. The purpose here was only to answer a very limited and local question:
what was the specific role of Europeans (especially the French) in the definition
of territories? To finally answer, I would reassert first that one needs to distinguish
two groups here. For the first group—Schaeffner, Hoérée, Baresel, Burian, and
some others—the dilemma was not to choose between, on the one hand, Gershwin and Whiteman, and on the other hand, Oliver, Armstrong, and Ellington.
What comprised jazz for them was only the Fisk Jubilee Singers, Roland Hayes,
Paul Whiteman, Ernst Krenek with his *Jonny spielt auf*, and composers of fox-
trots, understood through written scores. These authors of course partly missed
the point, whatever contours one would define for it, but put some obvious claims
(technical among others) on the table. Others writers, headed by Robert Goffin
and Hugues Panassié, made a contribution that consisted of a more balanced
knowledge of the music of the day, even if their knowledge of its historical
dimension was more than questionable. But it becomes obvious that they were
not the only, nor the first, ones to do so. Therefore, it appears to me that it is not in
keeping with the reality of the music and its commentary to say that Europe,
located far away from the music as it was actually played and left unmarked by the
tradition of commentary tradition, "discovered" jazz.

NOTES

The first part of this article, and more generally this research, owes much to Karl Koenig
and his amazing compilation of musical texts: *Jazz in Print (1856-1929): An Anthology of
Selected Early Redings* (Hillsdale: Pendragon, 2002).

1. Spaulding, 1863, in Koenig, *Jazz in Print*, p. 3.

2. Ibid., p. 5.

3. Ibid.

4. Anonymous, 1900, in Koenig, *Jazz in Print*, p. 60.

5. Anonymous, 1901a, in ibid., p. 67.

6. Anonymous, 1901b, in ibid., p. 636.

7. Sherlock, 1901, in ibid., p. 638.

8. Ibid., p. 66.

9. The article first appeared in German in a periodical called *Die Musik* and was
translated the following year and published in *Metronome*.

10. Kühl, 1902, in Koenig, *Jazz in Print*, pp. 75-76.

11. Jelly Roll Morton claimed to have written "New Orleans Blues" in 1902. See, for
example, Hardie, 2004.

12. Seagrove, 1915.

13. Niles, 1926a, p. 5.

14. Ibid., p. 6.

15. Ibid., p. 14.

16. Among them are Gustav Kühl's article from 1902, quoted above, and an article about ragtime in the *London Times*, February 8, 1913, by Arnold Bennett.

17. "[Murray Pilcer and Gaby Deslys] danced on this storm of rhythms and drums a kind of tame disaster" (Cocteau, 1918, p. 433).

18. Ansermet, 1919, as translated in Walser, 1999, p. 11.

19. Which may to some extent be considered normal for a renowned conductor (Ansermet was at the time in London to conduct Diaghilev's Russian Ballet Orchestra).

20. Ansermet, 1919 [my translation], p. 125.

21. Ibid., p. 128.

22. Ibid., p. 129.

23. Ibid., p. 130.

24. Spaulding, 1863, in Koenig, *Jazz in Print*, p. 3.

25. Ibid., p. 131.

26. Ibid.

27. Andrew Fry, for example, talks of the "the casual racism of an earlier era—less ill-intent than ignorance." Another of his statements makes me more uncomfortable. Denouncing, with good reason, the highly problematic late text by Ansermet (*Les fondations de la musique dans la conscience humaine* [The Foundations of Music in Human Consciousness]), published in 1961, Fry declares: "Thus jazz history has, for decades, celebrated the text of a man who was not only fairly ambivalent about the music, but whose extraordinary, racialized historiography trapped jazz in an unending cycle of its folk tradition." Can we criticize a text for positions adopted by the same author forty-two years later? I would also add that, even if one may not agree with the 1919 Ansermet's vision of the possible future of jazz and believe that, on that point, he was wrong in his predictions, we have to acknowledge that, for one thing, this future was not so easy to envisage, and, for another and most significantly, it was a question that cropped up again and again throughout the 1920s. Ansermet (again in 1919 but not in 1961) was in a sense initiating this important debate we have talked about. Finally: if one declares, for example, that blues evolved less than jazz, would it be an act of "racialized historiography trapping blues in an unending cycle of its folk tradition"? This is often the problem with that particular approach to what looks like the well-known "hermeneutics of suspicion," as Paul Ricoeur called them: one is quickly trapped in this double bind. On the one hand ("jazz will not evolve"), one risks being accused of regarding this music and its musicians as primitive. On the other ("jazz will evolve"), one will be considered Eurocentric for being unable to perceive music other than in the ideological framework of Western art music, or within a linear evolutionary scheme.

28. Same for Schaeffner's or Hoérée's texts quoted hereafter.

29. For a taste of actual racist positions in France during this period, see the end of the present article.

30. See Fry, 2008. This would not prevent Ansermet, on the other hand, from including

Marian Anderson singing Negro spirituals, as well as Mozart, in some of the concerts he organized in 1934 in Switzerland (see Tappolet, 2006, pp. 132–35).

31. Schaeffner and Coeuroy, 1988. Schaeffner is the actual author of the book. Coeuroy had collected responses to jazz from a series of personalities of the day, and commented on them in an appendix.

32. Baresel, 1926.

33. Osgood, 1926.

34. Whiteman, 1926.

35. Knowlton, 1926.

36. Niles, 1926b.

37. Handy, 1926.

38. Schwerké, 1926.

39. Copland, 1926.

40. Egg, 1927.

41. Bernhard, 1927.

42. Hoérée, 1927.

43. Schaeffner and Coeuroy, 1988, p. 14

44. Ibid., pp. 73–74.

45. Ibid., pp. 70–71.

46. Ibid., pp. 109–10.

47. Ibid., p. 103.

48. As a point of comparison, that same year, 1929, Abbe Niles cited in a report on jazz records by Duke Ellington, Red Nichols, Joe Venuti, Eddie Lang, Frankie Trumbauer, Donald Lindley, Red McKenzie, Eddie Condon, Paul Whiteman, Nat Shilkret, Ben Bernie, Rube Bloom, the Original Wolverines, Wilton Crawley, Seger Ellis, Clarence Williams, Louis Armstrong, Peg Leg Howell, Bessie Smith, and Clara Smith (Niles, 1929).

49. Hoérée, 1927, p. 216.

50. Ibid., pp. 217–18.

51. Ibid., p. 218.

52. Ibid., p. 227.

53. Ibid. *"Avoir le cafard"* could indeed be translated accurately as "having the blues."

54. It is interesting to note that Hoérée cites the possible origin of the word "jazz" by referring to the well-known story of a supposed musician in Chicago named Jasbo Brown. Hoérée tells the story as coming from a "Roger Graham, music publisher in Chicago" but does not name any other source. It seems this story had first been told in an anonymous article in *Current Opinion* from August 1919, entitled "Delving into the Genealogy of Jazz," itself citing "the *New York Telegraph*, Broadway's own gazette" (Anonymous, 1919). There is little chance of Hoérée's having read this article. But another fact indicates that one of Hoérée's main sources—as it was for other French (and European?) authors—might have been *Jazz* by Paul Whiteman. Indeed, the story is told in Whiteman's book (Whiteman, 1926, pp. 17–19), but the "music publisher in Chicago" is here a promoter called Joseph Gorham. If this is true, then in a sense, Whiteman would have been the one who passed on the information.

55. Hoérée, 1927, p. 213.

56. Although Catherine Parsonage seems to think that they were available in England as early as 1919 (Parsonage, 2003, n. 2, p. 324).

57. See Miller, 2005.

58. In Burian, 1928, p. 9, translated and quoted in Matzner, 2001, p. 182.

59. Burian, 1928, p. 10, in Matzner, 2001, p. 182.

60. In Matzner, 2001, p. 183.

61. Milhaud, 1924, *in* Koenig 2002, p. 359.

62. Milhaud, 1927, *in* Brierre 2000, p. 18.

63. An allusion to Jean Cocteau playing the drums at the Gaya, soon to become Le Bœuf sur le Toit.

64. Auric, 1979, pp. 171–72.

65. Goffin, 1932.

66. Panassié, 1934.

67. From the Brabant, a part of Belgium.

68. Goffin, 1932, p. 11.

69. Ibid., pp. 11–12.

70. An allusion, of course, to *Le jazz* by Schaeffner and Coeuroy.

71. Goffin, 1932, p. 13.

72. Panassié, 1934, p. 25.

73. Ibid., pp. 25–26.

74. Kennedy, 1987, p. 37.

75. Ibid., p. 38.

76. Or at least that is the way his son, Pryor Dodge, describes it in the collection of his father's articles that he edited (Dodge, 1995, pp. ix-x).

77. Dodge, 1995, p. 3.

78. Ibid., p. 7.

79. Dodge, 1995.

80. Ibid., p. 16.

81. Ibid., p. 25.

82. Henry Prunières (1886–1942), French music critic. Founded *La Revue Musicale* and author of, among other writings, a history of music. He was a very early enthusiast of jazz.

83. Ibid., p. 26.

84. In the same context, we could also have mentioned Robert Donaldson Darrell and his several reviews of Duke Ellington in the *Phonograph Monthly Review*, starting in 1927 (Tucker, 1993, pp. 33–40).

85. Like Robert Goffin and other French-speaking authors, Panassié uses the misspelling "Mississipi," with a single "p."

86. Panassié, 1934, pp. 55–56.

87. Sargeant, 1975, p. 45.

88. Ibid., p. 9.

89. Let us note only how omnipresent he is in these commentaries—in France, obviously, in Europe, and the United States most probably. Even if one does not wish to

reevaluate the music, it is evident that Whiteman was central to this musical world at the time under consideration.

90. Howland, 2009, pp. 147-48. I would agree even more with the last sentence of this statement: "Evidence suggests that part of Ellington's compositional development involved the adaptation, expansion, and ultimate transcendence of a formal model that was popular among his white arranger peers. The wholly American tensions of race, class, and cultural identity that unduly attach themselves to this observation create an unfortunate potential for misunderstanding" (p. 147).

91. I developed this point in chapter 17 of *Analyser le jazz* (Cugny, 2009).

92. To give a final example of this, I shall quote a passage from a music initiation book published as late as 1935. Hugues Panassié was involved in some of the articles in the index, but not in this section on jazz (the author may have been Émile Vuillermoz): "One cannot ignore the numerous jazz composers, the most representative of whom is the American George Gershwin (1898), author of the famous *Rhapsody in Blue* and of the operettas *Tip-Toes, Lady Be Good,* etc. . . . Otherwise, specialists in jazz composition are generally anonymous and lend their themes to musicians enjoying popular success, such as Irving Berlin, Holländer, Erwin, Friml, Abraham, Goodwin, Brown, Vincent Youmans, author of the famous *No, No, Nanette,* Romberg, etc. Let us also note the most famous jazz groups, those of Paul Whiteman, Jack Hylton, Ted Lewis, Duke Ellington, Ray Ventura, etc., who have maintained a well-crafted repertoire and who continue to uphold the rich possibilities of a musical form that has paid its dues to excessive popularization" (see the collection from 1935, pp. 105-6; Ray Ventura was a famous French bandleader of the 1930s).

93. Lloyd, 2006, p. 29.

94. Ibid., p. 33.

95. Ibid., p. 31.

96. Ibid., p. 36.

97. Actually, they worked together since Bullard managed the Grand Duc in Montmartre where Bricktop made her Parisian debut as a singer-dancer. She was about to become one the most famous figures of Paris nightlife throughout the 1920s and '30s. The successive nightclubs she managed were centers of life for a very rich American society traveling in France and sometimes living there for a while, including figures such as F. Scott Fitzgerald and Cole Porter.

98. Bricktop and Haskins, 1983, p. 127.

99. Ibid., p. 238.

100. Davis, 1989, p. 129.

101. Ibid., p. 218.

102. Zwerin, 2000, p. 40. Even as late as the end of the 1950s, Juliette Gréco recalls terrible situations in everyday Parisian life when she was with Miles Davis. I personally experienced a very embarrassing display of brutal racism with the blues player Lucky Peterson in France in 1995. Most of today's musicians of African, West Indian, or Arabic origin can tell many such stories.

103. André Suarès, in Panassié 1946, pp. 66-67. Some of Suarès's writing was also brutally misogynistic. Yet it is not a little paradoxical to note that, born of a Jewish father,

Suarès was pursued by the Germans and the French Milice (militia) during World War II. On some other matters—literary, for example, but also political—he could be regarded as progressive.

104. Which they knew mainly from recordings—perhaps that explains why the first general discography of jazz was put together by a Frenchman, Charles Delaunay (Delaunay, 1936).

105. DeVeaux. 1991, p. 532.

106. See Mazzoletti, 2004.

107. See Parsonage, 2003 and 2005.

BIBLIOGRAPHY

Allen, William Francis, Charles Pickard Ware, and Lucy McKim. 1867. *Slave Songs of the United States*. New York: Simpson.

Anonymous 1856a. "Songs of the Blacks." *Dwight's Journal*, November 15, 1856.

Anonymous 1856b. "Slave Funerals." *Houma (LA) Ceres*, January 17, 1856.

Anonymous 1856c. "The Lilliputian Musicians." *Charleston Mercury*, November 22, 1856.

Anonymous 1899a. "Ragtime." *The Shreveport Sunday Judge*, 1899/05/04.

Anonymous 1899b. "Syncopated Music." *Brainard's Musical Journal*, Autumn 1899.

Anonymous 1900. "Ragtime." *The Musician*, March 1900, in Koenig 2002, p. 60.

Anonymous 1901a. "Syncopated Rhythm vs. 'Ragtime.'" *American Musician*, July 1901, in Koenig 2002, p. 67.

Anonymous 1901b. "Suppression of Ragtime." *American Musician*, July 1901, in Koenig 2002, p. 63.

Anonymous 1919. "Delving into the Genealogy of Jazz." *Current Opinion* 67, no. 2, August 1919, pp. 97–99.

Ansermet, Ernest. 1919. "Sur un orchestre nègre." *La Revue Romande*, Lausanne, October 15, 1919, no. 10, pp. 10–13. In Tappolet, 2006, pp. 125–32.

Arom, Simha. 1985. *Polyphonies et polyrythmies instrumentales d'Afrique centrale*. Paris: Selaf.

Auric, Georges. 1979. *Quand j'étais là . . .* Paris: Grasset.

Ballanta-Taylor, Nicholas J. G. 1925. *St. Helena Island Spirituals, Recorded and Transcribed at Penn Normal, Industrial and Agricultural School, St. Helena Island, Beaufort County, South Carolina*. New York: Schirmer.

Baresel, Alfred. 1926. *Das Jazz-Buch*. Jul Heins. Zimmerman.

———. 1929. *Das Neue Jazz-Buch*. Wilhelm Zimmerman.

Barton, William E. D. D. 1898. "Old Plantation Hymns." *New England Magazine*, 1898/02, 25, 4, pp. 445–56.

———. 1899a. "Hymns of the Slave and the Freedman." *New England Magazine*, 1899/01, 19, 5, pp. 609–24.

———. 1899b. "Recent Negroes Melodies." *New England Magazine*, 1899/02, 19, 6, pp. 707–19.

Bechet, Sidney. 1978. *Treat It Gentle: An Autobiography*. New York: Da Capo.

Bernhard, Paul. 1927. *Jazz, eine Musikalische Zeitfrage*. München.

Brailoiu, Constantin. 1949. "Le folklore musical." *Musica aeterna*. Zurich: M. S. Metz, pp. 277-332.

Bricktop, with James Haskins. 1983. *Bricktop*. New York: Atheneum.

Brierre, Jean-Dominique. 2000. *Le jazz français de 1900 à aujourd'hui*. Paris: Hors collection.

Cocteau, Jean. 1918. *Le coq et l'arlequin*. In Cocteau, Jean, *Romans, poésies, œuvres diverses*. Paris: Le livre de poche, 1995.

Collective. 1935. *L'initiation à la musique: À l'usage des amateurs de musique et de radio*. Paris: Éditions du Tambourinaire.

Copland, Aaron. 1926. "Jazz Structure and Influence." *Modern Music*, November/December 1926, in Koenig 2002, pp. 495-96.

Crozat Converse, Charles. 1899. "Ragtime." *Etude*, June 1899.

Cugny, Laurent. 2009. *Analyser le jazz*. Paris: Outre Mesure.

Davis, Miles. 1989. *The Autobiography*. New York: Simon and Schuster.

Delaunay, Charles. 1936. *Hot Discography*. Paris: Jazz Hot.

DeVeaux, Scott. 1991. "Constructing the Jazz Tradition: Jazz Historiography." *Black American Literature Forum* 25, no. 3, 1991, pp. 525-60.

Dodge, Roger Pryor. 1929. "Negro Jazz." *The Dancing Time*. London, October 1929, in Dodge 1995, pp. 3-8.

———. 1934. "Harpsichords and Jazz Trumpets." *Hound & Horn*, July-September 1934, in Dodge 1995, pp. 12-26.

Dodge, Pryor (son of Roger Pryor Dodge). 1995. *Hot Jazz and Jazz Dance: Roger Pryor Dodge, Collected Writings, 1929-1964*. New York: Oxford University Press.

Egg, Bernhard. 1927. *Jazz Fremwörterbuch*. Leipzig: W. Ehrler and Co.

Fenner, Thomas, and Frederic Rathbun. 1874. *Cabin and Plantation Songs as Sung by the Hampton Students*. New York: Putnam's Sons.

Fry, Andrew. 2008. *Remembrance of Jazz Past: Sidney Bechet in France*. Queen's University: Belfast.

Goffin, Robert. *Aux frontières du jazz*. Paris: Sagittaire, 1932.

Handy, W. C. 1926. *Blues: An Anthology*. New York: Albert and Charles Boni.

Hardie, Daniel. 2004. *The Ancestry of Jazz: A Musical Family History*. Lincoln: iUniverse.

Harney, Ben. 1897. *Ben Harney's Ragtime Instructor*. Chicago: Sol Blum.

Hoérée, Arthur. "Le jazz." *Revue Musicale*, October 1927, no. 12, pp. 213-41.

Howland, John. 2009. *Ellington Uptown: Duke Ellington, James P. Johnson, and the Birth of Concert Jazz*. Ann Arbor: University of Michigan Press.

Johnson, James Weldon, and J. Rosamond Johnson. 1925. *The Book of American Negro Spirituals*. New York: Viking Press.

———. 1926. *The Second Book of Negro Spirituals*. New York: Viking Press.

Kennedy, Raymond F. 1987. "Jazz Style and Improvisation Codes." *Yearbook for Traditional Music* 19, pp. 37-43.

Knowlton, Don. 1926. "The Anatomy of Jazz." *Harper's*, March 1926, in Koenig 2002, pp. 457-61.

Koenig, Karl. 2002. *Jazz in Print (1856-1929): An Anthology of Selected Early Readings.* Hillsdale: Pendragon.

Kühl, Gustav. 1902. "The Musical Possibilities of Ragtime." *Metronome* 19, March 1903.

———. "Ragtime." *Die Musik,* vol. 1, August 1902, translation in Koenig 2002, pp. 74-76.

Liuzzi, Fernando. 1927. "'Jazz' e 'Anti-jazz.'" *Nuova Antologia* 251, pp. 70-76.

Lloyd, Craig. 2006. *Eugene Bullard: Black Expatriate in Jazz-Age Paris.* Athens: University of Georgia Press.

Martin, Denis-Constant, and Olivier Roueff. 2002. *La France du jazz, Musique, modernité et identité dans la première moitié du XXe siècle.* Marseille: Parenthèses.

Matzner, Antonín. 2001. "The Beginnings of Theoretical Reflections on Jazz in Bohemia 1918-1962." *Musicologica Olomucensia* 6, pp. 179-192.

Mazzoletti, Adriano. 2004. *Il jazz in Italia dalle origini alle grandi orchestre.* Torino: EDT.

Mendl, Robert William Sigismund. 1927. *The Appeal of Jazz.* London: P. Allan and Co.

Milhaud, Darius. 1924. "Jazz-Band et instruments mécaniques—Les ressources nouvelles de la musique." *L'esprit nouveau* 25, July 1924, in Martin and Roueff 2002, pp. 178-81.

———. 1927. *Études.* Paris: Claude Aveline, in Brierre 2000, p. 18.

Miller, Mark. 2005. *Some Hustling This!—Taking Jazz to the World 1914-1929.* Toronto: Mercury.

Niles, Abbe. 1926a. In Handy 1926, pp. 1-41.

———. 1926b. "Blue Notes." *New Republic,* February 3, 1926.

———. 1929. "Jazz 1928: An Index Expugatorius." *Bookman* 68, no. 5, January 1929, pp. 570-72.

Osgood, Henry. 1926. "Jazz." *American Speech* 1, no. 10, July 1926, pp. 513-18.

Panassié, Hugues. 1934. *Le jazz hot.* Paris: Corrêa.

———. 1936. *Hot Jazz: The Guide to Swing Music.* New York: Whitmard and Sons.

———. 1946. *Douze années de jazz (1927-1938).* Paris: Corrêa.

Parsonage, Catherine. 2003. "A Critical Reassessment of the Reception of Early Jazz in Britain." *Popular Music* 22, no. 3, October 2003.

———. 2005. *The Evolution of Jazz in Britain, 1880-1935.* Aldershot: Ashgate.

Ping-Robbins, Nancy R. 1998. *Scott Joplin: A Guide to Research.* New York: Garland.

Ramsey, Guthrie P., Jr. 1996. "Cosmopolitan or Provincial? Ideology in Early Black Music Historiography, 1867-1940." *Black Music Research Journal* 16, no. 1 (Spring 1996), pp. 11-42.

Sargeant, Winthrop. 1975. *Jazz: Hot and Hybrid.* New York: Da Capo.

Scarborough, Dorothy. 1916. "The 'Blues' as Folk-Songs." *Journal of the Folklore Society of Texas,* 1916.

Schaeffner, André, and André Coeuroy. 1988. *Le jazz.* Paris: Claude Aveline, 1926, new edition Paris: Jean-Michel Place.

Schwerké, Irwing. 1926. "Le jazz est mort! Vive le jazz." *Le guide du concert,* March 12-19. 1926.

Seagrove, Gordon. 1915. "Blues Is Jazz and Jazz Is Blues." *Chicago Daily Tribune,* July 11. 1915.

Sherlock, Charles Reginald. 1901. "From Breakdown to Ragtime." *Cosmopolitan* 31, no. 6, October, pp. 631–39.

Spaulding, H. G. 1863. "Under the Palmetto." *Continental Monthly* 4, no. 2, August, pp. 188–203.

Szwed, John. *Early Jazz History and Criticism Bibliography*, http://jazzstudiesonline .org/?q=node/396.

Tappolet, Claude, ed. 2006. *Ernest Ansermet, correspondances avec des compositeurs américains (1926-1966): D'Aaron Copland à Virgil Thompson, les grands maîtres du Nouveau Monde*. Geneva: Georg.

Tucker, Mark. 1993. *The Duke Ellington Reader*. New York: Oxford University Press.

Walser, Robert. 1999. *Keeping Times: Readings in Jazz History*. New York: Oxford University Press.

Whiteman, Paul. 1926. *Jazz*. New York: J. H. Sears and Co.

Wynn, Neil, ed. 2007. *Cross the Water Blues: African American Music in Europe*. Jackson: University Press of Mississippi.

Zwerin, Mike. 2000. *Swing under the Nazis: Jazz as a Metaphor for Freedom*. New York: Cooper Square Press (1st ed.: *La tristesse de Saint Louis: Swing under the Nazis*, New York: Quartet, 1985).

JÜRGEN ARNDT

15 / EUROPEAN JAZZ DEVELOPMENTS IN CROSS-CULTURAL DIALOGUE WITH THE UNITED STATES AND THEIR RELATIONSHIP TO THE COUNTERCULTURE OF THE 1960S

I.

n 1979, the *Neue Zeitschrift für Musik* devoted a whole issue to European jazz. It was a way of reaching a wider public outside the jazz scene, drawing attention to developments since the 1960s, which were often encapsulated in the slogan "emancipation." Joachim Ernst Berendt summed up this view in his article: "European jazz has liberated itself. The time has passed when jazz musicians on our side of the Atlantic always imitated only the latest fashions from America. As part of the process of musical and social emancipation in the 60s, the European jazzers returned to their own forms of expression."[1] And Ekkehard Jost confirmed in his essay in the same issue:

> The history of jazz in Europe up until the mid-60s is characterized by the collective effort of European musicians to understand the creative processes taking place in the USA through a more or less significant phase shift. . . . From 1965 onwards, the ratio of European music to its American models gradually changed; in the late 60s, the jazz press started to think about an emerging European type of jazz.[2]

Which "type" Jost had in his mind became clear not only from his subsequent comments, which mainly concerned the trio of Peter Brötzmann, Fred van Hove, and Han Bennink, the Alexander Schlippenbach Quartet, and the Globe Unity Orchestra. This "type" was revealed also through the musicians who had the opportunity to speak in the aforementioned issue of the *Neue Zeitschrift für Musik*: Peter Brötzmann, Alexander von Schlippenbach, Jost Gebers, Willem Breuker, Misha Mengelberg, and Gunter Hampel. It provided a focus for the artistically advanced and radically improvisatory efforts that had developed particularly in the context of the so-called new music.

This emphasis underlines the importance of a German perspective—perhaps also a Continental European perspective. But what about the British point of view? Certainly there had been in England, too, developments in improvisation that included the sound patterns of "new music": for example, Derek Bailey, who was inspired by the particular sounds of Anton Webern. But the British perspective adds another important line of development: here we must mention John McLaughlin, another English guitarist, one shaped by the intense blues scene in London and no less a contributor to jazz. Stuart Nicholson emphasizes in his study of jazz rock the special significance of European jazz musicians: "When jazz rock emerged at the end of the 1960s, it was the last coherent radical jazz movement (and the only movement in jazz where European jazz musicians played a major inceptive role)."[3] Alyn Shipton confirms this point: "The earliest moves toward jazz rock began not in the United States, but in Britain, in the same musical melting pot of rhythm and blues, traditional jazz, skiffle, and bebop from which the 'British invasion' rock groups of the 1960s emerged."[4]

It is apparent that European jazz musicians have been successful in a number of respects at establishing particular signatures: in blues-based as well as advanced concert music. Both these trends are based essentially on intercultural dialogue with contemporary developments in the United States. They owe their distinctive characteristics not to a rejection but to an increasingly intense engagement with African American musical culture and developments in avant-garde art not only in Europe but also in the United States.

On the one hand there is the blues, traveling from the Mississippi Delta to the industrial city of Chicago, interpreted at once in a traditional and a modern style, and the extension of the blues into modern jazz since the 1940s. Muddy Waters and Miles Davis are representative of these trends. McLaughlin recalls his activities in the early 1960s: "I started with Alexis Korner. Alexis had everybody in his band at some point. But then I listened to Miles Davis. . . . Miles formed a new school, and I knew at once: This is my school. I kept playing rhythm and blues and it was great because we were playing real jazz solos. It was blues but at the same time it was much more than the blues."[5]

On the other hand, there was a focus on artistically advanced developments in jazz, which had a close affinity with the new music. Bailey remembers the music he played in the 1960s with the trio Joseph Holbrooke, together with drummer Tony Oxley and bass player Gavin Bryars:

Simplified, the position was that Oxley provided the connection and interest in what were then contemporary jazz developments—from Bill Evans through John Coltrane and Eric Dolphy to Albert Ayler—while Bryars' interest was in contemporary composers: Messiaen, Boulez, Stockhausen, Cage and their followers. This combination of interests, enthusiasms, obsessions, which of course overlapped in all directions, led logically and organically to a situation where the only way to pool our efforts and the only comprehensive expression of this confluence was through a freely improvised music.[6]

Among the composers listed is John Cage. The avant-garde composers in the United States owed their independence from the representatives of new music in Europe to Cage and his circle in the so-called New York school (Morton Feldman, Earle Brown, and Christian Wolf). American artists maintained their edge through the radical perpetuation of Cage's art concept—for example, the Fluxus movement.

So European improvisers, looking for their own identities in the domain of art (music), drew their impulses not only from Europe but also from artistically ambitious developments in the United States.

II. Counterculture

Since the late nineteenth century, the United States has been a template for cultural self-awareness in Europe. According to historian Hartmut Kaelble,

> The USA has been . . . an economic or a social and cultural or political (role) model, and often all at once. All the same, the US model ran counter to European feelings of superiority towards any other society worldwide and towards its own peripheral societies in Southern and Eastern Europe. These feelings had persisted since the 18th century. Therefore, the debate over the USA played a very special role in European's own self-image.[7]

However, this role has changed over the years: at the beginning of the twentieth century, the United States became the most significant challenger to the postulated superiority of Europe. Since World War I, Europe's self-image had been in crisis. Only in the 1960s and 1970s did European self-confidence gradually recover: "The deep crisis of Europe's self-image gradually receded, as from this time onwards the European standard of living improved and at least in Western Europe it was possible to establish peace within the region and a working democracy."[8]

It is evident that this changing relationship to the United States was fundamental to the reception accorded to jazz in Europe. In the same way, it is clear that the development of European self-confidence in general since the 1960s provides the broader historical context for the developing self-confidence of European jazz musicians. Moreover, there is another, even more profound link between European and U.S. cultural developments that benefited both jazz and European music: the counterculture.

From the African American civil rights movement to the anti–Vietnam War protesters, from the Beat Generation to Fluxus, from the hipster to the hippies, the counterculture provided many cultural reference points that European jazz musicians could tap into.

344

Perhaps the most significant metaphor in this respect comes from Norman Mailer's essay "The White Negro," published for the first time in 1957 and reprinted in 1959 in the writer's collection *Advertisements for Myself*. Mailer—influenced by Jean-Paul Sartre's existentialism and Sartre's liking for jazz—invented the "white Negro" as the "American existentialist—the hipster." "The presence of Hip as a working philosophy in the sub-worlds of American life is probably due to jazz and its knife-like entry into culture, its subtle but so penetrating influence on an avant-garde generation, that post-war generation of adventurers."[9]

Mailer created a special literary identity and characterized the hipster as a "ménage-à-trois—the bohemian and the juvenile delinquent came face-to-face with the Negro."[10] The image of the "white Negro" is replete with clichés: of the bohemian living outside society, of rebellious youth and the African American with his supposed physically oriented vitality. The African American, Mailer suggested, had "to live with danger from the first day . . . and so he kept for his survival the art of the primitive, he lived in the enormous present, he subsisted for his Saturday night kicks, relinquishing the pleasures of the mind for the more obligatory pleasures of the body."[11]

Despite the obvious stereotype, Mailer's use of the expression "white Negro" to describe this contemporary phenomenon was apt. From a European American perspective, the phenomenon revived certain character traits of the former bohemia. Mailer ascribed to the bohemians an adolescent life force, manifested through an inclination to revolt, perhaps even adventurous-felonious revolt. In this way, Mailer gave a social context to the "white Negro," helping the bohemian to relate once again to society, even if this relationship consists of turning *against* society.

By linking African Americans with bohemia, Mailer imparted to the "white Negro" not only a suggestion of oppression but also in particular—and in contrast to the former image of the psychologically more instable bohemian—a certain physical presence and "primitive" nativeness.

Mailer drew together in his literary conception of the "white Negro" contemporary phenomena such as the civil rights movement, rock and roll, and the Beat Generation. In fact, Mailer constructed his "white Negro" mostly from fragments of cliché. At the same time, though, he offered a point of identification, an idealized image for white middle-class youth in the United States and Europe who fulfilled the most important function, protesting against cultural traditions and social conventions during the 1950s and 1960s.

By now, there is a well-established body of research on the former counterculture. Sociologist Andreas Reckwitz sums up the main elements:

In the 1960s, the real counterculture was established in urban centers and university cities, where several lines and "scenes" were connected loosely but recognizably. The political student movement represented liberal-leftist, socialist and anarchist thinking. The hippie subculture . . . was linked to the sexual revolution and the alternative international community movement.[12]

These different movements were linked by a common orientation: the counterculture did not refer to it as an established identity but as something diverse and forthright. They rebelled against the technical rationality of the modern age and against certain social roles. The counterculture sought authenticity beyond social conformity. Even in daily life, the aim was to apply nonconventional aesthetics. This intended broadening of perceptions led to aesthetic self-stylization on a daily basis, involving apparently irrational, sensually orientated, often risky actions centered on the body. It was white middle-class youth in particular who were the backbone of the counterculture:

> That the countercultures . . . primarily focused on youth rather than artistry as a criterion of difference did not distance them from the preceding cultural-aesthetic counter-movement, but enabled them on the contrary to develop a radicalized model of aesthetic subjectivity, only marginally reliant on art in a narrow sense and thus completely transforming art into daily life.[13]

Similar radical artistic movements can be found in the literature of the Beat Generation (Jack Kerouac, William Burroughs, Allen Ginsberg, etc.) and in the intermedial "happenings" of the Fluxus school (George Brecht, Allen Kaprow, Nam June Paik, etc.), which questioned the separation of art and everyday life.

The counterculture movements were looking for directness and nativeness as an alternative to the technically originated rationality of the modern age. Hence, the counterculture's attitude was as manifest in experimental art projects as it was in blues-oriented rock music. Rock now became a canvas for the projection of creativity, rather as jazz had been before. There was still a singular fascination with African American music, especially among Europeans. Neil A. Wynn sums up his reflections on African American music in Europe:

> For [Jean-Paul] Sartre and others in pre- and post–World War II Europe, black music was also attractive because it was a "vehicle" of American culture in all its immediacy and all its uncompromising energy. To an even greater extent, jazz offered a release from the drab hardships and spoke of another world. At the same time, ironically, in its liberation and identification with the African American minority, it was a mode of protest.[14]

In the 1960s, the blues in particular was regarded as a source of nativeness and, at the same time, could be presented as a "mode of protest" against modern employee culture. In addition to the American and European enthusiasm for the blues, the avant-garde art movements were looking for directness and nativeness as alternatives to the technically driven rationality of the modern age. An exciting alternative emerged for jazz musicians in the United States, just as it had in Europe. On the one hand, it could bring musicians closer to the elevated world of art; on the other hand, it connected them to older African American music traditions like blues and gospel music, and it chained them to rock. ?

III. Blues

In recent accounts of British jazz history, from Stuart Nicholson to Alyn Shipton, a line of development shows how intense dialogue between blues and jazz around 1960 eventually paved the way for jazz rock in the second half of the decade. These developments occurred in England in particular, and especially in London. Molds were set, and stages marked, on the way to jazz rock by bands such as Alexis Korner's Blues Incorporated, the Graham Bond Organization, Cream, Soft Machine, Colosseum, Nucleus, etc.

The blues discussion, from the Mississippi Delta blues of Robert Johnson to the Chicago blues of Muddy Waters, was what essentially defined British rock music. This discussion was particularly significant for the circle around Alexis Korner. The link between blues orientation and the counterculture was obvious. As Paul Stump writes: *what* ?

> What helped the cause of the blues revival was that the values it represented to the revivalists were synonymous with the bohemian values that became identified with the 1960s . . . modern jazz, bebop, hard bop or at least r'n'b offered something ostensibly primal. Here was the soundtrack beyond suburbia—a world that a young rebellious spirit could call his own. . . . This was music, it was imagined, that came straight from the heart. A blues boom of both Chicago and Delta varieties was well underway [in] London at the turn of the 1960s.[15]

Through a nostalgic recourse to the blues, and its creative offshoots in London, drawing on the recent development of rhythm-and-blues and soul (Ray Charles), rock music gained a more rebellious type of sound, much more rebellious than rock and roll ever had. Bands like the Rolling Stones incorporated into their music as well as their image an extrovert, physically explicit, and especially provocative sexual character.

Jazz, and especially its younger, modern forms, were an essential element of the London scene at that time. Traditional blues and modern jazz were in direct dialogue with each other. As Stump puts it, "Rhythm and blues was firmly entrenched in the bohemia of late fifties London alongside cool jazz. Both were consonant with the overriding concern of bohemia—a dedication to the purest liberation, and by extension, expression of the soul."[16]

Shipton specifies: "The key innovation in Korner's band was that over a straightforward rhythm and blues beat, with simple harmonies, he added a hard bop saxophone section, usually of Dick Heckstall-Smith and Art Themen, but sometimes with multi-instrumentalist Graham Bond on alto as well."[17] This is rarely documented, though, on records from the first half of the 1960s. At least the available examples, like the soul-jazz title "Sappho," recorded by Alexis Korner's Blues Incorporated in 1963, testify to the presence of jazz.[18]

On the first album by the Graham Bond Organization, a remarkable description of the music as a "startling fusion of rhythm and blues and modern jazz" can be found in the anonymously written liner notes.[19] But the tracks on this album do not display this kind of fusion. Apparently aware of the participating musicians' jazz experience, the anonymous author concludes: "Ginger Baker, Jack Bruce, and Dick Heckstall-Smith have all played in various jazz groups. But as renegade jazzmen they turned to rhythm and blues with such fervency, and played with such a combination of skill and emotion, they quickly built up a massive following in live appearances up and down the country."

The Sound of 65 is not a fusion, but rather a blues or rhythm-and-blues album, opening programmatically with Willie Dixon's "Hoochie Coochie Man." Even more evident are the jazz origins of the album There's a Bond between Us, recorded in November 1965. You can hear this all the more clearly in the opening and closing instrumentals, "Who's Afraid of Virginia Woolf?" and "Camels and Elephants." However, the album's style is clearly rhythm-and-blues-oriented, with an explicit reference to Ray Charles, whose "What'd I Say" features at the beginning of the LP's second side.

Rather than the Graham Bond Organization's recorded repertoire, the band's concerts might have provided more evidence of a jazz influence. The tracks on the albums mentioned are too short to allow for improvisational freedom, which might have emerged during the band's performances. The linkage of blues and rock in a manner akin to jazz became manifest when bassist Jack Bruce and drummer Ginger Baker left Graham Bond in 1966 to form the band Cream with Eric Clapton.

In fact, Cream sounds more like a loud, aggressive rock band than like a modern acoustic jazz group of the 1960s, although Stuart Nicholson is right in stating,

Clearly, any rapprochement with rock posed problems of authenticity in balancing the sounds associated with rock and jazz improvisation. Yet a working model of what a jazz-rock "fusion" might sound like was revealed by the English band Cream, formed in July 1966. Combining former jazz musicians Jack Bruce on bass and Ginger Baker on drums with blues purist Eric Clapton on guitar, they broke open the temporal limits of blues and popular songs with long, extended improvisations over rock rhythms. When the band toured the USA in 1967, *Rolling Stone* magazine pointed out that Cream "had been called a jazz group." Indeed, during their tour many critics credited Cream with combining jazz and rock: "The healthiest development in popular music these days is the extraordinary convergence of jazz and rock," said *Life* magazine in January 1968.[20]

Nicholson refers to Richard Saltonstall's review of Cream's first two albums, *Fresh Cream* and *Disraeli Gears*, published on January 26, 1968, in *Life*. Saltonstall mentions several times the relationship between rock and jazz in the context of Cream, and he concludes with the words: "But what is significant is that, throughout, these British rockers have displayed the spontaneity, sophistication and mood of rebellion that originally belonged to jazz."[21] There are other examples of a comparable reception from contemporary journalists. Claude Hall observes in a review of a 1967 Cream concert in New York for *Billboard* magazine: "The Cream, a trio from England, proved themselves . . . in their opening here at the Café Au Go Go [New York], to be one of the best rock groups around. Also, they should certainly rank high among jazz groups and among blues groups." Hall also comments: "Whether it is called rock or hip jazz or rocking blues, it is today's music. And the Cream is at the top."[22]

These journalistic perceptions of Cream's music correspond entirely with the band's own notion of what it was. Alyn Shipton adds: "It is significant that [Cream's] earliest appearances were in a jazz context, and certainly in 1966, Bruce and Baker still thought of themselves as jazz musicians."[23]

Jack Bruce says as much in various interviews. "Thinking back on that band, it was really a jazz band, there was so much improvising by the time it evolved," he recalls. "We started off playing four- or five-minute tunes, but by the time we got to San Francisco in '67, it had started to stretch out. It became almost like an Ornette Coleman band, with Eric not knowing he was Ornette Coleman, Ginger and me not telling him."[24] There is probably a good deal of British humor in Bruce's claim that Clapton did not know what was going on. But the bassist's enthusiasm for Ornette Coleman is genuine:

It's something that actually goes back to when I started out as a jazzer in the early 1960s. . . . Back then, I was really keen on saxophonist Ornette Coleman, and his band that I particularly liked, had no pianist. I also played quite a lot with jazz trios, so I took that idea into the rock arena, if you like. There are a lot of things I like about it but mostly it's the freedom aspect I enjoy. When you play with keyboards, you get locked down into set chord structures, whereas this way, you can really get into something spontaneous and explore a contrapuntal approach, if that doesn't sound too high-flown, which is how I like to play.[25]

Of course, Eric Clapton was not completely unaware of the jazz influence in Cream's musical style: "The Cream was really a jazz group, a jazz-rock group."[26] On the band's second album, *Disraeli Gears*, Clapton hears "a magical combination of blues, rock, and jazz."[27]

Shipton defines as the main characteristic of Cream's music "the repetitions of riffs—of which *Sunshine of Your Love* is perhaps the best known—that then opened up into a vamp for long-drawn-out improvisations. By and large Cream did not cycle its way through thirty-two measure songs, but adopted different structures that involved the simple 'hook' of a catchy rock theme being combined with the opportunity for open solos. That was to be a central idea in jazz-rock—albeit one, as Bruce says, that came from jazz in the first place."[28] An even more precise description of Cream's musical approach would be: variability of sound design refers to the complexity of jazz. This is reflected in the varied course of the music and also in the vertical linkage and integration of guitar, bass, and drums. The result is a continuum in which all three musicians constantly alternate between foreground and background. It is by no means a hierarchical relationship, one in which Clapton improvises solos while Bruce and Baker accompany him. There is not so much one prominent soloist as closely linked interaction between the three musicians. The process of continuous change is maintained and advanced through permanent interaction.

John McLaughlin took a very similar route through the British blues and jazz scene to that of Jack Bruce and Ginger Baker. McLaughlin also played with Alexis Korner and later in 1963 in the Graham Bond Quartet with Bruce and Baker. In 1970 a live recording of this quartet, playing three titles at the Klooks Kleek club, was released on the album *Solid Bond*.[29] Bond plays alto sax exclusively and Bruce the double bass. Together with McLaughlin and Baker, they make up a swinging modern acoustic jazz ensemble, comparable neither to the latter Graham Bond Organization nor to Cream. The repertoire is Sonny Rollins's "Doxy," a call-and-response blues waltz written by Bruce ("Ho Ho Country Kicking Blues"), and an up-tempo blues from Bond and McLaughlin ("The Grass Is Greener"). They serve as the starting point for longer, open improvisations from all four band members.

Shortly afterward, Bond formed his Organization and leaned more strongly toward traditional blues, or rather rhythm and blues, switching to Hammond organ and voice/vocals. Dick Heckstall-Smith took over on the saxophone.

McLaughlin left the Bond group. In the years that followed, though, he crossed paths with Jack Bruce in particular. In 1968, McLaughlin took part in the recording of Bruce's album *Things We Like*.[30] In 1970, Bruce appeared with Tony Williams Lifetime, along with McLaughlin and Larry Young on organ. They recorded the album *Turn It Over*[31] and toured together in Great Britain late that year. In 1970–71,[32] McLaughlin and Bruce were both on Carla Bley's recording of *Escalator over the Hill*.[33]

At the end of his time with Cream, Jack Bruce recorded, as noted above, a progressive jazz album in August 1968, *Things We Like*. The original intention was to use a trio with Bruce on double bass, Heckstall-Smith on saxophone, and Jon Hiseman on the drums. The first two tracks, "Over the Cliff" and "Statues," feature this lineup. The influence of Ornette Coleman, mentioned before by Bruce in the context of Cream, was evident in the group sound but also in the polyphonic mesh of improvisation. McLaughlin was involved in the remaining six pieces and added a fundamentally different, distorted sound color with his electric guitar. The open approach to improvisation persists in the six pieces with McLaughlin. Beat-oriented passages or pieces with a succession of solos (as in the "нскнн Blues") alternate with metrically unrestricted and polyphonic improvisations (in the rubato "Ballad for Arthur" or the rapid pulse of the title track, "Things We Like").

In January 1969, McLaughlin formed his own band and improvisational concept, recording his debut album *Extrapolation*.[34] Together with saxophonist John Surman, bassist Brian Odgers, and drummer Tony Oxley, McLaughlin plays his own compositions such as "Arjen's Bag," rerecorded later as "Follow Your Heart." Uneven meters (such as 11/8) and melodic passages based on distinctive guitar riffs become a characteristic of McLaughlin's music. Moreover, the familiar idiosyncrasies of his improvisatory approach, with extremely fast tone sequences and rhythmical accents, emerge clearly through McLaughlin's choppy and hard-struck chords. The titles of the compositions, especially at the beginning and end of the album, refer programmatically to the contemporary counterculture. McLaughlin presents the basic musical action by opening with the album's title track, with its abrupt changes between different musical styles and sonically dense fast passages. The term "extrapolation" does not allude just to one clearly defined musical area. McLaughlin uses electric guitar almost exclusively on this album, but the last track, "Peace Piece," is recorded without accompaniment and played on the acoustic guitar. This choice of instrumentation reflects the contemporary political backdrop of the peace demonstrations against the Vietnam War.

Shortly after he recorded *Extrapolation* in London, an exciting year brought McLaughlin to the American center of jazz-rock. Arriving in New York in February, McLaughlin took a big step forward in his career. Drummer Tony Williams invited him to join his fusion trio Lifetime, together with organist Larry Young. The album *Emergency!* was recorded on May 26 and 28, 1969, becoming a milestone in the history of jazz-rock due to its high-energy, intense sound design.[35] Nicholson places Tony Williams in a complex musical context between jazz and rock. He refers to the link with Cream in particular: "In many ways, Lifetime were an abstraction of Cream, with their 'power trio' approach to improvisation, albeit closer to the edge than the blues-based improvisation of the earlier band, a group which Williams is on record as having admired."[36] McLaughlin's contribution to Lifetime cannot be overstated. In Tony Williams's opinion, McLaughlin was not just an unknown European teammate but the one and only guitarist who could provide a significant musical impetus. It is not so surprising that Nicholson should interpret the album *Emergency!* as a continuation of McLaughlin's *Extrapolation*: "As *Emergency!* revealed, Lifetime was a logical extension of the ideas worked out in England by McLaughlin on *Extrapolation*."[37]

But McLaughlin's extraordinary impact in 1969 goes even further. Shortly after his arrival in New York, Miles Davis had already invited McLaughlin at the end of February to join a studio session, which spawned the album *In a Silent Way*.[38] In August of 1969, McLaughlin was in the studio with Davis again. They recorded the album *Bitches Brew*,[39] for a touchstone of jazz-rock. In an extremely short period, McLaughlin was not only accepted as a musician in New York but also forged a new musical development specific to this time.

But he was not the only European in Miles Davis's musical orbit in New York. European jazz musicians such as bassist Dave Holland and in particular pianist and keyboardist Joe Zawinul from Vienna, who was already well established on the U.S. scene for some time, made a significant mark on the epochal albums *In A Silent Way* and *Bitches Brew*.

In the 1970s, McLaughlin, Holland, and Zawinul succeeded in advancing the evolution of jazz development further, shaping styles and leading successful bands. While Holland formed the mostly free-improvising quartet Circle with Anthony Braxton, Chick Corea, and Barry Altschul, from 1970 onward Zawinul headed up—together with Wayne Shorter—one of the most important fusion bands, Weather Report. In 1971 McLaughlin formed his Mahavishnu Orchestra, an equally important jazz-rock group.

The Mahavishnu Orchestra consisted mainly of European musicians. Besides McLaughlin, there was the Czech keyboardist Jan Hammer and the Irish bassist Rick Laird. Hammer came to the band on the recommendation of Miroslav Vitous, and McLaughlin knew Laird from before in England. In fact, Jean-Luc Ponty, another European, was meant to play the violin in the group; however, Ponty did not join the Mahavishnu Orchestra until 1974. Instead, the violinist's role went to the only American in the band, Jerry Goodman from Chicago. Drummer Billy Cobham from Panama supplied the percussive power.

The name of the band came from McLaughlin's former Indian guru Sri Chinmoy. He not only gave the guitarist the Indian name "Mahavishnu," but also suggested using the name for the group. The engagement with Indian culture, both music and religious beliefs, was an important facet of the counterculture in the 1960s. Reckwitz connects the contemporary interest in African American blues with the debate over Eastern religions and cultures: "The cultural-revolutionary context encourages a playful 'othering' of the subject, that now seems emblematic: the other of black culture . . . the other of Far Eastern cultures—for example, the self-control required in meditation techniques."[40]

Meditative Eastern practices open up alternative conceptions to the rational modern world of Europe and the United States. They aim to expand consciousness and perception, a motivation very much in line with risky drug use. Nicholson mentions this association in particular with regard to McLaughlin: "Mahavishnu was a microcosm of the sixties preoccupation with alternative religions and philosophies. Often bad experiences with drugs were behind a search for alternative paths toward spiritual enlightenment—which in many instances became a case of substituting one habit (drugs) for another (Eastern religion)."[41]

Velocity is one of the core musical characteristics of the Mahavishnu Orchestra. McLaughlin radicalized his perception of sound once again: the musicians performed with virtuosity individually and as a band. The high-speed playing resolves into calm passages, intensifying the effect of the velocity even more. The orientation toward common musical frameworks such as beat and form loosens in favor of a highly differentiated process, both composed and improvised, coupled to extraordinary meters, which leads to tightly focused swirls of sound. This happens independently of the different musical styles found on the first album, *The Inner Mounting Flame*, recorded in 1971:[42] the faster, riff-based pieces like "Meeting of the Spirits," "The Noonward Race," or "Vital Transformation," the slower, blues-oriented "Dance of Maya," or even the acoustic trio (guitar, violin, and piano) that plays "A Lotus on Irish Streams" at the end of side one of the album. The swirls of sound generated by the group are a challenge to the control of both the players and the listener. They aim at an awakening beyond analytic understanding. The last piece on the album is, appropriately enough, "Awakening." This track brings the musical action to a special peak, as it consists almost entirely of a sound swirl.

British Bands like Cream were extremely successful on an international scale, as was John McLaughlin with his different musical excursions around 1970. These examples illustrate the great significance of European musicians in the developing links between jazz and rock in the 1960s and at the beginning of the

1970s. Bands from Cream to the Mahavishnu Orchestra made an essential contribution to the musical development of the counterculture.

IV. Fluxus

Since the late 1950s, the European embrace of the blues had occurred mainly in England, and especially in London. Around 1960, there was a unique situation in England, characterized by Shipton as a "musical melting pot of rhythm and blues, traditional jazz, skiffle, and bebop."[43] This situation was the starting point for the aforementioned developments. As far as continuing the improvisatory tradition of Fluxus was concerned, there was no such geographical concentration. References to Fluxus were significant in England, West Germany, and the Netherlands.

In a way, John Cage constituted—together with other New York school composers and the radical continuation of their efforts in the Fluxus movement—the aesthetic opposite pole to the blues within the counterculture. Once again, the basic artistic impulses had their origins in the United States. However, their relationship was with the European new music. In the 1950s, the new music was particularly influenced by the ideas of Anton Webern and involved figureheads such as Karlheinz Stockhausen, Pierre Boulez, and Luigi Nono.

This distinction is clear from the memoirs/memories of bassist and composer Gavin Bryars, who was part of the free improvisation scene in London during the 1960s. Around 1965, Bryars played in a trio called Joseph Holbrooke, together with guitarist Derek Bailey and drummer Tony Oxley. While playing in this band, Bryars tried to integrate Cage's ideas into the music:

> But it was the case that the only outlet for this thing we were doing was through a situation, and a music really, that was based on jazz. By about '65 though, I was barely interested in jazz at all. At that time I got the '61 Cage catalogue and I ordered things every week through the local music shop. So I was getting all those pieces and studying them and there was something strange about trying to reconcile that information with what we were doing. I had also got Cage's *Silence* by this time and the ideas in that had quite a strong effect on me and at the same time I was studying composition with George Linstead. So I was actually listening and thinking about and studying classical music far more than anything else.[44]

In the late 1960s, having worked with Cage in the United States, Bryars intensified the impact of Fluxus in London.[45] He was playing improvised music with Bailey, percussionist Jamie Muir, and pianist John Tilbury, and Bryars was responsible for the anarchic element characteristic of the Fluxus movement:

There was an aspect of improvisation, but I was also aware of the post-Cage musical world, Fluxus and things of that kind, where you would get the anarchic element involved. You would also get the early La Monte Young territory of undifferentiated activity going on for very long periods. I saw that area of composed music as also being part of improvised music—and vice versa. It wasn't any different to me.[46]

In addition to the circle around Bailey, the improvisatory ensemble AMM was the main link to the ideas of John Cage. AMM was formed in London in 1965 by guitarist Keith Rowe, saxophonist Lou Gare, and drummer Edwin Prévost. Pianist and composer Cornelius Cardew joined the ensemble in 1966 and brought avant-garde concepts to bear on the ensemble's improvisatory processes. Prévost explains:

Victor Schonfield—who organised concerts of avant-garde musics in those days, and was the first critic to write about our work—once called AMM "John Cage jazz." The ideas of John Cage allowed any sound source material into music and encouraged a zen-like sense of "nowness" that superseded formal appreciation (and its attendant philosophy) of the western music tradition. But Cage always maintained a strong hold on the way "his" music was to be made. . . . AMM opted for the freedom to work collaboratively that is absent from the Cage agenda.[47]

Thus, the improvisational development of Cage's concepts and those of the Fluxus movement was not only about a simple transfer of ideas but about individual adaptation and the creative consequences that ensued.

However—as already mentioned—the embrace of Fluxus by improvisers was not as focused on England as the interest in the blues. Improvisers from the Netherlands and West Germany, such as pianist and composer Misha Mengelberg and saxophonist Peter Brötzmann, were directly involved in Fluxus performances.[48]

"Fluxus did not have a program; it stands for nothing," said Mengelberg. "Fluxus only means current. I felt that there was a very intense connection to Dadaism, and in my opinion, Dada was the most brilliant art movement of this century."[49] Misha Mengelberg's nod to Dadaism has a historical lineage: Marcel Duchamp brought Dadaist ideas to the United States. Those ideas inspired many artists, particularly Cage, who counts for many as the intellectual/spiritual "father" of Fluxus because he introduced "happenings" and used chance as a compositional tool.

Moreover, Fluxus was very important to Peter Brötzmann. Interviewed in 1968, he said:

Working with [Nam June] Paik 2, 3 years ago, I saw many things that went far beyond the activities of Stockhausen. . . . This is the direction of Cage, continued through the Fluxus movement, although at this moment it is [at the beginning of 1968]—it died two years ago. But those things were very important. Things George Brecht did, for example.[50]

JÜRGEN ARNDT

The main point of the Fluxus movement, as in Dadaism, was to blur the borders between art and life, between art and daily routine. A very well-known example by the American George Brecht is called *Word Event* and includes as its "partitura" (score) just the word "Exit." Performances can occur anywhere. In February 1963, Brecht's *Word Event* was the closing piece at the Festum Flexorum Fluxus at the Kunsthochschule in Düsseldorf. Owen Smith reported: "The evening concluded with a performance of Brecht's *Word Event*, in which the performers turned off all the lights and left, leaving the audience alone in the darkened room."[51] After a while, the audience realized Brecht's piece by leaving the venue.

Although the Fluxus movement started in the United States, promoted by Cage and with prominent American representatives such as George Brecht, Allan Kaprow, and George Maciunas, in Europe it found significant like-minded artists like Joseph Beuys or Wolf Vostell. Many exceptional Fluxus events therefore took place in Europe. Both American and European artists were involved in these events, such as the aforementioned Festum Flexorum Fluxus.

In the previous decade, Cage had caused a stir at the Donaueschinger Musiktage festival in 1954 and particularly at the Internationale Ferienkurse für Neue Musik Darmstadt in 1958. Donaueschingen and Darmstadt were regarded as strongholds of the international new music scene. Cage drew attention with his concept of "indeterminacy," leaving compositional and interpretive decisions to chance and giving broad leeway to the performer. In this way, sounds and noises should be isolated from subjective perceptions and functional or semantic attributes. Cage's performance in Darmstadt had a huge impact on music history, because he began to make serial composers such as Pierre Boulez, Karlheinz Stockhausen, and Luigi Nono, who tend to achieve a high degree of compositional control, think again. Even before the European emancipation in jazz began in the 1960s, U.S. composers were challenging the dominance of their European colleagues in the field of new music.

In his lectures in Darmstadt, Cage integrated performance elements unrelated to his textual explanations. In 1958, Mengelberg took courses in Darmstadt and was impressed with Cage's lectures: "[Cage] was smoking six cigarettes at a time but also manipulating them, burning them or laying three on an ashtray and burning the fourth. I remember the manipulation more than the lecture. His talk was also interrupted by David Tudor playing. I remember thinking that the lecture, manipulation and playing should appear as a single entity."[52] Mengelberg was quite right in his spontaneous assessment and could see the inspiration or confirmation to lend his own music a stronger connection to everyday life. This became one of his major concerns within the Fluxus movement. Accordingly, Mengelberg was very comfortable in the Fluxus environment. "This was the first time for me where I had the impression with everything I tried musically—sense and non-sense—that there were other people in the world doing these things and talking about them. There, I felt more or less at home."[53]

Peter Brötzmann was linked to Fluxus not via the new music but through his close association with the fine arts. Brötzmann's first studies were in Wuppertal at the former Werkkunstschule:

Finally, I also dropped out of high school and switched to the Werkkunst-schule. We actually had a Werkkunstschule then in Wuppertal: it was a school for applied art. But at the time there were also independent classes in painting, sculpture, etc. That was a small remnant of the Bauhaus style. So the school accepted me and I studied graphics, commercial graphics and painting. Actually, that had been my aim. I had a lot of fun with music, but that was just a sideline [to my art studies].[54]

Brötzmann made direct contact with Fluxus, particularly the Fluxus artist Nam June Paik, in Wuppertal:

In those days, Wuppertal had this magnificent gallery, the "Galerie Parnass." Paik, who had just been thrown out of every German music University, settled near Cologne. There he had a garage where he could store all of his electronic stuff, and a German housewife, cooking fried potatoes for him. His first big exhibition was actually at the "Galerie Parnass." I got this job, because I hung around there anyway and because gallery owner Jährling needed some people to help him out with this exhibition. That was—and I realized it only over the intervening decades—a very important time for me. Because Paik was already a very, very important man. When I met him and when I had the pleasure of working for him, he was engaged in a number of many musical installations, like prepared piano and others things. Those were smaller, technical pieces. And the first TVs were already around him. I am not sure if he really knew already what he was doing when he fumbled around with the TVs, but that was the beginning of his great "TV career."[55]

For Brötzmann, transferring Fluxus strategies to jazz-oriented improvisation techniques was an obvious step, because of the importance of music to Fluxus, especially in the case of Paik. "The encounter with the Korean artist Nam June

Paik, a student of John Cage and a representative of the Fluxus movement, deeply influenced my development. I realized that we had to break open conventions and clichés if we wanted to go further."[56]

Thus, the Fluxus movement, with its origins in the United States, gave vital impetus to the independent explorations of European jazz musicians such as Brötzmann and Mengelberg. The musical and improvisational approaches of Brötzmann and Mengelberg were similar in their degree of radicalism, but they took different paths in terms of specifics.

Mengelberg presents his music as quite quotidian. He is especially interested in the seamlessness between art and life in the form of play and daily routine, something the Fluxus movement sought to achieve:

> One of the things that inspires me in making any gesture, musically and theoretically, is its relation with daily life, in which there is no such thing as an exclusion. One moment I met you and the next I am washing dishes or playing chess. So many facets on many levels, whether you like them or not. Of course, I don't mean daily life transformed into music but in certain respects there are parallels between the music and daily life. For example, in the respect that very vulgar things are happening near to very aesthetic things: people go pissing one moment and have deep philosophical thoughts the next. Or maybe both at the same time. . . . The sort of improvisation I am interested in is the sort that everyone does in their lives. They improvise in taking six or seven steps to the door, scratching their heads with one or two fingers.[57]

Mengelberg regards art not as something special, as something separated from life: as such, he maintains a more embryonic style of piano playing. Mengelberg's technique could be seen as "jingling." That is why he does not behave as if he has to perform a concert, even if that is exactly what he does. Instead, on the concert podium Mengelberg acts like someone who just sits down at the piano and is surprised by what comes out of his pianistic "backpack" or sees what happens if he tries out new sounds, even if the result is boring monotony. This is an everyday approach, but it calls for the same amount of knowledge, ability, and concentration as a conventional artistic act, if presented as an artistic program.

Mengelberg is aware of this: "Actually, there is only one kind of method—no, I don't want to call it a method. . . . I try to avoid certain musical formulas. So, I know they are here, they are used by many musicians, but I don't want to use them."[58]

Mengelberg tries to leave these "certain musical formulas" behind not through a step forward but a step back—to before there was a mature stylistic specification. In the post-stylistic context of art history in general and music history in particular, which became manifest through the avant-garde activities of Cage and the
Fluxus movement, Mengelberg becomes a pre-stylist with his "jingling" piano

playing: often his improvisations show a gradual, sometimes tough, but aimless jingling progression, which can specify a certain sound or play eclectically with undeveloped style clichés or stylistic quotes from jazz and other musical genres.

Mengelberg was inspired by Thelonious Monk to hesitate while gradually "jingling forward." But in contrast to Monk, who—while focusing on individual sounds—always tries out those sounds in a new way, Mengelberg operates at a conceptual level. This brings his improvisations close to the principles of the Fluxus movement. In the end, the aim of closing the gap between art and daily life is fulfilled at a theoretical level only if the concepts and their reception are compelling enough, and not just through individual art products or their performance—as was demonstrated by the example of Brecht's *Word Event*. As such, the conceptual approach inspires the artistic realization. In terms of theory, Mengelberg's preparatory work can be located in a specific improvisational technique: the hesitation, going back to Monk, is the basis for the conceptual residue. Therefore, musical movement is never fluent in Mengelberg's improvisations.

The consequences of Peter Brötzmann's experiences with Fluxus were different but no less radical than those of Mengelberg. Brötzmann's expressive, highly energetic style attacks the musical sound. He extends the sound from within until he reaches his limits and goes beyond them. Thus, not only is identifiable pitch often lost, but there are pronounced tone fluctuations and extreme vibratos, which almost seem to alter the notes. The sound fluctuations do not keep the sound moving but threaten to break it from the inside, as Brötzmann's musical textures also starts to waver. The sound becomes a kind of a breaking cluster. Brötzmann combines his sound design with a loud noise. He produces this noise by simultaneously using his vocal chords, singing, speaking, or even screaming: "It is probably pivotal that I see the use of the instrument as an extended opportunity to speak. Instead of playing, I would sometimes prefer to sing for the whole evening—if I were confident with that. It is easier for me with an instrument in my hand."[59] Brötzmann's simultaneous singing does not produce several voices like that of Albert Mangelsdorff, with whom he often played. Mangelsdorff adds new tones to his trombone sounds, but Brötzmann blurs the individual sounds, giving them an explosive feel.

Brötzmann's characteristic musical procedure is not intended as pure instrumental technique. His music is full of expressive gestures; it underpins an existential concern: "Playing for me means a form of survival, yes."[60]

Since the 1960s, Peter Brötzmann and Misha Mengelberg were the most obvious examples of jazz musicians including Fluxus impulses as an essential component of their respective improvisation techniques. Sometimes they improvised together, especially in larger ensembles. In 1979, they recorded together in a trio, releasing the album *3 Points and a Mountain*.[61] The third musician was

Han Bennink, drummer, multi-instrumentalist, and fine-artist. From the start of the 1960s up to the present day, Bennink has played with Mengelberg in a variety of ensembles, from duos to the ICP (Instant Composers Pool) Orchestra. Particularly since the *Machine Gun* recordings in 1968, Bennink has been working with Brötzmann—in the 1970s especially—as part of an ongoing trio with Belgian pianist Fred van Hove. Fluxus was a key inspiration for Bennink too: even elements of the performance environment (walls, the ground, and other resonant objects encountered more incidentally) can become instruments for him. Bennink's energetic play is expressed more and more through unexpected accents and quasi-explosions of sound. On the other hand, in opposition to the sound, there are theatrical-scenic acts. These subversively question, in a playful, humorous way, the sincerity and autonomy of art. In doing so, they lend the performance a quotidian flavor that can be seen as related to Fluxus.

The consequences of Fluxus, in terms of the advanced further development of jazz in Europe, did not occur in isolation through the relevant scenes in England, the Netherlands, and West Germany, but also shaped the intense exchanges between musicians from these countries. Mengelberg, Brötzmann, and Bennink were among the most active and influential improvisers since the 1960s. They developed close links between advanced improvisation movements that have their origins both in modern jazz, and in the western counterculture.

V. *Fluxus to Blues*

The search for directness and nativeness as an alternative to rationality of purpose, with its origins in the technical developments of the modern age, underlined the avant-garde movement as well as the orientation toward the blues. This is why the counterculture could have the same influence on experimental art projects as on blues-oriented rock or jazz-rock.

European jazz musicians succeeded in developing their own characteristic styles by engaging in intense dialogue with American cultural phenomena, not by turning away from the achievements of American jazz musicians. Above all, the European musicians who succeeded in establishing themselves in the United States, particularly the English musicians, were successful internationally. This goes for the successful U.S. tours by Cream, but also for John McLauglin's involvement in Tony Williams Lifetime, his collaborations with Miles Davis, and eventually the formation of the Mahavishnu Orchestra. From the second half of the 1960s, European input was highly significant even for jazz in the United States, and particularly in the field of jazz-rock.

The process took a bit longer in the realm of free improvisation. Since the

1980s, both Misha Mengelberg and Peter Brötzmann have been stepping up their direct improvisatory dialogues with American musicians.

Mengelberg turned again to the music of Thelonious Monk and Herbie Nichols, interpreting their compositions, among others, with the American soprano saxophonist Steve Lacy and trombonists Roswell Rudd or George Lewis, but also with the ICP Orchestra.[62] Among these retrospective jazz activities were trio albums such as *Who's Bridge?* recorded in 1994, and *No Idea* in 1996, as well as the quartet recording *Four in One* in 2000.[63] These albums are especially remarkable in terms of European-American dialogue. On the one hand, Mengelberg underlines his relationship with American jazz; on the other, the albums are notable for the involvement of younger American improvisers. New York avant-garde musician John Zorn initiated and produced two of the three albums, conscious of the increasing importance of improvisational contributions from Europe since the 1960s. The same applies to the aforementioned quartet album, *Four in One*, made with American trumpeter Dave Douglas. This collaboration confirmed the growing acceptance of Mengelberg in the United States as well. There is further evidence: since the 1990s, Mengelberg has stepped up his concert performances in the United States. In 2006, he toured the States with the ICP Orchestra, prompting enormous interest in the media; high-profile newspapers such as the *New York Times* reported on individual concerts. In 2007, *Down Beat* magazine even published a detailed account of the forty-year history of the Instant Composers Pool and the current orchestra members.[64]

Since the 1980s, Brötzmann has played with a number of well-known free-jazz improvisers from the United States, for example drummers Andrew Cyrille and Rashied Ali or pianist Cecil Taylor.[65] Some of these many projects and ensembles are particularly outstanding: the group Last Exit during the second half of the 1980s, with Brötzmann and Americans Sonny Sharrock (electric guitar), Bill Laswell (electric bass), and Ronald Shannon Jackson (drums); the quartet Die Like a Dog in the 1990s, with bassist William Parker from New York, drummer Hamid Drake from Chicago, and Japanese trumpeter Toshinori Kondo; the Chicago Tentet, active from 1997 to the present day as an alliance between representatives of the Chicago improvisation scene, such as saxophonist Ken Vandermark, trumpeter Joe McPhee, cellist Fred Lonberg-Holm, and bassist Kent Kessler, as well as other European musicians such as saxophonist Mats Gustavsson from Sweden.[66]

Brötzmann and Last Exit in particular can be seen as an illustration that the choice between embracing the blues and a Fluxus orientation is not intended as an either/or. Neither direction excluded the other; rather, they crossed paths again and again. The musicians in Last Exit combined melodically, metrically, and tonally disconnected passages with beat-oriented rhythms and riffs. Brötz-mann's and Sharrock's improvisations often went from gliding sound cascades to cries, while Laswell and Jackson increased the intensity through rock and jazz rhythms or rolling drum patterns, typical of Jackson. But they also include primarily melodious as well as rhythmically and metrically open passages. Despite their radicalism, Last Exit remained traditional in a way. Blues was the basis, given prominence in Jackson's vocal interludes. He would pay homage to Ma Rainey, the most significant blues singer of the 1920s other than Bessie Smith, or to Willie Dixon's blues classic "Big Boss Man," which became famous in 1961 through Jimmy Reed's version.[67] Beyond these clear but mostly fragmentary quotations, the improvisations were often anchored in the blues. As far as Sharrock and Jackson are concerned, the fundamental blues orientation is hardly surprising: just think of Sharrock's tribute to blues guitarist Blind Willie Johnson on his first album under his own name, or his role in Miles Davis's soundtrack for the Jack Johnson movie. Ronald Shannon Jackson was born in Fort Worth, Texas, and grew up there, like Ornette Coleman, in a blues-oriented "land-scape." But what was the reaction of Peter Brötzmann, playing saxophone, molded by free jazz and Fluxus? In 1986, Brötzmann not only confirmed his affinity with the blues through his membership in Last Exit, but also underlined his own approach: "The music [of Last Exit] has to do with blues, sure. I feel very comfortable with that shit. . . . I'm not an American and I'm not a black guy. But I think I've had my own experience of the blues. I have no problems with that area. I would be ready to work with a good rhythm and blues group, too, anytime."[68]

In the 1960s, the embrace of the blues and concepts developed by Fluxus formed two essential reference points for European jazz musicians within the counterculture, which was also particularly shaped by American influences. This resulted in many creative improvisational dialogues, which did not leave the initiative to American musicians as was previously the case, but made possible independent contributions from many European musicians, contributions that played a significant part in the development of jazz.

NOTES

1. Joachim Ernst Berendt, "Beobachtungen über den Unterschied zwischen der amerikanischen und der europäischen Jazz-Szene," *Neue Zeitschrift für Musik* 140, no. 3 (1979): 231.

2. Ekkehard Jost, "Über den Anfang vom Ende des Epigonentums und über die Überwindung der Kaputtspielphase im westdeutschen Free Jazz," *Neue Zeitschrift für Musik* 140, no. 3 (1979): 237.

3. Stuart Nicholson, *Jazz-Rock: A History* (New York: Schirmer, 1998), xv.

4. Alyn Shipton, *A New History of Jazz* (New York and London: Continuum, 2007), 606.

5. John McLaughlin, in Joachim Ernst Berendt, *Das große Jazzbuch: Von New Orleans bis Jazz Rock* (Frankfurt/Main: Fischer, 1982), 146.

6. Derek Bailey, *Improvisation: Its Nature and Practice* (New York: Da Capo, 1993), 86.

7. Hartmut Kaelble, "Wie die Europäer Amerika sahen: Die USA und das europäische Selbstverständnis im 19. und 20. Jahrhundert," *Amerika und Europa: Mars und Venus? Das Bild Amerikas in Europa,* ed. Rudolf von Thadden and Alexandre Escudier (Göttingen: Wallstein, 2004), 45.

8. Kaelble, "Wie die Europäer Amerika sahen," 43.

9. Norman Mailer, "The White Negro: Superficial Reflections on the Hipster," in *Keeping Time: Reading in Jazz History,* ed. Robert Walser (New York and Oxford: Oxford University Press, 1999), 243.

10. Mailer, "White Negro," 244.

11. Ibid., 244.

12. Andreas Reckwitz, *Das hybride Subjekt: Eine Theorie der Subjektkulturen von der bürgerlichen Moderne zur Postmoderne* (Weilerswist: Velbrück Wissenschaft, 2006), 454.

13. Ibid., 453.

14. Neil A. Wynn, "'Why I Sing the Blues': African American Culture in the Transatlantic World," in *Cross the Water Blues: African American Music in Europe,* ed. Neil A. Wynn (University Press of Mississippi, 2007), 14.

15. Paul Stump, *Go Ahead John: The Music of John McLaughlin* (London: SAF, 2000), 15.

16. Stump, *Go Ahead John,* 15.

17. Shipton, *New History of Jazz,* 606.

18. Alexis Korner, *Kornerstoned: The Alexis Korner Anthology, 1954–1983,* 2 CDs, Castle Music: CMEDD1026 (2006).

19. Graham Bond, *Sound of 65* and *There's a Bond between Us,* CD, BGO: BGOCD500 (1999).

20. Stuart Nicholson, "Fusions and Crossovers," *The Cambridge Companion to Jazz,* ed. Mervyn Cooke and David Horn (Cambridge et al., 2002), 220.

21. Richard Saltonstall, "Rock and Jazz in a Creamy Mix: Two by 'The Cream,'" *Life,* January 26, 1968, 12.

22. Claude Hall, "Cream: Group That's Cream of Rock Crop," *Billboard,* October 7, 1967, 20.

23. Shipton, *New History of Jazz,* 607.

24. Giles Smith, "Returning to Bass: In the Sixties, Jack Bruce Helped Cream to 30 million Record Sales," in *The Independent,* August 29, 1992, www.independent.co.uk/arts-entertainment/rock—returning-to-bass-in-the-sixties-jack-bruce-helped-cream-to-30-million-record-sales-now-the-singer-and-bass-player-is-back-with-his-own-band-giles-smith-met-him-1541322.html (accessed September 13, 2010).

25. "Jack Bruce. Rockin' the Blues," *Edinburgh Festival Magazine,* August 3, 2009, www.edfestmag.co.uk/jazz/festival-jazz-featured-events/jack-bruce (accessed September 13, 2010).

26. Nicholson, *Jazz-Rock,* 22.

27. Eric Clapton, *Clapton: The Autobiography* (New York: Broadway Books, 2007), 87.

28. Shipton, *New History of Jazz*, 608.

29. Graham Bond, *Solid Bond* (1963/1966), CD, Warner: 8122-79906-5 (2008).

30. Jack Bruce, *Things We Like* (1968), CD, Polydor: 065 604-2 (2003).

31. Tony Williams, *Turn It Over*, LP, Polydor: 2425 019 (1970).

32. For more details on Cream's tour of Great Britain in 1971 see: Nicholson, *Jazz-Rock*, 142.

33. Carla Bley and Paul Haines, *Escalator over the Hill* (1968, 1970/1), 2 CDs, JCOA 839310-2.

34. John McLaughlin, *Extrapolation* (1969), CD, Polydor: 841598-2.

35. The Tony Williams Lifetime, *Emergency!* CD, Polydor: 849 068-2 (1991).

36. Nicholson, *Jazz-Rock*, 141.

37. Ibid., 142.

38. Miles Davis, *The Complete in a Silent Way Sessions* (1969), 3 CDs, Sony: c3k65362 (2001).

39. Miles Davis, *The Complete Bitches Brew Sessions* (1969), 4 CDs, Sony: C4K 65570 (1998).

40. Reckwitz, *Das hybride Subjekt*, 463-64.

41. Nicholson, *Jazz-Rock*, 149, parentheses in original.

42. Mahavishnu Orchestra, *Original Album Classics: The Inner Mounting Flame, Birds of Fire, Between Nothingness and Eternity, Visions of the Emerald Beyond*, 5 CDs, Columbia: 88697172532 (2007).

43. Shipton, *New History of Jazz*, 606.

44. Bailey, *Improvisation*, 91.

45. See Ben Watson, *Derek Bailey and the Story of Free Improvisation* (London: Verso, 2004), 95.

46. Watson, *Derek Bailey and the Story of Free Improvisation*, 96.

47. Edwin Prévost, *No Sound Is Innocent* (Matching Tye: Copula, 1995), 12.

48. For further studies of Mengelberg and the Fluxus movement see Jürgen Arndt, *Thelonious Monk und der Free Jazz* (Graz: ADEVA, 2002), 203-15.

49. Peter Niklas Wilson, *Hear and Now: Gedanken zur improvisierten Musik* (Hofheim: Wolke, 1999), 154.

50. Siegfried Schmidt-Joos, "'Weil viele Dinge geändert werden müssen': Ein Interview mit Peter Brötzmann," *Jazz Podium*, April 1968, 129.

51. Owen Smith, "Developing a Fluxable Forum: Early Performance and Publishing," *The Fluxus Reader*, ed. Ken Friedman (Chichester: Academy Editions, 1998), 4-5.

52. Kevin Whitehead, *New Dutch Swing* (New York: Billboard Books, 1998), 15.

53. Wilson, *Hear and Now*, 154.

54. Peter Brötzmann, Interview by Jürgen Jung, *Bayrischer Rundfunk*, March 6, 2006, www.br-online.de/download/pdf/alpha/b/broetzmann.pdf (accessed September 28, 2010).

55. Brötzmann, interview by Jürgen Jung.

56. Bert Noglik, *Jazz-Werkstatt international* (Berlin: Neue Musik, 1981), 195-96.

57. Bailey, *Improvisation*, 131-32.

58. Peter Niklas Wilson, "Meister des Moments: Der niederländische Pianist Misha Mengelberg im Gespräch," *Deutschlandfunk* (radio broadcast), May 22, 1998.

59. Noglik, *Jazz-Werkstatt international*, 208.

60. Ibid., 194.

61. Peter Brötzmann, Misha Mengelberg, Han Bennink, *3 Points and a Mountain*, FMP 0679 (1979).

62. Roswell Rudd, Steve Lacy, Misha Mengelberg, Kent Carter, Han Bennink, *Regeneration*, Soul Note: SN 1054 CD, 1982; Misha Mengelberg, Steve Lacy, George Lewis, Arjen Gorter, Han Bennink, *Change of Season (Music of Herbie Nichols)*, Soul Note: SN 1104 CD, 1984; ICP Orchestra, *Two Programs: The ICP Orchestra Performs Nichols–Monk*, ICP 026, 1984 and 1986.

63. Misha Mengelberg, *Who's Bridge?* (Avan 038, 1994); *No Idea* (DIW 619, 1996); *Four in One*, Songlines: SGL SA1535-5, 2000.

64. See Nate Chinen, "ICP Orchestra's Experimental Jazz Swings at Tonic," *New York Times*, March 23, 2006, www.icporchestra.com/reviews.htm (accessed October 29, 2010). See also: Michael Jackson, "Going Dutch: ICP's Coincidental 40-Year Journey," *Down Beat*, April 2007, 38-43.

65. See the discography of recordings by Peter Brötzmann, www.efi.group.shef.ac.uk/mbrotzm.html (accessed September 28, 2010).

66. For further studies of these bands with Peter Brötzmann see Jürgen Arndt, "Misha Mengelberg und Peter Brötzmann in improvisatorischen Dialogen zwischen Europa und den USA," *Jazzforschung/Jazz Research* 42 (2010), Graz: ADEVA 2010, 35-60.

67. Last Exit, *The Noise of Trouble*, Enemy: EMY 103, 1986; *Cassette Recordings 87*, Enemy: EMY 105, 1987.

68. Steve Lake, "The Living End: A Candid Exchange of Views and Verbals among the Members of the World's Last Music Group—Bill Laswell, Ronald Shannon Jackson, Sonny Sharrock and Peter Brötzmann," 1986, http://web.archive.org/web/20021108221021 (accessed September 28, 2010).

TONY WHYTON

16 / EUROPE AND THE NEW JAZZ STUDIES

yes I
read
this

right

I n his 1988 article "Some Problems with Jazz Research," Lewis Porter described the way in which jazz scholarship had, until that time, been largely an amateur pursuit. Porter suggested that the growth and development of jazz and black music studies in the United States would eventually transform the way in which the music was discussed and understood (Porter 1988, 204). In the postwar period, when jazz had been the subject of professional study, writings had borrowed heavily from the field of formalist musicology and echoed the analytical methods developed in relation to Western classical music. Musician scholars such as Gunther Schuller, for example, argued for jazz to be recognized as art, demonstrating a passion for great jazz through the discussion and analysis of landmark recordings. From the 1950s on, these efforts, coupled with the writings of critics such as Martin Williams and Marshall Stearns, signaled a move toward the creation and celebration of a jazz canon in the United States, a body of masterworks that constitute the core of the jazz tradition. For example, Williams's *Smithsonian Collection of Classic Jazz*, and his collected writings grouped under the title *The Jazz Tradition*, embodied this aesthetic by reifying jazz history and presenting the music as a unified and unproblematic continuum of periods and styles.

good

Come the 1990s, the professionalism that Porter described resulted in a growth in new musicology, where a new generation of scholars began to question the methods that had been used to date. Bruce Johnson, for example, examined the problem of jazz scholarship and the way in which formalist musicology, coupled with a focus on jazz recordings, denied the importance of orality/aurality in jazz (Johnson 1993). Equally, scholars such as Robert Walser challenged the logic of using formalist methods developed in classical music to explain jazz, and suggested that new methods of transcription and analysis were required to capture the intertextual and signifying qualities of the music (Walser 1993). The 1990s offered a sea change in the development of jazz research, with scholars challenging the ground upon which jazz history had been written to date. Writings such as Scott DeVeaux's "Constructing the Jazz Tradition: Jazz Historiography" and John Gennari's "Jazz Criticism: Its Development and Ideologies" offered groundbreaking examinations of the discourse of jazz history and served to shape subsequent writings on the subject. DeVeaux's work highlighted the political function of jazz historiography and the ideological implications of canon formation. In describing the tradition as a construct, his work destroyed any claim to a natural or

yup

very good

organic development of jazz history. Instead, DeVeaux explored the way in which history and the notion of tradition are often constructed to serve the needs of the present and to reinforce the myths and values of certain writers, commentators, or groups. Together, these writings signaled a shift in approach for musicology toward what later would be described as the New Jazz Studies. From the 1990s on, the study of jazz has been opened up to different methodological and disciplinary interests, and the New Jazz Studies has marked an investment in cultural and critical theory and a commitment to cross-disciplinary or interdisciplinary perspectives. Edited volumes such as Krin Gabbard's *Jazz among the Discourses* (1995a) and *Representing Jazz* (1995b) and Robert O'Meally's *The Jazz Cadence of American Culture* (1998), for example, demonstrated how the study of jazz could be enriched by perspectives from outside formalist musicology. Drawing on writings from film studies, African American literature, fine art, and cultural studies, these texts illustrated how traditional understandings of jazz could be revised and examined in new ways.

Today, the portrayal of jazz as a coherent and unproblematic tradition is confronted head-on by New Jazz Studies scholars. The history of the music is subject to conflict and contestation; jazz is a critical discourse that has changed and adapted over time, feeding into issues of race, gender, class, identity, and place. The New Jazz Studies draws attention to the political and ideological backdrops in which jazz is created and, most importantly, the discipline has given rise to voices that were previously excluded from jazz history, from women to the musicians themselves. Today, the New Jazz Studies encapsulates a vast array of critical positions, and yet, despite this plurality of approach, the engagement with jazz outside of American contexts has been limited. Ironically, in dispelling several mythologies about jazz, the New Jazz Studies has arguably failed to engage with the global spread of jazz and the intercultural exchanges that have occurred in the music since its inception.

Resisting Essentialism:
Toward a New European Jazz Studies

There has been a long and complex history of jazz criticism in Europe, as other writings in this volume discuss. Despite their centrality to the creation of a body of writings on jazz, historical writings emanating from Europe are, largely, described as being overly romanticized and limited in their representation of jazz either through fetishistic desires for otherness, primitivistic accounts of musicians, or the ideology of European modernism.[1] Moreover, writings that discuss the critical relationship between Europe and America have, until recently, tended to reinforce journalistic codes, and established mythologies and binary oppositions between the two continents and the interplay between musicians working in different contexts. Typically, European writings are discussed as important historically but of little use today or downplayed as being irrelevant to the spread of "authentic" jazz culture in the United States. James Lincoln Collier's *The Reception of Jazz in America*, for example, arguably commented more on Europe than it did on the reception of jazz in America. Collier devoted the bulk of his text to refuting or downplaying the role that European writers had in "discovering" jazz and challenging the idea that Americans did not appreciate jazz as an indigenous art form (Collier 1988).

More recently, the formation of an authoritative jazz canon has served to reify jazz, detaching the music from popular culture and broader social and geographical exchanges. In addition, the neo-traditionalist agenda has continued to resist musical Eurocentricity (although it often draws on other European art forms to legitimize jazz's cultural value), and jazz history is frequently represented in African American exceptionalist terms. Although I understand the desire to create a critical discourse for evaluating jazz in its context and the need to separate jazz from the paradigms of classical music, the denial of European influence misunderstands the dynamics of cultural development and exchange. For example, when the New Jazz Studies scholar and musician George Lewis promoted Eurological and Afrological theories in the mid-1990s, there was an inevitable loss of complexity and sensitivity to the intercultural dialogue that has existed throughout jazz history (Lewis 1996). Indeed, I would argue that by continuing to present Europe as a "bleached continent," to use Paul Gilroy's term, colonial-imperial power structures and simplistic binaries remain intact and it becomes impossible to move beyond very straightforward and oppositional descriptions of U.S. and European scenes. Gilroy argues that the synonymity of the terms "white" and "European" cannot continue, particularly given that nationalist ideals persist through a sense of absolute ethnicity and racialized difference. To counter this perception, Gilroy suggests a new way of thinking about European culture:

> The feral beauty of postcolonial culture, literature, and art of all kinds can be used to complicate this picture, but they cannot provide an antidote to the problems that make culture and ethnicity so widely and automatically resonant. Something larger, bolder, and more imaginative is called for. We need to see how the presence of strangers, aliens, and blacks and the distinctive dynamics of Europe's imperial history have combined to shape its cultural and political habits and institutions. (Gilroy 2004, xiv)

Within this context, Gilroy advocates a complex and sophisticated understanding of cultural impact and influence, where notions of whiteness and blackness are challenged alongside a revision of European history. Gilroy argues that we would be able to challenge the fantasies of the newly embattled European region as an ethnically pure or politically fortified space by, among other things, developing an understanding of Europe's openness to the colonial worlds it helped to make. Similarly, Bruce Boyd Raeburn's work on New Orleans culture echoes Gilroy's desire for revisionism, providing a useful way into understanding the complexity of cultural exchanges between U.S. and European musicians and writers. On the one hand, Raeburn's work demonstrates how jazz in New Orleans was not born out of racial purity but a number of complex cultural exchanges and influences, including a significant European influence. On the other hand, the reification of New Orleans style as racially pure was largely spearheaded by the work of European jazz writers such as Hugues Panassié, Robert Goffin, and Charles Delaunay, who interpreted jazz either as the soundtrack to the modernization of industrial Europe or as a fetishized Other (Raeburn 2009a and 2009b). This paradox typifies the complexity of exchange and interplay between U.S. and European writers and musicians.

For the remainder of this chapter, I want to explore ways in which the themes raised so far could play out within the context of a New European Jazz Studies. Using Stuart Nicholson's book, *Is Jazz Dead? Or Has It Moved to a New Address* as a starting point for a discussion of the politics between European and U.S. jazz scenes, I demonstrate the potential for new insights and illustrate how the New Jazz Studies could add a depth of investigation and critical engagement with jazz as a cultural practice in Europe today. Indeed, the following examples comment on a range of themes that are of direct relevance to New Jazz Studies work today, from cultural mythology to colonial/postcolonial history, from ethnography to race, from essentialism to the commodification of blackness, from issues of class and gender to the questioning of authenticity, from the significance of positionality within criticism and discourse to identity and community.

Nicholson and the Nordic Tone

Since its publication in 2005, Nicholson's *Is Jazz Dead?* has had a wide-ranging influence on the jazz industry, not only being cited by scholars of jazz studies but, perhaps more significantly, receiving a significant amount of press coverage for its pro-European stance among musicians and arts professionals. In demonstrating the global and "glocal" impact of jazz, Nicholson uses a language analogy to describe the way in which local jazz dialects emerge and are flavored by national characteristics, describing jazz as the product of local scenes, environments, and cultural sensibilities. Nicholson describes the way in which jazz has been claimed

and adapted within a global context; however, when discussing the transcultura-
tion of music, surprisingly, he falls back on national traits and cultural stereotypes
in his description of jazz from around the globe. For example, Nicholson uses the
testimony of musicians to reinforce the fact that Australian jazz is "open," has a
"big throatedness" coupled with a little bit of "bravado," whereas in Scandinavia,
the music is "angst-ridden," expressing among other things, a sense of "Nordic
chastity" (Nicholson 2005, 188, 197). When describing Scandinavian jazz and the
production of the "Nordic tone" in particular, Nicholson constructs a problematic alternative to the American mainstream. For Nicholson, the Nordic tone
represents a refreshing, "pure" antidote to the contrived and formulaic American
mainstream. The music is principled and authentic in that, in coming from the
North, it "brings an awareness of the closeness of man to nature" (Nicholson
2005, 197–98). Nicholson suggests that there is a certain internal drama at play in
Scandinavian art and this somehow reflects the intimate sensibilities of the people whose identity is determined by the landscape they live and work in. For
example, Nicholson describes the music of Jan Gabarek as "an ordered calm in
the often frantic world of jazz, projecting the stark imagery of nature in the frozen
north" (Nicholson 2005, 207) and goes on to state that the Nordic tone can be
heard in the playing of musicians from all Scandinavian countries.

Although, on the surface, Nicholson's work reads as an important sideswipe at
the hegemony of the neo-traditionalist agenda in the United States, his writings
do not move beyond a simple inversion of the jazz-as-American/jazz-as-global
binary and, as such, arguably replace one form of essentialist narration with another. The description of the pure, frozen, natural, and open North as a contrast
to the urban, corrupt, contrived jazz of America also suggests a model of European culture that is not far removed from an age-old colonial spirit. Whether
intended or not, Nicholson portrays Scandinavia as an ethnically pure landscape
devoid of corruption and the negative influence of the United States. Despite the
continued discussion of cultural exchange and the collaborations between Scandinavian musicians and African American jazz artists within his book, Nicholson's
continued emphasis on the innate sensibilities of Nordic musicians inevitably
contributes to the ideological and imperial bleaching of Europe discussed above.

In the context of wider European culture, where national sentiment is often
used to promote xenophobia and fear of "otherness," I would argue that jazz's
ability to encourage transnational collaborations and styles is one of its significant
features. Indeed, one of the central qualities of jazz, as I see it, is the music's
ability to transcend national and geographical borders and to challenge cultural
stereotyping.

Jazz, Race, and Postcolonial Europe

Other types of essentialist ideology masquerading beneath a celebration of pluralism can also be found within the testimony of musicians working within the current European jazz scene. For example, consider the following two statements featured in Nicholson's book by the British saxophonist Courtney Pine on the pluralism of the British jazz scene today:

> I really believe your environment helps shape what you do as an artist. . . . It really has to be about the musician's natural experience—if you have a classical musician and you ask him to play Bob Marley he's going to sound weird, but if you are going to play something of that musician's natural background that's going to be very natural. (Quoted in Nicholson 2005, 172)

> There was a time when we would basically find an icon from America who's current and emulate him, but now we're not happy with that. . . . So now I feel comfortable enough to present my cultural heritage, so when you see me you know I listened to Bob Marley, you can hear some Caribbean stuff in there, you hear European stuff in there, you can hear some African stuff and you can hear that American thing as well. (Quoted in Nicholson 2005, 176)

Pine's second statement seems to reinforce the breaking down of boundaries and the celebration of the multitude of influences that are open to musicians today. And yet, when it is compared with the first statement, we can begin to see how boundaries are constructed around who can and cannot lay claim to a supposedly authentic voice within this pluralistic context. By continually placing emphasis on innate sensibilities (or the "natural" disposition of musicians) and denying classical musicians' access to the music of Bob Marley, Pine's pluralism comes with certain caveats; musicians must express some natural sensibility to the music they are performing, and therefore European classically trained musicians are insincere if engaging with the music of Bob Marley. If we accept this reading, at its most basic, the statement reinforces Eurological and Afrological distinctions discussed above without acknowledging the complexity of cultural life and identity politics in postcolonial Europe today. Furthermore, by continually emphasizing the word "natural," Pine's statement conflates the cultural background and lived experience with innate ability and sensitivities.

To unpack this further, I want to respond to the challenge set by Guthrie Ramsey in his article "Who Hears Here? Black Music, Critical Bias, and the Musicological Skin Trade" and write myself into my criticism. Ramsey argued that by moving toward a degree of self-reflexivity—recognizing how subject positions shape the study of music and supposedly objective readings of music—

great (handwritten)

mention this (handwritten)

scholars can rejuvenate the discourse of black studies and its underlying political imperatives and "shed light on the complex reception histories of black music" (Ramsey 2001, 40). Thinking of my own subject position in relation to Pine's comments, I am puzzled by his constant emphasis on the natural and subsequent exclusion of musicians from accessing black culture based on a presumption of their background and training. My formative experiences as a child growing up in Stockwell and Brixton, South London, were fairly typical of most kids living within inner-city settings and participating in state education today. Only when I attended university did I realize that my education was unusual when compared with that of my peers from other parts of the country. Where most children were singing hymns or listening to Bible stories, my schooling involved, among other things, a variety of musical influences alongside Caribbean folklore in the form of trickster stories of Anansie. As a Londoner with an East End family, I was subject to a melting pot of cultural influences ranging from Bob Marley to jazz to music hall, and my peer group engaged actively with different kinds of music and cultural experiences. As a musician who went on to receive "classical training," I'm left wondering where my experiences sit with Pine's reading of playing things that are "natural." While I am not laying claim to having authentic black roots, my childhood experiences were typical of most kids growing up in inner-city London today who encounter the full spectrum of life in a modern metropolis.

Pine's words, when coupled with my own experiences, provide an opportunity to interrogate concepts of whiteness and to problematize the notion of the essential black subject who expresses a "natural" affinity with the music he or she performs. From my subject position, I would argue that Pine's words infer an exclusivity of ownership of black culture and a denial of the complexities of cultural influence and identity politics today. As Stuart Hall discussed in the late '80s and early '90s, we must, on the one hand, retain an understanding of the ongoing politics of race and institutionalized racism but, on the other hand, not let this hold us back from dispelling the myth of the essential black subject. Hall, Gilroy, and others have discussed the historical imperative for defining race as an organizing category in Britain. Strategic essentialism, in effect, helped to express a common experience of racism and marginalization. And yet, once the category of race became hegemonic over individual racial and ethnic identities, there simultaneously developed a need to displace and reorganize cultural strategies and call an end to the notion of the essential black subject. Hall argued that in order to transform the politics of representation and liberate ourselves from the monolithic construct of race as a sociopolitical category, it is important to acknowledge and celebrate the existence of new ethnicities and to understand a diversity of subject positions. He states that "black" is a "politically and culturally constructed category, which cannot be grounded in a set of fixed trans-cultural or transcendental racial categories and which therefore has no guarantees in nature" (Hall 1996, 443). And yet, the friction between race as a social construct and racism as an everyday experience is not easily resolved. As Henry Louis Gates Jr. suggests: "It is important to remember that 'race' is only a socio-political category, nothing more. At the same time—in terms of its practical performative force—that doesn't help me when I'm trying to get a taxi on the corner of 125th and Lenox Avenue" (Gates 1993, 38). Despite these frictions, the destabilizing and challenging of the essential black subject is an inevitable and necessary step in changing the cultural and political landscape. By celebrating diversity and different subject positions, we move away from simple reversals of black and white, natural and unnatural, authentic and inauthentic, and, indeed, classical music and Bob Marley. The challenge to simple reversals is perhaps best summed up by bell hooks, who, in clear reference to the Gates anecdote above, challenges the notion of race as a unified experience:

> Privileged black folks who are pimping black culture for their own opportunistic gain tend to focus on racism as though it is the great equalizing factor. For example, when a materially successful black person tells the story of how no cab will stop for the person because of color, the speaker claims unity with the masses of black folks who are daily assaulted by white supremacy. Yet this assertion of shared victimhood obscures the fact that this racial assault is mediated by the reality of class privilege. However hurt or even damaged the individual may be by a failure to acquire a taxi immediately, that individual is likely to be more allied with the class interests of individuals who share similar status (including whites) than with the needs of those black folks whom racist economic aggression render destitute, who do not even have the luxury to consider taking a taxi. (hooks 1994, 150-51)

Hooks's comments here not only offer a challenge to conventional binaries, foregrounding class issues in debates about race and identity, but also comment on the way in which common manifestations of blackness are contested and negotiated within black culture.

Destabilizing the Essential Black Subject: Jazz and the MOBOs

In the context of exploring the continually shifting boundaries of race, the British jazz scene offers several interesting examples of the complexities and tensions surrounding the questioning of the essential black subject and the way in which race politics is experienced in everyday situations. One good example of the contested category of race came in 2006 when the organizers of the Music of

TONY WHYTON

Black Origin (MOBO) awards removed jazz from its awards list. This move sparked a protest of words and action by Jazz Services, the United Kingdom's national jazz agency, and Dune Music, a British company devoted to the promotion and recording of predominantly black jazz artists (and, as such, a company with the most to lose from the exclusion) and empowering black performers. The national press featured articles about the controversy of the MOBOS and the exclusion of jazz from the ceremony, quoting figures such as Courtney Pine, who stressed the music's integral links to black history, and covering the demonstration that took place outside the Albert Hall, the venue for the 2006 ceremony, led by Dune artist Abram Wilson.

On one level, the exclusion of jazz from the MOBOS demonstrated how movable a construct race is. Jazz might be considered black music historically, spelling out the "origin" in the Music of Black Origin, but at the time of the award ceremony, the music wasn't considered central enough to black cultural experience to be included automatically within the awards list. Although jazz was reinstated in following years, its absence from the MOBOS demonstrated how destabilized the essential black subject had become and also how disturbing this instability was for British jazz artists for whom race was central to their identity. To be a black British jazz musician excluded from the MOBO awards was difficult to take, as if the awards provided access to an exclusive club, an essential body of genuine artists. For black British jazz artists, to be excluded resulted in a challenge to their authenticity, the legitimacy of their blackness, and the centrality of jazz to the development of popular music. As Pine stated: "The Mobos was the only thing that recognised jazz in that way [a music of black origin]. Jazz was the stepping stone for rock 'n' roll, rhythm and blues—all popular music. Folks have got to know that we've been excluded" (quoted in Baracaia, 2006). This situation could obviously have provided black British jazz artists with an opportunity to offer alternative modes of representation that rejected the limited categorization of blackness found within the MOBOS and other media contexts. Indeed, the MOBO rejection could have led to a challenge to cultural stereotypes and an empowering of musicians to speak from a variety of positions. Ironically, however, I would argue that when understandings of race become displaced and fragmented in this way, there is an inevitable desire to reassert race as an essential category. As Anthony Cohen suggests in his book *The Symbolic Construction of Community*, community is felt at its most intense when the boundaries by which we define ourselves are challenged or eroded (Cohen 1993, 98). Furthermore, when existing paradigms, infrastructures, and media representations of racial identity are so strong, it is difficult to envisage alternative ways in which black subjects can define themselves, especially when championing a music that has limited representation within broader cultural spheres.

374

interesting!

n)le

find this for me!

Although jazz's exclusion from the MOBOS fed into debates about the destabilization of the essential black subject, the incident fed into much larger issues concerning the music industry and marketplace. Indeed, arguably the protests had more to do with jazz's loss of media representation and the music's dwindling market share than they did about racial identity. Building on this, the exclusion of jazz also feeds into what bell hooks describes as the "commodification of blackness," the Western capitalist codification of black culture that has continued to limit and control the representation of black subjects. For hooks, class politics, as well as racial interests, lie at the heart of the limited representations of blackness, as black culture frequently becomes synonymous with the underclass, urban living, and/or ghettoized communities. When discussing the filmmaking of Spike Lee, for example, hooks describes the way in which the director has had to conform to limited modes of representation in order be successful:

> Since his agenda is to succeed within that system as much as possible, he must work it by reproducing conservative and even stereotypical images of blackness so as not to alienate that crossover audience. Lee's work cannot be revolutionary and generate wealth at the same time. Yet it is in his class interest to make it seem as though he, and his work, embody the "throw-down ghetto" blackness that is the desired product. (hooks 1994, 150)

In light of hooks's comments in relation to jazz and the MOBOS, the perception that the music no longer conformed to the norms of commodified blackness could also have played a part in the exclusion. Arguably, jazz was bad for the MOBO awards' street cred, as it offered a different range of cultural significations, class interests, and manifestations of black experience. On the exclusion of jazz from the awards, the artist Corinne Bailey Rae questioned the linking of black music with urban experience:

> The assumption that all black music has to be urban is a really ignorant way of thinking about black music. Black people and black music have affected all popular music of the twentieth century, from Jazz to soul to hip hop to reggae to pop. . . . Music by black people does not mean it has to come from an urban perspective.[2]

Here, Rae acknowledges the multifaceted nature of black experiences today and comments on the limitations of institutional and media representations of race.[3] However, despite these informed words, I would argue that jazz's reinstatement in the awards from 2007 came with certain restrictions, namely that award winners from 2007 onward reinforced some form of commercialized urban ideal.[4]

Jazz and New European Identities

TONY WHYTON

Considering the examples outlined above, I am not only interested in artists who actively seek to challenge stereotypical representations, but, perhaps more importantly, I argue that it is necessary to take a step back and examine why race as an essential category continues to have currency in today's postcolonial world. If we acknowledge that the essential black subject has been displaced and fragmented and replaced by a variety of subject positions or individual ethnicities, the question of why race continues to play a central part in identity construction is complex, not only born out of our sense of the past and shaped by our history, a product of long-established paradigms and representations, but also linked to something aspirational or a type of becoming, how we want to be perceived and identified. Building on this, I argue that instead of viewing identity as something fixed, we should think about it as dynamic and discursive. Viewing identity as a form of becoming, it is important to ask why the sociopolitical category of race is foregrounded over other identities within today's postcolonial context. Like British trombonist Dennis Rollins, who suggested in an interview as part of the Open University's *What Is Black British Jazz?* project that he feels free to "try on" different identities and can "go into black" when it suits him, the use of race as a defining category has a multitude of functions that can empower musicians, enabling them to explore different subject positions. Identity within this context is not restrictive but dynamic and in flux.

Returning to Nicholson and supposed Scandinavian sensibilities, I would argue that the same rules of identity formation apply. The Nordic tone is a cultural construct that serves a variety of purposes and reinforces certain values and beliefs—it says as much about the way in which Scandinavia is promoted and represented today as it does about the past. More important, and integrally tied to identity formation, is the need avoid talk of national culture in jazz as something essential, and I would suggest that the strategy of resistance to African American essentialism should also be applied to European contexts; the Nordic tone, for example, is not an expression of some collective Scandinavian consciousness. Indeed, we need to distinguish between codes and conventions that have developed within specific cultural, social, and politically determined contexts, and music as some kind of natural sound with inherent qualities. I would argue that the assumption that musical codes and conventions represent some kind of deep-rooted national consciousness is deeply flawed and ignores the complexity of identity formation today. As Dave Hesmondhalgh states:

> *The local is increasingly affected by the global*: Partly as a result of this increasing movement of cultural texts, but also because of other, wider factors, cul-

tural identities are increasingly complex. . . . Many texts are now based not on the interests, concerns and culture of particular nations, but on those of a variety of nations, or of sections of people who share a transnational culture. (Hesmondhalgh 2007, 219)

The challenge moving forward is to understand the way in which jazz continues to develop amid changing social, cultural, and political conditions without our readings of the music, and the expressions of the musicians themselves, being contained by those conditions. Like Stuart Hall, who in his study of black British cinema celebrated the wealth of representations of black subjects in films such as *My Beautiful Laundrette*, I eagerly await the day where other types of jazz identity are foregrounded either to complement or to challenge existing figurations. How vibrant would the European jazz scene be if we had artists championing "gay black British jazz" or Urban Nordic Noise, or musicians playing "carbon-neutral jazz" or "vegan jazz," "a pride-in-being-university-educated jazz," or "economic downturn jazz"? This vision is also not very far removed from the experiences of musicians bound up within the context of the current black British jazz scene, as bassist and bandleader Gary Crosby observes: "I believe we are all working towards a British jazz scene that is so reflective of Britain today, that's what we are all working towards. Its emphasis was really Black community, whereas now it's musicians of any skin colour or any background, playing to any environment" (quoted in the "What Is Black British Jazz" podcast, 2009). In suggesting a new model for changing European culture, I am attracted to Paul Gilroy's argument that, as well as being sensitive to the problematic issue of race within Europe's colonial past, we need to move on from the anticolonial sentiment and reified concepts of race and class that have dominated postwar discussions of European civilization, toward judgments that are "more alive to the ludic, cosmopolitan energy and the democratic possibilities so evident in the postcolonial metropolis" (Gilroy 2004, xi).

Europe and the New Jazz Studies

Over the last ten years, there has been a gradual growth and interest in applying New Jazz Studies methods to European cultures. Several critical studies, monographs, and edited volumes have been published that examine the way in which jazz has played out in contexts outside the United States, and there is a growing acknowledgment of the vibrancy and critical potential of investigating jazz in different European settings.[5] This significance of jazz studies in Europe is perhaps most firmly evidenced through the growing number of national and European jazz research projects that have been supported in recent years. For example, the

United Kingdom's *What Is Black British Jazz?* project (funded by the UK's Arts and Humanities Research Council in 2009) and the pan-European *Rhythm Changes: Jazz Cultures and European Identities* (funded by Humanities in the European Research Area in 2010) are large-scale projects that bring together a range of researchers from different disciplinary backgrounds, from music to sociology, from media to cultural studies. Through the funding of projects such as these, there is an acknowledgment that jazz is integral to European life, and that by understanding more about development of jazz cultures we can gain insights into the complexities of identity formation today and the critical exchanges between American and European artists, writers, and audiences. As a research area still in its infancy, European New Jazz Studies offers the potential for groundbreaking insights into cultural politics of jazz past and present, examining topics from cultural identity to mediation, from migration to cultural exchange. Within this context, a New European Jazz Studies should engage with national, transnational, and transcontinental exchange as a critical discourse, resisting essentialist ideologies and examining the way in which jazz cultures obtain their meaning in the function that the music has for its musicians, audiences, and industry.

NOTES

1. See, for example, Ted Gioia, *The Imperfect Art: Reflections on Jazz and Modern Culture* (Oxford: Oxford University Press, 1988).

2. *Daily Mail Online*, 20 September 2006, www.dailymail.co.uk/tvshowbiz/article-40 6103/Jazz-musicians-protest-cold-shoulder-Mobos.html.

3. The limited representation of blackness is perhaps seen at its most extreme within gangsta rap. As rapper and producer Andre Romelle Young (aka Dr. Dre) states, "It felt funny going in the studio talking about 'this bitch' and 'this ho' and how 'I fucked this girl' with a wife at home. But then, I have to look at it like entertainment, and I have a set fanbase, and there's certain things they want to hear. They wanna hear Dre be Dre." See Ekow Eshun, "The Rap Trap," in *The Guardian* [weekend supplement], 27 May 2000.

4. The MOBO jazz winners were Soweto Kinch in 2007, YolanDa Brown in 2008 and 2009, and Empirical in 2010.

5. For examples of these writings see E. Taylor Atkins (ed.), Jazz Planet (2004), George McKay, *Circular Breathing: The Cultural Politics of Jazz in Britain* (2004), and Jeffrey H. Jackson, *Making Jazz French: Music and Modern Life in Interwar Paris* (2003).

BIBLIOGRAPHY

Ashcroft, B., G. Griffiths, and H. Tiffin, eds. 1995. *The Post-Colonial Studies Reader* (London and New York: Routledge).

Atkins, E. T. 2003. *Jazz Planet* (Jackson: University Press of Mississippi).

Baracaia, A. November 2006. "'Jazz Warriors' Plan Protest at Mobos," *Evening*

Standard, www.thisislondon.co.uk/music/article-23367429-jazz-warriors-plan-protest-at-mobos.do (accessed 1 November 2010).

Cohen, A. 1993. *The Symbolic Construction of Community* (London and New York: Routledge,).

Collier, J. L. 1988. *The Reception of Jazz in America: A New View* (New York: Institute for Studies in American Music).

DeVeaux, S. 1991. "Constructing the Jazz Tradition: Jazz Historiography," *Black American Literature Forum* 25.3, Literature of Jazz Issue, pp. 525–60.

Gabbard, K. 1995a. *Jazz among the Discourses* (Durham, NC, and London: Duke University Press).

——. 1995b. *Representing Jazz* (Durham, NC, and London: Duke University Press).

Gates, H. L. Jr. 1990. *The Signifyin(g) Monkey: A Theory of African-American Literary Criticism* (Oxford and New York: Oxford University Press).

——. 1993. *Loose Canons: Notes on the Culture Wars* (Oxford and New York: Oxford University Press).

Gennari, J. 1991. "Jazz Criticism: Its Development and Ideologies," *Black American Literature Forum* 25, pp. 484–523.

——. 2006. *Blowin' Hot and Cool: Jazz and Its Critics* (Chicago and London: University of Chicago Press).

Gilroy, P. 2004. "Foreword: Migrancy, Culture, and a New Map of Europe," in Raphael-Hernandez, H., ed., *Blackening Europe: The African American Presence* (New York: Routledge,), xi–xxii.

Gioia, T. 1988. *The Imperfect Art: Reflections on Jazz and Modern Culture* (Oxford: Oxford University Press).

Hall, S. 1996. "New Ethnicities," in David Morley and Kuan-Hsing Chen, eds., *Stuart Hall: Critical Dialogues in Cultural Studies* (London and New York: Routledge), pp. 441–49.

Hesmondhalgh, D. 2007. *The Cultural Industries*, 2nd. ed. (London: Sage Publications, 2007).

hooks, b. 1994, *Outlaw Culture: Resisting Representation* (New York: Routledge).

Jackson, J. H. 2003. *Making Jazz French: Music and Modern Life in Interwar Paris* (Durham, NC, and London: Duke University Press).

Johnson, B. 1993. "Hear Me Talkin' to Ya: Problems of Jazz Discourse," *Popular Music* 12:1, pp. 1–12.

Lewis, G. 1996. "Improvised Music after 1950: Afrological and Eurological Perspectives," *Black Music Research Journal* 16.1, pp. 91–122.

McKay, G. 2004. *Circular Breathing: The Cultural Politics of Jazz in Britain* (Durham, NC, and London: Duke University Press).

Murray, A. 1970. *The Omni-Americans: New Perspectives on Black Experience and American Culture* (New York: Outerbridge and Dienstfrey).

——. 1978, *Stomping the Blues* (London: Quartet Books).

Nicholson, S. 2005. *Is Jazz Dead? Or Has It Moved to a New Address* (London and New York: Routledge).

O'Meally, R. 1998. *The Jazz Cadence of American Culture* (New York: Columbia University Press).

O'Meally, R., B. Hayes Edwards, and F. Jasmine Griffin, eds. 2004. *Uptown Conversation: The New Jazz Studies* (New York: Columbia University Press).

Porter, L. 1998. "Some Problems in Jazz Research," *Black Music Research Journal* 8, no. 2 , pp.195-206.

Raeburn, B. B. 2009a. *New Orleans Style and the Writing of American Jazz History* (Ann Arbor: University of Michigan Press).

———. 2009b. "Stars of David and Sons of Sicily: Constellations beyond the Canon in Early New Orleans Jazz," *Jazz Perspectives* 3.2 pp. 123-52.

Ramsey, G. 2001. "Who Hears Here? Black Music, Critical Bias, and the Musicological Skin Trade," *Musical Quarterly* 85:1, pp. 1-52.

Schuller, G. 1986. *Musings: The Musical Worlds of Gunther Schuller; A Collection of His Writings* (Oxford and New York: Oxford University Press).

Walser, R. 1993. "Out of Notes: Signification, Interpretation, and the Problem of Miles Davis," *Musical Quarterly* 77:2, pp. 343-65.

Williams, M. 1993. *The Jazz Tradition* (Oxford: Oxford University Press).

TONY WHYTON

17 / REVISIONING HISTORY LIVED
FOUR EUROPEAN EXPATS, THREE MEN AND ONE WOMAN, WHO SHAPED ONE AMERICAN LIFE IN TWO AMERICAN CULTURES

M y time in Europe doing interviews and research for my book *Northern Sun, Southern Moon: Europe's Reinvention of Jazz* (Yale University Press, 2005) exposed me to many variations on the trope of American "expats"—mostly African American musicians who lived and worked full time in Europe as expatriates—and those who toured there regularly and often enough to have a comparably consistent presence and influence. Many European musicians told me about hearing their first jazz on the Voice of America radio station, or through their contact with American GIs, or at clubs and festivals that presented visiting Americans and/or expats.

When my friend and colleague Dr. Franya Berkman recently invited me to speak to her Lewis & Clark College History of Jazz class in our home city of Portland, Oregon, about the "free jazz" period spanning the late 1950s and the '60s, I found myself rooting around on iTunes and in memories of my own childhood and early years as a fan and budding young trombonist-composer-arranger on the West Coast during those decades. I wanted to give these Oregon students a glimpse of their specifically *regional* music-cultural history, as I had lived it. While at that time I certainly didn't know or think of the influence of anyone or anything European as seminal to my formative years in this American music, the hindsight of my prep for this talk alerted me to how deeply some European expats in America did influence my not-atypical coming of age in even its most Afrocentric aspects.

Once this premise is in play, it suggests a broader survey than I will present here. A German (Alfred) Lion and (Francis) Wolff raised me and many other European-American "wild children" in their den (Blue Note Records), teaching us how to understand and speak African American music's language as fluently as, if not more so than, our own more native musicultural tongues. Turkish-born Ahmet Ertegun and (especially with the jazz side) his brother Nesuhi did the same with their Atlantic Records, redirecting the inroad African American music had made into the first part of the century's mainstream culture as "jazz" to the second half's even vaster grassroots of R&B and rock genres. Also, the first serious books about the music most of us read then were by two Frenchmen, Hugues Panassié and André Hodeir.

My background was even more jazz-specific than that general milieu, in ways both cultural and musical. It started me off in the thick of the West Coast jazz scene (the one most popular in Germany then, as it happened), shaping my knowledge, tastes, and aesthetics down some lines rather than others as a result. That led me to associations with some *people* rather than others when I started working as a musician and writer about the music.

To summarize it, I would start with the bromide that the West Coast scene was the "whitest" and most Eurocentric part of the American jazz culture in the 1950s–'60s era, in part for certain reasons having to do with Hollywood's draw of modern composers for film work, and of the most formally trained and disciplined musicians for studio work At the same time, for the same reason, it was more conducive than its East Coast and Deep South counterparts to the flexible aesthetic of the music's structure, function, and voice needed to accommodate both the Third Stream and the "free jazz" breakthrough's assertion away from the "jazz" rubric altogether, and down from a momentum of the pre-1960s "black uplift" and "jazz-as-modernist-avant-garde" to one of an African American presence in the Maverick school of American experimentalism-cum-world-music— which may yet prove a thicker and ultimately more fruitful and enduring branch than jazz-as-genre in American music history. (I pointedly don't assert such advantage over the midwestern scenes, to which the West Coast scene is more linked in ways I will touch on ahead.)

The four European expats I will discuss all played key and direct roles at different times in the evolution of that part of American music I engaged with at different stages of my own personal and professional growth, and those engagements defined the quality and shape of the part of my identity in the music I see as most deeply American.

In chronological order of their influence:

- Russian immigrant music theorist Joseph Schillinger, dead five years before I was born, set forces in motion in American music that I was shaped and swept along by for years before I became aware of them and of how prevalent their idiosyncracies of vision would prove to be in my own arc from student to professional

- Austrian immigrant keyboardist Joe Zawinul was the first white musician to break through the color barrier my youthful internal radar of such things had devised within the music, and then among the first to further break down the similar wall between "acoustic/jazz" and "electric/rock" in my mind—all at a time when the same meltdowns were happening in the culture at large, and

382

MIKE HEFFLEY

altering my own personal courses as a budding European-American musician in the '60s and '70s

- German immigrant vibraphonist Karl Berger cofounded with vocalist-percussionist-dancer-choreographer (and fellow German and wife) Ingrid Sertso and Ornette Coleman in Woodstock, New York, the Creative Music Studio from the 1970s to the mid-'80s, which hosted and nurtured the musicians and music I would become most involved with as musician, journalist, and scholar from the 1980s on, especially through my most focused work with Anthony Braxton and the German FMP community
- British immigrant pianist and music journalist Marian McPartland launched the National Public Radio (NPR) show *Piano Jazz* in 1978, which has become my primary resource in my own recent turn from sometime public trombonist-bandleader to privately practicing pianist pondering his next public options

The nature and scope of the crucial formative influence of the first of these people will not be readily apparent until I do a fair bit of stage setting, so bear with me.

Bitter Roots (1948–1961)

Most of my work as a journalist and scholar of music has focused on either the current moments of any given time, or on history before my time. Before engaging the in-between zone of "history I have lived," a summary of my own European lineage may be in order.

The first Heffley (then spelled "Haffelee"), given name Johan Carle, from Germany's Black Forest, started my father's side's now-populous American clan after crossing the Atlantic on the English ship *William* in 1735 at the age of twenty. Irish ancestors joined themselves to that clan, including one past matriarch named Woods born on the boat coming over. English and Scots-Irish came through my mother's side. All were predominantly working class throughout their generations, and, true to their national stereotypes, music, literature, eros, war, and drink found more than marginal expressions in their various lives.

One of the interesting perks of living to the age of sixty-two is that (1) part of what is now "history" to many (even to me) is also part of my own life remembered, and (2) this age seems to activate more memories and reflections of that part than have surfaced in most of the other years *since* it happened. I can (as can most, I presume) reenter the states of mind and knowledge and awareness of the world that were my lived experience at the time, especially when I hear the music I listened to then.

I was born in Richmond, California, in 1948. My father had served as a marine in the Pacific during World War II; his marriage to my mother shortly thereafter ended when he moved to Hollywood to become an actor, before I was old enough to remember him. He disappeared from my life until I was thirteen (though I grew up watching him on TV); when we were reunited, he played a big part in my (re-)education about both race and music, about which ahead.

Richmond was and is a rough town. Mostly working class, the demographic established then and still holding comprised a black underclass (35 percent) and a Latino (25 percent) and white (20 percent) lower-to-middle class. The remaining 20 percent is a mix of Asian and Native Americans and other ethnic groups who migrated there in the thousands to work in the major wartime and postwar industries of shipbuilding and oil refining. All have experienced some economic and social rise since that time, especially the African Americans, but not enough to significantly change the dangerous face and feel of the place (recently ranked sixth among cities in the nation in crime rate) of 103,000-plus across the Bay from San Francisco. An initial strong presence of the railroad's Pullman Porters helps to explain the African American majority and the prevalence of blues and jazz in Richmond and its neighboring East Bay bedroom communities, Oakland the largest among them.[1]

My mother's father, who moved his family from Commerce, Oklahoma, to escape his killer job and hated boss in a lead and zinc mine (the same kind of job worked then by the father of my mom's childhood classmate, baseball legend Mickey Mantle) was among them. This was part of the poor-white exodus to the state that started in the Dust Bowl years, a mini-version of the last century's Great Migration of blacks in its American mix of desperation and hope. My mother was hired as a secretary at Union Oil soon after she graduated from Richmond High School.

That side of my family, from Oklahoma and Missouri, was not as brutally racist as the worst of the southern redneck culture that spawned many of the Richmond whites, but they were close enough to it in worldview, tastes, and affect, along with the rest of that culture around us, to infuse the first thirteen years of my life with the sense of poor-white fear and loathing provoked by living in a predominantly black urban town in a rapidly changing society. (One of my earliest TV-fed memories is a nightmare of being captured and eaten by cartoon African-tribal cannibals.)

I can still clearly recall an awareness of Richmond as a town where most of the blacks lived in the most ghettolike (unincorporated) area, called North Richmond, which I just seemed to be born knowing was a dangerous no-man's-land, never to be entered day or night. Indeed, my family moved away from their first Canal Street digs up to the then-whiter neighborhood on 10th Street when it was time for my birth, expressly to get away from their black neighbors. Physically, the part of town my family lived in during my first five years was not so different from the black part; we lived in what was called federal housing—cheap, projectlike apartments to house the influx of migrant workers.

I remember a visceral sense of physical aversion to black skin, hair, and features themselves, an aversion that could easily turn to panicked revulsion if challenged or breached—not something I recall feeling so violently about the brown skin and other features of Asians or Latinos (or Mexicans, as we called them then), who numbered more regularly among my neighbors and playmates. I remember, on the occasional trip to San Francisco, the shock my family would express at the sight of an interracial couple, especially a black man with a blond woman— something that seemed as unnatural and disturbing as the occasional man with earrings and/or long hair then. I do remember sporadic friendly brushes with some black kids at school—but I also remember them never going very far before some adult in my family nipped them in the bud, subtly or otherwise. I remember no one ever conveying sensitivity by replacing the word "nigger" with "the N word"; they just said it when they wished to, casually, maybe switching to "Negro" or "colored" when in mixed or polite company.

Overall, until the gradual processes of discovering folk, blues, and jazz records at my local library a year or two before Ornette Coleman's first LPs showed up there, and of getting old enough to reassess the worldviews and prejudices I was born into in light of the civil rights movement taking up more and more of the evening news, my childhood gestalt framed white America as definitive, good, right, and the one to which nonwhite minorities aspired, in every way. I saw it as open and designed to accommodate those who cared enough to enter it fully, just as it was open to the poor and rustic who were also intelligent and talented among its own lower-middle classes (like my family). I saw those ethnic minorities who failed to embrace and enter it so as roughly equivalent to my own fellow whites who were too stupid, lazy, and/or criminal to do so—like I myself would be if I let myself be less than all I could and should be—and I saw blacks as the most distant outliers among those aspiring minorities. Yes, there were some "good ones" and even great ones among them, but they were the exceptions who proved the rule.

I hadn't thought so far as to figure out why that was—looking back, it all just looks like classic racist culture, though at the time it felt more like classic *classist* culture, European style—but my deepest sense was that this group of people was the most "other" to the (white) American "self," and had the farthest to go and most to overcome to rise from its "lowest" to any American heights. The classism was racialized to blackness, as if touching it, let alone embracing it as equal, would cause a fall from the higher social status of whiteness.[2]

All of that changed most radically, thoroughly, and suddenly when I met my father.

Better Fruits (1961–1968)

Wayne Heffley's career as actor and author is documented on the International Movie Data Base (IMDB) website. He came from the German-Irish lower-middle-working-class demographic that matched my mother's "Okie" roots; his birthplace of Shafter, near Bakersfield, in rural California, was in fact a stop point of arrival of the migrant Dust Bowl Okies immortalized in John Steinbeck's *Grapes of Wrath*, and his earliest sexual fantasies were about some of their exotic (to him) gypsy-like maidens.

However, he was made of headier stuff, and educated and cultivated himself (informally, autodidactically, no college) to become a serious man of arts and letters. By the time I met him, in 1961, he was an established Hollywood actor, a man on his fourth of five wives (my mother was the first), and proud owner of a library of hundreds of books and LPs of classical and film music. Through my frequent visits to his Hollywood home and voluminous letters between Richmond and there, he woke and tutored the creative-intellectual part of me on that material, and I then moved on my own into the jazz and more modern and American sides of Western art music that he had yet to get to, which I then helped him do in our exchange. Golden years, until about 1968.

About halfway through them, in 1965, seventeen-year-old Mike Heffley made his first extended trip away from his family home in Richmond to the Berklee School of Music in Boston on a *Down Beat* magazine-sponsored scholarship to a summer session there. I won it on the strength of an audition tape of my original composition-arrangement for big band and sextet recorded live by the older local working musicians I had connected with, performed in concert at my high school. I had learned how to score such music through Berklee's correspondence courses, advertised in *Down Beat*; I learned how to perform it by listening to and playing along with jazz records at home, transcribing both their written and improvised lines by ear, starting with Louis Armstrong's Hot Five and Hot Seven recordings and working my way up through Fletcher Henderson, Count Basie, Benny Goodman, and others, then into bop and cool jazz records. I would get together with like-minded music students and older locals after school hours in ad hoc rehearsal bands to play these transcriptions, because no American high schools or colleges at the time offered any instruction in such music in their formal curricula.

My frequent visits to my father in Hollywood during the first half of the 1960s gave me an added edge to compensate for this deficiency in American music education. During the three to four years I was getting my jazz-trombone and theory chops together on the side in that way, my father used his Hollywood connections with agents who worked with musicians as well as actors in the film business to give me some seminal formative experiences: frequent visits to the jazz club Shelly's Manne Hole, where the drummer-proprietor would come by our table to autograph my LPs of him and share solicitous and encouraging words, and would coax other guests to do the same (pianist Bill Evans is the one I recall most to this day, and Gerry Mulligan, with his music from the films *I Want to Live*, *A Thousand Clowns*, and *The Subterraneans* already branded on my brain); trips to the Monterey Jazz Festival, where I saw Los Angeles–grown Charles Mingus's epic and astonishing performance of *Meditations on a Pair of Wire Cutters*; Duke Ellington's *Sacred Concert* at Glide Memorial Church in San Francisco, the Modern Jazz Quartet playing from their French-classical-chamber-toned LP *Fontessa*; I devoured *Birth of the Cool*, *Sketches of Spain*, *Porgy and Bess*, and the other Miles Davis–Gil Evans masterpieces; my fellow Californian Dave Brubeck (like Miles, a landed gentry, horse-ranch country kind of guy at heart) was the man of the hour; and I couldn't get enough of the pianoless quartets of Gerry Mulligan with Paul Desmond and Chet Baker, as an improvising horn player's perfect school in practical counterpoint.[3]

From this rich schooling-out-of-school, my formative years imbued me with a sense of musicianship as marketplace and functional craft as much as high and cutting-edge art, and of jazz as squarely located in the modernist incarnation of Western art music's own interdisciplinary, programmatic, and intercultural aspects.[4] Shelly Manne, for example, did a concept album called *The Gambit*, based on aspects of chess; Asian and Latin influences were strong in the West Coast scene, as were literary voices, through the San Francisco–centered Beats.

Those European composers who had incorporated jazz's early sounds in their work were also part of this Los Angeles *Umwelt*. Stravinsky was a familiar figure in our own part of town, and a great companion there of the writers my father admired (W. H. Auden and Aldous Huxley, and Dylan Thomas before them and my time there, in the early '50s before he died). My first college music classes at UCLA were in Schoenberg Hall, named after its illustrious former faculty member (Theodor Adorno and Hanns Eisler had also been serious presences in the LA music/academic culture in the '40s). Darius Milhaud was a name I learned through exposure to Brubeck, just as Stockhausen would later become familiar to me through Anthony Braxton—and the African Americans I was most focused on then (MJQ pianist John Lewis and Miles Davis, through their landmark work on *Birth of the Cool*, recorded at Hollywood's physical landmark, the Capitol Records building), seemed more a part of that California cool blend of country, sunny beach, jazz-classical-movie/modern-concert music, car-on-freeway culture than the hardscrabble, drugged-out club scenes of frantic-manic bebop set against elitist-exclusionary conservatories on the East Coast; more so too than what seemed (on the margins of my own radar then) like the more scuffling and depressed blue-collar and segregated cultures of the Midwest and Deep South.

What does all this have to do with Joseph Schillinger? It was in large part the fruition of an American music culture in my time that his work and vision in the 1930s and '40s had seeded as thickly as the recordings and concerts of American jazz musicians were sowing on European ground then. I would not learn until years later how seminal Schillinger was to all of this West Coast (specifically Hollywood)/San Francisco/Chicago/Boston axis (comprising four of the eight cities, counting nearby San Jose as San Francisco, with certified Schillinger teachers of some six hundred students in 1947). The Berklee School, of course, was first called the Schillinger House, when instituted in 1945 by Schillinger's student Lawrence Berk to teach the master's ideas about the arts, and his system of composing; and the cream of the crop of Hollywood arrangers and composers and popular songsmiths such as George Gershwin, Vernon Duke, Glenn Miller, Oscar Levant, and others were students of Schillinger in his time.[5]

By the time I and thousands of young American jazz geeks like me came along in the '50s and '60s, the pulp-pop magazine and correspondence-course culture of *Down Beat* and the Berklee School was up and running as a grassroots curriculum, pedagogy, and institution to supplement a German classical/conservatory model rooted in nineteenth-century America, shared by both the K-12 public school system and higher education, that systemically excluded jazz as worthy of its attention; that, and the hardscrabble world of a hypersegregated music business deemed the opposite of "legit" (to call up an abbreviation of "legitimate" then commonly used to describe "serious" European and American Europhiliac music), would have constituted my only music education, sans Schillinger.

The musical potential and aspirations of a poor white boy were thus nurtured along with those of anyone else who could take the inexpensive courses. When in Boston, I not only got to learn all things jazz directly in performance and composing-arranging classes from the likes of John LaPorta, Herb Pomeroy, Alan Dawson, and other great musicians there; I also had weekly private lessons in classical technique and repertoire from one of the Boston Symphony's brass players.

Also in 1965, a much more seasoned and savvy thirty-five-year-old pianist-composer-arranger named Muhal Richard Abrams was launching another grassroots initiative to similarly fill this gap in American music education for his own South Side Chicago community: the Association for the Advancement of Creative Musicians (AACM), a not-for-profit corporation with a mission to promote "creative music"—a rubric that served to integrate both composition and improvisation as equal aspects of an American music that had been drawn and quartered into "legit" composition on the high and "jazz" and "popular" riffraffery on the low end of its racial/cultural/social hierarchy.

George Lewis's monumental *A Power Stronger Than Itself: The* AACM *and American Experimental Music* describes Schillinger's influence on Abrams then in a way that tells both why it laid the foundation for African American music's way out of the minstrelish "jazz" box and how intertwined that music has always been with traditional and modern Western art music:

> [Charles] Stepney, a house arranger for Chess Records . . . introduced Schillinger's books to Abrams. . . . Everywhere he went over the next four years, Abrams kept these two massive tomes at the ready, teaching himself the complete system and developing new ideas under its guidance. . . . While serialism based its rule sets firmly on the chromatic scale, and bebop harmony revised Wagnerian chromaticism, the Schillinger system made few presumptions concerning materials. . . . As a budding painter who had already explored the synaesthetics of Kandinsky, Abrams was excited about Schillinger's construction of a necessary, ordered connection between sense, science, emotion, reason, and the natural world. *These ideas resounded with Abrams' own explorations of the connection between music and spirituality.* (pp. 59–60, my emphasis)[6]

I bring this Chicago connection to Schillinger—specifically with that mention of Abrams's concern with "spirituality"—into my West Coast-cum-personal history because one of the earliest major musical influences on me after my school days in the San Francisco Bay area and Boston was a bassist/reedsman named Donald "Rafael" Garrett. Garrett was Abrams's friend and fellow Chicagoan in the music, and had formed with him the Experimental Band there in the 1960s, a precursor group to the AACM, then had moved to San Francisco. After an aborted first semester at UCLA as a composition major, I returned to San Francisco to try to start gigging when I saw some of my peers there getting somewhere doing so. The main one, an Oakland bassist my age named Joe Halpin, whom I'd met at Berklee, had landed a regular spot in pianist Denny Zeitlin's trio, along with Oakland drummer Oliver Johnson, who went on to record with Braxton and play with Steve Lacy in Paris for many years. Joe and I rented a house together with another musician, and Joe and Oliver frequented Garrett's sessions with other local players for his working band the Rafael Garrett Circus.

That connection exposed me to two major streams of the music then from Garrett's insider perspective—John Coltrane's (and therein, one might argue, "jazz's") final years, and the AACM's first ones. Garrett often played with Coltrane's group when it came to town, and is on several recordings done then (when Eric Dolphy died in Berlin, the latter's bass clarinet was in Garrett's possession). I was still pretty young and on the sidelines of all this as a player, but as a nearby vicarious observer I got plenty of the kind of information I needed to understand what was happening in the music I cared most about, what it did and didn't have to do with me, and so how to proceed in my own self-development, and why.

In short, the burst of glory I saw especially in the recordings Coltrane made with Garrett (*Kulu sé Mama, Om, Live in Seattle*) and in his work with his more regular group and wife Alice at the time, and in similarly ecstatic/cathartic expressions by Albert Ayler, Pharoah Sanders, and Sun Ra, was part and parcel of the cultural moment of San Francisco/America/world circa 1965–70: marijuana, LSD, the rock (several of them formerly "folk") groups playing there and then, the sunbursts of utopian hope followed quickly by the flashburns of its deaths (Coltrane and Ayler, in the music, like King, the Kennedys, and Malcolm, in the politics, and Jimi, Janis, and Jim Morrison in their part of the music).[7] It was irresistible and overwhelming in its moments, but more as spectacle than participatory experience for me, in ways directly tied to racial identity.

Before Ornette and Cecil, my initiation into the music as a young white fan was framed by an (unconscious, unarticulated) assumption of "black uplift": jazz was integrated, part of American modernism, a tent big enough to hold both white and black identities, and the latter comprised its strongest voices by virtue of their mastery, not repudiation, of the Western formal-harmonic-melodic-metric system. From James Reese Europe to Louis to Duke to Bird to Miles, Mingus, and early Trane, the changes of Common Practice harmony, the AABA blues and song forms and more complex additive structures, and the meters of 4/4 and 3/4 time constituted the foundation of whatever buildings they designed and brought to life, for whatever functions, in both improvisation and composing/arranging. Even my first exposures to the challenges of those fundamentals, by Ornette and Cecil, didn't shake them loose in me. Ornette's first bands were in Los Angeles, and, as mentioned above, featured my man Shelly Manne on drums, and were endorsed by MJQ pianist John Lewis. The first Cecil Taylor I heard was on an LP bylined by Gil Evans (*Into the Hot*, Impulse, 1960); although the latter was present mostly in name only, the point is that both of these first contacts were more like guests being hosted in a house by people I was already familiar and comfortable with. Their departures from chord changes, form, regular meter, etc., still fell under the category of "interesting dissonance and experiment" employed to express a black identity still framed by a white Western tradition/aesthetic. Moreover, they still seemed couched within music as ecumenical/secular avant-garde modernist art, not do-or-die spiritual possession or trance that felt so exclusively "other" in spirit. When that black uplift turned to black power, and when nonviolent bids to integrate turned to riots and revolutionary rhetoric rejecting integration "into a burning house," and when the music I'd grown up with and was well into engaging as seriously as I could then turned to reflect those turns, I felt forced to stand back and reassess, even while still gripped by it.

Preceding and overlapping these revolutionary shifts was Cannonball Adderley's group with Joe Zawinul on keyboards, who penned the band's 1966 popular hit "Mercy, Mercy, Mercy." It added a flavor to the mix that helped me resolve the identity issues challenging me on the music's more fiery front lines, even while leading to a different kind of dead end (albeit through important changes and lessons).

Late-'60s Shakeups (Race, Music, Money)

Brian Glasser's 2001 book *In a Silent Way* about Zawinul is replete with comments from Cannonball, George Duke, Orrin Keepnews, and others about how surprisingly black/funky/soulful—choose your nonwhite compliment—the pianist was. As it happened, I was privy to this revelation from Cannonball in real time in the 1960s when he voiced such things in interviews and stage patter.

I had listened to Cannonball for years, and was pleasantly surprised to see his characteristically soul-jazz tune hit the pop charts, and his group more generally enjoy more commercial success than other jazz groups. At the time, it felt like the success of a strategy to move beyond bop and cool—both limited to small jazz audiences—and find a wider popular audience, and to do so via the more "down home, rootsy" black sound evoking soul and gospel (naturally enough, in the rising tide of civil rights and black power; Mingus had done it best and for long, but that kind of popular cachet had never seemed an option he would enjoy or be inclined to reach for).

As a side note to continue the thread of European modernism's/Schillinger's influence on not only jazz but black popular music as well, consider this from Yusef Lateef about his time in Cannonball's quintet with Zawinul:

> We never use the word *jazz*—that's a misnomer—but we would study scores of composers for the orchestra, the sonata allegro form and so on. We'd study classical music, but also Baroque and Impressionistic music, everything from Bach to Ravel to now. Sometimes it would be he [Joe] and I, sometimes as a group. Sometimes Cannonball would lecture on Stravinsky—*The Rite of Spring*, etc. We were concerned for the development of our music. We were interested in Stravinsky's melodies, harmonies, rhythm, the nuances. And of course many European compositions—like Dvorak's ninth symphony or Debussy's *Golliwog's Cakewalk*—are based on African-American folksong and music.[8]

Glasser also reports that although the original (*Capitol Records*, 1966—my emphasis) LP that Zawinul's hit tune was on stated in its liner notes that it had been recorded live in a Chicago nightspot called The Club, owned by one of Cannonball's friends, it had in fact been done in a Hollywood studio to which an audience had been invited and supplied an open bar to simulate the sounds of an enthusiastic bunch of fans. My kind of story, wish I'd heard it back then . . .[9]

All this new (to me) info from Glasser's book confirms the one epiphany I did have about race and the music at the time—a sea change in my own emerging adult consciousness comparable to the one from redneck Richmond to literate-liberal Hollywood culture that meeting my father incurred—when I heard Cannonball talk in interviews about this white guy with the funny name from Vienna as being the composer of "Mercy," and as playing out his role as the band's pianist with as much "soul" as any African American to that soulful manor born, which relieved the confusions about race and music the zeitgeist and my background were torturing me with.

To make this long story less long, Joe Zawinul's appearance on that part of the scene then (after emigrating to America in 1959 on a scholarship to the Berklee School, by the way) was the first of many such examples to come since that blew away the notion of identity-essentialism in the music—that there was a "black thing" or a "white thing" in any immutable sense that determined and constrained where any of us could go as musicians or people. As I read about his background in Viennese classical music culture, and as I read more about Cannonball's background as an educator and son of educators, I grew out of the vision of American music as polarized between intuitive, spontaneous black and educated, foresightful white; Europhiliac and Afrocentric; composed and improvised; formal and "free." All of that was there for all of us here, points on a spectrum unbroken for the taking and shaping.[10]

These musical reflections of hierarchies of class in our culture included another one that was breaking down with the rest of them then, that between folk, rock, pop, and jazz. Zawinul played a role in that shift for me and my time as well, after the racial one, when he composed "In a Silent Way" in response to a winter night in Vienna upon his return visit to his family home there after his long and triumphant time abroad in search of his musical glory. He did so simply by playing the same role in Miles's band as he had played in Cannonball's—providing the title track to an album that was part of a larger breakdown of genre/social borders. With "Mercy, Mercy, Mercy," the crossover was from small jazz to large pop audience; with "In a Silent Way," it was that as well, and also from acoustic jazz to the electric jazz-rock "fusion" of the time.

What Schillinger had started with his syncretistic ideas about the arts (including electronic and electroacoustic music—he was one of the first Hammond organ owners, and worked closely with electronic instrument pioneer Léon Theremin) and his populist ways of propagating them in America, Zawinul stepped up to embody and activate simply by being, like Schillinger, an "other" from that same Western classical culture who could morph into the African American "self" so seamlessly as to show that what was going on here was indeed the power of music to transcend all its local/traditional aspects and converge and converse in any one of them globally.[11]

That said, once one has been liberated, one must decide which of all possible tracks to commit to, and why. In my case, the thing both of these crossovers had in common was their bid for commercial success, and careerist context. I was a child of my time and place then, which in my case meant (1) the aforementioned San Francisco hippy/Berkeley-Oakland-revolutionary/marijuana-and-LSD spirit of things trumped what we called the "plastic" (phony, shallow, materialistic) LA-cocainish commodification of those same things—the latter was assimilationist vis-à-vis an Establishment we still looked to bring down politically, socially, culturally—and (2) that was even more keenly true for me at age twenty, in 1968, because I was individuating then from the strong ego and influence of my father with an ego and will to match his, being the proverbial acorn fallen close to that redoubtable oak. Embracing the Hollywood work ethic for the arts, especially music, would have betrayed my own budding identity and world in favor of my father's, for all its formative influence. This position dented not a bit my profound respect for Miles and Zawinul as musicians, and for the actual music each was making in his new electric playground (or, indeed, for my father); I just knew it wasn't going to be my scene, any more than was the high holy road of a trance music divorced from my own real identity and affinities (or even one married to them, for that matter).

Following my heart and soul that much away from what they *weren't* took me to the next and major journeyman part of what they *would become* for the next few decades, and for the first years as a solid and ripening adult. Enter Herr Berger.

Parallel Paths (1970s–1990s)

Heidelberg-born (March 30, 1935) Karl Berger is the only one of these four expats I've had any personal contact with. I met him by phone in 2008 when he graciously agreed to an interview in conjunction with my project then for producer Michael Cuscuna to write the liner notes for his Mosaic Records' reissue of Anthony Braxton's historic Arista recordings circa 1974–80. Berger was important to those recordings not only for his contributions as a vibraphonist to parts of them, but far more for his role as cofounder and manager of the Creative Music Studio (CMS) in Woodstock, New York, where Braxton also lived as his neighbor and worked and workshopped as a regular at the CMS to create much of the music on those recordings.

393

As with Schillinger, I was unaware until after the fact of the importance of Berger's work then to my own life and work in the music. Unlike Schillinger, his influence was contemporary, a kind of parallel stream to my own. By that I mean that the nature and direction of my involvement with the music in the Pacific Northwest through the decades of the 1970s–'90s was more similar to his vision and activities at Woodstock than to those of most other musicians and music activists then (except, naturally, those in our overlapping circles), especially those of any white Americans.

When I moved to Eugene, Oregon, in 1971, then married and had a child by 1973, I met there a couple of kindred brothers in the music around my age who were also settling down to start new families, leaving behind similarly more colorful urban lives in our shared area of American music. Arzinia Richardson and Malinké Robert Elliot were both from St. Louis, and had been early founding principals of the Black Artists Group (BAG) there, which had close ties and overlapping band members with the AACM. We discovered each other early on, and collaborated throughout the '70s and '80s in fostering and growing a Pacific Northwest scene along the lines of our respective backgrounds and momentum.

For bassist Arzinia (he had toured Morocco with Ornette, among other similar gigs) and me, that meant working as local musicians (and music journalist, for me) and hosting radio shows at the local community college station KLCC; for all three of us (Malinké was a playwright and administrator) it meant bringing in the musicians of our circles whom we thought most important and least supported by mainstream entertainment and culture industries/networks. Over those decades, these included Sun Ra and his Arkestra, the Art Ensemble of Chicago, the World Saxophone Quartet, Julius Hemphill's (ad hoc) Ducktown Minstrels, Ornette Coleman's Prime Time, and similar artists and groups.

As an informed jazz buff, I was aware of Berger's history as a vibraphonist. I knew he had associations with Don Cherry and Ornette, had played with many other great musicians, and was doing something interesting in Woodstock, but it was a marginal awareness until I spoke to him, in 2008, for the Mosaic liner notes.

"The 1970s was the golden age for the CMS," he told me, "especially between 1976 and 1982. The practice of the big labels like Arista at the time with Anthony—of focusing on one or two more adventurous artists and really promoting them heavily—had the effect of drawing more people into the music of CMS generally. More students would enroll to come and learn this music. The student bands became big, good resources for composers, Anthony especially. They helped him copy the parts for his Four Orchestras project, and were on hand to play through work as it was written, allowing him to hear it. In the days before computers, that was quite a luxury."

As with Schillinger and Zawinul, American musicians, journalists, and scholars have embraced Berger's work and sensibilities not only as a full-fledged expression of the American musical soul and family, but as a leading, seminal one therein. According to his website (www.karlberger.com/quotesaboutkarlberger), "The way Karl plays the vibes he should be president of the United States," said Dave Brubeck; and "The thing that struck me as unusual about Karl Berger when I first heard him playing at the Mercer Arts Center in the 1970s was how much at home he sounded with some of the best young players in the New York jazz scene. To my ears then, most European jazz musicians were derivative at best, and often out of touch with the leading American improvisers. But this guy from Germany played as if he'd grown up in New York. How could that be?" Peter Occhiogrosso wrote in the *Village Voice*.

What Berger and Sertso did and continue to do is put this thing called "creative" music in the context of "world music," beyond the constrictions and problematic nuances of "jazz," "avant-garde," and "experimental" rubrics.[12] "As the CMS grew during that time, the more it became the world music center," he says. "More people from different traditions came in, and the world music genre was on the rise. Particularly the summer sessions had a lot of Brazilian, Turkish, Indian, African people there, who were bringing their own music in. We didn't have our large facility until '76. The countercultural aura of Woodstock drew a healthy cross section of talented musicians, too—people who had gone through the conventional music education, training, and professional situations and weren't satisfied with that. This was their chance to get an intensive eight-week exposure to the best players in the kind of direction they wanted to take their music. Dave Holland lived nearby too, and Cecil Taylor heard his first large-ensemble work with the student orchestra. Again, that was a real luxury for composers in the days before computers."

The "creative" rubric constitutes something like shared DNA between Berger's work and mine in those years. When I met Anthony Braxton in 1988 and got the chance to bring him to Oregon to perform his music with a band of regional players, I called and billed that band, on his suggestion, the Northwest Creative Orchestra (NCO). "Creative" for both music and orchestras had long been the tag of choice to bypass and transcend "jazz" or "free jazz" among AACMers and like-minded peers; it described an approach reflecting Schillinger's (for example, penning a line of music from the contour of a big city skyline, or from the morning's stock market numbers), quintessentially in Braxton's music (though I never heard him mention Schillinger as an influence)—synaesthetic, "scientific" in the tone of its idiosyncrasy, interdisciplinary, populist, accessible through all ethnic/cultural vernaculars but not racially essentialistic (what Braxton calls "trans-idiomatic").[13] The resulting CD of the performance (*Eugene*, Black Saint, 1989) garnered five stars from *Down Beat* and opened the door to further such projects with Andrew Hill, Oliver Lake, Vinny Golia, John Carter, Julius Hemp-hill, Ursula Oppens, and others. What Berger had been doing with and for some of those same musicians and their colleagues in the Northeast—offering a work-shop band à la Abrams's and Garrett's Experimental Band of skilled and savvy players to showcase ambitious works by under-supported masters of the idiom (or trans-idiom) in sore need of it—our NCO was stepping up to do in the Northwest, where the culture and audience for such music was even less enlightened and populous.

"Anthony told me when I saw him recently in Switzerland that he felt very grateful for the CMS period, and thought that it helped him develop his stuff," says Berger. "Anthony was a regular at CMS during those years. He workshopped a lot of the music on the *Creative Orchestra Music* record with the students. We had a kind of orchestra rehearsal every afternoon, always about 20 or 25. He would come for a week. He was a regular there for as long as he lived in Woodstock, starting in 1973."

The "world music" rubric and direction was another, major part of abovemen-tioned shared DNA. The NCO entered the arena around the same time as the emergence of world music as a genre of the pop music industry, of the promotion of multiculturalism in culture industry grantors, and of the neocon movement spearheaded by Wynton Marsalis, Albert Murray, and Stanley Crouch through Jazz at Lincoln Center in New York. I felt my own long-cultivated background in this thing called (albeit problematically) "jazz" at a fork in the American-cultural road: everything troubling about it was coming to fruition in the neocon branch, and all the things about the music that made more sense to me were likewise coming to a head in the work of Braxton, Berger, the AACM and BAG artists, and my own NCO.

After our initial success with the Braxton project, I was inspired by the vision expressed in this review of our CD to set off on a path that would forge a comple-mentary alternative to the Jazz at Lincoln Center scene:

Picture yourself in a perfect jazz world where every city with 100,000-plus inhabitants has a resident orchestra that can play the music of visiting compos-ers like Anthony Braxton, Carla Bley, or George Russell. Sound unlikely? I thought so too until I heard Eugene's Northwest Creative Orchestra with Anthony Braxton. . . . What an amazing realization of a dream this record is.[14]

Dreaming just that dream, of establishing the NCO in my home town then to take its place with the already well-established Eugene Symphony, Eugene Op-era, and internationally acclaimed Bach Festival there, I incorporated it as a 501(c)3 and got the best grants by playing up the interdisciplinary, educational, and multicultural potentials of my projects—Japanese American music and history with Andrew Hill, African history of the slave trade with John Carter, music and visual art with Vinny Golia, etc. I settled into that process of establishing us so, with an eye to making it my life's work and comfortable passion—a career (in spite of my younger self's upturned nose at the concept) niche that felt truly "creative" to me, organic and viable. The more I learned and thought about what Karl Berger was doing on the other side of the country, the more I dreamed of us and like-minded colleagues taking the music in our much more interesting and richer direction from America *to* America and the world with love, countering the neocons who so annoyed us then.

As things developed, though, my work as a journalist and scholar of the music outpaced and outshone my work as a musician, both by choice (as I aged) and circumstance (the world accepted and rewarded my writing more heartily than my music). The "world music" side of that work I channeled into a Ph.D. in eth-nomusicology (as Braxton's graduate teaching assistant at Wesleyan University), culminating in my current professional focus on an international improvised mu-sic scene fed by the folk and court traditions of many cultures; the nonprofit side veered into the grants I got for the second such entity I (co-)incorporated (with Braxton), the Tri-Centric Foundation, to fund Braxton's projects, and into grants I proposed for myself individually, for my writing projects; and the personal-musician side shifted away from being a public trombonist in (occasionally) Brax-ton's bands and other contexts to cultivating privately my piano playing . . . which had begun in earnest with an association with singer-pianist Meredith d'Ambrosio . . . which in turn led me to the work of my most recent and ongoing influential expat.

Music to Stay Young Growing Old With
(the Whole Time . . .)

To close the circle opened here, reaching a certain age seems to awaken memo-ries, even to revive the real power, of one's earliest years. In my case, they were marked by absent males and several generations of females (single mother, single grandmother, sister, and an aunt just ten years older whose excellent piano rendi-tions of American songbook standards were part of my first up-close exposures to music). Abovementioned current professional focus—my third book, well under way, is primarily about women artists; and abovementioned private piano playing is primarily informed by the history of solo piano stylings of those standards, and of my own compositions of music and lyrics to build on that tradition and repertoire.

Born to a musical family in Boston, it so happens that it was Meredith who first made me aware of who Schillinger was, and his foundational role in the Berklee College and in the Tin Pan Alley sources of her material. She and I became friends and neighbors when she lived in Eugene for part of the 1980s, and writing articles and reviews of her music got me into her vast and exquisite body of work (as a painter as well as a musician—yet another offshoot of the synaesthesia). She's covered the best of that tradition from the Gershwins, Vernon Duke, Yip Harburg, Johnny Mercer (who was also cofounder of Capitol Records), Alec Wilder, Harold Arlen, Noël Coward, Hoagy Carmichael, and Jerome Kern to their more contemporary torchbearers such as David Frishberg and Fran Landesman.

I had the thrill of composing a song and lyric for her, which she improved upon to suit her style and recorded ("Once upon a Tempo," on *It's Your Dance,* Sunnyside Records, 1985). That experience opened another possible door for my working life in the music, but it too was swept aside by the connection with the NCO and my work at Wesleyan with Braxton. I kept it up as a private hobby, and as I gradually lost interest in working as a public trombonist, playing solo piano and singing lyrics grew to feed my personal need to make music, which has never waned in private.

Unlike the three men expats, Marian McPartland (born Margaret Marian Turner in Slough, England, 1918) has been on my jazz radar screen since I first came to the music, and has come to burn brighter rather than dimmer there over time. My connection with Meredith brought McPartland's National Public Radio (NPR) show *Piano Jazz* to the forefront of my attention, but any *Down Beat* subscriber and reader of the rest of the jazz press in the '50s and '60s would be aware of her as an interviewer of other artists and a writer about issues related to the music, as well as a major player in her own right. Specifically to my region, she launched a forerunner of *Piano Jazz* from New York's WBAI-FM in 1964 that was carried by Pacifica Radio's West Coast stations.

When I started to acquaint myself with her history and work back then, she already carried a rich part of American music history. That part includes several tropes already introduced here: her foundational classical training (at London's Guildhall School of Music and Drama), her synaesthesia ("The key of D is daffodil yellow, B major is maroon, and B flat is blue"),[15] her Chicago connection (her American husband cornetist Jimmy McPartland replaced Ravel-besotted "In a Mist" composer-cornetist Bix Beiderbecke in the Wolverines, a territory band of mostly Chicagoans). Her print and broadcast journalism of the music, and the more specialized columns for *Down Beat*'s Music Workshop series (1968–72) about more technical-analytical aspects of it ("How to Comp," "Voicing Piano Chords," an analysis of Coltrane's "Giant Steps," to name a few), bore the authority and insight of a player, something rare in that field and an example of what I aspired to become.

Now in her ninety-second year, she's proven herself to be the gold standard for any and all of us facing the prospect of aging well within a life in this music. For women, she's modeled a balanced empowerment as both artist and entrepreneur (starting her own Halcyon label in 1969); for me personally, she's one of those rare people successfully answering the question Karlheinz Stockhausen posed, which haunts all of us blessed/cursed with longevity: as we get older, how do we integrate our present with all that has come before? (my paraphrase)—in countless daily ways. One most recent is her inclusion of Ornette Coleman's classic "Lonely Woman" on her latest CD *Twilight World*. Seeing that reminded me of Louis Armstrong's 1970 rendition of Pharoah Sanders's "The Creator Has a Master Plan." The continuum is as trans-generational as it is trans-idiomatic in the lives I hope to emulate.

With any luck, like her around her sixtieth year, I am just about to late-bloom into the final and most fertile and productive third of such a life. Her *Piano Jazz*—to which she invites fellow pianists each week to add their music to hers in live duets, and to take turns playing solo, and to talk about it all—is the longest-running show on NPR. As I look ahead to the horizon of my (hopefully) golden years, the top of my "bucket list" as a musician is to create music I can play on the keyboard, some with words I can sing, to make a body of that kind of solo work . . . and to inform that process by mining the archives of Ms. McPartland's shows as thoroughly as I mined Braxton's work as a scholar and musician, and the ideas and visions of the part of American music that schooled and spawned his work before that, and the West Coast "jazz" culture and its close "classical" cousins before that. Perhaps (icing on that cake) even to join her as a guest on her program, if I come up with the goods to share in time.

Retroflection

Dr. Berkman and I agreed on the pedagogical richness of a prop I brought to my talk about that "free jazz" section of her Jazz History class: a copy of the "New Jazz Chronology" from John Gray's indispensable research tool *Fire Music: A Bibliography of the New Jazz, 1959–1990* (Greenwood Press, 1991). It starts with the 1954 Supreme Court *Brown v. Board of Education* decision that ruled segregation of schools unconstitutional, followed by Charlie Parker's death in 1955; it ends with the 1969 shooting deaths of Black Panthers Fred Hampton and Mark Clark by Chicago police, and Albert Ayler's body found in New York's East River. The entries for the fifteen years between them made a similar weave of political and musical history, chronicling the end of colonialism in Africa and the rise of the civil rights movement and its arc through the Black Arts movement and Black Panther Party along with the emergence of Ornette Coleman, Cecil Taylor, Albert Ayler, John Coltrane's later recordings, the AACM, BAG, and similar groups and artists.

My mostly apolitical account here has reflected the affect of the music itself, as I lived it then, have observed it in its major actors, and look back on it now—but more out of a surfeit than an absence of social-political consciousness. The phrase "the personal is political" became most popular through the women's movement that ignited around the end of Gray's chronology, but it was in the air before that, and applied then and now to my own coming-of-age-cum-aging in the music. It is patently obvious that the music discussed here has been an African American cultural expression reflective of and inextricable from the social movements of Gray's purview. However, even with the occasional overtly programmatic statements (by Max Roach and Abbey Lincoln, Charles Mingus, Archie Shepp, John Coltrane, most famously) it always rode high above the level of the political propaganda or identity of any kind of party hacks or transient activists, instead turning such issues and events into more timeless artistic statements. Mostly, the totality of its bodies of work stood and spoke so eloquently and powerfully in accord with the spirit and positions of the political bodies and work that no professions of alliance were necessary; they went far better without saying.

My own retrospective introspection about my racist roots has been matched by an amplified resonance since the election of our first African American president, as I've watched the rise of the Tea Party and other right-wing voices. Like Jimmy Carter,[16] my old redneck eyes have recognized this same nasty spirit sporting its colors and flexing its muscles, after decades of relatively more dormancy. Still, now as then, one persists in hope toward one's light.

Then, as now, the evil arguably greater than racism was/is the classism that keeps people of all races in poverty while the rich get obscenely richer. Martin Luther King and Malcolm X both worked their ways through the racial issues to those of class and economics in their short times of engagement, and I need only invoke the headlines of the last few years to evoke the current face of that ongoing struggle. My own ongoing connection to the more world-music-fed jazz/improvised/experimental music scene constitutes my connection to my own continuity with that American-cum-global struggle.[17]

The importance of that fact to my thesis here is, again, the reminder my four European expats are that the musical-sociopolitical drama is not parochially American—or is so only if we qualify American culture as the soil in which Europe and Africa were transplanted to eventually bear the best fruits and flowers of their respective cross-pollinating souls. My initial youthful sense of the classical world of composition, developed in Europe and continued in America, *deigning* to cede a worthy match in the more improvisational, rhythmic, and timbral-textural palette of jazz was not entirely a symptom of my white racism or Europhiliac bias; it simply had yet to be tempered and balanced with the complementary conscious-ness of the African side's comparable leverage in that American exchange. At its best, American music has fulfilled the richest potential of each tradition through the contributions of the other; geniuses from Armstrong to Ellington to Tatum to Monk to Abrams to Braxton have embodied aspects of Europe's musical crafts-men from Adolphe Sax to New Orleans German brass bands to visionary com-posers from Scriabin to Schoenberg to Ravel to Schillinger as brilliantly as have composers from Ives to Stockhausen to Cage; they've done so in a collusion of peers and equals with the four who happened to touch my own life as told here, and with many more like them. On their side of the pond, these "many more" have taken the music that started out as specific to the black communities and cultures in America and claimed and customized it for their own versions of resistance to oppressive powers and systems, and of positive retooling of their classist classical traditions.

The latter point is important, lest readers surmise from this a reduction of the music to a reactive response to top-down pressure, thus more derivative and contingent than original. As George Lewis noted, Schillinger's system appealed to Abrams because it was descriptive rather than prescriptive, offering a theory and methodology that would accommodate rather than arrest and constrain individual inspiration and originality. This requires not only a faith and trust that such individuation comes with its own inherent order, but also a working knowl-edge of said order's details and patterns as *reflecting* a universal order, not as *deviating* from it destructively.

When Schillinger spoke of a "mathematical basis of the arts," it was descriptive because his mathematics (however questionable in spots) were *applied*—empiri-cally based in material reality (celestial mechanics)—rather than the *pure* mental abstracts (number theory) mathematicians employ when they find it useful to.[18] Their technical details are beyond my scope here, but fields such as chaos theory, fractal geometry, and theoretical cosmology are all recent examples of applied rather than pure mathematics that resonate with the organic way Schillinger's music-theoretical mind worked in his writings and music, as also Braxton's (I feel in a position to assert), as also my own and the minds of many other writers and musicians who say things like "the characters in my plays/novels have wills of their own," or "I really don't know what I'm doing when I play my music; it's more like the music plays me." A descriptive system simply charts what one knows to be there; a prescriptive system is one that is imposed as a bodiless abstract on a body as if the latter were a chaotic and formless mass in need of such an abstract's infinitely detailed imposition. Such a system starts its life as descrip-tive of the body's own order and detail and form, and is best left to continue as such, living and letting other such systems/bodies live—but it is often, disastrously, turned to prescriptive ends by those who would wield power and control unduly.

Schillinger—cofounder with American folk patriarch Charles Seeger of the American Musicological Society—was fascinated by his ancient Caucasus roots, and while the neocons were prescribing "jazz" as America's "classical music," Albert Ayler's complete recordings were being packaged and presented by the folk label Revenant Records, and drummer Sunny Murray was saying this:

> Record sales, market research, they don't take into account what we're playing. *Folk music.* Louis Armstrong, Chick Webb onwards . . . it's really folk music, American folk music. You go to Armenia or Greece or Turkey and listen to folk music and it *is* folk music, because there's never been commercial marketing and profiteering done on it. Where American jazz is concerned, the originality has been diluted because of profiteering and exploitation and the music hasn't been allowed to revise itself constantly enough.[19]

and Anthony Braxton this:

> The attempts to house it, to write it out, in many ways involved reducing the vibrational spectra of the music. I think the music we call jazz, so-called jazz, really brings it out, *folk music brings it out* [my emphasis—M.H.], all of the musics that are close to the community and allow for individual presence bring out this dichotomy between the rational system [what I'm calling prescriptive—M.H.] and the three-dimensional system [what I'm calling descriptive—M.H.].[20]

Looking back and forward on all this, it seems I've made and charted for myself a version of that old European path of the *amateur*. The concepts of career and commerce, with their fool's-gold pressures and rewards, seem to have left me cold. My main musical heroes couldn't sell out if they wanted to; even the most celebrated, in and out of academia, are chump change, financially and culturally, compared with pop and classical money-makers. On the aristocratic side of that European tradition, I'm in the music sheerly for the love of its power to evoke and invoke, in their fullest and most refined glory, life's highest majesties and mysteries, rather than for fame or fortune; on the folk side, I'm moved by a similar passion for it as the heart's blood of daily life's ups and downs, rites and play, and celebrations and laments (high art and folk art—two sides of the same coin once we cut the classism loose). My work as both musician and writer about the music that fills that bill for me in private has had its public moments, but they've come and gone like foam on the private sea, and I've let them, indifferently, like a member of the ancient Chinese literati playing his *qin* alone at home.

I don't know if anything I do from this point forward will turn from private to public again; today's Internet technology offers the option of such a turn much more viably than platforms only a few years past now, so we will see. I do know the music has taken me just where I want to be, especially in my inner life, and continues to feel like it's doing so. I also know myself as part of the European side of a cosmopolitan American family that has found its real love and health, above and beyond even while in the thick and the muck of its challenges of dysfunction and pathology.

NOTES

1. See Vincent (1995, 197) for a description of the Richmond scene that foregrounds the role of women running the nightclubs. Oakland, of course, gave birth to the Black Panther Party, which also had a strong presence in Richmond (I occasionally sold its newspapers as a young hippy on the streets in Berkeley then).

2. For an interesting glance back at the way scholars such as those in this book wrote about race and class and black music at the end of the 1960s, see *Black America*, an anthology edited by John Szwed (1970). Its interest lies in the fact of Szwed's still-current voice and work in the field, a source of fascinating compare-and-contrast between now and then.

3. These recordings set me up for Ornette's first pianoless quartet album, with Manne on drums, *Tomorrow Is the Question!* Ornette would not record with a piano again until the 1990s.

4. George Lewis (2008, 248) cites a 1977 British jazz journalist's description of the MJQ's 1957 concert at my ancestor's Black Forest venue of the Donaueschingen Festival of Contemporary Music as having "thoroughly overshadowed the premiere of Igor Stravinsky's *Agon*," and German critic Joachim Ernst Berendt's citation of German classical music critic K. H. Ruppel's assertion that the concert's "continent-wide importance . . . to the acceptance of jazz on the European concert stage recalled the impact of Benny Goodman's 1938 Carnegie Hall event." These observations reflect two things about the music's impact at that time in Europe: (1) it was a New World competitor against Old World culture's avant-garde within Western modernism, and (2) it foreshadowed the soon-to-come postmodern version of the competition, between postcolonial liberations and lasting gasps of segregation, apartheid, and imperialism.

5. See Brodsky (2003, 45–73) for a comprehensive overview of Schillinger's life and work. Pease (2010) sheds light on Schillinger's impact on Berklee's early curriculum. More specific to Hollywood, "he helped solve the problem of artistically coordinating soundtrack with film track" (Brodsky 2003, 45), and "these investigations eventually developed into a more systematic method of musical scoring for film sequences" (49).

6. See Cowell ([1930] 1996) for the book Lewis says Stepney applied, along with the Schillinger texts and "the work of Gyorgy Ligeti, to his landmark work for Ramsey Lewis, the Dells, the Rotary Connection and Minnie Ripperton, Phil Upchurch, Muddy Waters, and Earth, Wind, and Fire" (58).

7. Alice Coltrane would extend that energy in her subsequent work, both into more Indian directions and via her treatments of Stravinsky. See Berkman (2010) for her important new words in this conversation.

8. Glasser (2001, 77).

9. See Cuscuna (1998) for a full account of the 1966 session and of his 1995 reissue of it.

10. See "Race and the Embodiment of Culture" (in Szwed 2005, 77–90) for an erudite corroboration of my epiphany.

11. David Ake (2010, 121–40) applies Stuart Nicholson's "glocalization" rubric in his essay "Negotiating National Identity among American Jazz Musicians in Paris."

12. See creativemusicstudio.org for Berger's own account of this, and for news of his most recent activities in Istanbul, Turkey, in collaboration with Italian jazz activist Francesco Martinelli, and for news of his project to archive the CMS's many live recordings of musicians from Asia, Europe, and South America circa 1972–86. See Sweet (1996) for an intimate firsthand history and profile of the CMS, one full of its most colorful and illustrious cast of character studies, by one of its resident students.

13. Brodsky's description of Schillinger could almost replace his name with that of Braxton and still feel substantively on target in many of its specifics. Schillinger enjoyed the respect and affection (as a "master composer equal to Beethoven" [p. 51]) of compatriots Dmitri Shostakovich and Vladimir Horowitz, and of Nicolas Slonimsky, whose *Thesaurus of Scales and Melodic Patterns* became the practice bible of Coltrane and Frank Zappa, among many others. Schillinger scorned academia as professional pedantry and was shunned by it in return, though he clearly had the scholar's mind and calling; he developed his own often impenetrable terminology, and generally went his own way through his own life's ups and downs more successfully than not, in terms of finances and the respect of those he cared about, as well as fulfillment of his own work he *most* cared about. See Lock (2008) for a current and comprehensive look at synaesthesia in Braxton's work; Szwed's "The Local and the Express: Anthony Braxton's Title Drawings" (2005, 215–19); and Broomer (2009) for a similarly fresh investigation on another such aspect paid much and close attention not only by scholars of Schillinger and Braxton but by them, in their own respective voluminous writings on music: time as music's "canvas."

14. Bannister (1992, 14).

15. Balliett (1977, 289).

16. See Naughton (September 16, 2009).

17. This from recent news shows a side of European influence in America opposite the one my four expats have shown: Timothy Egan (*New York Times*, December 16, 2010) wrote, "At the same time, the gap between the rich and poor, and the concentration of wealth owned by those at the very top, has never been so great. After examining these trends, *The Economist* wrote that 'the United States risks calcifying into a European-style class-based society.'"

18. See Norris (2011) for a spirited critique of the overreaching presumptions of empirical certainty expressed by Stephen Hawking and other theoretical physicists about science's trumping of philosophy as an epistemology.

19. Warburton (2000), answer para. 29.

20. Lock (2008, para. 10). Braxton's own music history classes at Wesleyan included as much that was categorized as African American "folk" material as "jazz," and he voiced preference of Alan Lomax's work over John Hammond's, for its agenda of cultural preservation rather than commercial commodification. Ake's "Race, Place, and Nostalgia after the Counterculture: Keith Jarrett and Pat Metheny on ECM" (pp. 77–101) captures well that link between West Coast and midwestern jazz cultures I alluded to above, as does Lewis's book (p. 24) on the connections between 1950s Chicago and Kansas City styles.

BIBLIOGRAPHY

Ake, D. *Jazz Matters: Sound, Place, and Time since Bebop.* Berkeley: University of California Press, 2010.

Balliett, W. *New York Notes: A Journal of Jazz in the Seventies.* New York: Da Capo Press, 1977.

Bannister, G. *Eugene (1989).* Seattle: Earshot Jazz, p. 14, 1992.

Berger, K. n.d. *Creative Music Studio.* Retrieved December 24, 2010, from creativemusicstudio.org.

Berkman, F. *Monument Eternal: The Music of Alice Coltrane.* Middletown, CT: Wesleyan University Press, 2010.

Brodsky, W. "Joseph Schillinger (1895–1943): Music Science Promethean," *American Music* 21/1 (Spring 2003): 45–73.

Broomer, S. *Time and Anthony Braxton.* Toronto: Mercury Press, 2009.

Coleman, O. *Tomorrow Is the Question!* (Contemporary S 7569), 1959.

Cowell, H. *New Musical Resources.* Cambridge and New York: Cambridge University Press [1930] 1996.

Cuscuna, M. "The Cannonball Adderley Rendez-Vous." 1998. www.cannonball-adderley.com/2683.htm (accessed December 24, 2010).

D'Ambrosio, M. *It's Your Dance.* New York: Sunnyside Records, 1985.

Egan, T. *New York Times.* December 15, 2010. http://opinionator.blogs.nytimes.com/2010/12/15/the-tears-of-john-boehner (accessed December 22, 2010).

Gioa, T. "Marian McPartland Plays Ornette Coleman (and Everything Else!)." March 12, 2008. The Jazz.com Blog, www.jazz.com/jazz-blog/2008/3/12/marian-mcpartland (accessed December 22, 2010).

Glasser, B. *In a Silent Way: A Portrait of Joe Zawinul.* London: Sanctuary Publishing, 2001.

Gray, J. *Fire Music: A Bibliography of the New Jazz, 1959–1990.* Westport, CT: Greenwood Press, 1991.

Hansson, C. "Marian McPartland, Jazz Pianist: An Overview of a Musical Career." 2008. http://clarehansson.com/marianmcpartland (accessed December 22, 2010).

Heffley, M. *Northern Sun, Southern Moon: Europe's Reinvention of Jazz.* New Haven, CT: Yale University Press, 2005.

Lewis, G. E. *A Power Stronger Than Itself.* Chicago and London: University of Chicago Press, 2008.

Lock, G. "'What I Call a Sound': Anthony Braxton's Synaesthetic Ideal and Notations for Improvisers." In *Critical Studies in Improvisation/Études critiques en improvisation* 4[(1)] (2008).

McPartland, M. *Twilight World.* Beverly Hills, CA: Concord Jazz, 2008.

Naughton, P. "Racism Is Driving Anti-Obama Protests, Says Carter." *Times Online.* September 16, 2009. www.timesonline.co.uk/tol/news/world/us_and_americas/article6836592.ece (accessed December 22, 2010).

Norris, C. "Hawking Contra Philosophy." In *Philosophy Now: A Magazine of Ideas.* March/April 2011. www.philosophynow.org/issue82/Hawking_contra_Philosophy (accessed March 8, 2011).

Pease, T. "The Schillinger/Berklee Connection: A Perusal of Lawrence Berk's Notebooks." 2010. www.berklee.edu/bt/122/connection.html (accessed December 24, 2010).

Sweet, R. E. *Music Universe, Music Mind: Revisiting the Creative Music Studio, Woodstock, New York.* Ann Arbor, MI: Arborville Publishing, 1996.

Szwed, J., ed. *Black America.* New York and London: Basic Books, 1970.

———. *Crossovers: Essays on Race, Music, and American Culture.* Philadelphia: University of Pennsylvania Press, 2005.

Vincent, T. *Keep Cool: The Black Activists Who Built the Jazz Age.* London and East Haven, CT: Pluto Press, 1995.

Warburton, D. "Sunny Murray." November 3, 2000. www.paristransatlantic.com/magazine/interviews/murray.html (accessed December 22, 2010).

18 / UTOPIAN SOUNDS
MIMESIS AND IDENTITY IN
EUROPEAN JAZZ TECHNOLOGIES

Utopian Machines

J azz music and modern music technologies, whether electric, electronic, or digital, have at least one thing in common: they both come to us from America. The United States still leads in these two sectors today and continues to produce both in industrial quantities. However, although the history of jazz has been told many times, that of music technologies has only been dealt with on occasion and has rarely been looked at in relation to a single musical genre. We will here take a look at the history of some developments in European jazz (including some European jazz musicians who worked elsewhere) and how these were connected to the introduction of certain technological developments.

To begin with, we must remember that the history of music technology in the twentieth century began with straightforward amplification, followed by sound effects and then by the development of synthesizers, which widened the field of application enormously. The move from analog to digital technologies opened up an almost infinite series of further possibilities, to the point of being able to use small home computers as recording studios, sound libraries, and sound-processing tools. If we look at the history of electrical, electromagnetic, and electronic application to musical instruments and amplification, we find ourselves viewing an almost entirely American panorama. Indeed, U.S. patents cover nearly every development in this field, from the triode valve (1906) to the prototype of the transistor (1947), from the Telharmonium (1893) to the Hammond organ (1935), from the Rhodes electric piano (1942, developed and marketed by Fender in 1969) to the Moog synthesizers (Moog modular 1963, Minimoog 1970), from the analogical sequencer (1971, marketed in 1976) to sequencer software controlled via Midi (first seriously diffused in 1996). The electromagnetic pickup for the electric guitar (1931) was also American, as were tape delay effects such as the Echoplex (1959), the programmable electronic drum machine (1969–70), and the Lyricon (about 1972)—the first reed instrument specifically designed in electronic form.[1]

Some, however, would question the apparent American supremacy in music technologies, in the same way that people have questioned whether jazz is really from New Orleans. The European contribution to the history of music technology is in fact of significant importance, just as the Italian, French, Irish, or Jewish factors are when looking at the origins of jazz. It could be argued, therefore, that the real father of the valve was a European; that a grand piano with electromagnetic pickups was constructed by Bechstein Pianofortefabrik in 1931, and that the first electronic applications for the saxophone were designed by the French engineer Jean Selmer, whose factory bears his name. In 1965, Selmer designed the Varitone, but the Selmer factory sold fabrication and distribution rights to the American company Electro-Voice. The instrument immediately gained an enthusiastic follower, Eddie Harris, and was also used, albeit less frequently, by other American saxophonists such as Sonny Stitt and Lee Konitz. The original idea behind it was nevertheless European.

In reality, the history of music technology tells the story of a two-way exchange of ideas and inventions between Europe and the United States. The American (and later the Japanese[2]) designers and companies should be given credit for developing models capable of being mass-produced at increasingly contained costs, which could then be marketed and exported all over the world to be used in music everywhere. The Europeans, on the other hand, remained largely outside this industrial movement for decades, with the exception of just a few portable electronic organs, guitar amplifiers, and analog monophonic synthesizers, which were nearly all of British or Italian production.

In contrast to the prevailing commercial standards of the time, therefore, European music technologies were the exception. We all know, however, that exceptions do not always prove the rule. Indeed they can often outline the narrative evolution of specific identities. As early as 1759, for example, when the *clavecin électrique* (electric harpsichord) was constructed in Paris, it was the Europeans who first realized that electricity could be used to create instruments that could imitate or perfect those that already existed. Later on, it was again European imagination that dreamed up how to create sounds that had never previously been heard.

The production of sounds generated by nontraditional instruments using primitive and progressively more sophisticated technologies constitutes one of the most interesting chapters in the history of twentieth-century music in Europe. As early as 1913, the Italian futurist Luigi Russolo invented the Intonarumori, and, to cite just the most famous examples, he was then followed by the Russian Lev Termen (Léon Theremin) with the Theremin (1919); the French Maurice Martenot, who invented the Ondes Martenot (1923–28); the German Friedrich Trautwein, who invented the Trautonium (c. 1929); and the Rhythmicon, the true prototype of the electric drum, again invented (1930–31) by Termen. Even though these inventions lacked circulation on the other side of the Atlantic, they all bear witness to European imagination and represent the foundation of a new "technological" approach to music. The fathers of electronic music are also nearly all European: the French Henri Pousseur, the German Karlheinz Stockhausen, the Hungarian György Ligeti, the Greek Iannis Xenakis, and many Italians as well (Luciano Berio, Franco Evangelisti, Bruno Maderna, Luigi Nono, Pietro Grossi). Even Edgar, or Edgard, Varèse, as the double spelling of his name here shows, was a Parisian who grew up and was educated in Italy and France and who only later became a naturalized citizen of the United States. Some of these founding fathers had studios at their disposal, which were equipped for sound experimentation and were often linked up to national radio stations, such as that of Berio and Maderna in Milan, Stockhausen in Cologne, Pousseur in Bruxelles, Grossi in Florence, Nono in Freiburg, or the IRCAM Parisian studio of computer music, founded by Pierre Boulez, who had used electronic music together with other composing techniques like serialism and aleatoric music since the 1970s. In those studios ideas and techniques were perfected by these composers, but their tools were hardly ever shared outside their working studios or serialized for commercial purposes and distribution. Instead, they were sooner or later reinvented or reapplied by American industries and then by the Japanese. Nevertheless, the first tape-generated echoes and tape delays were used by Pierre Schaeffer and Stockhausen a long time before their commercialization by the Echoplex company. Giuseppe Di Giugno, the Neapolitan physicist who together with Boulez and Berio founded IRCAM, worked for years on the construction of the 4X system, the first entirely digital workstation built for the analysis and synthesis of sound in real time, finally completing the project in 1979. It was such a big, costly, nontransportable and non-serializable machine, however, that it was outclassed by Yamaha's DX7. Even if the DX7 was less sophisticated and less ambitious, it was based on more or less the same principles, it was economical and transportable, and as a consequence it completely dominated the market.

In the end, the history of music technology in Europe represents the history of a utopia. Although appearing for the first time in jazz during the '70s, this utopia has ancient roots touching on some fundamental aspects of European cultural identity.

Electric Dawn

European jazz grew out of the phenomenon of acculturation, that is, local adaptation and imitation of a foreign but dominant language. A dialectic process between *mimesis* and *identity* is activated in every process of acculturation. Django Reinhardt was probably the first musician to set up an authentic European jazz style, partially based on native traditions and features; but he was also the first great jazzman in Europe to use imported technology such as the electric amplified guitar, turning it into an original sound. The first instrument to undergo a profound transformation in the twentieth century to the point of actually creating a new musical language was in fact not the keyboard, but the guitar.

Reinhardt's contribution to the electric guitar has never been properly studied. His first recordings on the instrument were carried out in 1947. He had just come back from a tour in New York, where he had played with Duke Ellington at Carnegie Hall, performed for one month at the Café Society Uptown and made his acquaintance with modern jazz. On his return he immediately began to display an interest in the most varied forms of artistic expression. During that year, he premièred at the Boeuf sur le Toit with his first painting exhibition, he was asked to do the soundtrack for the film *La fleur de l'âge* by director Marcel Carné (the film unfortunately was never realized), and some of the most important dance companies in Paris prepared choreographies based on his music.

Django's electrically modified instrument also inspired him to original forms of expression. These, however, were faced with a big obstacle—they could not be reproduced in his official recordings. The recording technology of the age did not allow for sudden changes in dynamic range, and, moreover, the balance achieved between the various instruments of an ensemble that is today known as "mixing" was then carried out by physically placing the musicians at different points in the studio with respect to a single microphone. A potentially aggressive instrument like the electric guitar, therefore, had to be kept under control not only by the technicians, but also and above all, by the musicians who were themselves playing.

Despite these heavy limitations, Django found ways to make the most of his electrified instrument in the recording studio. He concentrated on certain details of the sound where the electric guitar had greater expressive potential than the acoustic instrument. In "Gypsy with a Song" (1947),[3] for example, he made use of the greater sustain guaranteed by the amplified instrument for a very quick and extended vibrato. An acoustic instrument using a microphone placed at a safe distance could never have captured this with high definition. It was only when playing live, however, that Django was free to radically explore the electric guitar. Earlier, Charlie Christian, in his memorable recordings at Minton's Playhouse in 1941, had introduced dissonant bi-chords (that is, minor thirds and major sixths), which lightly saturated the loudspeakers of the old valve amplifiers, giving an early taste of the expressive quality shown by rhythm-and-blues and rock 'n' roll guitarists that would later dominate the '50s. But Django dared even further. He emphasized very strong octave bi-chords (using the technique that was later perfected in a "more polite" style by Wes Montgomery), and he liked bringing his hand down strongly on full six-string chords, which sent the loudspeakers of his amplifier into flagrant distortion. We can hear an example in "Swing Dynami-

410

que,"[4] part of a live recording carried out in February 1947 in an old cinema for a French radio program. In order to record the concert, the French engineers used the Philips-Miller system. This was a Euro-American technology dating back to before the early tape recorder, already used for cinema recordings since the '30s and adopted by many radiophonic studios because it enabled the recordings to be longer than those on the 78s. It offered Reinhardt the possibility of recording his performances with the same freedom he had when playing live, without being limited in terms of dynamic contrast and without saturating the overall sound of the group.

It was the first time distorted sound like this had been heard in 1947 Europe, if not in the entire world, but it was too early for this new sound to inspire new expressive horizons, and the most radical Django exploits were just episodic. Django Reinhardt used sudden peaks of euphoria and moments of violent ex-pressionism in a softer, more contained and balanced tonal context, alternating rapidly between these two moods. He could play with formidable strength in his right hand and used very hard plectrums, but he loved to alternate between a delicate and powerful approach, rapidly contrasting dynamics and tonal shades while playing. Nevertheless, Reinhardt's style as a whole foretold the approach to modern guitar playing.

In those years, as well as in the '50s, Reinhardt's approach to the electric guitar was not appreciated by the critics, and it wasn't until 1959 that the German musicologist Joachim Berendt understood how much Django's style was appro-priate for the electric guitar. Berendt sensed that the "the melodic lines he initially played on the normal 'acoustic' guitar seemed to invoke the technical and expressive possibilities offered by the electric guitar."[5]

The new guitar sound offered by Reinhardt when playing live was destined to remain isolated for many years, until the arrival of rock 'n' roll when guitarists exploited "overdrive," the natural effect resulting from the saturation of an ampli-fier's cone. This was only perfected in the second half of the '70s, however, on the arrival of the "fuzz box" (an electronic effect for the production and controlled distortion of amplified sound, which radically altered the waveform), followed by many other guitar effects in the next few years. Looking back, we can see that meaningful use of electric guitar distortion was introduced around the mid-'60s by English bands and musicians such as the Rolling Stones (Brian Jones, Keith Richards), the Beatles (John Lennon), and the Yardbirds (Jeff Beck). Django Reinhardt, however, even if an isolated example, gave European jazz historic supremacy in the development of a personal and evocative sound through the use of simple and efficient musical technologies, which were at that time still at a primitive stage.

Strings and Symbols

GIANFRANCO SALVATORE

It was rock music, however, that was responsible for the first true exploration into the depths of "technological" sound, which jazz, some years later, benefited from. At the center of this scene was Jimi Hendrix, an African American with strong blues roots who began his solo career in England on a quest for sound experimentation and who contributed to the perfection of the majority of technological devices for the electric guitar. Hendrix's importance should be measured against the fact that the electronic effects he introduced would have an impact not only on rock guitarists, but also on other important instrumentalists of future jazz-rock. Examples include the wah-wah pedal (used by Miles Davis on the trumpet in 1970 and then, in two years, by the whole of his band, with the obvious exception of the drums[6]); the Octavia or octave generator (the Varitone was able to generate a similar effect for jazz saxophonists); the fuzz box used to regulate distortion, as well as a variety of echo and phasing effects—forerunners to the digital delay and harmonizer, which benefit from the enormous resources unleashed through signal processing and multiplication.[7] This technology was applied to electric organs as well (in England, for example, by Mike Ratledge of the Soft Machine) before the birth of synthesizers.

Thanks to Hendrix's experimentation with sound, the electric guitar was introduced, first in England and then in the United States, to a sound spectrum of expressive qualities that, although unsupported by the harmonic language of jazz, was of a substantially wider and more incisive nature than the sound of the American jazz guitar. In the immediate aftermath of the Hendrix whirlwind, the expressive evolution of electric guitar technologies inevitably continued to develop in England, where Hendrix had begun his experimental journey. After Charlie Christian, the American electric guitarists in fact pulled back toward softer and less imaginative sounds, and for a long time the guitar played little part in the main developments of jazz history, even though it was in the hands of some great musicians. It was in fact Europe that brought new inspiration to the string instruments of American jazz.

We must here introduce the first in a small series of important European jazz figures who, when moving to the United States, had a momentous impact on American jazz and on its sound. John McLaughlin was a musical figure of particular importance. His first recording on the electric guitar in the United States was *Devotion* (1970).[8] It showed coherent continuity with respect to Hendrix's innovations, both in terms of the harsh guitar sound (which the English musician then softened in favor of greater lyricism) and in his choice of drummer, Buddy Miles, one of Hendrix's most important collaborators. Within a year, however, McLaughlin had taken advantage of the formal aspects and methodologies he

412

had picked up during his discontinuous but important discographic collaboration with Miles Davis from 1969 onward. He found a synthesis between his main cultural and musical influences, the Spanish flamenco and the Indian raga, combined with an inspiration that tended toward mysticism, previously expressed in jazz by the music of John Coltrane.

In order to achieve this synthesis, however, McLaughlin had to resolve a problem with sound. To make his guitar play with the expression of a saxophone, or even a sitar, he needed something beyond the physical structure of the guitar. He needed a virtually infinite sustain, free from decay. This problem had been battled with for years, and it had been eventually resolved by another English guitarist, Robert Fripp (leader of King Crimson, forerunners of "progressive rock"), through a combination of manual and electronic techniques, using the "controlled feedback" introduced by Hendrix and combining it with a special series of pedal effects. Within the aesthetic context of the Mahavishnu Orchestra, the group with which McLaughlin consecrated his unique sound and style, this sustained guitar sound had to interact, often in very fast and virtuoso exchanges, with two other instruments, Jerry Goodman's violin and the Minimoog synthesizer of Jan Hammer from Prague, another European who emigrated to the United States in 1968.[9]

This continual exchange, especially between guitar and violin, may remind us of the European precedent, Reinhardt's Quintette du Hot Club de France: a brilliantly virtuoso dialogue, dominated by the sonority of the plectrum and the bow, combined with arpeggios and scales in the medium-high register. Hammer's synthesizer enhanced the dialogue with a third voice—almost as if Django had Stéphane Grappelli's violin and Hubert Rostaing's clarinet both playing with him in the same band.

In the Mahavishnu Orchestra, however, the dialogue was three way, and a "Djangoish" interpretation of their work is too simplistic here. The interplay in McLaughlin's band between the electric guitar, violin, and synthesizer was characterized by a mimetic type of approach where the three instruments imitated each other, both in terms of sound and style. This approach has strong symbolic value. The three instruments strove to build a single identity, with the guitar and the synthesizer imitating the fluid legato continuity of the violin. Their dialogue, characterized by a virtuoso and "transcendental" style (in Liszt's sense of the term), developed constantly toward a climax. Working together as one, the three instruments used to establish a mounting tension that grew until it became almost unsustainable, to then explode cathartically in progressions of scales, which tended relentlessly toward the highest register of each instrument.

In the music of the Mahavishnu Orchestra, the guitar, violin, and synthesizer imitated each other to such an extent that their identities could almost be confused with one another both in terms of sound and style, and the critics and the public interpreted this in a mystical light. McLaughlin, who was then a follower of the guru Sri Chinmoy, was in fact expressing an interior journey of a deeply symbolic nature, inspired by the fundamental principles of Hinduism. One of these was the concept of Trimurti, a notion expressed by a Sanskrit term that means "having three forms" and which refers to the triple aspect of the supreme divinity: creator, conserver, and transformer (Brahma, Vishnu, and Shiva). Although the inspiration came from India, this tendency toward symbolic representation in musical projects expresses the typical utopian and visionary mentality with which European jazz musicians tended to approach sound technologies.

The jazz guitarist who most sensed the possibility of symbolically portraying his own expressive world through electronic sustain and reverb was, after McLaughlin, the Norwegian Terje Rypdal. As with McLaughlin, Rypdal's fundamental source of inspiration also centered on the violin's sound and expression. In his first recordings, he would sometimes actually use a violin bow on the strings of the guitar,[10] but later on, he chose to use a volume control pedal, which he found useful for eliminating the "attack" sound produced by the impact of the plectrum and for creating fade-ins (unsurprisingly his second instrument was the flute). More recently, he began applying the slide technique to a similar expressive end. His electric guitar consequently produced a very pure, ethereal sound, which Rypdal used on several occasions in dialogues with Miroslav Vitous's bowed double bass.

Michael Tucker, jazz critic and professor of poetics at the University of Brighton, emphasizes the importance of the often desolate Norwegian countryside as a source of inspiration for the local artists. He comments that throughout the nineteenth century "European artists, thinkers and travellers . . . lovers of the North sought a sublime, healing experience of landscape," and underlines that "by the beginning of the twentieth century, the idea of the North as a key to the renewal of inner life had acquired a magnetic aura—partly through the landscape itself, and partly through the "Nordic" art and literature, music, architecture and design which that landscape has helped to inspire."[11]

In describing the "visionary quality, typical of Nordic poets," but which belongs to Scandinavian composers and jazz musicians as well, Tucker highlights three aspects: "the striking quality of an existentially open, sometimes angst-ridden quest which is apparent in much of the most notable Scandinavian culture of the past century and a half"; "the problematic legacy of Protestantism in Northern Europe," which is reflected in the work of "painters and poets, thinkers and film makers"; and "the ancient, mystery loving and animalistic wisdom of the pagan and polytheistic Nordic world."[12] Tucker's argument, however, does not take into consideration how the quality of *tones* contributes to the creation of musical symbols and metaphors. The Nordic countryside would not have its particular poetic quality if its narrow fjords and wide spaces were not illuminated by a special light that cannot be found anywhere else in the world, a light that is able to profoundly influence the psychology and mood of the Norwegians. It is a cold and melancholy light.[13]

In pieces such as "Rainbow" (in his eponymous debut album *Terje Rypdal*, 1971),[14] where the title alludes to the use of the bow but also to the humid and dusty consistency of the sound, Jan Garbarek's strongly reverbed soprano sax joins the exchange between Rypdal and Vitous. Even if each instrument manages to maintain its own timbre and pitch, they share the same luminescence. The resulting texture is like a subtly woven, iridescent spider's web, or a series of laser rays that interweave in the sky. Interestingly enough, the Norwegian guitarist's and the Mahavishnu Orchestra's debut albums were issued almost contemporaneously, both independently focusing on mimesis between one instrument and another. But at the same time, Rypdal's tone-color fabric seemed to reflect something that belonged intimately to him: the light of his land, transformed into soundscape.

McLaughlin and Rypdal seem to revive a philosophical cornerstone of the European musical tradition, mainly found in Italian and German Baroque, where the idea of mimesis and imitation is deeply rooted in the symbolical (*ut pictura poësis*) or rhetorical (the "doctrine of affects"—*Affektenlehre*) concepts of art and music. A Promethean utopia, indeed, but one that has expressed itself also through simple, self-referential episodes throughout the history of music, where musical instruments have played at reciprocally imitating each other's sound. It is enough to look at lesser-known masterpieces from the Baroque era, such as *Capriccio stravagante* by Carlo Farina (1626), where an ensemble of violin, viola, viola da gamba, cello, and *basso continuo* imitated the fife, trumpet, clarinet, drum, and Spanish guitar. This sophisticated game was a genuine offshoot of the hyperbolic stylings and larger-than-life approach of the seventeenth century. It represents an authentic exchange of musical identity, rooted in instrumental virtuosity and in illusionism typical of the Baroque era.

Mimetic approach to sound is also inherent in blues and jazz, but in the symbolic world of the black diaspora, the philosophical foundations of orality (the classical Logos, or the *nommo* of the African tradition[15]) constitutes a cosmic principle before existing as a communicative principle. In fact, throughout the history of blues and jazz, when a musical instrument imitates anything, it is almost always the human voice. Examples of this can be found in the African talking drum, the bottleneck technique applied to the blues guitar, the wah-wah mutes for trumpets and trombones in classic jazz, or the vocal-like duets of Charles Mingus's double bass and Eric Dolphy's bass clarinet in the famous

mind/body binary here *what?* *bring ! not fond of this binary* *(primitivistic reading)*

GIANFRANCO SALVATORE

"What Love."[16] Such music has an onomatopoeic feel, a feel of concrete discourse, of direct communication and an almost carnal articulation. It is the exact opposite of the European mimetic approach, which tends either to intellectualize the musical discourse into a sophisticated divertissement, or to exalt the more-abstract symbolic components.

European and African mentalities differ substantially from one another, the former being more individualistic in nature, based on a different symbolic tradition, and tending to express its inherent cultural outlook in a variety of forms and symbols through the latest available technologies. McLaughlin and Rypdal, for example, employ a range of solutions to develop the idea of an exchange of sonic identities between instruments. In the trinitarium symbolism of the Mahavishnu Orchestra, this exchange is rooted in mystic meaning. In Rypdal's music, on the other hand, an icastic tension prevails, which aims at soundscape and vision. In "Rainbow," as in many of the Norwegian guitarist's following works, a texture of sounds is created—sounds that are similar enough, yet different enough, to successfully interweave into a multicolored tapestry. Electronic effects on all three instruments stimulate a wealth of overtones, which symbolize optical refractions and reflections, as if sounds are teasing and playing with light. Even in his more recent symphonic compositions where Rypdal extends his conceptual and tone-color ideas to the string section, the musician's poetic approach generally tends to produce immaterial and translucent sounds.

"National sentiment" and landscapes apart, the tendency to conceptualize musical expression through philosophical and abstract, or representative and figurative, ideas, is strongly rooted in the European tradition and makes up a profound aspect of its identity. This tendency is nurtured by a visionary conception of music that develops sound and form around a mimetic and symbolic approach and at times aims for synaesthesia—sensorial short circuits of acoustic and visual perception.[17] Whereas religious emotion, cathartic techniques, and magic were employed in ancient times, in the modern age scientific and technological research have taken their place. The ancient and modern world would indeed seem to be in stark technical opposition to each other here—irrationalism versus technocracy—but the apparent contradiction is less dramatic than would at first appear, as we shall now see.

Inspired Keyboards

During development of European music over the ages, a visionary tendency often surfaces with a strong underlying immaterial and symbolic conception of music. Paradoxically, this has frequently been expressed through the application of machines and physical, electric, or electronic principles. But it is not at all

416

unusual to find examples of a symbolic, or even religious approach to the use of machines in the history of European musical technologies.

We are looking back at a long story, which began in the ancient Mediterranean where European thought and imagination were born. The first developments took place in the Greco-Roman civilization, where art and science made up a single *tekhne*, where music was seen as numbers, and numbers were the key to both the cosmos itself and to its representation. The Renaissance and then Baroque civilization brought these ideas into the modern age, thanks to artists who were also engineers or alchemists, such as Da Vinci or Bosch, and musician-architects who built tonal labyrinths, such as Bach. This integral part of European cultural heritage finally found new expression in modern industrial civilization with the early avant-garde artistic movements of the twentieth century such as Futurism or Bauhaus.

It is significant that the first electric musical instrument in history was made by a theologian and was dedicated to the pagan god of altered consciousness and intoxication, mystic vision and mystery sects. The instrument was the Denisdor, invented by the Czechoslovakian Václav Prokop Diviš (1698-1765), a Premonstratensian priest and natural magic theorist. The inventor-theologian drew inspiration for the instrument's name from his own surname, which he associated with the name of the Greek god Dionysus (evoked though the French *Denis*). Diviš was a pioneer of European research into electricity and is most remembered because he is believed to have invented the lightning rod independently of Benjamin Franklin.[18] So Diviš was part of a long string of European inventors ahead of their time, who were, however, outclassed by their American colleagues. Probably toward the end of the 1740s, Diviš also made his "Denis d'or," which was mentioned for the first time in a written source in 1753[19] and which unfortunately no longer exists. The instrument was a sort of electric harpsichord with fourteen registers, able to imitate both chordophone and wind instruments through the electrification of its tailpiece. The first keyboard instrument in history to use electric technology therefore also represents the desire to "miraculously" (or rather "mechanically") imitate another instrument, providing us with an example of a utopian ideal nurtured at the crossroads between religious and technological culture.

The first electric harpsichord (or *clavessin électrique*), invented in 1759 by the French Jesuit Jean-Baptiste Thillaie Delaborde, also had something magical about it in the eyes of its maker. In a paper published in 1761," Le clavessin électrique,"[20] Delaborde not only described the instrument in technical terms illustrating its musical possibilities, but also underlined the fact that if played in a dark environment, his electric harpsichord could bewitch the listener with the brilliant sparks it produced during performance.

In these early experiments, we can already see signs of a utopian idea, which is profoundly European where music exists and manifests itself "sub specie technologiae," an acoustic vision of imaginary worlds—a vision that dates back to the "philosophical toys" of the Baroque era, the mechanical parts of which often included a keyboard. The eighteenth century not only introduces us to Diviš and Delaborde but to another French Jesuit as well, Louis Bertrand Castel, who invented and constructed the *clavecin oculaire*—a keyboard instrument capable of producing colors in relation to musical notes based on Athanasius Kircher's and Isaac Newton's theories. Inventions such as these started off a whole series of eighteenth-century "color organs" that were capable of generating interaction between lights and sounds and which were almost always produced by English inventors, such as Frederick Kastner and Alexander Wallace Rimington. Some of these inventors were also concert performers, others painters, but none of them became as famous as a Liszt or a Da Vinci. Nevertheless, the entire "son et lumière" experimental scene of the twentieth century, from Scriabin's *Prometheus* to Pink Floyd's light shows, was either directly or indirectly based on their assumptions, offering a heterogeneous but coherent chain of artistic and technological experiments that spanned Futurism, Bauhaus, and abstract expressionism.[21]

This whole creative tradition, devoted to the visionary elaboration of existing instruments, of instruments that imitate others, of instruments producing lights and sounds together with music or generating new and previously unheard sounds, would never have been possible without the convergence of the symbolic with the technical, humanistic with scientific culture, art with utopia.

Various symbolic worlds meet here. In one of these, music imitates other arts (poetry, theater, even cinema) by exalting the representative power of sounds, thus enabling music to express itself in a way capable of evoking a visual experience through listening. The whole concept of "program music" came from this, as did the descriptive musical style of Romanticism, the "tone poem" form, and Debussy's impressionism and symbolism.

In yet another symbolic world we find the quest for direct visual stimulation through sound and hallucinatory experiences of synaesthesia and sensorial short circuit. Although these are natural phenomena, Europeans have often tried to simulate them artificially throughout their cultural history, as in the "special effects" of the Eleusinian mysteries in ancient Greece, the supportive role of emotional ritual music and somber temple lighting in myriads of religious cults (including that of Catholicism), the "colored organs" of the eighteenth and nineteenth centuries, the French concept of *son et lumière* in historic venues, and the Anglo-Saxon light shows at the heart of the psychedelic culture where liquid slides were projected simultaneously to the music, as well as some further examples in late-'70s' English and American rock.[22]

These two worlds are both based on the idea that music is a powerful tool for creating illusions and daydreams, although the techniques and styles used can vary significantly. In the symbolic world of musical machines, on the other hand, the job of the "dream machine" is carried out by special instruments that vary according to the era. Over the course of history, mysticism or romantic dreaminess has been attributed to various European musical instruments: the ancient Greek Apollonian lyre and Orphic kithara, the Dionysian *aulos*, which made its way to the Greeks from the East, the Renaissance *lira da braccio* and later the harp used in symphonic orchestras and musical impressionism. The modern-day equivalent of these instruments is the synthesizer, and like the other "dream machines" that came before, it carries something "different" with it, something alien, an aura of "otherness." In fact it is no coincidence that science fiction cinema has used the synthesizer more than any other instrument.

In American jazz and jazz rock, however, the synthesizer has often been used in a completely different way—as an instrument for hyper-realistic mimesis, for larger-than-life imitations of instruments typical of African American culture such as the harmonica and the blues guitar. The possibility of modifying the physical nature of sounds, together with the "pitch bend" function, has encouraged imitations of these sounds and styles in monophonic synthesizers ever since they first existed. The '70s and '80s saw the success of Chick Corea's pseudo-guitar style, based on long portamentos and glissandos, openly and directly inspired by John McLaughlin, and that of Herbie Hancock, which was closer to the funky style guitar blues-licks.[23] Although the use of synthesizers in this way preserves the cultural identity of African American music by maintaining its aural archetypes, it has little to do with creative experimentation and has never been part of the different symbolic approach with which European sensibility expresses the relationship between the musical and visual worlds.

The greatest innovators of the synthesizer are actually those who have looked at it as a new instrument in its own right and not as a substitute for something else. It is unanimously agreed that the most important of these, the greatest synthesizer artist and "poet" in jazz, was the Austrian Joe Zawinul, another European jazz musician who made his career in the United States.

Already pioneer of the electric piano, Zawinul has a very significant history as a musician. "I have never been a real pianist,"[24] he told me in the summer of 1985, a comment that may seem astonishing, seeing as he was the pianist and only white musician in one of the most important modern jazz bands, that led by Cannonball Adderley, for almost all of the 1960s. Zawinul, who passed away in 2007, was born into a farmworkers' family in a small village near Vienna, and played the accordion for years as a country boy. I had the privilege of exchanging opinions with Joe Zawinul and absorbing his ideas for over twenty years. Since the very first time I met him in France, he always made a point of emphasizing how his passion for the synthesizer came from within, based on an innate idea, his own exclusive way of conceiving music, which he had had before synthesizers even existed. "Originally, I was an accordion player. I had an Italian accordion, a Paolo Soprani, with a lot of registers, and that was my first synthesiser. . . . I could change the sounds, choose a basic sound and modify it, create the sound of a real oboe or a bassoon for example, bringing out their specific tone-colours and musical qualities . . . and all this when I was just a boy."[25]

This key idea housed various other undeveloped ideas within it, ideas destined to form his personality as a creative musician. The first of these was a symphonic conception of the keyboard—he viewed it as a mechanical means of triggering other instruments' sounds. As a boy in Austria, when he placed his hands on a keyboard, his instinctive desire was really to produce the sound of an orchestra. This would appear to coincide neatly with the European concept of mimesis, but in reality there was a hint of "magic" about it, typical of the rural origins of a creative genius like Zawinul: what a symphonic composer only does in his mind— composing at the piano but "thinking" the other instruments—an accordion player actually puts into practice, by playing out whichever instrument he imagines on the keyboard. Twelve years after our first meeting, Zawinul extended this to the church organ: "Yes, I've always thought the accordion was the beginning of a great revolution, but I also think the church organ with its different registers was the first synthesiser."[26]

But Zawinul never thought of the accordion or organ as passively mimetic instruments, however. Indeed, the second idea that grew out of his primary experience as an accordion player was centered on the possibility of modifying sound through personal expressiveness (using traditional keyboard instruments), or through programming synthesizers. I think this is what he meant when he once told me: "There is a big difference between using pre-programmed sounds in your instruments and sounds that you actually create yourself. What I mean is that you create your own instrument."[27] This brings us to the third idea that defines Zawinul's poetics: he considered digital processing of sound to be the necessary prerequisite for all his musical creations. Zawinul boasted that he had never bowed his head thoughtfully over manuscript paper, waiting for an idea. In his daily creative practice, composition and improvisation coincided completely (he recorded all of his improvisations at home), and all he needed was a sound that inspired him. When composing, his structural decisions were directly inspired by tone-color possibilities, the exact opposite of the concept of "orchestration" as an option in the classical tradition. Zawinul described his modus operandi to me like this: "For me, sound is the first thing. . . . When I wake up in the morning, I turn on my instruments and I want to listen to something. So I start to play around a sound, and when I get something I like, I memorise it in my machines, and then I start playing, and I compose and that's it."[28]

This is why Zawinul said that he had never been a "real" pianist: "For me, playing the piano has always been like having my wrists handcuffed.... The piano is always the same. It doesn't matter who the pianist is or how they play, you always hear the same sound."[29] Although he occasionally went back to the piano to please his friend Friedrich Gulda, with whom he publicly performed and recorded Johannes Brahms' *Variations on a Theme by Haydn, op.56.* Zawinul never stopped rejecting the instrument at heart, even though it had brought him success in the American jazz scene. In the summer of 1986, he was alone on tour in Europe presenting his album *Di-a-lects*,[30] which was about to be released. During his live performances, he would interweave loops, textures, and melodies to create dense orchestrations, making creative use of the sequencer and, in particular, various electronic drum machines, which he enjoyed playing, as he put it, "one against the other." I was there at the Ravenna jazz festival for one of his concerts during the Italian tour, when the truck carrying the many instruments he needed didn't arrive in time for the sound check. The festival organizers asked him to substitute his performance with a solo piano concert, but he refused indignantly, even at the cost of having to pay a fine. It was a clear example of artistic integrity, but also of the uncomfortableness he felt for that old instrument that could produce "only one sound."

This discomfort had already begun to show itself when he was a young jazz pianist still working in Europe. "My first encounter with electronics was in 1948, in Austria. I was playing in an American club and on the floor below in the same building there was a chapel with a Hammond B3 organ in it which I threw myself into playing with a passion—I was already thinking about different sounds from the piano."[31] Twenty years later, he moved from the piano to the electric piano, but "I processed the sound using a wah-wah pedal."[32] Then he met Mike Nock, the New Zealander pianist and synthesizer player, who was one of the pioneers of jazz rock in the United States. Nock gave him a ring modulator, an effect that, when applied to an electric instrument, radically transforms its sound by multiplying and modifying the signal: "and from that moment on, I began playing in a different way. But my experimentation with sound also involved the piano, which I hadn't abandoned altogether and which I often played as 'prepared piano,' putting all sorts of things on the tailpiece: pins, tape, tambourines."

Zawinul's first approach to "synthetic" sound was in fact with effects obtained through an unconventional use of the piano. In "Milky Way," one of the pieces in the eponymous debut album by Weather Report[33] (Zawinul's most famous band), "the introduction was based on chordal resonance obtained by holding down the piano keys and the pedal, while Wayne Shorter played a note on the soprano sax above the tailpiece, making it vibrate in sympathy. Then I cut out all the attacks of the notes from the tape. It wasn't possible to do such things with synthesizers at the time, but I did it all the same, with acoustic tools."[34]

The synthesizer was the only instrument that could put all of Zawinul's ideas on musical creation into practice: his symphonic vocation, his personal creation of sounds, and his approach to musical composition stemming from choice of tone colors. He was clear about the unique nature of this instrument: "We have to clear up a misunderstanding: the synthesizer has nothing more in common with a piano than a trumpet or a violin or any other instrument has. The only thing it has in common is the keyboard . . . for all the rest, the synthesizer is a completely different instrument, actually, it's much more than just a single instrument."[35] Even though he had spent most of his life in the United States, Zawinul as a European musician sought a multiple identity in the synthesizer, an identity arising from its virtually infinite variety of sounds.

Over the years, Zawinul, like Miles Davis, wanted to contaminate the visionary electronic/symphonic conception of his music with the typically African American ideology of *funky*, based on a beat that is not only measured and articulated but also dramatically contracted and outlined: a beat that dissolves the mind into the body, stimulating prenatal memories, the pleasure principle, the libidinal consciousness. He Africanized (rather than Americanized) the European vision he had pursued in the first years with Weather Report and became the creator himself of a multiple identity, culturally identifying with the technology of the synthesizer as a "producer of synthesis." In the end, Zawinul achieved a unique blend of European visionariness and black physicality: another utopia, unique in its genre.

Echo, Narcissus, and the Musique Mécanique

In the work of these jazz musicians, music is not just about the art of sound. It is also about working on identity—identity of musical instruments, of the arts, of sensorial experiences, and the way these are handled within the relationship between music and reality, music and imagination. As we have seen, mimesis, a typically European poetic technique, is often involved in this process. Instruments imitate other instruments; sound imitates light; melodies, harmonies and rhythms become capable of visual, poetic, narrative, and dramatic expression. In all these cases, European cultural identity is expressed through a continuous reworking of its objects' and instruments' identity in a constant dialectic between tradition and innovation. We often encounter the archetype of metamorphosis throughout this cultural and aesthetic process—an archetype that stems from both mythology and the unconscious, and finds creative elaboration in a tradition

422

spanning from Ovid to Kafka. The utopia, here, is that of transforming an identity that is, in itself, always partial or temporary and constantly in progress, saving nonetheless its main cultural roots and symbols—which include the myth of metamorphosis. In other words, this utopian identity coincides, in Europe, with a conception of identity as a *process*.

In the process of elaborating a cultural identity of its own, European experimentalism in electronic jazz also began exploring the simultaneous multiplication of a player's own identity. This phenomenon originates from the ancient utopian concept of the one-man band, which began when the ancient Greeks inserted little cymbals into the frame of a drum in the late fifth century BC.[36] It then continued into Medieval times with "pipe and tabor" players (who used one hand to play a little drum that had a shoulder strap and the other to play a three-holed straight flute) and later was applied mechanically in Baroque organs with the multiplication of manuals (that is, keyboards) or, stylistically speaking, with multiple counterpoints played on a keyboard by a single musician. In the twentieth century, recording and sequencing technologies have taken over this role, enabling musicians to play in counterpoint to themselves and multiply their own musical identity.

This narcissistic utopia has been expressed through two main techniques. The first is the multi-tracking technology, which consists in rerecording over previously made recordings. A single musician can record his own performance, then record another over that while listening to the first recording in real time. This layered construction can be continued to a virtually infinite level. The first jazz musician to pioneer the use of this technique was Sidney Bechet playing all instruments on his 1941 recordings of "The Sheik of Araby" and "Blues for Bechet."[37] Later on, Lennie Tristano overdubbed himself on piano (three parts on "Descent into the Maelstrom," 1953, first issued in 1979; four parts on "Turkish Mambo," 1954), followed by Bill Evans (two entire albums based on piano duets and trios "with himself") in the following decade.[38] A few saxophonists also experimented with the technique.[39]

The idea was welcomed more enthusiastically in Europe, where this modus operandi had roots in centuries of one-man bands. In European jazz, one of the leading figures in this sphere was the saxophone and bass clarinet player John Surman, whose first solo album, *Westering Home*,[40] in 1972, was a milestone for the application of multi-tracking in jazz. Toward the end of the '70s, the idea was perfected both in terms of form and content in the new series of albums that Surman began releasing with ECM where the musician successfully combined new musical technologies with his experience as an avant-garde jazz musician, while maintaining a genuine European spirit.

Perhaps the first thing we notice about his recordings is that Surman does not play the synthesizer like a keyboard player would. His synthesizer is linked to a sequencer, a sort of digital recorder (today available as software for computers), in which short or long patterns are programmed and memorized and can then be reproduced, also cyclically if desired. Surman creates loops resembling a sort of iterative *basso continuo*, often based on broken chords, programming the synthesizer with acoustic instrument sounds (recorder or church organ), and on top of this he improvises with the bass clarinet or the soprano saxophone in a rhapsodic style. The unique aspect of this style is that it sounds neither classical nor jazz, but rather has a surreal taste of folk about it. Surman's use of a sequencer applied to the synthesizer reminds us of the so-called organetto di Barberia from the eighteenth century, invented by an Italian, Giovanni Barbieri, and still used by buskers at the beginning of the twentieth century—a mechanical organ with many pipes and bellows, which can reproduce melodies engraved on a rotating cylinder by turning a handle. It is also called a barrel organ. Surman's sequencer and the organetto have this in common: they both use a preprogrammed tool (it doesn't matter whether it is mechanical or electronic, analogical or digital) that triggers a modular or strophic sequence on the sound machine, while another instrument may play melodically over this background. This way of using music technology revives an ancient European tradition—*musique mécanique*, the history of which has been reconstructed in recent years largely thanks to the recovery, collection, and study of "musical machines" of the past. Here I would like to mention the Musée de la Musique Mécanique at Gêts, in Haute Savoie, which has a collection of 550 items, and two Swiss institutions: the Musée Baud di L'Auberson in French-speaking Switzerland and the Museum für Uhren und mechanische Musikinstrumente in Oberhofen on Lake Thun, in the Swiss canton of Berna, which also has some instruments with orchestral and percussive sounds for playing so called "jazz band" programs (mainly ragtime and fox-trots).

In street festivals associated with some of these museums, where there is no set musical program and musicians can play wherever and whenever they want, it is common practice for amateur musicians passing by to stop at one of the mechanical instruments and improvise in their own traditional style on the popular instruments of the local tradition. Even if unintentionally, Surman seems to have adapted these kinds of urban folklore, in a more cultured and "artistic" style, while maintaining the same feel as the *musique mécanique* thanks to the contrast between the mechanical sequence, improvised parts, and acoustic sounds "re-thought" in a technological light.

Surman's talent also lies in his ability to electronically manipulate the "out" signal, that is, intervening with various effects that elaborate the sound after it has been created by his wind instruments. His use of digital delay is remarkable. This is an electronic device that produces a repetition of the sound signal sent to it and can be regulated in terms of timbre, delay time, feedback, digitally simulated reverb of artificial environments (open or closed, tiny or huge spaces), and cyclicity of repetition (even to infinite). We are basically looking at a perfected version of the old tape echo, which, thanks to digital technology, can make use of a variety of techniques to process the sound and also offers the chance of structuring peculiar patterns into shapes and forms.

This creative practice also had some isolated American precedents, in particular John Klemmer, who began experimenting just after he had left the Don Ellis and Oliver Nelson big bands. In this period, just after the mid '70s, various young white saxophonists, all influenced heavily by Coltrane, were interested in exploring a wide range of music—from the Far East to the Beatles, from rock to electronic music. In his introduction and solo in "My Love Has Butterfly Wings" (from the 1969 album *Blowin' Gold*[41]), for example, Klemmer created rhythmic and dynamic tensions by playing "against" himself using electronic repetition of various phrases from his solo as background to new phrases.[42]

Surman's approach is very different, however. By regulating the digital delay and linking it up between the amplification system and the microphone, he obtains a cyclical repetition of notes performed on the saxophone (using all or just some notes selected with a pedal), thus creating an accompaniment by himself for his own solitary melodic lines. This mechanical process may appear banal in itself, but it is the way Surman uses it within a very precise poetic style that makes the difference. When listening, you can easily hear how much this technique recalls both the ancient "drone" and the concept of the canon. Thus Surman rethinks in technological terms a musical concept with clearly European roots.

It is also important to remember that electronic effects and their technology were not designed specifically for jazz, but rather for various types of popular music, from more serious rock to blatantly commercial music. These "backing technologies" were only ever taken seriously in Europe, where experimentation was pushed to the extreme and where their potential was studied with the aim of creating form, rather than from a purely decorative perspective. Luigi Nono, for example, used multiple digital delays, harmonizers and flangers, together with micro-tonal transpositions available thanks to the French technology Publison (commonly known as the "Infernal Machine") in the Experimentalstudio of the Heinrich-Strobel foundation at Freiburg. Using these resources, he was able to conceive the ambitious sound project *Prometeo* (1984–85) and realize further works in the second half of the decade (the composer died in 1990). In these, the sound of every instrument was amplified and electronically modified, and the player had to predict and interact with the repetition of his own sound signals, which were often reproduced with very long delays and with radical modifications to the sound spectrum of the acoustic instruments used.

The idea that fragments of discourse can be repeated to produce artificial dialogues, absorbing a meaning from this sort of narcissistic mirroring, is deeply linked to European cultural tradition. The Greeks dramatized this idea into a myth, that of Echo and Narcissus. Echo was a nymph, punished by the goddess Hera, and as a result she could only express herself by repeating the last words spoken by someone else. Narcissus was a young man in love with his own image, who rejected the love-smitten Echo. The nymph's unrequited love eventually consumed her until there was nothing left but her own voice, which still resounds in the woods and the valleys. Italian fifteenth-century poetry was the first example of an art to make use of this myth as a technique for formal invention. In one *rispetto* by Angelo Poliziano (1479) for example, Echo replies to the god of the woods, Pan, using the technique of internal rhyme. The nymph's words, "amo" (I love), "Un solo" (Only one), etc., arise from repetition of the ends of the god's questions.[43]

In general, we can detect the archetypal mark of the natural phenomenon of echo in all types of imitation in polyphonic music—in the way secondary voices imitate the main voices and especially in canon and fugue. Less common examples of the echo technique as immediate repetition of a motif or an instrumental phrase but at a softer volume began to appear at the start of the fifteenth century with Josquin des Prez and, more specifically, in poetic and musical forms that focused on the "echo" technique. Composers such as Giovanni Gabrieli (*Canzon à 12 in Echo*) and Sigismondo d'India (*Ahi! chi fia che consoli*) expressed themselves using the "echo madrigal" form, as did composers later on such as Rameau in his work *Impatience*, Scarlatti with *Giardino di Amore*, or Gluck's masterpiece in act 1 of *Orfeo ed Euridice*. The technical device employed in these poetic forms is always contextually linked to its mythological and narrative roots and constantly communicates a sense of melancholy.

The same narcissistic melancholy saturates Surman's explorations of similar forms and techniques through the use of contemporary technologies. Comparable topics in the African and African American contexts are profoundly different. In Africa, for example, the natural phenomenon of echo is a source of social amusement for people in company. The Baka pygmies of Cameroon play with the echo of the forest, letting out their typical yodel (*yeyi*) and developing polyphonic variations based on the naturally resounding echo of their call[44]—a game with nature played by the people who live in direct contact with it. In traditional African American music, the ecclesiastical foundation of the antiphonal matrix, the liturgical and participatory significance of call and response, and the euphoric potential of the riff transform the natural pattern of echo into the social rite of "echoing"—in the repetition of a preacher's key words, for example, or big band sections that mirror each other. Features of individuality and otherness are thus turned into an expression of community. Surman, on the other hand, multiplies his own sound, integrates his own various sonorous identities and is able to keep himself company while remaining alone.

Nevertheless, some of the fundamental values of jazz are still expressed in Surman's poetics, as they are in other European technological utopias. In 1987, I was artistic director of a festival in Rome, aptly titled "Hi-Tech Jazz." I invited John Surman to come and play a solo concert, commissioning him with a performance for reed instruments and synthesizer. He had not undertaken an exclusively solo performance like this for many years. After the concert, he told me where he thought electronic music and jazz met: "With the invention of the digital sequencer, we were given the possibility of developing patterns, and I thought I would treat them as a riff." By way of example, he sang some typical riffs from a swing orchestra, and commented: "It's simply a groove, a repeated phrase, a figure that I can bounce about and repeat to create swing, then I can work on that. . . . We're talking about something that jazz musicians have *always* done: playing on a structure which repeats itself, but contrasting the repetition by way of variations."[45]

This meeting ground between European poetry and African American values is even more evident, in my opinion, in the way Surman uses electronic effects. For example, in "All Cat's Whiskers and Bee's Knees" (*Withholding Pattern*,[46] 1985), for baritone sax and delay, the English musician develops his improvisation by regulating the repetition frequency of the electronic delay on the rhythms and notes he produces in real time. As a result, he is allowed to create a bass line or a spontaneous harmonized passage. But most of all, in overlapping new or repeated phrases with the help of technology, he also creates pure swing, that most typical element of jazz. Surman swings on himself, or rather on his own echo. He single-handedly combines the stylization of an archetype originating from a myth, the polyphonic technique born out of European history, and a typically jazz sensibility.

In the wake of Dionysus and Prometheus, Echo and Narcissus, the great Da Vinci and the more humble artists and inventors of utopian sounds who have today almost been forgotten, European jazz continues to reformulate myths and archetypes arising from the deepest strata of its cultural identity. We are confronted with a musical creativity that draws inspiration from thousands of years of history, but that pushes continually forward into the future.

NOTES

1. Apart from a few books that are listed in the bibliography, studies concerning historical electronic instruments and prototypes are only found in specialist magazine articles of various nationalities, which often have limited circulation. For quicker access to informa-

tion, see the *Grove Music Online*. General information is also available in specific and usually accurate Wikipedia entries. A chronological review with useful dates can be found at http://120years.net/nav.html. The Conservatory of Friburg (Switzerland) offers the useful website www.synthe.ch and has a historical collection of electric and electronic instruments dating from the eighteenth century to today.

2. From the Yamaha FM digital synthesizer—the famous DX7 keyboard—and the first digital delay pedal by Boss, both marketed in 1984, up until the EWI "Electronic Wind Instrument" series, and the EVI "Electronic Valve Instrument," finalized by the Japanese firm Akai at the end of the 1980s, although designed by the American Nyle Steiner during the 1970s.

3. CD, *The Chronological Django Reinhardt 1947*, vol. 2, Classics 1046.

4. LP, *Rythme Futur*, Vogue Jazz Legacy, 500108.

5. Berendt, 1979, 275.

6. See Salvatore, 2007, 142, 157, 163

7. For Hendrix's pioneering use of electronic effects see Heatley 2009 or the appendix to Shapiro and Glebbeek 1992.

8. A recent CD reissue is Celluloid CELD 5010.

9. This first lineup of McLaughlin's Mahavishnu Orchestra recorded four seminal records: *The Inner Mounting Flame*, CD Columbia CK 65523, first published in 1971; *Birds of Fire*, CD Columbia/Legacy 66081, first published in 1972; *The Lost Trident Sessions*, CD Columbia/Legacy 65959, recorded in 1973 but first published in 1999; and *Between Nothingness and Eternity*, CD Sbme Special Mkts 32766, live recording (1973), first published in 1974.

10. He was preceded in England by a rock guitarist, Jimmy Page from Led Zeppelin, whose interest in electronics also led him to experiment with the Theremin.

11. Tucker, 1998, 185.

12. Tucker, 1998, 186

13. The same light also inspired the pianist Keith Jarrett in the choice of title for his 1974 album *Luminessence* (CD ECM 1049 ST), a play on words joining the concepts of "luminescence" and "essence." This was the same year he asked the Norwegian saxophonist Jan Garbarek to collaborate with him when he formed a "European Quartet" with two Scandinavian musicians as the rhythm section, Palle Danielsson from Sweden and Jon Christensen from Norway.

14. CD ECM 1016.

15. Jahn, 1989, 132.

16. *Charles Mingus presents Charles Mingus* (CD Candid 79005).

17. For artistic simulations and semantic mechanisms related to the phenomenon of musical synaesthesia, see for comparison Salvatore 2005 and Salvatore 1999.

18. See for comparison Cohen and Schofield 1952, with objections by Hujer 1952.

19. *Tübingische Berichte von gelehrten Sachen*, 30 July 1754, p. 39.

20. Delaborde, 1761 (reprinted with the same title by Minkoff, Paris, 1997).

21. Salvatore, 2005, 30–37.

22. Ibid., 37–44, 51–57.

23. It was George Duke, however, who came closest to perfecting the faithful reproduction of the soloist guitar sound.

24. Salvatore, 1986, 12.

25. Ibid.

26. Salvatore, 1998, 82.

27. Ibid.

28. Salvatore, 1986, 11.

29. Ibid., 12.

30. CD Columbia CK 40081.

31. Salvatore, 1990, 47.

32. Ibid.

33. Weather Report, *Weather Report*, first released in 1971 (CD Sony 48824).

34. Salvatore, 1998, 83.

35. Salvatore, 1990, 45.

36. See Salvatore, 2011.

37. CD, *The Chronological Sidney Bechet, 1940–41*, Classics 638.

38. Bill Evans, *Conversations with Myself*, first released in 1963 (CD Verve 821 984–2), and *Further Conversations with Myself*, first released in 1967 (CD Universal UCCV 9344).

39. Zoot Sims in 1956 on the album *Zoot Sims Plays Alto, Tenor and Baritone* (CD Fresh Sound FSRCD 434); Paul Desmond and Gerry Mulligan in 1962 on "The Way You Look Tonight" (*Two of a Mind*, CD RCA Bluebird 09026606401).

40. FMR CD16-L795.

41. LP Cadet LPS 321.

42. Tom Scott was also doing something similar in that period. He also came from the Ellis and Nelson big band and was influenced in the same way as Klemmer, even though he soon became more involved in pop and funky music.

43. "Che fai tu, Eco, mentr'io ti chiamo?—Amo. Ami tu dua o pur un solo?—Un solo" (Poliziano 1985: 193).

44. Compare "Song for Gathering Mushrooms" in the collection dedicated to Cameroon in the UNESCO record series (CD Auvidis/Unesco D8029).

45. Salvatore, 1987, 35.

46. CD ECM 825 407–2.

BIBLIOGRAPHY

Berendt, J. E. *Das neue Jazzbuch*. Frankfurt am Main: Fischer Bücherei GmbH, 1959.

Cohen, I. B., and Robert Schofield. "Did Diviš Erect the First European Protective Lightning Rod, and Was His Invention Independent?" *Isis* 43, no. 4, 1952.

Delaborde, J.-B. Thillaie. *Le clavessin électrique*. Paris: Minkoff, 1997; first published in 1761.

Delaunay, C. *Django mon frère*. Paris : Eric Losfeld Éditeur, 1968.

Dobson, R. *A Dictionary of Electronic and Computer Music Technology*. Oxford: Oxford University Press, 1992.

Heatley, M. *Jimi Hendrix Gear: The Guitars, Amps and Effects that Revolutionized Rock 'n' Roll*. Minneapolis, MN: Voyageur Press, 2009.

Hujer, K. "Father Procopius Diviš: The European Franklin," *Isis* 43, no. 4, December 1952.

Jahn, J. *Muntu: African Culture and the Western World*. New York: Faber and Faber, 1989 (1958).

Levenson, T. *Measure for Measure: A Musical History of Science*. New York: Touchstone, 1994.

Poliziano, A. *Poesie italiane*. Milan: Rizzoli, 1985.

Salvatore, G. "Joe Zawinul: Quindici anni dopo." *Tastiere* 1, no. 5, 1986.

——. "John Surman: 'Antimusicale l'elettronica? È un utensile per l'artista vero.'" *Musica Jazz* 43, no. 11, 1987.

——. "Joe Zawinul: Pianoforte/Sintetizzatore." *Piano Time* 7, no. 91, 1990.

——. "Incontro con Joe Zawinul." *Liberal* 1, no. 10, 1998.

——. "Sinestesie nella terminologia musicale e coscienza del mondo." In G. Stefani and S. Guerra Lisi, eds., *Sinestesia Arti Terapia*, CLUEB, Bologna, 1999.

——. "Orpheus before Orpheus: The Myth of the Magic Citharode." *Spring Journal* 71, Fall 2004.

——. "Let There Be More Light: Il teatro musicale dei Pink Floy." In G. Salvatore, ed., *Pink Floyd—The Wall: Rock e multimedialità*, Stampa Alternativa, Roma, 2005.

——. *Miles Davis: Lo sciamano elettrico*. 2nd enlarged ed. Rome: Stampa Alternativa, 2007.

——. "Fuori gara: Il tympanon fuori e dentro la polis." *Rudiae*, special issue, 2011 (forthcoming).

Schrader, B. *Introduction to Electro-acoustic Music*. Englewood Cliffs, NJ: Prentice-Hall, 1982.

Shapiro, H., and C. Glebbeek, *Jimi Hendrix: Electric Gypsy*. London: Mandarin, 1992.

GIANFRANCO SALVATORE

HERBERT HELLHUND

19 / ROOTS AND COLLAGE
CONTEMPORARY EUROPEAN JAZZ
IN POSTMODERN TIMES

Our time, often described as the "information age," has put knowledge of nearly every aspect of the present, the past, and the possible future at our fingertips. Our civilization's advanced information technology has put the furthest corners of the world within our reach and has suffused what were once multiple strands of cultural tradition with a global network of generally available "cultural knowledge," elements of which can be individually selected and combined.

It is no secret that this trend—particularly in the Western world—does not exactly lead to deeper cultural consciousness and understanding. A less obvious corollary effect, however, is the structural erosion of traditions (in the sense of continua of cultural praxis) in the modern information society.

"Without argument . . . the vast reorganization in our circumstances has quietly, while we were looking the other way, dismantled anything resembling a tradition."[1] This statement refers to literature, but it could well apply to Western music since the '60s and thus to jazz—this broad applicability is itself a hallmark of the boundary-transcending nature of postmodernism. Nevertheless, the economic and media-related wave of globalization has its counterpart: a tendency toward appropriation at the regional or local level through evaluation and selection, of, and combination with, "homegrown" elements, a process of differentiation that has acquired the name "glocalization." This is in effect the simultaneity of old and new, and a sort of mixture of distant and local forces.

It would, however, be too easy to view this gallimaufry of individual tastes and approaches as nothing more than a blight on the face of traditional culture. Its gradual development into a range of mixtures of, and interconnections between, established principles points to a certain culture-historical inevitability. Jazz has also exhibited these phenomena for some time now—a time in which development kindled from within the music, accepted for so long as an axiom, has come to a halt.

Up until the 1970s, the story of jazz is a straightforward narrative. It is one in which there may be changes of emphasis, or national outlook, or definition. It may be viewed in a way that avoids establishing a canonical framework of artists and works, by looking at the social, commercial, or intellectual aspects of that narrative, but there is a clear sense of development, of the music moving forward.[2]

This claim begs the question: what conditions led to the drying up of music's developmental drive from one epochal style to the next? We also have to ask: what has replaced this strict course of development, and what compensates for the loss of musical rules and norms that once arose from generally accepted musical goals or ideals?

As far as European composed music is concerned, recent decades have seen a lively debate about how to view developments since the 1960s. The term *post-modern* has been at the forefront of this debate and has often sparked, or been the object of, major controversies. Among the questions that have been raised are the following:[3]

> What is the relationship of the postmodern to the modern (a concept already included in the term): is it a continuation, a revision, a new interpretation, or an opposing position?
> Is not each element of the modern succeeded by the postmodern, as a result of further development or the emergence of contradictory tendencies?
> Is postmodern a category of style or of time?
> Is the pluralism observable since the 1960s an expression of pure arbitrariness or a necessary consequence of growth in the available methods?
> Should the willingness to include in composed music previously despised popular genres be viewed as part of a process of dehierarchization, a reconciliation of so-called higher and lower culture, an intercultural discourse? Or does it point to a "phenomenon supported less by artistic necessity and more by feel-good ambitions,"[4] to a "postmodern license to do actually anything . . . a variety store for arbitrary use"?[5]

Behind these positions, stated with such combative élan, obviously lies a particular understanding of history, the premises of which must either be confirmed or damaged. However, it is also apparent that principles of artistic production once held sacred have begun to wobble, and that the meaning of this wide-ranging paradigm shift labeled "postmodernism" is anything but clear.

One astounding feature of the postmodern debate is its diffusion into the most diverse cultural areas: in addition to music, the debate takes in architecture, visual art, literature, the social sciences, and the humanities. In approximately three decades of discussion, a wide variety of authors and commentators have offered their opinions. The German social scientist Jürgen Habermas, for example, spoke of the "modern as unfinished project," thus depicting the postmodern as a restorative phase after the political upheavals of the 1960s and '70s. Jean-François Lyotard's historiological concept of a series of "grand narratives" led to the conclusion that "history in the modern era, associated with the experience of progress and freedom of mankind, has lost its credibility and as such must be viewed as having come to an end."[6]

Composers qualified elements of their own work in retrospect: Pierre Boulez, for example, compared his previous strict adherence to the rules of serialism (which he himself had considered historically imperative) to a two-year-long tunnel.

As diverse as the fields of this debate are, one constant applies to them all: the end of progress in the direction of a single historical goal is universally held to be a fact, raising the question of what the consequences will be of this loss of unshakable historical rigor.

Let us turn now to our subject, contemporary European jazz, which can be broadly defined as the music of the European jazz milieu from the latter decades of the twentieth century up to today. This generous definition not only allows us to consider developments in the work of individual members of this artistic community; it also avoids the obsolete linkage of the idea of contemporaneity with an avant-garde that aims at completely new goals. This connotation has, to a great extent, been lost both to jazz and to the composed music of the present day. In addition, as Ekkehard Jost[7] so vividly put it, "European jazz" as a material category is useless: the milieu comprises a large number of very different approaches, from which a few—mostly regionally defined—focal points emerge as criteria for differentiation both internally and in comparison with American jazz. These criteria will be discussed later in more detail.

Jazz in Europe, significantly more than in the United States, has found itself in a continuing process of differentiation brought on by the revolution sparked by free jazz in the 1960s. This development has fostered a multitude of trends—often completely individual, often subject to regional or temporal boundaries. Here, as in composed music, the term *postmodern* is often bandied about without sufficient definition. The following will attempt to catalogue a few of the most prominent symptoms and their causes, in order to achieve a general outline of the concrete conditions and effects grouped under the postmodern label, which is tossed around far too often.

No present (defined here not in the punctual sense but as the time period enclosing a set of currently important trends) has ever seen the kind of *stylistic pluralism*—space for so much parallel and cooperative activity between old and new elements of the jazz tradition, but also between elements of completely different musical idioms and fields—that exists now. An overwhelming amount of available material shapes the contemporary market for production. All the many

433

styles of jazz and its various fusions form part of the great mass of accessible material, but so do elements of ethnic and folk traditions as well as the huge base of popular music and European concert music, all of it at our disposal—and often quite easily available. Anything goes? Let us look back to a time before these materials were in polyidiomatic supply:

> Material development in jazz grew, for a long period of time, with a striking vitality founded on a dual principle of expansion and differentiation. Innovations continually forced musicians to take a position; where that position was positive, a process of absorption, analysis and further development occurred, without which the wide diversity of individual, group or regional styles present in all of the great stylistic epochs would not have become a reality. In addition, the old was constantly giving way to the new—with the complete exploration or exhaustion of each trend serving to drive the differentiation process. . . . The length and constancy of this process of differentiation and change allowed people to become accustomed to it, to see in the process a sort of natural law. . . . After this, a new, grand perspective would have been overdue—but it was and is nowhere to be seen. Is that because the possibilities both of tonality and its negation have been used up? Because all imaginable expressive media have been explored to the point of depletion? Because no musical parameter, rhythm or formal design is showing signs of any meaningfully new development? The unmistakable truth is that the engine of material advance, long believed to be perpetual, is getting weary.[8]

Thus, out of numerous present and available idioms ensues a single situation marked by a general lack of direction.

Each musician must adopt a position in this situation, but the positions are anything but self-evident. Since there is no longer a compelling direction to musical development in jazz, there is no longer any compelling perspective for the jazz musician.

"The overabundance of material, easily perceived as a form of material duress, misleads many musicians to a markedly defensive, selective attitude, only a small step away from dogmatism."[9] Spurred by a love of great recordings from the past—for example, the hard bop era—and with the sense that following this path will put them in a safe place, musicians dedicate themselves to a particular direction, often underpinned by a purist ideology. But dangers lurk on this path: in emulating the heroes of days past, the musician comes close to the epigonism that prevailed in European jazz until the beginning of the 1960s, a condition long thought to have been overcome. It has to be said also that the current, academically supported conservatism in jazz, coupled with a growing army of young standards-playing jazz musicians, has made this a widespread, if not general,

434

tendency. Let us call exponents of this trend *neoconservatives*. Can they ever hope to achieve what they aspire to amid the reality of a music whose material-historical spring has sprung and whose socio-musical evolutionary conditions belong firstly to a different cultural context and secondly to another age?

"In a retrospective situation, everyone can play the notes and stuff, but they don't have the magic, because they've become so homogenous that something's lost. In our day, we would play, and then the technique would come to fit whatever we wanted to play. But today they develop the technique first, and then play in a kind of chronological isolation."[10] One can assume that this statement from pianist and composer Andrew Hill (in 2000) refers primarily to young American and not European jazz musicians—but the symptoms are very similar.

If these—excuse the paradox—backward-looking champions of the modern are numerous, they are nonetheless not the typical exponents of jazz under the sign of stylistic pluralism; these exponents exhibit a willingness to embrace significantly greater idiomatic openness than the proponents of a bygone modernity. However, in their acceptance of complex or changing perspectives, these more open-minded exponents face several problems at once. They must find or create connections between disparate musical genres without becoming arbitrary. In realizing their music, they must often deal with diverse challenges both to their technical resources and their ability to interpret credibly such multifaceted material. This tension between a variety of interests and the need to convey them convincingly has gradually given rise to a new type of contemporary jazz musician. That musician is not an eclecticist, always searching for something new, nor is he/she the determined representative of an avant-garde, uncompromising in his or her own unwavering position. Instead, he or she is something of a *generalist*—one might almost say a role player. This musician can play over complex changes as easily as in a free jazz context, is familiar with the European musical tradition (both concert and folk), is often extremely well informed about current pop-music trends, and—often being both a composer and instrumentalist—is able to operate expertly through very diverse media. These musicians see themselves as innovators, not to say avant-gardists. However, as clearly defined as the artistic position of the "classical" avant-gardist was, so is that of his/her contemporary descendant completely undefined. The avant-garde has a tough time in this polyidiomatic present. How should it position itself, when no clear direction is apparent? What material should it choose in the face of musical parameters that are largely exhausted?

Another, rather curious symptom of the times is a widely dispersed inclination toward recycling and revision, an interest in reflective repetition of different areas of the musical past, resulting to some extent in music that is composed and improvised over other music. The tagline for a contemporary jazz festival in

Cologne during the early '90s read, not without a certain irony, "Post This, Neo That." This slogan jokily expresses the fundamental duality of the situation: a more or less concealed historicism on one side; an avid interest in recombination on the other—although the effect of contrasts in creating tension can be just as intentional as the search for harmonious syntheses. However, this historicist component is mostly devoid of any of the respect accorded by a museum; the basic interest in revision or reinterpretation of the old usually precludes it. Instead, older elements are removed from their original framework, juxtaposed with newer or other old clichés from the most diverse sources, and simultaneously recomposed and adapted for use in a heterogeneous, individually defined context. It is the work of an *arranger*—not in the conventional sense, but in a new and more general way, focused more on the conception and notation than on improvisation. This process has always played an important role in the jazz context, but the role has now notably expanded.

Arrangement as integration: this aim is as old as jazz itself. The head arrangements in New Orleans jazz merged blues and ragtime; later, the so-called swing style included elements of the New Orleans and Chicago styles, as well as fashionable dance and Broadway tunes, often played by smaller ensembles. Paul Whiteman, who fashioned his own hybrid concept of "symphonic jazz" out of old-time jazz and light orchestral music combined with the glamour of Broadway overtures, is an extreme—but also extremely successful—example of this drive to mingle the multicolored realms of the musical imagination. As Manfred Straka attests, there was a veritable boom in big bands appropriating European concert music during the swing era. Interestingly, it was "not the famous orchestras of Afro-American leaders ... but in particular [those] of white ... leaders [that were] dominant in that movement."[11]

This trend was strengthened and brought to the fore by the work of numerous jazz musicians of the 1950s. The interest shown in the music of Johann Sebastian Bach by Gerry Mulligan, Lennie Tristano and his circle, and John Lewis and his Modern Jazz Quartet—never in the sense of a direct appropriation of Baroque stylistic features, but rather in the use of linear voice leading—points to a desire to connect and, furthermore, to combine. It would seem here that disparate realms of musical thought and feeling, fostered by a "doubled" socialization in jazz and the European-influenced musical tradition, sought to amalgamate. The openly declared intention of the so-called Third Stream movement at the end of the 1950s, which numbered (once again) Mulligan and Lewis among its most prominent figures, was to unify these two spheres. Ten years later, in spite of all the commercial interest in jazz-rock fusion, musicians such as Chick Corea, Keith Jarrett, John McLaughlin, Joe Zawinul, and even Miles Davis once again showed evidence of this musically motivated desire for "progression through integration."

European musicians in the 1960s, released from the influence of modern jazz by free jazz, began to discover their own ways of integrating components of their European identity, described by Bert Noglik as "substreams"—at first tentatively exploring this mode of thought under the influence of their American predecessors but soon doing so with more confidence. There began a process of examining these American influences, partly appropriating and partly negating them. Free jazz had a huge—even dual—significance in this process: on the one hand, liberating self-expression; on the other, serving as a source of direct musical inspiration. However, the rapidly growing pool of individual, specifically European approaches was now informed by a consciousness of domestic musical traditions.

Some highlights of this trend will now be presented; the individual positions of a few European musicians will be described, without attempting to depict their circumstances in detail. In order to assess the similarities and differences within this ongoing process, we will look at Germany, then at England, Austria, France, and Scandinavia. A brief, very selective consideration of the respective developments will be followed by a few comments on the area of media production and marketing, using the ECM label as an example.

In 1965, the Gunter Hampel Quintet recorded the LP *Heartplants* (MPS CRM 603). Appearing on the date were trumpeter Manfred Schoof, pianist Alexander von Schlippenbach, bassist Buschi Niebergall, drummer Pierre Courbois, and Hampel himself on vibraphone and flute. This recording has attained the status of a historically significant document of European jazz musicians on their way to artistic self-determination. The musical conception, ranging from an adaptation of the Modern Jazz Quartet's style to open modality, free atonality and structural elements that borrow from "new music" and twelve-tone material, will not be discussed further here.[12] We are more concerned with the protagonists' intentions and their way of verbalizing them, as exemplified in the liner notes: "I want to find a way towards free atonality—in other words, tonal equality—coupled with swinging rhythm. . . . We are looking for new musical paths on which we can assimilate and ponder the impressions and experiences of this world" (Hampel). Niebergall explains his piece "No Arrows" in terms of a basic dramaturgical arc combined with twelve-tone methodology; Schlippenbach, who had previously studied composition in Cologne with Bernd-Alois Zimmerman, comments on his piece "Iron Perceptions": "This piece is the starting point for our ideas about structural jazz. It is based on a graphic score in which the musical structures have been turned into visual patterns. The usual symbols serve only as compositional elements, side by side with other tools."

After Hampel's group split up, another ensemble was formed under the direction of Schoof, including Schlippenbach and Niebergall as well as saxophonist Gerd Dudek and Jacky (Jaki) Liebezeit on drums. The 1966 LP *Voices*, whose

437

opening track is entitled "Roots and Collage," "reveals . . . no insecurity what-soever, instead bearing the unmistakable character of a definitive musical state-ment about the confidence with which musicians can now wield the new creative tools of jazz. Although it is marked by a highly developed compositional frame-work and careful consideration of formal detail, this music is anything but overin-tellectualized—instead there is a fine balance between construction and improvi-satory freedom, mental labor and full-force expressivity."[13] In the cover notes (LR 41.005), Schoof adds:

> Our music is polyrhythmic. Tempi are not defined metrically. The drums provide a polyrhythmic texture. The structure of this texture underpins the laws of rhythmic respiration. Each instrument in our quintet is simultaneously a rhythm and an accompanist. Melodies are formed in a free twelve-tone scale. The richness gained in material expands the possibilities for composition and improvisation. The group is an organism. The freedom of the individual de-velops within the group interplay. The more this interrelation is achieved, the better and more focused this music will be. We link the various compositions without any breaks. In this way we can intensify the focus, and this manner of playing comes close to the symphonic form in which everything is connected to form a whole.

The train of thought in both jazz and European contemporary music can hardly be more clearly articulated than in Schoof's comments here. The desire to explain music in an almost academic manner, a common feature of the elec-tronic avant-garde at the time but less so in jazz, is also evident in the notes for the subsequent LP *Manfred Schoof Sextett*, one of a series of studio recordings of the "new music" (!) released on Wergo: each recorded piece is accompanied by a brief written protocol.

The quest for authenticity through consciousness of one's own musical-cultural roots is also evident among other members of the German improvising avant-garde at the time—remarkably often in terms of their recourse to modern composed music. Alexander von Schlippenbach (whose Globe Unity Orchestra, formed in 1966, could hardly have come to fruition without the prototype of Ornette Coleman's 1960 recording *Free Jazz,* and certainly not without John Coltrane's 1965 *Ascension*) had this to say about the interest in European com-position: "We listened to Bartók's string quartets; *Pierrot Lunaire* was like a drug. The end of the line in atonality—inadmissible in a Schoenbergian sense—was the magic formula. An utter pandemonium of new sounds, forms and rhythms emerged."[14] The gesturally reticent, intensely expressive tonal language of Anton Webern was a particular inspiration to the mission to practice free improvisation in an artistically independent manner. The trombonist and cellist Günter Christmann formulated this urge in terms of the "Authority of music—something which in my opinion is nowhere as clear as in Webern. . . . As much as possible, I would also like to produce only the necessary tones. In this respect, experiencing Webern's music is for me an enormous stroke of luck"[15] The examples of Albert Mangelsdorff and the "power play" improvisers led by Peter Brötzmann and Peter Kowald suggest the differences of approaches adopted by German musicians searching for freedom in the 1960s. While Mangelsdorff actually never broke decisively with American jazz (his oft-quoted credo "for me it's got to swing"— something he demonstrated masterfully—speaks for itself), Kowald's "Kaputt-spielphase" style, a relatively violent musical jailbreak, implied the negation of all previous musical obligations and the desire for a new age of freedom.

Musicians in England were also interested in modern European composed music and particularly in that of Webern, although they largely had to disregard the composer's strict compositional style—a precursor to serialism—when improvising. Tony Oxley: "We left the musicological discussions alone for the most part, made less of the compositional methods. In its place we paid more attention to the aural impressions, which we then attempted to recreate in an improvisational context."[16]

Sound research, non-linear music, and non-idiomatic music have become established terms in describing the initial years of multifaceted and highly original development in England. The oscillating cascades of sound (realized through circular breathing) produced by saxophonist Evan Parker belong as much to this picture as the strangely archaic-sounding aesthetic of the group Azimuth, with Norma Winstone, Kenny Wheeler, and John Taylor. Barry Guy's London Jazz Composers Orchestra has been an integral part of British orchestral free jazz for decades. The ensemble incorporates constructive principles from contemporary composition as well as—occasionally—early music ("Harmos" is made up of uniquely processed material from Monteverdi's *Marienvesper*). Since the 1990s Django Bates has exhibited, with his virtuosic, self-referential eclecticism (for example on the CD *Summer Fruits and Unrest*, 1993) possibilities for big bands that lie outside both free jazz and the American tradition.

Conceptual and stylistic variety achieved through individual positioning in a poly-idiomatic context: this quasi-solution to the problems of postmodernism has also been demonstrated in Austria for decades. Two contrasting examples in the field of orchestral jazz or jazz-related music are Franz Koglmann, and Mathias Rüegg's Vienna Art Orchestra. Koglmann, a flugelhornist and composer, as well as a festival and label programmer, represents the artist as polymath. After starting out in mainstream jazz, he turned to free playing in the 1970s, recording with renowned musicians such as Steve Lacy and Lee Konitz. Soon, though—guided by his interest in European art music—Koglmann found his way to a conception

439

that was substantially compositional. *Schlaf Schlemmer, Schlaf Magritte* (1984), recorded by the Pipetet, the ten-person ensemble formed by Koglmann in 1983, shows that its leader's conception is equally beholden to jazz and to modern orchestral composition. Koglmann also takes inspiration from visual art (Schlemmer, Magritte) and from literature—for example, by translating poetry into music: "I read a poem, I read it again and again, then I sing it, until a melody forms.... If it works, the first step of the composition is accomplished."[17] The 1986 festival *Jazz op. 3*, produced by the Wiener Musikgalerie under the artistic direction of Koglmann, revealed its intentions in its subtitle: "The Secret Love for European Modernism."

Mathias Rüegg is much more interested in reverse engineering than Koglmann—arrangement, compositional reinterpretation, idiomatic transformation. These processes require templates, however. *From No Time To Ragtime* (1983) includes arrangements from diverse periods of jazz history, rendered in the unmistakable musical language of the Vienna Art Orchestra. They range from the orchestra's version of an Anthony Braxton composition to a Joplin ragtime reworked from Rüegg's perspective. On *The Minimalism of Erik Satie* (1984), Satie's compositions provide the framework for reflections that generally end up quite a long way from their starting points. Rüegg found the pulse of the postmodern zeitgeist: the orchestra's performances in the 1980s at both jazz and classical (!) festivals attracted capacity and wildly diverse audiences. It played on other continents, while Rüegg and the orchestra, respectively, won the *Down Beat* polls in the arrangement and big band categories.

The name of a musicians' collective whose declared mission is to research an imaginary folk tradition (ARFI—Association pour la Recherche d'un Folklore Imaginaire) has probably inspired the community of jazz writers no less than the musicians themselves. The musicians of the ARFI, whether in their best-known formation, the Workshop de Lyon (a quartet with two reed players, bass, and drums), or in the larger ensemble La Marmite Infernale (nomen est omen!), have described their improvisational concept in various ways, including the following: "to play with the memory of sounds produced a moment ago; to play with musicians, in a complex relationship with the listener, the viewer; ... establishing emotional connections, creating a new folklore—these are all developmental levels of musical improvisation."[18] The goal here is not a regression to old, crude folk forms but the creation of a new folk tradition—whatever that may be. The recordings of the Workshop de Lyon give the impression of an improvisational method aimed more at being understood than displaying virtuosity: themes and improvisations alike are often built on patterns, and the musicians are not afraid of redundancy. The themes are often constructed like songs, and the atmosphere is generally dancelike, at times tending toward the rustic as a result of the somewhat superficial percussion. The horn stylings are less reminiscent of bebop than of spirited French dances and marches; without the generous space given to improvised passages, one would not necessarily conclude that the music had anything to do with jazz.

One of the most prominent European jazz musicians working today, Louis Sclavis, is an exponent of the Workshop de Lyon approach. Some elements of his early years with the group have remained in Sclavis's own concept—both enshrined and transformed. Pattern organization in the themes, accompanying voices, and improvisation is often the preferred method, while a reedy timbre dominates the melodic aspect—if only due to Sclavis's virtuosity—and at fast tempos there is a certain tendency toward rigid, on-the-beat phrasing. Nonetheless, Sclavis is not only an outstanding instrumentalist and improviser—probably the most significant bass clarinetist since Eric Dolphy—but also an exceptional musical conceptualist. In his music, as in his playing, the American modern jazz tradition is relegated to secondary status; Sclavis's inspiration comes from a universe of musical sources—classical music, jazz, real and imaginary folk music, rock, musette, tango . . . and he weaves all these influences into an individual synthesis. His project *Ellington on the Air* (1985) transformed the Duke's music into something unique, while his ensemble recording (collectives have always formed an important part of Sclavis's music) *Les Violences de Rameau* (1996) generates similarly imaginative and highly unusual associative spaces. Sclavis unmistakably demonstrates the artistic potential of today's musically synthetic thinking.

Mention of the "Nordic tone" in jazz usually denotes musicians associated with the Norwegian Jan Garbarek or a succession of younger musicians influenced by Garbarek and his associates. If these musicians do actually exhibit a particular tone, what are its characteristics and where does it come from? The English saxophonist John Surman commented:

> My introduction to Norwegian Jazz came during the Montreux Festival in 1968, when I heard Karin Krog's Quintet with Arild Andersen, Jon Christensen, Jan Garbarek, and Terje Björklund. They had a sound that stood out from many of the "free jazz" groups around at the time, especially in the way they were using a sense of "space" in the music. . . . From a musical standpoint, one of the features of jazz in Norway that I found really interesting was the way in which the musicians seemed able to use tunes from their folk music tradition as a basis for improvisation.[19]

Garbarek, who initially—as with so many other European musicians—followed American models (in this case, Albert Ayler and particularly John Coltrane), did not make the connection with folk music at the end of the 1960s without assistance.

Unlikely as it may seem, Jon [Christensen], Arild [Andersen], Terje [Rypdal] and myself, thanks to Don Cherry's open mind, had the opportunity to deal also with Norwegian folk music forms. During this period, the custom in Norway was to invite famous visiting American musicians to do a session at the radio station. And as Don was playing with us, he came up with the idea that we could also invite some folk musicians. Now we knew quite a lot of the folk musicians, and would hang out with them in the clubs in Oslo, but the idea of playing together hadn't arisen. At Don's insistence, one of them was contacted, a female singer, and she came to the radio studio. Nothing at all was prepared beforehand, Don just organized everything on the spot, very smoothly and easily, and we played—and the combination of folk music and improvising sounded so *right* to me. I think from that moment on, the idea of having a folk music aspect or folk musicians involved in this music was always there in my mind.[20]

The assumption that the Norwegian scene would not have existed had ECM not focused international attention on its artists is an overstatement. However, this scene would certainly have been markedly different without ECM. Manfred Eicher's interest may have started with the aforementioned musicians, but the association between this early preference and the conspicuous presence on the ECM label of Norwegians, Swedes, and Finns such as Jon Balke, Nils Petter Molvaer, Trygve Seim, Arve Henriksen, Bobo Stenson, Anders Jormin, Eward Vesala, and Iro Haarla is no accident. The question here concerns the significance of ECM's selective criteria and the label's clear affinity with the jazz-related music of Scandinavia.

To begin with a comparison: the American label Blue Note was characterized by a one-dimensional, almost exclusive focus on hard bop, the leading jazz style of the 1950s and '60s. If there is such a thing as a postmodern answer to Blue Note, it is certainly the polyglot ECM. However, the omnivorous, category-blind versatility of the ECM catalogue should not be confused with lack of discrimination: the label—meaning Manfred Eicher, the *spiritus rector*—is extremely particular.

Asked in an interview about the typical ECM sound, Eicher replied: "The musician has a sound; for me that sound is already there before the microphones are set up. Color, dynamics, articulation, the whole architecture is always there before the recording. We don't fabricate an 'ideal sound.' The ECM sound is influenced by my preferences; these are the basis of the decision as to what music gets recorded. You could perhaps say that, through the choice of program, a programmatic sound is created."[21]

ECM is all about the studio sound. Thanks partly to his engineers, Martin Wieland in Ludwigsburg and Jan Erik Kongshaug in Oslo, Eicher has achieved a subtlety in rendering musical structures—from individual timbres and their inter-action to imaginary landscapes—that has set a new standard for recording tech-niques that are at once documentary and gently interpretive. "In musicological terms: sound becomes a primary parameter, takes its place alongside rhythm, harmony, melody and form, aligns itself closely with expression. Details, illumi-nated as clearly as possible, connect to become images in perfectly structured aural spaces."[22]

This Norwegian music tends toward a serene, melodic character, as described by Surman. In contrast to the majority of American jazz, it does not eschew silence and has a much better grasp of the suggestive possibility of rests—features that sit well with the subtle tastes of ECM's producer. Taken together, a series of tendencies (not to say constants) emerges that can be appended to the aforemen-tioned conventional parameters.

Let us first look at meter and rhythm. Medium or slow tempos are in the majority; the time signatures are more varied than in modern jazz, so reliant on 4/4 time—but not as complex as the many contemporary styles that favour odd or constantly changing meters. The rhythm of both the solo and accompany-ing voices is differentiated significantly from the meter. Delicate and extremely transparent, many of the recordings present a finely structured image akin to chamber music. These tendencies are reinforced by the fact that mostly small groups find their way into this studio. Swinging jazz grooves are less frequent than dance-like rhythms in duple meter; these often create an additional "eth-nic" component through the choice of instruments as well as the shape and characteristics of the music. This component is emphasized by the frequent use of percussion instruments of highly diverse provenance; these instruments not only enliven the rhythmic action but, due to their sound character, are also extremely well suited for integration into finely structure soundscapes.[23]

The harmony is dominated by smooth progressions, modality, and simple diatonics, in contrast with the complexity and wealth of dissonance often found in modern jazz. Tonally free passages, for example in recordings by the Art Ensemble of Chicago, are even more clearly subject to the primacy of sound. Sound as criterion: some observers speak here of the greatest possible purity, others of typical ECM prettification, catering to hi-fi gourmets.

Melody, functioning also as the link between rhythm and harmony, is a central component of this music. "The melody voices are sometimes meditative, often songful, highly expressive. They show a preference for song-like structures, en-riched by excursions into improvisational fantasy—these voices, with their expres-sive facets and instrumental timbres, provide excellent material for the engineer and producer behind the big window in the studio."[24]

These factors fall a long way short of characterizing the diffuse notion of "Nordic jazz." They are, however, factors that emerge with a frequency beyond mere coincidence, and they are fit for use as criteria in attempting to describe what this notion represents.

The aural image combines with rhythmic, harmonic, melodic, and instrumental factors to form an aesthetic complex that binds together the enormous idiomatic variety of the ECM oeuvre, itself an expression of Eicher's desire for synthesis.

Jazz of various stylistic colors, jazz with ethnic components, jazz juxtaposed with European composition both old and new,[25] composed music from various style epochs—ECM is practically omnipresent, even in areas not related directly to the music: the label's cover art has also become a regular journalistic and sometimes even academic theme. Let us just note the following: if, as is often claimed, a stylized "Idea of the North" pervades the ECM aesthetic, then it is

not only as manipulation of sound but also as visualization. The record sleeves and now the CD covers showed and show that very clearly. As well as a series of covers whose art often comes in monochrome pastels with contrasting letters, following a sort of neutral aesthetic, there has been a long-running design scheme with photographs that convey this aesthetic even more explicitly: pictures of archaic-looking nature scenes, mostly empty of people, lit in the stringent formal language of black and white photography, occasionally also in flat, pastel colors—as if looking through a veil into another reality.[26]

The availability through the media of both old and new, and access to material that is spatially and culturally remote, have become hallmarks of our time. The enormous global stream of information has eroded traditions; global influences have overlapped with their local reception. In European jazz, the end of the American stylistic dictatorship has made possible an overabundance of individual artistic positions. Responses to this situation are undogmatic and synoptical, shaped by a free choice of material that can be accepted or discarded, often with an eye to personal cultural roots. Consciousness of the European art-music tradition plays a major role, as do links to real or imaginatively extrapolated folk traditions; the relationship with the jazz tradition is a matter of personal choice. Musicians and producers are faced more than ever with decision processes regarding a plurality of influences. The postmodern is a matter of vision and revision, (re)discovery and eclecticism, roots and collage.

NOTES

1. Wain, in Shipton, *New History of Jazz*, 873.

2. Shipton, *New History of Jazz*, 873.

3. See Hiekel, "Postmoderne im Musikdiskurs," 1–16.

4. Ibid., 5.

5. Ibid., 6.

6. Ibid., 5.

7. Jost, "Über das Europäische im europäischen Jazz."

8. Hellhund, "Gibt es eine Avantgarde im zeitgenössischen Jazz?" 49.

9. Ibid., 50.

10. Andrew Hill, in Giddins, *Visions of Jazz*, 883.

11. Straka, "Kompositionen der abendländischen Kunstmusik im Repertoire von Swing-Ensembles," 49.

12. Compare Jost, *Europas Jazz*, 42.

13. Ibid., 62.

14. Schlippenbach, in Noglik, 1988, 528.

15. Ibid., 527.

16. Ibid.

17. Koglmann, in Wilson, *Reclam Jazz Klassiker*, 753.

18. Jost, *Europas Jazz*, 428.

19. Lake and Griffiths, *Horizons Touched*, 35.

20. Ibid., 22.

21. Messerschmidt, "Beiträge von ECM-Bassisten zur Weiterentwicklung des Europäischen Jazz," 54.

22. Hellhund, "Der Norden, eine Himmelsrichtung oder eine Ästhetik," 37.

23. Ibid., 37.

24. Ibid., 38.

25. Compare Wilson, "Traumhochzeit oder Mesalliance?" 107.

26. Hellhund, "Der Norden, eine Himmelsrichtung oder eine Ästhetik," 36.

BIBLIOGRAPHY

Giddins, Gary. *Visions of Jazz: The First Century*. Oxford, 1998.

Gioia, Ted. *The History of Jazz*. New York, 1997

Hellhund, Herbert. "Gibt es eine Avantgarde im zeitgenössischen Jazz?" In Arndt, Jürgen, and Werner Keil, *Jazz und Avantgarde*. Hildesheim, 1998.

———. "Der Norden, eine Himmelsrichtung oder eine Ästhetik: ECM und der Jazz Skandinaviens." In Kern, Rainer, et al., *Der Blaue Klang*. Hofheim, 2010.

Hiekel, Jörn Peter. "Postmoderne im Musikdiskurs: Einige einsichten und Ansichten." In Flechsig, Amrei, and Stefan Weiss, *Postmoderne hinter dem eisernen Vorhang*. Bericht über das Symposium in Hannover, 2009.

Jost, Ekkehard. *Europas Jazz*. Frankfurt, 1987.

———. "Über das Europäische im europäischen Jazz." In Knauer, Wolfram, ed., *Jazz in Europa*. Darmstädter Beiträge zur Jazzforschung, Bd.3, Hofheim, 1994.

Lake, Steve, and Paul Griffiths, eds. *Horizons Touched: The Music of ECM*. London, 2007.

Messerschmidt, Ulrich J. "Beiträge von ECM-Bassisten zur Weiterentwicklung des

Europäischen Jazz." In *Jazz und Europäische Musik, Jazzforschung/Jazz Research* 36, Graz, 2004.

Noglik, Bert. "Substreams: Die verborgene Moderne in der improvisierten Musik Europas." In Shipton, Alyn, *A New History of Jazz*. London, 2002.

Straka, Manfred. "Kompositionen der abendländischen Kunstmusik im Repertoire von Swing-Ensembles." In *Jazz und Europäische Musik, Jazz Forschung/Jazz Research* 36, Graz, 2004.

Wilson, Peter Niklas, ed. *Reclam Jazz Klassiker*. Stuttgart, 2005.

———. "Traumhochzeit oder Mesalliance? Alte Musik und Neuer Jazz." In *Jazz und Europäische Musik, Jazz Forschung/Jazz Research* 36, Graz, 2004.

Wolbert, Klaus, ed. *That's Jazz: Der Sound des 20. Jahrhunderts*. Darmstadt, 1988.

CONTRIBUTORS

JURGEN ARNDT (GERMANY) is a professor at the University of Mannheim and author of *Thelonious Monk und der Free Jazz* (2002). His research is dedicated to jazz, popular music, and new media.

ARRIGO CAPPELLETTI (ITALY) is a pianist and composer, and a professor at the Venice Conservatory. He has written the books *Il profumo del jazz* (1996) and *Paul Bley* (2004).

LUCA CERCHIARI (ITALY) is a professor and archivist at Padua University and the author of *Jazz* (1997), *Scott Joplin's* Treemonisha (2001), and *Miles Davis* (2001), among other titles.

VINCENT COTRO (FRANCE) is a professor at the University of Tours and has published many articles the book *Chants Libres: Le Free-jazz en France 1960–1975* (1999).

LAURENT CUGNY (FRANCE) is professor of music at Paris Sorbonne University and the author of *Electric Miles Davis* (Dimanche, 1995) and *Jazz Analysis* (2008).

MARTIN GUERPIN (FRANCE), currently of the Paris Sorbonne University, doctoral research program, concentrates on the influence of jazz on French music in the interwar period.

JOHN EDWARD HASSE (USA) is a pianist, record producer, and curator of American Music at the Smithsonian Institution. He has written or edited numerous books, including *Beyond Category: The Life and Music of Duke Ellington* (1993) and *Jazz: The First Century* (1999).

MIKE HEFFLEY (USA) is a musician and musicologist, and has published *The Music of Anthony Braxton* (1996) and *Northern Sun, Southern Moon: Europe's Reinvention of Jazz* (2005).

HERBERT HELLHUND (GERMANY) is a musician, musicologist, and professor at the University of Hannover. His research is dedicated to jazz, rock, and music pedagogy. Among his writings is *Cool Jazz and West Coast Jazz* (1985).

DAVIDE IELMINI (ITALY), music critic, has written many articles and essays, and the book *Giorgio Gaslini* (2009).

EKKEHARD JOST (GERMANY), musician and radio producer, has been a professor for many years at the University of Giessen. His books include *Free-jazz* (1975) and *Europas Jazz 1960–1980* (1987).

FRANZ KERSCHBAUMER (AUSTRIA) is professor at the University of Music and Performing Arts at Graz, author of *Miles Davis* (1978), and editor since 1980 of *Jazzforschung/Jazzresearch*.

RAINER LOTZ (GERMANY) is a record collector and producer, researcher, and author of many books, including *Hitler's Airwaves* with Horst Bergmeier (1994) and *Black People* (1997).

CATHERINE TACKLEY PARSONAGE (UK), a professor at Open University, Milton Keynes, has written many articles and essays, and the book *The Evolution of Jazz in Britain, 1880-1935* (2005).

BRUCE RAEBURN (USA) is curator of the Hogan Jazz Archive at Tulane University, New Orleans. He has published numerous articles and the book *New Orleans Style and the Writing of American Jazz History* (2009).

GIANFRANCO SALVATORE (ITALY) is professor at the University of Lecce. He has published several books on jazz and popular music, including *Charlie Parker* (2005) and *Miles Davis* (2007).

ALYN SHIPTON (UK) is a music critic for the BBC, bass player, teacher at the Royal Academy of Music, and author of books on Fats Waller, Dizzy Gillespie, Cab Calloway, and of *A New History of Jazz* (2001).

MANFRED STRAKA (AUSTRIA), former teacher at the University of Music and Performing Arts at Graz, has written many articles on jazz history for the magazine *Jazzforschung/Jazzresearch*.

TONY WHYTON (UK) teaches music at the School of Media, Music and Performance at the University of Salford. His books include *Jazz Icons: Heroes, Myths and the Jazz Tradition* (2010) and, as editor, *Jazz* (2011).

INDEX

453